EXPERIENCE IS AN ARCH

Brian William John Gregg Wilson, 1990

Experience is an Arch

A Pedagogue's Swansong and Family Memoir

by

Brian W. J. G. Wilson

> I am a part of all that I have met;
> Yet all experience is an arch, wherethrough
> Gleams that untravelled world, whose margin fades
> For ever and for ever when I move.
> Alfred, Lord Tennyson, *Ulysses*

The Memoir Club

© Brian W. J. G. Wilson 2007

First published in 2007 by
The Memoir Club
Stanhope Old Hall
Stanhope
Weardale
County Durham

All rights reserved.
Unauthorised duplication
contravenes existing laws.

British Library Cataloguing in
Publication Data.
A catalogue record for this book
is available from the
British Library

ISBN: 978-1-84104-169-8

Typeset by TW Typesetting, Plymouth, Devon
Printed by Biddles Ltd, King's Lynn

To Sara

*And for our children
and
our grandchildren*

The lights begin to twinkle from the rocks;
The long day wanes: the slow moon climbs: the deep
Moans round with many voices. Come, my friends,
'Tis not too late to seek a newer world.
Tennyson, *Ulysses*

I have heard the mermaids singing, each to each.
I do not think that they will sing to me.
Eliot, *The Love Song of J. Alfred Prufrock*

  Soft you, a word or two before you go . . .
Speak of me as I am; nothing extenuate,
Nor set down aught in malice.
Shakespeare, *Othello*

All saints have a past; all sinners have a future.
Chekhov

Contents

List of illustrations		ix
Acknowledgements		xi
Chapter 1	Introduction – Faithful Lives; Unvisited Tombs	1
Chapter 2	The Commonplace Books – Jewels Five Words Long	6
Chapter 3	Parents I – Father	13
Chapter 4	Parents II – Mother	24
Chapter 5	Antecedents I – Wilson Family Connections	41
Chapter 6	Antecedents II A – The Gregg Family Tree	49
Chapter 7	Antecedents II B – Gregg Family Connections	60
Chapter 8	Early Childhood – the Invasion of Malaya	70
Chapter 9	The Palace, Armagh – Sanctuary	75
Chapter 10	Mourne Grange – An Educational Idyll	85
Chapter 11	Sedbergh – *Dura virum nutrix* – a hard nurse of men	97
Chapter 12	The Army	110
Chapter 13	Christ's College, Cambridge	121
Chapter 14	Radley College – Lotus Land?	137
Chapter 15	The Combined Cadet Force – Leadership Training?	150
Chapter 16	The King's School, Canterbury	158
Chapter 17	An Academic Interlude – JACT Ancient History: Author and Examiner	173
Chapter 18	Sara – A Marriage of True Minds	179
Chapter 19	The Hollins Family – Some Ramifications	190
Chapter 20	Anna and Emma – *Pignora amoris*	201
Chapter 21	Audrey – The Macafee Connection	215
Chapter 22	From Eastbourne to Campbell College	224
Chapter 23	Campbell College I	235
Chapter 24	Campbell College II – Familiar Matters of Today	247
Chapter 25	An Evin Macha – The Navan Fort Initiative Group	265

Chapter 26	St Mary's, Wantage – 'The Female of the Species …'	280
Chapter 27	In Retrospect	290
Chapter 28	Retirement – Rejoining the Community	299
Chapter 29	Swan Songs – Cruising with Swan Hellenic	311
Chapter 30	Church Activities – Parishes and Religious Broadcasting	326
Chapter 31	Cleeve, Somerset – Grandchildren and Other Commitments	338
Chapter 32	The Arch of Experience – Gleams that Untravelled World	350
Chapter 33	In Conclusion – *Respice*; *Prospice*; *Sursum corda*	359
Chapter 34	Envoi – Final Thoughts; Last Words	363
Appendices – Family Trees and Connections		365
I	Macgregors	366–7
II	Greggs of Cappagh	368
III	Wilson, Martin, Ronaldson, and ? Cody	369
IV	Wilson, Ronaldson, Strong	370
V	Wilson, 'Other' Wilsons, Woods, Brabazon	371
VI	Hollins, Fennell, and Brontë connection	372
VII	Hollins, Lennox, Andrews, Garrett, Drennan, Eggar, Duffin	373
VIII	Somerville Family	374–5
IX	The Maddens of Mallow	376
Index		377

List of Illustrations

Between pages 68 and 69

Father 1930
Dr Steevens' Hospital, Dublin – Resident Staff 1922
Mother 1930
Mother 1960
Mother and Father – engagement photograph
Mother's Bridesmaids
The Gregg – Somerville wedding
The Gregg – Wilson wedding
Granny Wilson ('Gan')
Grandpa William Wilson
Gan and Grandpa Wilson
At Trumroe – Gan and Grandpa
Father's sister, Mabel Ronaldson, with Sybil
Father's brother, Arthur Wilson (Uncle Artie)

Between pages 148 and 149

The Palace, Armagh – a painting by Lesley Gregg
John Gregg, DD, Bishop of Cork
Robert Gregg, DD, Archbishop of Armagh
Grandfather, John Allen Fitzgerald Gregg, CH, DD (*The Birley Portrait*)
Frances F. Gregg, founder of St Luke's Hospital, Cork
Dr Katharine Gregg, Missionary Doctor
Hilda C. Gregg, authoress (Sidney C. Grier)
At the Palace, Armagh: Brian, aged 2, with Grandfather
At the Palace, Armagh: Brian, aged 17, with Grandfather
Samuel Owen Madden and Mabel
Samuel Fitzgerald Madden
Owen Madden

William Madden
Castletownshend – a view of the village
Castletownshend – a family picnic in the 1920s

Between pages 228 and 229

The Cambridge University Rugby Fives Team, 1960
Grandfather's Rugby Fives Trophy from Cambridge
The King's School, Canterbury – the Norman staircase
Sara – pastel by Juliet Pannett
Anne Neilsen Trist, Sara's sister – pastel by Juliet Pannett
Sara Remington Hollins – engagement photograph
Arthur Remington Hollins
The Wm Hollins Mills at Pleasley Vale
The Vale House, Pleasley Vale
Ted Hollins with his brother Dick
Ted Hollins marries Jane Fennell, 1936
Ted Hollins gives away his daughter Sara, 1969

Between pages 308 and 309

Anna Wilson marries Dr Robert Adams, 2003
Emma Wilson marries Patrick Hales, 1998
Granny Sara Wilson
Our Grandchildren
The Sara Wilson Tapestry
Audrey (my sister) and Alistair Macafee
A happy coincidence of Academic Honours
The Macafee Cousins
Campbell College, Belfast
Horas non numero nisi serenas
A Ripe Old Age

Acknowledgements

I have had so much help from so many quarters that my fear is that I shall leave someone out. On the technical side my particular thanks must go to Dr Jennifer Soutter, my editor, for her expert guidance and meticulous supervision of the text, and to Lynn Davidson and the staff of The Memoir Club for their patient assistance and very professional support.

I hope that within the text I have acknowledged the source of the illustrations whose provenance is still accessible; many are very old dating back to the 19th century. Particular thanks are due to the Bolsover District Council for permission to include a fine aerial photograph of the old Hollins mills at Pleasley Vale; to Jewel Smith (our family's senior surviving member) for many of the old photographs of the Gregg and Madden families and of Castletownshend; I wish I could have included far more, because they offer vivid reminders of days gone by; and to David Macafee for a fine wedding photograph of my daughter, Anna, and her husband; special thanks also to Simon Painter, of Simon Painter Photography, for generously allowing me to make a collage of his four fine photographs of the Macafee cousins at Anna's wedding.

The quotations from my favourite authors and poets show a certain predilection for writers from earlier centuries, who are beyond the reach of mortal communication; but whether past or present, all are, I hope, acknowledged in the text. Where I have been unable to seek permission for their use, I hope at least that their presence in my personal quotation books and inclusion here will be taken for the compliment which I intend – and an apology for my lapse.

My sources of information are varied. Family memory is a significant element and here I have had tremendous help from Jewel Smith, whose remarkable memory has been a source of much family material; from Stuart and Sybil Strong and Pat Gunkelman, our 'American cousins,' for information about the Wilsons and the Ronaldsons; from my cousins, Christina Hoare and Julian Somerville, for information about the Somerville family and reminiscences of Castletownshend; from Annie Stephens and Alicia St Leger of Cork for details of the Jennings family; from Anne (Sara's sister) and Richard Trist, for fascinating details about the Hollins family; to Audrey, my own sister, and Alistair Macafee, for details of the Macafee and Lowry connections, and to Audrey again for much hard work delving into the clutter of our family archives for material and photographs. She it was that re-discovered the lost family tree.

Finally, above all, my thanks go to Sara, my wife, for her encouragement and support. She has always read everything I have written, and her fine critical judgement has been a great source of confidence to me in persevering with whatever project I have had in hand. Were it not too flippant a tribute, I might be tempted to describe her as my Macavity – the 'hidden paw' that guides my pen. Suffice to say that she above all has been my inspiration.

CHAPTER 1

Introduction – Faithful Lives; Unvisited Tombs

> *Come, let's away to prison:*
> *We two alone will sing like birds i' the cage.*
> *When thou dost ask me blessing, I'll kneel down*
> *And ask of thee forgiveness. So we'll live,*
> *And pray, and sing, and tell old tales, and laugh*
> *At gilded butterflies; and hear poor rogues*
> *Talk of court news, and we'll talk with them too,*
> *Who loses, and who wins, who's in, who's out;*
> *And take upon 's the mystery of things,*
> *As if we were God's spies; and we'll wear out*
> *In a wall'd prison pacts and sects of great ones*
> *That ebb and flow by the moon.*
>
> Shakespeare, King Lear's Valedictory

THIS IS SURELY ONE OF THE GREATEST farewell speeches anywhere in literature. An old man makes his peace with the child he loves, with his God (perhaps), and with himself; sees all in due proportion; bids farewell to life; and resigns himself to his final days in a frame of mind which believers might well call a state of grace. What better quotation with which to start a set of reminiscences?

The sort of people who write their autobiographies usually seem to be either politicians seeking to carve their niche in history by an exercise in self-justification, in the hope that history will be kinder to them than they deserve; or genuinely high achievers, whose drive for success includes an irrepressible desire to ensure that their success is recognised, applauded, and (ideally) envied by their contemporaries; or celebrities, whose merits are so modest and moment of glory or notoriety usually so brief that they (and their acolytes) must use every means at their command to attract the attention of a fickle and rather foolish public, in order to keep their image bright while they separate their admirers from as much of their hard earned cash as they can in the shortest possible time.

I hope none of these are my motives. I am not a politician; I do not think of myself as a high achiever – indeed, if I was writing my end of term report, I would describe my career as 'slightly disappointing'; I have never been a celebrity, though I share with many celebrities a deep sense of insecurity and lack of self-confidence. But in my case it derives, I suspect, from childhood, where like many others at a crucial stage of development I lacked a fixed abode, because we

1

were refugees from the Japanese invasion of Malaya, and was deprived of a father, because he was interned for three and a half years in Changi jail in Singapore by the Japanese. In addition, again like many others, the fear of Hitler as an ever-threatening bogeyman loomed over my childhood imagination at a time when every problem or complaint evoked the universal response – 'you must realise there's a war on . . .'.

But I realise, now, how very little I know of my own antecedents and how much I wish I knew more. My father, Cecil Samuel, never spoke of his own upbringing, let alone his experience of internment – indeed, I fear he was so traumatised by his experiences as a civilian prisoner of war that he never spoke of them at all, and found it quite difficult to talk to me about anything very personal, a feeling which was entirely reciprocated in what must have been a very typical father/son relationship. The loss is entirely mine: he was a fine man, whose great strength of character and physique brought him through his ordeals and whose great integrity and firm adherence to principle made him indifferent to popularity and uncomfortable with the narrow-minded, rather bigoted society in Northern Ireland, where, perforce, after the war he completed his career. I wish I could have got to know him better. In a belated effort to understand what he had endured, I read Brian MacArthur's *Surviving the Sword*, a horrifying account of the ordeals endured by the FEPOWs, the military POWs under the Japanese in the Far East. It made me wonder how any man could go through such suffering and not be driven mad. That my father came home and resumed his work as a consultant surgeon reinforces my admiration of his fortitude, both physical and mental.

My mother, by contrast, was tremendously family-minded and the history of her family, the Greggs, is probably synonymous with the history of the Protestant Church of Ireland, of which they were very distinguished members. But she lost her mother just after the war ended, and both her brothers, Claude to pneumonia while a cadet at Dartmouth, and John, also an interned civilian prisoner of the Japanese, who died tragically at the hands of the Americans, when the Japanese freighter in which he was being transported as a prisoner along with many others to Japan, was torpedoed by them in 1943. Brian MacArthur's account of these 'hell-ships' leaves one wondering only how many of those unfortunate prisoners welcomed death as a blessed release from their torments. As for the American genius for scoring 'military own goals' and being indifferent to 'collateral damage' in warfare, it has had a long history since those times!

So by mischance I became the senior male member of the Gregg family in the main line and was always conscious of what felt like a responsibility to my mother to live up to my inheritance. Of that, more anon.

As a result of circumstances, therefore, what might have become in happier times a widely extended family was reduced to my father's sister, Mabel Ronaldson, married to William (Uncle Billy), a farmer in Westmeath, and their children (Sybil and Cecil); my father's brother Arthur (Uncle Artie) who emigrated to America and was never mentioned in our family, though he married and had two children; and the two Gregg girls, Margaret, my mother, and her sister Barbara, who married Michael Somerville. Barbara's children, Christina and Julian, were the only cousins who meant anything to me in my childhood, though occasional visits to Claremount in Mullingar brought me into brief contact with Sybil and Cecil, both significantly older than I, at an age when such differences rendered them somewhat more distant than the Olympian gods. There were also various other more or less distant and more senior relatives whom I never really got to know, since they seemed to live somewhat inaccessibly in the south of Ireland. Barbara's two novels, *We are Besieged* and *Footprints on Water* still give something of the flavour of what life was like for them and their kind in the declining years of the Protestant Ascendancy. Uncle Michael's aunt, Edith Oenone Somerville, of Castletownshend, Co. Cork, gives us a much more comic – and famous – account of the same era in her immortal *Experiences of an Irish RM*. Now in old age I find that there were more relations than I thought and I regret my lack of contact over the years. No doubt it is a subconscious motivation for this attempt to research my origins and tell my story.

I wonder if it is the decay of traditional religion, with its promise of eternal life, which has encouraged the increasing interest of the current generation in its origins. It is almost as if, without our confidence in a future, we seek a kind of spurious immortality from the past and the long line of our ancestors from whom we derive. Perhaps, rather, it is our obsessive interest in ourselves, very much a characteristic of modern society, which has stimulated this interest, reinforced by the modern pseudo-science of psychology, which has encouraged us to blame our inheritance, whether genetic or cultural, for our shortcomings and failures, and inculcated a desire for self-knowledge and self-understanding as a source of the absolution once provided by a now increasingly inadequate church. Steven Pinker, in his splendid book *The Blank Slate*, has demolished such nonsense once and for all, showing clearly that 'the fault, dear Brutus, lies not in our stars but in ourselves that we are underlings'. We are what we are because we so choose to be, whatever the excuses modern psychology and the current fashion for counselling may choose to dredge up for us. To explain is not to absolve; we can choose to rise above our inheritance. To blame our inheritance, environment, or circumstances is simply a cop-out.

Whatever the causes and effects, growing up in Lisburn, a dreary, God-fearing and, in my boyhood view of it, God-forsaken Ulster town, some nine miles from Belfast, I had no extended family with whom to play, and only the companionship of my beloved sister, Audrey, and a very few friends, most of whom lived in more fashionable areas on the far side of Belfast in North Down at a time when public transport or my bicycle were the only means of seeing them. Lack of relatives, boredom, and loneliness are in many ways my strongest recollection of boyhood holidays. Term time at boarding school was different.

Suffice to say, I have put this book together in case my children, and even grandchildren, ever want to know more about their origins, to have some idea from whence they are sprung, and the influences that worked upon their parents and grandparents, and gave them their own genetic inheritance. I hope they will derive from it a healthy pride in their family, and in those relatives and forebears who have each added their small portion to the story of our island nation. We are, every single one of us, small miracles of survival, since by chance and good fortune every one of our ancestors has survived innumerable dangers and enjoyed what Othello called 'hairbreadth 'scapes i' the imminent deadly breach'. Each of us could, in theory and if we had the necessary records, trace our families back to Lucy, the common ancestor of all mankind if the palaeontologists are right. For that reason alone it is a profound privilege to be alive and almost a duty to keep the line going.

My first title for the book was *Ramifications*. Etymologically it means 'making of branches' and it seemed suitable, because I very much wanted to give some account of the activities and memories of the various branches of our family, as well as setting down the story of my own life, the forces that impacted upon it, and my observations in old age of events and circumstances that shaped it. As a classicist I have always felt a kind of kinship with Ulysses, not for his many wiles, nor for his heroism in battle

> far on the ringing plains of windy Troy,

but rather for

> That grey spirit yearning in desire
> To follow knowledge like a sinking star.

Tennyson's great poem is for me one of the finest in the language and conveys better than any I know through the character of Ulysses that feeling of always wanting to learn more, to discover the mysteries of life, and seek the God whom my mother once memorably described as an 'eternal mind expanding ever to elude'. That surely has to be the meaning and purpose of any human life. So I picked as my title a line that best encapsulates this thought.

The title has, also, a second association for me, because it seems a kind of symbol. The most important event of my life, beyond peradventure, was my marriage. When we were getting serious, but before we were engaged, Sara and I went off to Connemara for a holiday together (separate bedrooms, of course, in those days of innocence and utterly respectable behaviour), and on our wanderings through that wonderfully wild and empty landscape with a wind blowing and clouds on high in 'mighty adumbration', we came to a bridge across a stream and climbed down to have a look. As we sat there on a rock beside the chuckling waters, the setting was glorious, the moment magical. Sara confessed later that she had said to herself, 'If the sun comes out, he will propose.'

It did; I did; and all else is secondary.

But those lines from 'Ulysses' forever symbolise for me that untravell'd world of marriage, which gleams always beyond the moment of the here and now, whose joy knows no ending, and whose experience gives to every man a glimpse of heaven. As Robert Frost puts it in his lovely little poem:

> Never again would birds' song be the same.
> And to do that to the birds was why she came.

If, *en passant*, this account also offers to the social historian a small window into the life of a vanishing world, it will be a kind of unintended bonus. I have written it as I would a tale for my children, but if others find they wish to eavesdrop, I am content that they should. It is written almost entirely from memory – I have never kept a diary and the moves to a number of different domiciles have slimmed down the amount of memorabilia, which as a family we have been able to retain. So there will be errors of historical fact and family circumstance, I have no doubt. Such errors will derive from a faulty memory rather than malice, and if offence is caused thereby, I crave pardon from my victims. No doubt I shall, like the soldiers of Agincourt in Henry V's glorious speech 'remember with advantages what feats I did that day'. But my intention is to seek to tell the truth unvarnished, and if it is the duller for that, I regret it but will at least have remained true to my calling as an ancient historian.

This is an autobiography, but I hope it honours the members of an ordinary family who, each in their own way, lived their lives faithfully, seeking no particular glory for themselves but only to do their best 'in that state of life unto which it pleased God to call us', as the old Catechism put it. One or two were quite distinguished; but most of us lived hidden lives, loved I hope within our families, but beyond that content to live out the 'noiseless tenor of their way' along the cool sequestered vale of life. Sufficient memorial for most of us the closing lines of George Eliot's *Middlemarch*:

> The growing good of the world is partly dependent on un-historic acts: and that things are not still with you and me as they might have been is half owing to the number who lived faithfully a hidden life, and rest in unvisited tombs.

CHAPTER 2

The Commonplace Books – Jewels Five Words Long

The only end of writing is to enable the reader better to enjoy life – or better to endure it.

Dr Samuel Johnson

We read to know that we are not alone.

Anon

THE NEAREST THING TO A DIARY that I possess is a succession of Commonplace Books and these provide at least some reflection – hardly a record – of what I was reading and how I might have been thinking over more than fifty years. At the age of fifteen, and much too young by modern standards, I entered the Classical Upper Sixth at Sedbergh, devoid of any knowledge of science and without any O Levels (predecessors to the GCSE), because a doctrinaire government had ordained that no one could sit them until the age of sixteen, by which time I was taking my A Levels. Of all this, more anon. But the first thing I was instructed to do was to purchase from the school bookshop a very large, and what seemed very expensive, hard-backed exercise book. Inside the front cover I was ordered to inscribe four Greek words or phrases: *thauma* (wonder); *sophrosune* (sobriety/restraint); *gnothi seauton* (know thyself – words also inscribed above the entrance to the Oracle of Apollo at Delphi); and *meden agan* (nothing in excess). Not a bad set of signposts for life.

Greek was always my first love, but I was better at Latin, having started it early enough to have a firmer grasp of its grammar and syntax. So at some later stage I added to my frontispiece two Latin apothegms: *carpe diem* (seize the day – words immortalised years later in that wonderful film, *The Dead Poets' Society*, and penned by Horace, a poet whom to my sorrow I never really got to know) and Boethius' lovely sentiment, *superata tellus sidera donat* (earth conquered gives the stars), thereby adding a religious dimension to what would otherwise be a set of entirely secular mottoes for good living.

Thereafter into that book went anything that appealed to me plus, of course, anything that appealed to the Master of the Classical VI, Peter Newell, a tyrant and slave driver, but an inspirational teacher with an absolute commitment to ensure that in Classics, if in nothing else except rugby football, standards of scholarship at Sedbergh should always be of the highest possible. I learned to work hard – too hard, actually, and it left my broader education deficient and deprived me of the enquiring mind, which I rediscovered only in later years. Every week we learned a passage of Latin, Greek or English by heart and woe betide if we proved unable to reproduce it on demand. Every week my Commonplace Book expanded with some items that I was commanded to like and many more that genuinely appealed to me.

I opened my account with four lines of my own choice, the start of Milton's 'Lycidas', which had caught my imagination at an early age at my prep school, where I was made to learn them by heart along with lines from his 'L'Allegro' and 'Il Penseroso'. By a sad coincidence Milton's poem, perhaps the pinnacle of a long tradition of European pastoral poetry which began with the Greek Theocritus, is a lament for a college friend, drowned on a crossing of the Irish Sea. In my final year at Sedbergh I too lost a close friend in the Classical VI, Richard Bromley, drowned by blind mischance while crossing a river in spate on the school CCF assault course. So Lycidas came to have an extra meaning for me as a result. By a nice additional coincidence Milton was one of the greatest of the alumni of my own Cambridge college, Christ's, and I am still the proud possessor of a block of the myrtle tree from the Fellows' garden, under which he is said to have composed that poem. Grandfather Gregg was an Honorary Fellow of the College and gave it to me, having received it, I imagine, at some point by virtue of this high honour. It has remained for me a kind of talisman ever since.

> Yet once more, O ye Laurels, and once more
> Ye myrtles green with ivy never sere,
> I come to pluck your berries harsh and crude,
> And with forced fingers rude
> Scatter your leaves before the mellowing year . . .
> For Lycidas is dead, dead ere his prime,
> Young Lycidas, and hath not left his peer:

I must have written it down in my Quotation Book from memory, since I now find I left out the fourth line. Yet so ingrained is the habit of memorisation from those early days that as I typed it here, I reinserted the missing line without deviation or hesitation. Imagine my pleasure when I read Ian McEwan's novel, *Saturday*, and found that a central episode and the relationship of two of the main characters turned on the ability learned in childhood to recite great poetry. But at £5 per twenty lines, his heroine, Daisy Perowne, had more mercenary motivations than any that pertained to me. Amongst other mild eccentricities, I made it my business to collect 'definitions' of poetry, knowing full well of course that you cannot define the indefinable, but the effort might enhance the capacity to appreciate it. Here is A E Housman on the subject, and he knew a thing or two about poetry.

> I can no more define poetry than a terrier can define a rat, but I think we both recognise the symptoms which it provokes in us. One of those symptoms was described in connection with another object by Eliphaz, the Temanite, in the book of Job (4.15). 'A spirit passed before my face: the hair of my flesh stood up.'

Though I never read English as an academic subject and feel lamentably ill-educated in my reading, I have loved language and literature, especially poetry, for as long as I can remember. When I was working on my translations for *The Age of Augustus*, published in 2003, I had to make a stab at translating a fair amount of Latin poetry from that period. It also required a short introduction explaining why poetry can be a useful body of source material in the study of history. I reproduce it here because it says something of what I feel about poetry generally.

> Ezra Pound once famously remarked that 'poets are the antennae of the race'. Such an assertion, if true, would be sufficient to justify the inclusion of poetry in a volume of source material for the history of any period. But it is not the function of the poet to deal in facts, to record information, nor (usually) to report events. That is the task of journalism – an altogether humbler trade.
>
> Poets deal in perceptions, moods, emotions, responses, desires, hopes, fears. Historical virtues such as accuracy, objectivity, comprehensiveness, balance, exactness (save of language) are not for them. Ambiguities, suggestiveness, compression to the point of obscurity, image and association, echo and overtone, implication not explication, metaphor, simile, symbol, intensity of feeling – these are the poet's virtues and the would-be historian must be aware of them before he can use such material effectively.
>
> If, then, the reader seeks to know not so much what happened or even why, but rather what it felt like at the time, what were the responses and perceptions of sensitive and articulate contemporaries (the 'antennae people') to the events in which their lives were inextricably entangled, then the poet's value is considerable. Could we, for example, fully understand the enormity of the suffering of the First World War without the War Poets? Or the intensity of the feelings of Irish Nationalism without Yeats?
>
> But always we must read with care. The Roman Poets were, after all, what we would now call the 'spin-doctors' of their time. They identified themselves with the regime of Augustus and wrote in part at least to serve its purposes. But they were also great artists and no great artist can be entirely constrained by the wishes of his patron – his integrity will prevail and he will exploit constraints to enhance his creation by transcending the limitations imposed upon him. So it was with the Roman 'court poets', most notably Virgil. We must take the poets in the context of their time – a time in which men had grown tired of civil war and turned to Octavian/Augustus as to a god in gratitude for the gift of peace and as the source of inspiration for old values restored and new ideals espoused. To such feeling the poets helped to give expression.
>
> What then is the translator's task? This is a source book – not a work of art. Should he not, therefore, seek simply to convey meaning as accurately as possible, without regard for that inexpressible element which distinguishes poetry from prose? There, alas, is the problem. Meaning in poetry is not like meaning in prose; poetry is many-faceted, subtle, inapprehensible. Prose conveys information; poetry suggests response. The translator cannot himself write poetry – those who think they can nearly all conspicuously fail. The best a translator can do is to seek to convey

something of the meaning and feeling of his original in a form which, while seeking to convey the poet's perceived intention, at the same time declares to the reader 'this was not prose and should not be read as prose'. This is the primary justification for translations which retain the poetic format and such devices as rhythm and metre, assonance, alliteration, and rhyme, metaphor and enriched language, and other 'poetic' features. The translator is saying, simply: 'my poet once sought to convey to you a range of ideas, emotions, responses, aspirations in the most moving, beautiful and persuasive way he could. Do not therefore read my piece as prose; do not imagine either that I think I am a poet. But by poetic devices I hope to remind you constantly that once, long ago, a great poet was at work and is speaking to you now. Your analytical skills as an historian are not enough. You must bring to bear on your material sensitivity, empathy, imagination and insight – and, if you can spare it, just a touch of sympathy for your humble servant, the translator.'

Of all the elements of my education for which I most bless all those who taught me, the habit of compulsorily learning poetry (and prose) by heart is perhaps the greatest, along with Latin Prose Composition. Sadly, the curse of fashion, which has always bedevilled education in our country, has ensured that the practice has largely ceased and our children are the poorer for it. English literature must surely be one of the most richly endowed of all literatures and there is no way that one can make even a tiny portion of it truly part of oneself without committing it to memory. Such an exercise not only gives one a share of some of the world's greatest riches, it sharpens the imagination, widens the perception, deepens the understanding, heightens the intuition, extends the vocabulary, and stimulates a love of the beauty of words. It builds into the mind a sense of the rhythms of expressive language, a love of sound, a sympathetic awareness of meaning and underlying suggestion, and by the strange alchemy of the human brain, the capacity years later to conjure as it were out of thin air a compelling turn of phrase or a powerful expression of feeling, which may convey one's thoughts, win the attention of others, or even move the hearts of men.

Thanks to this great gift, I have ended up with an enjoyment of language and a love of words, which have been both useful to me professionally and a source of unending pleasure all my life. If you need convincing of the pleasures I describe, read *You English Words* by that lovely novelist of the English countryside, John Moore, author of the Elmbury trilogy. He will quickly demonstrate to you that I am not indulging in a display of 'ostrobogulous piffle'. My old friend, Don McClen, took this a stage further and actually published privately his own anthology, which he called *The Heart of Things* – a copy of which holds an honoured place upon my shelves. I might yet seek to follow suit. Shortly before his death another old mentor and friend, S S Sopwith (S'pwith), one of the great schoolmasters and teachers of English at Shrewsbury and then King's Canterbury, a relative of the family who built the Sopwith Camel, the First World War fighter plane flown by my beloved Biggles, gave me his last copy of his own small anthology, *An English Sampler*, a gem of a book subtitled 'Essential passages of prose and poetry in English Literature'. The habit of anthologising is one that should be practised by all who love English.

The first compulsory insert in my Commonplace Book was the lovely description from Virgil's *Aeneid* (VI. 305–316) in which he describes the ghosts of the recently dead crowding to the banks of the river Styx in the hope that Charon, the grim ferryman, will row them safely over into Hades. He likens them in their multitudes to the autumn leaves that fall with the coming of the first frosts of winter, and this image inspired Tennyson's glorious lines, 'Thick as autumnal leaves that strew the brooks/ In Valombrosa . . .'. Virgil's sonorous concluding lines convey by sound alone a deep sense of yearning for the unattainable. This once inspired a Latin-less scholar, clearly blessed with a poet's ear, to say that he could not translate the words but that the sound to him was reminiscent of the words of the psalmist (Ps 137) 'By the rivers of Babylon, there we sat down, yea, we wept when we remembered Zion'. It later became a rather wonderful pop song. Listen to the vowel sounds of the last line in your mind's ear and see if they have the same effect on you.

Stabant orantes primi transmittere cursum
Tendebantque manus ripae ulterioris amore.

There they were standing, begging to be the first to cross the flood,
And stretching out their hands in yearning for the further shore.

The next pieces were my own choice, Isaiah's famous prophecy (35 1–2; 6–8) 'The wilderness and the solitary place shall be glad for them and the desert shall rejoice and blossom as the rose . . .', in the Authorised Version of course, not the dreary banalities of modern translations. This was followed by Winston Churchill's, 'We shall prove ourselves once again able to defend our island home, to ride out the storm of war and outlive the menace of tyranny, if necessary for years, if necessary alone' (nearly all monosyllables, please note, and all the better for it; good English is simple English, enriched only from time to time by the occasional word of Greek or Latin origin), and then Arthur Hugh Clough's 'Say not the struggle naught availeth . . .', quoted by Churchill himself I believe in a speech, when the news came through that America was joining the Allied war effort. 'Westward look, the land is bright.'

In whole or in part I can still recite all these, though sadly the onset of old age and what Churchill called 'the surly advance of decrepitude' means that they are beginning to fade like the glimmering landscape of Gray's 'Elegy in a Country Churchyard'. But I continued, more or less faithfully, to add my entries to that book from September 1952 until in December 1964 it was filled. It is a record of all sorts of things, from *bons mots* to long passages, which caught my fancy at some particular moment. Some have little or no merit; some reflect an at times childish taste or juvenile sense of humour. Others remind us of the words of Keats in his poem, 'Endymion',

> A thing of beauty is a joy for ever:
> Its loveliness increases; it will never
> Pass into nothingness; . . .

And that for me is what the whole collection is — a thing of beauty and a joy for ever. As Keats (again) observed in his 'Ode on a Grecian Urn',

> Beauty is truth, truth beauty, — that is all
> Ye know on earth and all ye need to know.

I am now into my third volume and for me each is an immensely precious reminder of a lifetime spent in the teaching, reading, and enjoyment of language. Caliban may have told Prospero that 'You taught me language and my profit on it is I learned to curse'. But Caliban got it totally wrong — as you would expect of a brute beast. Language is what raises us above the beasts of the field; a love of language is one of the greatest blessings that a teacher can offer to a child. In that I have been quite singularly blessed.

Interestingly, I was to discover forty years later that my grandfather, too, kept a Book of Quotations. He was a far greater scholar and had a superbly honed mind, cast in the analytical or perhaps judicial mould. Indeed had he not been Archbishop, as he admitted himself, to be Lord Chief Justice of England would have been his ultimate ambition. He too had the habit of learning by heart. But where I practised it sporadically, he did it systematically and assiduously all his life. When, at my confirmation, he gave me my deceased Uncle John's Greek Testament, he also gave me a tiny book of spiritual exercises called *The Daily Round* (passed to my godson and nephew, Jeremy) and inscribed it entirely from memory with the famous words from the end of the Epistle to the Philippians: 'Finally, brethren, whatsoever things are true, whatsoever things are honest . . . etc.' I can still quote it in English. He did it in Greek, and of course he got all the accents right too — as every gentleman should, naturally. Here is H W Chandler in his *Preface to Greek Accentuation*, dated 1881.

> In England at all events every man will accent his Greek properly who wishes to stand well with the world. He whose accents are irreproachable may indeed be no better than a heathen; but concerning that man who misplaces them, or worse still, altogether omits them, damaging inferences will most certainly be drawn — and in most cases with justice.

Standards have clearly lapsed lamentably since those glorious days, and even in my school-days signs of this decline were apparent, since accentuation was in the process of becoming an optional extra.

There is a fascinating comment on my grandfather's Quotation Books in George Seaver's biography (pages 32–33). He notes that the entries date most frequently from his curate's years – a time when, no doubt, he was still studying and reading widely as his knowledge and understanding grew. They do not, he suggests, show any profundity of thought; nor do they reflect the range and wealth of his reading. Apart from his unexpectedly keen interest in the nature and purpose of Art, the meaning of Beauty and the function of Imagination, much inspired by Ruskin, they come largely from the poets and prose-writers of the 19th century, 'but of European philosophers there is no quotation, save one from Plato's *Gorgias*'. Seaver suggests, probably rightly, that 'these gleanings from the harvests of other minds are made with a view to corroborating a faith which is already assured and has never been seriously assailed by the tempests of doubt; has never known with Browning what it is to "... stoop into a dark tremendous sea of cloud"'.

Grandfather was still learning by heart and reciting almost to the end of his life. George Seaver tells us that at the 1958 Lambeth Conference, of which he was by right of seniority the Father, in a debate at the plenary session on the subject of alterations in the wording of the Psalter he 'amazed the assembly by repeating from memory phrase after phrase of the Greek version of several different psalms in support of a certain suggested English rendering. The whole assembly stood and spontaneously accorded him round after round of acclamation.'

All this I write by way of explanation for the fact that, if I appear to be over-inclined to scatter quotations through this memoir, it is not that I want to indulge in a sort of academic showing off. But these things are so much part of me that they arrive unbidden from the storehouse of my memory and will act, I hope, as a sort of seasoning to the otherwise rather turgid diet of my own prose. For me language is a great delight and poetry one of life's great joys. My sorrow is that I was less well grounded in English literature than I would have wished. But it remains for me an enchanted garden, into which like a child, I am at times almost afraid to venture and in which I still get lost. But perhaps if you know what gives profound pleasure to another, you may feel you know and understand him just a little better.

Such is the spirit in which I offer others a chance to share what has always mattered to me. But if an excess of quotation irritates, you can always skip them, viewing them rather as one might the illustrations in a children's book, adornments possibly but not necessarily essential to the text itself. But for me they are,

> ... Jewels five-words long
> That on the stretched forefinger of all Time
> Sparkle for ever.

CHAPTER 3

Parents I – Father

I wanted to grow up and plough,
To close one eye, stiffen my arm.
All I ever did was follow
In his broad shadow round the farm.

I was a nuisance, tripping, falling,
Yapping always. But today
It is my father who keeps stumbling
Behind me, and will not go away.

Seamus Heaney, 'Follower'

MY FATHER, CECIL SAMUEL WILSON (1897–1977), was born at Sharvogue, Mullingar, Co. Westmeath, which is about as near to the centre of Ireland as you can get. Of his antecedents I know little. There was on his shelves a photograph of himself, his mother, 'Gan', and his father, William, whom I never saw, but he looked like a typical Victorian gentleman, severe rather than genial, with a big, drooping moustache, a dog, a walking-stick, and, I think, plus fours. They were seated on a garden bench in the garden of the family farm, Trumroe, Castlepollard, Co. Westmeath.

I always understood that the Wilsons hailed from Yorkshire and probably came over with the Elizabethan settlements of the 16th century, but it could I suppose have been as part of Cromwell's army, though I would prefer the former! No doubt many such adventurers saw Ireland as a way of bettering themselves, if not making their fortunes, and no doubt also their Protestant affiliations will not have endeared them to the local population. That the Wilsons were part of the local 'gentry' by the time that William Wilson acquired his farm, Trumroe, in Castlepollard, was evident enough and I remember at least one visit to the Pakenhams for tea, though the connection with the famous tree-hugger Thomas Pakenham (Lord Longford) was one that I never made until years later. But they were comfortably off rather than rich, and certainly not sufficiently prosperous for Cecil, my father, to have much hope of making a living from the family farm.

Seeking your fortune overseas was the lot of all enterprising Irishmen, and like the Scots they emigrated in large numbers both to the New World and to the further reaches of the British Empire. Rather like his Elizabethan forebears, Grandfather William Wilson had also gone abroad to seek his fortune, in this case to the Kimberley mines in South Africa. But he always had a longing to return to Ireland to farm, though Gan adored South Africa and would happily have remained there. I wonder if perhaps Cecil had caught from his parents something of the excitement and hopes of those fortune-hunters of the great South African mining period, because he loved the novels of Francis Brett Young, *They Seek a Country* (about the great Boer trek) and *City of Gold* (the Johannesburg gold rush). He too sought his fortune abroad, and went out to join the Malayan Medical Service, first as State Surgeon in Selangor, and later in Kuala Lumpur. He would probably have ended his career there had not the war intervened. No doubt, too, as a Protestant in a poor and less than tolerant Roman Catholic country he probably had to recognise that he might well have had no great future at home.

He was British and proud of it; and doubly proud to have been a British Colonial servant and to have lived a significant part of his life in the service of the Empire. He would have been moved and pleased by Nirad Chaudhuri's generous dedication to his autobiography, which Don McClen sent me after we found that we shared a contempt for those who spend their days denigrating the Empire's achievements and apologising for it.

> To the memory of the British Empire in India, which conferred subjecthood on us but withheld citizenship; to which yet every one of us threw out the challenge: *Civis Britannicus sum* (I am a British citizen), because all that was good and living within us was made, shaped, and quickened by the same British rule.

Yet Ireland remained always his first love and I am sure he would have settled there if he could. But the active discrimination in the society of the south (as in the north, but in reverse) would have been a considerable disincentive. The Irish novelist, John McGahern, though himself a Roman Catholic, in his autobiographical *Memoir* gives very vivid glimpses of the level of tyranny exercised by the church in that country. 'Individual thought and speech were discouraged', he says, and 'by 1950, against the whole spirit of the 1916 Proclamation, the state had become a theocracy in all but name. The Church controlled nearly all of education, the hospitals, the orphanages, the juvenile prison systems, the parish halls. Church and state worked hand in hand.' What I learned about at second-hand from my family is entirely consistent with this account.

Whether religious or political, my father hated bigotry of any kind and the perceived tendency in his adopted Northern Ireland for jobs to be fixed for friends or relatives or co-religionists was something he found intolerable. But the South was no different, and my mother told me that he even gave up his membership of the Masonic Order, because he was ashamed of its inherent corruption and the way as an organisation it was more interested in working for the advantage of its members than of society at large. He disliked the Orange Order for much the same reasons. Whether these were his motives for going to work abroad I cannot be sure; but from what I learned later of his attitude to religious and political discrimination I am inclined to think so. Membership of any order, whether secret or otherwise, he felt robbed its members of their independence and integrity; and the only association of which he was willing to remain a member was the Friendly Brothers of St Patrick. From there he derived some cherished friendships, and when I myself became a member I was assured by a venerable member that 'we may not do much good, but we certainly do no harm'. From all I saw I think I could agree.

William Wilson had four children, Arthur, Cecil, Mabel, and Millie, his second daughter, who died in South Africa of infantile diarrhoea – a fact that I only discovered in 2005 from my aunt Mabel's family in America. The effect on Cecil and his siblings is unknown; he never mentioned poor Millie. But then he never mentioned his father either. I don't know why, except that Victorian fathers and sons probably had little inclination to communicate and in this my father was distinctly Victorian. Perhaps, too, in common with his generation, which had seen so much suffering, he felt that overt evidence of inner emotion was not something to be indulged in. No doubt, too, the experience of POW camp will have taught him to keep his thoughts to himself.

He was always quite clear about the role and status of the paterfamilias, and he never that I can remember helped in any way with household chores – even the washing-up. Rarely either did he seem capable of rational discussion within the family; he was never willing to concede an argument. One disagreed at one's peril. He was bound by a strong sense of duty; insistent on good manners, on politeness to and appreciation of employees and subordinates (in this he was very Irish and very un-British, since the Irish lack the English obsession with class and status), and courtesy to the point of chivalry to women; he was also very clear about how he thought a gentleman should behave, including opening doors for ladies and for elders and betters, giving up one's seat to ladies and the elderly in a bus etc., and how one should be dressed. He was constantly irritated by my typically adolescent habit of wearing my socks at half-mast, and by my resolute refusal to wear sock suspenders, despite his repeated encouragement. It never seemed to occur to him that the very terminology made it totally unacceptable. Only girls wore suspenders! More positively, and with characteristic generosity, he insisted on buying for me at the age of eighteen full evening dress, dinner jacket, and morning suit – all bespoke from Gillies, the best tailor in Belfast. I had little occasion to use the first, except at the Cambridge May Balls, but the last (still almost as good as new) I wore to my own wedding and to those of my daughters. I can still squeeze into it after some fifty years.

So firmly inculcated in us was the idea of good behaviour that my sister Audrey still remembers how, at the age of about seven, he came into her bedroom one day without knocking and she rebuked him as a 'very naughty man' for so doing. When he said, 'but I came in very quietly' she reiterated that he was 'still a very naughty man'. He used to tell the story against himself with great delight years later.

Yet when integrity and good manners clashed he could be stupidly bloody-minded. In an attempt to establish contact with relatives (Wilson cousins) whom we had not seen for years, my mother invited them to lunch. They were good-living, church-going, and teetotal. My mother, with the best of intentions, decided that they would probably expect us to say grace before meat and so she asked him, 'Would you say grace, Cecil.' Back came the reply, 'I have never said grace in my life and I don't propose to start now.' Mother, nothing daunted, said grace herself and we all sat down to the most agonisingly uncomfortable lunch party I can ever remember. Integrity – admirable; but the quiet courtesies and unimportant hypocrisies that help life move smoothly on defeated him on this occasion. Was he right? I doubt it.

His father, William, must have died relatively young, since Gan survived him by many years. As a widow she kept the family farm going for a number of years before age compelled her to retire to live with her daughter, Mabel, at Claremount, Mullingar. She had always had a very soft spot for Mabel's daughter, my cousin Sybil, who used to bicycle over to Trumroe from Claremount (about twenty-two miles) and go to church with her by pony and trap. Gan gave Sybil her leather-bound Prayer Book and Hymnal, and this has passed on through the family first to Daphne and now to her daughter, Clare. I like the idea of family heirlooms, especially those that are old but have little monetary value. Passed down through the generations they can be cherished for their associations and the memories they evoke with little fear of theft.

Until she sold the farm Gan ran it with the help of a couple of faithful retainers, whose names I am ashamed to say have long since escaped me – though 'Frank' and 'Sherwin' generate certain vibrations, visual and mental. My childish recollection has Sherwin desperately shabby, clad in a long black coat with oversized boots turning up at the ends, and walking with a kind of shuffling waddle. He slept, I was convinced, in the stables, and the pony was his particular charge. If true it is rather less shocking than it would seem now. Ireland was an agricultural country, and like most such countries, very poor. Farm workers were badly paid and poorly cared for, beyond good farmhouse meals in the big farm kitchen. But given the poverty, even square meals and a roof over your head of some kind must have represented a significant bonus to your minimal wages.

I was made to learn as a young boy a haunting poem by Padraic Colum, 'The Old Woman of the Roads', which I still remember began with the words

> Oh to have a little house,
> To own the hearth and stool and all
> The heap'd-up sods upon the fire,
> The pile of turf against the wall.

It ends on a similar note.

> And I am praying to God on high,
> And I am praying Him night and day,
> For a little house – a house of my own –
> Out of the wind's and the rain's way.

It haunted my childhood imagination for years. There must have been so many living in similarly dire poverty for whom such words would have rung desperately true. Again John McGahern's *Memoir* reflects this with painful clarity for the period even as late as the 1950s.

I remember no other workers, but for a farm of some 240 acres, workers there must have been. There was an orchard, in a fine walled garden, if I remember rightly, grazing land – I have no recollection of any cereal production – and a bog, the source of turf for fuel. There was a pleasant farmhouse; a stable yard at the back; a tall stand of elms (or beeches) and long walks across the fields to the bog, which must have been a source of game as well as turf. Father enjoyed shooting and fishing, and used to reminisce fondly of Lake Derravaragh and dapping for trout (or was it salmon?) in the mayfly season. He had a quick eye for a snipe, though I have no recollection of his ever shooting anything except vermin – jackdaws, magpies, and the like. After his experiences as a POW, he could hardly bring himself to shoot even those, though he kept his beloved 12-bore until the day he died.

For Protestants schooling in Ireland caused something of a problem. By repute even in my young days Catholic schools were brutal, and the more recent emergence of revelations about sexual scandals (which would have been wilfully concealed by the Church authorities until the last years of the 20th century) have reinforced the unwholesome picture. Protestants were, too, a tiny segment of the population and if they wanted to bring up their children in the traditions of their own faith, it was well nigh inevitable that they would have to send them to a Protestant boarding school. Wilson's Hospital in Mullingar would have seemed an obvious choice, since it was well established, having been founded in 1761 by Andrew Wilson, another of the Westmeath Wilsons, with whom as yet I have been unable to establish any family links, though I remain certain they must exist. I once took an archery team from Campbell College down there to compete and got a very nice feeling about the place – it seemed warm and friendly. It went coeducational, but only as recently as 1969, when it 'married' Preston School, Navan. For reasons unknown Cecil was sent further afield, to board at Sligo Grammar School, and later to Mountjoy, in Dublin, before reading medicine at Trinity College, Dublin, and going on to train as a surgeon. To the end of his days he remained convinced of the superiority of the TCD medical training over that of Queen's University, Belfast. He felt its products were more broadly educated and better trained. Such an opinion, amounting to a prejudice, will not have helped him in his relations with his Northern Ireland medical colleagues, particularly in the contentious scrabbling for merit awards, which can sometimes disfigure relationships within the profession in small communities, but as far as I know he was largely indifferent to such matters.

His greatest disappointment was to have developed appendicitis just as his FRCS(I) exams were approaching and so he missed the opportunity to gain what for a surgeon was a prerequisite for advancement to consultant status. I do not know whether this was because he could not afford to repeat a year financially or because in this examination there is no second chance. Instead he went on to take a yet higher qualification, his M.Ch. (Master of Surgery), and then went to work at the Mayo Clinic in Rochester, Minnesota, USA, at the same time as his lifelong friend, Nigel Kinnear of the old Adelaide Hospital, sometime president of the Irish Royal College of Surgeons, and later one of Stuart Strong's special mentors. The other two medical friends whom he mentioned often and remained close to were Ninian Falkner and Sir Ian Fraser, both men whom he admired greatly. Dad always admired surgeons of courage and was somewhat contemptuous of those who were not. Nigel certainly was 'one of the lion-hearted pioneers of vascular surgery' (to quote J B Lyons in his account of the lives of Presidents of the Royal College), who 'recognised it as one of the major surgical challenges of the second half of the 20th century, and set about tackling it', taking on the risks that more timid colleagues tended to eschew. After his time at the Mayo, Father took up what was to be his substantive career in the Malayan Medical Service. However, my mother gained her FRCS(I) some years later and she was always able to bring him to the College of Surgeons' dinners as her guest – a position which at times clearly irked him, though he enjoyed the events.

Reverting briefly to his schooling, Sligo he remembered with great affection, and in rare moments of reminiscence he would talk warmly of the headmaster, called Smylie I think, who was clearly much loved and something of a father figure to his boys. He told me little else, except that there was a mention of picnics on 'the Lake', presumably Lough Gill, made famous by Yeats' poem, 'The Lake Isle of Innisfree'. Whence came his love of music and an almost totally concealed skill at the piano, I do not know; but musical he certainly was. But from Sligo and Mountjoy (of which he never spoke) he must have derived his great love of rugby football, which became a sore trial to my mother and myself in later years. Week after week we were dragged off to watch dreary club rugby matches at Ravenhill, in the days when the game was little more than a boring struggle between battling forwards on rain soaked pitches, rarely enlivened by any open three quarter play. Jackie Kyle, the great Irish fly-half, was his particular hero, not only for his brilliance as a runner but also for his instinctive and uncanny knack of 'turning up unexpectedly under a blade of grass' to rescue a situation in which his team had been wrong-footed and caught out of position.

From his obsession with the game, sadly, derives my own dislike of it, a dislike increased by association with many of its exponents, encountered at school, university, and among fellow-teachers, who seemed (with honourable exceptions) to be loud, crude, beer-swigging and mindless. He, of course, was a wing three-quarter, which did require some degree of skill; I was by contrast doomed by a certain stoutness of physique to be a forward in those days when forward play required little skill or coordination. I might have learned to enjoy the game as a back, but I was temperamentally ill-designed for the brutish struggles of the pack, where thuggery and cheating on the blind side has always been part of the game. So when it was decreed that I should go to Sedbergh, instead of the 'family school' Shrewsbury, where they played soccer, my dislike of the game became intense. At Sedbergh rugby really was the school's religion and I hated it.

Though by profession he was a surgeon, in his heart of hearts I am sure my father was a country boy and a lover of the countryside. When he returned after the war, he hoped to work in the Irish Republic. But he found that as a Protestant medical practitioner in what in those days was a less than tolerant Roman Catholic country, the Church dictated health and welfare policy, and for Protestants work was not easy to find. It is hard to appreciate in these more liberal times, when the churches of both denominations have forfeited power along with respect and persuasion, how totally dominant then was the position of the Roman Catholic church in Ireland, with strict censorship of books on the Index, and the wicked *Ne Temere* decrees, which ordained that in a mixed marriage the children must be brought up in the Roman tradition. This ensured that in time the Protestant population would decline and constituted a kind of licensed religious ethnic cleansing, which would probably not now be tolerated under the European Convention of Human Rights. My parents used to be very indignant about it all, but it was a brave family in those days that was prepared to face the wrath of the local parish priest and his congregation, and not many did. It is little wonder, then, that the Protestant population of the Republic has declined to its present tiny numbers. As a boy with little knowledge or understanding of such political matters, even I can remember the headlines on one memorable occasion when church policy forced the resignation from government of a liberal health minister (was he called Noel Browne?), who had dared to challenge the Church's position. But most politicians ran scared of the Church, because it could command their votes from the pulpit in the name of God and His church.

I was too young to have been properly aware of the anxious peregrinations of my parents, as they tried unsuccessfully to find an appointment in the south of Ireland. What I thought of as simple visits, or even holidays, to relatives and friends in the south were probably part of this unhappy process and certainly my sister, Audrey, remembers vividly three very happy months staying with the Ronaldsons at Claremount, while our parents went job-hunting. In the end my father was advised that it would be almost impossible to get a post there. As a result he even contemplated returning to run the family farm. But desperation rather than conviction would have been his motive, for he was a brave and brilliant general surgeon and would have been very unhappy to abandon his profession. By a strange coincidence one of his former theatre sisters, a Miss Jackson, lived in retirement in Sedbergh, about fifty yards from my boarding house. She used to ask me round to tea from time to time and told me once that he had 'the most beautiful hands of any surgeon' she had ever worked with. Sadly

I never had a chance to watch him operate, for I would have liked to understand what she meant by 'beautiful hands' in the surgeon's craft, but I read somewhere that the traditional qualities of a great surgeon are that he should have 'the heart of a lion and the hands of a lady'. And that is the nearest I have ever come to understanding what she meant.

In the end, though never comfortable with Northern Ireland bigotry and intolerance, he found a post there in Lisburn, as senior consultant surgeon at the Lagan Valley Hospital. So to Lisburn we moved from our temporary wartime home in Armagh, and there we spent the next fifteen years. By all accounts he was greatly loved by his patients, on whom he probably expended rather more devotion than perhaps he managed to give to his own family, except when they were genuinely ill. Then suddenly all his gentleness and kindness took over and one felt embraced in the warmth of his concern. I was rarely ill, but once I got jaundice and once mumps (with complications!) and his love and care was palpable. He was, in fact, a dedicated healer of men, a 'beloved physician', and to that calling he committed all his reserves of physical and emotional energy. He was no less committed to the training and welfare of his staff (innumerable housemen continued to write to him from all over the world when they had left for higher positions) and I remember well his pleasure in their achievements, as well as the pride and delight with which he reported once that he had persuaded the management committee of the hospital to build a tennis court for the nursing staff and a solarium for the patients.

How great a strain his work proved I never really guessed. He had been a big man, physically strong, and a fine athlete. He returned from POW camp weighing seven stone, and it is remarkable that he could recover sufficiently to carry the burden which he did. He worked very long hours, was rarely home before 7 or 8 p.m., and then often spent a couple of hours reading up in preparation for the next day's operations, with a 'stinger' (a long whiskey and soda, traditional evening drink in Malaya) beside him – but never more than one.

The stress showed itself in uncomfortable and sometimes rather distressing quarrels with my mother, who endured his irritability with saintly forbearance. He was a good, but instinctive bridge player; she a calmly logical one. Family bridge (often night after night) was one form of relaxation for him and a nightmare for us. I have never since played the game, because the arguments to which the inevitable post-mortems gave rise and the allegations of stupidity or carelessness remain for me a kind of childhood horror. He had a short fuse when crossed or challenged, and my prevailing memory of our relationship was one of apprehension, never of physical violence since he never in his life raised a hand to me, however much I deserved it; but he had a searing tongue when roused and was capable of cruel remarks that cut to the heart. To my contemporaries I would have seemed mildly extrovert, being both good at games and reasonably clever; but I was in fact a timid child, desperate only to please, and was very much aware of how often I seemed to fail to do so. To this unsatisfactory state of affairs I would attribute much of the serious lack of self-belief, which has afflicted me all my life.

I loved reading; so did he, but he seemed to find it deplorable that any healthy teenager should spend so much time curled up with a book. But of course he never had time to enjoy recreations with the aforementioned teenager, beyond dragging him off to rugger matches on a Saturday afternoon, or family golf on Sundays, which was somewhat less of a trial I admit. He wanted me to become a fisherman – another sport he had greatly enjoyed in his younger days. It would have been a wonderful way of getting to know each other better. But he never took me; instead I was sent off on my bicycle to find some fairly distant river, armed with his old greenheart trout rod and a box of flies. After a bike ride of an hour and a half or so, and another hour and a half of tangled lines, and some harmless ribaldry from local children coming out of school, I gave up without even setting a fly upon the water and went home. And that was pretty well the end of my fishing career, apart from mackerel fishing while on holiday in Castletownshend, where I once caught seventy-six mackerel in an hour, rowing backwards and forwards through a huge shoal that had come into Castlehaven Bay. But that wasn't true fishing and I am sorry I never discovered its delights. It is the kind of tranquil, almost contemplative occupation to which I would be temperamentally well suited. The episode offers an obvious lesson to all fathers of sons: always say 'why don't **we** go and . . .'; never, 'why don't **you** . . .'.

He retired in 1962 and bought Ballycrenan, a lovely house in Helen's Bay overlooking Belfast Lough. It cost the princely sum of £10,000 and I well remember him saying with some anxiety that it was more than he felt he could really afford, but that my mother had so set her heart on it that he could not bear to disappoint her. It was a rare moment of insight into the other side of his character – his love for my mother and his great generosity. At Ballycrenan he maintained, with her somewhat more expert help, a delightful three-acre garden and perhaps found in a sort of return to horticulture, if not agriculture, something of the contentment, which the stresses of his professional life had denied him. He certainly seemed much more at peace with himself and was always a gentle if undemonstrative grandfather, with the interesting peculiarity that, though a medic and married to a gynaecologist, he was genuinely offended by mothers who breast-fed their babies in public. He was in many ways still a Victorian in outlook and when, for example, finally and rather too late, he brought himself to tell me the facts of life (at the age of sixteen plus) the relief he felt was manifest, when I told him that we had been given a full lecture on such matters by the headmaster of Mourne Grange, my prep school, before we finally left the school. 'That was very good of him' was his only comment, and we left it at that.

In accordance with his abiding commitment to physical fitness, he continued to watch rugby and play golf, which he loved, to the end of his life. He had played to a handicap of about eight in his prime, and had been the long-driving champion of the expatriate community in Malaya, once credited with a winning drive of some 325 yards. His sporting ability was brought home to me long before, when he played in the annual parents' cricket match against Mourne Grange in his first year back from POW camp. He cannot have held a bat for ten years at least and yet I vividly remember my pride when he scored twenty-five runs in quick time including a sizzling cover drive that reached the boundary in about half a second. He was solemnly presented with the customary 'broomstick' (a bat cut down to the width of about two inches) with which to continue his innings, but I don't think he achieved the stump, which was the reward for reaching forty.

Late in life from 1969 onwards the Troubles of Northern Ireland tormented him and we had many disagreements about the underlying causes. I shared his abhorrence of their atrocities, but my perception that there were grievances on the Nationalist/Catholic side, which had enhanced the influence of the IRA and required at least a degree of understanding of their activities, enraged him. He, of course, had seen an earlier IRA campaign in Dublin in the 1916–1922 period, so he knew from first-hand experience just how nasty their campaigns could become. In the end, characteristically, he forbade me to discuss the matter. He lacked the academic cast of mind, and a dispassionate search for truth through reasoned argument was something of which he was incapable. He much admired ex-Irish Fusilier Sir Gerald Templer's handling of the Malayan insurrection; but he failed to make the parallel connection with the Northern Ireland situation. Templer set himself to win hearts and minds as well as defending the vulnerable from terrorists. British policy, so often seen (sometimes with justification) as betrayal by the population of Northern Ireland, was the same. You cannot win insurgency wars by brute force and technological superiority alone – a lesson the USA has yet to learn.

I have little doubt that I was influenced in my views by the magazine *Fortnight*, a new publication in Northern Ireland at the time, which sought to bridge the gap between polarised political opinion by reasoned analysis of the sources of division between the two communities, started if my memory serves me correctly by a friend and contemporary from Cambridge, who was in fact an academic lawyer with one of the most original casts of mind that I had come across. I don't think any of my friends or family ever read it – reasoned analysis of the Northern Ireland problem was not a strong suit, often for understandable reasons.

To have picked up the threads of a damaged career so successfully; to have lived to eighty after all that he had endured; to have survived the barbarity of internment under the Japanese – all this is no mean achievement, and a tribute to his physical and spiritual strength, but also to the devotion of my mother who had to share the burden of his recovery. To the end of his days he would speak with profound affection and admiration of his namesake though no relation, Bishop Wilson of Singapore and later Birmingham, with whom he claimed to have been proud to share a cell. The Bishop's immense religious conviction, spiritual strength, and legendary courage and Christian forgiveness under torture held the camp together and gave so many of its inmates the courage to endure. My father remained a practising Christian to the end of his days. Though he had little time for ostentatiously pious types, he had an instinctively sound judgement of character and was quick to recognise genuine goodness when he saw it. His beliefs were, I am sure, tempered by a robust common sense, which I would like to think I might have inherited. My mother told me once that in discussing the Christmas story and the birth of Jesus he had remarked to her that he had a sneaking suspicion that 'perhaps after all Joseph had something to do with it'. I have long shared his suspicions.

In a rare moment of self-revelation he told me once (with typical matter-of-fact understatement) that in Changi he had been in charge of one of the camp's illicit wireless sets. The Japs knew they existed and had instituted a systematic search for them, which was getting alarmingly close to him, and would certainly have led to his execution. He was saved by the dropping of the two atomic bombs on Hiroshima and Nagasaki, which brought the war to an unexpectedly abrupt end. There can be no doubt that, whatever the cost to the Japanese, the result was to save far more Allied soldiers' lives than they destroyed of Japanese. It also gave the world more than half a century so far of relative peace through 'the balance of terror', which has at least ensured that another world war between any two great powers was almost unthinkable. For this I have always admired the moral courage of Harry Truman, the American President, who took the truly tough decision, which gave us that peace and brought my father home. Even in my youth I always held the CND movement in contempt for their naïvety and lack of willingness to face the brutal facts of wartime horrors and the cruel dilemmas of policy which war imposes upon political leaders.

An inveterate smoker all his life, to the despair of my mother, he would vehemently deny that there was any connection between smoking and lung cancer or bronchitis, claiming never to have seen any evidence of its effects on any of the patients on whom he had operated, though in the end he did start smoking mild cigarettes. He was an asthmatic, for whom the simple sight of a horse or a cat would set off a fit of sneezing, and he suffered from bronchitis regularly. But it is perfectly possible that the sedative effect of smoking combined with his obsession with physical exercise did more to extend his lifespan than shorten it. He got pneumonia at the age of eighty and died peacefully in hospital in the early hours of the morning somewhat sooner than expected; in fact my mother was at home and asleep. That too was characteristic: he would not have wanted to cause a fuss or be a nuisance. I placed his ashes in the family grave in Mayne churchyard, near Castlepollard. Sadly the church itself, at which we must have worshipped as a family in my childhood, though I have no memory of it, is closed. But Dick Kilroy, an old friend and brother officer in the Royal Irish Fusiliers, was acting at that time as a kind of honorary churchwarden and made the committal possible. Later he did the same for my mother, whose ashes rest beside those of the man she loved with such almost sacrificial devotion.

CHAPTER 4

Parents II – Mother

Remember me when I am gone away,
  Gone far away into the silent land;
  When you can no more hold me by the hand,
Nor I half turn to go, yet turning stay.
Remember me when no more day by day
  You tell me of our future that you planned:
Only remember me; you understand
It will be late to counsel then or pray.
Yet if you should forget me for a while
  And afterwards remember, do not grieve:
  For if the darkness and corruption leave
  Some vestige of your thoughts that once I had,
Better by far you should forget and smile
Than that you should remember and be sad.

TAKEN FROM MY ANTHOLOGY, this poem by Christina Rossetti, though probably not so intended, serves well to express the love of any child for its mother, and the pain of loss.

My mother, Margaret Dorothea Gregg (1907–1991), whom I adored this side of idolatry, was a remarkable woman. When she died, the *Belfast Newsletter* and the *Belfast Telegraph* carried obituaries of her, but neither made any attempt to do more than present a relatively cursory factual record. But a close friend and neighbour asked me if I could write an appreciation of her, which he could use as the basis of his own article for the *Irish Times*, which was duly published on 5 February 1991.

Obviously I was constrained by editorial necessity and it was written in some haste. But neither in length nor quality does it match my mother's own wonderful and deeply moving tribute to her father, which constitutes the final chapter of George Seaver's official biography, commissioned by the Church of Ireland. It is as fine a piece of biographical writing as I have read anywhere, and I photocopied the whole of it into my Anthology. Her education may have been slanted towards the sciences and her training medical, but hers was a generation at ease in the arts as well as the sciences, since in those days doctors were still allowed to be roundly and properly educated, illegible perhaps, but certainly literate.

But, for good or ill, this is what I wrote.

Margaret Wilson, MA., MB., FRCS(I), who died at her home in Donaghadee on New Year's Day at the age of 83, was the eldest daughter of one of Ireland's greatest Anglican Archbishops, John A.F. Gregg, Archbishop of Armagh from 1940–1959.

Inheriting her father's formidable intellectual powers, she was something of a pioneer for the role of women in that most conservative of professions, Medicine. She graduated in 1931 from Trinity College, Dublin, with first places in Midwifery and Surgery, and as winner of the Professor of Medicine's Prize. She then became the first woman to gain the Hudson Scholarship at the Adelaide Hospital. In 1936 she married Cecil S. Wilson, M.Ch., of Castlepollard, himself a graduate of TCD and by then a consultant surgeon in the Malayan Medical Service. She became a Consultant Gynaecologist in Kuala Lumpur, but the Second World War put an end to a career that might have culminated in high academic or professional distinction.

Her husband and her brother John (a civil servant in Malaya with the Colonial Service) were both taken prisoner by the Japanese, while Margaret escaped with her two young children, Brian and Audrey, taking refuge with her father in the Palace at Armagh for the duration of the war. Because her mother was crippled by arthritis, Margaret assumed many of the responsibilities of an Archbishop's wife, though she continued with a limited part-time practice at the Armagh Infirmary.

Her husband survived the horrors of Changi gaol in Singapore and on his return home was appointed, in 1947, Senior Consultant Surgeon at the Lagan Valley Hospital, Lisburn. It was at this stage that, putting duty before inclination with the unflinching clarity of judgement, which was a family characteristic, she decided that her first obligation was to her husband and family. She abandoned any serious attempt to return to her medical career and instead offered herself to a life of public service, such as the Girl Guides, where she became a County Commissioner, to committees of the Royal Victoria Hospital and of the Welfare of the Handicapped, and as a Magistrate in the Juvenile Courts.

But to the end of her life it remained a matter of disappointment that despite her wide experience and abilities she was never called upon to serve the province in some more challenging way. Her surprisingly shy nature may account for this, or, perhaps, that severe intellectual clarity which was intolerant of the petty dishonesties and self-seeking, which often mar the world of public committees. Perhaps, too, her breadth of sympathy and experience gave her a vision and understanding unsuited to the more parochial outlook of many of her contemporaries. Suffice to say, the province lost the services of a remarkable woman. The gainers were, of course, her family, who found in her a devoted mother and grandmother, a rock of strength in adversity, and a wife totally dedicated to a husband who had suffered much at Japanese hands and depended deeply on her support.

In an age of militant feminism such devotion to duty might seem extraordinary; but to her duty was always an imperative, and having decided where her duty lay, she set herself to live out the implications of her decision wholeheartedly and without the self-indulgence of regret. And in the end it brought her fulfilment of a kind and a heart at peace.

That summary of an admirable life, which for obvious reasons never received the acknowledgement it deserved – on this earth at least – offers a useful starting point.

Since it was written for public consumption, it says little of her as a mother, a grandmother, and matriarch of our family. As a mother she was as near perfection as I can imagine. She held the household together. After the war, and living in Lisburn with my father battling to regain his health and his professional career, she was the rock on which the home was built. We had lost everything in Malaya, and I don't think money was particularly easy, even though my father must have been earning a reasonable salary.

Before the war she had acquired none of the conventional home-making skills which tradition required of women in those un-emancipated days. She taught herself to cook; she kept hens and maintained the garden, from which we got a plentiful supply of vegetables and eggs (of which she sold the surplus). I remember her sweating for hours and hours over two sheepskins, which she had decided would make nice bedside mats. She read up how to cure them, bought a couple of pelts, and proceeded to do so. She was the practical one who made repairs and kept things going. Dad couldn't even mend a fuse. We did not have a washing machine; all the washing was done by hand and in the holidays I always helped, doing the wringing while she scrubbed. A television in those early postwar years was unheard of; a portable wireless for my twenty-first birthday present was the height of luxury. Briefly in Lisburn we had a living-in housemaid, because it was almost *de rigueur* in our social class, but she got rid of her very quickly, either as part of an economy drive or because she could not bear to have someone else always in the house – and anyhow, she could cope. But she did accept the help of a wonderful 'daily' called Mrs Edith O'Lone, who was a gem and remained a friend of the family for years.

She had given up smoking during the war, characteristically deciding that it was a waste of money, and turning from a forty-plus per day smoker into a non-smoker overnight. That was typical of her strength of character: if she decided that something had to be done, she simply did it, however difficult or unpleasant. She even handed in her diamond engagement ring in response to a government appeal for diamonds to help the war effort – and regretted it ever after. When I turned seventeen and could drive a car, she used the money saved to buy a second car for family use, which was the start of our family's love affairs with Morris Minors, Minis, and Morris 1000s. For understandable reasons for the rest of his life my father refused ever to buy a Japanese car. Meanwhile, deprived of the professional career which I am sure in her heart of hearts she would have liked to return to, she gave her spare time to good works. Of these she said little, partly out of natural reticence – she was never one to parade her virtues – but partly because my father (for doubtless psychological reasons which he himself probably could not have explained) was almost jealous of her activities and inclined to mock them, in a way which lacked the gentleness of affectionate teasing. I think he resented her having any sort of life of her own.

Of the activities which I knew about, without actually knowing what she did: she was on the Northern Ireland Council of Social Services; on the Catering

Committee of the Royal Victoria Hospital; she was a County Commissioner of the Girl Guides – and I always thought the uniform was very smart! She was for a time at least a Governor of Alexandra College in Dublin. She was a magistrate in the Juvenile Courts in Belfast, and I always remember the sympathy she felt towards some of those who were up in front of her. One story she told was of a young lad charged with some sort of reasonably grievous offence; she noticed that when he got up to leave the dock he carefully put his chair straight – 'so I knew that he had been well brought up and probably broken his mother's heart.' She was like that – she noticed and had a profound sympathy for those who had gone astray. It may be that which made me terrified of ever letting her down; I could not bear her to be disappointed.

When my father retired in 1962, aged sixty-five, we moved to a lovely house bought, I think, from the family of Charles Brett, our family solicitor, called Ballycrenan in Helen's Bay. It was a fine brick house, set in three acres, and looking down over Belfast Lough. Now I think for the first time, with the stress of work over, in Yeats' words, they managed to find some peace there, where . . .

> . . . peace comes dropping slow,
> Dropping from the veils of the morning to where the cricket sings;
> There midnight's all a glimmer, and noon a purple glow,
> And evening full of the linnet's wings.

My father mellowed; my mother had a home she loved in a village she liked; the evening if not the midnight of their lives gained something of a glimmer; both their children were in decent jobs, whatever Dad thought of my choice of career; and life took on a certain degree of harmony. When Audrey and I got married, in 1969 and 1970, and then the grandchildren arrived in rapid succession (Audrey delivering at the rate of two to my one) Mother found a new purpose in her life and was a wonderfully supportive, if somewhat spoiling, granny to Audrey's four. Sadly we saw rather less of her because we were living in Eastbourne, but holiday visits were a pleasure, despite a slight anxiety not to disturb and overtax their hospitality. Emma once, in a fit of misdirected affection, bit Granny rather sharply on the bottom, which produced an impressive explosion of discomfort and wrath and an instinctive clip around the ear, if I remember aright, and left us all treading on eggshells for a few days. But all in all they were happy days.

When my father died in 1977, a year after I had come back to Campbell (a school to which he was nearly sent as a boy and of which he was tolerably pleased to see me as headmaster), Mother sold up – to my great regret, since I would have done almost anything to keep a hold of Ballycrenan – and very sensibly bought a bungalow in Donaghadee, about three hundred yards away from Stramore, where Audrey lived. It meant that, while still fit, she could help with the four grandchildren, who at one stage were all under four, as a useful supplement to

Nanny Sey, who had looked after the Macafee family since time began, but was beginning to age.

I think she found real happiness and satisfaction in her new role and location, and her mind remained as sharp as ever, her interest in both family and the world at large unimpaired. This happy state continued for nearly a decade when, inevitably, Old Age crept up on her almost unawares and with it his ungodly ally Senility, though fortunately not in his most extreme form. There followed in those last few years the usual battle between love and necessity, practicality and the desire to let her stay at home. She made a brief attempt, greatly against her will, to take the place in a local nursing home which we urged her to accept. It did not work and she reverted to her house with the aid of a succession of living-in Irish aunts, whose patience she sorely tried and whose lives she occasionally and ineffectively threatened with her walking stick. She died of a stroke on 1 January 1991; Audrey was with her. I, alas, was not. But I have to say that it must have been a blessed release for her – and I am afraid for us. She had become very hard to handle.

I lament her passing with every fibre of my being. Some of her last words to me were of concern for my happiness, at a time when she was herself deeply unhappy. Her care was always for the family and never for herself. I don't think she ever really got over my early retirement from Campbell College, and my return to England was the final straw.

Her ashes rest in Mayne churchyard in Westmeath, beside those of the man she loved so well and cherished so devotedly. May they both sleep the sleep of the just, and find eternal joy beneath the everlasting arms.

Of her childhood I know little. She always thought of herself as a Cork girl and she was born in 1907 in the rectory at Blackrock, a suburb of that city. Her father had been appointed to the incumbency of Blackrock parish in September 1906, having earlier been Curate and Residentiary Preacher of St Fin Barre's Cathedral, Cork, a small Victorian architectural gem, built by his grandfather, also John Gregg, Bishop of Cork, whose marriage to Elizabeth Nicola Law gave us our long connection with the Law family, including (distantly) Field Marshall Bernard Law Montgomery.

Margaret was born a year later and remained a somewhat sickly child for the first year of her life; in fact she nearly died in her first month. Cork she always loved, and Castletownshend, a small erstwhile fishing village in the far west of the county, no less. There the family regularly holidayed, and there she used to stay also with her father's cousin, Canon Owen Madden, Rector of Castlehaven, a brilliant ex-Cambridge mathematician, who became a sort of second father to her. There too her Cousin Jewel Smith (née Evans), Owen's niece, was a frequent visitor and they became lifelong friends. Later my parents also took the family there, for blissful holidays staying at The Castle, which the Salter-Townsend family ran as a guest house, and where playing with their four children (Geraldine,

Robert, George, and Anne if my memory has not played me false) I learned to row a boat and play billiards. Later again I took my family there on several occasions, either renting Fanny's Lodge or the Red House, and once staying in the Mall Cottage, Uncle Brian and Aunt Biddy Somerville's lovely home, halfway down the hill.

My grandmother, Anna Alicia Jennings, to whom my mother bore a remarkable likeness in old age, came from the Sarsfields, an old Cork family, famed in Irish folklore as members of the Wild Geese, who fled from Ireland after the 1691 Penal Laws to serve in the armies of the Continent. She was the youngest of four girls in a family of seven, and according to George Seaver, quoting my mother, 'was the daughter of a not very business-like Cork businessman who died early, leaving Rose, his wife, to repair the family fortunes by competent management'. She did this to remarkably good effect, sending the boys to Cambridge and the girls to good English schools.

Anna herself went to Clifton (in whose junior school years later my own daughter Emma was to teach), travelling to Bristol from Cork by boat in what cannot have been comfortable circumstances in those days. Instead of going to university, which she had hoped to do but was prevented by weak eyesight, she worked in the Cambridge Settlement in Bethnal Green, which gave her a wonderful insight into the depths of misery endured by the poor of those days, and was of course invaluable experience for a rector's wife. She grew up at Brookfield, a fine house, built by Tom Jennings, Anna's uncle, which stood in its own grounds well outside the city boundaries in those days. Did Thomas, father of Meg, Muirne and Eithne, take in his brother's family after his early death? It would account for George Seaver describing her as a 'daughter of the house', and the 'aunt' of Meg and her sisters.

I remember Brookfield well, since I stayed there on more than one occasion when we visited Cousin Meg (Rose Margaret), one of the three Jennings sisters. I always enjoyed the tale of how her father (?grandfather), who built Brookfield, kept a boat on the roof, some three storeys above the ground. Being in his religion of a somewhat fundamentalist persuasion he was, apparently, convinced that Armageddon was due and with it a second flood. He clearly had every intention of himself taking the role of a second Noah, presumably without the full complement of necessary animals, and apparently saw no inconsistency in thus seeking to thwart the purposes of the Almighty to rid the world of sinful men. My cousin Christina tells me also that 'the walls, built of hideous yellow firebricks (clearly he feared fire as well as flood) were so thick that no one could angle a gun to cover the inside of the ground floor rooms', and that the house was 'built to withstand a siege, with an enormous water tower built into the roof'.

Annie Stephens (née Rycroft), a former editor of the *Bangor Gazette* (later the *North Down Spectator*, for which she still writes an occasional column, 'Gleanings from Cork'), is a great friend of Audrey's through their connection with the St

Luke's Home in Cork. She has forwarded to me the following information about the Jennings family, very kindly collected by Alicia St Leger, a historical researcher, who is also (like Annie) a pillar of St Fin Barre's Cathedral.

Information about the Jennings family
2006
(Alicia St Leger)

In the early 19th century Thomas Jennings established the Brookfield Chemical Works to manufacture lime and magnesia at the western end of what is now College Road in Cork. Jennings was already a vinegar manufacturer and the company had also produced bleach at one stage. The company later manufactured mineral water and raspberry cordial. By 1910 the Jennings company had premises on Brown Street, in Cork city centre.

Thomas Jennings was associated with the founding of Queen's College, Cork (now University College, Cork) in the 1840's, as was Francis M. Jennings, who may have been Thomas' son. Some of the land on which the university was built was purchased from the Jennings estate.

The Jennings family owned the land at the western end of College Road and in the later 19th century built a large family residence there. The house, called Brookfield House, was built of an unusual yellow coloured firebrick and had a stone staircase. It is said that the person who built the house had a fear of fire! [And of flooding – see my note above – BW] The house is still in existence, but has recently [2005] been surrounded on three sides by modern university buildings. The Brookfield property is now used by the nursing faculty of the university, while the remaining portion of gardens now contains student residences and a hotel. Brookfield House originally had large gardens surrounding the house, with beautiful mature trees. Some of the trees have survived recent building works.

A Thomas Jennings died in March 1935 – he was a descendant (grandson?) of the Thomas Jennings who established the chemical works. He had three daughters:

Rose Margaret (Meg) – unmarried
Muirne – married Bernard Gedge, no children. They lived at Brookfield House
Eithne – first married Rev Warburton E. White (rector of Kanturk, possibly Kinsale?) and second married Ted Pope. No children.

Muirne and Eithne were twins.'

(Here Alicia St Leger's account of the family ends)

Cousin Eithne Jennings (later Pope) lived in Kinsale, County Cork, but I never met her. Cousin Muirne at that stage lived in London, having married Bernard Gedge, a stockbroker, and they were extremely kind to me on several occasions, having me to stay (at Manor Fields, Putney) and acting as surrogate aunt and uncle at a time when I had few relatives in England. They inherited Brookfield at some point and lived there until Bernard died, and Muirne went into a retirement home. Having no children, they left a generous bequest to the cathedral, and Brookfield itself to the University of Cork – an action for which my mother never forgave them, and for which she blamed Bernard, suspecting him of seeking to acquire merit on earth through the one bequest and in heaven from the other, at the expense of the family's money, not his own! I can offer no judgement in the matter beyond noting that there is a clear and long-standing connection between the Jennings family and the university, which puts a somewhat different slant on the decision to make the bequest.

My mother says of Granny Anna Alicia that 'she was a splendid person, immensely kind and supremely sensible, efficient, imperturbable in a crisis, and an admirable housekeeper and administrator' – which was just as well, since Grandfather had little time for silly women, whom he found 'beyond comprehension'. He greatly admired, by contrast, the 'wives of the rectory', who often brought up their families on small stipends and in difficult circumstances, with minimal recognition for the noble (and unpaid) work they did for their parishes. Admiration butters no parsnips, and my own perception of the church's exploitation of its womenfolk, and in these latter days no less of its often impoverished and greatly reduced congregations, is rather less charitable.

Cousin Jewell Smith, from the Madden side of the family, remembers Anna Alicia rather differently. She remembers her as very kind to her personally, but 'a rather untidy heap of a woman, the antithesis of Grandfather, with an amazing collection of chins and a tendency to organise everyone, obstinate, not an intellectual, very forceful'. (Well she might be after years in Bethnal Green and as a schoolgirl regularly crossing by herself to England on the Cork/Bristol ferry). An amusing story illustrates what might have seemed a mean streak in her character too. Jewel recalls how she 'was taken for a drive once to collect eggs and was struck by the incongruity of the Archbishop's wife (as she then was) with a chauffeur driving around Irish cottages to find eggs at a penny the dozen cheaper than they could be bought in the local shops'. But then, of course, the Jennings family were from 'trade', and in those days that provenance carried a certain implication of inferiority. But in trade no doubt you soon learned the hard way one of life's more valuable lessons: that if you look after the pennies the pounds will take care of themselves. And of course the Bishop's wife had once been the wife of a curate and then a rector, when there were fewer spare pennies to go round. Old habits of thrift I have no doubt died hard and my own judgement would perhaps be somewhat less critical.

My mother was in due course sent to school as a boarder at The Manor House, Brondesbury Park, North London, where she became head girl and captain of games. I have no idea of the date but I assume it was around 1920. By one of those strange quirks of coincidence, at that same school was another girl with Irish connections (through the O'Brien family) called Joan Hamilton. She later married a Canon of Durham Cathedral, Michael Ramsey, who shortly afterwards was appointed Professor of Divinity at the University of Durham, and ultimately Archbishop of York and then Canterbury. They remained friends and in touch throughout their lives, each of them sharing, as well as their school, a devotion to two of the greatest archbishops of the Anglican Communion.

When I joined the staff of the King's School, Canterbury, as House Tutor of Walpole House, my room looked out onto the rear windows of the Old Palace, the Ramseys' favourite retreat at weekends from the pressures of Lambeth. On the strength of this friendship with my mother and for no other reason that I could see, Sara and I were invited once with Anna, our elder daughter aged perhaps three, to lunch at the Old Palace one Sunday. All the social factors for which Michael Ramsey was famous – shyness, lack of small talk, amazing eyebrows – were well in evidence, though Joan was as relaxed and easy as he was uncomfortable. Owen Chadwick, in his biography, reports that though to their sadness they had no children, Michael himself was wonderful with children generally. But Anna defeated him. When we went into lunch Anna climbed onto the host's chair and ensconced herself at the head of the table, making it quite clear that she regarded this as her proper position. It would have required an artist in language to do justice to the Archbishop's reactions. He too knew his place and was not going to have it usurped, despite Joan's plea to him 'not to be so silly, Michael'. But the manifest distress that showed on his face was palpable when Sara, ever practical in such matters, simply picked Anna up and placed her where she belonged amid much tears and lamentation. Those immortal eyebrows went into overdrive; pain at a child's distress showed on his face; and I am sure that this great and good man was remembering with some dismay the injunction of Our Lord that he should 'suffer the little children . . .'.

The coincidences did not end there and one in particular has left me with a very soft spot for that school. Though a younger contemporary of my mother, also at The Manor House was Jane Fennell (later Hollins), a distant relative of the Brontë family, and whose brother John was to be Professor of Russian at Oxford University. She married Ted Hollins and it was their daughter Sara whom I married in 1969. Of all that more anon.

Another of my mother's greatest friends, Biddy Orr, from Northern Ireland, also went to The Manor House, thus giving rise to another of those family connections that endured throughout our lives. She married Brian Somerville, a regular army officer in the Royal Irish Fusiliers (where I too later held a short service regular commission). Though no blood relation, she remained to the end of her days my favourite 'aunt'; they were immensely kind to me when I was stationed as a potential officer trainee in Canterbury at the Buffs depot and they were living near Maidstone. Years later our paths crossed again, because she and Brian retired to Childrey, near Wantage, where I ended up as Deputy Head of St Mary's School. The wheel had come full circle and we were able to walk out to visit her and exchange reminiscences of younger days, especially Castletownshend, since she retained her remarkable memory until the end. She had a lively mind and was always interested in what was going on around her, and proved to be a wonderful source of gossip, often naughty but never malicious.

Aunt Biddy, I believe, introduced my mother's younger sister Barbara (who also went to Brondesbury) to Brian's brother, Michael, whom she married in 1935. The Somerville family (including Edith Oenone Somerville, famed as the author of *The Experiences of an Irish RM*) were, like the Townsends, Chevasses, and the Coghills, one of the old families of Castletownshend, the regular holiday haunt of the Gregg family. Their father, Admiral Boyle Somerville, had been assassinated by the IRA in 1935, in one of those brutally pointless murders of innocent victims with a British connection to which that organisation was inclined. Their excuse was that he had been helping to recruit local lads for the British Navy, at a time when there was little employment in the area and an organised boycott of English goods was increasing the general hardship for many families. A note found on his body claimed that no less than fifty-three had been helped in this way – too many for the IRA. In fact his 'recruiting' seems to have been no more than signing their application forms at *their own* request. But when would such niceties influence terrorists in time of armed struggle?

Very sadly Barbara was a severe diabetic and this must have contributed to her early death. Michael returned to England and bought an adjacent house to that of his brother in Childrey, and finally came to live in Wantage, where as a close neighbour he kept an eagle eye on all my family's comings and goings. He, too, was blessed with a phenomenal memory and was a walking encyclopaedia of family history. Sadly I never thought to ask him to record his memories until it was too late.

One story of his, which I do remember, albeit with less than total accuracy, was of his great aunt who as a young girl herself remembered handing Wellington his sword as he left a ball in Paris to fight the battle of Waterloo. It was something I used with pupils to illustrate the possibilities of oral memory as a source of material for historians.

My mother, Margaret, always regretted the fact that she did not go to Cheltenham Ladies College, where her formidable academic talent would have been recognised and wider opportunities opened up for her. But for reasons unknown, perhaps because her mother had hated the endless journeys across the water to school in Bristol, or because her father had become Archbishop of Dublin in 1920 and good Protestant schooling was now available locally, my mother left The Manor House and moved to Alexandra College, Dublin, of which later, as one of its more distinguished alumnae, she was for a time a governor. Her father, who had been translated from his position as Archbishop King's Professor of Divinity at TCD (1911) to become Bishop of Ossory, Ferns, and Leighlin (1916), had already had some contact with Alexandra College, where he had delivered a series of four addresses to the senior girls. He never talked down to the young, but certainly the girls would have found these talks a challenge. If they were able to follow his erudite arguments and discuss them with him, my mother need have had no doubts about the academic quality of the school. The first two pages of chapter six ('Bishop of Ossory') of Seaver's biography have a long extract, which gives a flavour of the quality of his talks. In this he discusses 'the scientific ideas of continuity, evolution and order in the physical universe' as evidence that 'Order is heaven's first law', and then sets against this the 'truth of divine immanence' and the proposition that 'natural law is no more than induction based on the observation of recurrent sequences of phenomena'. The vocabulary is entirely his. One suspects the good bishop would not have lasted five minutes talking to a modern sixth form.

Nevertheless, had my mother gone to Cheltenham the chances are that the whole course of her life would have been different. She might well never have met my father and I would not be here. These blind chances, which govern our very existence are extraordinary to contemplate. With the failure of the Olympian Gods in ancient Greece, thinking people began to invest the concept of *Tyche*, Chance or Luck, with the trappings of divinity, sometimes worshipping it as *Tyche Soteiria*, Our Saviour Chance, as the only plausible deity to explain the element of sheer random fortune and misfortune that seems to govern our lives. There are signs now in the early years of the twenty-first century, as conventional religion loses the adherence of thinking people, that something similar is happening once again. Matthew Arnold in 'Dover Beach', his wonderful poem about the ebbing of the Sea of Faith, describes it as

> Its melancholy, long, withdrawing roar,
> Retreating, to the breath
> Of the night-wind, down the vast edges drear
> And naked shingles of the world.

Where the educated Greeks and Romans turned to philosophy, the only solution that Matthew Arnold seems able to offer us is true love, and this too seems characteristic of the modern outlook, being one of the few things that can raise us above ourselves into a higher realm than the pursuit of pleasure and instant gratification which makes our age something of a wilderness of the spirit.

Mother was wonderfully open-minded on the subject of religion, fully prepared to discuss the problems of faith in a modern age, and she assured me on one occasion when we were talking about the Virgin Birth that 'we were already abandoning that in the 1920s'. From our discussions, often in letters, which sadly I never kept, I never forgot one resonant phrase she used of God as 'an eternal Mind, expanding ever to elude', and I have kept it by my side (so to speak) throughout my efforts to wrestle out my own far less adequate faith. She had a lovely analytical mind and fine way with words; she loved ideas and usually found in me, I think, a foil for discussion, which my father found irritating.

In 1920 Grandfather became Archbishop of Dublin at the relatively tender age of forty-seven. My mother never spoke much of her time in Kilkenny, seat of the Bishop of Ossory, Ferns, and Leighlin, surely one of the most poetic titles for any bishopric, but the move to Dublin and her time living in the Archbishop's Palace at 50 St Stephen's Green, must have been a source of great delight. Once they had reached the age of indiscretion and become students at Trinity College, Dublin, she and her sister Barbara (who read Modern Languages and also gained first class honours) found themselves at the centre of a wide and clearly delightful social circle, where she was always known among friends as 'Maggie Dublin', following the custom of Archbishops to take the name of their Episcopal province instead of their surname. As well as a brilliant academic, she was also a good athlete and like her father played a vigorous game of tennis (golf came later). There was sailing and swimming at Castletownshend on the family holidays, and (one must assume) the parties and dances, which we still associate with the 1920s, though mother never admitted to having been a flapper. There was also something of a craze for bridge. She was probably somewhat too seriously minded to go totally overboard amid the gaiety of the postwar (and post-civil war) period, and always felt that her younger sister Barbara (the first to marry, and a real 'honey-pot', according to Cousin Jewel) was the real attraction to the young men who clustered around.

Having a couple of older brothers John (b 1903) and Claude (b 1906) could in happier circumstances have been a wonderful bonus on the social side, but tragedy was to intervene. Claude died of pneumonia in 1928 at the age of twenty-two soon after joining Dartmouth Royal Naval College from Osborne. It must have broken her heart, for they were very close, and Grandfather's diary contains the simple but poignant comment, 'My little son' and then 'Hallowed be thy name'. I was always told that I closely resembled him, but the family portrait, painted from a photograph, suggests to me someone rather more handsome and distinctly more slimline. To their great shame I understand that the authorities of the Royal Naval College have never bothered to set up a memorial to those of their cadets who died while in training there. Claude cannot have been the only one and some small token of official sorrow for the tragedy of young lives lost and families bereaved should have been the least tribute they could have paid.

It is sad that sometimes the pressure of expectation and family comparison can lead to young men (and I dare say women) going off the rails. John, the oldest of the family, was a bit wild and at times an embarrassment to his father, though possibly a social asset for his sisters. He was handsome, witty, sociable, clever, a scholar of Shrewsbury, and then of the 'family college', Christ's, Cambridge, a fine athlete with a half-blue and selected as a 100-yard sprinter for the Irish Olympic team. But the company he kept was not always the best; gambling was for a time a problem; academically he disappointed; and only when he went down from Cambridge with an *aegrotat* did he settle down enough to spend a year in TCD working for the Civil Service Examinations. As a result he gained a cadetship in the Malayan Civil Service, narrowly missing selection for the Indian CS – which might have saved his life. He became a District Commissioner and Magistrate, and with his linguistic talent added to his Latin and Greek a working knowledge of French, Dutch, Tamil, Malay, and Cantonese. To add to the poignancy of his story, he fell in love with a Roman Catholic girl (whose name I never knew) in an era and in a country when mixed marriages were extremely problematical. With admirable self-sacrifice he seems to have felt that he could not inflict inevitable distress at such a marriage on his archbishop father and he never proposed. Malaya put time and distance between them but he never forgot her. His final request to my father, when they were both POWs, was to 'give her my love'. I wish I knew her name because I would have passed on the message. But I hope my father did.

Uncle John left me a legacy of some £500 (no mean sum in those days) in a will written on a scrap of paper while a POW, which some years after the war reached my father through a fellow prisoner. He had the embarrassing problem of asking his father-in-law, by then at Armagh and Primate of All Ireland, to hand over the money. It was then 'safely' invested in Government War Loan and by the time it came to me after Grandfather's death, it was seriously depleted. All the same, it started me on my life-long interest in the stock market and a hobby, which ever since has given me a great deal of pleasure, if limited profit.

Various family stories emanate from that Dublin period: Grandfather, very conscious of his duty to keep up appearances, driving to tennis matches clad in clerical garb to the waist (because it would be visible to the public) but wearing his long white tennis trousers beneath. Then there was his temporary arrest by the British army, because (according to George Seaver) he had been seen asking directions at the railway station from, of all people, the son of the republican leader Eamon de Valera, whom he closely resembled, and who years later, as Irish President, described him as his 'highly valued friend'. In those early days when, to the British, 'Dev' was still a terrorist, people had put two and two together, made at least five, and called out the army. In fact he had simply gone to have tea at a local hotel in Greystones with some old ladies and ex-missionaries, and had asked directions from a local bystander.

Mother looked back on that Dublin period as one of golden years of happiness and fulfilment, despite the events of the 1916 rebellion, the consequent struggle for Irish independence, and the ensuing civil war of the early twenties. She rarely mentioned those 'troubles' and I have no recollection of her describing her feelings at the time. However her sister Barbara's fine novel, *We Are Besieged* evokes the period well and is still worth reading. But the one thing Mother regularly talked about was her pride in the leadership, which her father, as Archbishop of Dublin, gave to the Protestant community of the South. He persuaded them that once Britain had ceded independence, it was their duty to cooperate with and acknowledge obedience to the new and lawful government. Hotheads may have counselled differently, but Grandfather was always clear that there was a god-given duty to obey legitimately constituted government (St Paul would have agreed) and his leadership may well have helped to avoid considerable bloodshed. Many eminent Protestants in the South had of course always been sympathetic to the idea of Irish nationalism, but he, certainly, helped to ensure a respected and honourable place for them in the new Free State, even though clerical and religious intolerance eroded some of the goodwill that existed at the start. If only there had been a similarly principled and far-sighted leadership of the Roman Catholic nationalist community in Northern Ireland, the country might have been spared a huge amount of bloodshed and heartbreak.

It was a measure of the respect in which Grandfather was held in the South that de Valera, when framing the Irish constitution, once called on him to ask how the Church of Ireland should be formally described. Grandfather said that the Roman Catholic church should not describe itself as simply the 'Catholic church' in Ireland, since Protestant churches were also 'catholic'. As a solution to this dilemma he pointed out that in the records of the Council of Trent the Roman church called itself 'Holy, Catholic, Apostolic and Roman'. The Church of Ireland, also catholic, but in Communion with Canterbury, designated itself the 'Church of Ireland'. He suggested that each should be described in the constitution in the form of words they themselves employed. De Valera accepted his advice and they were so designated.

Irish unity is the one subject on which I look back with profound regret. I personally had no problem with the idea, if arrived at honourably and honestly through the ballot box. I had the utmost objection to it being forced upon a reluctant majority by terrorism and undemocratic means. But I caused my mother enormous distress by my open-mindedness on the subject, which to her sounded as if I was an apologist for the IRA, which I could never have been. I had after all been a soldier during one of their less successful previous campaigns. But to defeat your enemy it is important to try and understand your enemy. Only so can you discover and undermine the sources of his strength. I felt that I could see 'where they were coming from', to use the modern cliché. To her it was treachery.

She wrote on one occasion in 1972 of her sorrow that my 'subversion had reached such a deplorable stage'. Like my father, she had lived through the troubles of the 1920s; her sister's father-in-law had been murdered by the IRA; her father had preached the duty of obedience to the law when the South gained independence, and she expected a similar loyalty to the Northern government; she had direct experience of the effects of Irish discrimination on her husband and her brother. She, my mother, had also lost friends in her own community and was living through the horrors of another IRA bombing campaign. There was I writing from the comfort and safety of my ivory tower in England, telling her of what she saw (wrongly) as my unthinking sympathy for the 'other side'. It hurt her terribly. To her the British government was guilty of a profound betrayal of its loyal people; they were selling Northern Ireland down the river.

I was in fact sufficiently sympathetic to this viewpoint that a couple of years later I wrote about it to my local MP, Ian Gow, a wonderfully conscientious and much loved Member for the local Eastbourne constituency. He summoned me to lunch in the House of Commons to hear my story. I sent him a long memo in preparation for our meeting, in which I detailed the feelings of local moderates in the province and in my covering note commented that 'it seems to me and my kind that Westminster has lost touch with the nation and I wish I could see more ways of changing the climate of opinion'. Sadly, I remarked, 'more tube-train and pub bombings seem to be the most effective way'.

That he largely agreed and was resolved, if the Tories got into government, to do something about it no doubt was a factor in his murder by the IRA.

Sadly, it is civil wars that too often divide families. Certainly my mother and her sister, Barbara Somerville, could not talk politics together, so diametrically opposed were their views on the Irish question. Barbara preferred the South and admired the Irish government, despite the murder of her father-in-law; my mother had great sympathy for the northerners, though Cousin Jewel remembers her in her younger days as having mildly republican sympathies. That her views changed radically is probably due to the influence of IRA atrocities in the North and her experience of southern intolerance and religious bigotry when her husband was looking for a job.

Echoes of ancient history: Thucydides saw and recorded similar divisions so vividly in his history of the Peloponnesian Wars, where I still find many parallels with our modern situation. In his devastating account of civil war in Corcyra (Corfu) in 427 BC, he records that 'words changed their meanings' and 'thoughtless acts of aggression became the courage you would expect from party members: moderation was a mark of cowardice; violent opinions could always be trusted; objections to them were suspect; family relationships were weaker than party allegiance; revenge more important than self-preservation; successful treachery a sign of superior intelligence'. And the cause of it all? Lust for power fuelled by violent fanaticism. In the struggle for dominance, he says, 'nothing was barred, and terrible were the actions to which men committed themselves. For war is a stern teacher and brings most people's mind down to the level of their actual circumstances.'

The only antidote is a sense of perspective, which the study of history can sometimes offer, and a willingness to contemplate the awful possibility that the other side may have some right on their side after all. Sometimes the distant view is clearer than the immediate. But it is very hard to accept this, when you feel you are in the front line of a brutal civil war. I still deeply regret the distress I caused someone so fair-minded and normally tolerant in outlook as my mother. For, as I said at the start of this chapter, I loved her this side of idolatry. But I have always tried to be fair-minded and to understand an opponent's point of view. Indeed a very good friend warned me in my early days at Campbell College as headmaster that 'here in Northern Ireland remember that fair-mindedness will always be taken as a sign of weakness'. I think I sometimes forgot this advice. But as Kipling observed,

> If you can keep your head when all about you
> Are losing theirs and blaming it on you,
> If you can trust yourself when all men doubt you,
> But make allowance for their doubting too; . . .
> Yours is the Earth . . .

Kipling understood the exigencies of empire and the savageries of war. He should be mandatory reading and learning for all school children. What he wrote of the British Tommy is no less true of government and the forces of law and order as represented by the British Bobby. In a war situation we love them only when we think they are on our side and looking after us, not 'them'.

> For it's Tommy this, an' Tommy that, an' 'Chuck him out, the brute!'
> But it's 'Saviour of 'is country' when the guns begin to shoot.

Mother graduated from TCD in 1931 one of the 'Forward Five' women undergraduates in a vintage period for women medics, though their collective soubriquet makes them sound more like the heroines of an Enid Blyton story. She won the Hudson scholarship to the Adelaide Hospital – the first woman to do so – and there gained her FRCS(I) and later went on to further training in Birmingham and Vienna, a city which she always remembered with affection and where she claimed to have existed perfectly happily and very cheaply on a diet of eggs and milk, for which her predilection lasted all her life and may well (along with butter) have done little to improve her condition in old age. Her diverse talents also won her a place on the university's women's tennis team and hockey second XI.

Her sister Barbara matched her for distinction, but as a linguist with a Senior Moderatorship in French and Italian and the Kathleen Burgess Prize in Italian. How the Irish Troubles of the early 1920s impacted on the two girls I cannot really guess; Mother spoke little of them, but living in Northern Ireland after the war until her death in 1991, she was enormously distressed by what must have felt like a repeat of those events of her early adult years.

Whether she was back in Dublin on leave or in a more permanent appointment I do not know. But another medical graduate of TCD, ten years her senior and already a consultant surgeon, came home on leave from Malaya for six months in 1936. Travel in those days by steamship was slow, and long leave was the only way in which colonial servants could find it worthwhile to come home to enjoy a proper holiday and regain touch with their families. His name was Cecil Wilson; tall; handsome; a fine athlete as well as a brilliant surgeon. Time was short for him; there seems to have been a relatively whirlwind courtship and engagement. They were married in St Patrick's Cathedral by her father, the Archbishop of Dublin, in what was apparently the 'Wedding of the Year'. Years later a very old friend of the family said to my mother, 'I always thought you were going to marry me.' 'So did I', said my mother. 'But you never asked me!' Now thereby must hang an unspoken tale of disappointment and (perhaps?) regret that might well make strong men weep.

That is where my own story begins, in Coronation year, 1937, on 16 June, in the Sepoy Lines Hospital, Singapore. I was christened Brian, with the addition of William after my paternal and John Gregg after my maternal grandfather. With a commonplace surname like Wilson, four initials have proved a useful attribute. Everyone remembers you, not for yourself or your personality, but because you have four initials. For some the pleasure of adding XYZ offers an additional source of childish amusement.

But let me first dispose of a little more family background.

CHAPTER 5

Antecedents I – Wilson Family Connections

Friends are God's apology for our relations
Hugh Kingsmill

BEFORE TURNING MORE DIRECTLY to my own story, I want to write into the record, so to speak, what I know of our family connections from family legend or occasional and desultory researches. Family history can be intensely boring to anyone but the closest members. Yet to discover connections not only with the famous and the infamous, but also with lesser figures who, in their own way, added occasional bright threads to the rich embroidery of human life can be a source of genuine pleasure to all but the most unimaginative.

For example, I know nothing about Buffalo Bill, beyond the fact that in my boyhood he was as famous as any Red Indian brave or cowboy hero portrayed on film by the late, great John Wayne. Born in 1846, he became sufficiently famous to get a brief mention in my small encyclopaedia as an army scout and Pony Express rider, who gained his nickname from his success in supplying the men working on the Union Pacific Railway with buffalo meat (in 1867–8 he is said to have killed 4,280 buffalo in eight months). He later made his name by touring the USA and Europe with his Wild West Show, which he started in 1883. He died in 1917.

His real name was William Frederick Cody and it was a strong family belief that he was a relative. My mother used to get a Christmas card each year from Dad's cousins, Helen and Jane Cody, two elderly sisters living in the USA, who she told me were related to him. Occasionally they sent me presents; one year it was a cowboy suit; another, they invited me to choose between a fine pair of brogue shoes and a Red Indian outfit. Those were the years of postwar scarcity and I still remember the silent disappointment of my mother at my entirely childish but very human decision to take the Indian outfit. They had sent photographs, which made it irresistible. But as ever, her integrity was total; it was someone else's gift and she made no effort to influence my choice.

Sadly, when I tried to establish what the exact connection was with our family, the official genealogist of the Cody family assured me that they came from the Channel Islands in about 1698, that he had a detailed family tree for all the offspring of the family since then, and that there was 'no Irish connection'. I have to believe him, yet I remain very puzzled by the existence of Cousins Helen and Jane Cody and the strong family legend that they were related to William F.

His sister, Helen Cody Wetmore, published in 1899 with a Forward by Zane Grey a biography of her brother, *Last of the Great Scouts*, deriving the family lineage from Milesius, King of Spain, whose three sons, Heber, Heremon, and Ir, founded the first dynasty in Ireland. The Cody family, she claims, comes from the line of Heremon and their home counties were Clare, Galway, and Mayo. She at least had no doubts about the Irish connection, but it clearly pre-dates the Cody connection with the USA and does nothing to invalidate the official verdict. His parents, Isaac and Mary Cody, had seven children, five daughters (Martha, Julia, Eliza, Helen, and May) and two sons, Samuel (a Wilson family name also), who died aged fourteen in a riding accident and William (again a family name), who married Louisa Fredirici at the age of twenty. He had at least three children, two girls, Arta and Orra, and a son, Kit Carson. I am still looking for Jane!

The alleged family connection derives from William Wilson of Mullingar, Westmeath, my grandfather, whose sister, Elizabeth, married an Edward Cody, also born in the year 1846. I had assumed, therefore, that Edward was in some way related to Isaac Cody, father of William, and that Jane was perhaps his daughter. This would account for Helen and Jane teaming up as two elderly widows, who sent gifts to their poverty stricken Irish relatives. Alas, I fear I may be wrong – but I am happy to let the legend live on and leave the puzzle to others. The internet entries would fill a volume on their own and the Buffalo Bill Museum, as well as Lee Norwood, the Cody Family genealogist, were very helpful to me and would no doubt assist in further researches. The Kansas Collection books acknowledge that the Cody family are 'Spanish-Irish', that on the maternal side they have links to some of the 'best blood of England', and several of the family emigrated to America in 1747. This could run and run.

When Cousin Stuart Strong sent me from America an old photograph of my Uncle Artie, I remarked to Sara, 'My goodness, he was a handsome man.' As usual the memory makes its own connections and it sent me straight back to my first Commonplace Book where I found, entered shortly after the poet's death, that delightful little poem by e e cummings (1894–1962) about Buffalo Bill. It is original in its content (which is suggestive of more than one meaning in the last two lines) and in its format (which I reproduce below, I hope correctly) and I still like to think of Cousin Bill and Annie (Get Your Gun) Oakley zapping pigeons together at their Wild West Shows 'justlikethat'. I was introduced to the poem by Michael Meredith, a colleague at Radley, who was freshly back from a period in the States and an enthusiast for American poetry. He went on to be head of English at Eton and the college librarian. He taught me more in a couple of years spent listening to his conversation than ever I learned from my teachers at school.

    Buffalo Bill's
    defunct
      who used to
      ride a watersmooth-silver
                stallion

and break onetwothreefourfive pigeonsjustlikethat
                                            Jesus
he was a handsome man
                    and what i want to know is
how do you like your blueeyed boy
Mister Death?

Apart from poor Millie, my father Cecil had two siblings: Arthur (Uncle Artie) and Mabel (Auntie Mabel). Arthur was never mentioned in the family and I grew up ever more convinced that he was some sort of black sheep, with a dark secret to conceal. He had gone off to America, like all the best and blackest of family sheep, and as far as I knew he was never heard of again. To my great surprise, only when I began to write this family memoir did I learn from my cousins Sybil and Stuart Strong that he had settled perfectly respectably in Georgia, USA, married Susan, a painter of considerable talent, and by her had two children, Susan and Moselle. I wish I had known more about him and his family and I remain puzzled as to why the families made no contact.

Auntie Mabel married William Ronaldson (Uncle Billy), who farmed Claremount, near Mullingar, about twenty miles from Castlepollard. He too had a brother, Arthur, who emigrated to New Zealand in the late 1980s and had a son, Ernest, probably named after Billy's other brother, Ernest, who was killed at Gallipoli. Was there any family lucky enough to be untouched by the appalling carnage of the First World War? Ernest and his wife Roma now live in Te Kuiti, NZ.

My memories of the various family farms, which I visited or on which I lived, tend to become conflated and impressions of life on one farm may well belong in fact to another. We were still (*circa* 1945) in the era of 'real' farming, with horses not tractors to do the hard work, and a far more labour intensive industry than modern farming has become. Now lonely men drive up and down huge fields in massive tractors, shut out from the natural world by the safety-cabs which the law demands, shut off from the sounds of living creatures by their I-pods; shut off from association with their fellow men by labour-saving technology, which has almost eliminated human beings from their work.

My childhood experience of farms at Trumroe, Claremount, and at the Palace in Armagh is very different, inextricably entwined with memories of real people, the farmers, the workers, and their children; of playing in farmyards, on haystacks, in hay barns and so on; of small fields fenced in by hedges, where we went gathering blackberries in autumn and looking for birds' nests in the spring; of vast cart-horses and massive implements of agriculture; of haymaking and harvesting; of the smells of hay barns and horses and manure. Farm work retains for me a rose-tinted memory of hard work done by the men, some help from the kids such as picking potatoes, and a highly sociable community. Laurie Lee's *Cider With Rosie* still has the power to evoke in me memories of what seems increasingly a golden childhood.

Some elements of Claremount specifically remain surprisingly vivid. Auntie Mabel and Uncle Billy first. She was a sweet person. I remember her as always smiling, always welcoming, with a lovely Irish accent from which one phrase echoes constantly, like T S Eliot's 'footfalls in the memory' – 'Och, the wee dote', she would say, whether of small child or tiny animal. 'Och, the wee dote.' Uncle Billy is less vivid, but fancy has him square-faced, strong-jawed, and of a ruddy countenance, like King David in the Bible. The thing I still remember was one occasion when we shared a bedroom, possibly because as a child I was afraid of the dark, or because our whole family coming to stay may well have put impossible demands on the house's bedroom accommodation. I am pretty sure there was no electric light, the house being lit with candles or oil lamps, whose smell still conjures up for me with absolute delight the long evenings when lamps were lit and the place acquired a rich romantic glow. I was long since in bed and 'asleep', but when he came to bed Uncle Billy simply knelt at his bedside and said his prayers, as a good Christian should. The absolutely simplicity of it all and the obvious normality of it left an impression on me forever after of a truly good man.

Water was derived from a well, I assume. Every morning someone used to pump a supply up to the header tank somewhere in the roof, which kept the house supplied. In addition there was one of those lovely long-handled pumps in the yard where you could pump a drink for yourself or the animals at any time. The dairy was pure enchantment: I was occasionally allowed to turn the handle of the 'separator' (I never heard it called anything else), which separated the cream from the milk. Some we drank – on our porridge; some went to make butter, but the churn was too heavy for me to turn, though I enjoyed beating the butter into large blocks; some was set aside for other purposes, but I know not what. The place was cool and fresh and spotless and magical. The mystery of turning cream into butter remains as strange as mediaeval alchemy.

There was a hay barn, and jumping from the upper levels to the lower was a sport for kings, but never entirely approved of, probably on the grounds of damage to good fodder not the absurdities of modern health and safety legislation. Hens as I remember it were everywhere and eggs could be found with something of the excitement of discovering buried treasure. The farmhouse looked out over big fields studded with huge trees, and dotted with contented cattle – I am sure they were Friesians, but I bet I am wrong. The orchard was filled with daffodils in the spring.

In the golden memory of childhood, life on those family farms reminds me of Virgil's descriptions in his *Georgics* of the idealised farmer's life, far removed I am sure from the daily and remorseless grind of the real thing. His most famous passage begins,

O fortunatos nimium sua si bona norint
Agricolas, quibus ipsa, procul discordibus armis,
Fundit humo facilem victum iustissima tellus.

O lucky farmers, too lucky if they could but recognise their blessings.
Far from the clash of armies Mother Earth herself
Pours out an easy living for them from the ground,
Due recompense for all their labours.

(Georgics 2.458)

But I prefer his tale of the old retired pirate from Corycum in Cilicia, pardoned by Pompey after defeat, and settled by him along with many others in the lands of southern Italy. Now that is the way to treat your erstwhile enemies. 'In defeat defiance; in victory magnanimity', as Churchill once observed.

'I remember', says Virgil, 'I once saw an old, old man – from Corycum he was. He had just a few acres of derelict land, not rich enough for ploughing with bullocks, unsuitable for pasturing his flocks, and useless for vines. But as he planted his herbs here and there amid the scrubland, with white lilies all about them, and vervain and scrawny poppies, in his mind he matched his wealth with that of emperors. Home he would come in late evening to load his table with a feast that cost him nothing. He was the first to pluck the roses in springtime and apples in autumn; and when bitter winter was still shattering the rocks with cold and halting the very rivers with its ice, there he was, already cropping the blooms of sweet hyacinths and grumbling that summer with its warm west winds was late again. That is why he was the first to gather an abundance of bees for his hives, the first to gather foaming honey squeezed from the honeycombs. His limes and pine trees grew extravagantly; and so fertile were his fruit trees that their early blossoms were matched in numbers at autumn time by the fruits they bore to maturity.'

(Georgics 4.127)

Sweet dreams of long ago! There was a dog, Jossum, and certainly one cat, since I vividly remember the one in hot pursuit of the other across the yard, travelling at barely less than the speed of light. The excitement was intense but over fifty yards the cat could match the dog and she escaped to safety up a wall and onto the roof – whence she hurled insults at her pursuer from a safe height. And then there was a pony (Johnny) and trap with gentle rides into town I suspect to do the shopping; and a jauntin' car, in which we all rode to church on Sunday. The smell of harness and horses is as evocative as ever, though horses generally have never been my scene. I was once given a riding lesson (not at Claremount) and left the saddle over the pony's head at its first hesitation and never rode again. I also inherited my mother's fatal finger for racehorses. If she backed a horse, she said, it usually died – a mild exaggeration, I have no doubt, but correct in principle. I am pretty sure she was responsible for the demise of the Queen Mother's horse, Devon Loch, which she would have backed out of loyalty for our wartime Queen. I seem to remember it dropped dead while leading in the National. Certainly the only horse I ever backed at a point-to-point led easily over the final fence and then simply turned smartly to his right and left the field. I don't bet, but in moments of wilder fantasy I have wondered whether I might have made a living by hiring myself out to others to spook the favourites.

Cousin Cecil, who inherited Claremount from Auntie Mabel, was a fine amateur jockey who rode at meets all over Ireland, and we used to watch for his results in the *Irish Times*. I think he turned the farm over to training racehorses. His own interest and the relative proximity to the Curragh – the mecca of Irish racing – must have reinforced the logic of his decision. He married Gabriel Mary Fox, whose family farm I think ran alongside Claremount. Sadly my working life has been largely in England and I have never met her, and have no recollection of having seen Cecil since my childhood. But, as the poet says, 'there will be time ... time yet for a hundred visions and revision ...'.

Cousin Sybil (Ibby) was, like Cecil, much older than myself and Audrey, and on our occasional visits she was usually away. She and Cecil existed like Olympian deities at a sort of distance from us kids. She was a very fine tennis player and the main farmyard had a tennis court at its centre, where no doubt she first learned to develop her skills. I remember her once only, when she was engaged to Stuart Strong, a graduate of the TCD medical school, who specialised in ENT and was, according to my parents, an 'absolutely brilliant' surgeon. Children notice such odd things. I remember only that he was tall, thin, and that he smoked. Who didn't in those days? When after fifty years I reported this to him, he admitted the offence. It can only have served to increase the sense of Olympian superiority, which a few years' difference in ages imposes on childish perceptions.

Stuart's story must be of great comfort to parents whose children have reading problems. He tells me that he was dyslexic and at the age of eight he could not read, since in those days dyslexia had not even been recognised as a condition. His aunt who had tried to educate him at home for three years declared him ineducable and he was packed off to boarding school, Kingsmead in Holyoke. His problem was that though literary academic courses (like logic and ethics at TCD) were impossible, 'if he could see it (and have a visual image of it) he could handle it'. Medicine suited admirably and the results were immensely distinguished.

His father had been at divinity school in TCD in 1897, but three weeks before graduation his own father (Stuart's grandfather) died and he had to return to the family farm and provide for four unmarried sisters. They were a Cavan family, mother being a Gray-Anderson from Belfast, whose father had come over from Glasgow to seek work in the linen industry. Strong churchgoers, they took their religion very seriously. The Strong household in Kells, Co. Meath had a great family Bible from which their father read at daily morning prayers; and from 1920 onwards his mother would invite 'an endless parade of missionaries on furlough from China, India, East Africa and so on' to visit. (Do I detect here the voice of a fed-up teenager?) Stuart met Sybil at an inter-varsity mixed tennis tournament in Cork and after a fairly long courtship (possibly not assisted by the somewhat daunting religious reputation of Moate House, the family home) they were married in 1950. They went out to Boston where, Stuart says, he was 'seduced by the progressiveness of the US medicine and medical schools', and there they have remained. Simon was born in 1956; Daphne in 1957. Both are themselves married, Simon to Sarah Stimpson, with three children, Hilary, Audrey, and Graham; Daphne to Laurence Foster with two, Maxwell Lawrence and Clare Ronaldson.

Not for nothing might this Memoir have been entitled *Ramifications*, since there is another branch of the Wilsons, which continues to be a source of much regret to me for my failure to make contact while I was living in Northern Ireland. As well as his sister, Elizabeth, who married Edward Cody, my grandfather William Wilson had a brother James, who married Annie Woods, the daughter of James Woods and Jane Brabazon, the daughter of Robert Brabazon and Fanny Moore. Hence the Brabazon link, of which I often heard mention in my childhood.

They had four children, William Robert (also known as 'Robin'), Maud, Samuel, and James Brabazon Wilson. Of these Samuel died young, in 1916; and William Robert (also known as Robin) stayed in Ireland in the family home, moving to the North with his parents in 1916. James Brabazon, born in 1902, married Emma Wilson, thus adding greatly to the confusion of our family tree, since there were now Wilsons on the male and the distaff sides. They emigrated to the States in 1928, taking James' sister Maud (Jane Katherine Elizabeth Maud) with them. She married another William Wilson, thus complicating the Wilson-Wilson family tree even further, since William Wilsons now existed on both sides of the family.

Pat Gunkelman, another of my American cousins, living in North Virginia and discovered in the course of my researches, is Maud ('Nana') Wilson's grandchild, the daughter of her eldest child, Verna Wilson Peters. Pat's son, Tad, has been reading medicine in Dublin, and trained at the Adelaide and then the Royal College of Surgeons. His rotations have even included a spell in Mullingar. His graduation has coincided with his marriage, with the reception at Powerscourt, in April 2006. Pat has two other sons and a daughter.

William Robert ('Robin') married Eileen Anne McGaughey, and they were the victims (I think) of my father's bad-mannered refusal to say grace at lunch, alluded to above. They had three children, Kathleen (who married Frank Weir), Alison (who married Ian Montgomery), and Philip Brabazon Wilson. Until I retired from Campbell College and began to work on the Navan Fort Initiative in Armagh, I knew nothing of Philip, even though he was my second cousin. He lived in Portadown and his house was called Sharvogue, after our grandfather's family home, where my father was born. Pat Gunkelman tells me that his mother called the house in Portadown 'Sharvogue' after their southern home, and that they had moved north in 1916 'to escape their neighbours' fate of being burned out'.

Some point of common interest (Navan perhaps?) must have brought us into contact. Philip worked for the County Armagh Education and Library Board and so we had a shared interest in things educational, but beyond a desultory correspondence we never managed to sustain the contact. Tragically he suffered a serious injury while working in the attic of his house and, though initially incapacitated, he ultimately died as a result of it, leaving a widow Lorraine and two children, Jonathan Brabazon and Anna Lesley Constance, whom (alas) I have never met.

Time and circumstance have prevented me exploring my father's childhood home as I would have wished. Family history is, I suspect, an old man's game and with limited years and energy remaining I am not sure how much more I shall discover. My first target remains Andrew Wilson of Wilson's Hospital, Mullingar. After that, we shall see.

CHAPTER 6

Antecedents II A – The Gregg Family Tree

I HAVE DIVIDED THE SUBJECT of our Gregg antecedents into two, because the ancient family tree which follows is long enough and contains enough historical interest to merit a chapter in its own right. It was copied 'from a handwritten account passed to Miss Kathleen Gregg, of Elm Grove, 65 Ranelagh, Dublin on 12 June 1936', and given by her to my mother on 2 May 1961. It was found with my mother's papers, though she died still convinced that it had been lost by George Seaver, to whom she had loaned it while he was writing Grandfather's official biography. I include it here, rather than in the appendices, because it is in narrative rather than tabulated form. It certainly offers strong support for the family claim to be descended from the MacGregors of Scotland and ultimately therefore from King Alpin.

The book itself is an old (?leather bound) account book bought from Pettigrew and Oulton of 36 Dame Street, Dublin, Printers and Stationers to the Bank of Ireland, and Account Book Manufacturers to His Majesty's Stationery Office. There is no indication of its date. But I note the present tense of the final entry (John Murray) – 'by whom he has a son, Evan John'. Is it significant? Was this originally done during Murray's lifetime? There is enclosed with the book a letter dated 8 October 1838 to R J Gregg, Paymaster Officer, from an illegible source, address 1 Kildon (??) Hse (??) sending him 'a painting of the Arms of MacGregor of Scotland from whom the Greggs of Ireland are descended, at least most of them. Can you pay the household?'

(Some names may be misspelt because the writing is not always clear; *editorial matter is in italics*)

Murray of Laurie, Perthshire Created Baronet, 23 July 1795

Though the royal descent of this most ancient clan might be traced from the chronicles of the Scottish kings to the remotest antiquity, we shall carry it no further back than their immediate and undoubted progenitor, **Prince Gregor**, third son of **King Alpin**, son of the celebrated **Achaius**, King of Scotland, who began to reign in 787.

1. Gregor had two sons, 1. **Dougallus** and 2. Gorbredus or Corbredus, from whom all the Macquaries or Macquaries, in Scotland, and Macguires in Ireland are descended. (Fordum, Andrew Winton, extracta de chronicis Scot.)

2. **Dougallus married Spontana, sister of Duncan, a king in Ireland, and their posterity got the name of Macgregor.** He died about the year 900

leaving two sons, **Constantine** and **Fruidanus**, from whom the Macfruidons, Macfruigons, or **Mackinnon**s, a numerous and warlike people are descended.

3. Constantine married **Malvina**, daughter of Donald, son of Constantine II, his namefather, who afterwards reigned under the name of Donald VI inter 890 and 904, and died greatly beloved of his subjects.

4. **Gregor de Bhraftich**, ie Gregor of the Standard, from his office of Standard-bearer to his uncle, King Malcolm I, son of Donald VI. He married Dorviegilda, daughter of the commander of the army, by whom he had two sons, **John** and Malcolm, of the Deers, so called from his having been a famous deer hunter, and keeper of the royal forests. He was succeeded by his eldest son . . .

5. . . . **John, vocatus Eion More Macgregor de Bhraftich**, who married **Alpina**, daughter of Angus or Aeneas, great grandson of Achaius, brother of Kenneth the Great, by whom he had a son . . .

6. . . . **Gregor Garubh**, or the stout, who married ------, a daughter of the ancient house of Lochow, predecessor of the family of Argyle. He fought under Duncan I in his battles against the Normans and Danes, highly resented the murder of the Monarch by Macbeth, and was a powerful promoter of the restoration of his son, Malcolm, Prince of Cumberland. He had two sons, **John**, and Gregorius obiit electus episcopus St Andred. He was succeeded by his son . . .

7. . . . **Sir John Macgregor**, Lord of Glenurchy, who was called Sir John, the Forward in Battle. He died about 1113, and left two sons, **Malcolm**, and Gregor, abbot of the monastery of Dunkeld. From him the MacNabs, or sons of the abbot, are descended. He lived to be the oldest bishop of his time, and died about 1169.

8. **Sir Malcolm Macgregor** of Glenurchy, married Marjory, daughter of William, chief of the army, and nephew of our Lord the King. (Sir Malcolm was a man of incredible strength. Being of the King's retinue at a hunting party in the forest, his majesty having attacked a wild boar or some other animal of prey, was like to have been worsted, and in great danger of his life; when Sir Malcolm coming up demanded his Majesty's permission to encounter it; and the king having hastily answered 'Een do, bait spair nocht!' Sir Malcolm is said to have torn up a young oak, and throwing himself between his Majesty and the fierce assailant, with the oak in one hand kept the animal at bay, till with the other he got an opportunity of running it through the heart. In consequence of which, his majesty was pleased to raise him to the peerage, by the title of Lord Macgregor, to him et heredibus masculis, and in order to perpetuate the remembrance of the brave action, gave him an oak tree eradicate, in the place of the fir tree, which the family had formerly carried. He was called More or Callum nan Caistal, 'Lord Malcolm of the Castles, because of the several castles which he built.)

He died about 1164, leaving three sons, 1. **William** 2. Gregor, called Gregor more graund; more because of his large stature, and graund, on account of his being ill-favoured or ugly; of him all the Grants are said to be descended. He was

Sheriff of Inverness about 1214; 3. Achaius, supposed to be the ancestor of the Mackays. Sir Malcolm was succeeded by his eldest son,

9. **William**, Lord Macgregor, who married filiam domini de Lindsay, and died 1238, leaving two sons and a daughter: **Gregor**, his heir, and Alpin, Bishop of Dumblane, from 1282 to 1290.

10. **Gregor, Lord Macgregor**, who joined Alexander II, 1240, with his followers, when that monarch went upon his expedition for the recovery of the western isles from Haco (?) of Norway. He married Marion filiam de Gilchrist by whom he had . . .

11. . . . **Malcolm, dominus de Macgregor**, strongly attached to the immortal Bruce, whom he is said to have relieved from the great chief at Lorn, at Dabriogh, and to have been mounted upon a milk white steed, and after this the King harboured in a large cave in Macgregor's lands, which to this day is called the King's Cave. He is celebrated by several bards. He died at an advanced age, 1374, leaving by Mary, daughter of Malin Macalpin, of Feunich, two sons, 1. **Gregor**; 2. Gilbert, from whom it is said the Griersons, of Lag, are descended; and several daughters.

12. **Gregor, called Aulin**, or Perfectly handsome, who married Iric, daughter of his Uncle Malcolm Macalpin, son of the said Malin, and died about 1413, leaving five sons and several daughters: 1. **Malcolm**; 2. **John, who became Lord of Macgregor**; 3. Gillespie, or Archibald, who married and had issue; 4. Gregor, of whom the family of Ruadbrudh, or Roro, are descended; 5. Dugual ciar, or mouse-coloured, whose tribe is now known by the name of Sliochd Ghregor a Chroic.

13. Malcolm died unmarried 1420 and was succeeded by his brother.

13. **John Macgregor of that ilk**, a man of very martial spirit. He married ------, daughter of the laird of Maclauchlan, a powerful and ancient chieftain in Argyleshire, by whom he had three sons and one daughter: 1. **Malcolm**; 2. **Gregor**, to whom he gave his estate of Breachdsliabh, whose heir now represents the family of Macgregor, as will be shown hereafter; 3. John. The daughter was Margaret, wife of Lauchlan More Macguarie, chief of that ancient family. John died 1461, and was succeeded by his eldest son . . . (*13. continues below after 17.*)

14. . . . **Malcolm**, who lived in the reigns of James III and IV. In his days the Macgregors lost many more of their lands. He married first ------, daughter of ------ Macintosh, by whom he had one son, **James**, and several daughters. And with a view to conciliate the difference between the two families, he married secondly Helen, daughter of Sir Colin Campbell, but was soon after murdered on the hill of Drummond, and great part of his estate seized upon. A mournful song his widow composed on the occasion is still preserved. By her he left an infant son, who survived his father only a few months. He was succeeded by his eldest son, . . .

15. . . . **James, laird of Macgregor**, who made a bright figure in the reign of James V and Queen Mary, to whom he was a hearty and powerful adherent. On

account of his loyalty he incurred the hatred of the Earl Regent and his party, by whom he and his clan were persecuted with incredible inhumanity. He had two sons, **Alexander**, and John who was killed at the battle of Glenfroon; and was succeeded by his eldest son, . . .

16. . . . **Alexander Macgregor, of that ilk**, who fought the memorable battle of Glenfroon, against the Colquhouns, Buchanans, and Gromes, 1602. Alexander having no lawful issue, and his brother John being killed at the battle of Glenfroon unmarried, the succession devolved on **Gregor** Macgregor, heir male in a direct line of Gregor, Second son of John, laird of Macgregor, of whom hereafter. Soon after Alexander's death there was a meeting in the old church of Strathfillan, where, in Gregor's absence, the tribe called Sliochd dhuil choir set up a chief of their own, in usurpation of his right; of which Gregor, 'who was a fine, daring fellow', having intelligence, hastened to the meeting; and carried with him **Gregor, a natural son** of the late Laird, a man of martial fire, who had been bred in his family, and had married his only daughter. Upon entering the church he found the new elected chief seated on a chair resembling a throne, above the rest, to him he immediately made up and threw him under his feet, and placed his son-in-law in the chair without a person daring to oppose him, and he was afterwards acknowledged chief of the whole clan, except by his brothers-in-law, when they came of age. (We have hereto subjoined an account of this affair; translated from the Latin history of the family of Sutherland, by Alexander Ross, Professor in the University of Aberdeen, in 1631).

> In the spring of the year 1602 there happened great dissensions and troubles between the Laird of Luss, chief of the Colquhouns, and Alexander, Laird of Macgregor. The original of these quarrels proceeded from injuries and provocations mutually given and received not long before. Macgregor however wanting to have them ended in friendly conferences, marched at the head of two hundred of his clan, to Leven, which borders on Luss' county, with a view to settling matters by the mediation of friends. But Luss had no such intentions, and projected his measures with a different view; for he privately drew together a body of three hundred horse and five hundred foot, composed partly of his own clan and partly of the Buchanans, his neighbours, and resolved to cut off Macgregor and his party to a man, in case the issue of the conference did not answer his inclinations. But matters fell out otherwise than he expected; and though Macgregor had previous information of his insidious design, yet dissembling his resentment, he kept the appointment and parted good friends in appearance.
>
> No sooner was he gone than Luss, thinking to surprise him and his party in full security and without any dread or apprehension of his treachery, followed with all speed, and came up with him at a place called Glenfroon. Macgregor, upon the alarm, divided his men into two parties, the greatest whereof he commanded himself, and the other he committed to the care of his brother John, who, by his order, led them about another way, and attacked the Colquhouns in the flank. There it was fought with great bravery on both sides for a considerable time; and notwithstanding

the vast disproportion of numbers, Macgregor in the end obtained an absolute victory. So great was the rout, that two hundred of the Colquhouns were left dead upon the spot, most of the leading men killed, and a multitude of prisoners taken. But what seemed the most surprising and incredible in this defeat, was that none of the Macgregors was missing, except John, the Laird's brother, and one common fellow, though indeed many of them were wounded.

The news of this slaughter having reached his Majesty's ears, he was exceedingly incensed against the Macgregors. They had not friends at court to plead their cause, and mollify his resentment, by making a fair statement of the case.

But instead of facts being placed in their proper light, everything was misrepresented in the blackest colours; and no person contradicting the insidious informations, the unhappy Macgregors were involved in inextricable troubles; for the king ordered the whole tribe to be denounced rebels, and proscribed. He further empowered the Earl of Argyle and the Campbells, to hunt them out, and drag them without any further tryal to punishment: nor indeed did they spare either industry or expenses in the execution of their commissions.

Pursuant to which there happened a remarkable conflict at a place called Bautshoig, where Robert Campbell, son of the Laird of Glenurchy, with two hundred chosen men, attacked sixty of the clan of Macgregor. In this action only two of the Macgregors, but of the Campbells no less than seven of their principal Gentlemen and many of the meaner sort fell upon the field, though they afterwards had the assurance to give out that they themselves had gained the victory. In a word, after many cruel murders and severe skirmishes, the Macgregors were in the end much humbled; and though many of them were killed, yet many more of the Campbells lost their lives on the occasions. But at length Argyle, by specious pretences and fair promises, enticed the Laird of Macgregor to come to a friendly conference, and then undertook to go along with him in person to court to be advocate himself and represent the case in such a manner that he made no doubt of reconciling him and his clan to King James. But all this was mere trick and deceit; for although he actually set out and proceeded in his intended journey as far as Berwick, yet he suddenly changed his mind, and returned to Edenbugh, where he caused the credulous old man and thirty of his relations to be publicly executed. By this exemplary punishment, Argyle imagined that he would not only put an end to the present troubles, but also open himself a door for extinguishing the whole name and tribe of the Macgregors. But things fell out otherwise than he expected. (Thus far Mr Ross.)

17. **Gregor the bastard**, in whose time this clan continued to be cruelly harassed by means of Argyle, the Earl of Montrose, chancellor, of whose tribe the Baron of Bucklivy, with many private men, were killed at Glenfroon; and of George Buchanan, Lord Privy Seal, who had much of the King's ear and bore an ill-will to the Macgregors for a like reason. To such a height of ferocity were matters carried that a price being set upon the heads of the clan by the Privy Council, two of their enemies, who had shared considerably of their estates, got bloodhounds, with which they hunted them, devouring and mangling them wherever they were found.

So keen and powerful were the conductors of their destruction, that a very severe act was made against them, whereby their name was proscribed, and all persons at liberty to mutilate or slay them, without being liable to law, nay, encouraged to it by a promise of their moveable goods and geer. In this situation the Macgregors continued till the solemn league and Covenant came in play, which, as their principal enemies were interested in, afforded them a respite. They were much courted to join the confederacy, upon promises of future friendship; but as a rebellion again Majesty had ever been detestable to them, and as they believed that the present purpose once served, the future friendship of the federates would at best be lukewarm, they declared 'That as they bore the crown on the point of their swords, they would not fail to use the latter in support of the former.'

Gregor the bastard being dead, Ewan, or Hugh, his son, and after him Malcolm, his brother's son, whose son, Gregor, and after him Archibald Macgregor, of Kilmaunon, his nephew, all of the bastard line, severally claimed the chiefship, but it was not acquiesced in by **Breachly, the real heir**, nor by any of the clan, excepting now and then by a few of Gregor a Chroic's tribe.

But as the issue of the bastard line are all extinct, we return to the **descendants of the first Laird of Breachly**, whose heir male immediately represents the house of Macgregor.

13. **John Macgregor** of that ilk, married ------ daughter of the laird of Maclauchlan, by whom he had three sons and one daughter, as before observed. [13. above]. **Malcolm** succeeded, but his heirs male failed in Alexander, [No. 16].

14. **Gregor More**, or the Great, the second son to whom his father gave the lands of Breachly, and in Glenurchy, with a numerous following of men. He lived in the reigns of James III and IV, and, grieved at the oppression of his family, raised his men and making several successful expeditions against their enemies, recovered possession of a large country, which his descendants enjoyed until the reign of James VI. He married Fuivola, or Flora, daughter of Macarthur, of Strachur (by a daughter of the family Argyle, ancestor of the present Colonel Campbele, of Strachur) by whom he had four sons and several daughters: 1. **Duncan, his heir**; 2. Gregor, a Captain of great reputation; 3. Malcolm, who married ------, daughter of Dugal Lamont of Strolaig, by a daughter of the family of Bute, by whom he had several children, from whence are some good families, and some landed commoners, in the adjoining countries, to this day; but during the general persecution, they lost their lands and took several different names as Ogilvie, Gordon, etc etc. 4. John.

15. **Duncan**, called the complete Hero, who acquired the lands of Ardchoil, and several others in Bredalbane, upon which he gave those of Breachly to his brother John. He married Mary, daughter of the Laird of Ardkinlass, by a daughter of the family of Argyle, by whom he had two sons, who survived him, 1. **Gregor**, 2. John, who was raised ot the knighthood, and was known by the title of Sir John Macgregor, of Glenrue.

16. **Gregor**, the elder son, married Isabella, daughter of Camero, of Strouhead, chief of the most powerful tribe of that name, by whom he had two sons and a daughter: **Duncan**, his heir, and Patrick, of whom the Drummonds, alias Macgregors of the Bows, and many other tribes are descended. More (??) was wife of Gregor, the bastard (No. 17) before mentioned.

Some disputes happened between this **Gregor** and Donnach a Dubh a Chruic, chief of a great family, about some marshes; a friendly meeting was appointed for adjusting the differences, but Duncan Dubh having hired eight assassins to conceal themselves in a closet where the meeting was held, on a certain signal they rushed out upon the too credulous and unguarded Gregor, who made a shift to get out of the house, and jumping into a deep pool, dragged several of the assassins after him; but from the number of stabs he had received, he was so weak when he got to the opposite bank, that the ruffians easily dispatched him. But not satisfied, Gregor's horse was sent as a token to his father; and though it is said that he dreaded some evil, he went and was murdered in the hundredth year of his age. Some mournful songs made on this occasion, are still preserved. Duncan Dubh seized upon the whole estate of this family, which with some interruptions, his posterity have enjoyed ever since.

17. **Duncan**, Gregor's eldest son, called Donach Abborach, from his having after his father's murder been carried into Lochaber by his mother's friends, as were his two brothers to Athol and Strathearn, by other relations, in order to save them from the like danger. He soon acquired such a reputation over all the high lands, that Duncan Dubh, dreading that he would make his old head answer for the murder of his father and grandfather, endeavoured by all means to bring about a reconciliation, which was at last effected by his acceptance of an offer made of his father's land, with several others in Glenlochry, in consequence of which the Duncans were sworn to an inviolable friendship, in presence of a numerous meeting of friends of both parties.

Duncan married first, Christian, daughter of the ancient family of Macdonald, of Keppoch, by whom he had a son, died young; secondly, ------, daughter of Macfarlane, of that Ilk, descended of the noble family of Lennox, by whom he had three sons, 1. **Patrick**; 2. Robert, who laid the plan of attacking the Colquhouns in battle, and to whose gallant conduct the success of that victorious, though unlucky day, is chiefly attributed, and his sword is actually preserved to this time; 3. Alpin, who married and had issue.

18. **Patrick**, who succeeded, was contemporary with Malcolm, grandson of Gregor the bastard, who aspired to the chiefship; but the clan unanimously followed this Patrick, whose valour and conduct qualified him for a leader. He joined Montrose, in the support of the Royal cause, with above a thousand of his clan. Mr Nisbet, in mentioning the loyalists, says, 'The Macgregors also, a clan inferior to none in bravery and activity, followed this chief.'

Patrick was in particular esteem with Montrose, two of whose letters are carefully preserved addressed to His Special and Trusty Friend, the Honourable

Patrick, Laird of Macgregor; that great man, in the strongest terms, expressed his hearty approbation of his unshaken loyalty, and assured him that 'His Majesty's affairs being once upon a permanent footing, the grievances of his family and clan should be effectually redressed.' But their chief hopes died with this great hero, though they were, in consequence of their loyalty, restored to their name, by act of Parliament, temp. Charles II.

He married Marian, daughter of Macdonald of Auchatrichatan, chief of the most powerful tribe of the Macdonalds in Glenco, by whom he had three sons, 1. **John**; 2. James, a major in the army, a man of great ambition, and being disappointed in his views went to America, where he married and acquired a great estate. He was at last killed by a party of rebel Indians; but some of his posterity still remain in a flourishing way, near New York; 3. Duncan died unmarried.

19. **John**, the eldest son, was a steady loyalist. In the time of King William, in an act entitled 'an act for erecting a justiciary in the highlands' is a clause rescinding Charles II's restoring the Macgregors (which is now considered as oppressive, and very little regarded) which so provoked the clan, that they were determined to be revenged on a great family in the neighbourhood, and to put John in the possession of the estate of his predecessors, in resentment of the cruel oppressions they brought upon the clan. But John, however sensible of their misfortunes, yet unwilling to be the cause of so much bloodshed, or to make the sons suffer for the actions of their fathers, argued the clan out of their resolution.

He married Ann, daughter of Macgregor, of Ross, by whom he had a son, **John**, and several other children.

20. **John, of Macgregor**, alias Murray, who amassed considerable property. It is said he was of essential underhand service to the attempt of 1715, but was cautious of embarking publicly, and therefore none of his clan took arm, excepting Dugal Cier's tribe, under the famous Rob Roy.

He married **Catherine**, eldest daughter of Hugh Campbell, of Lix, Esqr. By Beatrix, eldest daughter of Capt. Archibald Campbell, of Tory, Esqr., second son of the Laird of Dunstaffrage, by Janet, daughter and heiress of Robert Buchanan of Leny, by Margaret, aunt of Lady Jean Campbell, wife of George, second Earl of Panmure; and of Lady Ann, wife of John, third Lord Balmerino; and grand aunt of Lady Margaret Campbell, wife of Colin, Earl of Balcarvas; and of Lady Eleanor, wife of James, Viscount Primrose, and afterwards of John, Earl of Stair; and of Lady Mary Maude, wife of Charles, first Earl of Marr; and which Margaret was sister of John, first Earl of London, Lord High Chancellor of Scotland.

By this lady he had five sons, 1. **Robert**; 2. Peter, who married and left a daughter, Catherine, wife of John Gregorson, an officer in the second battalion of Royal Americans; 3. **Duncan**, who now represents the family, was sore wounded at the battle of Preston, in 1745, by which he is lame of a leg, and has a son, John, and a daughter, Drummond-Mary; 4. **Evan**, of whom hereafter; 5. John, who signalised himself at the siege of Carthagena, under General Wentworth, in 1740.

In the last war, at the attack of the French trenches at Ticonderago, he received two wounds by musket balls, yet could not be prevailed upon to retire, but marched on sword in hand, with the boldness of a lion, encouraging his men, till a third killed him on the spot; deservedly regretted by all his acquaintance.

21. **Robert**, of Glencurnick, assumed the name of Murray at the request of His Grace, the late Duke of Athol. He was attached to the interest of the Stewart family, and had the command of a regiment of his own clan in 1745, and mortgaged his whole fortune to forward it, which soon after his death was the means of carrying off the estate. When the Duke of Cumberland was informed that the Macgregors were in Bradenoch, Mr William Gordon, minister of Alva (himself of the name) was by the Duke's order sent to treat with the clan to lay down their arms and return home, with power from his highness, to assure that, if they complied, they should be restored to their name, and otherways favoured and countenanced by government: or if they would join his royal highness, that their commanders should have the same rank, and their promotion be esteemed the special care of his royal highness.

To which embassy, after holding a council of war, Glencarnock returned for answer: 'That he and his clan thought themselves highly obliged to his royal highness for the honour he had done them; but that, having embarked in this affair, they could not now desert it, whatever they might suffer should it misgive. That on the one hand, though his highness might love the treason, he must needs hate the traitors; and on the other, they would justly incur the odium of their own party: that therefore, they chose rather to risk their lives and fortunes and dye with the characters of honest men, than live in infamy and hand down disgrace to their posterity.'

After the battle of Culloden, the Macgregors marched in a body to their own country with flying colours, and then dispersed into small parties.

Soon after, the king's troop, conducted by an officer, burnt all the houses on Glencarnocks estate, carried off the cattle. Glencarnock having surrendered himself to General Campbell, Duke of Argyle, was, with the Earl of Kelly, and others, confined for several years in the castle of Edinburgh; during which time, he overcame, and by the violence of the fall broke the leg of, an English officer of great strength, who boasted that no man in Scotland could wrestle with him.

He married first, Christian, daughter of John Campbell of Roro, Esqr. By whom he had one daughter, Christian, wife of Capt. John Graham of the 42nd regiment, brother to Thomas Graham of Duchray, Esqr, and has issue. He married secondly Robina-Jacobina, daughter of the brave Major Donald Cameron, son of the celebrated Sir Ewan Cameron, of Lochiel, said to have died without issue male, for he had another daughter, Isabel, wife of Sir Archibald Sinclair. By the said Robina-Jacobina he had several children, all of whom died young, except John, who, like his ancestors, ambitious of military glory, went abroad a volunteer, under General Lord Loudon, and highly distinguished himself upon several commands. At the siege of Louisburg he gave signal proofs of his bravery; but having, with more boldness than prudence, jumped upon the breastworks to view the enemy, he was laid prostrate on the bed of honour, by a cannon ball, which carried off his head, deservedly regretted by all his acquaintance, and most sincerely lamented by his relations.

Glencarnock married, thirdly, Mary-Ann, daughter and heiress of William Drummond of Hawthornden Esqr one of the ancient honourable cadets of the most noble family of Perth, by Mary, Sister of Sir John Miln, governor of Guernsey, Bart., by whom he had no issue. He died at Edinburgh, Oct.1758, universally esteemed. We now return to . . .

21. . . . **Evan**, fourth son of John and brother of Robert, in whose regiment he was a major, and suffered exceedingly in the same cause. He was afterwards appointed an officer in the 88th regiment, and served in Germany, where his gallant behaviour on several occasions attracted the notice of the highest of the British army, and after the reduction of the 88th, he was put into the 41st regiment, lying in the island of Jersey.

He married Janet, youngest daughter of John Macdonald of Balgony, Esqr, by that celebrated favourite of the muses, the pious and charitable Mrs Alicia Mackenzie, aunt of Isabella, mother of Dunbar, Earl of Selkirk, and third daughter of the brave Major Kenneth Mackenzie, of Suddy, by Isabella Paterson, daughter of the Right Revd. John, Lord Bishop of Ross, by whom he had several children, 1. **John**; 2. James, died young; 3. Alexander, who married Frances, daughter of ------ Pascull, by whom he had Frances-Janetta, who died young; Evan-Edward-Hastings-Pascull; and Alexander, a Captain in the 90th Regiment of foot; 4. Peter, a Lieutenant-Colonel in the service of the East India Company, who married Eliza Futing (??); 5. Robert, also in the military service of the East India Company; and two daughters, Alicia and Peggy.

> 1. **John Murray, Esq Colonel in the East India Company's service, auditor General of Bengal, was created a Baronet, as above; married Anne, daughter of Roderick Macleod, by whom he has a son, Evan-John.**

Arms – Argent, a sword in bed, azure, and an oak tree eradicated in bend sinister, proper, in chief a crown, gules.

Crest – A lyon's head, crowned with an antique crown with points.

Supporters – on the dexter (alluding to the royal descent) an Unicorn, argent, crowned, horned, or; and on the sinister, a deer, proper, tyned, azure.

Motto: Een do, bait spair nocht.
Seat: Laurie, Perthshire.

(Note by BW: Here the main document ends. It is followed, in a similar but I suspect not the same, hand by a table (so called), which in note form summarises the above and then continues with the Gregg connection.)

The Gregg connection is not precisely established but seems probable. The biography of my grandfather by George Seaver offers an abbreviated account of the family tree probably based on that given above and I quote from it here, since it may help to make the account more comprehensible. It states that . . .

> In 1603 was fought the battle of Glenfruin between the Macgregors and the Colquhouns, as a result of which the former were proscribed. Many sought to restore their fortunes in Ireland under the names Gregg, Greer, Greir, Gregory, and other variants; and in the same century record is found of John Gregg and of his son (or brother) Jonathan Gregg of Cappagh. Jonathan's elder son Richard Gregg of Cappagh, born about 1700, married Eliza Robinet of Cork. Their fourth son, Richard Gregg of Cappagh and Ennis, born 1747 and died 1808, inherited the small family property. He married Barbara, daughter of William Vesey Fitzgerald of Ashgrove, Co. Clare and by her had twelve children. Richard Gregg died intestate and the property passed against his expressed wishes to his eldest son Richard 'in whose hands it did not increase'.
>
> His wife, who survived him was a Roman Catholic but was converted to the Protestant form of faith by her famous son John. She was also a sister of the Right Honourable James Fitzgerald, whose two sons were in succession the first and second Lords Fitzgerald and Vesey, of whom the first especially was to prove a good friend to his cousin John. (His second son, Robert, was the father of James Fitzgerald Gregg, born in Meath 1820, graduate of TCD in 1843, ordained in 1844, and was Vicar of Yoxford in Suffolk. He was Dean of Limerick from 1899 to 1905 and was an eloquent preacher of Evangelistic views).

CHAPTER 7

Antecedents II B – Gregg Family Connections

FROM MY EARLIEST DAYS, almost, I was aware of the importance of my Gregg family connection and the very high regard in which my grandfather was held wherever we went. This was not something inculcated into me by my parents. In fact from them I had no feeling that we were in any way different from any other 'normal' family. But even as a small boy I found that people outside the family seemed to be interested in me because of my grandfather. I was constantly told what a great man he was, what a great leader of the church he had proved, what a brilliant scholar he was, and how he had regularly 'defeated' the Roman Catholic hierarchy in religious and doctrinal controversy, thus defending the Anglican position and boosting the morale of his somewhat demoralised flock.

His little booklets, on the *Ne Temere* Decrees, which I have not been able to find or read, alas, and on the absurdity of some of the mythical accretions imposed by Rome on the early doctrine of the universal church (*The Primitive Faith and Roman Catholic Developments*), which I have read and found entirely persuasive, and above all his 'victory' in the Macrory correspondence in the *Irish Times* which, according to Protestant legend at least, led to Cardinal Macrory, the Roman Catholic Archbishop of Dublin, being ordered by the Vatican to desist from further public discussion with his formidable opponent, the Protestant Archbishop of that same city, because he was losing the battle – all these matters gave my grandfather an almost legendary status in Ireland in his lifetime. And even now, more than forty years after his death, elderly clergy at least still remember him with affection and admiration. My old friend and Rector, the late Canon John Barry, the immortal and inimitable 'Cromlyn' of the *Church of Ireland Gazette*, was but one of many in this respect. In at least two of his articles as recently as 2005 (both in my Commonplace Books) he mentioned him, once on the subject of the need for and the efficacy of prayer, and the other on his old saying that 'it may be that it is the true mission of the Church to disappear', which I had mentioned in *A Faith Unfaithful*, my own collected Sermons and Addresses.

To quote James McCann, his successor as Archbishop of Armagh,

> he was a unique person. Throughout many years of public life he wielded quite exceptional influence in the Irish Church and was a recognised leader of the Anglican Communion . . . His guiding hand held together the people of the Church of Ireland when the country was divided politically . . . and in later years he adapted himself in a remarkable way to the many changes that followed the ending of the Second World War.

The effects of all this on a boy of tender years were peculiar. Quite apart from any normal parental ambitions for me, as if by osmosis I felt a burden of obligation, indeed expectation, that I should 'do well' for his sake. It was an obligation entirely self-imposed, for neither he nor my parents ever gave expression to any such thing. But he had lost both his sons and I was therefore the senior male of my generation and I could not forget it. So when, in one of the great moments of my life and to my considerable surprise, I got a First in Part 1 of the Cambridge Classical Tripos, his comment to my mother that it was 'absolutely beautiful' was perhaps more important to me than any other expression of pleasure. When in Part 2 I ended up only with a 2.1, my sense of failure was palpable.

There is no need to say more about him. His official biography by George Seaver gives an admirable account of both his thought and his leadership of the church. His distinctions were legion: Doctorates of Divinity, Honorary Fellow of Christ's, his old Cambridge college, Editor of the *Wisdom of Solomon*, the dedication of a chapel 'to the glory of God and in memory of Archbishops Plunket and Gregg' in St Paul's Cathedral, Lisbon (the Irish Protestant church, through its bishops, had acted as a sort of foster parent to the repressed minority churches of the Iberian peninsula, Portugal in particular). His appointment as Companion of Honour by the Queen was a great surprise to him, for he was essentially a very humble man, but naturally a source of considerable pleasure at the end of a long life of service to the church. The medallion remains a family treasure.

What is worth saying is that the Gregg family have been associated with the Anglican Church of Ireland for two centuries at least and have served both God and His church in holy orders – or as missionaries in the case of the women – for all that time. As Seaver puts it, 'Gregg, Son & Grandson, Bishops and Archbishops to the Church of Ireland, have passed into ecclesiastical history'.

It all started with Richard Gregg of Cappagh and Ennis, who married Barbara Vesey Fitzgerald (aunt of the Lords Fitzgerald and Vesey). Their son, John Gregg (1798–1878) married Elizabeth Nicola Law and so by various ramifications related us to Bernard Law Montgomery, the victor of Alamein, and Henry Montgomery, an early Bishop of Tasmania. Stephen Law, Grandfather's cousin, was the senior partner of his highly respected legal practice in Dublin and was for many years the Gregg family's solicitor. He regularly brought his family on holiday to the Fort Hotel in Greencastle, County Donegal at the same time as us, and I always remember his wife, Cousin Ida, for her saintly sweetness of nature. Everyone adored her. Their son, Robert, was an ex-pupil of Campbell College, and one of the most brilliant literary scholars of his year at TCD, a sparkling conversationalist in a city famous for its wit. He died far too young, in his early fifties, and sadly I only knew him as a boy before his promise was fulfilled. His sister, Barbara, is a close friend of my sister Audrey, and godmother to her Margaret. She was, and I think still is, a distinguished and devoted social worker, dedicated to welfare work among the addict communities of her native city.

John Gregg, though the 'orphan child of the only Protestant family in one of the obscurest parishes in the most neglected county of Ireland' (his own words) was a brilliant scholar, a fluent Celtic speaker, a fine athlete, and such a powerful preacher that in 1835 Trinity Church was specially built for him near the Customs House in Dublin to accommodate the crowds of up to 2,000 (many of them poorer Roman Catholics, because he spoke Celtic) who flocked to hear him. He was made Bishop of Cork, Cloyne and Ross in 1862 and was largely responsible for the building of the new St Fin Barre's Cathedral, designed in the French Gothic style by Burgess, one of the most distinguished architects of the day. It is one of the architectural gems of Ireland and one of the few cathedrals where the same Bishop laid the foundation stone (in 1865), and saw it through to consecration (1870). He was the greatest pulpit orator of his generation and I still have three volumes of his sermons and addresses (*Memorials of John Gregg DD*), published by subscription in my shelves. His son Robert succeeded him as Bishop of Cork, and went on to become Archbishop of Armagh.

John Gregg had three sons and three daughters. The eldest son, my great-grandfather, John Robert (Vicar of Deptford and father of John A F, my grandfather), died of TB, having suffered all his life from ill health, which prevented him from realising the potential which the family believed to have been greater even than that of his distinguished younger brother, Robert Samuel. The second, William Henry, died young, aged nineteen. But the third, Robert Samuel (1834–1896), became Dean of Cork, then Bishop of Ossory, then of Cork, and ultimately Archbishop of Armagh.

Of John Gregg's three daughters, I know nothing of Elizabeth beyond the fact that 'she always had to be allowed to win at games, because she was the stupid one'. The source of this comment is unknown to me, but it sounds like a typically sisterly remark!

Frances Fitzgerald ('Fanny') was a remarkable lady. In 1872 she founded the Home for Protestant Incurables (humorously referred to locally as the Home for Incurable Protestants). The Victorians were content to call a spade a spade, but in the end political correctness prevailed and in 1966 the name was changed to St Luke's Home. It started, modestly enough, in Albert House, Victoria Road, Cork, with nineteen residents. By 1879 it had to move to larger accommodation on Military Hill, where the new Home was opened by Frances' brother, the new Bishop of Cork. In 1959 further accommodation (St Brendan's House) was added and yet another extension in 1962. Finally in 1993 the decision was taken to re-build on a greenfield site in Mahon, and in 1995 the new Home was opened by Mary Robinson, President of Ireland. Further additions followed, and now 120 residents are accommodated in four units of thirty each, one dedicated entirely to the care of sufferers from Alzheimer's. The founder's name is still honoured and the Home is a wonderful tribute to her memory. Finance was always a challenge, but the whole community has always been tremendously supportive, irrespective of religious allegiance. And at the moment of writing (February 2006) a huge bequest, thought to be worth some fifteen million euros, from a former resident has set St Luke's finances on a secure foundation for the foreseeable future.

John Gregg's third daughter, Charlotte Browne, married Samuel Owen Madden, later Dean of Cork, and father of Owen Madden, Rector of Castlehaven and Canon of Cork Cathedral, a brilliant mathematician and Senior Wrangler at Trinity College, Cambridge. All the male Maddens were called Owen (Irish: Eoghan), as far back as records go, and they were a very ancient Irish family, who lost their money and fell upon hard times. Owen (junior) lived in the Rectory at Castletownshend, which proved a haven of refuge for my mother and her sister Barbara, who holidayed there nearly every summer.

Another of Samuel Owen Madden's children was Geraldine Evans (née Madden, of course), whose daughter Jewel was a distinguished concert pianist, a great friend of my mother and of her sister Barbara, whom (like Aunt Biddy) she claims to have introduced to her future husband, Michael Somerville. 'Cousin' Jewel, who celebrated her ninetieth birthday in December 2005, married Dr Steven Smith, and lives near Crowborough, in a house with a glorious garden. She still has a remarkable memory, and is my most venerable source of material about the Greggs and their time in Cork. She was a bridesmaid to my mother and still remembers the occasion. Other bridesmaids included Clodagh Greenwood, Edith Synge, a niece of the great playwright, John Synge, whose grandsons, Lanto, Teran and Barty, I once taught at Mourne Grange when I acted briefly as a stand-in teacher, and Sheila May, an actress at the Gate Theatre, 'the only one whose good looks could not be ruined by the ghastly olive green dresses we all had to wear'. Margaret Griffith was the last of the team that Jewel could remember. She was a great character and friend of the family, whom I remember well, partly because of her extremely generous presents that arrived each Christmas. She used to join us on holiday at the Fort Hotel, Greencastle in County Donegal, and I still remember her as great 'craic', with shrieks of laughter and an irresponsible approach to the deadly serious business of bridge, which will have irritated my father immensely, and for which I could have forgiven her anything. They must have had a wonderful party after the ceremony, doubtless organised by Nigel Kinnear.

Samuel Owen Madden (senior) (1831–1891), the Dean of Cork, was the son of Owen Madden (1790 – 1853) and Sarah Tarrant. Owen, the father, was a bank director, a JP, and through his wife inherited ownership of the Mallow brewery. (In those days dowries were important, and it was often difficult for young ladies in straitened circumstances to marry – another factor in the decline of the great Protestant families). He was nicknamed 'The Rake of Mallow', and was suspected of having fathered half the county! So it was a prosperous and successful family. Sadly the son, Samuel Owen, the Dean, died at the early age of sixty, leaving behind a family of nine children, of whom the youngest was barely one year old.

The loss of a dean's salary must have been a severe blow to his widow, but the Maddens owned a lot of property around Mallow, which might have enabled them to manage adequately.

But then came the crowning blow: Gladstone's Land Act. In his first government he disestablished the Church of Ireland, which meant that Roman Catholic farmers no longer had to pay tithes to the church. He also pushed through his first Land Act, whose effects were symbolic rather than effective, but stated that any farmer evicted from his land, who had made improvements to it, was entitled to compensation. Then in his second government, in an effort to stem the flood of evictions resulting from the agricultural depression of the 1870s and 1880s, he passed the Arrears Act, which stated that any tenant paying an annual rent of less than £30 (a large enough sum in those days) no longer had to pay arrears. The Maddens lost heavily as a result, though they still managed to educate the boys at Repton and the girls at good English schools.

One of the girls, Geraldine Madden, trained as a nurse and then, quite possibly to get away from home, trained as a missionary in London ('delivering babies on newspapers behind Charing Cross') and went out to China with the CMS to serve on a mission station. It was staffed by missionaries of varying nationalities and from different church denominations. She disliked the Methodists and found American fundamentalists difficult, and after three months decided that she admired the Chinese rather more than the missionaries, and thought that they would have been much better off without Christianity.

She then became a theatre sister and her supervising surgeon who was training Chinese doctors, was a Dr George Evans. They married and their daughter Jewel (b 1915), mentioned above, is the source of much of this information. Sadly, of the Jennings family she knew little. They were, of course 'in trade' and therefore seen in those days as socially inferior to the Maddens. Rose Margaret (Meg) was 'a dear, who sadly never married', while of the twins Eithne was 'a strong character, who married Eddie White, the Rector of Kantul, and had a daughter, Elizabeth, who died tragically at the age of ten'. Muirne, she says, was a source of some anxiety to her family, being 'flighty', and susceptible to anything in trousers ('often gold-diggers of unsuitable age') until she met Bernard Gedge, who was 'very good for her and settled her down'. Anna 'brought money into the Gregg family and a good business head, which enabled them to manage even on a clerical stipend'.

From Jewel I learned, too, that my grandfather (son of John Robert, Vicar of Deptford, not Robert Samuel, Archbishop of Armagh) had three sisters. Katherine was one of the first woman doctors and very distinguished, just as her niece, my mother, was to become one of the first women surgeons to train in Ireland. She went out to India to work for the Church Missionary Society, but sadly died of cholera. There is a moving letter from a Mary Townsend to her mother describing her last illness and her funeral, from which I quote the following extract.

The coffin was covered with white, and many friends sent flowers. The authorities lent a gun-carriage; there being no hearse in Peshawar, I believe they usually do so. Miss Vines arrived late on Thursday night, and she thought you would like the grave to be in the English Cemetery, where it will always be guarded in case of any Frontier trouble, and not in the Christian Cemetery, which has before now been desecrated. The funeral procession left here at 4 o'clock. All the missionaries (men) acted as bearers, and they, with the native Christians, walked down behind the gun carriage until they got outside the City. They would have walked all the way but the distance was too great. Dr Lankester told me how struck he was with the reverent way the men of the City behaved while the coffin passed down, and we heard since that some of the leading men said on Friday to one of the English police officials, that she was not only such a good doctor, but such a good woman. All our nurses went to the funeral. We sent them down first, and all the missionary party were there, and several outside friends. The service was in English and was a great comfort to us all. We laid her to rest 'in the sure and certain hope of the Resurrection'. The Cemetery is at the edge of the Cantonments, under the shadow of the Frontier hills she loved so much.

It is a moving account of an admirable young woman, who won the love and admiration of all who knew her, and 'having lived faithfully a hidden life' died in the service of others, far from home, as so many others of her kind had done before and since, and now 'rest in unvisited tombs'.

Hilda Caroline, Grandfather's second sister, lived most of her life in Eastbourne. She wrote successful historical novels about India (where she had never been) and the Balkans, under the name of Sydney C Grier. Of the three volumes in my possession, my copy of *Berringer of Bandeir*, published by Blackwood in 1919, already lists some twenty-seven novels, a Modern East series, an Indian, two Balkan, a Century, an Island, and a Princess series, together with an edition of the *Letters of Warren Hastings*, price six shillings (about 30p). As a child Jewel remembers long views of her works in the library shelves, and being taken to tea with her once, in Eastbourne. She was intimidating both by reason of her intellect and her immense fatness, rivalled only by that of her cat, which was of similarly disproportionate size.

The third sister was Mary Penelope Valpy, so named after Richard Valpy, the famous classicist and headmaster of Reading Grammar School (a connection of which Grandfather was always particularly proud), and his wife Mary Penelope French, who was the great aunt of the famous Ronnie Knox ('Cousin Ronnie'), son of the Protestant Bishop of Manchester, the most brilliant scholar of his generation, who 'went over to Rome', and became a Monsignor. Mary Valpy married Martin Gurney, and used to act as chaperone to the Gregg sisters and Cousin Jewel, when they stayed with their unmarried cousin, Owen Madden (junior), in his Castletownshend rectory. Proprieties were clearly much more strictly observed in those days. She was religious, very fundamentalist, and 'a real horror and a pain', according to Jewel, but 'a tremendous personality' (presumably in the true Latin sense of the word, 'one to be feared and trembled at'). I dare say there was some compensation in the fact that she had three 'very good-looking boys', one of them presumably Cousin Jock (Brigadier Jock Gurney), whose name cropped up often in family discourse, though I never met him.

I have already said something of my mother's sister, Aunt Barbara, who married Michael Somerville of Castletownshend, in chapter 4. But it is worth expanding the Somerville story a little for the sake of completeness and because all through the Gregg story this remote little former fishing village in West Cork, a relic almost of old England and the Ascendancy, has figured as a sort of leitmotif. The Somerville connection with Castletownshend and West Cork goes back at least as far as the 1690s, when the Rev William Somerville (1641–1694) fled from persecution in Scotland in 1690, crossing to Donaghadee in an open boat with his family and his wife, Agnes Agnew, daughter of Sir Patrick Agnew of Lochinver. They eventually settled in Dublin. Their son Thomas (1689–1752) went to TCD and became Rector of Castlehaven, which of course includes Castletownshend. His son, Thomas II (1725–1793) married Mary Townsend of Rosscarberry. Known as Tom the Merchant, he made a fortune trading in commodities in the West Indies. He built the tower on Horse Island at the entrance to Castlehaven as a beacon for shipping, and built Drishane House as his home in the village in 1790. It is still in the family and I remember it as one of the 'great houses' of the village in my childhood. His son, Thomas III (1760–1811) married Elizabeth Becher Townsend (we later got to know the Becher family, who were descendants, when Brigadier (I think) Becher was stationed in Lisburn). Their son Thomas IV (1797–1882) married Henrietta Townsend of Castletownshend, and their son Thomas V (1824–1898) married Adelaide Coghill, the daughter of Admiral Sir Josiah Coghill and Anna Maria Bushe, whose father Charles Kendal Bushe was the Lord Chief Justice of Ireland.

From that union of Somervilles and Coghills sprang a distinguished line. Edith Oenone Somerville, author and artist, and Honorary Litt. D of TCD, was famed for *The Experiences of an Irish RM*, but less well known for her competence as an artist. I still have one of her paintings of Castlehaven and Horse Island, mentioned above; two Vice Admirals, Boyle (1863–1936), father of Michael, of the Royal Navy Hydrographic Survey, assassinated by the IRA; and Hugh, whose son Phillip, a Commander in the Royal Navy (1906–1942), won two DSOs and two DSCs but never married. Hildegarde married Sir Egerton Coghill, whose son, Nevill, won great renown as a Chaucerian scholar and translator of *The Canterbury Tales*. Nevill himself was godfather to a pupil of mine at King's Canterbury, Anthony Jones, whose parents (Kenneth and Anna) celebrated their silver wedding at the Carlton Towers in London. Nevill gave the speech with characteristic elegance and eloquence, while the music was by the Temperance Seven, one of the great groups of the sixties and seventies. Sara hates dancing and was pregnant with Anna, but I insisted that just once we must get onto the floor, because one day there will not be many people who can claim to have danced to the music of the Temperance Seven. I am prepared to swear they played 'Home in Pasadena'; but if they didn't, they should have.

Aylmer (1865–1928), their fifth child by his first wife, Emmy Sykes, was the father of Desmond (1889–1976) whom I remember well because he was the finest helmsman in the south-west, winning most of the races in local regattas, and he took me sailing more than once in his dinghy, *Coquette*. He married Moira Roche and their two sons, Christopher ('Dan') who still has a house down at the Rectory Strand at the lower end of Castlehaven, and Nicholas have between them given him six great-grandchildren, Harriet, Thomas, and John from Dan and Celia, Jennifer Pippa, Penny, and Robin from Nicholas and Jennifer.

Aylmer's daughter Elizabeth by his second wife, Natalie Turner, brought links with the Chavasses, another local family, through her marriage to Paul Chavasse, a captain in the Royal Navy. They also had a lovely house in Castletownshend, called Seafield, where there was, I think, a tennis court on which their children Timothy and Isobel used to play. They were six and two years my seniors, and therefore dwelt among the unreachable Olympian divinities of childhood hierarchies, but if my memory is not faulty, Isobel was a tall and striking redhead, to whom only John Betjeman could have done justice, while Timothy was kind enough on one occasion, aged perhaps sixteen and probably mildly contemptuous of his landlubbery cousins, to take my sister and myself on as crew in the local regatta for the Ancient Britons Race. In this, competing as 'Sea-Devils' and clad in nothing but seaweed and anti-wasp bluebag paint all over, and with our rowing boat rigged with a simple mast and sheet for a sail like an ancient Viking long ship, we were paddled heroically by Timothy into an undistinguished last place. Between them Timothy, who married Philippa Roche, and Isobel who married Robert Stileman, added another five to the splendid tally of Aylmer's eleven great-grandchildren. 'Happy the man that hath his quiver full of them.' Hal Chavasse, probably a cousin, was a Lieutenant in the Royal Irish Fusiliers, when I joined the regiment. He was to be decorated for bravery in picking up an IRA bomb and carrying it out of the barracks, thus preventing casualties at considerable risk to himself.

Michael Somerville, son of Vice Admiral Boyle, married Barbara, my mother's sister. A fine linguist, he went to Oxford where I believe there is a university of some minor distinction, served in the war, and then joined the French oil company, Total, where his linguistic skills were doubtless used to good effect. I remember him as infinitely kind, of exemplary patience and love for Aunt Barbara when her severe diabetes began to take its toll of her health, blessed with a prodigious memory and sharp as a razor even in advanced old age, always interested in family matters, and a limitless source of information about them. They are a remarkably long-lived family, and he it was who told me the story, already mentioned, of how the mother of his aunt as a young girl at a ball in Paris in 1815 handed the Duke of Wellington his sword as he set out for the battle of Waterloo.

Their daughter, Christina, I have never been able to forgive for being eleven days older than me! In our early days she was bigger too, which was doubly humiliating. When both families lived in the Palace at Armagh during the war, we squabbled a lot. Aunt Barbara once told me that I was a pain in the neck at that time – and I have to believe her. Modern psychology would no doubt find appropriate extenuating circumstances. I suspect that part of the reason why I was sent away to boarding school was to tame and civilise me. But I have no recollection of being other than a perfect child and as testimony to my innocence I still bear, almost invisibly, on my arm the scar where 'Kik' once bit me – probably under provocation, having been driven to distraction by my tiresome behaviour.

Kik, like her mother, had a distinguished academic career, getting a first in horticulture from London University. She married Simon Hoare, and they have three children, Patrick, Edward, and Francis ('Fran'). Simon was for many years a much-loved Rector of Carleton in Craven in the Yorkshire Dales, and is now a Canon Emeritus of Bradford Cathedral. If Castletownshend is the leitmotif of my tale, then the church connections of our families is most surely the main theme. Patrick has continued the tradition and was ordained Deacon on 2 July 2006 in Birmingham Cathedral, and is now a curate in Solihull.

Julian, Christina's brother, was born in Dublin during the war and his arrival as a new baby in the Palace in 1944 was a source of considerable excitement, though the mechanics of the arrival were as far as I know not a matter of any interest to us children. A pupil and Head of House at King's Canterbury, fortunately before I arrived on the staff there, he studied medicine at TCD, and until he retired was a Consultant in Urology in Halifax. He married Dione Powell, a high-powered anaesthetist, and they have two children, Nigel and Grainne, who married a Kiwi, Graeme Scott, and is now settled in Christchurch, New Zealand.

There are strong Somerville connections with Australia and New Zealand, through the Allen family, descendants of George Allen of Ferns, Co. Wexford (d 1663), who was forced to abandon his family estates on the borders of Sherwood Forest, after opposing Oliver Cromwell, and presumably settled in Ireland. Later descendants included Richard Allen, doctor to the Prince of Wales, later George IV. When he died in 1806 his widow, Mary, married a Thomas Collicott, who was later sentenced to death for defrauding the Revenue, but had his sentence commuted to transportation to New South Wales after intervention by the Duke of Kent, father of Queen Victoria. He was soon pardoned, and one of Mary's sons by her first marriage, George Allen, became a successful solicitor and set up his own firm of Allen, Allen, and Hemsley in Sydney. George's eldest son, also George (1824–1885), became Speaker of the NSW Legislative Assembly and was in due course knighted.

Father, ca. 1930, Cecil Samuel Wilson M.Ch.

Dr Steevens' Hospital, Dublin – Resident Staff 1922. Standing L. to R.: H.M. Martin, J.V. Williams, J.S. Glasgow, S.V. Jamieson, J.H. Stuart, C.R. Hillis, P.S. Bourke, W.H. Maguire. Seated L. to R.: W.E. Cullanan, Dr N.M. Falkiner, Dr C.S. Wilson (Resident Surgeon), E.D.F. Banks (Secretary), D.G. Thompson (Apothecary)

Mother, ca. 1930, Margaret Dorothea Gregg FRCS(I)

Mother, ca. 1960

Mother and Father, 1936, engagement photograph

Mother's Bridesmaids, 1936, '. . . the ghastly olive green dresses.'

Two Gregg Weddings

Barbara Fitzgerald Gregg – Michael Somerville, 1935. Mother (as her sister's chief bridesmaid?) is seated next to the bride

Margaret Gregg – Cecil Wilson, 1936. Next to groom: Horace Law, who gave mother away. Next to bride: Grandfather, then Archbishop of Dublin, who married them. Anna Gregg (Granny) is seated on his left

Granny Jeanette (Jennie) Wilson ('Gan') ca. 1900

Grandfather William Wilson, ca. 1900, in South Africa

Gan and Grandpa Wilson, ca. 1890

Gan and Grandpa Wilson at Trumroe, Castlepollard, Co. Westmeath, ca. 1930

Mabel Ronaldson (Auntie Mabel), ca. 1950, Father's sister. Centre: unknown; right, her daughter Sybil

Arthur Wilson (Uncle Artie), ca. 1925, Father's brother '. . . he was a handsome man.'

In 1895, a young Naval officer, Boyle Somerville, from Castletownshend, Co. Cork, visited Sydney with his ship and was entertained by the Allen family. There he fell in love with Helen Mabel, their youngest daughter. He took her for a walk on a nearby cliff top and only then discovered that she was already engaged. He seized her hand; pulled off the engagement ring; threw it over the cliff into the sea and asked her to marry him. She agreed. (I suppose it is the civilian equivalent of gunboat diplomacy). They were married in 1896 and lived in London until he retired from the Navy as a Vice Admiral, after a distinguished career. They went back to live in Castletownshend, at the Point House, until he was murdered by the IRA in 1935.

Such are some of the exotic connections of my cousins, Christina and Julian.

CHAPTER 8

Early Childhood – the Invasion of Malaya

AT WHAT AGE DOES A CHILD genuinely begin to remember events that have occurred? At what age does he begin to recognise the passage of time, except as measured by the regular onset of hunger? My own early childhood in Malaya remains with me only as a set of snapshots, dateless, timeless, and without sequence.

The very first memory is of being in bed, under a mosquito net, and a dim shape looming in the semi-darkness, and my absolute conviction that it was a tiger. There were, from time to time, tiger alerts and I knew that they were A BAD THING, as Winnie ther Pooh would have put it. I do remember once being forbidden to go out of the house for that reason, because there was a man-eating tiger on the loose. On this occasion I did not scream; I cowered and pretended to be asleep. I am sure that in fact it was my *ama*, my Malay nurse, whom I do not otherwise remember in any way at all, except that she always wore black, and presumably (since I had two working parents) she filled a similar role to that of a Victorian nanny, without quite the same capacity to inspire awe and affection in equal measure. So my very first memory is of terror and in those early years war inevitably brought a number of other terrors, which may have affected me in ways I cannot tell.

I was born in Singapore, at the Sepoy Lines Hospital, on 16 June 1937, Coronation Year. Why it was necessary for me to go there I cannot imagine. After all we lived in Kuala Lumpur (nearly 200 miles away, as the stork flies) and my mother was a gynaecological consultant there. Did she not trust her own hospital? Or was there, perhaps, some advantage in terms of nationality, even though at that time Singapore and Malaya were all one under British rule? No one ever hinted at any particular circumstances, though after the war, when Ireland was an independent republic, my parents were always very concerned to assert and safeguard our British nationality. It was drummed into me what a vital and precious document my birth certificate was, though in fact I had no difficulty getting copies from the authorities in Singapore. But it was probably more to do with Ireland than Malaya and became important when we settled in Northern Ireland and my father became an employee of the NHS.

We lived at 16 Clifford Road, Kuala Lumpur – where and how I got the address into my head I know not; but I have 'always' known it. I vaguely picture a pleasant, two-storey colonial dwelling with a covered porch in front, built into a bank of red clay, which the houseboys used to smear on their fingers and use instead of toothpaste. Where they lived or slept I have no idea. Three houseboys is my best tally, derived from another mental snapshot – performing consecutive somersaults at great speed like circus performers all along an upstairs landing or bedroom floor, entirely for my delectation. So we had at least four servants. Would that have been many or few for the white colonial professional classes of the time? Did we have a garden? Who tended it? How big was the house really? I can only guess. I do remember my father kicking a football over the roof to me at the back, but he was a good footballer and such a kick might well have flown over a veritable mansion. We lived there until I was four, so I must have had friends to play with and even gone to some sort of kindergarten, I would have thought. I have dim memories of playing, well, banging, a drum in some sort of children's band. That suggests some sort of institutional activity. My Uncle John was a regular visitor and, I gather, very fond of me.

There was a driveway up to the house, length uncertain, level, but of gravel or clay, not tarmac. It led to the main road into KL, down to the right, and beyond through jungle, which may well have been in fact no more than a tree-lined avenue. Up and to the left remained an eternal mystery. A dense wall of trees at the end of the drive is a clear memory, and the 'air-raid shelter' – a simple ditch or slit-trench with a corrugated iron roof covered with soil – on the far side of the main road, presumably under those trees. There was a distant bend down through the overarching canopy of trees, where once my father took me with some care to witness the capture of a rabid dog or maybe a hyena. It wasn't a tiger, so I had no apprehensions and a child's natural confidence in his father. They shot it.

Of my mother I remember absolutely nothing! She simply does not figure until our evacuation. Her *Baby's Journal* records that I was 'never entirely breast fed', which suggests a very busy woman, and that may be the explanation. I think that between myself and Audrey, born 11 November 1940, there was also a miscarriage, which gives my deduction some reinforcement. By the time she became a granny, my mother had convinced herself that I was a paradigm of all babies, so that it became a family joke that I was weaned in about a fortnight, potty trained in a month, eating red meat in half a year, and able to read at the age of one. Who am I to doubt my mother's memory?

Seventh December 1941, a date that will live in infamy in the annals of mankind, saw the bombing of Pearl Harbour and the entry of Japan into World War II, an act which made the European war into a truly world war. On 8 December the Japanese invaded Malaya and reached Singapore on 15 February, capturing 90,000 British and Commonwealth troops as well as an unspecified number of civilians, including my father and Uncle John. With characteristic ineptitude the British military commanders had long decided that Singapore could only be captured from the sea and all the defences faced in that direction. Nevertheless, the Japanese military achievement in overrunning and capturing a peninsula of some 200 plus miles in two months was remarkable, and the originality of their tactics, advancing by jungle paths and tracks, on foot and bicycle, totally defeated the ponderous and incompetent allied defences. Imagination was never a strong point in army leadership, and the old British army slogan (applied to officers as well as men) that 'you are not paid to think here' ensured that as usual we suffered innumerable initial defeats before sheer bulldog British grit allied to vast American resources finally won the war.

Of all this as a small child I knew nothing. I remember one bombing raid on Kuala Lumpur – very loud explosions not that far away as we crouched in our improvised air-raid shelter at the edge of the jungle. I remember standing in front of our house and being shown three tiny little British warplanes looping some very pedestrian loops in the distant sky and being told that they were Brewster Buffalos – well named, since their performance in the air would have barely improved upon that of the ponderous beast after which they were named. For all I know that was the sum total of the defending British air force and for the Japanese fighters I have little doubt that shooting them out of the sky was rather simpler than shelling peas.

We fled.

Of that chaotic journey down the peninsula to Singapore I remember nothing and was told little. The Japs were apparently hard on our heels; panic was in the air. Modern television pictures of refugees in many countries will make the modern generation far more aware of what such a rout entails. I assume we were in a car, which probably helped, but we had lost everything, including family silver, photograph albums (which my mother regretted even more, I think, than the silver), the securities and certainties of a British colonial administration, of which my parents were inordinately proud to be a part, and were much offended by those who began to disparage it during the fashionable liberalism of the sixties and seventies. Compared with the deficiencies of the colonial regimes of other nations, the British record and achievement stands as a beacon of enlightenment, tempered of course by a degree of self-interest, which it would be dishonest to deny. But it was a regime broadly benevolent in intention and practice and its legacy was relatively benign. For us, above all, a way of life and a degree of prosperity was lost and would never come again.

Colonial officers and civilian personnel had been ordered by the government to remain at their posts. Presumably they thought that Singapore was impregnable and that they would be needed to restore order and good government once the invaders had been seen off. My father and Uncle John, I assume, were locked up in Changi gaol, technically as civilian internees, but that spared them none of the horrors of Japanese brutality.

Farewells on the quayside are always poignant moments. I remember saying goodbye to my father, without the slightest idea of why he was staying or what he was in for. I remember the seemingly enormous bulk of the SS *Britannic* looming above us. I believe it was one of the last passenger steamers to leave Singapore and she remained forever in my mother's memory an object of deep affection. When the ship was finally taken to the scrapyard (in the seventies I think) she felt real sorrow at her going.

We were refugees, like any other, but at least we had a home to go to in Ireland, if we ever got there. There were regular boat drills; there was a major panic when a whale surfaced alongside and some of the passengers at least thought it was a German U-boat. It was crowded and uncomfortable and at the age of four small boys are particularly tiresome, I believe. Strange memories – I have no recollection of what I was doing to annoy whom, but suddenly on one occasion a strange man picked me up, carried me off to the cabin, and walloped my behind. A sense of betrayal by my mother (who alone was entitled to inflict such an indignity upon me) and a mild general apprehension of adults (presumably the object of the exercise) remained with me for a long time.

A happier memory, though no less evidence of my somewhat tiresome behaviour, was reported by my mother years later. She came down to the cabin one day to find that I had discovered the delights of female cosmetics and had decorated myself, the mirror, and heaven knows what else besides with her best face-powders.

'Brian, what have you been doing?' she exclaimed.

'Lots', was my succinct reply.

It covered the case, I think, though as repartee it is not quite in the same league as Albert Einstein who, it was said, never spoke a word until the age of four, when suddenly he announced to general astonishment, 'This soup is too hot'. Asked why he had never said anything before, he replied, 'Until now, everything was in order.'

These simple experiences seem to have affected me in later life. In my brief and totally undistinguished later career as a schoolboy actor and brief member of an amateur dramatic group, I always adored the smell of powder and greasepaint. As a traveller I have always also loved the sight of a vast and empty ocean sliding by outside the portholes of a great ship. I have travelled little on anything but cross-channel steamers, but even there I find the same sensations rise to meet my memories.

We reached the safety of South Africa and there my mother decided to wait to see if my father might get away and join us. It seems naïve now to think of it, but I am sure that in an era of less than adequate communications and in the turmoil of evacuation and wartime security, no one really knew quite what was going on. Hope, too, springs eternal and, as the Greek proverb says, 'it is a bad guide, but a good companion on the way'. We waited in hope but without reward for some six months.

We shared a bungalow in Durban with six other families. It must have been a nightmare for the parents but my only memory is of limited water supplies and sharing a bath with what childish imagination maintains was six other children all at once.

I wish that I could remember another, much more significant, event. I was apparently introduced to and shook hands with Jan Christian Smuts, the Prime Minister of South Africa, and one of the great leaders of the wartime Western alliance. The reason was that he was a very old friend of Grandfather's; they were fellow freshmen at Cambridge and shared digs for their first year. Both in due course became honorary fellows of the family college, Christ's. I assume mother contrived an audience with the great man, though it still seems extraordinary that he should have found time to meet an unimportant refugee family like ours.

We docked in Liverpool, having probably taken the long way round Ireland to avoid the U-boat threat in the western approaches to the English Channel, and thence by the mail boat to Belfast and home to Armagh. By then I was five, and my recollection of events begins to take on a slightly sharper, if still selective, focus.

CHAPTER 9

The Palace, Armagh – Sanctuary

*I have desired to go
Where springs not fail,
To fields where flies no sharp and sided hail
And, a few lilies blow.*

*And I have asked to be
Where no storms come,
Where the green swell is in the havens dumb,
And out of the swing of the sea.*

Gerard Manley Hopkins

ARMAGH IS A CITY SET ON A HILL, or rather upon two hills. Upon the higher stands the Protestant cathedral, St Patrick's, the first stone church in Ireland, founded in AD 445, somewhat dark and brooding. Upon the lesser hill, but (of deliberate purpose?) rising higher than the Protestant cathedral by reason of its two tremendous spires, stands St Patrick's Roman Catholic Cathedral, founded in 1840 and completed in 1873. Black Protestant though I am, I have to acknowledge that it is the more beautiful of the two, lighter and more graceful, with a lofty pointed ceiling and fine mosaic decorations. But what it lacks in grace the Protestant cathedral gains in sheer solidity, a symbolically suitable home for the Rock of Ages, and the archi-episcopal seat of my grandfather, the Primate of All Ireland, nicknamed the 'Marble Arch', a rock of scholarship and sound learning in defence of Anglican orthodoxy, against which the waves of Roman Catholic doctrinal innovation beat vainly and fell back. Nevertheless, he liked and got on well with his opposite number, Cardinal D'Alton.

It is a beautiful city, rooted in antiquity, predating Canterbury as a Christian foundation, London as a capital city, and Oxford as a university city. It was a centre of local power far back into legendary times. It was the home of Queen Macha, 600 years before the Christian era, and through her it is directly linked to nearby Evin Macha (Navan Fort), legendary capital of the Kings of Ulster, which figures in the *Táin*, Ireland's heroic equivalent to the Homeric Epic cycle, in which the legendary hero CuChulainn defended Ulster against the hosts of Maeve, the Queen of Connaught. Ard Macha, the Hill of Macha, gave Armagh its name.

But it was during the late eighteenth and early nineteenth centuries that the city gained most of the fine buildings, which made it such a gem of Georgian architecture. The Courthouse, the Prison, the Market House, the Observatory, the Robinson Library with its glorious Reading Room (originally planned as the nucleus of a later university, which sadly never came about), the Mall laid out with public walkways and lined with fine Georgian houses, the Royal School, and of course the Archbishop's Palace itself – all these gave it an air of real distinction unusual in the country towns of Ulster. Archbishop Robinson (appointed in 1765) and his successor, Lord John Beresford, were the inspiration behind the whole building programme, and also the encouragement of new developments in agriculture, which improved the economic health of the city and its surrounding countryside. The palace farm was intended to set an example of good practice.

Robinson, too, started and Beresford completed (in 1770) the new Palace in its 400-acre demesne on the edge of the city. It was a fine Queen Anne mansion with a basement and three upper storeys, with a large orchard in its walled garden, woodland, arable and grazing land, stables and farmyard, and accommodation for the farm workers and their families. It had a lovely little private chapel (1786), sadly neglected and used only as a storeroom, a large garden and greenhouse, chickens in an enclosure near the house, a stream at the bottom of the hill, and huge, eminently climbable trees, one a colossal spruce with branches down to the ground which could have concealed an army, one a beech with a low hanging branch ideal for swinging on. Part of the acreage was let out to two local farmers (Watson and Shannon are names that spring to mind) and the Golf Club had a nice little nine-hole course there, of which those living in the Palace were ex officio members.

For my mother it was doubtless a sanctuary; for a child it was paradise.

Living with my grandfather in the Palace as a result of the war were both his married daughters, my mother Margaret with myself and my sister Audrey; and my aunt, Barbara Somerville, with Christina and, later on, the newly arrived Julian. Her husband, Michael, rarely appeared since he was serving with the armed forces and war is a stern taskmaster. Grandfather's now bedridden wife Anna ('Granny') never left her bedroom and it was part of the daily ritual to visit her and say 'Good morning'. Domestic staff were, of necessity, somewhat curtailed by wartime economy, but the establishment still offered, as it were, a last echo of the gracious living expected of and by a prince of the church in earlier times. Apart from the chauffeur, Mr Totten, who lived up at the stables with his wife, there was the cook, Emily, who was inordinately fond of cats, and made a memorable oxtail stew at the drop of a hat (or even a cat during wartime emergencies?), but was not too good at anything else. The two housemaids, Bridget Power and Madeline Wills, were both utterly sweet and kind to us children, and patient I dare say beyond all deserving. On the top floor, with their own direct access by a stone staircase which probably served as a fire escape for the main household, were billeted an unknown number of American servicemen. They never impinged upon our consciousness beyond the fact that a Mr Woctor, I think it was, proved a generous source of sweets and chocolate for us and, I suspect, nylon stockings for the ladies. It was a big house and did not feel at all crowded. Let me take you on a tour.

You approached usually by the front drive, about half a mile long, which had a lodge and fine, pillared gates; then came the ruined Franciscan Priory (built *circa* 1264 and suppressed by Henry VIII in 1542) with its 'bare ruin'd choirs where late the sweet birds sang' (yes, I know Shakespeare's sonnet 73 refers to trees, but symbolically his reference to 'the twilight of such day/As after sunset fadeth in the west' also fits very well the decline and death of the old religion and so many of its lovely buildings at the hands of King Henry).

Next to it was the house of Mr Beale, the Steward, who ran the estate. Along the avenue before you turned down to the Palace itself were the stables, fine Georgian buildings in their own right and now a visitor centre and museum, but at that stage providing homes for the Kennedy family and the Tottens, as well as serving the usual functions of stables and barns.

There was a back avenue as well, again about half a mile, also with a lodge, where Joe Hinds, the gardener lived. Its final approach to the house was especially memorable. You crossed the stream where I used to sail my battleship and then came up the hill under a splendid line of noble beeches, sadly now felled, doubtless in the name of the idiotically destructive Health and Safety Act, which has eliminated the need for ordinary common sense and personal responsibility from the conduct of our daily lives. 'Aunt' Lesley, Grandfather's second wife and a former art teacher, painted the Palace and its chapel from beneath these trees and whenever I look at it I am reminded of Keats' lovely description of oak trees,

> Those green rob'd senators of mighty woods,
> Tall oaks, branch charmed by the earnest stars . . .

The main entrance to the Palace was a fine, spacious porch, supported by pillars and with cotoneasters growing up the sides. It bridged the excavated 'area' in which the house was set, whose banks were sufficiently distant from the structure to offer little impediment to light for the basement. You climbed stairs to enter the porch and more stairs to enter the Palace itself, finding yourself initially in the large front hall, its walls decorated with what Daisy Ashford would have called Ancestors, though strictly they were Predecessors. Archbishops of the recent and distant past looked down upon the visitor, who would not have noticed that behind a sideboard beside the door one portrait remained unhung and facing the wall. This was Grandfather's official portrait, done by an Ulster artist, Frank McKelvey, for the Church of Ireland. Grandfather disliked it very much – as did all the family. He refused to have it put up and I never saw it until I visited the Diocesan offices in about 2003; I understand his sentiments.

A far finer portrait of Grandfather, as Archbishop of Dublin, was painted in 1935 by Sir Oswald Birley, and this is reproduced as the frontispiece in George Seaver's biography. By a happy circumstance the sittings apparently went so well that the portrait was finished far more quickly than expected. So Sir Oswald painted a second and identical copy for the family. It remains in my possession and will pass on down the family until it is wanted no more. It is very fine and I have debated whether it should be offered to the Robinson Library, if they ever manage to bring to fruition the Gregg Memorial Reading Room which was, I believe, at one time planned for one of their most illustrious Primates. Other potential recipients include Christ's College, Cambridge or the National Portrait Gallery.

To the left of the hall was the study, first a sort of ante-room, and then the inner sanctum, dark, mysterious, lined from floor to ceiling with books. We rarely entered. There Grandfather worked all the hours that God sent, and then some, reading, preparing sermons and addresses, and corresponding by handwritten letter, nearly always by return of post, with a huge volume of people. He may have had a secretary at the Diocesan offices; I never saw one at the Palace. Next door was the drawing room, very much the 'best' room, used only on important occasions or for a formal tea party – with small sandwiches and cakes on stands and a lovely silver teapot with matching hot-water holder on a hinged stand, which we were occasionally allowed to tip, and with a small spirit burner beneath it to keep the water hot. A graceful iron staircase led directly into the garden. In the corner was a small display cabinet in which there was the most beautiful chess set I have ever seen, red and white, made from ivory, with real castles each with its slender flag pole, and every piece exquisitely carved. One piece was missing so it will have had little monetary value. But it was a thing of real beauty and if a child can covet, that was something I desired. To even touch it was most strictly *verboten*.

Then came the morning-room, light, spacious, looking out across the lawns to the rhododendrons (glorious for hide-and-seek) which embraced and sheltered them; very much the room in which we all lived and moved and had our being. Of its furnishings and adornments I remember only the fine ornate French clock, made by Japy Frères and shown at the Grand Exposition of 1855. It was presented in 1861 by his Ladies' Class to John Gregg, Grandfather's grandfather, when he retired as Archdeacon of Kildare to become Bishop of Cork, Cloyne and Ross. He was the one responsible for the building of St Fin Barre's Cathedral. Every Saturday morning Grandfather would solemnly wind it and I continue his practice to this day. It has now been going for over 150 years.

Finally from both morning-room and the hall double doors (designed for hiding between, though the grown-ups claimed that it was sound proofing) led into the dining-room, a really fine room, now the Council Chamber for the Armagh District Council. There were two large tables, one circular and large enough to accommodate us all for meals, the other larger still, oblong and appropriate for formal dinners. I never saw it used for that purpose – after all it was wartime. But before breakfast every morning the whole household, including the domestic staff, would gather there for a Bible reading and prayers – mercifully brief, presumably a shortened version of the daily Office. I never remember it as tedious or irritating;

simply part of the natural order of things. Then came breakfast, served in the traditional manner from hot chafing dishes on the sideboard.

Upstairs were at least six big bedrooms – possibly more. But the stairs themselves were much more important to me. Leading up from an inner, secondary hall, they were wide and relatively shallow with a landing as a half-way house. The banisters were wide and smooth, a source of endless delight, and I slid down them ad infinitum. Had I ever fallen from the top, it would have been a serious and possibly fatal accident. But it never occurred to me, and my mother was characteristically brave about allowing her children to take risks. Then I discovered that if I borrowed a large tray I could slide down the stairs themselves at a tremendous rate and with a most satisfying accompaniment of noise. I was virtually snow-boarding before it had even been invented.

Our other centre of indoor entertainment was the front hall itself. Its sofas and chairs supplemented by rugs and other paraphernalia allowed us to create the most wonderful dens and tunnels and obstacle courses. Never that I can remember did Grandfather even remonstrate with us at the chaotic disorder that we inflicted on the primatial residence nor at the noise, which I am sure we generated, in the course of our hilarious activities. He had lost two boys of his own and I would like to think that he derived some solace from having children about him once again. His public image was one of unbending rigidity reinforced by a degree of shyness; not for nothing was he nicknamed the Marble Arch, as I have already said. But to us he was the gentlest and sweetest of persons. Even when I broke a window once with a ball and was made to own up and apologise, forgiveness was immediate and absolute, though I confess that my initial trepidation and consequent relief was considerable.

The domestic staff lived, worked and slept in the basement. There was a huge kitchen, with an large Aga (or Esse) which presumably kept the hot water going as well. There was a pantry, scullery, a huge coal bunker with a tunnel leading out to the ice-house, which lay between the Palace and the stables. The estate had two such ice-houses, the other up in the woods above the steward's house. Neither was in use during my time, but ancient practice was for the estate workers to gather ice in the winter and store it in these underground repositories (which were very large) and insulate them with straw, so that a ready supply of cooling materials was available for either storage or refrigeration all the year round. They were always a bit scary, because it would be perfectly easy to fall into one and never be seen again – or so we were regularly warned by anxious mothers. Besides, we 'knew' they were full of white rats.

On the top floor lived the Americans. My dim recollection is of a large number of relatively small rooms. Originally they were probably used for the innumerable children of earlier Primates; possibly for the domestic staff. Other than under wartime pressures they were empty and unused. Once, amid considerable speculation and some shock, the skeleton of a tiny baby was discovered there, hidden in a trunk. It dated from long ago, presumably the private tragedy of some domestic servant, and I think the coroner's inquest required no further action.

In the heyday of Archbishop Lord John Beresford, who presumably had the resources to maintain the place in the style it deserved, the Palace must have been a very considerable establishment. My own emotional attachment to it remains powerful to this day. Its inevitable sale for economic reasons to the District Council for their offices was I suppose unavoidable; the church authorities simply could not afford the upkeep and they built as a replacement an undistinguished brick See House on the hill beside the Cathedral. But if more imaginative solutions could not be found, it would have been deeply appropriate if it had become the home and campus for Ulster's second university, thus restoring to Armagh its ancient mediaeval role as a centre of learning as well as religion. But politically, one suspects, Armagh was regarded as dodgy, and characteristic prejudice gave the NUU to Coleraine.

With Granny an invalid, in Dublin my mother had always acted as chauffeur on Sundays for Grandfather on his endless round of visits to the parishes of his diocese. Sunday at Armagh similarly remained the chauffeur's day off, and she continued to drive him on occasion. In his later years, with failing eyesight, he sometimes perforce drove himself, and the family lived in perpetual terror that he would have an accident and injure or kill some unfortunate pedestrian. Fortunately his guardian angel never deserted him and though I remember occasional terrifying but tortoise-like descents of the cathedral hill by car back to the Palace, no one came to any harm.

Mother also worked part-time at the Armagh Infirmary, whether out of financial necessity or because it kept up her professional skills. We never talked of money or finance in the family and in my teenage years I became mildly obsessed with how much I was costing them, without having the slightest idea of whether I truly was a burden. It affected later decisions, which I now sometimes regret. The Infirmary I remember because, unbelievably, I was in those days what the comic strip advertisements called a 'five-stone weakling', somewhat underweight and weedy. Would that I had remained so. What the comic strips offered as a remedy I do not recall, but as well as 'government orange juice', which I loved and which the enlightened authorities supplied for all children as a vitamin supplement, I was given liberal doses of Virol and Radio Malt, both of them utterly delicious and I am sure responsible for the fact that I soon became and have remained ever since something of a 'stout party' doomed to wrestle sporadically and somewhat unsuccessfully with a weight problem. I was also taken to the Infirmary, where clad in dark goggles like a wartime fighter ace, I was subjected to a series of doses of ultraviolet rays.

I went to school, as far as I know without trauma or demur.

As a result I proudly remain a former pupil of Armagh Girls' High School, whose kindergarten took boys and girls alike. It was there I presented my first girl-friend with an engagement ring, I am told, but fickle suitor that I was I confess that I do not even remember her name. The school was situated at the far end of the Mall in a lovely Georgian terrace and is now, very sensibly, married to the Armagh Royal School. Whatever the temporary drawbacks of coeducation for children in their mid-teens, the social experience of parity of esteem and an understanding of the different emotional and social development of the two genders can only be healthy. In my view the best schools in Northern Ireland in my time as a head were coeducational – Methodist College and Belfast Royal Academy – and it remains a matter of abiding regret that I failed in my efforts to take Campbell College in that direction.

Names begin to be added to the inventory of memory. Mrs Castell (possibly succeeded by Miss Acheson) was the redoubtable headmistress of Armagh Girls', one of many remarkable women who ruled the girls' schools of Northern Ireland. Of these Miss Ethel Grey of Bloomfield Collegiate in Belfast was perhaps the most formidable of all, the only human being, male or female, of whom the Rev Ian Paisley was said to be afraid. She ruled her institution (parents included) with a rod of iron (not literally, of course), but delivered order and academic success in no uncertain terms. The only thing I have in common with the redoubtable Ian Paisley is that we both placed our daughters under her care.

Miss Bowers was my class teacher. I loved sums and I dare say might have taken to mathematics had I remained in her charge for any length of time, because I was very good at them. But coeducation there ended at the age of seven and I was despatched to preparatory school, where maths teaching was, to put it charitably, not one of the strong points. I walked about a mile to school every day – or possibly bicycled when I learned to do so – certainly escorted by my mother, but with no concessions to the comfort and safety of the modern 4 × 4. No doubt it burned off energy and improved health, and in those relatively traffic-free days would have caused no concern for safety or security.

What I learned, apart from sums, I do not remember. I am sure I had long since learned to read, and the modern fashion of letting children discover reading 'in their own time' seems to me another of those fashionable idiocies which modern educationists have foisted upon a gullible government and public. For children, books improve communication, open the imagination, widen the capacities, and offer sheer delight – autonomously acquired and therefore doubly precious. They should start as early as possible, of course without turning it into drudgery for parent or child. I remember my own amazement when we delivered Anna to her first primary school in Eastbourne and received the strong impression of her teacher's considerable disapproval of the fact that she could already read. No wonder we have an increasingly illiterate generation of children, incapable of reading a whole book, whose only relaxation is the undemanding pap served up by popular television and the cult of celebrity.

Two figures loiter in the mind. The first is my sister, aged perhaps five, on her tricycle, racing down the high street of Armagh with my mother and myself in hot but somewhat ineffective pursuit. At the road junction, with a blind indifference to traffic, she cut the corner, entering the next street on the right-hand side of the road. On point duty stood an Officer of the Law in all his majesty, and this little scrap was duly taken into protective custody, while I fled back to my mother with howls of anguish because 'a big fat policeman has arrested her'. However, in those more genial days, a brief rebuke sufficed and on she went, wholly unreformed. In her nursing days in London she remained the terror of the town, according to Sara, who remembers her in her Mini racing round the city at high speed, but with rather more adherence to the rules of the road, and at no less high speed, though on foot, round the long corridors of St Thomas' Hospital, where she was known as Speedy Gonzales, or sometimes, the 'Atomic Bomb'.

And children do like naughty stories. A famous personage in Armagh in those days was a memorably gargantuan lady, who shall remain nameless. 'Why man, she did bestride the narrow streets like a colossus', followed as if in deliberate contrast to enhance her own magnificence by the tiniest of poodles. Legend had it that one day she went into Lennox, the local draper, and said to the assistant, 'I'd like to see a pair of knickers that would fit me.' Back came the immortal, if apocryphal reply, 'So would I.' History does not relate what happened to the assistant; but his riposte occasioned endless mirth and hilarity in us children for years after – and that surely is sufficient justification for his temerity.

Of wartime shortages I remember little: coupons and the rationing out of sugar, butter, and sweets; the mortification and unhappiness of my mother, when we returned by train from the South on a journey whose reasons remain lost for ever. Being, as ever, scrupulously honest, she declared to the customs officer that she had brought back some butter – a very precious commodity. He seized it and – as she bitterly commented afterwards – 'I am sure his family ate better for a few days'. Two postcards from my father, with bits blacked out by the censor; it is not a lot for some four years of life. So let me close the chapter with snapshot and doubtless rose-tinted memories of the rural idyll in which those childhood days were spent.

'I remember, I remember . . .' cart-horses, huge with shaggy ankles, a bit like modern teenagers in their fashionable footwear, ploughing in pairs, or singly bringing in the hay, the stacks winched onto floats with ratcheted levers which enabled two men to shift a whole stack onto the float by brute force; helping with the harvest, the clickety-clack of the reaper-and-binder pulled by horses with a driver and one man sitting beside him to collect and release due measures of corn (cut and neatly tied – how did a machine tie a knot?) in rows behind him, where women and children helped to build the stooks; days later, watching the men heave them onto carts and take them back to the farmyard, where (wonder of wonders) the early threshing machine, driven by a traction engine (or possibly a tractor with a belt drive) actually separated corn from straw and poured the one into sacks and spat the other out onto the ground for storage in the barns (my first encounter with technology). The corn piled up to dry in shifting heaps upon the granary floor. You could tread on it and find the hillside slide away beneath your feet; sensational! Potato picking, the strange little machine that flew round in a circle and spouted out potatoes in a never-ending stream, which we gathered into buckets and brought to the central heap, which was covered and protected from the winter colds and rain until required.

Memories: fooling around with the farm-workers' children – Geordie and Tommy Kennedy, I think; they taught me to eat berries from the barberry hedge beside the stables, to the alarm of my mother when she saw my lips and cheeks stained blue with the results; innocent days of romping in the hay, in days when it meant nothing more than that; hide-and-seek; tree-climbing; my first golf lessons and the only place where by sheer fluke at the short second hole I ever got a hole in one; Christina being taught to ride and I was given a go on her pony. It stopped; I didn't. I flew over its head and never rode again. I did the same on my tricycle roaring down the hill from the Palace and losing control, but nothing else. (When Emma did the same on her first bicycle on Stormont hill in Belfast, she lost her two front teeth and needed stitches); playing in the stream, small enough to be safe, big enough to float my battleship; rich in sticklebacks, captured in jam jars, and frogspawn in the springtime; vanishing at one point under rhododendrons, which hid one totally from sight; vaguely mysterious because it came from out of an unknown land and vanished into the piped watercourse beneath the city; falling off my pile of hassocks (erected for a better view) in cathedral matins into the aisle from the front (Palace) pew, to the delight of the choir boys and my mother's considerable chagrin.

Walks in the woods, where foxes replaced tigers as the source of childish terror. The magic of the first snowdrops and primroses; my own first garden, where I planted daffodils and still remember the excitement of their first appearance as green shoots, and a huge sunflower that grew by inches every day, which is what children really require if they are to be bitten by the gardening bug; gathering hens' eggs and watching them being preserved in water-glass and stored in big earthenware crocks; the long trudge to the Obelisk, the monument set on a distant hill within the grounds and visible from the windows of the morning-room; the hedgerows along the hill on which it stood were the best source of blackberries, gathered in autumn from among the hips and haws, whose colours still inspire emotion in me wherever I find them in these my own autumn days.

> Season of mists and mellow fruitfulness,
>   Close bosom-friend of the maturing sun;
> Conspiring with him how to load and bless
>   With fruit the vines that round the thatch-eaves run.
> To bend with apples the mossed cottage trees,
>   And fill all fruit with ripeness to the core; . . .

Once I could recite the whole poem, and it remains for me rich with the associations of autumnal glories in the countryside. It stirs the drowsy melancholy of happy times remembered and the sadly temporary joys of living closer to nature than I ever did again.

> Where are the songs of Spring? Ay, where are they?
>   Think not of them, thou hast thy music too –
> While barred clouds bloom the soft-dying day,
>   And touch the stubble-plains with rosy hue; . . .
> The red-breast whistles from a garden-croft;
>   And gathering swallows twitter in the skies.

Swallows, congregating on their telegraph wires ready to depart, exchanging gossip and reminiscences of summer days, are a bit like old men in their anecdotage twittering on about their golden memories as they too prepare for the long journey. It is for the young men to see their visions while the old men dream their dreams of yesteryear.

Chapter 10

Mourne Grange – An Educational Idyll

In April 1945, at the age of seven and three quarters, I became a boarder at Mourne Grange Preparatory School, near Kilkeel (then a highly prosperous fishing village, until the EC destroyed its fleet along with those of most of Britain's fishing ports) and at the foot of the Mountains of Mourne. An area of legendary beauty with a fine view of Slieve Bignian from the school windows, it was a perfect place to have a school. We were about two miles from the sea, and in summer the whole school would depart on bicycles to the seaside with all the main crossroads manned by senior boys to control traffic and see the cavalcade safely across – a genuinely responsible duty. There were picnics with Cowboys v Indians amid the bracken up in the hills; the eagerly anticipated annual bluebell walk through Lord Kilmorey's estate in May; and a special treat for groups of seniors, weekends camping down at Mrs Rooney's cottage on the Carlingford shoreline, where the good lady and her husband fed and maintained us on fabulously rich-smelling Ulster fries, and we ran harmlessly amok along the empty beaches, while just before bedtime Patrick Carey would tell us spooky ghost stories round the fire.

It was, naturally, the best prep school in Ireland, with contingents from the South as well as the North, but the war had not helped its clientele. When I joined there were thirty-seven pupils; when I left in 1950 there were eighty-four, I was head boy, and the school was celebrating its Golden Jubilee. It was founded and run for its first forty-five years by Alan Sausmarez Carey, an Old Salopian whose family hailed from Guernsey. He was tutor to the Earl of Kilmorey, whose estate was some half a mile up the road, and he helped him set up a school to prepare boys for entry to the best English public schools. Those planning to enter Irish schools like Portora were just about acceptable, likewise St Columba's; entry to Campbell College, Belfast was only for the lowest of the low!

Carey's wife, Florence I think, was a composer of minor repute, whose setting of 'St Patrick's Breastplate' remains in my view significantly superior to the traditional and rather ghastly tune to which it is normally sung. They were a doughty pair. He was a holy terror, armed always in class with a cane mainly though not entirely for effect, and liable to lose his temper at the drop of a hat or omission of a syllable; we were all terrified of him. But he certainly made us work. Mrs Carey was no less formidable, though she carried no armaments except her tongue, and a gimlet eye that would have stopped a charging rhino at a hundred paces. In absolute silence, she read to the whole school every Sunday evening for an hour and a half before bedtime – a totally admirable practice – from children's classics of the day, certainly *Lorna Doone*, *The Dog Crusoe*, and *Treasure Island*, among others; all well chosen, ripping yarns, and none too obviously improving.

Her son, Patrick, lived in awe of her and for this reason probably never married and ultimately took to drink, which proved his undoing. But that was after my time and for those five glorious years when Patrick returned from wartime military service, took over the school, galvanised it, and made it human and humane, the place flourished. He was, for me, one of the great schoolmasters of my experience, and I use the word schoolmaster advisedly. It is not snobbery to say that teachers teach; schoolmasters educate. Nor is it surprising that on the whole those who taught in the preparatory and public schools of England called themselves schoolmasters and saw their profession as a rather nobler and richer calling than that of any mere teacher. We were expected and prepared to work in term-time seven days a week and twenty-four hours a day, as required. We took games as well as taught our subjects; coached teams; ran clubs; supervised meals and break-times; we had no rights – only obligations, to our pupils, and to the head, whose word was law and who had more power over his subjects than any Prime Minister. I love the story of the headmaster of Eton (was it Alington?), who refused on the occasion of a royal visit to doff his academic cap to the Prince of Wales, explaining that he could not possibly allow the boys to imagine that there was anyone in the world more important than their headmaster.

Those were the days when you could still be an eccentric and run a school. Patrick Carey was a great eccentric, Falstaffian in shape and manner, somewhat larger than life, indefatigable, extraordinarily good company and a mighty quaffer of ale, as I discovered when I left the school and at his suggestion joined the Leprechauns at the age of fourteen, an Irish wandering cricket club, which aimed to bring good players to matches against schools in term-time, and ran a wondrously entertaining and boozy tour to central Ireland during the summer holidays. Somewhat pretentiously we thought of ourselves as the Irish MCC. The product of Shrewsbury and Oxford University, where he was a member of OUDS, drama was his passion, and though I was no thespian – or as he would have put it, 'you can act none', – from him I learned to love the theatre and all the glitter of the footlights, but to love no less drama in general and the plays of Shakespeare in particular. There was no nonsense about putting on plays that 'children will understand and relate to'. We did Shakespeare, interspersed with Shaw and JM Barrie *inter alios*. To my certain memory I acted in *Henry V* (holding a spear), *Twelfth Night* (I was predictably Sir Toby Belch), *A Midsummer Night's Dream* (who I was I know not, but not Bottom), *Julius Caesar* (Casca), *Androcles and the Lion* (the Call-Boy, in a green tunic, and forced to my considerable chagrin to plaster my bare legs with No 6 make-up, an embarrassingly fetching shade of pink!), *The Admirable Crichton* (the Honourable Ernest Woolley), and on the BBC Children's Hour in a play called *St Hervez and the Wolf*, my first broadcast and a tremendous thrill for which I think I earned the princely sum of £1.

It was an interesting sidelight on the man's imaginative generosity that the fee for that broadcast was divided up and entered into the pocket-money accounts of all members of the cast. A week later we were all summoned to his study and he pointed out, very gently, that not a single boy had bothered to say thank you for this largesse. It was not, he said, that he wanted to be thanked. But it was an immensely important thing always to remember to say 'thank you', when someone does something for you or gives you a nice surprise. It was so well done that I never forgot that lesson, and have always tried (I'm sure unsuccessfully at times) to apply it, particularly to subordinates who take trouble beyond the call of duty.

To counter the undoubted disappointment of getting rather minor parts, I had time and an excellent memory with which to learn all the good lines, and there was a time when I could recite most of them, rattling off Chorus' speech at the start of *Henry V* or the great speech before Agincourt, Antony's funeral oration over Julius Caesar, Orsino's opening to *Twelfth Night*, and others such, on demand. In the end I gained more than I lost from my inadequacy as an actor. A secondary but significant joy of being part of the MGDS (Mourne Grange Dramatic Society) was the opportunity for legitimate rule-breaking. We rehearsed till all hours, sometimes getting to bed around midnight, after raiding the school larder for late night refreshment, led by our headmaster. And then we were allowed a lie-in next morning. We always entered the annual Newry Drama Festival, and always won our class. Sometimes we went to the Dungannon Festival also and won there too. I have no recollection of ever failing to win and once I think we were deemed best in the festival. Adjudicators certainly included Cyril Cusack on one occasion; Hilton Edwards, another distinguished Dublin actor, on another. It was all utterly memorable experience, highly educational, but I have little doubt that in this mad modern age the authorities would have closed the school down for some specious reason under the Children's Act or on grounds of health and safety.

Patrick himself was a pillar of the Newpoint Players, a very good amateur theatre group based on Newry and Warrenpoint, whose productions were highly professional and often won awards at the drama festivals, which became part of the school's life, as well. Their star was one, Livingston Armstrong; Patrick Carey was a better producer and director than an actor. His energy was extraordinary. Having worked all day and half the evening, he would go off to rehearsals with Newpoint and be back in class next morning in good order. On top of that he was also a member of the dreaded B Specials, the police reserve who kept the country safe from IRA activity for many years, but were ultimately disbanded by Ted Heath. Unfashionable though it may be now to say so, in those days to the Protestant communities of Northern Ireland they were resolute and powerful defenders of the realm.

Behind every charismatic figure there is usually a devoted second in command, unseen and unappreciated except by those who know. He keeps the show on the road and performs all the dreary routine tasks that must be done; he is the practical one, who introduces a note of sanity to limit the wilder aberrations of his colleague's imagination, and his frown of disapproval is often enough to rein in extravagance or put a stop to folly.

Such was the great George Biddle.

Built like a mantelpiece, or rather in the shape of a solid cube, as broad as he was tall as he was deep, short, square, wide-shouldered, barrel-chested, without a neck, with enormous hands, and wrists like tree trunks (indeed school rumour had it that he had once been an all-in wrestler), a bristly moustache and Teutonic haircut, his wrath was like the wrath of God – indeed on dire occasions the Almighty probably took lessons from him. He was a combination of Poseidon, *enosigaios*, the Earthshaker, and Zeus, the Thunderer. Lightning flamed from his eyes; his face turned scarlet; thunder rolled about his brow; the back of his neck took on a fiery glow; and he would smite (his preferred terminology) us Philistines, not hip and thigh as the Bible recommends, but on the side of the head with considerable force and an absolute disregard for medical advice, had it been available in those days. Not for him the village bobby's clip around the ear; his smiting was serious and extremely painful. In these litigious days I have little doubt he would have been barred from teaching. For us such wrath came with the territory; he was an institution, feared at times certainly, but respected too, and viewed with affection, preferably from a safe distance. That was his only weakness; in those days it seemed entirely normal.

I admired him without reservation and Sara and I continued to visit him in Rostrevor, to which he retired, quite close to where Grandfather also lived in a somewhat more secluded retreat. He loved the school and served it almost till his dying day. He ploughed most of his hard-earned savings into it to such an extent that in the end he was made joint headmaster, a status which he richly deserved. Too old to serve, throughout the war he carried the school while Patrick Carey was away fighting and old man Carey was too old to do much more than teach a limited number of classes. A product of Giggleswick and (I think) Manchester University, he spoke in the somewhat stately and periodic mode of the 19th century and was in many ways a quintessential Victorian gentleman; he taught French and maths; gymnastics in our proper gymnasium, where I learned to climb ropes, vault, and use the parallel bars, but never mastered the art of the 'set-swing-off', the high bar which one gripped with one's legs before flinging oneself backwards without hands to certain destruction, only to swing round and up again and alight safely; he coached all games, of course; conducted morning PT before breakfast; helped maintain the vegetable garden, rolled and cut the cricket pitches; and he also kept the account books, striving to reconcile Patrick's inclination to spend with his own compulsion to economise. From him I learned a lot of French and some maths; with others I was less successful.

This is the tribute I wrote for him when, in my 'Thought for the Day' series on the BBC in 1981, I took as my theme for the week those men and women who live an almost sacrificial life, doing their duty faithfully and without recognition in the service of others.

> My friend George was a schoolmaster. He joined the staff of a small school before the war. He served it, first as master, then as assistant head, and finally as head, until it closed. During the war he taught all day, dug the vegetable garden half the evening, did the accounts for half the night, and was in the Home Guard too. He was the most unselfish man I've ever known. Nothing he did was for himself; he took no time for himself; he lived as if he took no salary for himself; he asked no reward and would have expected no credit. The only large sum of money that came to him he gave away. In later years he cared for and loved an invalid wife until the day she died – and would have been surprised that one should comment on it, since for him it was no more than his Christian duty and the tribute of his love. From all over the province and from the South his friends and pupils came to his funeral, all seemingly moved by the same emotion; this supremely humble and unselfish man had touched their lives for good and we were privileged to have known him.
>
> He was not a great man – as the world sees greatness. But, as a man, he was great. I think I would rather have that for an epitaph than the wisdom of Solomon or the riches of the Queen of Sheba.

You don't have to be mad to run a prep school, but it probably helps. You certainly need a resilience and flexibility which would challenge the capacities of a stoic and a saint combined. Finding staff was never easy; in the postwar period probably well nigh impossible. Some strange beings passed our way like ships in the night. But there were memorable characters as well – Arthur Butterworth, who I think went back to England to run a prep school of his own, and had a very fast bicycle (with gears!) on which he was quite happy to ride to Belfast and back in a day, as well as a splendid repertoire of Cockney and Victorian music hall songs, with which he used to regale us. 'My Baby Has Gone Down (pronounced *gorn dahn*) the Plughole' was one of my favourites. He too loved the theatre and taught English marvellously well. He was much moved by one of our productions and wrote a rather good sonnet for the school magazine in celebration of it. I was much impressed by it even at that tender age. It began,

> Shakespeare himself was in your hall last night,
> Mourne Grange, although you saw him not perchance
> While head on hands he viewed your humble stage . . .

Karl Mullen, young, enthusiastic, athletic, went off to be a missionary, I think. Harry Heather, a jolly man who had his own dance band, taught us music and singing; Bond Walker was a gentle, kindly, and immensely courteous artist, with a studio in the Mournes, from whom alas I was much too barbarian to learn anything at all – to my lasting regret. Willy Edgar taught carpentry, rather well, and shot me once – with an airgun using chewed up wood shavings for ammunition. It raised a mighty blood blister on my hand when he tried to demonstrate how accurate it was by firing between my raised finger and thumb. It never occurred to me to tell anyone! Some very nice ladies acted as matrons and ran the more junior classes, but perhaps because they were so much more civilised and 'normal' than their male colleagues, their names have failed to register in my memory banks, though Anne Henry and Judie Hannah may be approximations to the truth.

I was lucky and, maths apart, very well taught. I was clever and law-abiding, and therefore I am sure approved of by the powers that be. I was probably a little mark-grub, who liked coming top of his classes at the weekly mark-reading; to others I probably seemed a smug little prig. But marks, competition, the chance to win promotion to higher classes, instead of being locked by dint of age alone into the classes of one's sometimes slower peer group, as is the modern fashion – all this ensured that I was always stretched. I started Latin at once and Greek at the age of nine, having already been taught my Greek alphabet for fun over the dinner table by a prefect, Joe Cunningham, later Sir Josias, Chairman of the Ulster Unionists until his sadly early demise. By the time I left I was writing Latin verses and Greek iambics, and even occasionally showed a mild talent for writing English poetry and prose, which was given some scope in my capacity as editor of the school magazine.

It was a measure of the carefree times we lived in and the Head's determination to treat us as far as practicable as young adults in the making, that as head boy and therefore editor of the school magazine I was sent by myself to Newry, some twenty miles away, by bus to negotiate with the printer for the production of the magazine; there I met for the first time the mysteries of the compositor's art and the problems of typesetting before the days of computers and IT. On another occasion I was sent to greet visiting adults at the front door on behalf of the Head, who was temporarily occupied, and escort them to the drawing room and offer them a glass of sherry. They never forgot the episode and reminded me of it years later when I met them again. I was once told by Nicholas Colchester (later of the *Financial Times*) that his parents sent him to the Dragon School in Oxford, because above all others it treated its pupils as if they were members of a public school, and to Radley because there they were treated like undergraduates. Mourne Grange I always felt operated on similar principles.

Another joy was the school library, where as well as the conventional children's reading I first met the historical novels of G A Henty, surely the very best way of introducing any youngster to history, with ripping yarns set in authentically historical situations. There too I discovered Enid Blyton, whose books I enjoyed but now in retrospect see little of merit in, R M Ballantyne, Robert Louis Stevenson, Baroness Orczy, Arthur Ransome (who made me for life an armchair sailor – I still yearn to learn to sail adequately), W E Johns (creator of the wholly admirable Biggles), and John Buchan, the best of boys' story writers of that era, full of good adventures, with historically accurate settings instead of the silly fantasy worlds in which we now invite young children to disport themselves so unhealthily, and with heroes who were admirable human beings – a vast improvement on the amoral heroes of modern thrillers. Though of course *The Thirty Nine Steps, Greenmantle, The Path of the King, John MacNab* and the like were a wonderful read, most memorable of all was *Mr Standfast*, which subconsciously introduced me to the idea of levels of meaning within a story. I was already familiar with *The Pilgrim's Progress* and therefore was enchanted by the phenomenon of recognition and implicit symbolism which Buchan's version gave me. Walter Scott defeated me – Victorian verbosity was, I suspect, the problem.

Current affairs were mandatory; the methods of instruction simple to the point of brilliant. Breakfast was at 8.00 each morning and was eaten in silence for the first ten minutes, while the BBC news was relayed by loudspeaker to the dining room from the Head's study. The struggle for Europe was still raging, so the incentive to listen was probably somewhat higher than in times of peace. In addition, on permanent display, was a large map of Europe, and as the Allied advance continued week after week red rings would appear round the cities they captured. For whatever reason Leipzig was the name that captured my imagination and I used to watch fascinated as gradually the red rings and arrowed lines drew nearer until the great day came when the city fell. I have never been there.

Games naturally played a major part. The young need to burn off energy and perhaps the greatest betrayal of modern state education has been the failure to provide adequately for sport for young people. We played all the major team games, in preparation for public schools of whatever persuasion – soccer, rugger, cricket, but not hockey, alas, and of the more individual sports, tennis and athletics figured strongly; and boxing too, still regarded in those days as manly, teaching you to take hard knocks, and keep your temper. Golf and riding lessons were available for those who could afford it and were so inclined, and swimming (in the icy Irish Sea) was *de rigueur*. If, as occasionally happened, the whole school had passed the swimming test (thirty breast-strokes, unsupported), we were given a half-holiday. There was also a fives court and there under George Biddle, whose hands were made of cast iron, I first learned (bare-handed, of course) to play the game which has ever since been the source of some of my closest friendships and happiest memories. It was the Winchester variety, much the best of three types of fives. Rugby fives I have always regarded as caveman's squash, somewhat crude, though vigorous; Eton fives is for the devious, well suited to the school which bears its name and has inflicted us with more politicians than any school has any right to do; and Winchester fives, the happy balance between the two, with a small buttress just to complicate the issue, but plenty of scope for violently thrashing the ball about as well. At Sedbergh it was my salvation; at Cambridge my delight.

I was a decent cricketer and once even captained the Ulster Schools XI, for reasons I never understood, unless it be that coming from an English school I avoided local jealousies for the authorities. Had I gone to a good English prep school followed by a major public school, I think I could have been a genuinely good player. But both at Mourne Grange and Sedbergh the coaching was poor, the weather regularly wet, and as a batsman/wicket-keeper I never really learned my trade. It remains the game I love above all others and I would happily coach it until my dying day. Soccer I regarded as acceptable; rugby something to be endured; tennis I enjoyed; golf I preferred, but being disinclined to work at it, I never got my handicap below twelve; chess I discovered there, and under the club rules one had to qualify by being able to achieve checkmate with a king and two bishops – or one rook – a useful skill for all ages. I can still defeat my computer up to about level fifty out of seventy-two, which is graded 'Stronger', – one better than 'Intermediate', but not yet 'Advanced'.

I was not musical, but if accompanied I could sing in tune and play the piano to a very modest standard. So I sang in the chapel choir, which I enjoyed, and there I first learned to love the psalms, sung of course to the old familiar Anglican chants. Occasionally I even played the organ on weekdays at the daily service. The school chapel was delightful, with stained glass windows salvaged I think from Armagh, and equipped with a two-manual organ whose bellows was pumped by hand, offering a particularly valued means of escaping the Sunday service for those who could not sing (designated 'croakers'). I have always felt indebted to and impressed by the memory of it and the habit of daily worship, which remained with me (perforce) for the whole of my professional life as a schoolmaster, though sometimes the tedium of routine became extremely irksome. Chapel had genuine atmosphere and gave one a wonderful start to life as a worshipping Christian. We had a set psalm for each day of the week and they had to be sung by heart – to traditional chants and with the correct pointing, of course. I still carry them in my head:

Monday, Psalm 31, 1–6, 'In thee O Lord have I put my trust, let me never be put to confusion, deliver me in thy righteousness';
Tuesday, Ps 91, 1–8, 'Whoso dwelleth under the defence of the most high';
Wednesday, Ps 8, 'O Lord our Governor';
Thursday, Ps 23, 'The Lord is my shepherd';
Friday, Ps 15, 'Lord who shall dwell in thy tabernacle';
Saturday, Ps 119, part 2, 'Wherewithal shall a young man cleanse his way, Even by ruling himself after thy word'.

I promise you I have written them out from memory, including the numbers.

The Creed was said standing to attention, because old Mr Carey had once been so impressed by finding himself in a cinema in England where at the end everyone stood to attention for the National Anthem (those were the days!). He decided that this was a good practice, which should be imitated. On Sundays as well as writing the mandatory letter home – another habit which remained with me until the age of forty, when I was back in Northern Ireland and my parents were nearby – we had to learn by heart and recite the collect for the week. Most of the term-time collects remain in my memory, in whole or in part – but of course in the proper language of the 1662 *Book of Common Prayer*, not the modernised banality of the updated versions. We also sat routinely every year the so-called Synod exams, set and marked by the Church of Ireland, and invigilated by no less a personage than the local Rector, who never otherwise to the best of my knowledge darkened the doors of the school or its chapel. So without realising it, I became familiar with a useful portion of my Bible. I am sure I can still hear in my memory's ear George Biddle declaiming the story of 'Naaman, Captain of the Hosts of the King of Syria (who) was a mighty man of valour. But he was a leper.' All the language, the cadences, the grandiloquence is right. It remains my favourite OT story – as it was my mother's.

Small boys I suspect are usually aggressive, competitive, self-centred. I wonder if that is why I cannot remember making any close friends there, or whether rather it is the fact that most of us went on to English schools and we all lost touch. Even the names have largely vanished, thanks to the often trivial connections by which our memories work. Tom Andrews, because he seemed enormously tall, and who (though we did not know it) would ultimately become a distant relative by my marriage to Sara. Brian Hannon, my main academic rival, and a far better musician, runner, and actor than I, later became the Bishop of Clogher; Christopher Bland, followed me to Sedbergh and then went on to far greater things, as one of Britain's most successful businessmen; Joe Cunningham I have mentioned; he had a cousin Jamie, tragically killed in a tractor accident on his farm; Nigel May, whose father became Minister of Education in Northern Ireland and was probably responsible for the development of its successful education system. I always wondered why the Labour Party in its doctrinaire dislike of independence did not learn something from us, since there are no independent secondary schools in the province.

I remember a Clarke, because he was the only boy to have more initials than I, five to my four, A B D E A; Norman Mavitty because I seem to have kept on meeting him since; Richard Scott, because his family owned a big mill down in County Fermanagh and this seemed rather romantic; 'Bolo' Alexander, much larger and stronger than I, memorable because I faced him once in the boxing ring. At the first bell he simply rose from his stool, walked across and punched me really very painfully on the nose; I collapsed on the floor with a colossal nosebleed, and so ended probably the shortest bout in the school's boxing history (very educational, I'm sure); Nicholas Hudson because he was the only one whose family took me out on a Sunday, which my parents rarely if ever did; and I still remember a hair-raising dash home once over the Spelga Pass in thick cloud, as we hurried to get back before the deadline for exeats – those were the days when the fact of having driven at sixty mph was a genuine excuse for boasting; John

Houston, whose father was a bank manager, whose address and father's status always seemed impressive and exotic to a small boy: Northern Bank House, Limavady! Of the southern contingent, from Dublin came Bobby Blakeney, and P E Ward, nicknamed 'Potto' because his family had something to do with the Dublin zoo; from Achill Island T Kidd, who knew his Bible backwards yet found ordinary reading surprisingly difficult (dyslexia, I assume, but it had yet to be discovered by educationists); from Mayo came Tim Roberts, who got osteomyelitis, and for whom we prayed daily in chapel for weeks – with complete success, I am glad to say. I still remember his bowling action in cricket, which resembled nothing so much as a demented octopus trying to send a semaphore message. Like Virgil's ghosts, flocking to the shores of the Styx, once I begin, the names and some of the faces come crowding back.

> *Quam multa in silvis autumni frigore primo*
> *Lapsa cadunt folia, aut ad terram gurgite ab alto*
> *Quam multae glomerantur aves, ubi frigidus annus*
> *Trans pontum fugat et terris inmittit apricis.*

As many in number as the leaves of the forest
when they tumble and fall at the first chill frosts of autumn;
or as many as the birds which flock to the shore from the deep
when the icy blasts of winter drive them far across the seas to sunnier lands.

My father got back from Malaya at some point in that first term. I will never forget it, not for the excitement of seeing him – which came later – but because of the intense disappointment associated with the event. He rang up the school and asked if he could speak to me. It was obviously regarded as a special enough event for permission to be granted and I was summoned, mysteriously, to the Head's study to take my first ever phone call. Desultory words were exchanged with the strange voice at the other end, but he finished with the exciting news that he would 'see me on Sunday'. The whole school went out, as usual for the mandatory Sunday walk, in typical crocodile, and lasting a good hour and a half. I sat in the school dining-room in my Sunday best, with my eyes glued to the windows. An hour and a half later I was still there, distressed and disappointed. They were very kind; they rang the Palace and it transpired that what my father had actually said was 'we'll see you some day'. Of such misunderstandings are childhood tragedies born.

I finally did meet him when I returned to the Palace at the end of term. I remember the exact spot, at the top of the drive, outside the front porch.

'Do you recognise me?' he asked and I lied manfully,

'Yes, of course.' In fact I was as shy and awkward about it as if I was meeting a complete stranger. Those missing years had created a gulf which, sadly, I never felt able to bridge entirely.

I won a Minor Scholarship to Sedbergh, slightly disappointing, but better than an Exhibition. It was worth £75, which covered school fees for one term out of three. As far as I know my parents chose it entirely on the strength of Patrick Carey's recommendation; they never went to see it – travel was less easy in those days. It should have been Shrewsbury, the family school, but my father 'took a scunner' to the Head (was it Jack Wolfenden?) and refused to let me go there. Needless to say I was not consulted. It makes me think of Robert Frost's little poem: 'Two Roads Diverged in a Yellow Wood', which concludes with these words,

> I shall be telling this with a sigh
> Somewhere ages and ages hence:
> Two roads diverged in a wood, and I –
> I took the one less travelled by,
> And that has made all the difference.

A sad postscript

The tragedies of individual human lives are the stuff of drama and novels. But when reality takes the place of fiction, then the merely sad puts on the dark costume of the tragic.

I still lament the passing of Patrick Carey. I remember him best in the 1950s, on the Leprechauns' cricket tours to Carlow, the life and soul of everything, a figure larger than life, a born raconteur, a mighty toper, the dynamic behind our social evenings, a natural leader on and off the field. Mrs Doorley's Hotel in Bagenalstown (Muine Bheag – my Irish spelling is dubious, I fear) was the headquarters for those tours, with matches always liable to start two to three hours behind schedule, as the local farmers finally escaped their more serious duties to play against us. We had memorable battles against the Vicar's XI (led by Andy Willis, that much loved pillar of the Church of Ireland), where the Stephenson brothers were mighty hitters of the ball and could well have figured in the pages of *England their England*; who we played I barely remember – but it included Carlow, Mount Juliet, Collattin, and the like.

There was the remarkable match played on the grounds of the local lunatic asylum in Carlow, where play came to a halt from time to time to let the patients amble across the wicket on their sad peregrinations about the grounds, and where the asylum chapel provided a much more interesting hazard than the great tree inside the boundary of the St Lawrence ground in Canterbury. In error we were once put to change in their temporary mortuary, only to be received by a poor old gentleman in his coffin, laid out and awaiting his last rites; there is a more painful memory of another occasion when dear George Biddle (always the most reluctant of losers) was captaining our side in lieu of Patrick Carey and we batted for the first four hours, despite ever more desperate pleas from many of us to declare, leaving our opponents a bare hour in which to match our score. I was so ashamed I sulked on the boundary for the rest of the game, resolutely refusing my captain's invitation to bowl. There was the remarkable morning after the night before, a particularly celebratory final evening, when a deeply disturbed Patrick Carey summoned the team to the hotel window to confirm the existence of half a dozen large spotted dogs of somewhat pinkish hue, Dalmatians possibly, which were padding up and down the street and emptying the dustbins, convincing him that at long last a richly deserved bout of *delirium tremens* had overtaken him. Not all of us had indulged quite so deeply and we managed finally to set his fevered mind at rest.

In the end I was told he attempted suicide, but failed. I visited him in Purdysburn, the Belfast mental hospital, and heartbreaking it was to see the wreck of the man, empty of life, sitting at a table with a small oblong of wood, which they had given him to sandpaper – quite pointlessly. If that was therapy, God forgive the fools who deemed it so. He recovered to a point and was given refuge by a relative, a brother possibly, who lived in Cambridge. There I saw him once more, but he had abandoned the will to live or to communicate and was lost within himself in some sort of private agony.

He deserved an end as sweetly remembered by his friends as that of Falstaff.

> He's in Arthur's bosom, if ever man went to Arthur's bosom. A' made a finer end, and went away an it had been any christom child; a' parted even just between twelve and one, even at the turning of the tide: for after I saw him fumble with the sheets and play with flowers and smile upon his fingers' ends, I knew there was but one way; for his nose was as sharp as a pen and a' babbled of green fields.

The manner of his death I do not know and would not wish to know. He was a life force and that is how I would remember him. RIP.

CHAPTER 11

Sedbergh – *Dura virum nutrix* – a hard nurse of men

O Eton has her river, and Clifton has her Down,
And Winchester her cloisters and immemorial town.
But ours the mountain fastness, the deep romantic ghylls,
Where Clough, and Dee, and Rawthey come singing from the hills.

For it isn't our ancient lineage, there are others as old as we;
And it isn't our pious founders, though we honour their memory.
'Tis the hills that have stood around us, unchanged since our days began,
It's Cautley, Calf, and Winder that make the Sedbergh man.

The Sedbergh School Song

ABOUT A HUNDRED YEARS AFTER the foundation of Sedbergh School in 1525, by Sir Thomas Lupton, Provost of the Royal College of Eton, Thomas Hobbes coined his famous comment on the life of primitive man:

> No arts; no letters; no society; and which is worst of all, continual fear and danger of violent death; ... solitary, poor, nasty, brutish, and short.

Never one to let the facts stand in the way of a good story, I was tempted to make the phrase 'nasty, brutish, and short' my subtitle for this chapter, partly because I found it memorable, and partly because by the addition of a single letter 's' ('nasty, brutish, and shorts') I could apply the quotation neatly and pungently to my experience of Sedbergh. It would have been legitimate, but not entirely fair.

Yes, we wore shorts, except on Sundays, perhaps lest the Lord be offended. In fact our uniform was entirely navy blue: blazer, shirt (open necked, which was humane), long socks, and those shorts – which on eighteen-year-olds looked pretty silly, and was just one of the many Scottish fashions foisted upon their more civilised southern neighbours by those reared under their lamentable influence. I speak as one of Scottish descent, who subscribes fully to Dr Johnson's great dictum that 'the noblest prospect which a Scotchman ever sees is the high road that leads him to England'.

Brutish? Yes, to a degree. To suggest that there were 'no arts and no letters' would be untrue, because J H Bruce Lockhart, who had once been a great headmaster but was in something of a decline by the time I got there, had worked very hard to civilise the place. He was himself a man of many talents, a linguist who was made a Companion de la Légion d'Honneur for services to the French language, a good musician and a painter, as well as a rugby international of whom it was generally said with typical schoolboy generosity that he was the worst fly-half that Scotland ever had, and his son the second worst. My own knowledge of the game does not qualify me to comment on the claim. We had two orchestras; a wide range of arts and crafts on Wednesday afternoons were compulsory, as were art and music lectures for the sixth form as part of their general education. Drama, however, was lamentably unambitious, limited to occasional house plays and a school production every other year of a Gilbert & Sullivan opera.

But despite his best efforts, the prevailing atmosphere overall was pretty philistine, best illustrated by this brief welcoming dialogue with a senior on the day after my arrival as a new boy. X: 'What form are you in, Wilson?' Self: 'Upper IV A.' X: 'O God, a brain!' I might add that X was a bully – but there were not many like him.

I entered the school in January 1951. The details remain sharp and clear. First, my trunk, sent by PLA (Passenger's Luggage in Advance), in those uncomplicated days when British Railways were entirely reliable and a trunk sent a few days ahead could be guaranteed to arrive safely and on time. Then the boat from Belfast to Heysham, with the agony of stilted conversation for half an hour or more with Mother and Father until the almost welcome announcement, 'All those not travelling please proceed ashore.' The excruciating homesickness, every term, which never ceased until I went to Cambridge; some wild storms, which left me convinced that we could only sink, as had tragically happened to the Princess Victoria; sharing a double-berth cabin (bought for economy) with occasionally strange men, sometimes drunk, but never a threat, though in my innocence I would not have known what sort of threat they might have been; the desperately early arrival at Heysham, around 6.30 a.m., catching the train, changing first at Lancaster, then at Low Gill (later Tebay), and finally down the branch line to Sedbergh, with a mile-long walk up to the school. When the station was closed, we had to get out at Oxenholme, which then required a taxi across the fells to Sedbergh, but spared us the final walk. Getting to the school soon after 9 a.m. was miserable, because no one else arrived till mid afternoon.

And, on that first occasion, as it was for Eliot's Magi, it was bleak in the extreme. 'A cold coming we had of it,/Just the worst time of year/For a journey, and such a long journey: . . .' It was bitter cold and the wait on the open platform at Low Gill was icy. The ground was white with frost. Lupton House was uninviting in the extreme. The Irish contingent, about six of us, usually arrived together, but on this occasion, Eric McIldowie, who was to become a lifelong friend, was delayed by illness and my escort was a senior, whose obligations ceased as soon as we stepped in the door. Eric himself was the exact antithesis of myself, and perhaps that is why we got on. He was not interested in games, so at least we shared an antipathy to rugger, though he was a member of the school rifle team. He was a scientist, and rather a good one, always tinkering expertly with things electrical and mechanical. He went on to Oxford, and thence to Harwell for a time, before turning like me to teaching. A year my senior, he was a source of sanity in our slightly mad world – and in the holidays his mother regularly organised splendid Scottish dancing parties in Holywood, which helped me to overcome my shyness and learn to fraternise more comfortably with the fairer sex.

I was a term behind my now well-established peer group, who had joined in September, at the start of the school year. My parents had been persuaded by Mourne Grange that I was rather young and immature and would be better with an extra term in their more gentle surroundings. So, now, as one born out of due season, I was thrown in at the deep end, late and somewhat lost. I was placed in U4A, the scholars' form, and therefore again well behind the game, particularly in science which I had never done, and which I was allowed to abandon none the wiser after two terms.

So there I was, like Samson among the Philistines, 'eyeless in Gaza at the mill', not quite knowing what I was supposed to do or where to go. But I was no Samson and I found it tough and scary, though my first housemaster was kind. But he soon went off to be the head of Liverpool College. There were certainly scholarly men and good teachers on the staff – and my second housemaster had a first in classics, though he was among the least scholarly and intellectual of the clever men I have known. The saying that 'ideas, if they occur to him, he rejects like temptations to sin' could well have applied to him. Similarly, there were some very intelligent and able boys, the prefect for whom I fagged being one of them. He was a gentle, civilised, and very academic historian by the name of Robert Rhodes James, who became a Clerk of the House of Commons, an author of some distinction, Fellow of All Souls, and then MP for Cambridge. He always seemed embarrassed by the whole idea of fagging, and the only duty he inflicted on me was to clean his shoes. But, with such honourable exceptions, generally speaking there was a cult of toughness, the atmosphere was anti-intellectual, and the resulting products seemed too often to be hard, conforming philistines, with an unhealthy interest in rugby football.

The school motto, *Dura virum nutrix* ('a hard/harsh nurse of men') comes from Virgil's description of the early Sabines, I think, those rough, tough, coarse mountain dwelling tribesmen who formed the very backbone of the expanding Roman state and its armies. It was not inappropriately chosen. But Virgil himself had cribbed it from Homer's *Odyssey*, a passage where Odysseus tells King Alkinous of the Phaeacians who he is and where he hails from. Butcher & Lang's translation catches the flavour well.

> I am Odysseus, son of Laertes, who am in men's minds for all manner of wiles, and my fame reaches unto heaven. And I dwell in clear-seen Ithaca . . . A rugged isle, but a good nurse of noble youths. ('*trecheia all' agathe kourotrophos*').
>
> (Od.9.27)

Notice how Virgil's rendering has distorted the original. Homer's phrase 'good nurse of noble youths' (in Greek *kouroi*, young male figures, idealised in the funerary statues of early Greek art into some of its greatest achievements) has been turned into the 'harsh nurse of men'. The choice of the Latin motto rather than its Greek equivalent offers a revealing symbol of how Sedbergh to a degree lost sight of the educational ideal of nobility and nurture in the pursuit of toughness and hard living. It was in that respect still a very Victorian school, tough and proud of it.

I have no doubt that fifty years will have greatly improved and civilised the general ethos, and that the recent decision to go coeducational will have proved enormously beneficial. When I applied for the headship in about 1975 it would have been my proposal to the governors that we should look at the idea – my thoughts being that a 'marriage' with nearby Casterton Girls School was an obvious approach. Some boys had sisters there. I was interviewed, but fell at that first hurdle; I did not like them, nor they me. If I had suggested coeducation they would have run a mile.

I look back on my time there with very mixed feelings – I was a timid child, and certainly for my first three years one dominant emotion was a general sense of permanent apprehension; my regret is that, as a senior, I will have done little to alleviate such a feeling in others. One tends too easily to accept and replicate the ethos of any institution one belongs to.

> Into my heart an air that kills
>   From yon far country blows:
> What are those blue remembered hills,
>   What spires, what farms are those?
>
> That is the land of lost content,
>   I see it shining plain,
> The happy highways where I went
>   And cannot come again.

Something of Housman's ambivalence characterises my own memories, too. Schooldays, by convention, are the happiest days of your life. Not so my own days at Sedbergh, I am afraid. There were good things, of course, particularly those celebrated in the school song quoted above. The Yorkshire Dales, on the western edge of which Sedbergh is situated, amid the Howgill fells, are still a lovely part of the world, with Windermere and the Lakes some twenty miles further west, and the glorious expanses of the Dales stretching eastward. Sara and I have a couple of time-shares on Windermere (setting of my beloved Arthur Ransome's tales) and we have holidayed regularly near Settle, in Malham village, our most favourite place of all. My love of countryside – already well established – was reinforced by my time at Sedbergh. We had 'the freedom of the fells', in BL's (Bruce Lockhart's) oft-repeated slogan and those blue remembered hills are tinged with a sunshine which sometimes parted the darker clouds that loomed on the horizon.

But those hills were not a source of undiluted pleasure. I was a stout little boy when I got to the school, and lost seven pounds weight in my first term. Those fells were something of a purgatory, because of the endless compulsory cross-country runs on which we were sent, if for some reason rugger was 'off'. If we took too long on a given route, we were beaten for being idle. Uphill was torment; downhill fabulous, and I discovered the pleasure and mastered the art of scree-running and racing descents of hillsides, which have never left me. But I was good at fives and if I could book a court, then the run was excused, which is why I described the game as 'my salvation at Sedbergh'. To those endless hours in the fives courts I owe my three half-blues and captaincy of the Cambridge side. In my three years Oxford never beat us. Equally enjoyable was yard soccer, a far better game than rugger, and equally valid as a reason for not going on a run. Every house had a walled and tarmacked yard of considerable size, in which six-a-side soccer could be played ad infinitum (yard cricket in summer). The game was non-stop, since the walls ensured that the ball could never go into touch, and we played it by the hour, for pleasure as well as compulsory exercise.

The best time for the fells was the occasional extra half-holiday (one or two per term), awarded on the whim of the Head if fine weather made it appropriate. The rules were simple: by 4 p.m. you must be three miles away from Sedbergh. This put places like Cautley Crags and Cautley Spout, Calf Fell, or even Baugh Fell within the reach of even ponderous souls like me, and one could wander off with a few mates and simply enjoy the fresh air and the countryside. The nearest legal spot at which to await the hour of four o'clock was Danny Bridge in Garsdale, where there was also a small cave, where I dare say the ungodly enjoyed a crafty smoke – not an activity in which I ever felt the slightest interest. Occasionally our Housemaster and House Tutor, Austin Boggis (who introduced me to Puccini's *La Bohème*, 'Che Gelida Manina' in particular, by the simple device of playing his radiogram fortissimo late at night, with Gigli singing so gloriously that even my barbarian soul was moved), would take longer expeditions across Whernside or elsewhere, using two cars and starting from each side, exchanging keys in the middle when we met. Energetic souls indulged in feats of occasional madness such as running the twenty miles to Windermere (and back – possibly illegally by public transport).

Winder (see the school song above) was the school hill, looming over the town to a height of I think 1,500 feet. As a run, twenty-five minutes was par; take more than thirty and one was probably in trouble. Legend had it that one athlete for a dare did it in eighteen minutes during the twenty-minute morning short break in lessons, and got back in time for class – where he dropped dead. Of such legends are mythologies born. Calf (ninety minutes) was just too far, even for a half-day run, though it was occasionally imposed if the Head of House thought we all needed 'bracing up'. When the clouds were down and snow on the ground with a wind blowing, it was mildly threatening and very bracing. Once a plane was lost somewhere in the fells and we were all marshalled into a search party across Baugh Fell to look for it and I remember being deeply apprehensive lest we found it with a dead pilot inside. On such occasions failure can be a pleasure, and the walk, with classes excused, certainly was.

In the hills a few miles to the south-west was Lilymere, a lake of considerable size, which froze in winter. It was a time of year with little to commend it, what with compulsory morning cold baths (skip it and be beaten), cross-country runs, rugger with frozen hands, ice-cold dormitories etc. But if it really froze, a skating extra half-holiday with the whole school carried off in buses to Lilymere, tested for safety by staff armed with sledgehammers, was a time of utter exhilaration. There I learned to skate – adequately in a straight line, but not very expertly in the sudden turns required for ice-hockey, a game for the gods themselves. Never again will I move so fast over level ground, though skiing downhill with the help of gravity (which is cheating) may be faster. We could skate from end to end of the lake just for the hell of it; play ice-hockey – in shorts of course and without protective equipment of any kind (what would the sad demons of the Health and Safety Executive say nowadays?); staff would decorously figure-skate in various isolated areas; bliss was it in that hour to be alive.

By contrast come summertime and the living was easy. There were, as I remember it, no compulsory runs, though I cannot think why. I played cricket, which I loved, and ultimately captained the Colts XI, before apparently causing considerable shock by choosing to join the tennis club the following year, where I played for the school VI. I had been ill with mumps and came back late for the summer term. Finding the first XI already established and given no chance to win my place, in dudgeon I departed for the tennis club, only to regret my decision and return the following year to cricket and win my place and colours.

In summer too the rivers were low, where in winter under the endless rain that seemed to afflict the area they could turn into monstrous floods, rising fifteen or twenty feet in spate to overwhelm their banks and spread across the flood plains and threaten the bridges that spanned them, which never showed the slightest tendency to surrender to their power. In summer a calmer mood prevailed and river bathing became the preferred form of relaxation, in particular in the River Lune beside the viaduct, some two miles away, where shallow rapids turned in a moment into slow deep pools, where trout hung gracefully in the current, and salmon lurked, and adventurous lawbreakers would try to spear them with home-made harpoons. Occasionally bathing, but mainly sunbathing and gossiping on those river banks, by the waters of Babylon I sat down and slept. I don't think I ever read a book.

Almost more than the fells I remember those rivers with great affection. How I wish that I had learned to fish and joined the fly-tying classes, which were offered on Wednesday afternoons for arts and crafts. Instead I chose carpentry one year; picture-framing another; pottery the next; and declamation and debate the year after — an absolute waste of time, since we were taught none of the skills of speech making or debating. My father had long insisted that I learn public speaking if I got the chance; he was himself so uncomfortable making speeches that he would not even make the speech at Audrey's wedding. I suspect that he had an exaggerated sense of how easily the art could be taught, as well as a desire to make sure that I was not similarly handicapped. I always resisted this pressure, on the surprisingly mature grounds that once I had something useful to say I would be able to say it. On this occasion, I was proved right; it was a wasted year. No attempt was made to introduce us to the useful, if artificial, skills of rhetoric.

I see without surprise that all these, my strongest memories, have little or nothing to do with the development of my mind. *Mens sana in corpore sano* is supposed to be the ideal of education. My *corpus* was rendered *sanum* enough, I suppose. Certainly I was as fit as I have ever been, though in the famous annual Wilson Run, not named after me or any ancestor, I was the heaviest boy in the race, charged by the school doctor not to try too hard. Obediently I came second last, in 1 hour 45; the winner usually made it in about 1hour 15; the school record was 1 hour 10, and had lasted fifty years or more. Ten miles 'up hill and down dale, thorough bush, thorough briar', and plunging into 'deep romantic chasms' before struggling breathless up the other side to plough along the fell sides and over the lower slopes of Baugh Fell, it culminated in a final 2.5-mile road sprint back to the finish. It was optional to enter; but even I felt that I could not leave the school without competing once. I would not wish to do it twice.

So what about the *mens sana*? I wish I could be more positive.

I have said that I was thrown into the deep end and it might appear that the result was satisfactory. Five terms later I was in the Classical Upper VI, and in June 1953 after eight terms and barely sixteen years old I was sitting my A Levels, while taking four O Levels at the same time without having had any teaching. I read up the English literature set books in the week before the exam, and took English language, maths and French on the back of a good memory and what I had done in previous years. O Levels were regarded with relative contempt, though compared with modern, dumbed down GCSEs they were fit only for the higher echelons of MENSA.

Such accelerated promotion has its advantages. Clever children do not stultify and their capacity for absorbing knowledge in those early years is almost limitless. There were certainly some advantages in a school like Sedbergh, with its rather modest academic standard, since the system at least allowed me to escape rapidly from the boredom of the lower levels. I was not the cleverest boy in the school; nor was my promotion particularly noteworthy. Peter Hutchinson, the top scholar, consistently defeated me in the merit rankings all the way up the school, and could have gained an Oxbridge award, had he chosen to go there. But I was able enough to be thoroughly bored for my first two years, doing only enough to get by in all my subjects except science, where I should have been fascinated but in fact became rapidly disenchanted. Sadly, the subject was taught by a particularly uninspiring and rather stupid master, who totally failed to engage the interest of anyone in the class. He was a fine rugby player, which no doubt was deemed sufficient qualification for the job.

But I was, at least, spared the tedium of the modern system, which demands that every pupil remains with his/her age group for a year and progresses with them. This can be alleviated by setting, but even that is disapproved of by the purists and the proponents of mixed ability teaching, and the amelioration it offers is at best partial. The dogma of equality and the discouragement of élitism of any kind helped to ruin the first brave experiments in comprehensive education. Equality of any kind, whether in education or any other activity, is a denial of the observable facts of human nature, and ensures only equality of mediocrity in performance. One day élitism will return to the world of education, since all these things are largely questions of educational fashion and political dogma; they go in waves and we are still some decades away from inevitable changes in perception.

Precocity is a pejorative word for the fear which clever children inspire in stupider adults. I was not precocious nor was I rendered so; rather in fact I found that to spend time in class with those who were both clever and older in years was immensely stimulating, and if anything encouraged maturity. After all one sees more than enough of one's peer group outside the classroom for all social purposes. I was thrilled to reach the Upper VI and for the next two years worked as hard as I ever have done in my life, partly to keep up, and partly to satisfy the demands of that most exacting of taskmasters, Peter Newell, later headmaster of Bradford Grammar School and then the King's School, Canterbury, but at that moment Master of the Classical VI, the academic élite of a relatively unacademic school, though to do it justice in February 1964 *The Times* reported that a *Where* survey of the A Level results of the 'top' seventy-five boarding schools in the year 1961/2 had shown Sedbergh bracketed in seventh place with Westminster, for the average number of A Level distinctions per 100 boys. On A Level passes per hundred boys, it was much lower, at fifty-first. Bright boys did well; others not.

Educationally it was lamentable that I should have been able to get through school with no science, but in the early 1950s science had not yet acquired the 'must-have' status of later years. Those who planned to read medicine at university were, on the whole, the less able scientists, and probably better doctors as a result, since they retained their humanity in a way that clever scientists too often fail to do. Even arts graduates could still train as medics. The better scientists of my day went into physics.

Peter Newell was described to me, years later, as the dullest man ever to win a scholarship to Magdalen College, Oxford. With the wisdom of the years I can see that this was probably so; his teaching was mechanical in one sense, in that he drove his pupils extremely hard and made us learn the rudiments of Greek and Latin syntax and grammar, until we were expert in the rules and the exceptions to the rules, and could cite chapter and verse for both, with examples learned by heart, of course. I don't think I ever realised under his tutelage what it meant to be studying two great literatures. But by good fortune things changed in my final year, when he had moved on to higher things and was replaced by Anthony Reynell, who later went to Marlborough College as Head of Classics. Under Newell, classics was predominantly textual study, directed towards accuracy of translation, gobbits syntactical and literary, and the acquisition of vocabulary. As for ancient history, it was a necessary evil, a third A Level and barely taken seriously. That drama was about theme and character, form and structure, ideas and symbol, that literature might contain several levels of meaning, and be written in the context of historical situation, none of this meant anything to me. I was a mechanical digger of meaning in the most literal sense and Newell was the driver.

But my goodness I was grateful later, because my foundations were rock solid and the high-falutin' literary stuff could all be added afterwards, both in my final year and then at Cambridge. Reynell started it. Under him we studied the *Bacchae*, Euripides' greatest play, as an A Level set book and he opened my eyes to the meaning of the play and how a dramatist went about his craft. Ten years later, when I was asked to direct the Greek play at Radley, as successor to the immortal Charles Wrinch, it was natural that it should be my choice. It was the final and for me one of the most memorable events of my career there.

Dull though he may have been to his contemporaries, for us Newell sparkled, sometimes (naughtily) at the expense of his colleagues ('I am always in first gear; some of my colleagues are always in neutral;' 'I will not have you casting my pearls before your ... housemasters'), sometimes with epigram or apophthegm ('the grunt is no substitute for proper punctuation'; 'vague froth is no substitute for truth'; 'you should always joke about religion; you are much more likely to retain it if you do'; 'Juvenal takes the material of the *News of the World* and makes it literature'); or irrelevant asides which simply added to the fun and stimulus of the moment ('don't gossip; it's not orchestra practice'; 'I don't like the word 'benevolence'; it sounds like Father Christmas in a multiple store'; 'it's your funeral; I shall merely conduct it'; 'Kirkup is infallible – unlike the Pope').

He was absolutely dedicated to high academic standards, which cannot have made him the easiest of colleagues, but certainly maintained the high morale of the Classical VI, which under his aegis gained more Oxbridge awards than any other department in the school. No subject merited serious consideration except classics. 'Geography matters as long as you take it in your stride and don't study it as a special subject.' 'History and modern languages have not yet established themselves as serious and genuine vehicles of higher study.' 'General studies, in which a boy puts nothing in and gets precious little out.'

One of our more irreverent class members set himself to record these gems for half a term and made a collection of them – about 150 in all. He solemnly presented them to Newell, who was so amused that he had them copied and presented us each with a copy. Hence my brief selection above. In a fit of juvenile enthusiasm I was foolish enough to show them to my father, who normally had quite a good sense of humour. He made his displeasure absolutely clear and suggested that the man was a twerp, too childish to be allowed to teach us. In that he missed the true magic of the great teacher's craft. Not only must he organise and present his material in such a way that his pupils understand and remember it, and want to know more; he must also generate a kind of collective chemistry which ensures that everyone is delighted to be there and excited by the experience. However childish it all seemed in cold blood, at the receiving end it was certainly the greatest fun. Fun and hard work – the perfect recipe for schooling.

Only one other teacher really caught my imagination – Michael Thorneley. He had been house tutor in School House, when Bruce Lockhart was the housemaster (as well as headmaster). When BL retired, probably as a result of his influence Thorneley was appointed headmaster in his place. Internal appointments are pretty unusual in the public schools – and rightly so. They are sufficiently conservative and inward-looking institutions to need fresh blood at the top at regular intervals. The announcement absolutely flabbergasted the school (which had limited respect for the gentleman in question – the only sport he could play was figure-skating on ice) and it divided the staff. I remember walking back to my house after hearing it and just ahead of me was one of the older housemasters, a man endowed with a somewhat fiery temperament. He was absolutely apoplectic and the colour of his neck was a gloriously entertaining blend of scarlet and plum, and while he talked to his colleague he was literally and visibly spitting with rage. There was a movement among some of the staff to protest, vague murmurs of which reached us, but nothing came of it; they even asked Newell (by then at Bradford GS) to intervene but he wisely refused.

I only enjoyed one year of the new regime and predictably things went on much as before. But being taught English by the new Head was an enriching experience. There was an early setback to relationships when, in the somewhat satiric spirit in which we had been reared, A C Hogarth, aptly named, heralded the Head's entry to lessons one morning with a quotation from Shakespeare, a stage direction, appropriate enough perhaps, until mispronounced, deliberately – 'enter a Sewer', not as of 'one who sews with a needle' but as of 'that which conveys sewage'. The offended personage turned literally white with rage, which was quite exciting in an awe-inspiring sort of way, but impressively kept his cool, and the lesson began in an atmosphere of considerable unease. But no further repercussions followed. How very wise.

There was only one lesson of English per week – it was barely an academic subject of course by the standards of the times – and the methodology was strangely simple. Thorneley would recite some thirty or more lines, usually of Shakespeare, which we would take down in our quotation books as dictation, and then learn by heart for next time. But then he would talk fascinatingly about the context, often declaiming all the parts himself, explaining the dramatic situation, the characters, and the importance of the particular passage. Utterly memorable were the 'Homeric similes' of Arnold's 'Sohrab and Rustun' which still return to haunt my imagination fifty years later. We learned them all by heart, and in full.

> And dear as the wet diver to the eyes
> Of his pale wife who waits and weeps on shore,
> By sandy Bahrein in the Persian Gulf . . .
>
> For very young he seemed, tenderly reared:
> Like some young cypress, tall and dark, and straight . . .
>
> As when some hunter in the spring hath found
> A breeding eagle sitting on her nest,
> Upon the craggy isle of a hill-lake . . .

There were others too. Compelling in a different way was the psychology of Iago's corruption of Othello's love for Desdemona. The key passage is still with me. It begins:

> I: My noble Lord . . .
> O: What dost thou say, Iago?
> I: Did Michael Cassio, when you woo'd my lady, know of your love?
> O: He did, from first to last. Why dost thou ask, Iago?
> I: But for the satisfaction of my private thought. No further harm.
> O: Why of thy thought, Iago?

I could go on and on.

As with all the things I was compelled to learn by heart, I remain deeply grateful both for the acquisition of the lines, and for the greatly enhanced understanding of the plays and poetry from which they came.

School chapel was 'all right', but naturally enough a bit of a bore, especially when there were two services. Unlike my more worldly-wise brethren as new boys, I was tested and, as they saw it, foolishly demonstrated that I could sing in tune. Three right notes got me into the choir. BL often conducted the practices and I very much enjoyed it. I had no regrets until, like the typical teenage fool I was, when my voice broke I gave up and never went back. I enjoy singing, unmusical though I am. I should have remained in the choir and learned more. I should also have taken up the offer of music lessons, but I was deeply conscious of costs by then, I am not sure why, and knew that music lessons were 'extra'. I refused.

I also got confirmed, like everyone else, which is thoroughly sensible, whether one thinks one is a believer or not. It ensures that in later years you will know the way back, if you pass through the typical late adolescent atheist phase. In fact my religious development followed a different pattern, with most problems of belief coming later in life, when I began to think rather harder about the problems of the Faith. At the school stage, and even at university, I was a relatively uncomplicated believer with a slight tendency towards a sort of pantheistic view of God and His universe. The glorious natural setting of the school no doubt contributed and there were several moments when I was 'surprised by joy', though there was of course no one with whom I would have dreamt of turning to share the rapture. Most memorably once, emerging from Sunday worship at the back door of the chapel, I was confronted as always by Winder looming onto the gaze, but white with snow and absolutely glittering with sunlight against a blue sky. Of course there was a God! And I still think pantheism has much to commend it.

The same economic sensitivity that made me avoid music lessons led me to take the same three A Level subjects three years running. I had gained distinctions in Latin and Greek (equivalent of starred A grades nowadays I suppose) in my second year in the sixth, and at the very least should have added an extra subject to my repertoire. Instead I insisted on doing the same three again. The reason was finance: my parents had inadvertently failed to enter me for the State Scholarship in time. This, without means test, would have given me £75 per annum towards my university fees – a very significant sum. As with the decision not to take music lessons, no one asked me why; no advice was offered; no remonstration from my housemaster, who should have at least pressed me hard. My parents would I am sure have told me, even if it was not true, that the money was not a problem. Possibly also there was the Cambridge Scholarship exam to follow in December and so it may have seemed wiser to stick like the cobbler to my last. Once I had got my Exhibition, however, someone should have urged me to stretch myself a bit. My housemaster, Peter Marriott, was a genial soul, but somewhat indolent, and probably could not be bothered. I wasted my final two terms and though I passed A Level and got my State Scholarship, my performance was significantly worse and I gained no distinctions.

What matters most in one's schooling? I was certainly toughened, physically and probably mentally, by my experiences. But my confidence and self-esteem were less developed. I had learned to work very hard and to tolerate discomfort (which was useful in the army). I had reinforced my love of the countryside. I had played a lot of games, but never lifted a paintbrush, written a poem, or played a musical instrument. My best chance of becoming re-enthused was rapidly destroyed. Inspired, momentarily, by my first encounter with the slow movement of Beethoven's 'Pathetique', played to sixth-formers in cultural art/music appreciation lessons, I had bounced enthusiastically up to the Director of Music and asked whether it was possible to get a simplified version of the sheet music, which I could learn to play on the piano. 'Don't bother me now, boy; I'm busy', was the reply. I had not learned how to read a book properly; I had not discovered the excitement of ideas. Academically I was little more than a high-powered parrot.

Though I have always enjoyed sport, I regard the emphasis on sport in my school days as contributing to a serious retardation in my intellectual and imaginative development and personal maturity. Careers advice was unheard of.

But I had an Open Exhibition worth £50 per annum in Classics at Christ's College, Cambridge (Grandfather's and Uncle John's old college), and a Northern Ireland State Scholarship worth £75 per annum, enough to cover between them the fees for at least one term.

Like the father whose child asked him, 'What did you do in the war, Daddy?' my reply would have been similar, 'I survived'. In my early childhood, if not in my infancy, Heaven lay about me; at Sedbergh shades of the prison house had seemed to close upon the growing boy. Now he could begin to see the light again.

Is my verdict on my old school unduly harsh? I am not sure. But from all I hear, I would rather be there now than then, and I still wish I had gone to Shrewsbury.

CHAPTER 12

The Army

The Royal Irish Fusiliers – Princess Victoria's 87th/89th of Foot
Motto: Faugh-a-Ballagh (Clear the Way)
Organised as the county regiment of Armagh, Cavan and Monaghan in 1881

These, in the day, when heaven was falling,
The hour when earth's foundations fled,
Followed their mercenary calling,
And took their wages and are dead.

Their shoulders held the sky suspended;
They stood, and earth's foundations stay;
What God abandoned, these defended,
And saved the sum of things – for pay.

HOUSMAN'S MEMORABLE LITTLE POEM can be read in two ways. It has been argued that he had in mind the British professional soldiers of the First World War, and that his purpose was to honour them. But it can as easily be read as a denial of the conventional military values of honour, courage, dedication, and self-sacrifice; an assertion of the futility of fighting and war. I have always liked it, but when I set its thought against my own experience of military service I incline to the more cynical interpretation.

Having left school for the last time, I returned home presumably expecting a pleasant and rather lengthy holiday before going up to Cambridge in October. I had earned it. Relatively speaking my career had been exemplary; I had worked hard and played hard, had consistently good reports, been a school prefect, and won a scholarship.

I have no recollection of how or when it happened, but at some point, out of the blue, my parents told me that they had decided I was going to do National Service. Northern Ireland residents, for reasons that recent history will have made obvious enough, were not required to do it; there would have been rioting in the streets had it been compulsory. For the same reason my regiment-to-be had lost its claim to be the county regiment of Cavan and Monaghan in 1922, with the establishment of the Irish Free State. However, the parents had decided that I would 'volunteer'. There was no discussion; no attempt to ask my view of the matter, or even to examine the merits of going up to university first, as many did, and then going on to do their service; no consideration of the fact that the obligation on the rest of the UK would be ending shortly, which it did.

It is a measure of my father's inability to conduct a rational discussion, if there was any disagreement, that he presumably played it as a *fait accompli*. I am surprised that my mother went along with it. It is a measure of my own timidity, lack of confidence, and habit of obedience that I simply accepted the decision. I look back on it as a lamentable way to treat an almost grown-up son. If I was going to have to do two years in the armed forces, it was also a wasted opportunity. The Army offered many interesting possibilities (Engineers, Intelligence Corps, Signals, for example), and the RAF or the Navy would almost certainly have provided a more stimulating experience. But no; it had all been fixed behind my back, that I would join the PBI (Poor Bloody Infantry) in the shape of the Royal Irish Fusiliers. They were in a sense the family regiment, in that Michael Somerville's brother Brian was himself an Irish Fusilier, Armagh (Gough Barracks) was its home depot, John Law, a distant cousin was a serving officer in the regiment, and the CO of the Depot at the time (Major Jimmy Trousdell) was known at a social level to the family. It must have seemed an obvious choice, though I myself had no knowledge of the regiment or the connections.

The Powers-that-Be had invented what was called the Northern Ireland Short Service Commission. This was a one-year army commission, following the inevitable eight or nine months of basic training and officer cadet training, assuming one was selected for the latter – there was no guarantee. There was also a four-year commitment to service in the Reserve. The attraction, if one can call it that, was that provided one passed the War Office Selection Board (WOSB) first time, one would be out in twenty-one months and able to have a second long holiday before going up to university. Also, as a volunteer, one received a Regular's pay, which was nearly double that of a National Serviceman.

I wish I could say that the experience was of more than limited value to me. I probably grew up a bit. But two years is more than 10% of a young man's life and one would probably mature if one spent it, like Estragon, sitting on a mound under a tree chewing a carrot and waiting Godot. I learned few new skills, beyond teaching myself to touch-type in my spare time. I read several long (and to be honest rather tedious) classic Russian novels, played a great deal of poker with my brother junior officers, whom I liked. We had a problem, of course. It was the time of the Suez crisis and at one point it looked as if the regiment might be sent to Egypt. Fortunately, for once the Americans did the right thing and told the British and the French to behave. But the effect of the crisis was a serious shortage of fuel. There was little transport; we had limited opportunities for serious military training; we walked – sorry, marched – everywhere, which tends to slow things down; and being stationed in Germany with nothing much to do, the primary purpose of our existence was to stop the men getting fractious through idleness. The whole year was mind-numbingly boring and our existence seemingly pointless. We were, I suppose, the first line of defence against a Russian invasion, but I wonder if it had come to it how long we would have managed to hold up any advance.

If we were there to 'save the sum of things for pay' or anything else, no one told us.

I am back in snapshot narrative mode. Occasional moments are highlighted in my memory against a monotonous backdrop of pointless activity.

It is interesting to me that I can remember my first arrival at prep school, at Sedbergh, and at Gough Barracks; the one place I cannot remember arriving at was Cambridge, which was the one place where arrival was at least as good as travelling hopefully and did not feel traumatic.

The moment of my arrival was symbolic in that almost the first thing I saw was the corpse of a soldier who had committed suicide, on a stretcher and under a sheet, being loaded onto a one-tonner to be taken away. It was certainly a somewhat unexpected welcome. The next forty-eight hours were undiluted hell. Haircuts; issuing of uniforms and kit; inoculations, TABT, plus Yellow Fever (for reasons unknown) which left you feeling as if you had a severe bout of flu. Because this was a known reaction, we were allowed to spend much of our time in our barrack rooms, bulling our boots.

Only the army could have invented such a ludicrous system. Boots, especially toe-caps, had to be polished till they shone like mirrors. But when issued, the leather was entirely dimpled. Armed with a dessert spoon, a candle, and a tin of black boot polish, one heated the spoon on the candle and burned the boot polish into the toe-cap while pressing down so hard that the dimples were gradually ironed out. Thereafter a combination of spit and polish was required to work the boot into a high gloss shine. This was no quick process. My recollection is that after some five hours I had got almost nowhere. Weeks of effort brought me somewhere near to mediocrity. Greatcoat buttons were almost as bad. They had to shine, but were made of a specially designed non-shining brass. I was once put on a charge and sentenced to seven days CB (confined to barracks) for the heinous crime of having dirty buttons. My defence that I had spent some five hours trying to shine them was dismissed with contempt by my company commander. Justice, sweet reason, and common sense were not part of the army's code.

My fellow recruits seemed to be entirely London cockneys (as you would expect in an Irish regiment, this being the army), including one who was, by repute, the 'king' of the teddy boys. Almost the only recruit with whom I seemed to have anything in common was Harry Bates, a Wykehamist and a fellow Ulsterman, who like me was designated a potential officer and who, unlike me, decided at the end of his period of service to stay in the regiment and become a genuine regular. His genial companionship helped to make it all marginally more tolerable.

Gough Barracks, Armagh, the regimental depot of the Royal Irish Fusiliers, was set on the crest of a low hill above the Mall, frowning down upon the gaol, which by comparison was a surprisingly handsome piece of architecture. Only Dickens could have done justice to its awfulness, with its high walls crowned with barbed wire, its grim barrack blocks, and its married quarters, which from the outside looked like slum dwellings. The regiment had, of course, to its considerable embarrassment suffered the indignity of an IRA raid, which had robbed its armoury of weapons. The circumstances were never mentioned, but it gave us all a sort of frontier-town mindset: it was not going to happen twice.

At some point during my basic training it confronted me with an interesting dilemma. Guard duty at night was a serious business. In plimsolls for silence and fully armed with rifles and live ammunition, some of us patrolled the barracks, while others manned the defensive concrete strong points which commanded views of key locations. Our instructions were clear: any unidentified person was to be challenged to halt, and then to advance and be recognised. If they did not do so, the next command was 'Halt or I fire', accompanied by the action of putting a round up the spout. This drill was regularly practised and it was a serious matter if you failed to carry it out to the letter.

That night I was in the strong point covering the front gate and a view across the barrack square. I had seen the RSM, Regimental Sergeant Major, a being somewhat loftier than God, doing his rounds in the late evening, turning out the guard for inspection, and then proceeding onwards across the square. Did I challenge him or not? I knew perfectly well who it was, but did he know that I knew? He had passed from view behind a building before emerging into view again on the square. The drill was clearly laid down. Would it be a defence to say I knew who it was, when I could not claim that I could recognise anyone in the dark at that distance? In trepidation I took a deep breath and shouted, 'Halt'. He paid not the blindest bit of attention. I took a very much deeper breath, shoved a round up the spout, and shouted, 'Halt or I fire'. That stopped him dead, so to speak, in his tracks. 'Advance and be recognised.' It took him about ten years to advance from where he was to my position. I give him full marks. He simply said, 'OK, laddie', and went on his way. There cannot be too many soldiers who have threatened to shoot their RSM and lived to tell the tale.

My initial time in Armagh was mercifully brief. For reasons that were never divulged, it was the policy of the regiment to send its PLs (potential leaders – possible officers) to do their basic training at Wemyss Barracks in Canterbury, part of the Buffs' depot. The so-called PL wing there was commanded, most improbably, by a civilised and humane Commanding Officer, a Major Thomas. His unusual (for the army, of course) theory was that if you imposed too rigid or brutal a discipline, you knocked the confidence and initiative out of young men who were shortly to be trained as leaders. In his view officers were paid to think and to show initiative and this should not be discouraged. So the training there, though entirely orderly and disciplined, lacked the unthinking brutality of conventional basic training. The result was, so we were told, that a higher percentage of candidates from our unit passed WOSB (the War Office Selection Board) than from other units. Certainly we were never cowed by the mindless, stentorian bullies of NCOs that were commonly to be found in military establishments of those days. The training was good enough; we did enough drill to satisfy the most traditionally minded. Canterbury was a pleasant location. We saw little of it, though bar billiards in the Seven Stars was certainly one of the relaxations of choice. We also practised some of the leadership tests which we would encounter at the selection board, so that we were not taken entirely by surprise by challenges such as crossing a fast flowing river using two oil drums, three poles and a coil of rope too short to go round the drums, while carrying a five-ton block of concrete.

Basic training complete, I went off to the WOSB – a three-day ordeal, if I remember rightly – and was subjected to the usual battery of interviews, tests, leadership challenges and other inscrutable activities by which in their wisdom the army selected its officer material. My recollection is that out of eight or ten candidates in my panel, two passed. I was one of them. What merits they saw in me I am at a loss to imagine, beyond the good fortune of a public school education and a respectable accent.

Between passing WOSB and being sent to Eaton Hall Officer Cadet School I endured a period of about eight of the most tedious weeks of my army career. No one knew what to do with us. The gap was too short to send us to the battalion; too long to send us on leave. I spent several weeks in Canterbury doing fatigues and became extremely expert at lighting the stoves, which alone heated the offices from which the PL wing was administered. It was, in military parlance, a cushy number and I made no effort to find anything more constructive to do. Being paid for doing little was delightful. I was then reclaimed to the depot at Armagh and I remember nothing of my time there, presumably because they were as nonplussed as everyone else as to how to employ me. I have no doubt that in the all-regular professional army of today this sort of nonsense would not occur. National Servicemen, which in effect I was, must have been a nuisance.

Eaton Hall was a splendid location – a black, Gothic-looking pile, which would have served admirably as a film set for the abode of Count Dracula, but in fact was the seat of the Duke of Westminster, which had been commandeered by the army as an officer cadet school for National Service officers, while Sandhurst remained the élite establishment for the proper regulars. It had nice grounds and the usual array of Nissen-hutted accommodation for the trainees. Remarkably, though I never knew it, at the foot of the main staircase, hung Reubens' 'Adoration of the Magi'. It is now above the high altar in King's College Chapel, Cambridge, but at that stage it was simply there, in situ, and utterly vulnerable to the minor vandalism of passing officer cadets, especially at the end of every passing-out dinner. It was recognised for what it was by a young trainee officer cadet, who had a considerable knowledge of art. He very bravely drew the matter to the attention of the Commandant and it was removed to a safer location. He later went up to Christ's College at the same time as myself, and that is how I heard the story of its rescue. Those were complacent days as far as terrorism was concerned. There was the occasional mention of a threat, but not sufficient for anyone to decide to arm us with anything more effective than the pick handles with which we did our guard duty. After Gough Barracks, it all seemed a bit tame.

The NCOs who ran our lives were admirable men, impressive in bearing, deafening in utterance, absolutely dedicated to their job, and determined to make the best of us, even though, like all our predecessors we were the lousiest bleeding shower of miserable creatures that had ever passed through their hands or, in Jonathan Swift's immortal words, 'the most pernicious race of little odious vermin that nature ever suffered to crawl upon the surface of the earth'. Over sixteen weeks they wrought miracles of improvement in us! Though they were almost caricatures of any drill sergeant that one would have seen on film, they commanded our utmost respect. By contrast my platoon commander, a paratrooper captain of quite bovine stupidity, was an object of discreet ridicule and well-concealed contempt.

As I remember it, the training lasted some sixteen weeks, culminating in a week's battle-camp in Wales, which included a three-day exercise that was physically immensely demanding and nearly cost me my life. I was designated the Company Commander's wireless operator, which entailed following closely in his footsteps ready to transmit messages as and when required. In a howling gale with blinding rain, somewhere round about midnight, so wet, cold, and exhausted that I could hardly put one leg in front of another, armed with a rifle and with a very heavy wireless set on my back, amid the bogs of some god-forsaken Welsh hillside, I endeavoured to follow my boss across what looked like a muddy drain about six feet wide. He leapt it easily, being lightly equipped; I failed by at least three feet and disappeared up to my neck not in water but in oozy, slimy, all-enveloping mud, which seemed to suck me down. It must have been an old peat-cutting or some such. My boss, fortunately, heard my yell, which he well might not have done in those conditions, and just managed to grab the muzzle of my rifle and slowly, very slowly, drag me out. Since then, while walking on hills I have treated all bogs that I have encountered with absolute cowardice.

Only on one other occasion did I consciously face a serious moment of danger, and that was not in action either. By then I was commissioned and serving with the battalion in Germany. We were doing grenade practice with my platoon and I was standing on the range talking to my Company Commander with a collection of grenades beside me which we had just finished priming. From the next trench came the cry, 'Prepare to throw; throw!' My Company Commander, who was an old soldier, shouted, 'get down' and pushed me flat. The grenade exploded and the base plug whistled harmlessly over our heads. No harm done, but a very startled fellow officer looked out of his trench to apologise. It could have been unfortunate; but such things happen, though the modern media encourage the idea that they do not. Their headlines foster the fiction that nothing should ever go wrong, and that someone is always to blame; in fact, they are responsible for the modern tendency to be wise after the event, which helps to maintain their sales and feeds the lawyers, society's most parasitic and self-interested profession.

I was lucky – I never saw real action and was never tested under fire. For this I am grateful; I lack any inclination towards heroism.

Eaton Hall I remember with satisfaction rather than any pleasure. We worked hard and with a clear sense of purpose. My fusilier's *cawbeen* (Irish beret) and *hackle* (feathers) added something approaching the proverbial cubit to my stature, and selection as the right marker for my platoon on parade was a kind of minor distinction, which was gratifying. It meant I was considered co-ordinated and reliable. But I blew any chance of serious distinction, such as achieving the coveted Under Officer status, by a frivolous lecturette in front of the Commandant, which my platoon commander felt had made a fool of him in front of his boss. He had clearly been saving me up for the occasion, which he knew would come. It taught me a simple lesson about the cowardice and two-faced-ness of minor authority in the face of its superiors. Until that point, the lecturette exercises had been treated as of no importance – a laid-down element of the syllabus, which had to be gone through. There had been no instruction; and others before me had been trivial, flippant, frivolous, without any evidence of disapproval. None of us wasted more than a few moments on preparation for our five-minute talks. Suddenly I received a public and imperial reprimand for frivolousness.

One thing that the classroom element of our instruction did teach me was the value of the issued précis. The army has always been rather good at instruction; it teaches its soldiers, whether stupid or intelligent, with great efficiency. After every lesson we were given an excellent précis. It was a practice that I used throughout my teaching career, though I tended to issue them before the lesson and encourage pupils to add their own notes. The preparation of such précis is a useful discipline for the teacher and of great assistance to the pupil; it avoids substantial error in understanding or facts. It also means that a class can listen, concentrating on the essentials instead of just taking down what the teacher says almost verbatim. The difficult art of note-taking is a separate and no less valuable skill, but it comes later.

The passing-out parade was a great occasion, equivalent to graduation, and clearly intended to mimic the Sandhurst passing-out parade. I think the Adjutant rode a horse, but this may be fancy. I was now a Second Lieutenant, Her Majesty's Trusty and Well-beloved, the lowest of the low in the military hierarchy. I bought the mandatory trilby hat to wear with civilian clothes, so that I could acknowledge salutes from soldiers, who were expected to recognise an officer even in 'civvies'; opened my first bank account with the Westminster Bank, whom I have never left; spent a small fortune on the necessary dress uniform; acquired as part of an officer's equipment the fine Irish blackthorn walking stick, which has now been my faithful walking companion for fifty years; was sent on leave; and then went out to join the First Battalion of the Royal Irish Fusiliers, stationed in Wuppertal-Elberfeld in Germany. After ten months in the ranks, I now had a year of commissioned service ahead.

In ordering my dress uniform from Moss Bros at the high but manageable price of £25, I think it was, I had no idea what a tremendous crime I was committing. Only when I reached the battalion did I discover that this had to be ordered from the approved regimental tailor, at about four times the price, which with no private means I could not afford. Strong men trembled as they explained that General Sir Gerald Templer, the Colonel of the Regiment, could recognise the dud article at fifty paces, was liable to explode if he saw it, and would certainly tear the offending garments (literally) from the body of any subaltern seen so inadequately dressed. My only hope was that he never visited the battalion in the course of my time there. I am proud to say that under such fire I held my nerve and decided to chance it, while refraining from expressing the contempt I felt for such behaviour by such a lordly being. It was the action of a bully, inflicted on one who would be in no position to resist, and though I regarded the threat as very real, I felt that its realisation would be pathetic. Politely instructed to get myself properly dressed, I would have probably done so; such a childish exhibition of official disapproval was totally unnecessary. This boldness was very uncharacteristic of me; a small piece of my father's strong character had shown itself for once.

BAOR, the British Army of the Rhine, was originally the British Occupation Force of Germany after WW2 and its original function was to control the corps districts, which ran the military government of the British zone of occupied Germany. As the threat from Soviet Russia increased, BAOR became more concerned with the defence of the West than with the occupation of Germany. NATO was formed in 1949 and its primary combat formation was 1 (BR) Corps, and from 1952 onwards the commander of NATO's Northern Army Group (NORTHAG) was always the British Commander of BAOR.

BAOR had three elements – 1 (BR) Corps, the main fighting force, with HQ at Bielefeld, some 200 miles north-east of Dusseldorf, where the Rear Combat Zone was based, with the task of reinforcing the forward fighting formations. The British Communications Zone based at Emblem in Belgium was to control the ports and canals through which reinforcements from GB would be sent to the front. The size of the army varied between 65,000 and 125,000 troops, but was reduced in 1993 under the Options for Change policy to a mere 25,000, with the new title of BFG, British Forces in Germany.

Needless to say, in an army whose motto might well have been the famous lines about the Six Hundred, 'Their's not to reason why,/Their's but to do and die', it would not have occurred to higher authority to explain to the most junior of junior officers why he was there or what his function was in the greater scheme of things. Throughout my time in the army whether in the ranks or as an officer,

I saw no evidence that it had occurred to anyone that we were potentially intelligent beings who might be interested in understanding policy or strategy, and even better officers if we did.

We were part of BAOR and the Soviets were a threat, which we would have to resist. That was sufficient unto the day. We must expect tank assaults, which we were singularly ill-equipped to stop, and the possibility of nuclear attack, for which we practised digging very deep trenches for protection, twelve feet down and with six feet of overhead cover, with the access trench at right angles and facing towards the enemy, since the bomb was likely to be exploded behind our front lines and fall out would therefore be less likely to penetrate. It was an extremely tedious business.

As I have already said, it was the time of the Suez crisis, petrol was in very short supply, and training was essentially rudimentary. I remember long route marches over days, designed to keep us fit, led always by the Company Piper, Corporal Cullen, whose stamina was such that he could sustain his marching tunes hour after hour as we pounded along the highways and byways of middle Germany. Only once, on the army's main ranges at Sennelager during brigade manoeuvres, did we have a really exciting military exercise, riding into 'battle' at dawn on tanks after a night march, rather romantically guided by a line of dimly lit lanterns, which marked our route to the forming-up positions. There was the excitement of the assault and the pride that our regiment had undoubtedly accomplished its role faster and better than any other (how anyone could actually tell I have no idea). But just for those few days I caught a whiff of the excitement and romance of soldiering and had there been more of it I could have been tempted to remain. As it was the tedium and pointlessness of much that we did was such that I 'retired' after my year's service with the utmost relief.

Only two other enriching experiences remain clearly in my memory.

The first was a delightful three days' leave over the Queen's birthday weekend, in which John Leonard, a brother officer, and I took his ancient but splendid BMW (with manual throttle as well as accelerator – very posh) up the Rhine as far as the Rhine Falls in Schaffhausen in Switzerland. We slept under the stars in the vineyards; we ate what and where we could. We saw the Lorelei; spent a day in Heidelberg, which was fabulous; admired the fretworked spires of Freiburg; were impressed by the brooding darkness of the Schwarzwalt (Black Forest) and in particular the Mummel See, while finding considerable comfort in the eponymous gateaux of the area (*Kuchen mit Zana* became our daily catch phrase round about teatime); inspired by the madness of youth I vowed that one day I would float all the way down the Rhine on a Lilo; back down the Neckar valley until we rejoined the Rhine again at Mainz I think, and home via Koblenz and Koln. For one who had never holidayed abroad, because my parents subscribed to Uncle Matthew's dictum that 'abroad is bloody', it was an enchanting eye-opener.

The other experience was odder, but no less appreciated. The battalion was instructed to nominate an officer for a Religious Leader's Course, presumably because the chaplain's department had to justify its existence by running a certain number of such courses every year. The most junior and most expendable officer was inevitably chosen. It was me. The course was held in Iserlohn, a delightful part of Germany, hilly and forested, with innumerable waymarked footpaths for walkers. Of the contents of the course I remember little, except a rather good film for its time called *The Magic Box*, I think, which unfolded in glorious technicolor (still a bit of a novelty then) the wonders of creation with the implicit message that no one beholding such marvels could seriously doubt the existence of the Almighty. Very sensibly we were subjected to very little instruction, not much discussion, and no indoctrination. We were encouraged to take the afternoons off and to wander through the glorious scenery and contemplate its beauties. As a relief from the inanities of regimental life, it was a real blessing.

There was also one wasted opportunity, which I greatly regret, caused by my own naïvety and the regiment's failure to prepare me for the thing properly. A notice appeared on the Officers' Mess notice-board inviting anyone interested in making contact with a German family to volunteer. It was presumably part of a programme of getting friendly with the natives; the war had ended more than ten years ago; the Soviets were now our enemies; but we still had little or no contact with the civilian population, whose land we were occupying – or defending, depending on how you viewed it. I volunteered, was given the address down in Wuppertal, and duly set off along the famous *Schwebebahn* to meet my would-be host (Herr Willi Schenze, if I remember aright). I was horrified by the state of the town, which till then I had barely visited; ruins and rubble were still everywhere, with semi-destroyed buildings clearly being occupied as best the inhabitants could. It had not occurred to me what terrible suffering and dire problems the German population must have faced after the war. The family were clearly less than affluent but their hospitality was warm and friendly, though my total lack of German and their very limited English made the encounter difficult. On my next visit they introduced me to their daughter and then for a time made themselves scarce. In my innocence – Sedbergh had not prepared me for close encounters with the feminine kind – I smelled a rat and decided on no legitimate grounds that I was being set up for some form of matrimonial entrapment. I fled as soon as I decently could and never went back. An opportunity had been lost through poor preparation by the authorities, who should have provided some sort of basic language instruction and background guidance; and through my own immaturity. I am still mildly ashamed of myself when I look back on the episode, without actually feeling much to blame.

In July 1957 I returned to civilian life and prepared to go up to Cambridge. I had earned my living and been entirely responsible for my own destiny for two years, and perhaps I am unfair to say that it was all of limited value to me. To some extent it was indeed a formative experience. I had certainly matured and faced new experiences and some interesting challenges, including being (nominally at least) in charge of a platoon of men. I learned one valuable lesson: feed the horses first, then the men, and the officers last – in other words, always look after your subordinates before yourself. It is a lesson that seems to have been well and truly forgotten by modern captains of industry. I learned one lesson in military tactics, which also has useful applications in civilian life: the most dangerous moment on a patrol is the last mile, when you think you are safely home. You get careless. Be doubly careful. The habit of tidiness and importance of cleanliness once acquired has never really been lost either along with the old joke, 'if it moves, salute it; if it doesn't, paint it – white'.

The elusive quality of self-confidence is largely part of one's genetic inheritance, I suspect. But it can be acquired, or at least enhanced, by sympathetic training and a rich multiplicity of experiences recollected and reviewed in tranquillity. The army certainly gave me a whole new range of experiences, occasionally interesting, sometimes useful, more usually tedious, pointless, or uncomfortable. But the totality probably added something to my character, something to my ability to endure discomfort and wretchedness, and something to my capacity to cope with the unfamiliar. But all in all, it was not a lot to show for nearly two long years.

I liked my regiment; enjoyed the company of my brother officers; found little to attract me in mess life; and with all the typical arrogance of youth was on the whole unimpressed by the more senior officers, though some went on to distinguished careers. With regret I have to confess that I doubt if I gave back as much as I received; but as in my schoolboy career, I had done my best and worked conscientiously.

CHAPTER 13

Christ's College, Cambridge

College Motto: Souvent me souvient *(OF: I remember often)*

> *For we were nurs'd upon the self-same hill,*
> *Fed the same flock, by fountain shade and rill.*
> *Together both, 'ere the high lawns appear'd*
> *Under the opening eyelids of the morn,*
> *We drove a-field, and both together heard*
> *What time the Gray-fly winds her sultry horn,*
> *Batt'ning our flocks with the fresh dews of night,*
> *Oft till the star that rose at Ev'ning bright,*
> *Towards Heav'n's descent had slop'd his westering wheel.*
>
> John Milton, 'Lycidas'

I HAVE ALREADY EXPLAINED MY affection for Milton's poem, 'Lycidas', the lament for Edward King, his college friend drowned in the Irish Sea. His college was my college, so metaphorically speaking we were 'nurs'd upon the self-same hill', and here in pastoral mode he reflects something of the excitement of the shared exploration of ideas, the friendships of youth, and the long hours of the night spent in fierce argument and putting the world to rights, which is part and parcel of undergraduate life. The university experience has, or rather should have, little or nothing to do with getting a job, but everything to do with intellectual awakening and broad education. Under pressure from short-sighted governments, universities have abandoned this sacred duty, and offered their students training instead of education.

True education is a preparation for death, the moment of judgement for the life we have each lived. Education as preparation merely for the life of work is largely pointless. As Wordsworth puts it,

> The world is too much with us; late or soon, getting and spending, we lay waste our powers ... We have given our hearts away.

Plato in writing of the ideal education for our rulers says that

> when they are fifty, those who have come safely through and proved themselves the best at all points both in study and action must be brought at last to their true goal. They must lift up the eye of the soul to gaze on that which sheds light on all things; and when they have seen the Good itself, they must take it as a pattern for the right ordering of the state and of the individual, themselves included.

All would-be politicians should take note. It is sad, if not pathetic, to see young men and women going into politics as a career instead of doing something really useful first, gaining experience of the real world, and then bringing to the nation's legislature a moderation born of rich experience.

But it is the late Elizabethans who seem to have best expressed the value of academic education. Milton himself suggested that the aim of education is to 'know God aright and out of that knowledge to love Him, to be like Him, by possessing our souls of true virtue'. Here, too, is the great Francis Bacon on *Studies*:

> Reading maketh a full man; conference a ready man; and writing an exact man ... Histories make men wise; poets witty; the mathematics subtile; natural philosophy deep; moral grave; logic and rhetoric able to contend. *Abeunt in studia mores* (studies shape character).

Queen Elizabeth I herself endorsed this verdict:

> I pluck up the goodlisome herbs of sentences by pruning, eat them by reading, digest them by musing, and lay them up at length in the high seat of memory by gathering them together; that so having tasted their sweetness I may less perceive the bitterness of life.

Though much later, even Cardinal Newman maintained that

> if a practical aim must be assigned to a university, then it is the training of good members of society. For a university is an *alma mater*, knowing her children one by one, not a foundry, nor a mint, nor a treadmill. It is not and should not be an institution for instructing the masses.

Practical skills are acquired through apprenticeships to the masters of their crafts or professions. University study is not to be seen as a practical training for a career.

The early Greek philosopher Heracleitus (fl. 513 BC) wisely observed that 'the highest excellence is Thought'. Of royal blood, and true to his principles, he surrendered his kingship to his brother and wrote a treatise on the cosmos instead, which he placed in the Temple of Artemis at Ephesus, and of which fragments survive. He argued (like St John?) that Logos governs the universe, and equated it with transcendent wisdom and elemental fire. Such wisdom lies not in much learning, but in the awakening of the soul from the slumber of its private wants to an awareness of this cosmos, or world order. To listen to great teachers and share in their speculations is the beginning of wisdom, and is the true purpose of a university education. William Cory's translation of Callimachus' lament for Heracleitus, who must have been an inspired philosopher and teacher, reminds us of the true calling of all great teachers.

> They told me Heraclitus, they told me you were dead;
> They brought me bitter news to hear and bitter tears to shed.
> I wept as I remembered how often you and I

Had tired the sun with talking and sent him down the sky.
And now that thou art lying, my dear old Carian guest,
A handful of grey ashes, long, long ago at rest,
Still are thy pleasant voices, thy nightingales awake;
For death he taketh all away; but these he cannot take.

It is the penultimate line that starts a tear in the eye, for it expresses what must surely be the richest reward for any teacher, to have a pupil say of him (to translate it more literally), 'But your nightingales live on for ever; death can lay no hand upon them.'

At Cambridge I was singularly blessed. I had two Heraclituses, neither of them in my own college, but each in his own way hugely influential, and a good friend to me long after I had left the university. Within the college teaching system one had a Supervisor and a Director of Studies; for general pastoral care one had a Tutor. My Tutor was the well-known historian J H (Jack) Plumb, who took a close personal interest in his historians, but was relatively indifferent to pupils outside his own discipline. The classicists were a delightful pair of rather elderly dons, Sidney Grose (ancient as the hills, but exquisitely courteous in an olde worlde sort of way) and Arthur Peck (marginally less ancient, but a quintessential eccentric, who collected old lamp posts, was an expert on Aristotle, and had a room knee deep in books and documents, through which one struggled to find as it were a North West Passage to his desk, for discussion of one's latest essay or prose). Though doubtless brilliant in their specialities, their teaching was sufficiently pedestrian for me to complain formally to my Tutor, who refused to do anything about it. Whether fairly or not, I believed at the time that he was engaged in delicate political manoeuvrings to win the Mastership of the College, which naturally precluded the ruffling of any feathers or the loss of any potential ally. In fact he was defeated in his ambitions three years after I went down, in the election of 1963, by the Nobel Prize winner, Alexander Todd, and had to wait until 1978 to claim this ultimate accolade of academic ambition. C P Snow (also of Christ's and a friend of Plumb's) delightfully records such labyrinthine scheming in his novel, *The Masters*, which is a dimly concealed account of an earlier but similar political struggle within the college.

Fortunately Plumb, whom I never liked, for all his distinction as an historian, departed for a sabbatical year and his place as my Tutor was taken by a splendid English don, Graham Hough, who found a way round my dilemmas. Having got a First in Part 1 of the Classical Tripos, I was faced with the task of choosing my speciality for Part 2. My primary interest was in literature, but to choose this meant that I would be supervised within my college. So I opted for ancient history and to my unbelieving delight Hough said that he knew Moses Finley well, and that occasionally he was willing to supervise students who were not members of his own college (Jesus), if they had firsts. I could not believe my luck. This was my first Heraclitus.

Finley was the most exciting lecturer in the university; students from other disciplines flocked to hear his talks, which were delivered without notes from a couple of ideas on the back of an envelope, with vigour, eloquence, and in the manner of a thoughtful conversation, almost, between old friends. The sheer breadth of his reading was legendary, and when he declared in the course of a lecture that 'nowhere in the whole corpus of ancient literature will you find a single mention of this, that, or the other . . .', you believed him, because you knew he had read it all! He had been a professor at Rutgers University in the States; then a lecturer at Oxford before wisely transferring to the superior university; where he was Reader in Ancient History, and subsequently appointed Professor in 1970. In 1976 he was elected Master of Darwin College.

His range was extraordinary. His original speciality was psychology and American constitutional law; this he extended to economics and sociology before turning to ancient history. He had started to teach himself Latin and Greek at the age of twenty after marrying a classics teacher; he was familiar with German, French and Italian, and well read in the scholarly literature of those languages. Momigliano called him 'the best living social historian of Greece, and the one most prepared to face the methodological problems which social history implies'. We understood that he had been hounded out of the USA by that abomination of all civilised discourse and open-minded exchange of ideas, Senator Joe McCarthy; we did not know that he had formed the American Committee for the Defence of International Freedom among university teachers, in order to resist McCarthy's pernicious influence, and was dismissed by his university and came to England as a refugee from McCarthyism.

He was stimulating to listen to; refreshing in his ideas (he and Hough and several others had combined to try to revolutionise the teaching of arts subjects in the university); and he introduced a novel element of sociology and economics into the rather dry, traditional academic pabulum of the ancient history syllabus. He held seminars as well as giving individual tuition – an entirely novel approach, though probably common enough in his native America. The sheer intellectual enjoyment of listening to him teasing out the implications of his ideas was the thing we all remembered. America's loss was our enormous gain, and it was a fitting tribute to his genius as a teacher and scholar that he was knighted by the Queen and elected Master of Darwin, one of the university's research colleges.

He was a modern Socrates, and to have been taught by him I regard as one of the great intellectual privileges of my life. One of the most memorable moments of my undergraduate career was when he handed me back a long essay, about ten sides of A4, which I had written for him on the Causes of the Peloponnesian War. It had two words on it: 'My Congratulations' and one grade: alpha. It was a great moment, which I never forgot. He started me on my career as a translator by teaming me up with Pat Lacey of St Catherine's, later Professor of Ancient History at Auckland University, to produce a source book for late Roman Republican history. Pat was, of course, the brains behind the operation and planned the whole book off the top of his head in about forty-eight hours. But he was gracious enough to acknowledge that I had a better way with words, and I did nearly all the translating. Moses also got me a commission from Penguin Classics to translate Cicero's *Republic* and *Laws*, which alas I had to abandon when I got my headship, though I still have the text, and made me Secretary of the Ancient History Committee of JACT, the Joint Association of Classics Teachers, a post in which I served for ten years during an exciting (and ultimately rather sad) time in the evolution of classical studies.

For me his nightingales indeed 'live on for ever, and death can lay no hand upon them'.

Of my other Heraclitus, more anon. Christ's College, originally known as God's House, was founded in 1505 by the mother of King Henry VII, Lady Margaret Beaufort with the assistance of John Fisher, Bishop of Rochester, later to be burned at the stake for his allegiance to Rome. Christ's became a training ground for radical Puritans, among whom John Milton was to be a leading figure. Of its great alumni, apart from John Milton, the most famous name of which I was aware was Charles Darwin. I had heard of William Paley's *Evidences of Christianity*, without ever associating him with my college; Smuts and my grandfather were both honorary fellows, but I knew of them for family reasons. Todd, a Nobel Prize winner, and J H Plumb were leading figures in the college when I went up; of the reasons for their distinction I was unaware. C P Snow I knew of only as a novelist. Ian Ramsey had yet to become Bishop of Durham and was probably the most *papabile* of all potential Archbishops of Canterbury never to be so chosen, by reason of his untimely death. Of Rowan Williams I had not even heard until he was so chosen. As for the Master, Brian Downs, he was a remote and probably very shy character, whom I do not think I ever met and I certainly had no idea what his subject was.

Other colleges, such as Trinity and King's, had more distinguished academic pedigrees. But when I entered the college in October 1957, in terms of current all-round merit and a healthy mixture (both social, academic, and athletic) in its intake, Christ's would have been hard to beat. For this one man, the Senior Tutor, Dr C L G Pratt, whose subject was medical science, was largely responsible. We all believed he was hated for it by the academic purists like Plumb, whose narrow-minded interest in the things of the mind to the exclusion of all else might have produced more firsts, but would have robbed the college of much of its broad range of talents and interests.

There were many good legends about Pratt's method of selection, of which the most common was that when a candidate entered his room for interview, he would throw a rugger ball at him. If he dropped it he was rejected; if he caught it and drop-kicked it straight back into the waste-paper basket, he was accepted, whatever his academic merits. It was also believed that he deliberately left his front door unlocked at night, so that undergraduates out late who were prepared to risk it could get back into college, via his study window, without being fined for lateness. On one occasion a miscreant attempting the feat and tiptoeing through the study heard Pratt coming and hid behind a sofa. All was well; Pratt sat down and read a book. Three hours later he got up, yawned, and remarked, 'I don't know about you; but I'm going to bed', and left the room without looking back. He was that sort of man. His favourite poet was the very minor Thomas Lovell Beddoes; his favourite poem by that author, 'Dream Pedlary'. He once told me that he had always wanted to write a brief life of Beddoes. I like the idea of medical men civilised enough to love poetry. It is rarer nowadays than it would have been then; medicine has become too specialised for the broadly educated. I was delighted to discover recently that he is still alive and celebrated his hundredth birthday on 26 September 2006. I liked the man and I like the poem, of which I quote the first verse, *ex pietate* and in salutation.

> If there were dreams to sell,
>   What would you buy?
> Some cost a passing bell;
>   Some a light sigh,
> That shakes from Life's fresh crown
> Only a roseleaf down.
> If there were dreams to sell,
> Merry and sad to tell,
> And the crier rang the bell,
>   What would you buy?

During my time, in one memorable year, the college had nine, I think, of the University XV, and nine of the football XI. It boasted rugby internationals like Tony Lewis, Brian (was it?) Thomas, and Dave MacSweeney; Donald Steele, who was to make his name as a golf correspondent; Ian Balding, a rider and trainer of no mean repute; and others, I have no doubt, whose names have escaped me. Only in rowing were our achievements limited. I assume Pratt was indifferent to a sport which involves no ball and (absurdly) requires its participants to travel backwards at the highest possible speed they can muster. How can one take seriously a game in which the competitors cannot even see where they are going?

I made many good friends in the college and outside it. Pratt's eclectic mix of undergraduates gave the undergraduate body a very nice feel, a blend of ordinariness and ability which one was delighted to be part of. A measure of this quality was brought home to me on the one occasion on which my parents visited me there. In those civilised days one could hire at reasonable cost a private dining-room in college and have the chef lay on a dinner. I threw a drinks party of about thirty friends to meet the family and then a dinner party for a select dozen, served by white-coated waiters, and with the full service of wines and postprandial port. It was impeccably done; and my mates did their stuff. They all turned up smartly dressed in suits and charmed the pants off the parents, especially my father, who was deeply old fashioned in such matters, loved a sense of occasion, and was bowled over to find modern youth so entirely courteous, interesting, and interested. I suppose a year in an officers' mess had helped me to discover how things should be done on such occasions; I have always enjoyed ceremony and formal dinners, provided I am not responsible for the management thereof. Army guest nights were good fun, with the regimental silver on display, and the band and the pipers performing for our entertainment. I had also become president of the Goat Club, a college dining club, which met once a term for a formal dinner (without speeches), and this too helped.

To have impressed my father and given such pleasure to both my parents was reward itself, and well worth the four weeks' pea-canning in Norfolk with which I settled the bill. Finance was never easy. As a scholar I was entitled to rooms in college for all three years. This was a tremendous bonus for a somewhat shy character like myself, because those living out in digs were very willing to drop in for coffee after meals and so on. I was allocated a nice bedsit on the top floor of the new building for my first year; but for the following two years chose the ground floor of the adjacent Stevenson building, which gave me a separate bedroom, which could be kept clear of the tobacco smoke which I disliked even in those early days. It also meant that I was even more readily available to dispense coffee after all meals and people were always dropping in. The cost was modest; the social benefits considerable. In addition, I made a rule for myself that I would attend breakfast every day, whatever the circumstances. As a result I was always able to start work (or lectures) at 9 a.m. and by working at least five evenings a week was able to spend all afternoons playing sport or pursuing other forms of relaxation. It was a disciplined regime which gave shape and order to my daily existence.

I cannot remember exactly how my time at Cambridge was financed, or that of my friends. No one appeared troubled by finance, yet the only one who seemed comfortably off was Mark Coe, who was on an Army scholarship and ran a small car. He was to be cruelly murdered by the IRA in a bomb attack in Germany. Fees and accommodation were paid for by my father, helped by my scholarships. I am sure I was given an allowance; I know I overspent it. I may have had a few savings from my army 'career', but I am not sure how much. I knew that reading in the long vacation was expected and I always set myself one long reading task – the whole of Homer and the whole of Virgil were certainly two. But a job in the long vacations was also essential to make good the annual deficit. In my first year I went off with Bob Ewing, my closest friend, to Devon to see if we could get work on the buses. He was an ex-Inniskilling Fusilier and coincidentally had been my Junior Under Officer at Eaton Hall. The choice was unwise; Devon was an economically depressed area. But rejected at the main Plymouth depot, we got jobs based on Totnes with the Western National Omnibus Company. It was enormous fun; they were nice to work for; but the pay was hopeless: £8 per week, and no overtime. Out of this we had to pay for lodgings and food. At the end of eight weeks I had to ask my parents for money to get home.

But there was useful experience from it. I discovered Devon, or part of it; we walked the Dart from Totnes to Dartmouth on one occasion; on early shifts there was the romance of driving down the narrow Devon lanes in the early morning with mist hanging off the trees and countryside as green as my native Ireland; it turned my politics mildly pink, because if I, with no serious commitments, could not live on £8 a week, how on earth could a married man with a family? My sense of affront never developed into action; it simply remained as part of my subconscious reaction to the greed of great corporations and self-serving company bosses. But then they say that if you vote Tory at eighteen you have no heart; if you vote Labour at forty you have no head. Simplistic, of course; but there is something in it.

I still proudly claim to hold the national record for the largest number of standing passengers in a double-decker bus. In those innocent days I had not heard of health and safety; there was a cloudburst outside Paignton Zoo. There were hundreds of soaking people waiting for a bus; so I invited them on board, until they were packed so tight, standing upstairs and down, that we were incapable of movement inside, the bus barely so outside. Apparently the Fat Controller, in the form of the Inspector, saw the improbable sight of a bus down flat on its springs grinding its way back into Paignton and blew a gasket. If we had had an accident, I would have been very culpable indeed. I could not even collect any fares, because movement along the aisles was impossible. But the goodwill I gained for the company must have more than made up for the loss of revenue. I was reprimanded, kindly but deservedly.

But to balance my budget I could not afford another loss-making venture like bus-conducting. The following year Bob and I went off to work for Norfolk Canneries in North Walsham, in a factory which boasted the fastest baked-bean production line in the country, producing all the year round one million tins of baked beans every week (except in the brief pea-canning season). The basic principle was that the peas should be canned within four hours of having been harvested. This meant that a year's supply had to be produced in about four weeks and we all worked till the day's harvest was, literally, in the can. This meant hours of overtime, paid at time and a quarter after nine hours, time and a half after eleven. I discovered there the power of incentive and rewards, and countered the tedium of the work by calculating the money coming in after 7 p.m., measured at time and a half. The longest shift I worked was 38 hours on the trot, and the only drawback (on which I had not calculated) was that at 8 a.m. the following morning, the pay calculation started again at the basic rate. Nevertheless, I did this same job for two years running, because I earned even then the amazing sum of something like £100 per week, probably not far short of £1,000 a week in modern terms. It sorted out my overdraft very satisfactorily.

It kept my politics vaguely pink, this time not because of pay but because there was no contact between workers and management, whom we never saw. The foreman kept us at it; the management hid in their offices. I learned something about the importance in management of being seen about the place. I remember Jock Burnet, of whom more shortly, telling me about Jack Wolfenden, when he was head of Shrewsbury. He always, but always, even when he had business in London, made sure he was present in chapel every morning, before catching the 9.15 to the City. Even if no one saw him for the rest of the day, they felt he was about the place. It can seem very important for ambitious heads to take on outside commitments to develop their own careers, while persuading themselves that it helps to keep their school in the public eye. There is nothing more important than being on the spot, day in and day out.

I had often wondered how much I would forget of my classics in my two years with the army between school and university. To my great surprise, the answer seemed to be almost nothing. Thanks, I assume, to my excellent grounding in both languages, it all came flooding back. Intellectually I began to come alive, not only in my study of the classics, but also more generally. There were science lectures for arts students at which I learned a little of what Messrs Crick and Watson had been doing recently to unravel the sequences of the DNA code, as well as the more classical achievements of scientists, ancient and modern. At the university church, where Mervyn Stockwood presided as a stimulating, challenging, and sometimes enraging vicar, there were wonderful sermons/lectures from leading figures of the day. Among the more memorable were Nye Bevan and Malcolm Muggeridge, later canonised as St Mug.

What they had to say I have no idea, now. But at the time it was stimulating, and it made the church seem relevant and exciting to belong to. I had yet to develop a sufficiently independent mind to think out for myself where I stood on matters of faith and morals; I was still inclined to accept authority. And we talked and argued, earnestly and endlessly, in a way that would have seemed naïve and simplistic to more mature listeners. But it is only time, age, and bitter experience that teaches us that life is extremely complicated; that the truth is neither pure nor simple; that change and improvement are almost always bought at a price; and that many things cannot and some should not be changed at all. It is all very reminiscent of life in classical Athens in the time of Socrates, as described in the plays of Aristophanes, the history of Thucydides, and the dialogues of Plato. There was an intellectual excitement in the air. New ideas were burgeoning; the young were of course the first to adopt them and challenged their elders with all the arrogance of youth. The forces of Athenian conservatism rallied to the defence of the status quo; in the name of morality they denounced the new prophets; in the name of state security they sought to suppress iconoclasm; they found themselves a scapegoat in Socrates, who was actually opposed to much of the relativism of the age, and executed him for corrupting the youth of the nation and for failing to acknowledge the gods of the city. The similarity to what happened 500 years later to Jesus struck me even then. For rulers it is always expedient that one man should die for the people. It still is.

As for classical studies, I have had surprisingly few moments of regret for not having followed a new or more 'relevant' discipline. I was in a sense very narrowly educated, having been a specialist almost for the whole of my school life. But I now began to discover that I had of course been studying two great civilisations, two languages, two great literatures, two remarkable histories. Furthermore these two civilisations had shaped the culture of the West. As someone once put it, 'All that is good in western civilisation came from either Athens or Jerusalem.' Greek and Latin lie at the heart of all the Romance languages, but especially of the English language, which like Latin and Greek before it has become the *lingua franca* of the modern world. You cannot study English literature without knowing the literatures of Greece and Rome. The theology and language of the New Testament and the Christian church is shaped by Greek language and philosophy. The weakness of my education at Cambridge is not that I studied only classics, but that it was not part of the syllabus to follow the classical influence through into the literature and philosophy of the modern era, at least at a fairly superficial level.

The answer would of course be that you were now educated enough to do it for yourself. And for me, my choice of career did help to make good the deficiency just a little. By becoming a teacher of A Level students in a couple of schools with very bright pupils, I had to continue to educate myself as best I could for much of my career. Able colleagues in other disciplines helped, especially in my early years, when I had not become completely rigid in my thinking and dogmatic in my beliefs – a tendency of most pedagogues.

But the greatest weakness in my own conduct of my university career was that I was still really an overgrown public schoolboy, a sort of J D Marstock, as so cruelly but accurately described by Harold Nicholson in *Some People*. Games continued to matter; physical exhaustion was enjoyable; I wanted to try for a cricket blue but was not nearly good enough; but I played cricket for the college in the summer; hockey in the winter; fives and squash all the time. As I had done at school, I played too much sport and did not do enough reading round my subject. I was still an excellent schoolboy, but somewhat deficient as a true student and certainly not an intellectual, in that I worked hard for the purpose of getting a good degree more than for the love of my subject. I lacked originality and brought too little imagination to my studies – though I tried to develop these later.

Nevertheless, I got a first in Part 1 of the Classical Tripos. But it was the result of hard and disciplined work and a careful study of the syllabus, from which I selected with care a respectable minimum of material to cover and did so reasonably thoroughly. Only in later years did I come to see how damaging to one's intellectual development an enthusiasm for games can be. Certainly you make good friends, who share your enthusiasm, but do little to extend your thought. You fritter away precious years in becoming good at an activity where after the age of thirty your talent can only decline (apart from golf perhaps, the best of all games to learn at an early age) and for which it is possibly too late to find a substitute. Your horizon narrows; your vision focuses too closely on activities which too often retard maturity and have little value to society or the individual. I loved games; gained enormous fun from them. But I fear that Jack Plumb was probably right in his obsession with academics; Pratt probably wrong, though for the best of reasons. I have little doubt who was the nicer man and more rounded human being, so perhaps that final assertion undermines my whole argument.

My time at Christ's was undoubtedly the most fulfilling part of my education. Getting a first was a magical moment: characteristically, when in fear and trembling I went to inspect the lists published outside the Senate House, I started at the bottom with the 'thirds', and worked my way up through the lower and upper 'seconds', and then with utter incredulity found my name amongst the 'firsts'. The adrenalin rush was amazing: I went crazy; I could not stop running; I raced back to college, my shoes (loafers) fell off as I ran; I had to find someone to tell; I told Bill Cornwall, the Buttery manager and stood drinks all round; I ran round the Third Court; I rang home. It took about a day to simmer down and even with the disappointment of my upper second a year later, I never got over the sense that I had for once a real achievement behind me, and that for the rest of my life I had an antidote to my chronic sense of inadequacy.

But so many other good things happened to me there, all of which left me feeling that I was not wholly useless. It was a bonus that I had done my army service and was two years older than some, not all, of those who came up with me. It gave me the luck to be invited to join things and to organise things, which my inherent shyness would have discouraged. I was asked to join the May Ball Committee and became Secretary and then President thereof, with the painful duty in my final year of having to decide not to hold a Ball. The college hall was being repaired and renovated, and without it as a centrepiece, the ball would have fallen flat. Not everyone agreed. I was invited to join the Original Christian Minstrels, a glee club I suppose you would call it. Its sole and most entertaining purpose was to meet once or twice a term round a piano (brilliantly played by Richard Prentice) with a keg of beer and to sing the old music hall songs from the Victorian era onwards. The quality of one's voice was not a serious qualification or I would certainly not have been elected. I suppose what Johnson called clubbable-ness helped. I remained for ever after very fond of songs which were, I suppose, the pop songs of their day, but distinguished from their modern counterparts by the fact that they had good tunes instead of jungle beat and strumming chords, and decipherable words instead of animal yells and inarticulate eructations. Often, indeed, the words were witty, occasionally moving, but sometimes so excruciatingly sentimental that they were greeted within the

Minstrels with delighted acclaim for their sheer awfulness. The name of Scott Gatty was a name to be revered, as the collector of some of the best of them. As Secretary I had the challenging but enjoyable task of writing up the minutes in a manner which would amuse and entertain the membership.

By virtue of being Captain of the University Fives Club and representing my college in several sports, I was elected to the Hawks Club, thus gaining the privilege of wearing the most recognisable tie in the university and the wider world. I rarely made use of my membership, because the club was dominated by hearty oarsmen and noisy rugger players and I always felt uncomfortable there. There was a considerable snobbery among sportsmen and as representative of a very minor university sport, I simply did not rank. Such snobbery continues into adult life as well, if we can call it that, when we see the funny old buffers parading along the tow-path at Henley Regatta in their little caps and pink Leander scarves.

The Cambridge University Rugby Fives Club was based on Portugal Place, the home of all the university court games. It has now been replaced with a multi-storey car park but they have not rebuilt what was in my day a wonderful facility. Apart from changing rooms, there were six fives courts, three Rugby and three Eton; three squash courts, with some very distinguished international players in the university side; also I think racquets and badminton courts; real tennis was played elsewhere. Grandfather had been Secretary of the University Fives Club; I got my half blue (for a minor sport) in my first year and followed in his footsteps as Secretary the next, and was elected Captain in my third, when I played first string. We beat Oxford in all three years. I was invited to join the Jesters Club, the MCC of court games. The club had been founded by Jock Burnet and he remained President Emeritus until he died. He was also President of both University Fives Clubs. His 'day job', so to speak, was as Bursar of Magdalene College, though he was also a director of A & C Black, publishers of *Who's Who* and of the *Public Schools Year Book*, which he edited. The *Girls' Public School Year Book* was edited by his wife, Pauline, whose 'day job' was as chairman of the Cambridge Health Authority and a local magistrate. He was a governor of at least four public schools, Radley, Shrewsbury, Glenalmond, and Bromsgrove. He was the friend of headmasters and chairmen of governors all over the country, a source of wise advice and skilful recruitment, with a nicely wicked sense of humour. He had a finger in so many educational pies that one felt he was responsible for almost all appointments in the independent sector. One of us enquired at some point, 'Jock do you appoint everybody?' to which, quick as a flash, he replied, 'When I appointed you I began to think I could appoint anybody', a witticism taken in good part and harmlessly intended. He was an old boy of St Paul's and my own Christ's College; had served with the Air Ministry in the war; owned a bookshop for a time; gone into publishing; and then been appointed Bursar of Magdalene. He knew everybody. Intensely shy, he was the most skilful networker-in-reverse I have ever come across; he seemed to approach no one; everyone came to him.

He was widely read and a great collector of second-hand books, which filled shelves in every corner of the house at 28 Selwyn Gardens. He was the nephew of the great historian of Greek philosophy, John Burnet, and had something of that same philosophical cast of mind. Theology was an abiding interest and he persuaded me that every educated man should always have a theological book on the go, whatever else he was reading. I still try to.

Jock was to become my second Heraclitus, much assisted by Pauline, who was a sort of surrogate mother to many undergraduates. They were both devout Christians, and if ever a couple lived out the implications of the Christian gospel, that 'it is more blessed to give than to receive', they did. It is almost impossible to assess the good they did, the care they gave, the warmth and generosity of their hospitality, the hours they spent listening, talking, advising. They were a complete pastoral care system for many undergraduates, fulfilling much of the pastoral role that college tutors should (but too often did not) fill. Coffee and conversation was available at 10.30 a.m., almost daily, in his rooms in Magdalene, and I suppose I turned up once or twice a week for much of my last two years. Sunday lunch was by invitation with ten or a dozen crowded round the small dining-room table, but it was preceded by sherry at noon, for which open house prevailed. A gathering of twenty or thirty was normal; members of the fives clubs were regular visitors.

If Moses Finley gave me intellectual stimulus, made me a decent historian, and opened doors for me in the field of classics, Jock educated me in the wider sense both socially, in my general reading, and in a broader philosophy of life. He persuaded me to become a schoolmaster and sent me off to the Warden of Radley, Wyndham Milligan, who offered me my first job. He also sent him my predecessor and successor as Captain of Fives, Simon Langdale, who became head of Eastbourne College and then Shrewsbury, and Richard Morgan, who became head of Cheltenham and then came back to Radley as Warden. We have all remained great friends ever since, though our paths have diverged. I am godfather to Simon's Philippa; Margaret Morgan is godmother to my Emma.

He also introduced me to Launcelot Fleming, Bishop of Norwich and later Dean of Windsor, another sort of guru figure to my generation, with whom I occasionally went to stay. He was a dear man, once an Antarctic explorer, once a college chaplain, blessed with a wonderful capacity for making friends with the young and taking an interest in their careers. It seemed entirely natural that, after I was married, I should take Sara to meet him – the only occasion on which either of us can claim to have taken tea in Windsor Castle!

When I was wrestling with the idea of taking holy orders, Jock also passed me on to Bob Runcie, then Principal of Cuddesdon, later Archbishop of Canterbury, who wisely advised me to stick to schoolmastering, because my doubts about the church as an institution would have been uncomfortable, both for myself and the institution. Jock knew all the right people, not in the snobbish sense; rather, thanks to his wide acquaintance, he knew who would be best placed by reason of experience and position to give sound advice and assistance. He gave this sort of practical help to many and remained a friend to all of us long after we had gone down.

There were failings, of course, in the university's arrangements. For example, careers advice (apart from Jock, who was not entirely impartial in the matter) was still in its infancy. The University Appointments Board had little to offer, unless you already knew what you wanted to be. They gave me no help in deciding what career I might follow. The sort of work done even as little as ten years later by ISCO, the Independent Schools Careers Organisation was unheard of. ISCO's relatively simple psychological and aptitude testing was an enormous help in analysing aptitudes and possibilities, and I wish I had been subjected to the process. As a schoolmaster over many years I enjoyed taking my pupils through it and helping them to recognise their strengths and weaknesses, their aptitudes and abilities. It was time-consuming, but rewarding and each interview usually lasted about an hour and a half.

I had a cousin in Shell, who kindly arranged for me to meet one of their senior recruitment officers. But even at that high level, the lack of sophistication in the recruiting process was remarkable. In discussing what I would do and what sort of life I might have if I joined them, the only thing I was told was that I would travel to exotic places. No one suggested that working my way up a massive organisation and ultimately perhaps helping to run it would be a wonderful challenge to my brains and capacities. The idea that reasonably intelligent recruits would be attracted by the superficial glitter of 'travel' or even, in those slightly more idealistic times, big salaries seemed ingrained in those I spoke to. We all teased Mike Allen quite a lot for joining Unilever 'just to sell soap'. Much later, when as a head I found myself trying to get pupils interested in industry generally, I was fascinated by the sheer complexity of managing a modern organisation, and I know that if I had understood something of that I could have been tempted to join. It is the challenge to brains, powers of organisation, and personality that seems to me the best bait that industry can offer. By contrast, Jock's pitch for schoolmastering as a worthwhile and rewarding profession appealed readily to youthful idealism, and of course to someone like me with limited self-confidence it had the secondary appeal of the familiar.

My father was very disappointed and even several years later tried to get me to change direction. A great family friend, Ronald Kerr Muir, whom we got to know on family holidays in Donegal, again at the Fort Hotel, Greencastle, of blessed memory, has been a master at Oundle, I think, and had himself changed direction and was now a director of Courtaulds. He said that provided I was still on the right side of thirty he could probably help me to do the same. With a housemaster's job in my sights I turned him down. My father's bitter comment stayed with me ever afterwards: 'A man among boys; a boy among men.' It was a far more cruel observation than the traditional 'those who can do; those who can't teach', to which I always added, 'and those who can't teach become lecturers in education'. It is, in fact, a savagely demanding profession: you are a bit like an actor, but on stage for many hours every day; your audience always critical and potentially hostile; you probably have to perform seven or eight different 'dramas' each day, and re-learn your parts every week; it has been known to reduce strong men to tears. When, briefly, I had a small foray into the 'real world' as director of the Navan Project, I was amazed by how stress-free and relatively civilised commercial life seemed to be.

My friends seemed rather more organised about their futures, probably because they were somewhat more worldly-wise than I. Several read economics followed by law and, like Bob Ewing and others, were heading for the City law or financial firms. The most precise about his objectives was Chris Tugendhat. He knew exactly where he was going and how to get there. I envied him. He set out to become President of the Union (much more important to him than a good degree as an entrée into politics) and achieved it by good organisation rather than any great talent for speaking. His ultimate objective was politics, and he got there via journalism with the FT, and election as an MP, before ending up a European Commissioner. The utterly delightful Richard Luce (almost inevitably it seems with hindsight) ended up as some sort of panjandrum with the Palace. John Eardley was, I think, contemplating holy orders. Others, like Richard Boxall (Hepworth Ceramics) and Martin Cuss (OUP) headed for industry and commerce, which to me were a complete mystery. Alan Munro, a chemist, remained at Christ's as an academic, and ended up Master of the College – a consummation devoutly to be wished by any man.

But it was Norman Thompson who seemed to me to have achieved what my father – and with hindsight perhaps I too – might have wished. He was a brilliant mathematician (double first) who was captured for teaching by Ronnie Hoare's father (also at Christ's – was he his father's secret talent scout?) to join the staff at Strathallen, where he was headmaster. He then moved on to Gordonstoun, before escaping out to the 'real' world of industry and commerce, developing computer languages for IBM at Hursley. He combined this with working (to this day) as a tutor for the Open University and with research under Professor Kenneth Dover, a distinguished classical scholar at St Andrews, on some esoteric linguistic analysis as a means of identifying the authorship of ancient manuscripts. One way or another he also seemed to travel the world to learned conferences of every kind. When we left Cambridge in 1960, we opened an annual correspondence each Christmas and have sustained it ever since. I keep promising myself that I will re-read all our letters to see how the world has changed, but though the spirit is willing so far the flesh has proved weak. But my first impressions of teaching at Radley are recorded in the next chapter. Over the years we have met occasionally, but not as often as we should, partly because somehow in sympathy with the great Dr Johnson visits to Scotland have not tempted me.

It is sad to think how many friends are now mere names in the catalogues of memory. But in the modern world where jobs are often international and mobility the norm, it is probably inevitable. I am also, by temperament, a pretty hopeless old boy of any institution and avoid reunions like the plague. So I have no one really to blame but myself if old friendships are lost. One of my father's favourite little poems rises up before me in this connection; he often quoted it with quiet approval. Who wrote it I know not.

> From quiet times and first beginning,
> Out to the undiscovered ends,
> There's nothing worth the wear of winning
> Save laughter and the love of friends.

Our parents' professions probably shape our destiny more than we realise. Within their own field they know how to open doors and how the system works; so they can give good help and advice, though I have never forgotten my father's advice: 'don't touch medicine; it's no longer a profession. It's a trade.' But my sister went into nursing, none the less. I knew a bit about teaching and suggested to my daughters that if they had no clear idea about what they wanted to do, it was an excellent fail-safe qualification, offering opportunities for full- or part-time work, going abroad through TEFL, and so on. By then the Dip. Ed. was unavoidable, so the issue of whether it was worthwhile did not arise. I would have advised taking it simply to ensure that the state sector would be an option, though apart from the teaching-practice term it has little to commend it. No one in my day viewed it with anything other than the utmost contempt; most of us still do! If it were to be something one did after, say, five years' teaching and some experience of the classroom against which to test the educational theories propounded, sometimes by those who were classroom failures themselves, there would have seemed much more point to it. As it was, it never occurred to me to apply to take it.

My debt to Cambridge is great, for the intellectual excitement, the friendships made, the rich experiences enjoyed, and the building of a degree of personal confidence, which I had always lacked. I had a wonderful three years. I could have applied to do research and gain a PhD, but I was still acutely conscious of what I was costing my father; I had failed to get a first in Part 2 and was therefore unlikely to be seen as a star candidate; I had sufficient self-knowledge to believe that I had a very good second-class brain, rather than a brilliant first-class one; academe, increasingly attractive in later years, seemed a bridge too far; after two years as an independent salary earner in the army, I was impatient to get going.

To start a career at a school like Radley was immensely attractive, and I accepted Milligan's offer of a post in the classics department without hesitation and without applying to any other school.

Jock Burnet, the mighty hunter, the Nimrod of the independent sector, had struck again.

CHAPTER 14

Radley College – Lotus Land?

Now whosoever of them did eat the honey sweet fruit of the lotus had no more wish to bring tidings nor to return to his comrades, but there he chose to abide with the lotus-eating men, ever feeding on its fruits and forgetful of his homeward way.

Homer, *The Odyssey* IX.93

VAUGHAN WILKES, MILLIGAN'S PREDECESSOR as Warden of Radley, attached the epithet 'Lotus Land' to Radley, and in some ways it was well deserved, since for young staff it was too comfortable for our own good, and possibly the pupils' also. The title of the school song '*Lusimus*', a Latin word meaning 'we have played' might be seen as symptomatic. Set in 700 acres of the Berkshire countryside, between Oxford and Abingdon, its grounds laid out by Capability Brown, with the longest stretch of cut grass in England, much favoured by archers for long-distance shooting competitions, and with old Father Thames running sweet and serene through the water meadows in the shallow valley below, its buildings of mellow red brick set around the handsome mansion of the former Radley Hall, which formed its centrepiece, it could well have been the land which time forgot.

It was a young school, founded in 1847 by William Sewell, a brilliant and idealistic Anglican cleric, schooled at Winchester and Merton College, Oxford. Sewell had already founded one college, St Columba's, Rathfarnham, near Dublin, with the aim of creating a new kind of school, and also countering the domination of Roman Catholicism and fostering the decaying Irish church. Though it was initially a failure, it continues to this day, and some of the founding father's ideas are still enshrined in its ethos and in that of its sister school, Radley.

The focus of the school's life at St Columba's was to be the chapel, with mattins and evensong celebrated daily, and the saints and feast days of the church to be observed by the boys, and with fasting by the Warden and Fellows. The ethos was to be collegiate, with the Warden and Fellows standing *in loco parentis* to the boys, teaching and caring for them, for love of the work not for financial gain (indeed it was half-assumed that Fellows would have private means), and taking their meals with them, at the high table, much as in an Oxbridge college. The staffing ratio was to be unrealistically generous. Proper academic dress was to be worn and there was to be high emphasis on good manners and gentlemanly conduct, in marked contrast to the rather barbaric state of the public schools of the time. The curriculum was relatively enlightened. Religion and music took pride of place, together with the classics. But modern languages and history also figured, together with maths, science, drawing and Irish. The aim was to create a pleasant country-house atmosphere set in beautiful surroundings, the members of which were to be surrounded by beautiful things. Radley was to be an English St Columba's.

It was a lovely place to be and a lovely place in which to grow up. Beautiful surroundings must rub off on all but the most insensitive of souls, and beauty there was in abundance. My first visit, for interview, had been on a glorious autumn afternoon the previous year. I arrived by bus from Oxford station to see the wonderful chestnut avenue in all its autumnal glory, stretching up to the school and then on past the playing fields, and into the distance up the hill (Cheesers). After the somewhat more homely architecture of Sedbergh, the buildings seemed palatial; the Warden was charming; the atmosphere was one of peace and civilised living. Like everyone else coming there for the first time, I was captivated.

To a newcomer unfamiliar with the traditions of the school and the intentions of its founder, some things seemed peculiar and were often the subject of critical comment by keen young staff, who like young men in every age arrived in a mood to challenge before they understood. Teaching staff were all 'dons', an affectation which seemed pretentious; the boys all wore undergraduate gowns, which seemed silly; the houses were called 'socials' and the housemasters 'Social Tutors', which seemed quaint; major saints' days were celebrated by a slightly extended mattins, Ascension Day by the loss of a whole first lesson, which proved to the unbelieving that 'academics did not really matter'; after lunch every day there was a compulsory rest period on their beds for all the boys (like a kindergarten!); the salary was extremely modest – mine was a mere £750 per annum (£625 'all found' in term-time, which was valuable if you were unmarried). But there was no pension scheme and you had to go elsewhere in the holidays, so there was no chance of belonging locally. I was too innocent and too gentlemanly in those days to have even asked what I would earn. All the above would have made perfect sense, if Christopher Hibbert's excellent history of Radley College, *No Ordinary Place*, had been available as part of our non-existent induction programme. In time, of course, one came to understand, even approve of, some of these features. But initially it all felt a little precious.

After one term I wrote to Norman Thompson the first of the annual Christmas letters mentioned above.

Here are excerpts:

> The most difficult question (in your letter) to answer is 'How are you enjoying it?' My answer is 75%, but I don't expect to for a year or so. I feel still very much as though I do not belong; I am involved in little; I am not attached to a house; and of course, though this is to be expected, I am teaching badly. This applies particularly to English: I am faced with the job of teaching this to the Biology VI and I find it hell. I suspect that like you I am probably too conscientious and it worries me to do a job badly and I just do not know enough to teach a subject like that. The classics

side is not so bad, since I know enough to get by but this too is unsatisfactory since I am fighting to keep a jump ahead – a difficult job sometimes. My one resolve has been to make them work hard at all costs – since they may at least teach themselves something ... Extra-mural activities are countless – too much diversification of activity is possibly a failing here: and this may particularly be so in the athletic sphere. But as a breeding ground for hobbies and hobby horses it is a paradise and in principle I approve enormously.

The inmates are on the whole charming: boys are very nice if a little blasé, and regrettably endowed with too much money; the staff I like very much and they could not have been more charming, kind, hospitable, or helpful. The Warden is possibly too nice. The school is going up-hill rather than down-hill, I am certain. Under the new warden (7 years in office now) the academic standards have risen considerably and by Jove it was necessary, and they are still too low ... Symbols of advance, either in hand or just completed: 8 new classrooms, new Biology laboratories, modernisation of the theatre, new boat house, new athletics track, new ante-room for staff, giving us a drawing room as well as a dining room, a new swimming pool. Our starting pay is £775 per annum, which compares well with many schools, I think, and they take off £150 for keep of all kinds, including heat, light, mending, food, roof, laundry ... Don't broadcast my opinions; the school grapevine is terrific and things get about!

After more than forty years, this is how I remember it now.

The Warden, Wyndham Milligan (known to the boys as 'Gush' for his over-effusive manner), had been a very successful Eton housemaster, an ex-Guards officer, and a fine scholar (classics of course). He had come to Radley in 1954, so that by the time I joined in 1960 he was well established, and it was generally agreed that he had done much to improve the school. He had introduced a cautious and measured liberalisation, abolishing fagging, eliminating the bullying, which was a feature of so many public schools of the time, and tempering the obsession with sport which led to the domination of the community by the hearties ('bloods') of the main sports teams. He had defined the lower school curriculum much more precisely and introduced a tighter control of academic performance by fortnightly report cards, which he always read personally. Music was significantly improved, though he had a hang-up about drama. There was plenty of it, done to a reasonably decent standard (the immortal Peter Cook was an old boy and at least one master, the redoubtable Ivor Gilliatt, is instantly recognisable in one of the sketches of *Beyond the Fringe*). But I suspect that his Scottish background left him uncomfortable with the inevitable business of junior boys playing girls' parts and the better actors being encouraged to posture for plaudits and indulge in the mildly extravagant behaviour characteristic of the theatrical profession generally. He disliked sensuality of any kind, and his chapel sermons were often laced with half-disguised admonitions about the temptations of homosexuality, especially it seemed in summer, when 'the scent of new mown hay' presented such a particular and regular threat to his imagination that the phrase became a sort of common-room joke. Heaven knows what had gone on at Eton to induce this anxiety in him.

To a young 'don' he was a most supportive and encouraging boss. Not only was he accessible and affable; he trusted you, totally. He never inspected a lesson; he never interfered in the management of the department, which was ably run by Christopher Turner, later head of Dean Close and then Stowe. When I was having difficulties with a non-specialist sixth form English class, and one boy in particular, I went and asked for his help. He told me to leave it with him; he sent for the boy concerned and there were no further problems. He would regularly drop into the common-room of an evening before dinner for a sherry, and though he was not always comfortable in such a situation, it was not just gesture politics but a genuine attempt to stay in touch.

Though I say it as shouldn't, his appointments were outstanding, much assisted by Jock Burnet at Cambridge (who was an old friend and a member of the governing council), who sent him a string of able young men, at least thirteen of whom went on to headships in due course. Simon Langdale preceded me by a year; I joined the staff with Dick Usherwood, a fine teacher of chemistry, who remained at the school till he retired, and Ronnie Howard, a geographer, and the outstanding oarsman of his year at Oxford, a key figure in national and university rowing for years after. Ronnie brought David Hardy to join him a year later and the two made a most formidable team in coaching some of Radley's best crews; they won the Princess Elizabeth Cup in 1962. I had no idea that he was a Master of Wine and I remember David primarily as the most enthusiastic of biologists, who revived the department and was a mine of information on all things botanical and zoological, not least on a trip to Greece which we took in Richard Morgan's magnificent but elderly Mercedes, along with Peter Chamberlain, later a housemaster at The Leys. Michael Meredith, later to be head of English and librarian at Eton, joined a year later and was the most stimulating of teachers, a superb director of plays (I will long remember his production of Terence Rattigan's *Ross*), and a most generous educator of his less well read colleagues. Richard Morgan (after a false start in industry) and Anthony Hudson (later head of Pangbourne) followed, together with John Moore, a formidable academic and classic who went on to be head of King's Worcester.

Milligan had his weaknesses, of course. Who doesn't? For understandable reasons he did not get on very well with the more senior dons. It must be rare for any new head to be accepted by senior staff, who are probably entrenched in their ways, a bit tired, and feel somewhat threatened by the new broom. Social tutors in particular thought that he trespassed on their preserves, because of his encouragement of boys to come to him directly with problems, and his determination to get to know them all – which he did, and by their Christian names. They felt he was trying to be a super-housemaster, instead of a headmaster. These feelings were exacerbated by his willingness to be influenced by the younger staff, who had been his own appointments. Of these James Batten (later head of King's Taunton and his first appointment) seemed to have his ear to an unreasonable extent, and he held an unofficial but recognised position as the leader of the younger staff. On one occasion I myself went to the Warden in my youthful know-all mode and told him what I felt was wrong with his school, a litany of complaint to which he listened with the utmost courtesy instead of throwing me out on my ear, which is what probably should have happened. He was a very nice man. I happened to tell Simon Langdale what I had said, and I well remember his incredulity when an hour later at a meeting of the junior staff all my 'complaints' came back from the Warden's own lips, as if they were his own views. He did seem too often to formulate his opinions on the basis of what he had heard from the most recent visitor to bend his ear.

We all worried, too, about the money, which the school seemed to be spending somewhat lavishly. In those days inflation was not yet the bogey it was later to become, nor had anyone foreseen its remarkable capacity for wiping out debt. Hibbert's history acknowledges that neither Milligan nor his Bursar were particularly good at finance, but whether by unrecognised skill or sheer good luck (an essential quality in any great leader) events proved the expenditure fully justified. The inflation of the seventies (he retired in 1968) and the windfall sale of land to the fast expanding town of Abingdon more than rectified the situation, and with the improved management of finances under a new Bursar and much more financially expert council members, Radley was set up to become one of the best and most lavishly equipped schools in the country by the end of the reign of his successor, Dennis Silk, another of the long line of public school headmasters fostered by the C U Rugby Fives Club, though in this case he had a formidable collection of other distinctions in his armoury.

It is fair to say that Milligan laid the foundations of a great school, and Dennis Silk completed the process. If I had known in 1964 that Silk was coming, I would have stayed. As it was, for all Milligan's reforms, much remained as it had been. The school was inward-looking, comfortable perhaps rather than complacent, though it was that too, and promotion was extremely slow. It still had something of Wilkes' 'Lotus Land' about it. After four years, I could see no chance of becoming a social tutor for at least another ten or a dozen years. At that time I would be forty and I hoped to be a headmaster by then. Radley was not the place to be if you had any ambition. It was far too comfortable to be good for me; I felt it was dangerous to stay and I soon started to look around for something completely different.

Salaries were low; but the standard of living for bachelors was extremely high. The common-room (a term which in one sense embraced the whole of the staff, but in another the living-in bachelor staff, who were housed and fed there) was like a gentleman's club, or an officers' mess but with a rather more intelligent membership. It was situated in the Mansion, which also housed the bachelors' quarters, the school library, and the Warden's Office, though his secretary worked in a temporary building half-way down the drive, which may have helped to preserve her sanity. It was not a conventional staff room. It consisted of a comfortable drawing room with soft chairs and sofas, and the Warden would not tolerate any but the tiniest of notice-boards. If you had work to do, you went back to your rooms, which for bachelors were mainly on the upper floors of the same building, so it was no hardship. The separate dining-room next door served excellent meals, about which complaints were as regular as they were undeserved, since we were undoubtedly spoilt. It had a superb cellar, run by Tony Money, one of the nicest and most civilised of all the more senior members, an OR himself, and ultimately the presiding genius of the OR Association. Morning coffee was called 'Chambers' and announcements, if any, were mainly by the Warden. Dissemination of information was otherwise by notes in the pigeonholes, which were the only serious concession to the idea of a staff room for the transaction of business. One bright spark once got hold of the Warden's notepaper and circulated all the most pious members of common-room with a note asking them to be more diligent in their attendance at chapel. Result: religious outrage among the godly, and a reprimand for the culprit. A working room was added towards the end of my time, but I have vague recollections that it also housed the common-room Scalextrix set, which was much more fun and a source of considerable entertainment.

It was in every way a wonderful situation in which to start a teaching career, but it had one unattractive feature. The President of common-room was a scholarly and sometimes witty but extremely crusty old bachelor called Theo Cocks. He presided over meals with a curmudgeonly lack of grace and expected a degree of deference, which he did not deserve. We all sat at the long dining table (later replaced by three separate tables) in approximate order of seniority, feeling a little like Victorian children who should be seen and not heard. There we had to endure the dreary banalities of shop-talk among our elders and betters, or the trumpeting of a very rich but boring old social tutor, who had once been an accomplished music critic but (sadly) had been reduced by deafness to discussing little else but the virtues or follies of his charges at unendurable length and volume. Ronnie Howard's arrival transformed the situation almost overnight. After about a week, he breezed in one evening, slapped Theo Cocks on the back, and said, 'Hello Theo; I'm going to sit here', and sat down beside him. Precedence evaporated and the atmosphere of the place was totally altered. Ronnie was a big man, literally and metaphorically, and much too sensible to tolerate any more childish insistence on status. We were liberated.

I myself started in a bedsitter with the Gardiner family in their large house in the grounds. Staff housed on campus was part of Sewell's original vision, brought to complete fruition under Silk, who built a large number of residences for them. It is a good way to get more work out of them, since they become always accessible, together with their wives and families. Tony Gardiner was a retired social tutor, and still head of biology; the epitome of traditional Radley, but devoted to the institution and therefore more loyal to the Warden than many of his senior colleagues. His wife Peggy was a motherly figure with a genius for gossip, born of her intense interest in and love of the school, which they had jointly served for many years. I was merely housed there; meals were all taken in common-room, up in the Mansion. A year later I became an assistant tutor to Raymond King (G Social) with a small suite of rooms at the top of the house. These civilised conditions taught me how important it is for a teacher's self-respect that he or she be housed in conditions comparable to any normal adult in the world outside. I could have guests in without being ashamed of my surroundings. When I got to King's Canterbury, the contrast was a feature that depressed me more than almost anything else.

A more genial and congenial boss than Raymond it would have been hard to find. He smoked like a chimney; like the good historian he was, he found a wry amusement in many of the follies of his fellow men; he had a mildly shrewish wife, who found little pleasure in her role and made her unhappiness clear to him regularly – but, like Shylock on the Rialto, he 'bore it with a patient shrug, for sufferance was the badge of all his tribe'. I never saw him rattled or steamed up, except on one memorable occasion when he met me at his front door in evident shock and said, 'They've shot Kennedy.' He was approaching the end of his career, but he ran a cheerful house with as far as I knew no more problems than the norm. His lack of interest in sport and his generally laid-back approach irritated some of my younger colleagues. I found his sanity and ease of manner very reassuring. I still remember his amused description of a small error in one of his end of term reports, to explain which he was summoned to the Warden's office. 'I say, old man, aren't you going it a bit strong?' observed the Warden. 'However idle the boy is, I don't think you can write "He must do better, by Christ."' Raymond had inspected the offending document and recollected being interrupted by the fire alarm in mid-flow; he had failed to complete the final word: 'by Christmas'. He did not chuckle so much as breathe in and out in a sort of staccato, panting whisper, which on this occasion went on for some time. I remember him with great affection.

The classics department was a delight and I was assigned entirely to sixth form teaching, which was immensely demanding and a considerable privilege, since classics was still a relatively popular subject and we had classes of very clever boys, some of whom seemed much cleverer than I. In my first couple of years I worked incredible hours, rarely getting to bed before two, as I corrected work and prepared for lessons, and mastered sometimes unfamiliar texts. But it equipped me well to take on King's Canterbury, where they were even cleverer. The department was led by Christopher Turner, a kind, civilised and scholarly Wykehamist, with just a hint of that condescension of manner which is characteristic of the breed; a man of mildly evangelical tendency, but efficient, respected, and a sincere Christian. The Warden attended when he could. Theo Cocks, in his *persona* as a classical scholar, was witty and constructive – in his spare time he wrote the libretto for the dons' plays, whose improbable plots, excruciatingly laced with puns and other such *jeux d'esprit*, ensured that once a year we entertained the boys and made fools of ourselves in an entirely harmless way, most memorably when David Goldsmith, a stout, crew-cut mathematician and social tutor, with a brilliant if unorthodox approach to teaching, highlighted on the later TV series, came on stage dressed in a ballerina's tutu. Once seen, never forgotten.

John Evans was another headmaster to be – of the Strode School, Egham. A Salopian and a product of Trinity Hall, Cambridge, he had been a civil servant out in Nigeria, which gave him a maturity and wider experience than his more jejune associates, who were not above mocking him for it. He took over the department when Chris Turner left and ran it with clarity of purpose and total efficiency. With a lively mind and a considerable secondary interest in theology, he has remained a great friend to this day. We went with the chaplain, Godfrey Marshall, and Chich Thornton (in Greek, *tsits*), a mathematician with a good mind and a cynical contempt for all manifestations of keenness, for a wonderful holiday in Greece, in my case financed by a Henry Arthur Thomas Travel Award from Cambridge, which Moses Finley had encouraged me to apply for. It was my first visit to the country whose culture I had studied for fifteen years and I was enchanted. Our paths have crossed regularly in our differing careers. We met again when Simon Langdale brought him to Eastbourne as second master, as well as bringing me there as director of studies; then he took him on to Shrewsbury in another senior management role. He moved for a while to King Edward's Birmingham, charged with the development of a programme for recruiting the able underprivileged.

We met again when I was at St Mary's Wantage and he had retired to Sutton Courtenay, near Abingdon, and we used to go walking together until his legs began to let him down. His range of experience in state and private sector education was more varied than that of any other schoolmaster I have known. His wisdom lent proportion to my enthusiasms; his clarity of thought reined in my own wilder ideas; his robust common sense curbed some of the more extravagant assessments of his colleagues by his colleagues. The statement that 'Ronnie Howard is not a saint; he is a very good oarsman' collapsed one such edifice of mythological construction, to which some of us were prone. He was a considerable expert on Dylan Thomas, a fellow Welshman.

He gave me in my final year at Radley the most difficult and profoundly enjoyable task I undertook there. Charles Wrinch, a retired don and a most brilliant producer of plays, had retired from Radley village to the island of Jersey, and was no longer available to direct the biennial Greek play, done in Greek entirely by the classics department, unlike the more fashionable triennial Bradfield

Greek Play, where selected actors mouthed the Greek sounds parrot-fashion without understanding, and whose productions I found consistently wooden. Wrinch had produced and directed Euripides' *Phoenissae* in my first year – in modern dress, in which I trained the Chorus, costumed in military uniform; the *Birds* of Aristophanes in my third – a beautiful production with lovely bird costumes, done in the most sylvan of settings down by the lake below the Warden's house; and now, in my fifth and last year, and scheduled for my final weeks in the school, John asked me to direct Euripides' *Bacchae*, a task for which I was ill-equipped technically and by experience.

But for a classicist it was the most wonderful challenge. At last, instead of studying a dry text, one could actually try to bring a play alive, with very intelligent sixth-formers taking the main parts, actors clever enough to understand the Greek and the implications of the play as a whole, and good enough as actors not to need much instruction from me in a field where I knew I was deficient. If I told them what I wanted them to convey, they could do it better than I could show them. Their names remain with me, though I am shaky on the parts they played. Roger Harington (Pentheus), James Barraclough (Dionysus), Duncan Forbes (now a published poet and head of English at Wycombe Abbey) possibly played Teiresias, which would be appropriate, Jonathan Gaunt, and Guy Greenhous (already an expert on Offa's dyke). The lower school classicists formed the chorus of bacchanals. We played it in the small garden between the chapel and the dining hall, where the moving shadows of the large buttresses could be used to suggest the required earthquake by lighting effects, and the enclosing buildings gave the setting tremendous resonance for the sound effects (from Neilsen's Fifth Symphony, if I remember rightly).

On the merits or otherwise of the production I cannot comment; *The Times* reviewed it kindly, as it always did for school productions. On the experience of doing it I can say, categorically, that it was beyond question the most creative thing I had ever done. I was conjuring out of thin air, so to speak, a great drama, arguably the most powerful tragedy in the Greek canon, except possibly *Oedipus Tyrannos*. It came to life inside my mind, and the hours and hours of effort poured into exploring the meaning with the actors, and experimenting to try to suggest that meaning through the action and movement on stage, made me feel that in different circumstances I would have loved to make a career in the theatre – not as an actor, but as a director. I poured into it all the energy – imaginative, emotional, spiritual – that I possessed, and at the farewell party after the final production, I burst unashamedly into tears, largely fuelled by exhaustion and the joy of a task completed. Perhaps for the first time I had discovered that there is somewhere inside me, unrealised, a creative dimension which has never found expression. If there is to be an indictment of my own education, that is surely where it must lie. I would rather have written one great poem, or play, or novel, which men remembered, than reached the highest pinnacle of my profession.

I have always enjoyed coaching games. I became almost instantly master-in-charge of fives; it was a minor responsibility, but it was an encouragement for a new boy and we did play matches. I even coached rugby, at a modest level, but then took over the Leagues, all the non-team rugby, and tried to run it single-handedly, with boys for referees, instead of a somewhat reluctant staff, since naturally the keen ones all coached teams. It was a brave idea; we instituted proper refereeing instruction for the volunteers, and one or two emerged as very competent refs, though the challenge of managing a game of thirty unenthusiastic peers was considerable. In the end, sadly, we all agreed that the experiment had not succeeded and called it off. Getting boys to run things was something I was to try again at King's Canterbury, with the antiquarian society. It was so successful that membership burgeoned towards a hundred, and the headmaster lost his nerve and told me to stop it.

But of all the games I have loved, cricket remains the one I would gladly coach until I die, despite Lord Mancroft's description of it as 'a game which the English, not being a spiritual people, invented in order to give themselves some conception of eternity'. I started with the under-fifteens, but then Simon Langdale took over the first XI and asked me to join him on Bigside and run the second XI. He always thought about his sports in a way that I was too idle to do; I am an instinctive player of games and have never been able to take them seriously enough. Simon taught me everything I know about cricket coaching (which is still not a lot) and also improved my own performance as a batsman remarkably, by sorting out a few basic errors of technique in the nets. As a result I began to score more freely and faster as a batsman, and with considerably higher scores, which included a century in a game against, I think, the Cheltenham Common-room. The task of the second XI I saw as being to keep up the morale of those not selected for the firsts, and to challenge the firsts ferociously on our occasional internal matches. The method was to practise basic techniques endlessly, to teach constantly the importance of disciplined bowling to line, length, and field setting, and to raise the fielding to a level higher than that of the first XI. I would not now dare conduct the sort of slip-fielding practices we ran then and which did result in some almost miraculous catches in our matches. The damage done by health and safety legislation is a major discouragement to high achievement in school sport, as in much else.

Cricket is the most psychological of games, a battle of wills and wits as well as abilities. A lesser team will often beat a better by character and discipline. I had discovered this at Sedbergh in my final year, when I led my team to the inter-house finals with almost no talent beyond a collective will to win, through self-belief and playing to a preconceived plan. The side-effect was to make my housemaster believe for the first time that, even though I disliked rugger, I might have some leadership qualities. I look back on the coaching of games with almost undiluted pleasure. It lets pupils discover that you are human; you can share the enjoyment of a sport, learning to lose gracefully and even more important to win gracefully, which is much harder. But one must remember that it is only a game; winning is important, but only at the time, and should be forgotten immediately.

Other moments of delight still flash upon the inward eye of memory. I bought my first car, an elderly Ford Prefect, for about £150 from old Mr Gowring of Abingdon, in person: he had a good reputation as an honest man. A young schoolmaster of very modest means like me was hardly going to make his fortune, but he treated me as courteously as a much more prosperous client and did me proud; it was cheap and ran reliably; can one ask more? Gowrings became a quoted company on the stock market; I moved on to better cars. But I remember both car and garage with a sort of nostalgic affection, and for me Mr Gowring remains the antithesis of the conventional Arthur Daly picture of a car dealer. As Iago, extreme scoundrel though he was, puts it so powerfully to Othello,

> Good name in man or woman, dear my Lord,
> Is the immediate jewel of their souls.
> Who steals my purse steals trash, 'tis something, nothing;
> 'twas mine, 'tis his, and has been slave to thousands;
> But he that filches from me my good name
> Robs me of that which not enriches him
> And makes me poor indeed.

Robert Graves' lectures as the Oxford Professor of Poetry were another delight, as he criticised the editors of the Oxford Book of English Verse for doing their job like academics not poets. It was rollicking fun and provided me with one of the many definitions of poetry, which I have collected for my Commonplace Book through the years. 'A profession of private thought, reinforced by craftsmanship of words.' I have met worse definitions.

Common-room guest nights, and one in particular. My guest did not drive and I volunteered to go and collect him and deliver him home. It was a Thames valley pea-souper of a fog, and I shall never forget driving in my elderly Ford almost blind back to Radley, with my very distinguished guest, an Oxford professor, leaning out of the side window watching the kerb shouting 'nearer, further, in, out' as we struggled back. He was an old Christ's man, a great friend of John Brown, an ex-chaplain of Christ's and an early mentor of mine – whence the introduction. His name was Ian Ramsey, widely lamented by the church as the Archbishop that never was.

A deeply poignant moment: on the pitches on a golden autumn (?) afternoon, standing to attention (like the old soldier that I was) watching a small train disappearing up the line to Oxford and thence to Blenheim, bearing Winston Churchill's coffin to his last resting place.

Getting up early with several colleagues at five in the morning to hear the broadcast of Cassius Clay's fight with heaven knows who. It ended in one round, if I remember, and there was nothing to do but go back to bed. Staying up late to go out with David Hardy to look for badgers or listen for nightingales in Radley Little Wood. Holiday visits to the north of England to stay with Godfrey Marshall in his vicarage at Hayton, a practice which continued with Sara after we were married. He was the loveliest and holiest of men and his company a delight. On one memorable visit, aged seventy-plus, he took a group of us up Helvellyn along Striding Edge under cloud, and when we reached the summit he looked around and said, 'Let's go the other way down', and a cloud received him out of our sight. For all we knew he had gone over a precipice, but we followed in faith and all got back completely safely to Glenridding. He was one of the Marshalls of Patterdale, and his father had established a small plantation for him there at his birth. He knew the area like the back of his hand.

It was at Radley that I bought my first painting, too, and thus acquired a habit which has stayed with me ever since, though sadly I cannot afford to indulge it too often. Jeremy Holt, head of the art department, was a wonderful character. An athlete, a singer, as well as a painter, he cherished ambitions to do landscapes, but earned a supplementary living by portrait painting. He took a sabbatical year in America where, I believe, he painted John Kennedy among others. I fell for a Cotswold landscape of his when he held a small exhibition in the common-room. Hugely apologetically he told me that the price was £30, which for me was indeed big money, explaining that 'you are not only paying for the picture but for the ten years during which I earned nothing'. I have always remembered that when aghast at the prices of paintings in galleries I have visited. But undeterred I later bought two more, a pastel and a watercolour. They hang together on my walls and are precious reminders of a lovely man tragically killed in a car crash near his Cotswold home soon after.

Cricket in the holidays: Simon Langdale got me to join the Yellowhammers, a rambling club based on old Tonbridge and Radley pupils. They had a wonderful ten-day summer tour, based on Eastbourne College and Tonbridge School. We had some splendid games and I met some delightful people. It was good quality club cricket, probably slightly better than my talents deserved, but they were always glad of a makeweight. My favourite memory is hitting E W Swanton for four and hearing him grumble to a team-mate, 'Doesn't the fellow know it's the last over before lunch?' I had clearly breached some serious etiquette in the rule book of the Grand Old Man. The Jesters Cricket Club was another rambling club, playing at a rather less elevated level than the Yellowhammers, which suited me because I did get a chance to contribute more. Again, so many nice people played for them, including Edward Fox on several occasions, and our baby Anna made the early acquaintance of his daughter Amelia.

I regularly played with Michael Meyer, the great scholar of Ibsen and Strindberg, who seemed to have known every literary figure in the contemporary pantheon. He was wonderfully generous of his time and would willingly come

The Palace, Armagh, ca. 1950, with the chapel in the background. An oil painting by Lesley Gregg

John Gregg, DD, Bishop of Cork, 1875, Grandfather's grandfather. He 'built' St Finn Barr's Cathedral, Cork, laying the foundation stone and consecrating it – a very rare 'double'

Robert Gregg, DD, Grandfather's uncle. Archbishop of Armagh and Primate of All Ireland

John Allen Fitzgerald Gregg, CH, DD, my grandfather. Archbishop of Armagh and Primate of All Ireland. (The Oswald Birley Portrait (1935), painted when he was Archbishop of Dublin)

Frances F. Gregg (Grandfather's Aunt Fanny). Founder of St Luke's Hospital, Cork, 1885

Dr Katharine Gregg (Grandfather's sister) Missionary Doctor in Peshawar, India, ca. 1910

Hilda C. Gregg, ca. 1920 (Grandfather's sister). Authoress, writing as Sidney C. Grier

At the Palace, Armagh – Brian, aged 2, with Grandfather

At the Palace, Armagh – Brian, aged 17, with Grandfather

The Madden Family

Samuel Owen Madden and Mabel, 1877

Samuel Fitzgerald Madden, 1890

Owen Madden, 1877

William Madden, 1887

Castletownshend 1906 – a view of the village. Centre right: the Castle, where we used to stay, and the Parish Church above it

Castletownshend – a family picnic in the 1920s

and talk to classes on almost any literary topic. He inscribed a copy of his three-volume *Life of Ibsen*, with more generosity than truth, 'to Brian Wilson, a better batsman and classic'. He was himself a hockey blue from his Cambridge days. Sara has two vivid memories: one of being flat on her back in the rear seat of his sports car after a lovely dinner he gave us both in London – the reason being neither seduction nor a surfeit of drink, but the typical lack of space in the back of a Mercedes. Then, a visit to Eastbourne to talk to my sixth formers, when he stayed the night with us and was introduced to our Emma, a mere one year old. Michael with gin in one hand and a cigarette in the other, leaned over to look at her saying, 'Isn't she beautiful', and accidentally spilt his gin all over her. Emma never lost the taste for hard liquor, and years later astonished us when we took her out for supper as a sixth former at the college and she put away three Cinzanos in rapid succession without the slightest effects, thus demonstrating that she had inherited her grandmother's head for alcohol. My father always said my mother had the hardest head in Europe. Good times and good friends. The list could go on and on.

Radley had given me a wonderful start – teaching able boys; learning more about my subject through the sheer necessity of trying to keep well ahead of them; stimulating colleagues; congenial surroundings; a style of life that made us feel we were professional men, treated as professionals; working immensely hard on the typical 24/7 schedule of any member of a boarding school staff in a good school (though the changing climate of the times was to erode this ethos to a fair extent in the next thirty years); the academic standard had been improving steadily and on 17 February 1964 *The Times* reported that in the *Where* league table of A Level results for the top seventy-five boarding schools (to which I have alluded above in the chapter on Sedbergh) A Level passes, not distinctions, showed that in the number of passes per hundred boys in the school, Radley came sixth. It gave the fees as well, and Radley's fees were the sixth highest at £489 p.a. Ahead of it in this order of academic merit were Ampleforth, Epsom, Winchester, Oundle and Marlborough. Ahead of it in order of level of fees were Winchester (third in order of merit), Westminster (thirteenth), Harrow (fortieth), Charterhouse (thirty-ninth), Eton (fifty-first). We preened ourselves a little on these results. They seemed to give the lie to the old claim that Radleians were charming but ineffective; it also showed us that our hard work had paid off.

I had clearly had four good years' training in a first-class school, but I was getting comfortable. I had tasted the fruit of the lotus and found it alluring. It was time to move.

CHAPTER 15

The Combined Cadet Force – Leadership Training?

A Persian boy's education, which lasts fifteen years from the age of five, is only in three subjects: riding, shooting, and telling the truth. Before that age he is looked after entirely by women.

Herodotus 1.131

ONE OTHER AREA OF SCHOOL LIFE for which I offered my services, forgetful of the old army adage, 'Never volunteer', proved more interesting and rewarding than I expected – the CCF. One of the myths widely propagated about the Cadet Force was that it offered leadership training for young men who were destined to be the leaders of their country. It was the greatest nonsense and if anyone had given serious thought to leadership training it was not apparent in any of the training manuals that ever came my way. The British army of the First World War was rightly described as a body of 'mules led by donkeys'. Cadet Force uniforms, weaponry, and training seemed to have progressed little from then. The donkeys were still in charge.

The CCF had been compulsory at Sedbergh and was a complete waste of time. One attempt to create a more interesting training scheme had led to the construction of the assault course across the River Rawthey by Bertie Mills, MC, the 'mad major' of the Parachute Regiment, according to school legend. He at least knew something about real fighting and was a highly intelligent man, much too intelligent to have remained in the peacetime army. Tragically his initiative led to one tragic disaster in my time. My friend, Richard Bromley, on training with a 'commando' squad, was killed on that assault course, when in characteristic enthusiasm he got ahead of the pack and attempted the crossing on his own, with the river in wild spate, up about fifteen feet above normal and rolling great boulders down the stream, one of which cracked him on the head and pitched him into the water. It was an absolutely traumatic few days and I suppose it was the Celt in me at play; I still remember being absolutely convinced that I was going to meet his ghost in the section of the house where we were both prefects and asking to be moved elsewhere.

None of us were taught to shoot. A privileged few were able to go out on the school ranges; rather more were allowed a very occasional go on the .22 indoor range. Total boredom and an absence of any attempt to instil principles of leadership marked my experience. I became a sergeant; I cannot think why, what I did, or what was required of me.

There was little visible evidence that at Radley things would be any different and the contingent was, on the whole, officered by slightly more senior staff. The younger members of the 'keen' generation regarded CCF activities with contempt. The offer of my services was presumably welcome. The weakness of the system was the syllabus for the army section – always the largest part of any contingent, partly because the other two services (Navy and RAF) refused to support large sections, and the army got the dross. But the deficiencies of the military imagination and lack of serious commitment to support the Cadet Force contributed to the sense of futility. By contrast the Navy and RAF sections had a more interesting syllabus and the opportunity for more exciting activities at camp and so on. Most of the Navy could sail; a fair proportion of the RAF had opportunities to go flying.

But by the time I joined, partly as a means of discharging my four-year Reserve commitment, Arduous Training had come in. As a scheme it had its weaknesses, summarised by Ronnie Howard succinctly as 'doing not very difficult expeditions in as difficult a way as possible'. Nevertheless, as a way of exposing boys to challenging conditions and physically quite demanding tasks, it did fulfil a useful and educational purpose. Since leadership is fostered partly by the confidence born of a multiplicity of challenges encountered and overcome, it had the potential to contribute usefully to the problem of leadership. No one who has traversed the Brecon Beacons in late March with snow still on the hills and icy winds blowing will have any illusions about the difficulty; to do it as sometimes happens under cloud, relying totally on your compass, requires confidence, proper training, and good support; to have the task of leading and making decisions for a small group facing such challenges is valuable.

I well remember the agony of waiting at a checkpoint in bad weather, when teams failed to show up on schedule, and the anxiety of hunting through the late evening for those who had lost their way. There were no mobile phones then to summon help, and no way of knowing whether they were in trouble. The drill was to stay where you were; keep warm; get under cover; and wait. To complete the course, usually a week, meant that you had learned to set up and maintain camp; cook for yourself; keep kit dry; yourself warm and clean (relatively); to rely on your training and your comrades; and to complete the mission. A genuine degree of self-reliance and competence in difficult conditions was the reward. I am sure that the boys gained from the experience; I feel that I too gained quite a lot from helping to run it.

Then David Skipper left the RAF section to be head of Ellesmere, via a spell as head of chemistry in a London school, I think. I was asked to change my allegiance from army to RAF and to run the section, with promotion to the lordly status of Flight Lieutenant (VRT), equivalent of an army Captain, and rendering me for the second time Her Majesty's Trusty and Well-beloved. It was enormously refreshing; and we had some high-powered parents in the RAF, as useful names to drop when resources or help were required. The legendary Gus Walker, the one-armed international rugby referee, and Air Vice Marshall Grandy both had boys in the school at the time. I even managed on one occasion for the annual inspection of the CCF to persuade the Commanding Officer of Little Rissington, the RAF's Central Flying School, to let his Red Pelicans (predecessors of the Red Arrows) practise their aerobatics display over Radley on that particular morning. The Inspecting Officer was Gus Walker, and I remember with some pleasure his puzzled enquiry as to 'what are my Red Pelicans doing over here?' More modestly, the RAF liaison officer system ensured that a complete tiro like myself always had backup and help with equipment or to take a class, which I, who knew nothing of the syllabus, was rarely competent to do. Again I had recourse to my principle that, if possible, the leadership role should be filled by boys, turning my lack of knowledge to advantage by insisting that instruction was done by boy NCOs, since I was there to learn.

We once built, for instructional purposes, an amazing wind tunnel, complete with fan blower at one end and models of aerofoils suspended within. The problem was to find smoke with which to demonstrate the movement of air across an aerofoil. So I borrowed a smoke bomb from the army section, lit it, and waited for the fan to do its stuff, which it did – magnificently. But it was a very cold day, and cold air flows downhill, a useful secondary physics lesson. We laid a thick belt of dense fog all the way down the drive and across the main road from Radley to Oxford, bringing the traffic to a standstill with full headlights on, horns blaring, and minor chaos abounding for about half an hour. We did not repeat the experiment.

Camps were interesting and officers' messes much more welcoming than the army. There was a healthy classlessness about the RAF, which was in marked contrast with the inbuilt snobbery of the army – and for obvious reasons. When pilots are so dependent on their maintenance teams for their safety and survival, there is a limit to the degree to which they can afford to put on airs and graces. Teamwork is more important than hierarchy. The Flying Scholarship was, of course, the absolute plum reward for being in the RAF section, and a number of boys won one, thus learning to fly to private pilot standard at the expense of the RAF. Many more went to glider flying camps and gained the basic A and B qualification by going solo three times. In addition, everybody got a number of chances to go flying with the Air Experience Flight, often with pilots of the RAF Reserve, who took boys on sorties (with or without aerobatics) all over the place. One way or another, given a little flexibility from the school authorities over absences, quite a lot of flying went on. It was not leadership in the conventional sense; but if a multiplicity of experiences is an aid to confidence and confidence an aid to leadership, it helped.

There were good experiences for officers as well as cadets. At one camp I crashed a Lightning fighter into the ground from a height of 60,000 feet – but only in a simulator. It was extraordinary how the realism took hold of you as you watched the altimeter clicking down by hundreds of feet per second and you found yourself unable to do anything about it. But the most valuable experience they gave me personally was the opportunity to address my very real fear of heights and (believe it or not) of flying. A fair number of cadets each year were taken for gliding courses, and after the Flying Scholarship, these were the most coveted places. I was offered the chance to share their experience, and felt duty bound to accept. For me it was hair-raising and my first few flights under instruction scared the living daylights out of me. Aerobatics with my instructor in a Sedbergh glider almost finished me – he just wanted to show me the possibilities.

But came the dreaded moment when I was told I was ready for my first solo. The winch was attached; I gave the signal; and there came that shattering feeling of going at high speed almost straight up to 1,000 feet, like a kite in a high wind. As Pilot Officer Gillespie of the Royal Canadian Air force put it, and was so famously quoted by Ronald Reagan after the Apollo Shuttle disaster, I

> ... slipped the surly bonds of earth
> And danced the skies on laughter-silvered wings:
> Sunward I climbed, and joined the tumbling mirth
> Of sun split clouds ...

It is not quite true. I was pretty scared. The sense of having no feet on the ground is most peculiar; looking over the side to keep my bearings made me dizzy; the fear that I would not be able to detach the winch cable was inescapable; I repeated the mantra: 'level off – nose slightly down to increase speed – release;' it all went well and I was free. My instruction was to go left, left, and left again, before coming in to land. I knew I had plenty of height, but apparently went on a much wider circuit than the instructor expected; he looked a little disturbed when I reported back, and asked if I had not seen him signalling to me from the ground. As if ... ! I would have been much too scared to look anywhere much except straight ahead. I had been led to believe that the difficult thing was landing. For me that was the easiest – once I had the ground clearly in focus, I could relate speed to height to angle of descent without trouble and my vertigo disappeared. Two more solo flights and I had my A and B gliding licence. For a moment I knew what Yeats had meant by the magical phrase 'A lonely impulse of delight', when he wrote his lament for Major Gregory, 'An Irish Airman Foresees His Death'.

> I know that I shall meet my fate
> Somewhere among the clouds above:
> Those that I fight I do not hate,
> Those that I guard I do not love; ...
> Nor law nor duty bade me fight,
> Nor public men nor cheering crowds.
> A lonely impulse of delight

> Drove to this tumult in the clouds;
> I balanced all, brought all to mind,
> The years to come seemed waste of breath,
> A waste of breath the years behind
> In balance with this life, this death.

I do understand the soldier's creed, that 'one crowded hour of glorious life is worth an age without name'. But it is a depressing thought for those of us with other temperaments. I tried once to write a response to the final sentiment in Yeats' poem; it is not very good, but in the dreary routine of a pedagogue's existence, I derived some mild comfort from it.

> And if we few still left behind
> Shall ever to the stars aspire,
> Or even some rich beauty find,
> Or hope that sets the heart on fire . . .
>
> Then we should pray to God that we
> May share that impulse of delight,
> If only once, and thus may see
> Some hint of dawning in the night.
> Then in our little way we'll sink
> Back to some lonely corner cell
> And draw deep comfort, as we think:
> 'I too, though briefly, have lived well.'

G K Chesterton of course said it much better in his little poem, 'The Donkey', which has always moved me by its simplicity and the thought behind it.

> . . . With monstrous head and sickening cry
> And ears like errant wings,
> The devil's walking parody
> On all four-footed things . . .
>
> Fools, for I also had my hour;
> One far fierce hour and sweet:
> There was a shout about my ears,
> And palms before by feet.

What a fuss to make about an achievement which half a dozen sixteen-year olds at the school managed every year. To most people it would have seemed trivial. For me it was a very personal triumph over genuine terror. It was in its own way of similar importance to producing the *Bacchae* – a very private success in an entirely new area of experience. That the terror was not entirely fanciful is illustrated by the fact that the following year I lost a pupil, whom I had sent on one of these training camps; he seems to have flown his glider straight into the ground on his first solo; no one knows why, and the inquest found no cause for blame. The parents were as generous as the parents of Richard Bromley had been eight years before at Sedbergh. They said that their son had been thrilled to go on the course, and that at the moment of his death he would have been doing something that made him intensely happy. They held no one to blame. Such generosity of spirit would have made their son very proud. No one who works in schools ever quite gets over the trauma of the loss of a young life. My predecessor in the classics department at Radley had been in charge of the Naval section, and had lost a pupil in an accident with sheerlegs (I think they are called). Sometimes it is a fatal illness; at others an accident. It is inevitable that amid the changes and chances of this mortal life, these things will happen and children cannot be kept in cotton wool forever. But it is absolutely no comfort to agonised parents, horrified staff, or distraught fellow-pupils.

Here is a tiny poem by Callimachus, taken from the Greek anthology, one of the most moving I know for the economy and exactness with which it expresses the pain felt by a father bereft of his beloved son.

> Twelve years old was the son his father Philip
> laid to rest, here in this spot, his high hope, Nikoteles.

I use it always to illustrate the genius and economy of Greek. The word order is deliberate and precise and I have tried to retain it from the Greek. First word: the age, twelve, when a boy is just on the verge of leaving childhood behind and turning hope into fulfilment; then the juxtaposition of son followed by father, forever close; then the father's name, to be balanced at the end of the second line by his son's; the location, 'here' held over till the next line, to halt the reader in his tracks; the one comment, his 'high hope' (was he an only son?), with the Greek words full of the letter *lambda*, l, which lingers on the lips like a lost chord or a half-remembered dream, and which I have tried to suggest by the alliterative h's, like heaving sighs of sorrow; and only then at the very last, the child's name – all this contained in an elegiac couplet, a hexameter followed by a pentameter, to fit neatly on a grave stele.

I dedicate it to all those who have endured the agonies of such bereavement.

Another RAF initiative was in the field of leadership training and again it was a privilege to have been allowed to participate in a new experiment in cadet training. Someone in the training branch had clearly been giving some thought to how to train leadership and the rationale of their experiment was at the least interesting. How successful it was or could have been I have no way of knowing. As I remember it, the course involved a long weekend, Friday to Monday. The cadets were briefed and then put out onto the airfield at South Cerney to rig tents, cook, and organise themselves for the night. They were warned that emergencies might occur requiring them to move elsewhere at no notice and fulfil other tasks, repel enemy attacks or whatever. The emergencies happened; they got little sleep, and by morning they were pretty knackered. Training tasks continued all day and by evening they were almost done for. More 'emergencies'. By Sunday morning they were stressed and exhausted. That day they were set the sort of small leadership tasks that every candidate for WOSB is familiar with. Each cadet took the leadership role in turn and had to organise his team to complete a task against the clock, and with verbal pressure from the observer (mainly reminding him how little time he had left – very stress inducing). A good night's sleep followed and the next morning they were individually debriefed by the trainers and observers, in front of each other. There wasn't a sound on the bus home.

Now for the rationale, as I understood it: first, self-knowledge is an essential ingredient of leadership. You must recognise your own weaknesses and analyse them dispassionately. Secondly, weaknesses of character or capacity only emerge under stress (whether panic, loss of temper, loss of control, inability to think straight, failure to recognise the symptoms etc). Therefore would-be leaders must first be exhausted and stressed, before weaknesses will appear, allowing useful lessons in self-knowledge to be achieved; hence all the 'emergencies', which disrupted the first two nights' sleep. The debrief, leading to self-knowledge is the critical element of the exercise and is held over till the final morning when they have had a good sleep and are able to think seriously about the experience.

I dare say in this more psychologically aware era, much more subtle and sophisticated training can be and has been devised. But I felt that this was a coherent attempt to do something about the leadership training, which had long been claimed for army training but which really seemed to be little more than developing the capacity to shout 'rah rah rah' to the chaps, as you led them over the top to their deaths. I was sufficiently persuaded of the worthwhileness of the exercise to bring a group of cadets from King's Canterbury on the same course once I went there. If nothing else it will have added to the multiplicity of experiences which I do believe add to anyone's capacity for leadership, because of the self-confidence induced by the feeling that 'I have been here, or somewhere similar, before', and particularly if one is aware, thanks to a good debriefing, of where one's weaknesses were exposed on the previous occasion.

I never had anything to do with the Naval sections, but I helped out occasionally with the Radley sailing club and even in the relative safety of the gravel pits near Abingdon it was apparent to me that there was always risk, and where there is risk there must be skills reinforced by discipline, and where there are skills there is a need for instruction, and opportunity for seniors to learn by training juniors. If I ran a Naval section I would ensure that, whatever else, all members reached an RYA qualifying standard of some sort. Experience; skill; discipline; challenge – all these will contribute towards leadership skills.

I served my time in the CCF at Radley and then at King's Canterbury, thus discharging my Reserve commitment, which was part of my contract with the army originally. At Campbell College the CCF pipes and drums was a wonderful addition to the repertoire of worthwhile activities, with training delivered by Pipe

Major Wilson, late of the Royal Irish Fusiliers, and by seniors to juniors. It was not leadership of the conventional military sort, but there was considerable self-discipline within the ranks, leadership in the form of instruction, and they were good enough to give public performances all over the place in England as well as Northern Ireland. Our pipers competed successfully at the Scottish championships.

Multiplicity of experiences, once again.

I can say little about the Duke of Edinburgh's Award Scheme, which came on the scene after my CCF days were over. By introducing the element of service it added a valuable dimension to mere 'adventure training'. The structure and achievement targets gave the whole thing a much more coherent scheme of development and progressive measures of progress. It was admirably managed at St Mary's, Wantage, by Maggie Penrose, and I used to go out (again to the Brecon Beacons area) to help with the expedition work, mainly for girls who were going for the Gold standard. It was certainly challenging and no less worrying as we waited for groups to reach their RVs. Much good work was also done in service to the community under the same scheme, and it offered an excellent and more thoroughly thought-out supplement to the conventional cadet training which I had been familiar with.

Ironically, the best leadership training I have encountered would have turned Wyndham Milligan's hair whiter than it already was — drama. House drama competitions and the practical side of A Level drama courses both require of their youthful directors a level of skill, man/woman (one must be so politically correct these days!) management, tact, creativity, planning, and organisation sufficient to test the mettle of any would-be captain of industry. Adjudicators and examiners provide the debrief which the RAF scheme thought so essential. I have seen some wonderful productions and some that were unspeakable. From both the participants and the directors should have learned a lot. Better by far to have been the director of your house play than captain of the school rugger team.

Many, many good people have spent hours and years of their lives doing immensely valuable work in the service of youth training. It is largely unhonoured and unsung. There are no votes in it; no celebrity status; politicians can wring their hands and lament the disorderliness of youth and the collapse of discipline in home and school, but they do little to help those who work to make things better.

Could one end such a chapter with any other quotation than Cleopatra's lament for her soldier lover, Mark Antony, another of the Bard's almost magical passages?

> O! wither'd is the garland of the war.
> The soldier's pole is fallen; young boys and girls
> Are level now with men; the odds is gone,
> And there is nothing left remarkable
> Beneath the visiting moon.

CHAPTER 16

The King's School, Canterbury

To give up all this for God, Thomas, perhaps ...
But for Wales, Thomas? For Wales!

Thomas More to Thomas Rich in Robert Bolt's
A Man for All Seasons

FROM THE CIVILISED COMFORTS OF Radley, I went off to King's Canterbury, one of the two schools which claim to be the oldest in England, and appropriately one of the most uncomfortable to work in. My friends thought it was daft; Jock Burnet, I suspect, never quite forgave me.

The decision to move was correct; the choice of school was perverse, born of ignorance and naïvety, with a dash of ambition added. Five years in your first post is sufficient to make your worst mistakes, learn something of your trade, and move onwards, seeking promotion, and wider experience. I did not answer an advertisement; I simply wrote to the headmaster and asked if I could have a job. He told me I would have to wait a year and then I could come.

The choice of school was based on two simple considerations: there was a new headmaster, recently appointed in succession to the notorious Canon 'Fred' Shirley, who had come to the school in 1935 and finally retired in 1962. New heads always introduce what the Chinese curse calls 'interesting times' for their adopted institutions, but to watch them at work is good experience. In this case I actually knew the man. It was Peter Newell, my old Sedbergh Sixth Form Classics master, who had been a successful head of Bradford Grammar School, and had now taken on one of the most difficult tasks in education – following in the footsteps of a great headmaster.

I am afraid the task always seemed too much for him, almost as if he had been promoted, as Professor Parkinson would have put it, to his level of incompetence (though that is much too strong a word) presumably on the strength of his success at Bradford Grammar School, and also because he was a cleric, the need for which must have severely restricted the choices available to the governors of the school. In my naïve recollection of his personality and dynamism at Sedbergh, the possibility of his inadequacy never occurred to me. But to do him justice, almost anyone would have found the task of following Shirley impossible, though Newell's temperament probably made it doubly difficult for him. Though his undoubted virtues were undervalued by his staff, he always seemed to be a man under stress, despite the wonderful support and comfort of his wife Mary, one of the gentlest and kindest of headmaster's wives. It was as if every unexpected event was a threat, and even a simple expression of doubt or unusual request was a challenge to his authority.

More important to my calculations, however, was the fact that King's had a reputation as a highly successful school and for promoting young men early. Having 'lost' five years at Radley, I wanted to be a housemaster quickly, because within the independent sector that was the most reliable way to a headship. In that respect my judgement was correct: it only took me four years to become a housemaster, and at King's they regularly departed to higher things. The school had a good track record in gaining headships. What I had not realised was that the rapid promotion which I craved was also due to the fact that the school was so cramped and uncomfortable that young, unmarried men tended to get the housemasterships, because there was no room for married living quarters in the boarding houses. Shirley had run the school on the original Tesco principle, 'pile 'em high and sell 'em cheap'. It never occurred to me that housemasters, the most crucial staff in a boarding school, would exist in conditions that would have been unacceptable in most decent schools.

For their assistants, the house tutors, it was even worse. My own bedsitter was a room of modest size opposite the head of house's study, with whom I shared a loo. There were no other facilities; I used the housemaster's for bathing. Noise did not bother me; the lack of privacy, especially once I was courting, was more difficult, though the interest and encouragement from the boys was good for morale. 'How's it going, old man?' was the benevolent enquiry I used to get from Jeremy Carey, a delightfully fatherly head boy (and head of house) who always worked late, when he caught me sneaking back from London in the early hours. It seems to have been Shirley's policy to hire men young, unmarried and cheap, and to keep them in living conditions that were sufficiently uncomfortable to ensure that they would move on fairly rapidly; he could then buy in cheap replacements. The policy had originally been necessary, because when he was appointed his brief was to restore the finances of the school, which were in crisis, as well as building it up into a major educational establishment. In both those objectives he was undeniably successful but the discomfort was still part of his legacy.

Does the end justify the means? That Shirley lived for the school cannot be denied; that he wanted success for 'his' school is obvious. What is more debateable, as is probably the case with all great achievers, is the question of whether in this he was a devoted servant of a great cause or an egomaniac driven by a desire for success. In his case there were also deficiencies of character that might well not have survived in modern conditions. Legends about him abound, some doubtless apocryphal. Charisma he certainly had; many boys clearly adored him. But the picture I got of him from gossip and legend painted a thoroughly unattractive picture and his brooding presence still seemed to permeate the place. Contributors to Robin Pittman's *Fred Remembered* write of the air of menace combined with expectation whenever he was around – you never knew what would happen. He carried a cane in the sleeve of his gown when teaching and possibly enjoyed using it. Indeed one victim apparently claims to have been given thirty-seven strokes, though interestingly, as a measure of that charisma, he claims to have felt no sort of grudge afterwards, even though the experience was 'excruciating'.

Shirley's methods of dealing with his staff could be oblique. One member is said to have returned from the holidays to find that he had no teaching and no timetable – he left rather than be sacked, and thus presumably lost the contractual payment in lieu of notice he was entitled to. Shirley would probably have claimed that it was sound economics. When an early master in charge of rowing fell out with his Captain of Boats, 'Fred' remarked to a colleague, 'Well, you know why they don't get on, don't you? They are both in love with the cox.' Was it perceptive, or a revealing diagnosis? And of whom? He was professionally culpable in his habit of suggesting to the boys that he was 'on their side' and almost against the staff; more so for his act of taking thirty boys and several staff with him to King's from Worksop, his previous school, which he had also transformed, financially and academically. For this he was drummed out of the HMC. Like the legendary and proverbial Hippokleides, he probably 'could not have cared less'. Some years later his school had done so well that they had to bring him back. I myself found the HMC a similarly feeble organisation for all its pretensions. Shirley was something of a snob and cultivated top people, partly at least because anyone who would be useful to the school and enhance the quality of its clientele was fair game. He exploited his Masonic connections to the same ends.

The story (or was it merely legend?) that I liked best, appalling though it is when you think about it, concerns his 'promise' (alleged) to Somerset Maugham, that in return for a substantial donation to his new chemistry laboratory he would ensure that he was buried in the cathedral precincts. He was – beside the chemistry lab, which was not I am sure quite what the great author had in mind. But at least the school library was named after him.

Another illustration of his idiosyncratic approach, which for originality could border upon genius, was the appointment of S S Sopwith, always known as 'Spwith'. This splendid old man was related to Tommy Sopwith, builder of the famous Sopwith Camel, a WWI fighter flown by my boyhood hero, Biggles. 'Spwith' was one of the legendary teachers of English, far ahead of his time, who had been both housemaster and head of English at Shrewsbury. When he retired, presumably aged sixty, Shirley appointed him as housemaster of Galpin's, a post which he held with considerable success. After he retired for the second time, he was given rooms in the Precincts and there he lived until his death at the age of about eighty, a sort of *éminence grise*, a counsellor and mentor to younger staff, and still teaching occasional lessons to would-be Oxbridge scholars. I sat at the feet of this Gamaliel for many an evening and learned a lot from him. His *English Sampler* is a gem of an anthology of prose and poetry, very small, and each of the 120 selections very short, but each with a brief biographical note appended and succinct comment on the significance of the passage. He signed and gave me his last spare copy, which I had re-bound in green leather, green as his memory always will be. His introduction is a model.

> The first step in the study of literature is to learn how to read; that is, how to read so as to appreciate as fully as possible the writer's meaning and intention, his thought and mood. This can only be achieved by the reading and study of complete works, for a work of art is a unity and can be appreciated fully only as a whole ... One of the objects of this book is to present short selections of some of the masterpieces of both prose and poetry in our literature for such detailed reading and examination as may lead to a new understanding of what literature really is; and for learning by heart [Learning by heart – Amen, Oh blessed Spwith!] some of the passages from the varied store of our literary heritage ... It may be of some help to suggest the following method of discovering how to read a passage rightly: (1) make certain of the words which require special emphasis to make clear the logical meaning of the passage or to bring to light the associations which certain words are intended to evoke; (2) practise carefully the inflexion of the voice demanded by the mood – this is just as important in silent reading as in reading aloud; (3) note how the writer has employed the music of words to help convey his meaning ...

And so on. Simple, systematic, practical and clear: the art of the great teacher.

Here are the concluding lines of Arnold's wonderful poem, 'Sohrab and Rustum', and Spwith's comment upon them. It could serve almost as his own epitaph.

> But the majestic river floated on,
> Out of the mist and hum of that low land,
> Into the frosty starlight, and there moved
> Rejoicing, through the hushed Chorasmian waste,
> Under the solitary moon ...
>
> ... till at last
> The longed-for dash of waves is heard, and wide
> His luminous home of waters opens, bright
> And tranquil, from whose floor the new-bathed stars
> Emerge, and shine upon the Aral sea.

'Tragedy', he says in his comment on these lines, 'does not find its proper ending in tumult and passion, but rather in the contrast of the "vain turmoil" of human conflicts with the never-ceasing yet quiet movement of life ... The final lines of Arnold's poem form a kind of coda to the poem, in which the story of the river seems to reflect the bright hopes, the foiled searchings, and the ultimate attainment of the young heroic Sohrab.'

Shirley's qualities and his undoubted achievement made him a permanent topic of discussion among other headmasters – he seemed to be able to get away with some of the things they longed to do but did not dare. He even claimed that his governors could not sack him, because they did not pay him a salary. Certainly they used his canon's stipend supplemented by perks as part at least of his salary; but if anything they were probably simply frightened of him and the damage he might do to their school if he left. More important, he was extremely good at his job.

Nothing that I heard about Shirley's regime after I got there endeared him to me. As a canon he had continued to live in the precincts and must have been a real trial to his successor, whom he disliked and was happy to undermine. I met him once at his invitation in his old age and found nothing in his conversation or manner to attract me. I must have been a similar disappointment to him, since I was not yet sufficiently disillusioned to find fault with Newell, which is no doubt what he wanted to hear. I am sure I would not have lasted a year in his employment, being much too conventional and, I hope, blessed with some scruples where he seemed to have none. But as a corrective to my jaundiced and entirely second-hand view, based on the comments of those who knew him and had served under him, one should set the many generous tributes not only in Robin Pittman's memoir, but also in David Edwards' more substantial if somewhat hagiographic biography.

Peter Newell, by contrast, was honest, principled (though capable of deception, I have no doubt, like any headmaster), fundamentally kind, no less devoted to the school and his pupils, and immensely hard-working. He was probably better suited to the northern directness of his beloved Yorkshire than the more serpentine ways of a cathedral close in the devious south. He once said to me with a sigh that he seemed to be fated to install lavatories wherever he went – a more significant comment than it might seem. It illustrates his thoroughly practical approach and attention to mundane detail, and the fact that one of his problems was to make good some of the basic deficiencies of the previous regime, which would not have been much concerned with such trivialities. Shirley would have crammed in an extra bed instead of a loo. Newell was utterly dedicated; always about the place, thus obeying one of my fundamental rules for a head. Every afternoon he would take a walk round the playing fields, showing genuine interest in what was going on and using it as an opportunity to learn boys' names. He had no understanding of games or the challenges involved in coaching them; they were simply a useful way of keeping a large number of boys out of mischief; but they did have a bearing on a school's standing with parents, actual and prospective, so he took them seriously. I found a wry amusement in remembering his total indifference to games at Sedbergh.

Interestingly, I have no real idea what the boys thought of him. I suspect he puzzled them; he was clearly a nice man who cared about their welfare, but he was not easy to get to know and was much too concerned to defend his dignity beneath the gown and mortarboard in which he always appeared during school hours – an affectation which inspired a fair degree of snide comment in the common-room. There was a nice encounter once in the Green Court with a relatively senior boy, who at one stage in those liberal days affected Italianate sideburns almost down to his jaw line, well below the authorised level.

JPN: Higher, Pearce; higher!
Pearce: Oh, hiya, Sir, hiya.
JPN: No Pearce, higher – h-i-g-h-e-r.

No offence taken or given; no evidence of amusement on either side; but the effect on the sideburns was not totally insignificant.

The staff, by contrast, who were still mainly Shirley's men, disliked him for his formality, his inability to relax into his role, his rigidity, pernickety-ness, and unbending insistence on discipline and good order. With hindsight, I am sure this is in fact one of his real achievements. The period I was there, 1965–1973, saw schools across the country move from the acceptance of traditional hierarchal management (of staff as well as pupils) in a disciplined and orderly structure, inherited from the immediate postwar period, into a mood of challenge and response, a demand for greater 'freedom', which could degenerate sometimes into states of near anarchy. Everywhere the old rules and standards were challenged and often defied, whether in trivial matters like haircuts (which descended to the shoulder and looked frightful to any Orwellian 'right-thinking' person) or in more serious matters like drinking and drug-taking. Corporal punishment had always been reasonably effective and economical of time and effort, but was becoming unfashionable and would be illegal by the mid-eighties. Prefects were increasingly reluctant to impose order. Politicians, as usual, lost their nerve and increasingly caved in to the mood of the times or sought short-term solutions to long term problems. So did many headmasters, sometimes under pressure from their common-rooms. Newell adopted the position of the Ulster Unionists in a political context, 'No surrender; not one inch'. He kept his head, while all about were losing theirs, and certainly blaming it on him. Kipling would have applauded. King's remained orderly, disciplined, hard-working, and academically highly successful, and even drug problems were very rare. He handed it in on in good shape, and I even sent my elder daughter there for the sixth form – but under a successor.

But without a dedicated and supportive staff no head can get far. Newell had two problems: if he had a vision for the school's future, I was certainly not aware of it; he seemed content to hold the line – no more. After Shirley the lack of excitement must have been depressing for those who had known both regimes. Secondly, he seemed to have a congenital reluctance to praise, encourage, or thank. If things went right, he claimed the credit. If they went wrong, he distributed the blame and never shared it. He was, in that respect, a miserable man to work for. He disliked intensely absence from school for any reason. He was outraged when Archbishop Ramsey put me on a diocesan commission to make recommendations for education, mission, evangelism, and pastoral work. I suspect that the real affront was that a relatively junior member of his staff should have been so invited, instead of himself perhaps. He went out of his way to discourage it, though he baulked at the idea of actually vetoing the wishes of the Archbishop. When I asked for an afternoon off to attend the first meeting he granted it with sulky lack of grace and insisted on no repetition.

But the 'crime' for which I never forgave him and which finally cost him any residual loyalty I might have had, was when my sister got married. I asked for a night away from my house (I was a housemaster by then and it was admittedly early in a new term) to fly to Northern Ireland for the wedding, at which I was also proposing the bride's health, since my father had chickened out. He refused, graciously conceding me only the day (a Saturday!). Sara and I with Anna aged only a few weeks had to get up at some ungodly hour to catch the early morning flight from Gatwick and had to fly back the same evening, thus missing the previous evening's dinner and a chance to stay with my parents as an antidote to the inevitable sense of anticlimax that followed. This singular lack of generosity was entirely in character and I expect most of his staff would have similar tales to tell.

I could only contrast it with the generosity of Wyndham Milligan at Radley, and Simon Langdale at Eastbourne. They always encouraged absence for career development and were generous to a fault when compassion intervened. For example, while at Radley I heard on the morning news on the BBC of the death of my grandfather and his funeral the next day. My mother had deliberately spared me the knowledge that he was fading fast and I was taken totally by surprise. I went to Milligan, asked for permission to attend the funeral, caught the night boat to Dublin, on landing rang my old friend John Brown, by then Professor of Pastoral Theology at TCD and Principal of the Church of Ireland Divinity Hostel, and asked him where the interment was and how to get there. He rang the Archbishop of Dublin, George Simms, who was conducting the service, and he gave me a lift. The first my family knew of my intention to be present was when I turned up at the graveside. My mother was enormously moved by the effort, which I am sure was a great comfort to her. Milligan had made it possible. That is the way to treat your staff and I hope it was a lesson I learned from him. My lessons from Newell were, sadly, largely negative – but no less useful for all that.

The school itself had great strengths and in my view some weaknesses, apart from the problem of poor and overcrowded accommodation, which boys are usually adaptable enough to tolerate. Academically it was absolutely first-class. My possibly rose-tinted memory tells me that we never got less than twenty Oxbridge awards every year – a record which possibly only Winchester, Westminster, and

Manchester Grammar School would have matched. A and O Level results were excellent. The source of this excellence lay with the quality of pupils, of course, and obviously with the quality of staff, but partly also with the tutor system, by which every member of staff was responsible for about twelve to fifteen boys' academic work and expected to liaise closely with their housemasters on the subject. Pastoral oversight was a secondary but welcome addition. As always, some tutors were more diligent than others, but the overall effect (supplemented by systematic reporting every three weeks) was to ensure that the pressure to perform was constant and most boys worked pretty hard.

In addition Scholars were made a fuss of and given special status with purple gowns and two Senior Scholarships awarded each year to boys about to enter the Lower VI. These were extremely vigorously competed for and I had the pleasure and privilege of setting and marking the General Paper for that exam for many years and relished the challenge of trying to test abilities by setting questions for which no amount of swotting or coaching could have prepared them. Oxbridge colleges in those days still set store by the General Paper in their own exams, and so it was a kind of preparation for our cleverest candidates. All this meant that it was respectable to be clever and even hard working at King's, which helped to counter any peer group pressure in the other direction. It was a delight to teach there, even non-specialist subjects like divinity and English. The boys were clever, demanding, and challenging.

No less remarkable was the music, under Edred Wright, the Director of Music, where success built upon success and musicians distinguished nationally and internationally sent their musical sons to the school. The second orchestra was perfectly capable of performing a full symphony; the first orchestra did so regularly. Not being a musician I am hardly competent to offer a more expert assessment of that quality, but there is no doubt that we were what would now be called a centre of excellence for music, and the quality of concerts given at the summer arts festival (King's Week) was extraordinary.

Drama was not as good as people seemed to believe, to anyone at least who had seen what could be done in school productions. Guy Boas, I think it was, argued much the same point in a book on drama, possibly when discussing the capacities of Shakespeare's boy actors. Schoolboys and girls bring a freshness to their acting which can be captivating. In fact I found our productions ponderously worthy, but dull, and in some senses almost over-rehearsed. Schools tend to myth-making and the myth of King's drama seemed to me just that: a myth. Good but not special, even when for the production of *King Lear* the great Paul Schofield was enlisted by Sopwith to give a little help to our Lear. But King's Week was an excellent vehicle for drama as well as music, and productions were always competent.

The third area of excellence was sport. The Assistant Bursar, Colin Fairservice (a wonderful source of sometimes scurrilous stories about Shirley) had played cricket for Kent in his day and his primary task was to run the games. He was the finest coach of rugby and cricket that I have known. How he did it, I have no idea, though in Shirley's day it will have helped to have had the headmaster bellowing on the touchline and not above tripping an opposing winger with his walking stick, if he looked like scoring. Colin was no track-suited rugger bugger. He always maintained that the higher you went in sport, the more the key to performance lay with the mind not the body. His willingness to conduct practices unchanged and armed with an umbrella rather than a whistle showed that he practised what he preached. He produced sides whose results were remarkable in both games, and in one year three boys in the cricket XI had batting averages of over 100. If my memory is correct they were David Gower, England and Leicestershire; Charles Rowe, Kent; and Brian Hamblin, Oxford University. I still boast that I 'coached' David Gower for a fortnight, when I ran the Colts XI; but 'coached' overstates the matter. He passed through my side for a fortnight *en route* for the first XI in his first year at the school. I was also his housemaster for a term, but he always seemed almost too grown up for his contemporaries and was quickly promoted to his senior house.

We also had outstanding squash teams year after year, thanks to the fanatical coaching of Dennis Ball, later head of Kelly College, while rowing was remarkable for its results in conditions which made it extremely difficult to achieve much. But David Goodes, a fine musician also who ran the second orchestra, was in charge of a wonderfully happy and effective boat club.

My own small contribution was to run the hockey for several years, but neither as player or coach was I anything much to write home about. But I did fully subscribe to the Fairservice doctrine that success in higher levels of sport was a matter of brains as well as brawn and I think I improved the performance of our not very successful hockey club, to the extent that in one year we were the Kent champions. It may sound absurd, but when I took over a very demoralised first XI I was influenced by what I had read of Field Marshall Sir William Slim in the Burma campaign. He too took over a demoralised army, who had reached such a pitch of despair that they believed the Japanese invincible. His solution was to instruct his commanders that they were only to fight engagements with overwhelmingly superior numbers, so that they were bound to win. A company would take on a small section; a battalion a platoon; a brigade a company, and so on. Once the myth of Japanese invincibility had been demolished, they could fight on more appropriate terms. It worked and the tide of battle turned. I adopted a similar principle. We would play to avoid defeat at all costs. Instead of the conventional two-man defences, I introduced a third (sweeper) and sometimes even a fourth defender. We treated a draw as a victory. It was dull but it did the trick. I also urged the team to watch first division soccer and see how men moved off the ball and into space; we talked tactics by the hour with chessmen on a table over coffee. I only wish I had been a better and more experienced player and that

I had come to the game twenty years later, when the rule changes had created a much more exciting and watchable sport.

And that was it. To a regrettable extent King's offered limited opportunities for minor sports, and a poor repertoire of societies for such a large school full of able boys. As I have briefly mentioned in an earlier chapter, I was asked to take charge of the Somner (antiquarian) society and chose as my boy secretary one Simon (I think) Blackmore. He was a brilliant organiser and an enthusiast for industrial archaeology. We followed my usual principle that boys should run everything. We established a series of sections specialising in different areas: industrial archaeology; Roman Britain; the cathedral and its history; brass rubbing; coins; the Walpole Collection; and what else I can't remember. The response was terrific and membership I think got to a hundred and we even produced our own calendar of events. In one sense certainly the society was like the hundred-headed hydra, and barely under control. Able boys with intellectual energy to spare and given their heads will tend to get carried away. We laid on a wonderful exhibition for one Speech Day, of which I was immensely proud, and for which I would claim little credit since the boys did it all – and I got none. Predictably Newell lost his nerve and I was instructed to limit our activities. Anything that seemed too successful frightened him.

Nevertheless, there were good aspects to my existence there. I went straight into Walpole House as house tutor to Richard Meredith, later headmaster of Giggleswick and then Monkton Combe. He was a man of boundless energy and enthusiasm, a wonderful boss who gave me my head as a tutor, contrived to find responsibilities for me that would widen my experience, such as becoming knowledgeable on the subject of American university entrance, because initially two of my tutor set were targeted on American universities, preferably Harvard. Despite a certain difference in theology, since he was moderately evangelical, we saw eye to eye on pretty well everything else, and I found myself enjoying once again the whole business of being associated with a boarding house, despite the discomforts of the accommodation. He had a very lively mind, could tease and be teased, was still a bachelor at that stage and little older than I (rapid promotion again at King's). We both got married while at the school, and have remained excellent friends ever since. Hazel is godmother to my Anna; I godfather to his James.

His successor at Walpole, Robin Pittman, was tough enough to force Newell to create married accommodation rather more reasonably tolerable for a married housemaster than what the Shirley-conditioned Merediths had to put up with. It is always easier to negotiate reasonable terms and conditions at the start of one's tenure of office. Once established, they tend to take you for granted. By then I was a housemaster up at Riversleigh, the junior boarding house. Robin brought a degree of imaginative civilisation to what had been a rather Spartan establishment and was a highly successful housemaster until he too moved on to a headship, first at Queen Elizabeth's Hospital, Bristol, and then at St Peter's York. By then I was at Campbell. He was another of the really close friends I made at King's, and again, he is Anna's godfather; I am Katy's.

I sometimes wonder if the fact that so many of us disliked Newell helped to make us all friends, in alliance against the common enemy, so to speak. But it was not as simple as that. I cannot easily define my own feelings about him or those of the common-room. He must have seemed a somewhat dreary replacement for Shirley, to those who liked the latter. I personally was torn by ancient loyalties and the fact that he was exceedingly kind to me, especially when I was wooing Sara. He took a paternal interest in the affair and had her to stay on a couple of occasions, since obviously there were no guest rooms in the boarding houses. But in the end for the reasons given above he forfeited my affection, which he could so easily have maintained.

It may also be that the relative discomfort in which we all lived, by marked contrast with (say) Radley, encouraged us to find sources of relaxation and pleasure outside the precincts of the school, which enabled us to enjoy each other's company. Incompetent actor though I was, the actor's craft and director's skills always interested me, and I joined a rather good amateur dramatics group called The Priory Little Theatre, from which I gained a lot of fun and learned a little about drama. I remember many a cheerful evening at the Roma Antica Italian restaurant, or the Greek taverna next door, where Christopher Copeman (a brilliantly creative teacher of English at the junior school, whose inscribed anthology, *As Large as Alone*, I still possess, and from whom I first heard the name of Michael Morpurgo) could sometimes be persuaded if in his cups to demonstrate his skills as a Greek dancer. The Wife of Bath, a restaurant not a lady of the night, was for special occasions, and appropriately expensive on a teacher's salary. I played hockey reasonably regularly for the Canterbury third XI and some club cricket with a rather good local Sunday club called Highland Court, graced by players from the Kent Squad and one or two distinguished names like Mike Denness and John Shepherd. I was out of my league, but enjoyed my role even as a humble makeweight.

Of our marriage I shall tell the story two chapters on; for now it may be taken as read, but with a nod of gratitude to Newell for his encouragement. I had once as a pupil translated a phrase in Demosthenes rather idiomatically for him, and it remained a sort of in-joke between us. The great statesman was chiding the Athenians for their dilatory approach to facing up to the threat from Philip of Macedon — Churchill would have understood perfectly. The Greek (*epeidan ti genetai*) means literally — 'whenever what happens?' which I had rendered 'What are you waiting for?' Having seen Sara off after a visit, Newell turned to me and said, 'What are you waiting for?' 'Ah! *Epeidan ti genetai?*' I replied.

He clearly approved of Sara, and (since that is the way heads' minds work) her qualifications as both a nurse and a trained caterer may well have caught his attention. She was ideally qualified for Riversleigh House, which took in fifty-five new boys each year, and catered for them at breakfast and supper as well as housing them. It was a mile away from the main school and always somewhat independent. Its housemaster, George Robertson, had just been appointed to a senior house, and would need replacing. It must have seemed an attractive proposition. Potential housemasters are always two a penny; but to have on its staff as house matron a highly qualified paediatric ward sister from St Thomas' who had also trained at Great Ormond Street was a real catch. I would much rather have waited for the offer of a senior house, especially since we were only just married (in March 1969) and the offer was for September. But a bird in the hand is always worth two in a bush when you are a young-ish man in a hurry, and I accepted it with some alacrity. I did assume that I would get a senior house reasonably quickly, but Newell's mind did not work like that. Sara was too useful; I was probably too liberal. After four years I was therefore only too happy to accept Simon Langdale's invitation to join him at Eastbourne College, where he had just been appointed headmaster. The fact that this absolutely enraged Newell was by then icing on the cake.

I suspect that Newell felt he had made a mistake in appointing me to Riversleigh. I had long felt that King's was in every way too rigid in its outlook and almost Victorian in its management of boys. The junior houses, in particular, had had two very traditional housemasters with whose methods I was out of sympathy. The key to the happiness and success of young boys coming into a new, large school was, I was sure, that they should feel happy, relaxed, and confident in an atmosphere which was as home-like as it could reasonably be. I certainly felt that parents in particular very much appreciated this approach. It soon became clear that Newell did not, though to do him justice he limited his interventions to oblique indications that my colleagues (senior housemasters) did not approve, though one (Chris Miller of Linacre) was entirely sympathetic, and therefore the source of most of the prefects I appointed. One of them, Mark Henry Reacher, beloved of both our children, was to become Emma's godfather, a young man with a delightfully characterful mother and a memorable turn of phrase – he once described my mother as 'clearly not the biodegradable sort'. Sara was a huge bonus in this area. Not having been reared in boarding schools and being therefore unfamiliar with their traditions, she could see the absurdity of many of the sacred cows that grazed upon our pastures. She liked children – all children – and was a perfect mother figure to our whole family of fifty-five youngsters, and a source of confidence to me that my 'liberal' ideas were not entirely wrong-headed.

My first cardinal sin was to allow the boys to wear casual clothes in the house and its quite extensive gardens; this was not allowed in the main school, for fear that visitors would see the boys in scruffy dress and conclude that the school was undisciplined. Discipline is an obsession with heads, governors, and a certain kind of gossipy parent in almost every public school, many of whom expect schools to apply standards of discipline to their children that they themselves are too feeble to impose. Some like Newell become paranoiac on the subject. Man's (and woman's) tendency to extrapolate from the particular to the general also ensures that if one pupil steps out of line, the whole school is 'going to the dogs'. Our boys had a tedious daily walk of a mile each way to and from school; they were well out of the limelight; and the uniform was extremely uncomfortable. Casual clothes were simply common sense. I stuck to my guns and on a visit one evening, courteously prearranged perhaps in the hope that I would spare him the embarrassment of seeing this enormity by having them all in uniform that evening, Newell was forced to concede that it all seemed very pleasant and orderly. But I'm sure he didn't like it.

We had our crises. I still remember Sara, heavily pregnant and with no cook on a Sunday for the boys' breakfast, having to boil seventy-five eggs. Her solution was to suspend them in boiling water in a set of blue string bags. Unfortunately the dye ran and blue eggs were not flavour of the month. Ultimately we had to go Continental – which no one seemed to mind (croissants or rolls seemed mildly exotic). But crises apart, she quite enjoyed the challenge of trying to feed boys on what they liked – and my memory is that they fed like fighting cocks, especially because budgetary constraints were generously unspecific.

Another crisis was not so amusing. An unfortunate lad, who had lost his mother, slipped out one evening from the house for a crafty smoke in the local graveyard, and there came upon a tombstone with his mother's name on it. He had no idea she was buried there (nor had I) and he had a sort of brainstorm and took off into the blue yonder. Fortunately for my professional reputation he was quickly missed. But having notified the police we waited up till all hours for news. It was a great relief when the London police rang to say that he had been found and was being held safely until I could collect him. Failing to miss a boy is one of a housemaster's real nightmares; it can happen through sloppy roll-call procedures, or deliberate conspiracy, but also sometimes by sheer mischance. My own daughter Anna illustrates the point. As a sixth former at King's, she took an afternoon out in London once without permission to meet Nicola Cunningham, an old friend from Northern Ireland. Her bag was stolen, but she got back safely to King's without being missed. The bag was recovered later and returned to me in Belfast by the police – a very alarming moment. A huge policeman in full body armour rang our doorbell one day. 'Are you Mr Wilson?' 'Yes.' 'Do you have a daughter called Anna?' 'Yes.' Heartbeats up to 180 per minute. 'Her bag has been sent to us by the London police.' By sheer good luck for her, the only address in the bag was her home address. I debated shopping her to the authorities, but decided on balance against. But we had a few words on the phone. It made a very good story at her wedding, with Nicola present.

Discipline with junior boys was hardly problematical, though as in any community the occasional spate of theft or bullying needed attention. Sadly it was my experience that too often one could clearly see why the victims of bullying had been picked on, even though the perpetrators had to be confronted. Theft is almost worse. It can destroy community feeling and is very difficult to counter. No amount of urging will get young people to be careful with their possessions; sometimes the theft is simply a loss through carelessness; too often it is reported too late. One's best chance of catching a culprit is when one is informed within an hour of the loss. When these conditions applied, I would go through the whole rigmarole of a police-type investigation: locker searches; interrogation; and everyone under tight supervision and with no talking instructed to write down where they were at the time stated and who they saw and who saw them. This would often eliminate a majority. Then I would cross-check the stories with each other and look for discrepancies. Too often even this yielded no results, but it made waves and showed that the authorities took the matter seriously.

It was an enjoyable four years and being outside of the precincts gave us a degree of independence, which others envied. The gardens were lovely and the lawns spacious enough for croquet and just lying about in the sun; the four prefects (usually Lower VI and prospective prefects for the following year in their senior houses, and therefore enthusiastic about the job) became family friends; the team of domestic staff were similarly part of the family and were often a great help with our two children. Anna and Emma were both born while we were at Riversleigh and both were christened in the crypt of Canterbury Cathedral – very atmospheric. There was a wonderful team of domestic staff, some of whose names remain firmly fixed in our minds, like those of anyone's favourite nanny: Mrs Henley and Mrs Whidditt, the evening and morning cooks; Mrs Rye, who ran the linen room; and May (we never knew her as anything else), whose spotless loos were her pride and joy. The down side of the job was that the boys left after a year for their senior houses, just when you felt you were beginning to know them properly, and you had to start all over again. But it did mean that in my four years I saw four generations through my hands.

It would be difficult not to say something about the cathedral, the mother church of the Anglican Communion but also the school chapel, as one new boy told his parents in his first letter home '. . . And we have a Cathedral in the grounds.' My comments are based on impression more than knowledge, naturally. The Dean and Chapter at the time did not have a good reputation. Though we liked the Dean as a person, he was regarded as weak and the Chapter as quarrelsome and divided. Trollope would have found plenty of material there. The school services were no doubt often as tedious to the boys (and some staff) as they probably are in any boarding school.

And yet . . . and yet . . . Anna, I think, remembers 'Cath' as one of the high points of her time at King's. I still miss hugely the glory of mattins in the choir, with the whole school in full-throated voice for the singing of Standford's *Te Deum*, and some memorable carol services, especially one that opened in a darkened choir with Palestrina's Advent Responsory, sung by an unseen voice, 'I looked from afar . . .' to which the whole choir – and it was a good one – burst into a stupendous response. Memorable moments. The influence upon developing youngsters of a routine of worship, seriously intended and properly conducted, may turn them off from religion for good. But I suspect that the real cause of such disenchantment is the climate of the times combined with the church's failure to make the faith credible to a modern scientific age, rather than the perceived effects of 'compulsory worship'. Newell rightly pointed out that it was in fact not compulsory worship, only 'compulsory opportunity for worship'.

So what was my verdict on the school, which I had served for eight years? Undoubtedly a good school; effective; well ordered; it knew what it was trying to do. *Which?* would have called it 'good value for money'. I am not convinced that it was as good as Eastbourne for the 'ordinary' boy or one who needed bringing out. There was an element of 'sink or swim' about it, though this may not be entirely fair. In terms of what I regarded as my apprenticeship for a headmastership, I think I learned more about what not to do than otherwise, though I did recognise the value of the tutorial system, regular report sheets, Arts Week (which I tried to emulate at Campbell), young housemasters with energy and commitment, and areas of excellence (academics, some sport, music) which set the standards by which other activities were judged. But the demeaning effect of Newell's approach to man and woman management, and the school's lack of commitment to giving their living-in staff decent conditions in which to do their job, reflected badly on the governors and the head, but well on the professional commitment of those who taught there. The decision to take sixth form girls and later to go fully coeducational I would totally applaud; the massive improvement in conditions instituted by later regimes makes me pretty certain that my strictures are now out of date. I hope so.

CHAPTER 17

An Academic Interlude – JACT Ancient History: Author and Examiner

SOME TIME IN 1966, SOON AFTER joining King's, I went (in the holidays, of course!) on a week-long conference about the teaching of ancient history. I am not sure when the Joint Association of Classics Teachers (JACT) was founded, but the conference was held under their auspices and fronted by John Sharwood Smith of the London Institute of Education, who was (as far as I know) the driving force behind JACT and the man to whom all classics teachers are indebted for his part in the battle to save their subject. He was truly inspirational and wholly practical in his ideas and advice, and worked tirelessly for the subject. His name must be familiar to every teacher of classics in the last forty years.

The keynote speakers were my old supervisor, Moses Finley, and his Oxford counterpart, Peter Brunt, the Camden Professor of Ancient History. They were advocating a new style of teaching for the subject, which would require an entirely fresh syllabus, new text books specifically written for that syllabus, and a new style of examination. Ancient history had always been the poor relation of the classical studies. It was taught, not so much as a historical discipline with concern for sources and the evaluation of their evidence, but rather as a largely narrative and rote-learned subject, where one regurgitated what the text books told us – usually the *History of Greece* by either Bury or Hammond, and the *History of Rome* by Myres or Salmon, supplemented sometimes by the relevant books of the Cambridge Ancient History. If one used an ancient source in support of a statement in an essay, it was, as it were, by the fortunate accident of having read the appropriate book of Thucydides or Livy as part of one's Greek or Latin course. I have no doubt that in some enlightened schools they did rather better, but the evidence of the first few years' examinations of the new syllabus would suggest that my picture is broadly accurate.

The Finley/Brunt thesis was that the traditional approach to ancient history teaching was simply not historical study in any meaningful sense. First of all, the long 'outlines period' was a nonsense, since inevitably no student could hope to do much more than learn the narrative and repeat it on demand. That some sort of outline was needed was accepted, but the consensus was that as long as it was at least 100 years, it would suffice. This would then be backed up by more detailed study of coherent topics, where detailed reading of sources would be encouraged.

Next, documents are essential to any historian and the ability to assimilate and evaluate them a *sine qua non*. By great good fortune the source documents for the study of the two great periods of Greek and Roman civilisation were also in their own right great literature. It was as if Shakespeare were the primary source for the history of the Tudor dynasty. It would be a joy to do Tudor history, if that were so. Indeed at King's I remember a delightful evening where the reverse process applied. A L Rowse, the great if controversial historian, gave a lecture to the sixth form on Shakespeare from the historian's perspective. This inspired me to read his book, *William Shakespeare*, in which he sets each of the plays in its historical context, showing how its ideas and language reflect contemporary events which had affected the poet's outlook. I have found it a great help in understanding the plays I have studied. But for ancient historians it is simply the other way round: the great classical writers, however wonderful as literature, must also be studied as documents.

There were also many important sources which no classicist would be likely to have read, and it would be essential for significant extracts from these to be collected, along with more familiar material, and presented cheaply as source books for students. You can't be a historian without studying and comparing a large number of sources, but access to them was difficult because some of the authors are singularly dull, and very few, if any, pupils would be able to read Greek and Latin fluently enough to cover an adequate range. The study of classical languages was already in serious decline in all but the very élite public and grammar schools.

From the recognition of this reality LACTORs were born, original sources selected and translated for ancient historians who did not have the languages. They were produced initially by the London Association of Classics Teachers (LACT), the OR at the end standing for Original Resources. LACTOR No 1, *The Athenian Empire*, was culled from Hill's *Sources for Greek History* and sold out within a few months. There are now eighteen LACTORs at least, and I may already be out of date. It seemed important that the production of these source books should be a joint exercise between a university don and a practising teacher, the one to provide the width of reading and knowledge of the subject which an authoritative collection would require; the other to ensure a degree of realism in the quantity, quality, and presentation of the material selected.

Forty years later these principles still apply. The cooperation between don and teacher in the production of source material continues to this day. In 2003 LACTOR 17, *The Age of Augustus*, emerged as the largest and most ambitious of all LACTORs to date, with over 400 pages. It was the result of collaboration between myself and two academics, initially John Rich of Nottingham University, who was responsible for the structure of the book and selection of most of the material, and then Melvyn Cooley who took over editorial control.

As well as LACTORs, Chatto & Windus, the publishers, who had always been great friends of classical studies, agreed to bring out a series called *Ancient Culture and Society*, with Finley as the general editor, relatively short and inexpensive, covering some of the main topics in the new syllabus, but with a clear emphasis placed on the relevant sources and their evaluation. The great scholar A H M Jones produced his *Augustus* in rapid time almost off the top of his head; Brunt took on *Social Conflicts in the Roman Republic*, and in conjunction with John Moore, by then head of classics at Radley, an invaluable edition of the *Res Gestae* of Augustus with translation and lengthy supporting notes. Brian Warmington did *Nero: Legend and Reality*. They remain an excellent series, and I still have on my shelves copies of all the LACTORs and almost all the *Ancient Culture and Society* series.

There was huge enthusiasm. A subcommittee of JACT, the Ancient History Committee, was set up. Answering a call for volunteers to help, I had said simply that I was happy to help as office boy, filling envelopes and posting them, with the result that by accident rather than design I became its secretary for the first ten years. The committee set to and produced a new A Level syllabus with lengthy supporting guidelines and reading lists for teachers; the old Oxford & Cambridge Board (now subsumed into OCR, to no one's advantage that I can see) gave us every encouragement and acted as examining authority for the so-called JACT Ancient History Syllabus, on behalf of all boards, while continuing, as did others, to run its own traditional ancient history syllabus as well. We ran an excellent week-long training course for teachers at Eliot College, Canterbury, the administration of which fell to me, while Finley and Brunt sorted out the academics. It was quite stressful and Sara reminds me that I suffered some sort of 'turn' and had to be sent home (just down the hill) to recuperate.

The academic basis of source-based and documentary study which was pioneered in 1966 is now enshrined in the latest ancient history syllabus, which is treated as a history subject, not a classical. It was first examined in 2001, I think, when it superseded the original JACT syllabus, established after the 1966 conference. Of course by now it had to be formally approved by the lunatic bureaucracy imposed by government to control all examinations, which were perfectly adequately managed before by the individual examining boards. This was due to the (partly justified but not really very important) perception among teachers of inconsistency of standards between examining boards, which could be denounced as 'unfair', and this naturally soon made the issue political. The inconsistency never really mattered; those to whom it was important made it their business to know the relative status of the different boards; others just got on with whatever syllabus suited them best. Whenever governments interfere in education, things get more and more complex, and nearly always less and less satisfactory. They can't resist the urge to tinker under the idiotic belief that you can standardise something as richly diverse as education. Standards certainly do not rise. The system is now so cumbersome that, had it existed in 1966, I doubt if JACT could ever have started on the project.

I think one of the most rewarding features of the whole JACT enterprise was the way in which, because there was a real crisis, teachers and university dons united in a common cause, where in the past they had tended to operate in two separate spheres of existence. As well as the names already mentioned, George Cawkwell (University College, Oxford) and Michael Crawford (from Christ's, my own college) are two others which come to mind, while John Roberts, head of classics at Eton, and Kit Haworth of High Wycombe Grammar School were two of the main driving forces on the teachers' side behind all our activities.

From these beginnings emerged the JACT Ancient History Bureau, intended to offer practical advice and help to teachers at O Level rather than A Level. It was managed for a time by Mark Greenstock, another classicist from Radley (and later Harrow) recruited into the organisation. In a much later incarnation I returned to the fray as its treasurer. Inevitably as classical languages continued to decline, the next step was the emergence of a Classical Civilisation A Level syllabus for those who found the languages inaccessible but literary rather than historical study more to their taste. I liked it and taught it at St Mary's Wantage. So the battle for the survival of the classics was protracted, at times almost inspiring, but in the end and probably inevitably the subject has continued to decline. As a young teacher I was already lamenting the fact that the subject was too difficult for pupils under modern conditions, when it had to take no more than its fair share of period allocations. Relevance is of course a factor in pupils' perceptions, though my own view is that all arts subjects can be said to be irrelevant in the narrow and mercenary sense, classics no more so than English literature or history. But once it becomes too difficult, pupils will vote with their feet out of sheer demoralisation. There is a danger that the same thing could happen to physics and chemistry, though they have the bonus that their relevance seems incontrovertible. But relevant to what? People do not ask that question often enough.

All this involvement in the evolution of classical studies was excellent experience for me and invaluable for the development of my understanding of my subject. You can only hope to continue to teach well (and I am not sure I did) if you continue to progress in your knowledge and appreciation of the subject you love. I decided that I would teach more effectively if I also had a better understanding of how the subject was examined. I wrote to the Oxford & Cambridge Board and offered myself as a marker of A Level in any classical subject, preferably ancient history. They took me on; the subject was sufficiently small for there to be no huge problem in coordinating marking; consistency they said was always the most important quality, since if one marked consistently statistical analysis would soon show if one was too severe or generous, and adjustments could be made. After my first year I passed muster and continued to mark for them for a number of years. The money was trivial and no one in their right mind would do it for the rewards. To this day payment is pathetic – at best one may average two to three papers an hour when in full flow, earning no more than £6 an hour for the work – about the same as for stacking shelves in a supermarket. But it is interesting to see how standards vary and how over the years they rise or decline and it does keep one aware of developments in one's subject.

In due course I became Examiner in Charge of Ancient History for Cambridge Locals, with the very interesting task of setting papers as well as marking them. Later again I became first a Moderator and later Chief Examiner in Latin A Level for NISEC, the Northern Ireland Schools Examination Council. And for a couple of fascinating years I acted as outside Moderator for the Classical General Paper set by Cambridge University for classics candidates. I marked Classical Civilisation for UCLES and for a short spell O Level 'Nuffield' Latin for the SUJB, to give me some idea of how the subject was being handled under the new Cambridge Latin Project. I have now reverted to my humble beginnings and still mark A Level Ancient History for OCR. It is a demanding but interesting activity, almost enjoyable, a source of mild intellectual stimulus and genuine professional interest.

But Moses Finley had not finished with me yet. My next assignment was to produce a source book to be used as a set text for the late Republican period in Rome. It was published by the OUP in 1970 and thirty-five years later is still on the reading lists. Moses explained his idea very simply. JACT needed a source book; he had a tame don who was willing to plan the work, select appropriate passages, and give a general oversight to the work, but he had not the time or energy to do more. Thus I met the delightful Pat Lacey of St Catherine's, at that time a lecturer in ancient history at Cambridge, later Professor of Ancient History in Auckland University, New Zealand, a man with a deep knowledge of the work of Cicero in particular. He roughed out the design of the book in about forty-eight hours – it is something you can do if you know your subject – and *Res Publica: Roman Politics and Society According to Cicero* was born.

My task was to translate into readable but accurate English the passages selected by Pat Lacey to illustrate the theme of the book. It was a stimulating exercise; I found that I seemed to have a knack for translating, which was a particular source of pleasure to me because Grandfather had been the editor and translator of the Wisdom of Solomon for the Revised Standard Version of the Bible and I liked to think that in my own little way I was following in his footsteps. Pat Lacey was generous enough to say that I was better at it than he, and that he thought I should do almost the whole of the book. He kindly agreed to do the Letters; I did the rest. When OUP lost interest, the Bristol Classical Press took it on, and the book has remained under their imprint ever since.

The classics editor at OUP had been another Christ's contemporary, Martin Cuss, and he had an idea for another classical series for younger readers and students, under the general heading '*Stories from* . . .', consisting of selected tales from the great classical authors, Herodotus, Ovid, Livy, and so on, and to offer them as short, illustrated softbacks to schools and the general reader. The idea was excellent; the execution sadly did not seem to work, and I am not sure why. I took on *Stories from Herodotus* and having made the selections asked David Miller, a colleague at King's, to join me because collegiality can make for a better product provided you don't quarrel – which we didn't; we were both working extremely hard as usual and it would divide the labour. Herodotus is a gift, full of good stories; Martin got a set of excellent illustrations; and the result I thought was a very satisfactory product, which sold adequately for some twenty years, but is now out of print. I bought up the final copies. It remains my ambition to bring out a second edition, with the addition of stories from Thucydides (and possibly Xenophon). For whatever reason, after Livy, Ovid, and Herodotus the series came to an end. When that fabulous film, *The English Patient*, came out, I tried to get OUP to resurrect the book, since I felt that the Herodotus connection had commercial possibilities; but they weren't willing to play.

Much later, when the new 2004 syllabus was being developed, JACT decided that they needed a new source book for the special subject 'The Age of Augustus'. This was a very ambitious undertaking; it was intended to be genuinely comprehensive – a sort of one stop shop for the subject. I was asked to work with John Rich of Nottingham University on the usual basis. He would provide the brains and the expertise in selecting source material, literary and otherwise; I would do the bulk of the translating. We got a bit bogged down because John had too many commitments, but then Melvyn Cooley took over the supervising editor's role (and some of the translating) and the book, *The Age of Augustus*, was finished at great speed and came out in 2004. It too is a recommended text and source book. As a result I have the peculiar pleasure of being an examiner in a subject where two of my books are recommended texts and finding excerpts from them quoted on exam papers for comment and interpretation.

I shall leave till later *A Faith Unfaithful*, published in 2005, since it concerns religion rather than classics. I have digressed somewhat from my story when in mid-career at King's and I must pick it up from there. I had fallen in love, and despite the problems presented by my job at King's and courting at a distance, I was managing to slip up to London every fortnight or so to see Sara, much helped by a very tolerant Richard Meredith who covered for me when necessary.

In the spring of 1968 I had popped the question, when we took that holiday in Connemara together which I mentioned in the Introduction, but with extraordinary forbearance Sara had agreed that we would keep it a secret for a while and not get married until *Res Publica* was ready for press. I am ashamed to think how long I kept her waiting – well over a year, I think. We went public with our engagement in the summer holidays, when the translating side of the work was done, and finally made it to the altar at Chelsea Old Church on 29 March 1969.

CHAPTER 18

Sara – A Marriage of True Minds

Shall I compare thee to a summer's day?
Thou art more lovely and more temperate.

SHAKESPEARE'S SONNET 18 (whoever it is addressed to) is generally agreed to be one of the finest love poems in our language. For myself I find greater depth and feeling in that other sonnet, number 116,

> Let me not to the marriage of true minds
> Admit impediments. Love is not love
> Which alters when it alteration finds,
> Or bends with the remover to remove:
> O, no! It is an ever-fixèd mark,
> That looks on tempests and is never shaken;
> It is the star to every wand'ring bark,
> Whose worth's unknown, although his height be taken.
> Love's not Time's fool . . .

I find similar sentiments expressed in what I might call lyric prose in Dr Iannis' advice to his daughter Pelagia in Louis de Berniere's lovely novel, *Captain Correlli's Mandolin*. Indeed I wonder if it does not capture the true nature of that most amazing of human phenomena even more fully and more accurately. 'Love is not breathlessness', he says; 'it is not excitement, it is not the promulgation of promises of eternal passion . . . that is just being "in love", which any fool can do. Love itself is what is left over when being "in love" has burned away.'

The whole speech combines the wisdom of the old with something of the lyric quality of poetry, and catches as well as anything I know the essence of what love really means. When you have found such love, as I said in my Introduction, 'all else is secondary', and, as Dr Iannis puts it, your roots 'become so entwined that it is inconceivable that you should ever part'.

In thirty-seven years Sara and I have never quarrelled, nor even raised our voices; I sometimes get steamed up about things; Sara never does; she remains always the still centre of my turning world, where all is peace; we have shared good and bad times together without recrimination; we have been blessed with two children whom we adore and who appear to reciprocate that love; and if that love has been earned, hers has been the sweet patience of which I have had the luck to share the harvest. For Sara has a genius with children of all ages. Her love for them is of that unconditional quality that children recognise by instinct and respond to, and is born of a delighted joy in all their ways. She is a peacemaker among peacemakers and where she is sweet harmony prevails.

> To gild refined gold, to paint the lily,
> To throw a perfume on the violet,
> To smooth the ice, or add another hue
> Unto the rainbow, or with taper light
> To seek the beauteous eye of heaven to garnish,
> Is wasteful and ridiculous excess.

Like the man says, extravagance of compliment can pall and quickly engender disbelief. Those who have not been as blessed in their love as we may find it hard to imagine that such a love is possible. For those who know it can be, there is no need for me to over-egg the pudding. In the words of the ancient Latin formula of marriage:

> She says, '*ubi tu Gaius, ego Gaia*', 'where you are Gaius, I am Gaia'.
> He replies, '*ubi tu Gaia, ego Gaius*', 'where you are Gaia, I am Gaius'.

We are as one and always have been.

My sister Audrey trained as a nurse at St Thomas' Hospital and having done the Integrated Health Visitor course at Southampton University, she returned to St Thomas' and became a theatre sister. She went into a hospital flat in nearby Walcott Square, No 42, to share with three other hospital sisters, Veronica Bazeley from intensive care, who tragically died young of an infection caught while nursing in the Middle East, Sheena Ross, a sister tutor, also in intensive care, who remains another of our great friends, and Sara Hollins, a paediatric sister on Helen ward at the Royal Waterloo, though she later moved back to St Thomas' to become 'Sister Seymour'.

Aged about thirty by then and mildly disenchanted with my job, having passed through the honeymoon period at King's Canterbury, like many young-ish men I was wondering if I would ever meet 'the right girl'. In the era of Jane Austen it was primarily a problem for young women, who had no escape into careers and depended entirely on social proprieties to meet appropriate suitors. Nowadays the problem seems almost reversed. Despite laments about 'glass ceilings', which still have an element of truth about them, for young women the world's their oyster, and they often have other fish to fry than seeking husbands. Mine was a world in transition, half-way between the two. I grew up in a time when formal dances and dance cards were still perfectly normal practice. I was taught to ask for 'the pleasure of this dance' and to escort my partner back to her place when the dance was over, usually with all the other girls and if possible close to the open fire. Bed and seduction was still only for cads and utterly unthinkable to anyone properly brought up. I was also shy – Sedbergh had not helped, though our housemaster's wife had heroically volunteered to act as partner to all of us in turn during house ballroom dancing lessons. They did not last long – and it must have been hell for her.

Audrey turned up trumps. I was introduced to and went out with all her flat mates in turn, and liked them all. Whether by chance or Audrey's design I know not, but Sara was the last on the list – and that was it. The Italians have an expression for it, something along the lines of 'he has been thunderbolted'. I think I came across it in *The Godfather*, a rather good thriller about the Mafia, which I used to get pupils to read in order to understand the nature of *amicitia* in ancient Latin society. The word is conventionally translated 'friendship' but has nothing to do with friendship in the modern sense, everything to do with the Mafia concept of family: a nexus of relationships of favour and obligation, demanding respect for status in the pecking order, patronage and loyalty to the patron, obligations imposed by favours received and not yet reciprocated, and a range of relationships like those within the Cosa Nostra. Somewhere there the thunderbolt struck even the flint-hearted Don Corleone – and that was that.

My Latin is good enough; my Italian non-existent. But I have no doubt that in that most beautiful and expressive of languages they describe love's thunderbolt better than anyone else. Even more fortunately, for me it never struck again. It may not yet have been love to the exacting standards of the good Doctor Iannis, but I was most certainly 'in love'.

Poor old Catullus, conventionally regarded as the greatest Latin love poet, never seems in fact to have got beyond the 'being in love' stage; an erotic poet he was, perhaps; a poet of love, no. But he catches something of that early thunderbolt moment, when he first fell head over heels for the lovely but abominable Clodia, the wickedest woman in Rome. The circumstances are totally different; the initial symptoms not dissimilar.

Lingua sed torpet, tenuis sub artus	I am tongue-tied; down my limbs
Flamma demanat, sonitu suopte	A thin fire seeps; with a ringing all their own
Tintinant aures, gemina teguntur	My ears resound; and black night closes
Lumina nocte.	Over my two eyes.

Give me Tennyson every time for true romanticism. Like him, I could have exclaimed so easily,

   Sweet is every sound,
Sweeter thy voice, but every sound is sweet;
Myriads of rivulets hurrying through the lawn,
The moan of doves in immemorial elms
And murmuring of innumerable bees.

Working in a boarding school it is not easy to pay court to the lady of your dreams. I lacked Othello's rich experience of adventure with which to woo my lady with rare tales of derring-so. Pea-canning in Norfolk or bus-conducting in Totnes lack something of the resonance and romance of slaughtering dragons or slaying the infidel. Fortunately, to the best of my recollection, she was somewhat more reticent than Desdemona's father in 'questioning me the story of my life'. I had no need to speak of 'most disastrous chances', nor of my

> ... moving accidents by flood and field;
> Of hairbreadth 'scapes in the imminent deadly breach
> And portance in my travel's history.

No mention either of

> ... antres vast and deserts idle,
> Rough quarries, rocks, and hills whose head touch heaven,
> And of the Cannibals that each other eat,
> The Anthropophagi, and men whose heads
> Do grow beneath their shoulders.

Instead I confined my 'witchcraft' to the purchase of a new car, going distinctly up-market to replace my mother's much loved but ageing Morris 1000, which I had bought from her, with an Austin 1100. The long commute to London when the day's work was over became a little easier, though whether such decisive expenditure impressed the lady I am inclined to doubt, in the light of experience.

My recollection is that on these occasions we divided our time between going to the theatre, almost always the National, where I found the architecture exciting and the productions memorable. What we saw I do not remember though I think we must have seen *Rosencrantz and Guildenstern are Dead* two or three times. Alternatively we dined out, always at the Bistro Mayfair, a delightful little dive where you got a pleasant dinner, a juke box, and a tiny, overcrowded dance floor on which you could barely move, but this was not a serious problem in those days of close encounters of the more affectionate kind. Our favourite tune – you do have to be as corny as any soap opera just occasionally – our favourite tune was 'A Whiter Shade of Pale', and I can never hear it in its modern re-issued format without remembering those enchanted evenings. Under the right circumstances I am a sucker for sentimentality.

The old song says that 'A man chases a girl until she catches him; he runs after a girl until he's caught; he fishes for a girl until she's landed him; it all turns out exactly the way she thought.' Oh the wily ways of women; only once did she let slip the secrets of her craft. One night in the Bistro Mayfair, quite early on, I managed to leave a blob of cream (or was it a smidgeon of gravy?) on my cheek after a particularly appetising dish. Almost before you could say 'A Whiter Shade of Pale' she had her handkerchief out and leaning across the table she was wiping the offending area clean. I submitted without demur. Older and wiser heads than mine would have recognised the symptoms of anticipated ownership, and would have cried, like Coleridge,

> ... Beware! Beware!
> Her flashing eyes, her floating hair!
> Weave a circle round him thrice
> And close your eyes with holy dread,
> For he on honeydew hath fed
> And drunk the milk of Paradise.

I had fed on honeydew and was bewitched. I am sure that all day long and for many months I sang the songs from *My Fair Lady*, surely the greatest of all musicals of all time, but to tell the truth, beyond that chronology goes totally askew. At some point I met Sara's parents; she met mine; we went on holiday to Connemara and the sun shone all the time; we travelled up the west coast of Ireland staying here and there *en route*. What happened in the intervening year between engagement and marriage I have absolutely no idea. The pavements had always 'stayed beneath my feet before', but now I felt as if I had taken wings. I finished translating *Res Publica* in a burst of energy; corrected proofs; taught; resigned from Walpole House and was accorded comfortable accommodation for the only time in my career at King's, a 'set' (sitting-room, bedroom, bathroom) in Lardergate in the Green Court; found a flat up near the hospital (where Sara would work) at 5 Ethelbert Road, where I lived for a term (largely on joints of cooked ham bought from the local delicatessen) in a house which had been the boyhood home of the landlord. He was so bowled over by my determination to rescue the garden and make the place really civilised that I think he would have granted any request within reason from his new tenants.

We were married in Chelsea Old Church, on 29 March 1969, by the vicar, the Revd Leighton Thompson, a kindly and benevolent soul who wisely (I thought) made little attempt to preach to us but simply took us by the hand as it were, and led us to the gates of heaven. The reception was in the Basil Street Hotel; my best man was my oldest friend John Deane, nobly flying over from Ireland to do the honours that I had done for him some two years previously; Bob Ewing, my closest friend from Cambridge days, was my senior usher; Audrey was Sara's bridesmaid, to whom she bequeathed her bouquet, with very satisfactory results. We honeymooned first in the Cotswolds at the Bay Tree in Burford, before departing to Ireland for a week's stay in the Lake Hotel, Killarney. There we explored an area of my native country which I loved and where every year my parents were wont to take an early holiday, proudly claiming that they were always the first in the year to take a boat trip down the lakes. I bathed one day in an icy Atlantic under bright sunshine out of sheer exuberance; I played one round of golf there for old times' sake, with Sara caddying for me – I am amazed that I got away with it, since it must be Western man's equivalent of those Giles' cartoons of black clad Middle Eastern ladies carrying water pots on their heads following in a line behind their lord and master. I don't think I ever asked her to do it again! But the effect was remarkable and I have never played such a round or will again, finishing in two over par, but with nobody to witness the achievement. Since my new wife did not understand the mysteries of that most agonising of games, where you move from joy to despair in an instant, her evidence would not have carried weight.

They say that the Secretary of the Lord's Day Observance Society faced a similar problem once, when he rather naughtily played a round of golf on a Sunday. The archangel Gabriel, sitting as usual up there on the right side of God, nudged his master and said, 'Look!' 'I see it', said the Great Golfer in the Sky. But when the sinner drove the shot of his life, some 450-yards to the green, and scored a magical hole in one, Gabriel thought his master had lost the plot. But the ways of the Almighty are wilier than ours. 'It's quite simple', he remarked. 'It's Sunday. So who's he going to tell?'

We probably dropped in on Ballycrenan *en route* for home; and then, back to Canterbury and 5 Ethelbert Road, where we made the happiest of starts to married life, albeit for only one term, before we moved to Riversleigh.

And we have lived happily ever after.

To go back to the beginning. Ted and Jane Hollins, Sara's parents, were living at Bleak House, Guiseley, on the outskirts of Bradford. Ted was working at Salts Mill as a time-and-motion expert. Jane, who had been used to the rich social life of London, hated it and the choice of Bleak House for the name of their home, though probably mere coincidence, would have conveyed her feelings accurately. She suffered from acute depressions, and the dreary Yorkshire weather (which I too remember as a boy) cannot have helped her general feelings of despair. They had two daughters, Anne Nielsen and Sara Remington (named after their paternal grandmother and grandfather respectively). They lived there until Sara was about seven years old, when they moved south to Angmering in Sussex, to be near Jane's mother (Granny Fennell) in the hope that she could help with the children and that an improved climate would alleviate her condition.

Sara's elder sister Anne had the misfortune to suffer from *retinitis pigmentosa* (an affliction which gives its victims either total blindness or at best keyhole vision) and this too required endless medical investigation to try to find a cure and establish a cause. In fact it seems to have been sheer bad luck. Though she always retained her limited vision, she was registered as blind, and had to be sent away as a boarder to a specialist school from the age of six, poor child. This may have been an influence in the development of very differing temperaments, Anne being outgoing and gregarious, Sara tending to be rather more reserved and somewhat shy. Their parents were impressively robust in their upbringing: Anne was never given special treatment and both girls were encouraged to compete with each other – whether such sibling rivalry is a good thing is debateable. For Sara and me the lack of such competitiveness between our two daughters has been a joy; they have always been simply the greatest of friends. Anne trained as a physiotherapist and worked for a time at the Radcliffe in Oxford, and was even required on one occasion to treat the notorious Robert Maxwell. After she married, she continued a limited private practice while bringing up her two children. More recently she has worked as a senior counsellor for the Samaritans. Her robust acceptance and conquest of her disability (as some would call it) is a tribute to her own strength of character as well as her parents' admirable determination that she should manage it and refuse to feel like a victim of it. I never heard her complain about it.

Anne married first – appropriately enough as the elder – but if the competitiveness encouraged by their parents came into play, she won that race. Richard Trist, her husband, graduated from Oxford University in jurisprudence and went into local authority administration, ending his career as Chief Executive of Portsmouth, a city with which his family had long-standing connections, his great-grandfather, Jacob Owen, having built All Saints, Landport – a 'Waterloo church', paid for by vote of Parliament to provide places of worship for the heroes of Waterloo when they returned from the wars. New homes were being built for them on the outskirts of towns and cities where no ancient churches existed. Jacob Owen later was appointed chief engineer and architect to the newly-appointed Board of Works in Dublin in 1832. One of his sons built the Belfast zoo; another, Thomas Ellis Owen, was the architect of much of Southsea, and built St Jude's church, largely at his own expense, having been persuaded to do so by his brother, the vicar, to help sell his houses.

He was a wonderfully supportive husband, and like ours their marriage has been blessed with children, Isabel and Lawrence, and grandchildren, and has lasted for nearly forty years. They recently had a splendid celebration of Richard's seventieth birthday for all the extended family and friends in Brighton, at the very successful Seven Dials restaurant, established by their Metcalfe cousins. More recently Anne has fought a heroic battle against cancer with that same courageous determination to live life to the full that has always been one of her most admirable qualities.

Sara was tall, slim, and beautiful (well, he would say that, wouldn't he?). But Juliet Pannett's portrait dated 1966, when she would have been twenty-seven, catches something of that beauty, which is only potentially apparent in Michael Leonard's earlier portrait of 1955, when she was sixteen. I never saw her in her tall Nightingale cap and dark blue sister's uniform; rather than beautiful, I suspect she might have seemed mildly formidable, nearly six foot tall and probably looking slightly more.

Her record as a student nurse was outstanding. She was trained at the Nightingale School, where she was the gold medallist of her year; then she went on to specialist children's training at Great Ormond Street, where again she was the top nurse. They did not award gold medals to already qualified nurses, but Sara won the silver medal, the highest award open to her. No wonder they took her back at St Thomas', first as a charge nurse on Lilian Ward ('the best training in the world'), and then after several years at the Royal Waterloo as 'Sister Helen' back to St Thomas' again, briefly, as sister in charge of Seymour ward, 'Sister Seymour'.

They always said that she should have trained as a doctor; she had the ability and the diagnostic instincts, and when she was the school nurse at St Mary's, our very enlightened school doctor, Rick Godlee, came to trust her judgement completely. Once or twice in her diagnoses she picked up things that might easily have been missed. So accurate was she that I have only one example of her fallibility and that was when I myself got appendicitis in 1970. I am suspected of having mild hypochondriac tendencies (probably due to having medical parents who were never impressed by any of my boyhood ailments) so when I complained of sharp stomach pains but ate a hearty breakfast, Sara was somewhat dismissive of my assertion that it was my appendix. By bedtime she had come round to my way of thinking and sent for the doctor. It was taken out that night, having already perforated and developed into an abscess, which lasted for about three weeks, before I was well again. It is so nice to be able to hold her only known error over her, and I remind her of it if I ever feel the need to keep her in order.

When I was courting her, I am glad I had no idea how distinguished she was; it might have frightened me off. As it was, one of the things that I am sure helped us to get on, and then to cement our marriage was the fact that she had such a lively and interested mind, and I soon came to have a deep respect for her intelligence. I always felt that she was more than a match for me intellectually, though I may have had a better formal academic training thanks to the luck of a university education, which she surely deserved and would certainly have enjoyed. In her literary judgement she was streets ahead and I never wrote anything or made a speech anywhere that I did not first submit to her acute inspection – and I think I almost always took her advice. She had her father's analytical brain as well as her mother's artistic instincts, and the combination was invaluable. To feel respected is to feel good about oneself and is conducive to a high morale; such mutual respect for a mind as well as love for a person can be a tremendous force for harmony in a marriage, unless you are the sort of person who always wants to dominate.

Rather than send her to the village school (which was always retained nevertheless as a threat for poor performance at school) her parents sent Sara to West Preston Manor, a local fee-paying establishment. Whether economics dictated the decision, or an old-fashioned view that women's education should be confined to the traditional 'goodness, music, and French', we cannot say, but it was not a very academic school. Sara was the only girl in her year group to stay on for A Levels, which she took in one year, failing history but passing English literature. It has been her great love ever since and she is far more widely read than I am. Her primary interest lies in the novel, classical and modern, where I would incline to drama and poetry, so in fact our interests complement each other. If she tells me to read a book I try to do so. More recently she has acquired my long-standing interest in theology, and I am delighted to find her sharing my enthusiasm for a liberal approach to the subject, as exemplified by the work of Bishops John Spong or Richard Holloway. Our theological standpoints are very similar.

It was in Angmering that Sara at a regrettably tender age had a brief foray into a life of crime, forgery and theft being what the police call her MO, her *modus operandi*. She started to bring good reports back home from her teachers, which gave her parents considerable delight, until they discovered that she was being somewhat extravagant rather than economical with the truth. The school's reaction was very enlightened: they pointed out that Sara was desperate to please them and to win their approval, and that they should be pleased rather than angry about it. I do so sympathise with her: I too was almost a driven child in a similar desire to do well at all costs and terrified of bad reports.

Graduating to higher levels of criminal endeavour, and encouraged by the vicar's daughter (she says – shades of Adam in the garden of Eden?) she helped her to raid the local church's donations box. They spent the proceeds immediately in the village shop, thus showing a singular lack of money-laundering expertise in what was, as far as we know, their first heist. The most painful part of Sara's punishment was being compelled to go back to the shopkeeper, whom she did not like, apologise, hand back the goods, and recover the money. By contrast, the vicar's reaction to the news of his daughter's peccadillo was to laugh uproariously, no doubt following the injunction of his lord and master that he should forgive unto seventy times seven. The combination of her own failure and the manifest injustice of her accomplice's escape from retribution seems to have been enough to set Sara on the path of virtue ever after. What became of the vicar's daughter history does not relate.

The school failed to unlock their pupil's outstanding potential, which was fortunate for me; had they done so we might never have met. Though she wanted to train as a nurse, Sara had to fill in a year because the Nightingale School only took in trainees from the age of nineteen. For her this was a tremendous blessing. She was sent to 'Rannie's' for a year, Miss Randall's School of Domestic Economy, in Eastbourne. Miss Randall was a distant relative of the family and this may have encouraged the choice. For Sara it was the first time she had been away from home, and it was like liberation. She enjoyed the course, made good friends there, learned at some length and among other more useful accomplishments how to iron a gentleman's handkerchief, and chose as a special subject institutional catering, which would prove extremely useful later at Riversleigh. She again came away with the top prize for students of her year.

For both of us Eastbourne has always held entirely happy memories, as it had for my grandfather before me. Though only briefly a pupil at the college before moving up to Bedford, he returned to the town year after year for his holidays, which he would spend watching the tennis tournaments in Devonshire Park. For Sara it meant freedom and a very useful training and when she returned some years later with me to join the staff of Eastbourne College, there were other young families, a friendly staff, and no responsibilities for a boarding house. There we were able to enjoy our children's early years among good friends in a lovely location. Not for nothing is Eastbourne called 'the suntrap of the south'. Sara used to walk the children regularly to Gildredge Park to play, and there she made the acquaintance of Jennie and Andy Weldon and their two daughters, Jane and Kate, of almost identical ages to our two. The friendship of our two families has lasted a lifetime at parents' and children's levels.

What a wonderful collection of skills my future wife had acquired. Medical skill – despite her inadequacies as a diagnostician of appendicitis; child-care skill – little about being a mother could disconcert her; she had seen it all before, and she was a truly wonderful mother of our children; catering, both at the institutional and domestic level. She is a brilliant cook as well as an expert caterer; household management – she could do a lot more than iron a gentleman's handkerchief; artistic and decorative instincts, which manifested themselves in our shared delight in buying pictures, as well as similar tastes in furnishing and décor; widely read – so she could extend my literary education; a knowledge of art – where she educated me in a way that neither school nor university had managed to do. And rather as the army gave me a kind of disciplined efficiency in the conduct of routine chores of every kind, so too St Thomas' and Rannie's together with her own iron will gave Sara a similar determination and speedy efficiency in the ordering and management of everything she turned her hand to. She could do more than most people in rather less time.

She had been a wonderful children's nurse, but once she had had children of her own she felt unable to return to her first love, simply because suddenly the suffering of sick children seemed more than she could bear. It came too close to home. So she brought to the hospice movement and the care of the dying her great gifts of healing and her infinite capacity for listening with compassionate attention to the pain of others. She worked first as a volunteer in the newly founded Northern Ireland Hospice and then, when we returned to England, at the Sue Ryder Home in Nettlebed.

Hers is a genius for the loving care of others, for skills count for little in the balance when weighed against the wholeness of the person. It is impossible to describe how much her love and companionship have meant to me over the years, amazing that she had so much to give to others too. She it is that made our home a place of peace and harmony; she cherished our children and taught them how to love and be loved, and to imitate her gentleness; her heart was, as it were, the hearth that warmed the home; she asked so little for herself, and yet she gave so much, comforting and cajoling, re-building morale when it was down, encouraging when things went wrong, supportive in time of conflict, tolerating with a grave good humour the masculine stupidities which I share with my kind. Like all those whose lives she touched, I am the better for having known her. She is my laurel tree, a symbol which the poet Yeats used to stand for all that is fresh and good and deeply 'rooted in one dear, perpetual place', – my heart.

Men, it seems to me, are pretty primitive creatures, the legacy no doubt of their ancient role as territorial hunters, forced by nature to violence of method and competitiveness of temperament, and cursed with an egocentric stance towards their fellow men. It is the genius of womankind to counteract those failings, derived from man's early role which dates far back behind his emergence as *homo sapiens*, which is very recent in evolutionary history. Our species has been male-dominated for far too long, and the results have been deplorable, politically, socially, morally, and economically. The folly of the feminist movement, inevitably led by the more aggressive and dare I say masculine of the female species, has been to seek to play a man's role in a man's world, instead of moulding by a gentle seduction our sad and idiotic masculinity to a greater femininity. There is, I fear, no other way to save the world. Leave it to men and we will in due course wipe each other out, because where men rule, competition rules instead of cooperation, and the result is usually war. Given the weapons of mass destruction now available, the race will soon die out by internecine struggle, if we cannot find a better way.

The home-maker must become the rule maker also, not in the Thatcherite mode of playing the real man among a collection of rather sad political nonentities; but by showing men how to live cooperatively and creatively in a way that men have never done before. They say that the hand that rocks the cradle rules the world; they are wrong. It doesn't; but it should. But for us, the blessed members of her family, it surely always did. Yeats' fine poem, 'A Prayer for My Daughter', catches something of the flavour of those rare qualities, of which I feel the utterly undeserving beneficiary.

> May she become a flourishing hidden tree
> That all her thoughts may like the linnet be,
> And have no business but dispensing round
> Their magnanimities of sound,
> Nor but in merriment begin a chase,
> Nor but in merriment a quarrel.
> O may she live like some green laurel
> Rooted in one dear perpetual place . . .
>
> And may her bridegroom bring her to a house
> Where all's accustomed, ceremonious;
> For arrogance and hatred are the wares
> Peddled in the thoroughfares.
> How but in custom and in ceremony
> Are innocence and beauty born?
> Ceremony's a name for the rich horn,
> And custom for the spreading laurel tree.

CHAPTER 19

The Hollins Family – Some Ramifications

It's time to tell a little of the story of Sara's family, whose considerable ramifications include connections with Northern Ireland, which I found to my great surprise were a lot stronger than my own.

The story of the Hollins family is almost synonymous with that of the textile industry of the East Midlands. They derive from Ashby-de-la-Zouche, Leicestershire, where they had been in the brass industry for generations. There (according to F A Wells, *Hollins and Viyella*) Humphrey Hollins died in 1695, leaving his son, also Humphrey, a 'shop of tools belonging to my trade'. In 1724 the family moved to Nottingham, and in 1789 we find Henry Hollins, his grandson, advertising for a journeyman brazier and tinplate worker in the *Nottingham Journal*.

But already Henry Hollins and four colleagues had formed a partnership in 1784 to start a cotton mill in Pleasley, a small Derbyshire village, trading as Cowpe, Oldknow, Siddon & Co. The fifteen-acre site which they leased for forty-two years at £42 per annum, lay along a stretch of the River Meden and included a dam for power, an old corn mill, a forge, and the associated machinery. In 1827 they bought the property outright. When Sara and I visited it in 2003, we were told by the caretaker that the name of Hollins is still an honoured memory. The site, with its huge mill buildings and associated millpond, remains there today, a magnificent 'museum piece', a lost corner of Britain's industrial history. The old Hollins house, the Vale House, where Sara's father Henry Edmund, 'Ted', was brought up, was still standing, though half-derelict, but there was no trace of the original corn mill. The beauty of the spot gives a somewhat less depressing picture than you might expect of the 'dark satanic mills' of William Blake's 'Jerusalem'.

Of the partners, Henry Hollins (Sheriff of Nottingham in 1767) was an established local figure whose father had been mayor of the town in 1762. He would have had in his own firm the skilled manpower to build the required machinery. Cowpe, aged twenty-five, the chief executive, was a considerable technician and probably built some of the machinery himself; Oldknow, Paulson, and Siddon were experienced businessmen, with strong connections to the drapery trade.

It was a time when cotton had become very popular, especially for stockings, and many experiments were being made into industrial methods of spinning the yarn by power-driven machinery, to counteract the deficiencies of handspun thread, which tended to be too uneven and weak for weaving. Wool, the traditional material was too hot in summer; silk too expensive; cotton was ideal for people of 'middling circumstances'. Wide international markets were opening up and with improved machinery the price of cotton thread was coming down. Paul patented his device for roller spinning in 1738; Hargreaves of Blackburn his spinning jenny in 1764; Arkwright his roller spinning machine in 1768, which he tried out in Nottingham before moving to Derbyshire to use water power from the River Derwent instead of horses. In all this Derbyshire and Nottinghamshire were active competitors to Lancashire. There were serious problems with patents rights and Arkwright was unable to defend his invention adequately, and it is possible that Hollins and his colleagues took advantage of this in their own designs.

They were enlightened employers for the time, being usually ahead of legislation in their care for workers. By 1791 they had about forty apprentices accommodated in an apprentice house with a schoolroom and 'a middle-aged woman to have care and management of the boys and girls'. They were kind and generous too. In 1986 Anne Trist met Margaret, daughter of Swetenham who was Arthur Hollins' gamekeeper. She was once a parlour-maid at the Vale house, and when she was married Arthur Hollins sent his own best car to take her to and from the church. Ted Hollins, too, had another story of how the chauffeur would be sent to buy gin for the house and a blind eye was turned when he tucked a bottle under a bush in the drive for his own later consumption. By contrast, the firm once caused five children to be committed to jail for leaving their employment – so the story of their benevolence is not entirely one-sided.

They also established a reputation for quality, which endured for over a century and may have protected them during the inevitable periods of recession to which all industry was subject. They were always innovative: they pioneered the concept of integrated production, the branding of products such as Viyella and Clydella, targeted advertising and the development of niche markets for designer and fashion goods. They installed a steam engine as an alternative power source to water in 1804, and constantly reinvested profits in new machinery and equipment. They also introduced in 1917 an early example of a profit-sharing scheme for their workers.

Henry bought out Cowpe in 1797 and his son, Henry II, took over management of one of the mills. He also started the long tradition of a Hollins living in the Vale House, Pleasley, beside the works. It was a fine, three-storey house, but sadly by now (2006) it may well have been demolished, since it was described in a recent report as 'unstable, requiring demolition'. Though for a time he left to join his brother Charles elsewhere, Henry II returned on the death of his father in 1825, taking over the management and bringing in his eldest son Henry III. He also changed the name to Hollins, Siddon, & Co.

Siddon died in 1846 and Henry II and his son Henry III both died in 1848. William Hollins, a younger son of Henry II, had been managing the firm since 1841, but now aged only thirty-two he took over the whole firm, which became simply William Hollins & Co. A fire had recently destroyed the old mills; under

William they were rebuilt and modernised, with new machinery like the self-acting spinning mule and combing machines, and an improved working environment. Water was still the cheapest source of power, but when water levels were inadequate, steam was used instead, since cheap coal was now available from the Derbyshire coalfields.

Commitment to innovation continued, with the firm's early exploitation of merino wool from Australia. Blended with cotton it produced a fine, strong yarn which made a fabric smoother and more comfortable than pure cotton, cheaper and less liable to shrink, and well suited to the hosiery trade. The decision to specialise in mixed yarns was the making of the firm. In the official catalogue of the Great Exhibition of 1851 they are described as 'William Hollins & Co, Manufacturers of Merino, Cashmere, and cotton hosiery yarns, used in the Midland counties for the manufacture of hosiery and on the Continent for knittings and hosiery purposes'. They tried silk, without success, and then moved into dyeing of mixed yarns, developing a specialised unit for high quality work. They established mills in Nottingham and prospered in the good times and survived during the economic recessions.

William did not die until 1890, but Henry Ernest, the able son of William's elder brother Edward (who also had cotton mills in Lancashire) joined the firm in around 1865. When they became a joint stock company in 1882, with limited liability for the first time, he became managing director and led the company with great distinction almost till his death in 1920. His younger brother Claude was company secretary and his son William assistant manager at Pleasley, living in Uplands, another house on the mill estate, since William still lived in the Vale house.

Though hugely successful, it was still very much a family business. On William's death in 1890, the company was reconstituted with William's son, William II joining the board, and Henry Ernest's brothers, Richard Arthur and Claude serving as directors. As well as internally generated expansion financed by profits, they began to expand by take-over. They bought the Via Gellia mills in Matlock as a going concern, specialising in the spinning of merino yarns, as well as others in the Nottingham area – partly at least for defensive purposes against competitors.

It was a time when markets were less than stable, American tariffs were a problem, merino was expensive and demand in decline. Hollins began to experiment with different mixtures of wool and cotton to find the right formula for weaving into cloth and by 1891 one of their Glasgow weavers had produced cloth of an acceptable standard. And so Viyella was born, taking its name probably from the Via Gellia factory in Matlock, and with its trademark registered in 1894. Profitable almost from the start, it was sold through retail outlets that were prepared to accept what was in effect a system of retail price maintenance, in an era when it was almost unheard of. The South African war and the development of khaki Viyella gave added impetus to a product, which was never cheap but stood for quality. It became the cornerstone of the firm's prosperity, though it never generated the increasing profits which its potential suggested. William Hollins became a public company in 1908 and their name became virtually synonymous with Viyella.

In 1916 Henry Ernest resigned as managing director, though he continued as chairman till 1919. He died in 1920 and is buried in Barbon in Westmoreland (Cumbria), where for many years Jo Hollins (who changed his surname to Gibson) had his family home. Indeed there is a family plot in the churchyard there, marked off by a hedge, with no less than fifteen gravestones commemorating either Hollins or Gibson family members. Henry Ernest had married an heiress, Mary Anne Gibson, the daughter of Joseph Gibson and Anne Remington of Whelprigg, near Barbon. Whelprigg itself is a Tudor mansion now owned by Henry Bowring, a descendant of the original Joseph Gibson and Anne Gibson, who built it in 1834. It rates a mention in Simon Jenkins' *England's Thousand Best Houses*. Henry and Mary Anne Gibson had five sons, Charles, Joseph, Arthur, Denis, and Esmond. Family mythology records that he dictated careers for each of the sons. Joseph was required to change his name to Gibson in order to inherit the Gibson family wealth; Arthur was required to take over the family business; Henry married Mary Wilson, who was known as 'Gamma'.

Arthur Remington Hollins, Sara's grandfather, whose qualifications seemed impeccable, succeeded his father in both offices at Wm Hollins. Sadly his technical abilities were not matched by qualities of general management and leadership, and following serious financial problems for the firm in the recession of the early 1920s, he was ousted as chairman and MD in 1923, though he remained a large shareholder and a member of the board until 1924. He moved to London and set up a small business with Jack Garrett, his brother-in-law.

So the family left the Vale House in 1924, but over seventy years later, in 1998, Ted Hollins remembered two events in Pleasley, which were etched forever in his memory. His daughter Anne recorded them from his tape-recorded 'letter' to her and (with slight abbreviations and minor editing) this is her account.

> About 70 years ago a new boiler was required for the powerhouse [at Pleasley] and it had to come along the road by the lower dam. The road is right on the edge of the dam and then turns left, mounts a very small slope, turns right to the boiler house, and then home and dry. So as to be really well clued up, the chaps who were handling this [massive piece of machinery], which was being towed by a tractor, parked it a hundred yards away overnight, so as to gather their forces or ideas together. And the next day, returning to it [they found that] it had sunk into the road, not badly, but badly enough. Apparently they couldn't extract it without putting down metal sheets and jacking it up – which they did, and eventually got it moving again. Then we came to the left turn into the boiler house slope, and the tractor went more – and I was there watching it as a boy and thoroughly enjoying it – the tractor went more and more slowly as it took the strain of trying to pull the boiler up the slope, until it finally came to a stop. And then, not just like that, they

put the brakes on the tractor. But it made no difference – well it must have done – but the front wheels of the tractor slowly rose up into the air and the boiler pulled the whole contraption back down to the bottom of the slope. At that point I had to disappear ... and I didn't see the outcome, but they obviously had to get another tractor – I suppose one to push and one to pull. I wish I had been there to see it all coped with.

It was a period when firms that could afford to do so had complete equipment – boiler, power house, dynamos – the whole lot. I can't think of all the attachments, but anyway the result was that the whole thing was a self-contained unit and with no need to call on outside power for anything. Sir Titus Salt did it, the Lever Brothers did it, Viyella did it, and whether it paid off or not I simply don't know. There probably wasn't power there anyway, and it would have been very expensive to buy it in on a cable. Which may have been the reason – I just don't know.

My father [Arthur Remington Hollins] was a great believer in powerful action on any problem that might arise. The water supply – which was again part of the complex – got clogged up with pondweed and pondweed blocked up the supply of water to the boilers and so it had to be dealt with very radically. My father put on gumboots that went right up to his waist – I don't know what they were called – and marched into the whole thing with a [supply of] dynamite. He laid the dynamite in the weed area and then decided to trail a wire back to the side of the mill, only to find that he couldn't get out, and sunk into the mud from so much standing to do what he was doing. He was a fairly heavy man, so that he couldn't get out. Anyway, they towed him near to the shore and naturally the wall around the area was appreciably higher than the water and the mud. So somebody had a bright idea: they got a ladder and poked it under his arms and told him to hold on while they sat on the other end of the ladder [like a seesaw]. Then he slowly oozed up out of the mud and was removed satisfactorily, ready to have another go another day.

When he did set the dynamite off, it was very spectacular and covered the windows of the Vale House with nice rich mud and Gertrude, [the housekeeper] whom you didn't know, rushed out in a fury complaining that now all the windows had to be washed ... But the mill had its own fire department with machinery for putting out fires, so they trundled that up to the house, hosed down the windows while Gertrude watched in rage and irritation, and everything was put back in order.

Shortly afterwards Arthur Hollins was appointed managing director at Salts Mill, Saltaire. He was allocated an enormous house, Milner Field, though he had to furnish it himself. Soon after they moved in his wife, Anne Neilson (née Garrett), caught pneumonia, possibly due to the damp in the house, and died in January 1926. Their two sons, Henry Edmund ('Ted'), and Dick were just eighteen and fourteen, and still at school. Arthur himself died three years later, having fallen ill while on a fishing trip to the west coast of Scotland. Ted and Dick set up home in Ilkley with the family retainer, Gertrude, as their housekeeper. Under different circumstances Henry Edmund ('Ted') might easily have worked at Pleasley, but in fact joined Salts Mill as one of the early pioneers of time and motion studies in factory management.

It was a technique also being applied to the Hollins business by William's grandson, Henry IV, who was an assistant director in charge of production at Pleasley. There appears to have been some disagreement at board level over how best to measure costs, and this may lie behind Henry's decision to resign in 1935, thus severing the last connection of the family with the firm.

It is a fascinating story of one of Britain's manufacturing dynasties, whose industry has suffered more ups and downs of fortune than many. Sadly it has now been almost totally superseded by the cheap labour and new technologies of the emerging nations, but the Hollins connection is something to be very proud of.

In St Michael's Churchyard, Pleasley, there are at least five family graves, with headstones commemorating some eleven members of the family.

Henry Edmund, Sara's father (always known as Ted) was born in 1907. His mother Anne Neilson was the daughter of Edmund Garrett, whose marriage to Frances Andrews brought connections to several well-known Northern Ireland families, including the Andrews family of Comber. Indeed, I believe Ted and his brother Dick have their names inscribed in the Andrews' family Bible, while the shared Drennan connection was sufficiently significant to the family for Dick to be christened Richard John Drennan.

John Andrews, Frances' father, had married Sarah Drennan, daughter of Dr William Drennan, a staunch Presbyterian with liberal and nationalist sympathies, committed among other things to winning equal rights for Roman Catholics. He was even a founder member of the Society of United Irishmen, but gradually withdrew, when they became a secret society whose methods he disapproved of. In 1807 he moved to Cabin Hill, owned by his sister, Martha M'Tier, and described by her as 'a small genteel house at a moderate rent in a tolerable situation' on the outskirts of a Belfast, which she complained 'was crowded with rich upstarts skipping from the counter to their carriage'. There his son Tom, brother of Sarah, died young at the age of eleven, and was the subject of a moving biography, *Little Tom Drennan*, subtitled *A Portrait of a Victorian Childhood*. There is still a memorial stone to Little Tom in the Cabin Hill grounds, and his father in a lament for the child invoked his spirit to return to Cabin Hill 'to be its good genius still and sanctify the place'. That it should one day become a preparatory school for boys seems entirely fitting.

William was extraordinarily active in public life. As well as his medical practice, he had political interests, and was a moving spirit in the foundation of 'Inst', the Royal Belfast Academical Institution. He was also the author of the famous Drennan letters, written to his sister Martha over a span of more than twenty years. She had originally bought Cabin Hill in 1785 with her husband Sam, sold it in 1789, but returned to it in 1800 as a widow, sharing it with a friend, and handing it on to her brother William in 1807. He lived there till his death in 1820. Its most interesting moment came almost exactly 100 years later when it was rented for a year (in 1921, after the partition of Ireland) as a residence for Sir James

Craig, the first Prime Minister of the newly established Government of Northern Ireland, with the billiard room converted to a cabinet room and the lodge a guardroom for the special constabulary. It became the preparatory school for Campbell College in 1929. And until her recent death Esme West Watson, née Garrett, still called the family home in England 'Cabin Hill'.

Sarah Drennan was also a descendant of John Hamilton, the Sovereign of Belfast in 1684–5, whose daughter Martha Hamilton married Robert Lennox and fashioned the wonderful Lennox quilt, which hangs in the Ulster Museum. Sarah's other brother, Dr John Drennan, had a daughter Maria, who married Adam Duffin. Their nine children included Celia, and Sylvia, better known as Molly, whom we were able to visit in her old age in Newcastle, and whom Patricia Gray kept a kindly eye on until Molly's death; Celia married a Colonel Randall, the brother of the redoubtable Miss Randall, founder and proprietor of the Eastbourne College of Domestic Economy, always known as Rannie's, where Sara spent a delightful year, as did Anne Mahood, Alistair Macafee's sister.

Sarah and John Andrews had a son, Tom, the architect of the ill-fated *Titanic*, and a daughter, Frances, as stated above, the wife of Edmund Garrett (1850–1936). The Garretts had five children, of whom Anne Neilsen married Arthur Hollins, Ted's father; Emma Frances married Norman Eggar; and John ('Uncle Jack') married Mary Jamieson.

Of the Eggar offspring, Patricia married John Gray, who chaired the Northern Ireland Electricity Board. They retired to Dundrum, near Newcastle, and lived there till his death. She was ladies' captain of the Royal County Down Golf Club and a Visitor for Magherabery Prison. She then moved to Devon to be near her daughter, Belinda, and her grandchildren and we still visit her there as opportunity offers. She remained our children's favourite 'cousin', and we have many happy memories of visits to Dundrum, playing games (especially Racing Demon, where Patricia could not bear to lose), tricks and leg-pulls, and one particularly happy occasion when Anna and Emma were going through their adolescent 'gothic' phase, whose more visible symptoms were hair dyed black and black clothes. Patricia greeted them on the steps of the bungalow almost unrecognisable in a black wig, shawl, and dress.

Gillian Eggar married Douglas Strachan, and by a strange coincidence their daughter Rosemary married Tim Wilson, son of my father's cellmate in Changi gaol, Singapore, Bishop Leonard Wilson.

Uncle Jack Garrett's offspring included Esme, who married Colin West Watson, Zaidee, who married Dick Godfree and has been a wonderful godmother to Sara, and Henry Edmund Lennox, who married Rachel Hartland, and ended a distinguished army career as (doubtless) the very model of a modern Major General.

Clichés such as 'small world' leap to mind when one considers how many interconnections there have been in our two families. But the Andrews' mill in

Comber was one of the biggest in the province, so it is not perhaps quite so surprising that a connection developed, probably through the initial chance acquaintance forged by business and commercial contacts. At this stage one can do no more than hazard a guess. Similarly the Cabin Hill connection surprised us all when we first discovered it.

Ted Hollins himself had one brother, Richard (always known as Uncle Dick). He was a highly successful stockbroker and a 'fun' uncle to the children. On our visits to his home on St George's Hill, Weybridge, his favourite magical trick was to operate his garage doors by remote control on the command 'abracadabra', much to the amazement of Anna and Emma, to whom he seemed a very potent wizard indeed, with a much appreciated secondary trick of making gifts of extra pocket money appear out of thin air as they were departing.

He married Kathleen Leonard, a widow, whose son by her first marriage is the very distinguished painter, Michael Leonard. His picture of the Queen, 'Corgi and Bess', commissioned by the Reader's Digest and now in the National Portrait Gallery, appeared on the magazine's front cover and is a gem. His portrait of Sara as a teenager is striking perhaps, rather than beautiful. We have a more flattering pastel drawing of her by Juliet Pannett, an old friend of the family. Dick and Kathleen had a son, Brian, who is something of a wizard with engines and shares his uncle Ted's youthful passion for very fast cars.

Little is known about the early life of the two Hollins boys. Their mother died when Ted was in his early twenties and Dick still in his teens. There was a family retainer, Gertrude, the housekeeper, of whom Ted always spoke with affectionate respect. Amongst her other duties in those days would be helping lady visitors to unpack, since no 'proper' lady would have done so for herself. So Gertrude was able to assess and report on the suitability of the girl-friends who came to stay, after carefully checking the state of their underwear! Sara's expert view of the matter is that in a thrifty Yorkshire household, however upmarket, carefully darned would undoubtedly have scored more highly than brand new.

Ted certainly was a vigorous young man, with a passion for fast cars, his favourite being a Hispano Suiza of which he was very proud and spoke of often. It did cause him problems when their step-grandmother, 'Gamma', developed a passion for being taken for a drive in their sports cars and began to make a nuisance of herself. The boys cracked the problem by contriving to lock the steering wheel so that the car went round and round in circles. They then invited the pestilential lady for a drive. She hopped in; they set the car going and then hopped out, leaving her helplessly and indefinitely circling the driveway. Dante, who consigned all of earth's most pestilential people to the circles of hell, would surely have approved. Whether this cured the good lady's addiction history does not relate.

Ted was also an enthusiastic potholer and when we began to holiday at Malham he confessed that he knew it well and had stayed, as we did once, at the Buck

Inn. He had climbed down Gaping Ghyll and other famous sink-pots in the area. Presumably in his earlier days he had explored the Peak District as well. Very surprisingly he was exempted from military service with the RAF, because it turned out that at some unspecified point he had had TB – or because of his flat feet according to another family legend.

He never worked in the family business, though he loved to return to the Pleasley area on holiday, escorted and chauffered in his riper years by Sara. He said little about his links with the firm, yet his name was familiar enough to the caretaker when we visited the site.

By contrast he spoke with great enthusiasm of his time at Salts Mill in Saltaire. They were very enlightened mill owners who built a model village to house their workers and were well ahead of their time in the provision of welfare services for them. He clearly approved. His own job was to do time and motion studies with a view to increasing efficiency, inevitably incurring a degree of suspicion among the workforce. The task appealed to his logical and analytical mind and he was very happy there. He was always a thinker, determined to make up his own mind and not run with the crowd, whether in abstract matters like religion or more practical affairs such as investment and the stock market. Had circumstances not forced him to move south, he might have become a leading figure in industry, since he was highly enough thought of to be invited to accept a job in the USA, but he felt unable to take it because of his wife Jane's poor health. Evidence of how highly he was thought of at Salts can be found in letters from 1941 from the firm applying for him to be placed in a reserved occupation and excused call-up, because he was 'unique'. The company (who claimed that they were engaged in 50% government work and 15% export) stated that 'he cannot be replaced, as it would take years of training'. His official designation was production and efficiency manager.

Jane Fennell, Sara's mother, was born into a family with distant connections by marriage to the Brontës. Her great grandfather, the Rev John Fennell had married Jane Branwell, whose niece Maria married Patrick Brontë, father of the Brontë sisters. He later married an Elizabeth Lister. In the light of the Hollins connection with spinning and textiles, it would be nice to think she was connected to the inventor of the Lister nip-comb, which separated and straightened raw wool, but I have no evidence of it, beyond the fact of the family's proximity to Bradford.

Jane herself was highly artistic, not in the formal sense, but in her remarkable creativity and appreciation of beauty. Very sadly she suffered from manic depression, which was a cruel affliction to her personally and a heavy burden for her husband. Her mother had been something of a society beauty and Jane inherited her beauty and being naturally gregarious enjoyed the social life of London. She had a brother, John, who was very brilliant and ultimately became Professor of Russian at Oxford University, marrying Marina Lopoukhine, and having two children, Nicholas and Juliana. Jane was introduced to Ted by her cousin, Christopher Hodgson, a great friend of his, who lived in Scarborough and presumably knew him socially or from business. He assured him that he had 'just the girl' for him, and so it turned out.

Their marriage lasted for sixty years (1936–1996), and amid the trials and stresses of Jane's illness, Ted remained a devoted and utterly faithful husband to her, caring for her in the down phases and steadying her when she was on a high. What enormously impressed me as a suitor for Sara's hand was how thoughtfully sympathetic he was to her affliction, which he explained carefully to me, and which he was determined to understand and manage with all the skill that medical science could offer in those days, and endlessly seeking new treatments which might alleviate the condition. The effort was a severe drain upon him, physically and emotionally, but I never heard him complain. If there is a heaven, he will assuredly go there for his love of her and his saintly commitment to his marriage vows ('in sickness or in health'). No man could have done more; most would have done less; some, too many in this modern era, including the highest in the land, would have probably cut and run.

Jane herself was heroic. I really wonder if I would ever have guessed there was anything wrong, beyond an occasional moodiness, if I had not been told about her illness. She was absolutely remarkable in her determination to put on a good show, and she remained impeccably groomed and always charming in her hospitality. Only to those in the know would a certain artificiality of manner have been a sign that all was not well. No doubt the family paid the penalty later. She was a dear and anyhow for being Sara's mother I would have forgiven her anything.

It was Jane's illness that brought the family down to Angmering, in Sussex, where they bought Robin Hill and set themselves up as market gardeners, an activity in which they could both share and which meant that Ted need not leave home to go to work. Jane had found the north of England deeply depressing (who called their house in Guiseley 'Bleak House', I wonder, and why?). Sara remembers how they came south by stages, staying for unspecified periods of time with relatives *en route*. In many ways there is a parallel with my own family's peregrinations, while my father looked for a job on his return from the war, as there is in reverse with my mother's no less faithful care for my father, whose POW experience had so deeply damaged him.

Jane's mother, Sylvia (née Mitchell) was already living in the village, in a lovely house, Garden House, with a fabulous garden, which she tended expertly as well as lovingly. She was a great help in looking after the children when Jane was in one of her down phases. Sylvia herself was a tremendous personality and the greatest fun. She was a sculptor of distinction and her bronze statue, 'Pan With Pipes', was exhibited at the Royal Academy. In her youth she had been a devotee of the theatre and had an interesting and extensive collection of autographed theatre programmes and memorabilia, which we passed on to a theatre museum.

The many acquaintances and friends she made there were often invited down to Garden House for weekends, and Sara well remembers some of her exotic visitors, and exploring their bedrooms and belongings in their absence, egged on by Alice, the cook.

Recklessly extravagant, like the prodigal son Sylvia 'wasted her substance', though not necessarily on riotous living. Only when she was down to her last few thousands did she consent to allow Ted to take over her investments and rebuild her capital. This he did with great skill, and in time equilibrium was restored. But for all her lack of prudence, she was also a woman of entrepreneurial spirit. She used to buy up old cottages in the village and renovate them, before selling them on for a profit. But she was undone by her own temperament: when things were going well she was always inclined to 'have a bust'; then, when she had gone too far she had to 'pull in her horns' and start again. It must have been exasperating to look after her affairs; but she was great fun to know.

Uncle Jack Garrett came to live in nearby Angmering-on-Sea, close to the beach. He was a true eccentric of whom I remember little, though we visited him on occasion to pay our respects. He was something of a recluse, and trial to his wife, Mary, who attended faithfully to his slightest whim. Esme, his daughter, continued in the same tradition, proving no less devoted in her care for him. The one thing I remember is his garden, seemingly filled with nothing but the darkest and gloomiest collection of evergreens I have ever seen.

Though the Hollins' family name has been lost from this side of the family, as from mine the Gregg name has gone, there are at least other branches of the Hollins clan, whom Sara and I have never met. Time may one day reveal them to us.

That was the family to whose star I had the great good fortune to hitch my wagon. What was it Claudio says to Beatrice in *Much Ado About Nothing*?

> I were but little happy, if I could say how much. Lady, as you are mine, I am yours;
> I give away myself for you and dote on the exchange.

CHAPTER 20

Anna and Emma – *Pignora amoris*

THE PHRASE *PIGNORA AMORIS*, pledges or tokens of love, derives from one of the Latin poets, probably Ovid though I would prefer it to be Virgil. It has always stuck in my mind, not only as a convenient ending for a hexameter line, if you are composing Latin verses, but also as a felicitous description of the gift of children, one of the greatest blessings that can be showered upon a marriage. I wish I could remember the context from which it comes, but though I have searched both memory and dictionary, I cannot place it.

Naughty old Francis Bacon says that, 'the noblest works and foundations have proceeded from childless men, which have sought to express the images of their minds, where those of their bodies have failed. The care of posterity is most in those that have no posterity.' He may be right, though Shakespeare, if no one else, suggests that he may not be. But given the choice between great achievement and having children, I would settle for children every time! 'The joys of parents are secret', he observes. 'And so are their griefs and fears. They cannot utter the one; nor they will not utter the other. Children sweeten labours; but they make misfortunes more bitter.' But, as the ghastly modern advertisement has it, 'They are worth it.'

Despite the anxieties that all parents go through from time to time, our children have been the source of our greatest joys. We have always been a close-knit family and the happy chance that brought them both to Bristol has meant that our own move to nearby Cleeve village has ensured that we have never lost touch and have the added blessing of getting to know our grandchildren in a way that many grandparents never do. It makes for the greatest happiness, for us at least. The gods have been unutterably kind to us, and I would like to think that in some small measure they have made recompense for my grandfather's tragic loss of both his sons.

Anna was born on 8 July 1970; Emma on 2 June 1972, and I was categorically forbidden by Sara to attend their births in the Kent and Canterbury Hospital. Nor, I confess, had I much desire to do so, regarding the current fashion for birthing fathers as little more than a temporary fad. I am not sure that it is anything to be proud of, but when they each arrived into this world I was fast asleep at Riversleigh. So both girls spent their early years in a boys' boarding house with a working mum, but at least her job kept her in the same building and therefore never out of reach. Anna was the easiest of babies; Emma rather less so, though Sara's post-puerperal depression did not help. She defeated it with her usual iron self-discipline, but for mother and child it was a difficult time.

The Riversleigh boys were always interested and genuinely concerned for their welfare, one reporting to us that Emma had discovered how to move a pram with the brakes fully on, when he found she had almost reached the front gate *en route* for the London road and heaven alone knows where; but then she was technically proficient from an early age. Another told Sara in some alarm that Anna's pram had been shut under our garage door and that she was not to be seen. The pram was nearly perpendicular wedged under the roll down doors, which a well-meaning boy had closed for the sake of our and her security. Anna was unharmed, huddled in the bottom of the pram and fast asleep. Mercifully such alarums and excursions were few and far between. If a role model for a happy family were needed, I hope we provided it. Both children were christened in the lovely crypt chapel of Canterbury Cathedral, Anna by James Trevelyn (Sara's cousin by marriage) and Emma by Peter Newell, in token of our long friendship, despite its ups and downs. They were beautiful babies – does any parent ever think otherwise? – Anna having the most lovely eyes and Emma the curliest of curly blonde hair, which made us wonder sometimes if we should have entered her for a Miss Pears Soap competition.

Sara was the most competent of mothers, combining the duties of house matron, caterer, and motherhood with seemingly effortless efficiency. Though our two-bedroom flat at the top of the house was small, she managed them both with complete aplomb, Emma being promoted from our bedroom to the drawing room in her carry-cot once we were ready for bed. Nights were not too badly interrupted. Interestingly enough, when there were difficulties getting them to sleep in the afternoons, it was the folk wisdom of the staff of Riversleigh which introduced Sara to the simple magic of fresh air. Thereafter come rain, snow, gale or blizzard, the children spent their afternoon rests outside in their prams and slept like logs. She passed on the same trick to Emma in due course, and Imogen and Arthur have been similarly hardened to the rigours of the English climate. For Anna it has been more difficult, with a temporarily very noisy building site beyond their garden.

With Anna aged three and Emma one we moved to Eastbourne College, living at 20 Grange Road in a rather more spacious flat on the end of a day-boy house, but without tutorial responsibilities there. It was a superb location, overlooking the main cricket field and just below the Meads, the smart residential end of town. I could reach my classroom in one minute; the sea was about ten minutes' walk away; the shops about the same. Devonshire Park and the Congress Theatre were even nearer, at the end of the main campus. The Downs and Beachy Head were reachable by a brisk walk or a quick five-minute drive. We could not ask for more.

Of the school and my work there, more will follow. Suffice to say that it was the happiest and most civilised of all the schools I taught in, its attractions much enhanced by the fact of being located in a town and thus without a feeling of being cut off from the outside world. The presence of sixth form girls and a substantial number of day-boys increased the overall feeling of normality.

Our three years there were perhaps the happiest of times for all our family. For Sara there were relatively recent recollections of Rannie's; for me the pleasure of working with Simon Langdale, an old friend and a very able boss, who set the school on its now highly successful path after a period of some difficulty. There were lots of staff with young families; plenty of children's parties; new friends made, as well as old friends rejoined.

Of the new friends made, perhaps the greatest were the Weldons, Andy and Jennie, and their daughters Jane and Kate. They moved soon after we met to a lovely old Victorian house on the edge of the village of Chiddingly. Andy had built a pond where he kept ducks and Jennie, an enthusiastic rider, had a horse in their five-acre field. They had an adorable dachshund called Lizzie – a real character. It seemed an idyllic country existence, with plenty of village activities to busy themselves with – Andy on the village council giving short shrift to the idiocies of local planners and village politicians, while Jennie was for a time chairman of the governors of the village school. Andy and I saw eye to eye on most things – not least the lunacy of all authorities and the inadequacies of state sector education; and I still remember his complaints about the sheer lack of ambition for its pupils evinced by the local comprehensive school where the girls had been studying. In short order he removed them both and sent them to Moira House, an independent girls school in Eastbourne. The results were dramatic; they both did very well. Kate ended up as head girl and both have had successful careers.

Jennie and Sara shared a love of reading and a naughty sense of humour, while I suffered regular mockery from her for my sartorial eccentricities. Jennie taught EFL for a number of years at a language school in Eastbourne, with hilarious accounts of her dealings with her pupils. Even when we moved on to pastures new, we stayed in touch with visits and by correspondence, and for one memorable week we looked after their house while they went on holiday and I learned to care for Primrose, Jennie's beloved horse, of whom even I became quite fond in the end, though I am terrified of all equine manifestations. The idea that I might one day be learning what every boy scout knows, which is how to remove stones from horses hooves with that special implement on his scout knife, would have amazed me. Kate and Emma still stay in touch after all these years.

Of the old friendships renewed, Sue Davies was one of our oldest and dearest. I had known her since her time at Wycombe Abbey in Shelburn House with Audrey. Bob Ewing and I, with amazing daring, had once dropped in to say hello while we were passing through the town, and I still remember the consequent fluttering in the dovecots we caused and how we were smartly ordered out into the grounds to take the air well away from temptation while Audrey was extracted from her tennis game to meet us. O those days of long lost innocence! Sue had become the Warden's secretary at Radley to both Milligan and Silk, and then feeling the need for a change came down to Eastbourne to join Simon's team. There she remained with successive heads until her retirement. She seems as busy as ever, running with characteristic competence her Old Girls' Association and the local National Trust, as well as researching the college archives on behalf of the Old Eastbournians. She also learned to play golf, which I have no doubt she took to easily, given her natural sporting abilities.

Her father, Roy, was a dear man and a distinguished scientist, with whom I used to have interesting conversations about faith and religion. Coming from diverse directions – he a very able scientist and I a mere classicist and arts man – we were none the less in broad agreement about what was credible in the Christian faith and what was not. Like me, he seemed to be wrestling with the problems of belief, and had corresponded with a number of fellow scientists on the subject. As always, I found it very comforting when scientists seemed to be of a like mind to myself. I still have some of his letters in my files and I quote several of my letters to him in *A Faith Unfaithful*.

Sue's sister Jill and her husband Etienne Dreyfous generously allowed us once to stay in the guest apartments of their lovely house near La Rochelle, where we were regularly visited by hoopoes on what remains a memorable holiday. So our connections with the family go a long way back.

John Evans, also ex-Radley, but now a retired headmaster, joined as Second Master.

Though my nominal salary had increased, my real salary was reduced by the loss of free living enjoyed by housemasters in most boarding schools. We started Anna (aged about three-plus) at the Chelmsford Lodge nursery department, an excellent local prep school, which was located about two streets away from us, but which she remembers with less affection than Emma does. But at five we transferred her, probably for financial reasons, though I can't remember, to the Meads Church of England Primary School. By then she was well able to read – an accomplishment which they were less than appreciative of, to my surprise.

Certainly she was not stretched and gained little beyond a degree of socialisation, which for Anna was never a problem anyhow. She was intelligent, articulate, gregarious, and made friends easily. I remember only three things from the school's comments on her: first their reference to her 'constant worried little frown' (she is a bit of a worrier, like her father); secondly that she was 'not very autonomous'; and third the fact that she had 'not yet grasped the concept of the oneness of one'. Such a formidable philosophical achievement might well defeat greater brains than those of a child of five and I dismissed it as teacher's gobbledygook designed to obfuscate and confuse innocent parents with the appearance of expertise. She was certainly well able to count, so it was a deficiency that caused me no great anxiety. She read enthusiastically, and has remained a voracious reader all her life. I am sure it is one of the best things a parent can do, to get their children reading at as early an age as possible without unduly forcing them. No wonder we have an illiterate generation reared almost since birth to dependence on TV for entertainment.

Anna was not going to make a lot of progress at that school, but after four terms we moved to Northern Ireland, and the prep department of the local girls grammar school, Bloomfield Collegiate, soon resolved that problem. Though state primary education has improved over the last twenty years, there is nothing to touch a good prep school for giving children a really useful start to their schooling, but within Northern Ireland the state system was much stronger at primary level than in England.

In due course Emma followed in Anna's footsteps and was lucky enough to come under the care of the immortal, much loved, and wonderfully successful teacher, Miss Joseph. Precocious as ever, Emma soon had her first boy-friend, Alexander Halliday, the son of a fellow classics master at Eastbourne. I always took care to teach girls with the door of my study open so that Sara could act as a sort of unofficial chaperon – even in those days a sensible and professional precaution. On one lovely occasion, when I was taking an ancient history tutorial with a couple of sixth form girls in my study, Emma came racing out to Sara in the kitchen saying, 'Hush, Mummy, don't say a word; don't even breathe. Listen! Daddy is telling the girls about Alexander. He says he's Great.'

Sara, meanwhile, ever a glutton for punishment and with Anna and Emma now at school, set up a small pre-school playgroup, which was a great success, and enabled her to maintain her skills with very young children and of course helped her establish contacts with other families.

Three golden years flew by.

Despite the troubles in Northern Ireland, which frightened me rather less than those who were unfamiliar with the province, when my promised three years at Eastbourne were up I applied for and was appointed to the headship of Campbell College. So in January 1977 we moved ourselves lock, stock and barrel to the College's lovely 100-acre campus on the eastern edges of Belfast, just below the Stormont Parliament buildings and with a fine backdrop of the Craigantlet Hills behind. It was a lovely spot in which to bring up children. The grounds were expensive to maintain and therefore somewhat neglected, but they still retained much of their beauty from the days when they were part of the Belmont estate. There was a fine avenue of superbly stately beeches, as tall as any I have seen, in which a colony of herons nested every year – said to be the largest urban heronry in Britain. Each year their arrival, within a week of 31 January, as regularly as clockwork, was the surest harbinger of spring. Their noisy nest-building, with much clacking of beaks and squawking of argument, was a source of considerable entertainment; their even noisier feeding habits with their young still more so. One year, at the request of the biology department, we adopted two nestlings, which had been jostled or pushed out of their nest; the boys came over to feed them; we gave them house-room; the children christened them Henry and Rumpus. To the best of my knowledge they both survived.

Fine forest trees abounded; there was a small ornamental lake, mildly polluted and increasingly filled with detritus, but pretty for all that. Treecreepers nested in the magnificent Wellingtonias; there was at least one nesting sparrow hawk; a badger den; foxes; in fact the whole place was a miniature nature reserve, probably the more so because it had been somewhat neglected, little disturbed except by the boys' illicit nicotine brigade. In effect we were living on a large private country estate, which is ideal for children in many ways, but can contribute to a certain sense of isolation, because friends can't easily drop in, which for teenagers is as essential as oxygen. But the school swimming pool was an excellent source of pleasure, exercise, and acquaintances. The inimitable Billy Graham, one of two Billy Grahams on the long-serving support staff of the school, ran swimming lessons for children in the school pool, as well as helping with the school team under the management of Fred Parkes, a member of the Campbell staff but also an Irish international swimming coach. They were soon taught to swim and both have remained fast swimmers, despite motherhood and years of neglect of their technique.

Schools were the first issue. We had researched the local schools as best we could at a distance and with the help of my mother. The Northern Ireland grammar school system, for which they were of course too young when we got there, was the typical aspiration of all parents, and a system that delivered excellent results for its pupils. But all the local schools ran 'prep' departments, which would obviously give us a degree of priority provided the girls passed the dreaded eleven-plus. When it approached we also took the precaution of seeking a provisional place in a secondary modern school with an excellent reputation and an outstanding head; but fortunately this proved unnecessary. Both girls passed comfortably.

The choice of local school was difficult. Sullivan Upper, in nearby Holywood, run by a very long-standing and brilliant head, John Frost, was academically the most attractive, with the bonus that it was coeducational; we misread his fair-minded account of the pros and cons as a brush-off, and since he was a good friend I always enjoyed teasing him for so unkindly turning down my two children for his school. It never failed to get an embarrassed protestation of innocence out of him. Methodist College in the centre of Belfast had a good academic reputation, but was enormous and by repute somewhere in which you sank or swam. The Darwinian principle of survival of the fittest did not seem to be quite what we wanted. Both these schools would have involved a daily bus journey, unless we took them by car, and this we preferred to avoid.

That left two local girls grammar schools, Strathearn and Bloomfield. The general assumption was that we would choose Strathearn, because it had the social cachet, but that is something to which we were both indifferent. It also had a disappointing reputation for academic results, which Audrey Lamb later did much to improve. But it was good at games and with hindsight I think that I somewhat undervalued this aspect of a girl's education. Bloomfield Collegiate, by contrast, run by the formidable Ethel Gray, was highly disciplined, very hard-working, and with very good results. I doubt if Ethel set much store by games or other extracurricular activities, and this in my view was a weakness. But if one had to choose, work was the priority. We chose Bloomfield and had no regrets. Anna was lucky – she found herself in a year group of delightful girls, some of whom have remained faithful friends to this day. Emma had a more difficult group, of whom several seemed to be positively unpleasant. Northern Ireland women are tough – they have always had to be. In children a similar toughness can turn easily into the kind of mental bullying which causes distress. But that's the luck of the draw and unless the circumstances are extreme parents should encourage their children to 'hang on in there'. Life is not always kind and it is as well to get used to the fact. At some point we wondered about a change of school; Sara was more resolute than me and she was, as usual, right. The girls got excellent O Levels and were well set for their sixth form careers. Emma, in addition, had shown considerable musical talent at piano and violin; indeed, her violin teacher, Harry Cawood, told me that she just might have made a career out of it. I am glad she did not. Unless you reach the very top, it can be a pretty soul-destroying existence.

We had promised them £500 each, if they did not smoke until they were 18, and another £500 if they held out till 21. When they came of age I was £2,000 richer than I might have been. No such bribe was offered for refraining from alcohol, and under-age drinking was the norm, with little evidence that hotels and pubs (or parents, one has to concede) were making much of an effort to stop it. The Northern Irish, like the Scots, have never learned to drink in moderation, but Anna and Emma and their friends were pretty restrained in their drinking habits, and never came home the worse for wear. It is possible that the fact of always being collected by us may even have helped to restrain them. Despite the Troubles, they enjoyed a reasonable nightlife, but we always arranged to pick them up in town or from whatever hostelry they and their friends were patronising, and to insist on absolute punctuality at the rendezvous. They were pretty good about it, though I do remember once having to brave a totally jam-packed pub in Newtownards to extract one of them, when she was late.

Only one event caused any real anxiety. Emma went to the cinema in Belfast one night and the IRA exploded a huge 1,000 lb bomb not far off. She was very frightened, thinking the roof was falling in, and suffered a degree of anxiety for some while after. Waiting to collect her at a nearby car park against a background of considerable activity by the security forces, my feelings are best left to the imagination. Relatively speaking drugs were not much of a worry or problem at that stage in Belfast. The paramilitaries had not yet decided that they were a good source of revenue, and so they were pretty savage to those found dealing in them. It is my recollection, possibly wrong, that the police told me that the drug squad in the late seventies was only six strong in Belfast. Dublin, by contrast, was soon to become by repute at least the drug capital of Europe and it is my impression that in Belfast, as in every major city in Britain, drugs are now a serious problem.

As I remember it, when offered the choice, both girls decided that they would like to go to boarding school for their sixth form years. I was firmly in favour, since it seemed to me a good preparation for university to spend a couple of years away from parents but in a protected environment, learning to cope (not least with boys) on their own, and broadening their acquaintance. I do not remember considering single sex schools, but if they had demanded it I might have agreed. What I would not have considered would have been the boarding departments of the local grammar schools. Apart from Campbell itself, it seemed to me that they were little more than dormitory facilities, lacking anything of the ethos of a traditional English boarding school, and there was no point in going there. When I began to think about what I knew or had heard about English schools, I realised that I had serious reservations about many of them. At least I knew roughly what we would be getting from the schools I had taught at, so in the end the choices were limited to King's Canterbury and Eastbourne College.

By now Newell had left King's Canterbury and been succeeded by Peter Pilkington, who had done a wonderful job in upgrading the place and making the 'plant' somewhat more appropriate to modern conditions. He had also proved to be a good man to work for and the general atmosphere had lightened. Sadly he had just moved on to St Paul's, but Canon Phillips, the new head whom I never met, was unlikely to have much impact for good or ill in his first couple of years, so this was not a problem. King's had taken its first and only girl, a classicist, into the sixth form while I was there; but though they were not yet fully coeducational as they are now, the girls had a substantial presence. It seemed a good choice and to the best of my knowledge Anna was happy there, got good A Levels, and went on to St Andrews University to read English. My only grumble was that, whereas the school bent every effort to get boys into the university of their choice, they seemed somewhat less committed to doing their best for girls. St Andrews was not her first or second choice and I saw little evidence of any effort to ring round in support of her. They rejected my advice to try for Christ's, the family college, and her attempt to get into Newnham proved unsuccessful. In fact after an unhappy first year she enjoyed St Andrews too, and got a good degree (a 2.1), though I was disappointed by the university's poor pastoral care and what seemed to me limited amenities (barring a reasonably well known golf course) and depressing black stone, that gave a dreary atmosphere to that somewhat unimpressive little town. Edinburgh was probably just too close and sucked away most of the more civilised sources of cultural interest. I am sure Anna saw it all rather more positively.

When it came to Emma's turn, the choice was the same: Eastbourne versus King's. She chose Eastbourne and won a sixth form scholarship. But for girls doing sciences in mixed classes, experience seems to suggest that there is often a problem of confidence and self-esteem. Teaching such classes requires subtle skills and sensitive teachers. Boys are competitive, aggressive, pushy; girls often gravitate to the back of the class and settle for a quiet life, contributing little and losing motivation, and failing to perform as well as they could. Emma was unlucky enough to suffer in this respect from poor teaching and her A Levels were not as good as she might have hoped. But helped by the fact that she had three A Levels in maths and sciences, she was accepted by Reading University to take a degree in psychology. The pastoral care in Nugent House, the girls' house, under Euan Clarke and then Philip Cantwell, was good – better, I felt, than at King's. Emma was very happy there and had a great time.

Chance rules so much in our lives. If Emma had been as well taught in her sciences as she was in her maths by my old friend and colleague, Duncan Bowles, she might have gone to a different university to read a different subject. If so, she would never have met Paddy. And that I am sure is the very best thing that happened to her. As we are told in *The Rubáiyát of Omar Khayám*,

> 'Tis all a chequer board of nights and days
> Where Destiny with men for pieces plays:
> Hither and thither moves, and mates, and slays,
> And one by one back in the closet lays.

In fact, with hindsight, the sciences may possibly not have been the best choice for her at A Level, though she has a very good analytical mind; but she is also highly creative. If so the fault must be largely mine, since I am sure I pushed them, because girls with science A Levels were still a valuable and relatively rare commodity. As with all choices, whether parental or pupil, one makes the best judgement one can at the time, and there is little point lamenting mistakes, if mistakes they are. But I sometimes wonder if she might have been happier studying subjects on the arts side, possibly with a philosophical slant to take advantage of her analytical talents.

By the time the two girls were at university, we were back in England where I was deputy head of St Mary's School, Wantage (again, more anon). The school accommodation was not really adequate, though with limited resources it was probably as good as could be expected. It was a three-bedroom house, but with only one living-room and no study for me to work in. And of course we had too much furniture. When I retired from Campbell in 1987 we had bought (with a mortgage of course, and some help from my mother) a lovely house on the Glenmachan estate, less than a mile from the school, while I worked on the Navan project. For £90,000 we got a brand new four-bedroom, three-reception, two-garage, detached house with a large garden (about one third of an acre) and fine forest trees all round us, many with TPOs on them. When we moved back to England, two years later in 1989, I sold out for £95,000, when the housing market was at its height there (though still depressed in Northern Ireland). This was only enough to buy a small two-bedroom town house with no garden. It was a fairly brutal re-introduction to English house prices in South Oxfordshire, but we felt it essential to get on the housing ladder; it had the additional merit that it was situated next door but one to our house-to-be, in Alfredston Place, a new award winning development across the road from the school.

We thought that Anna (at St Andrews) and Emma (still a sixth former) would find it liberating to occupy this new little house, while we lived next door but one in the school property. They could take all meals with us, or none, entirely as they chose, and would be able to enjoy a typically student existence. In fact the experiment did not work very well, and for the only time in their lives there was a degree of friction between them. There was nothing we could do about it until, sadly, my mother died and her legacy enabled us to take out with confidence a much larger mortgage (of £100,000 – which was for a schoolmaster a ferocious figure) in the knowledge that if the worst came to the very worst, I could sell all my inheritance to repay it. By then, of course, house prices were very depressed and my £95,000 house had dropped by one third in value to £70,000.

But in the same two-year period the developers had failed to sell a single one of their badly over-priced big town houses in Alfredston Place that were the crowning glory of their development. They had dropped their prices steadily but to no effect. I was able to get a brand new, four-bedroom, three-bathroom (two *en suite*), two reception town house, with two car ports and a balcony, and with a small but attractive garden at the back for only £125,000 – also a reduction of one third from the original asking price of £185,000. The firm, I think, later went bust – and I was not surprised. The girls got the two big bedrooms at the top of the house, which gave them space to study and live, and escape from us if they wanted to; Sara and I took the smaller ground floor *en suite* bedroom; I got a study, and the living-room was so big that there was plenty of room for a dining-room on the elevated platform (intended for a grand piano!) at one end, if we wanted to be smart and not eat in the kitchen. It was a tremendous improvement in our circumstances, the final gift of a devoted and wonderful mother whose tender and loving concern for us had never flagged, however far away we seemed to be. We lived there enormously happily until we finally moved to Somerset in June 2000.

Then came the problem of careers. Life is so easy for those who have always known since an early age that they wanted to be an engine-driver or a doctor or a trapeze artist, or whatever. For such the mechanics are simple – find out the qualifications needed and get them. For those with maths, especially with sciences in support the key to opening most doors, there are plenty of options, which is why I was so keen for Emma to study them at A Level. For those who have no idea what they really want to do, there is a problem; doubly so, if their chosen subjects are on the arts side. A degree – any degree – is a help. It proves to a possible employer that you are capable of thinking and of working consistently to meet a challenge; and though the final examinations are not the Day of Judgement, they are not a bad approximation, since all your sins of omission and commission return to haunt you with a vengeance.

For boys at least there are fewer complications, such as having children. Get good A Levels; get a good degree; get a qualification; get started; be flexible and prepared to change if you find you have made a mistake; the money is nice, but at the early stages it is better to find out who you are, what you like, and where you want to go. Even in 1977 I was saying to pupils only half jokingly that if it's money you want, leave and train to be a plumber. It was quite prophetic, it seems to me, but now the Poles have cornered that market, ever since their country joined the EC. For girls job satisfaction is quite important; flexibility essential. My advice to the children was that, if they really had no idea what they wanted to do, train to be a teacher. You will never be rich; but you will with any luck work among civilised and educated people, who are similarly not too obsessed with money (like lawyers and city folk), and are willing to work for others as well as themselves. Taking a teaching qualification gives you an extra year to sort out your ideas; the ability to teach requires that you learn to organise your thoughts, articulate them clearly, and present them logically. That is not a bad training for almost anything. The holidays can be a bonus; the hours are broadly reasonable; there is equal pay; and the teacher's pension is indexed and backed by government. In addition, especially if you have the luck to speak English, you can go abroad and do TEFL; you can certainly get part-time employment; and if ambitious you will earn a reasonable professional salary.

The girls both took teaching qualifications, Anna at Canterbury and Emma at Brookes University, Oxford. Emma chose to specialise in the younger age groups; Anna with the older, teaching English to A Level and so maintaining and developing her long-standing love of literature. Anna started out at Meon Cross, near Fareham, but the school had no sixth form and she felt it wiser to move on, first back to Canterbury for the third time, to Kent College, and then to Bristol where she has taught for the last ten years at Redland Girls High School, which stands high in all the academic league tables. She has been very happy there and her results have been consistently impressive. Emma moved to Bristol to be with Paddy and found a job at Monkton Combe, with her old housemaster at Eastbourne, Euan Clarke, who had later been housemaster to David Macafee as well. He had recently moved to Monkton as head of their junior school. The commute from Bristol was not easy, and after a year she was contacted by Clifton Girls High School and invited to transfer to their prep department. By an odd coincidence, 100 years before, the Gregg family had had strong associations with both schools. At the time of writing (2006) both girls are full-time mothers, Emma out of conviction, Anna on maternity leave but preparing to return to teaching part-time.

Which brings me to the happiest topic of all: marriage. No parent can contemplate the marriage of a son or daughter with anything other than the utmost pleasure and delight. Of course there is a tendency for mothers to think no girl is worthy of her son and fathers no boy worthy of his daughter. We were spared any such reservations and totally enchanted that both our daughters seemed to have found the man of their dreams, husbands of whom we were soon extremely fond, and in-laws whom we genuinely liked! In an era when formal marriages seemed to be becoming less fashionable and the church less attractive to young people, whether as an institution or as the purveyor of a convincing faith, it was also a source of great pleasure to us that both sets of young people chose church marriages.

Emma met Paddy at Reading University, where he was reading land management. His family came from Cork originally – like all the best people – but his grandfather (Ernest James, born 1893) emigrated to Wales and there the family settled. He started as a face-worker in the early 1900s, but having been turned down by the army because of flat feet, he joined the Cardiff police instead, transferring to the HAC in 1916 (flat feet no problem!) and fighting on the Western Front before being posted to Murmansk during the Russian Revolution. After the war he became a partner in a cinema company, but sold up and started the family estate agency (E J Hales & Sons) in 1922. He married Kathleen Vanwye Senior and had three sons, of whom James Patrick (Paddy) was the youngest. Paddy joined the family business along with his brother Peter in 1956, and married Mary Josephine Matthew in 1962. They had three children, Andrew, Sally, and Patrick (Emma's Paddy).

They were a talented family of athletes one way and another. Paddy (senior) represented Wales at golf and reached the last eight of the British amateur championship in 1965. Mary was the daughter of Harold Stanley (Stan) and Josephine Matthew, and her maternal grandfather, Arthur Gould, was the first superstar of Welsh rugby, captaining Wales no less than eighteen times. As a result of a newspaper campaign he was presented with a house for services to Welsh rugby, which led to the other three home countries refusing to play Wales in 1897, if Gould was selected, on the grounds that he was now a professional – the start of 100 years of debate in Wales over professionalism generally. Paddy (junior) became an accomplished skier and was the British Junior Mogul champion in 1989, placed third in Britain, and represented his country in Europa cup competitions. He has recently turned his energies to triathlon instead. A chartered surveyor, he was a director of MEM, and now of Savills, who took them over.

Emma and Paddy were married on 4 April 1998, in the chapel of St Mary's School, Wantage, from which I had retired the previous summer. Roger Clayton Jones officiated, a former senior chaplain of the British army and then the much loved 'padre' of the school. Very sadly, he died unexpectedly, only a couple of years later and much too young, to the shock and sadness of all who knew him.

He had been a wonderful colleague, a passionate fisherman, a fine producer of plays, a superb pastor, and a tremendous support to his invalid wife, Jo. I will remember him with great affection and admiration, not least for his robust approach to his faith and fine gift of preaching sermons that were short and compelling.

I had considerable trouble extracting permission from the Lambeth authorities to hold the wedding in a school chapel, despite the full support of John Salter, the vicar of Wantage, and the fact that the school chapel had been, so to speak, my parish church for the last eight years. The archbishop had a policy of refusing permissions for weddings anywhere other than in parish churches, and as a result I am sure he lost a great deal of goodwill for the church, and the allegiance of some at least of its members. It was mean spirited and ungracious, at a time when the church should have been delighted that anyone wanted to be married under its auspices. I was disgusted, but persistence won out in the end. I got my way; they got their fat fee for doing nothing but obstruct our wishes.

On 19 September 2001 Emma and Paddy presented us with our first grandchild, Imogen Brianna; two years later with our second, Arthur Gregg, and I was deeply touched that the family name of Gregg will be carried on into yet another generation. My mother would have been so pleased too. They are, both of them, blessed with the sweetest of natures and we are lucky beyond measure to have them close enough to see them regularly.

Anna met Rob Adams at a friend's wedding and there was a little bit of 'thunderbolting' here too (see chapter 18 if you have forgotten what I mean). Again the family have Irish roots. Rob's great grandmother was Lady Louise Geraldine Gaunt of the Martyn family of Gregan Castle in County Clare, which was of course the home county of the Gregg family also. This talented, adventurous, and fertile (!) family (Lady Louise was one of fifteen) achieved academic excellence in many walks of professional life, such as teaching, medicine and the law, with notable achievements in the arts and the Armed Forces.

His father, Michael Adams, was a respected solicitor in Salisbury, whose wife Judy was a French teacher and later a rehabilitation officer for the blind. His grandfather, Charles Kingsley Adams, CBE, was the director of the National Portrait Gallery, while his maternal grandfather, Seth Alan (Dick) Fox, was noted for his work in the colonial service and the RAF, getting an OBE for services to the National Association of Youth Clubs. His wife, Yvonne Patricia Fox (née Gaunt) was one of only 250 women to graduate from Oxford in 1937, and has herself written of her experiences in colonial Africa. His family tree includes a great-grandfather who was an Admiral, Sir Ernest Gaunt, KCB, KBE, CMG, who fought with Lord Jellicoe at the battle of Jutland, and later, as C-in-C Western Approaches, handed over the treaty ports to the newly established Irish Republic in 1922.

Rob is now a senior partner in his GP's practice. He and Anna were married on 25 July 2003 by Cathy Horder, our own vicar, in the mother church of our group of parishes, St Mary's, Yatton. I, or we, managed to forget the bride's bouquet, lovingly created by Sara, and despite my insistence in the weeks before the event that no daughter of mine was going to keep her groom waiting, however strong the tradition, since it was simply bad manners and bad organisation, on this occasion I had to swallow my principles, drive frantically back home to collect this essential item, and return – not only breaking the speed limit but also wilfully driving briefly the wrong way up a one-way road to get round a typical summer traffic jam, which might have added half an hour to my journey. As it was we were only about fifteen, possibly twenty minutes late, and at least everyone knew why; Rob had no need to fear he was being left in the lurch.

And on 14 November 2005 Molly Sara arrived to add to our complement of grandchildren. 'Happy the man that hath his quiver full of them.' So says the Good Book and 'Amen' say I.

Quite deliberately I have limited the story of our children to what is, I hope, a reasonably factual account of their life story. It will be for them to supplement it from their own perspective at some later stage if they so wish. This whole book is written primarily for them and their children, because I wish I had known more about the story of my own parents and grandparents and thought that one day they might feel the same. What little I do know I thought I should record, before senility or the garrulousness of old age (which they call anec-dotage) renders me a greater bore than I already am. It is not for me to second-guess the feelings and ideas of those for whom this tale is written. When I have finished this account, they will each be given a floppy disk of the text. If the spirit should so move them, it will enable them to complete a second edition for their children's children, by technologically simple additions to the original 'manuscript', and without the labour of having to write it all out again. They can even reveal what it was really like living with those 'pathetic old gits', their parents, by revealing their side of the story. This is merely mine. They both have something of a way with words and have both recently won short-story writing competitions in the *Bristol Evening Post*; I hope that one day time and energy will enable them to explore and exploit this talent. The magic of IT is such that by the time they decide to do so, they will almost certainly be able to speak their thoughts into a microphone and have it reproduced on the page without spelling mistakes or printing errors. In that at least I envy them.

Suffice to say that our two children are our pride and our delight; they have given us great joy and little anxiety, beyond the natural worry for the welfare of those we love. My prayer would be only that their children give them as much delight as they have given us. Enough said!

CHAPTER 21

Audrey – The Macafee Connection

LIKE ME, MY SISTER AUDREY was born in Malaya, on 17 November 1940, but she will surely remember nothing of the flight from the Japanese and our arrival in sanctuary at the Palace in Armagh. But though we both went to boarding schools and were thus separated for long periods of our early lives, we have always been close and I am devoted to her. She was an ally when things were difficult with my father; she was always a support and comfort; she was a good sport – really not bad (for a girl!) at playing boys' games in the holidays in Lisburn, when life quite often became tedious and I had few friends. She is a fine athlete and played a good game of tennis and golf, where she is a natural hitter of the ball, and could have gone far if she had had a mind to; I think in those days she was tactful enough to let me win, but that may be an example of what Shakespeare's Henry V called 'remembering with advantages' what feats I did that day. She would beat me at both now. On holiday at Portrush I led her into dangerous activities like climbing cliff faces and she was always game to follow, though once I also remember my mother having to rush into the sea to save her from being dragged out by the undertow of a big wave – an emergency for which I was not responsible. Undeterred, of course, she remains a fanatical swimmer still, and seemingly impervious to cold.

Above all, she found me the perfect wife. What more could a sister do?

I can claim to have reciprocated that last great favour, perhaps somewhat less decisively, since it took her rather longer to get round to settling the issue. The chronology defeats me, but at some point I went to a party in University Square, Belfast, given I assume by the Macafee family. There I met Alastair, a charming, somewhat serious young medical student, a couple of years older than me. I rather liked the cut of his jib, or the shape of his scalpel, or whatever is the appropriate metaphor on these occasions. As her chief scout, I reported back to Audrey that he would make a very satisfactory boy-friend, if we could contrive the contact, and when in later years she sometimes wondered whether the right match would ever turn up, I would remind her of the existence of this paragon, whom my spies assured me was as yet unattached. Anyhow, she hooked him in the end, and I remain very proud of my proven capacity as a talent scout.

We both remember the Palace with the utmost pleasure, though I have no specific recollections of our adventures together there. When we settled in Lisburn, Audrey went initially as a day-girl to the preparatory department of the local Friends School, Lisburn, one of the many excellent grammar schools with which the province abounded and which the rather doctrinaire Department of Education for Northern Ireland have been trying to destroy since at least 1975, if not before, and at long last look like getting their way.

'If it ain't broke, don't fix it.' What was 'broke' was the secondary modern system, not the grammar schools; but rather than trying to fix them, while continuing to offer excellent education to at least some pupils, they seem to believe now that it is 'fairer' to offer something worse to some in order to seem to be fair to the rest. I am told that they are about to impose a system of comprehensive schools on the province, just when the rest of Britain under a Labour government has decided that comprehensive schooling for all is not the ideal model for any education system. Ah well; I am glad I am old, as my old father used to say.

Just as I benefited from an initial period of schooling within the province, albeit as a boarder, because it enabled me to make some friends locally, so too did Audrey at Friends School, where above all others the name of Sally Kelso conjures up endless memories of visits to our house and Sally permanently afflicted with fits of giggles. Any self-respecting lad would have stumped off muttering 'stupid girls', but I have no recollection of any reaction beyond thinking it was rather charming. Audrey may well remember differently.

I suspect that I probably did need civilising and that boarding school was good for me. I have no memory of Audrey being in similar need. But the parents had also been to boarding school and presumably felt, along with many of their kind, that this was the right thing to do. I have to agree with them, though what is the right age to start remains debateable. To fill the gap between the eleven-plus entry to a grammar school and the thirteen-plus entry to an English boarding school, Audrey was sent for two years to the Manor House School, near Armagh. It was a success, I think, but she had always been destined for an English school as a boarder, and along with a fair number of Northern Ireland girls she was sent to Wycombe Abbey – a much better choice for her, I have to say, than Sedbergh was for me. Ever since she went there, it has gone from strength to strength, and is now one of the top two or three girls' schools in the country. Not only did she get good A Levels but she also captained the school tennis team and became an Irish lacrosse international.

She was always quick across the ground. My earliest recollection of her turn of speed was being in a field at Trumroe in Castlepollard on the family farm, helping my dad move sheep or cattle, and seeing her (aged perhaps five or six) travelling at little short of the speed of light down the road, screaming blue murder at the top of her voice. When I intercepted her (I'd never have caught her in a month of Sundays) she told me 'the man picked up a big stone and was going to murder me'. I instantly caught the panic, and my father who had been in the field with me arrived to find both of us hysterical. He took us to confront 'the man', who turned out to be an entirely friendly native, who had indeed picked up a big stone to wedge open the gate of the field to enable my dad to drive the cattle into the next one. I remained indignant that Dad seemed to find the whole episode rather funny; the man was simply bemused. I was already protective of my little sister – and I like to think that I have always tried to be thereafter. But her powers of acceleration clearly never left her and she represented Ireland on the wing, if I remember rightly, though sadly I never got a chance to see it.

We were both good at games, but neither of us sufficiently motivated to practise much, certainly not hard enough to win significant honours. Games in our day had yet to become the way to riches or celebrity and it would not have occurred to my generation that they might become a career in themselves. Of this I am glad, because for me the arrival of big money and professional sportsmen has destroyed the pleasure of watching competitive sport, where the participants seem all out to win at any cost, including too often surreptitious cheating, professional fouls, or disrupting an opponent's concentration by loud grunts with every shot or tantrums at the umpire. I am all for trying flat out to win when on the field of play, but I still believe in sportsmanship and prefer the principle that it is not the winning but the taking part that really matters. Only golf and billiards seem to me to have managed to retain the principles of gentlemanly conduct and sporting behaviour, which all true games players believe in. We played regularly in the annual tennis tournaments held by local golf and tennis clubs; we also played family golf (Mum and I versus Dad and Audrey) at the Royal Belfast Golf Club and also on holidays at Greencastle in Donegal, and unlike family bridge this could be good fun. As a family we were extraordinarily unadventurous in our holidays compared with what families do nowadays; but Dad needed just to switch off. Foreign holidays can be very stressful. He always took a month in the summer, of which the first fortnight did no more than start the path to recovery from the stresses of his work. Golf, swimming, picnics and exploring the countryside seemed to suit the parents well and we never ventured abroad. It was all very wholesome but hardly stimulating.

What took Audrey into nursing I know not, except that medicine was part of the family business, not only Father and Mother, but also further back in the Gregg family, where the women tended towards the caring professions. But she has always been a sympathetic and caring person, as well as immensely practical and competent at anything she turned her hand to, though I think she would acknowledge that she lacks my academic inclinations. Of course only the best would do, so training at St Thomas' Nightingale School was the obvious decision. All the best people went there!

The matron, Miss Turner, suggested that she took the Integrated Nurse/Health Visitor Course, as it involved university life, which she felt that Audrey would enjoy. She did, spending a very happy initial year in the Faculty of Health and Social Services at Southampton University, studying all aspects of health and public health, a course which she found fascinating.

The year gave her the opportunity to pursue her love of sport, and she gained her blue for lacrosse and half blue for tennis. She was thrilled to be selected to play for the Combined English University Lacrosse Team, which gave her a chance to play matches all over England. Hardly surprisingly, her practical efficiency and good sense also saw her appointed to the Committee of the Student Nurses Representative Council of which she became chairman in 1962–3.

This year was followed by three and a half years' nursing and obstetric training at St Thomas', before she returned for a rather dull nine months at Southampton to complete the health visitor qualification. Following this, she spent a year at the Royal Maternity Hospital, Belfast, to do her full maternity training, at a time when it was safe to cycle through any part of Belfast, day or night, delivering babies at home. While working at the Royal Maternity, and in bed with glandular fever, she received the news that she had been the top medallist of her year, and would receive it from the Queen Mother, to whom she would give the vote of thanks. She was made to work extra hours to earn the two days off to fly to London for this memorable occasion. Things never change!

Of her experiences she said little, but I believe that she regarded the health visitor qualification as simply a useful addition to her general nursing qualifications, though it was never her intention to practise as a health visitor. In due course she was back at St Thomas' and following as far as she could in her father's footsteps by specialising in surgery and becoming a theatre sister on Lockart Mummery's famous 'firm'. I have already mentioned her remarkable turn of speed, which in that august establishment soon earned her the nickname of Speedy Gonzales, or the Atomic Bomb. But they must have thought highly of her professionally, since in due course she was given a scholarship to travel for three months in America looking at theatre practice and writing a report for the hospital trustees. It enabled her also to re-establish contact in Boston with our Wilson cousins, Sybil and Stuart Strong, and that link has remained fresh ever since.

Cometh the hour; cometh the man.

I know little of the circumstances that brought Alastair Macafee and Audrey back into contact, but our much loved vicar and later bishop, George Quin, may have had something to do with it. After her scholarship to America, he arranged an evening gathering of young people so that Audrey could give a talk and slide show about her experiences. He purposely invited Alastair to attend, and made a particular point of introducing them. *Sicut columbae, sicut serpentes.* The rest followed – very slowly. But in the end it was the greatest source of joy to all the families on both sides when they announced their engagement. Alastair himself was (or was about to become) a consultant orthopaedic surgeon at the Ulster Hospital, Dundonald, and at the Musgrave Park Orthopaedic Unit in Belfast, and ultimately President (1995–97) of the Irish Orthopaedic Association, and then President of the Northern Ireland Medico-Legal Society (1997–98).

He was one of the old school of medical practitioners, whose patience and concern for his patients was to be seen not only in his healing skills but also his willingness to spend time with them, getting to know and understand them, to allay their concerns, and to treat them as human beings, not (as seems to be the modern practice) as 'units' on a factory production line, to be passed through the system as fast as possible in order to meet the latest and ever-changing targets imposed by an image-conscious, media-obsessed government. He was much admired and loved by all with whom he came in contact. That my rigorously old-fashioned father took to him immediately says much for the traditional principles with which he practised his craft.

I saw at first hand one example of his skill and human qualities at work. One of my pupils at Campbell College was caught in a practice scrum and suffered a broken neck. Paralysis was initially total. Fortunately the master coaching was one of our qualified PE instructors and he took all the correct initial precautions. Alastair was the consultant on duty at the local Ulster Hospital that day. The prognosis for such dire accidents is not particularly good and I have heard perfectly sensible people say that they would rather their children took drugs than learned to play rugger, such a dangerous game has it now become. Alastair manipulated the neck back into place and immobilised the patient, who for six months was in bed under traction. Ever so slowly feeling and mobility of limbs returned. I visited him at least once a week in the Musgrave Park Hospital, and his courage and stoicism were remarkable. His parents were wonderfully supportive too. The combination of determined patient, family support, and remarkable surgeon restored him to health. He got to Cambridge; stroked his college second VIII, and became (if I remember rightly) an official in the Patents Office. It was a wonderful story from which, I think, everyone came out with credit.

Alastair came of good stock, medical and judicial. His father, 'Prof' Macafee (Charles Horner Greer Macafee, to give him his full appellation) was by now retired, but had been a deeply loved and much admired Professor (subsequently Emeritus) of Obstetrics and Gynaecology at Queen's University, widely honoured within and outside the profession. He was made a CBE, a Deputy Lieutenant, an Honorary DSc (Leeds) and LL.D (Belfast), and an Honorary Fellow of the Royal College of Physicians of Ireland. He was known and loved throughout the province, and it sometimes seemed as if he had personally delivered half the children in Ulster, to judge by those who claimed to have had him in attendance at their own or their children's birth. He was a wonderful and wise old man, who talked with warmth, generosity, and humanity of his work and those to whom he had ministered. It was entirely characteristic that when he was widowed he retired to the small cottage in the garden of his home in Donaghadee, and handed over the house, Stramore Lodge, to Alastair and Audrey. There he remained, looked after by 'Nanny' Sey, a real personality, loved and admired by all who knew her, who had been the family nanny for fifty-seven years. She acted as his resident housekeeper until his death. Nanny remained in the cottage, watched over by Alastair and Audrey for another twelve years, until in failing health and almost blind, she decided to move into the local residential home in Donagadee, where she was wonderfully looked after and greatly loved by all the very caring staff. She lived there happily for another five years.

I never met Alastair's mother, Margaret Crymble (née Lowry), daughter of a famous Ulster medical name, Professor Charles Gibson Lowry (1890–1951), sometime Pro-Vice Chancellor of Queen's University and Professor of Obstetrics and Gynaecology at both the Royal Victoria Hospital, Belfast, and the Royal Maternity Hospital, which he was instrumental in establishing. On retirement he was made Emeritus Professor and subsequently Pro-Vice Chancellor of Queen's University. By a strange coincidence he received an honorary DSc from Queen's on the same day (8 July 1949) as my grandfather, Archbishop Gregg, received an honorary Doctorate of Divinity and we have a photograph of the occasion from the Belfast Telegraph Newspaper Library. Had they known, while sharing the same platform, that their respective grandson and granddaughter would unite the two families and that they would one day share the same grandchildren, it would have delighted beyond measure these two ornaments of their respective professions. C G Lowry's brother was at one time Home Secretary in the Northern Ireland Parliament and subsequently a high court judge. His son, Robbie, was to become Lord Chief Justice of Northern Ireland and then a Lord of Appeal in London.

Margaret, though something of an invalid in later life, shared the remarkable Macafee gift of inspiring love and affection in all who knew her. She even seemed to approve of Audrey, and that in a potential mother-in-law is a remarkable testimony to the qualities of both parties. Indeed Alistair tells me that she could lay claim to a place on my matrimonial scouting team. One of the last things she said to him, having recently met Audrey, was that, 'You should get to know her.' I'd been saying the same thing for years to her.

Alastair has a brother and a sister. His sister Anne, who had the bad luck to be a severe diabetic, was also a product of Rannie's in Eastbourne. She married David Mahood, a high-powered business man, with whom I was once a pupil at Mourne Grange. Jeremy, Alastair's brother, was a consultant obstetrician and gynaecologist, working in Leicester. He married Anne Sawyers and they had two children, Ian and Andrew. Five years after her death he was married again, to Doreen Hunter, recently retired as headmistress of Princess Gardens, now renamed Hunterhouse after an amalgamation with Ashleigh House, the school with which I had hoped that Campbell would effect a union.

Alastair and Audrey were married on 18 September 1970. I have already described the problems created by my headmaster at King's, which all but prevented me attending. Despite his efforts at obstruction, we got there in good time, with Anna aged five weeks, charming the local policemen who searched her carry-cot for bombs (we were into the Troubles by then) and then guarded her while we went to the church for the ceremony, which was conducted by dear George Quin, now a bishop and wearing (no doubt at my mother's request) my grandfather's pectoral cross for the occasion. George was as it happened also a governor of Campbell College, and married to Nora, a relative of the Macafee family. It was a lovely day and we had a good traditional wedding, a service, a marquee in the 'field' in the front garden of Ballycrenan, champagne, speeches, tea and cake – and away. Modern weddings by contrast have turned into marathons, as the party and the celebrations have increasingly tended to become more important than the marriage ceremony, while stag and hen parties have become as protracted as a Japanese water torture. No doubt in time this fashion, like all temporary phenomena, will change back again, when the appeal of simplicity reasserts itself. My speech proposing the toast of the bride was adequate to the occasion I hope, since years later it led to an invitation from Gavin Boyd to make an after-dinner speech at the Queen's Association Dinner, of which he was President at the time. As soon as I had finished, one guest, a rather humourless government minister, left claiming a pressing engagement. Whether the two events were connected I do not know, but I seem to remember I allowed myself some light-hearted though critical asides about government policy.

Within five years they had four children, all under four years of age at one point. Jeremy went to Campbell and on to Leicester, where after an initial foray into medicine, he returned to Queen's University, Belfast where he studied for his degree in physics and maths, following that with his PGCE. He has remained faithful to his Ulster origins all his life. He joined the staff of Bangor Grammar School, before abandoning the profession for the time being in disenchantment, fully understandably. He turned to financial planning and advice, passed all the necessary financial examinations in six months – one of the fastest ever – and is now a partner in a firm of financial advisers.

Margaret went to Strathearn and then on to St Leonard's in St Andrews, where she was head of house and got a Duke of Edinburgh Gold award, before going on to take a BSc degree in psychology at Newcastle University. She followed this with an MSc in occupational psychology at Nottingham, staying on at the university to manage a two-year study commissioned by the BMA. She then moved into the private sector, focussing on organisational development, ultimately joining the Bernard Hodes Group as their only in-house psychologist, with responsibilities in recruitment, psychometric profiling for senior appointments, and other such infernal complexities of modern recruitment practice. She is now working in the London Office of Kenexa, specialising in organisational development, dividing her time, she tells me, 'between global survey and talent management practices' and in 'the development of bespoke candidate assessment instruments'.

Of the twins, Barbara had a very successful early education at Glenlola Collegiate, where her musical and sporting talents were given a chance to flourish.

She then joined Margaret at St Leonard's for a short spell, before returning to Northern Ireland for her A Levels at Methodist College, Belfast, thus taking advantage of Northern Ireland's superb grammar school system. She returned also to her previous music teachers and gained Grade 8 in both flute and piano, while continuing also to play the violin. She went on to Dundee University, where she gained a BSc in physiology before switching to medicine, and then specialised in anaesthetics. She played tennis and hockey for university teams and was an enthusiastic member of the OTC for seven years. She is now a registrar in Belfast and has just crossed the critical hurdle in career progression by being awarded her National Training Number in anaesthetics, which could open the door to a consultant's post in due course, if all goes well.

David went to Eastbourne College, where he became head boy and went on to follow the family tradition at Nottingham University, reading medicine. He is now a senior registrar working in the Newcastle group of hospitals, specialising in colorectal surgery. He has gained his DM and is working for his Diploma in Medical Education, a subject in which he has a particular interest — hardly surprising in view of his genetic inheritance. He has also just become engaged to Vicky Ewan, a Specialist Registrar in Microbiology, and the wedding is planned for 31 March 2007, in Corbridge. We'll all be there (DV).

Of their views about modern medical training the less said the better.

With a 50% success rate in supplying the profession with its next generation of practitioners, Audrey and Alastair can be well satisfied that they have kept up the family tradition.

For me one of the nicest things about returning to Ulster in 1977 was that it allowed our children to get to know their four cousins. It was something the lack of which I have always been conscious and I am so glad that for Anna and Emma this deficiency has been made good. Living at a mere ten miles distance, and being of similar ages, they were able to see quite a lot of each other and they have all remained great friends to this day. For my mother, too, it was the greatest joy to be living close to Audrey and to be able to see and spoil her six grandchildren – which is the sacred duty of all grandparents, almost as important as knowing the names of all the 'really useful' engines who work with Thomas the Tank Engine, and how to operate a DVD remote control. When we all gathered at Stramore from time to time, it was amidst a lovely feeling of family harmony and undiluted happiness. I just wish my father had lived a little longer and been able to share more of our delight.

We all managed to fly over for Jeremy's wedding to Adele Boyle in July 2005, and this time we had no problems in joining them the evening before for a family celebration, or in staying for the wedding breakfast at the Culloden Hotel afterwards, currently listed in the top thirty hotels in Britain for weddings. We were staying there as well, in great comfort and with no problems about driving home afterwards. It was a wonderfully happy family occasion and reminded us, if reminder was needed, how important and enriching family connections can be.

In retirement now, and far too far away from us across that tiresome piece of water, which has always separated the members of our family, Audrey and Alastair remain as busy as ever. She has been inveigled into becoming the Lady Captain of the Royal Belfast Golf Club, of which she must have now been a member for over fifty years, as well as doing all her other good works, like helping to run the library in the Ulster Hospital and acting as a member of the committee of the local Abbeyfield Home for the Elderly. *En passant*, she also maintains their enormous garden, including a kitchen garden large enough to feed an army.

Alastair continues to keep up his medical connection by writing reports for law firms and insurance companies. He has meanwhile turned his hand to turning wood, and from time to time small ashtrays, bowls, birds, letter-openers, and other such delightful gewgaws made of exotic woods come our way, which we reciprocate by finding other examples of local wood-turners' craft to send him as additional challenges to his skill. They both play golf all over the globe, as far as I can see.

We both grow old disgracefully in tandem, each exercising our old man's time-honoured privilege of asserting to all who are prepared to listen that things are going from bad to worse, that the government has gone mad (which I suspect it has), that our respective professions are being ruined by the new generation, who haven't the slightest idea of standards or principles, and that in effect it has never been the same since the old Queen died.

Plus ça change, plus c'est la même chose.

CHAPTER 22

From Eastbourne to Campbell College

They are not long, the time of wine and roses

Anon.

There is a tide in the affairs of men
Which, taken at the flood, leads on to fortune;
Omitted, all the voyage of their life
Is bound in shallows and in miseries.
On such a full sea are we now afloat,
And we must take the current when it serves,
Or lose our ventures.

Shakespeare, Julius Caesar

CHAPTERS 20 AND 21 HAVE BEEN something of an excursus, hardly a digression, in which I have allowed myself to defy chronological order and cover the activities of our children and my sister's family, both of them far too cursorily to do them justice, but I hope adequately enough to give a sense of comprehensive coverage to my account of our families. In due course perhaps another generation may decide to continue the story in rather more substantive detail and even produce a second volume.

It is now time to return to the central theme. It is extraordinary to me that lines of verse learned at school should have such a profound capacity to influence one's approach to life and decision-making. I am sure my inherent pessimism, which has always seemed to reflect the outlook on life purveyed by the Greek tragedians, stems from my classical studies. Beware of hubris; appease the gods; look always to the ending; count no man happy till he is dead. Whenever things appear to have gone well, I have always had a pair of fingers crossed, metaphorically speaking, lest a jealous Fury or a chance impediment should make me stumble. I always expect misfortune to follow hard on the heels of good fortune. Temperamentally it prepares one for the worst, but it can also prevent one enjoying the best when it comes.

Other pieces of inherited wisdom derive from different sources. The passage at the top of this chapter from Shakespeare's *Julius Caesar*, has always been carried in my mind since prep school days when I was Casca ('speak hands for me') in the school production. Though uttered by Brutus to Cassius and though both were losers, it has always seemed the soundest of advice. He who hesitates is indeed quite often lost. So one side of me is usually ready to seize an opportunity when I see it, even if momentarily and in contradiction to my classics-based hesitations, it involves throwing my natural caution to the winds, and I suffer agonies of anxiety before any realisation. But I could never go the whole hog, as advocated by Rudyard Kipling in his much quoted poem, 'If',

> If you can make one heap of all your winnings
>   And risk it on one turn of pitch-an-toss,
> And lose, and start again at your beginnings
>   And never breathe a word about your loss; . . .

I would rather bank my winnings a little too early, as I tend to do on the stock market, leaving the final 10% to the other fellow, as they say. I would find it well nigh impossible to gamble my all. But sometimes you have to take the decision to go where Fortune seems to beckon. Going to Eastbourne College was a relatively easy decision; applying for and then accepting the offer of the headship of Campbell College was much more finely balanced, and with hindsight quite possibly a mistake, though it brought enormous pleasures with it as well as disappointments. In each case I took the plunge, and Sara, God bless her, came with me without a murmur of complaint.

In 1973 Simon Langdale, then a housemaster at Radley, was appointed headmaster of Eastbourne College. The two schools had always been close, ever since during the World War II Eastbourne had asked Radley to give them shelter, because they had to be evacuated from the south coast. Radley had replied 'yes' by return of telegram, and the relationship was cemented over the years by the fact that after the war their teams had continued to do battle in cricket and rugby.

Out of the blue I received a letter from Simon asking me if I would join his staff as head of classics and (after one term) as director of studies. This latter appointment was the clincher; I would not have gone as head of classics, simply because it was a declining subject and at Eastbourne a small department in a not very academic school. Compared with a housemastership at King's, which still had a strong Classical Sixth, it would have been a retrograde step. But with the added brief of trying to help stimulate an academic revival the proposition became much more attractive, and I said, 'yes' with little hesitation. Newell, my lord and master, was furious because, as he saw it, Simon was poaching his staff 'without the courtesy of asking'. He fumed and said he might go to the HMC, but I doubt if he would have done so. The more irritated he was, the more pleased I was. Relations were at a low ebb. There was no pleasure in working for him and I was glad to depart. As Brutus remarks to Lucilius, also in *Julius Caesar*, when he describes Cassius' lack of the 'free and friendly conference as he hath used of old',

> Thou hast described
> A hot friend cooling. Ever note, Lucilius,
> When love begins to sicken and decay,
> It uses an enforced ceremony.
> There are no tricks in plain and simple faith;

> But hollow men, like horses hot at hand,
> Make gallant show and promise of their mettle:
> But when they should endure the bloody spur,
> They fall their crests, and like deceitful jades
> Sink in the trial.

I do not think my performance had declined quite so far; after all, professional pride and commitment to my pupils demanded that I kept going till the end. But the zest and enthusiasm was gone, and I am sure it was in everybody's interest that I should take the current when it served and depart.

The college has now become fully coeducational; but at that time it already took girls in the sixth form and had a sufficient number of them (about sixty) to be more than just a token presence. Of the civilising effect of their presence on the boys I have no doubts, and despite inevitable differences of temperament and mental processes, I think it was good for the girls too. There can be problems if staff with dinosaur tendencies cannot adapt to their presence, as I felt happened in the science department when Emma went there some years later as a sixth former; but in general the whole place was a delight to work in – doubly so after the stresses of King's Canterbury. The presence of a substantial number of day-boys was also beneficial. The school's approach was to encourage them to take a full share in school life; they stayed and did prep in their houses after formal lessons; there were facilities for them to live in as boarders if their parents were away; they really had almost the best of both worlds – they were virtual boarders, but lived at home and so never lost touch with family life as well. Their presence was an additional touch of 'normality' in the somewhat artificial life of a boarding school.

By contrast with Newell, working for Simon was undiluted pleasure. He was an old friend, for a start, since he had been secretary of the Cambridge Fives Club when I won my place in the team. I was godfather to his daughter, Philippa, now a very distinguished freelance producer for the BBC and ITV. I had been an usher at his wedding to Diana. I had always admired the clarity of his thinking and strategic sense, as well as the tactical skills he brought to any sport he turned his hand to. Like Winnie Ther Pooh, my old hero, he liked to Think About Things. He always knew where he was going and how he was to get there. In addition, despite some very tough decisions, his personal relations with staff were as excellent as Newell's were bad. I was to discover also that he always delivered on his promises. In Diana, too, he had a wonderful helpmate and support. All the wives and families of the school instantly became part of her family, and her interest in everyone and everything was genuine and generous.

It is almost impossible to describe the pleasure and relief of finding oneself in a welcoming and friendly environment. The school had gone through a crisis, which had led to the departure of both head and his deputy, for reasons which I never understood, and into which there was no need to enquire. But it meant that Simon at least was welcomed with open arms, though I felt there was a degree of initial surprise at my coming in on the coat-tails of the new regime. But until my appointment as director of studies was made public, somewhere around half-way through that first term, there were no grounds for any serious suspicion. Simon's rationale for my appointment was generous in the extreme. He knew that his forte lay on the pastoral side and was kind enough to pretend at least that I was a better academic and would usefully complement his own abilities by trying to stimulate improved academic performance.

One of the features of the school that made it such a pleasant place to be was that it was (to use John Major's famous phrase) 'comfortable in its own skin'. Like any school, it had strengths and weaknesses. The major weakness was perhaps a very understandable complacency. The staff were comfortable; the boys and girls extremely pleasant; the plant was well maintained and the bursar ran a very tight ship; it was all very civilised. Inevitably there were some issues of discipline to be addressed – when are there not? – but in this area Simon was firm, fair, and consistent. It was a difficult time for all independent schools and increasingly sophisticated comparisons of performance were beginning to be made, so that it was essential to get, and be seen to get, good results not only academically but across the board.

My particular task was to look at the academic side and try to improve it. In such circumstances it is important first to define the problem. Exhortation to 'do better' is not going to help, if everyone thinks they are doing pretty well already. The memorable phrase used to me by one housemaster was that 'we may not be very good with the clever boys; but we do an excellent job with the ordinary ones'. Such a sentiment can be the kiss of death, not least because, if it becomes public perception, it is self-destructive. Parents will not send you bright pupils, the average quality declines, results quickly slide and you come to seem not very good for any pupils. I felt that if I could get a consensus that 'we could do better', that would be more than half the battle, since a problem acknowledged is half-way to being a problem solved, provided that you have conscientious staff and professional pride.

But the assertion 'could do better' needs to be underpinned by evidence with a reasonable claim to objectivity. In the same way, I have always felt that on pupils' reports the unelaborated statement 'could do better' is the sure sign of a lazy teacher who can't be bothered to think out precisely where deficiencies lie; it is also an insult to parents. It must be backed up by information about specific areas of weaknesses to which the judgement applies, and suggested remedies. I wanted, therefore, to find a way of deciding how good, or bad, we were for all our pupils, whether bright or not so bright.

So I set about trying to devise a system for evaluating 'value added' (though I did not call it that) long before it became the fashionable criterion of excellence in schools generally (this was still only 1973). We gave a general IQ test to all boys at entry and these I collated with their Common Entrance results, the one as a measure of natural ability, the other partly at least as a rough and ready measure of motivation. This matters almost more than ability, but rarely seems to be mentioned and is never assessed objectively. I even wrote to the NFER to ask if, as well as their IQ tests, they had a general test for motivation and attitude. I suspected that they had, but were not willing to release it to an 'amateur' like me. Professional psychologists had cornered this particular market. So I had to make do with exam results (Common Entrance and then O Level) as a crude measure of a willingness to work at a syllabus, and therefore to some degree at least evidence of motivation. I then correlated the IQ and CE results against the ISCO (Independent Schools' Careers Organisation) test results in the fifth form. These measured aptitudes, interests, and abilities for use with career planning. With O Level results as well I had a reasonable battery of information from which to try and predict future A Level results and to calculate what I estimated would be acceptable results for the year group as a whole.

Testing and ratification of prediction is the basis of all scientific method, and I was attempting to be 'scientific' (however crudely) in my approach to the problem of assessing performance. But the methodology was unproven and best presented as a performance indicator and not definitive. Later at Campbell College I used the same system with which to assess an even more disparate ability range. I once managed to predict our A Level performance to within 0.5% of the outcome. It could be a useful tool with which to persuade anxious governors that results were not necessarily as bad as they sometimes seemed.

As long as such assessments seemed credible, they could then be used to set targets within subject departments, if their heads so wished, and at least could be used as a basis for discussion if there were anxieties. I had not the nerve, and would not have wished, to insist in those early days that they should be mandatory. I was devising a tool for improvement; not a gun to hold at people's heads. I am not a great believer in hiring and firing, in the macho manner of captains of industry, where such aggressive treatment of employees may gratify an oversized personal ego, but does little for morale or the self-respect of the individual or their colleagues. Within the independent sector at least, most staff are extremely conscientious and hard-working and want to do well by their pupils. If they were not, they would not be in such a job. If they can see, objectively, that performance should improve they will usually seek to make the necessary improvement and often seek help in doing so.

More important for the immediate task was the fact that I had the ISCO results and subsequent A Level results from King's Canterbury, and managed to get hold of a set for Manchester Grammar School. These gave me a 'control' of sorts against two schools of known academic excellence. Though by then my loyalties were entirely with Eastbourne, I was forced to recognise that of the three, MGS had the brightest pupils overall, King's probably had the best results for boys of any given level of ability, and Eastbourne the worst results not only for the bright boys

The Cambridge University Rugby Fives Team 1960. L to R (standing): Antony Hole, Peter Mitton, Stuart Tovey, David Sharman; (seated): Michael Allen, Brian Wilson (Captain), Jock Burnet (President), Richard Morgan (Hon Sec), David Beevers

Tankard won by Grandfather in 1896 in the Cambridge Rugby Fives Doubles Tournament. Beside it, the last 'real' Fives ball made by Jeffreys Malings, master craftsman, given to the author by Jock Burnet

The King's School, Canterbury, ca. 1970. Norman staircase leading to Maugham Library. (An oil painting purchased by the author at a local exhibition)

Sara – pastel by Juliet Pannett, 1966

Anne Neilsen Trist (Sara's sister) – pastel by Juliet Pannett

Sara Remington Hollins – engagement photograph, 1969

Arthur Remington Hollins, Sara's Grandfather. Chairman and Managing Director of Wm Hollins & Co (1916–1923)

The Wm Hollins Mills at Pleasley Vale, Derbyshire. (Photo by permission of the Bolsover District Council)

The Vale House, Pleasley Vale. The Manager's House, where Sara's father grew up

*Ted Hollins, Sara's Father, with his brother Dick Hollins and friend.
Was the car his beloved Hispano Suiza?*

Two Hollins Weddings

Ted Hollins marries Jane Fennell, 1936

Ted Hollins (in the same morning suit) gives away his daughter Sara, 1969

but also for the less bright. I say 'boys' deliberately, because girls at that stage only came in at sixth form level and there was limited evidence on which to work, since what mattered was the value added from the bottom of the school to the top. After Emma's experience fifteen years later, had I been director of studies, I would have been working hard to find a method of assessing value added for the girls over the brief two years they were in the school.

I was satisfied that academic performance was a problem and some of my colleagues at least were able to agree. With a small working party of the more dynamic and enlightened heads of department, we worked out a plan of campaign for improvement, the details of which have long since escaped my memory. But the school has gone from strength to strength academically and I would like to persuade myself that I contributed in a small way to that advance.

The classics was a more difficult problem. In this modern age no one could expect a school to find room in the timetable to allow pupils the time to master the essentials of the two languages in the way they used to do in the 'good old days'. I was very much engaged in the attempts at the national level to modernise the ancient history syllabus and make it more academically convincing. Latin was another problem. The new Cambridge Latin Course was a serious and not unsuccessful attempt to bring the study of the language within the reach of average pupils with average timetable allowances. We committed ourselves to it wholeheartedly, with encouraging results in pupil enjoyment and morale. But the course needed quite a lot of refinement. Each unit was meant to take a year. The first unit was brilliant and pupils felt they were making good progress. By the time they reached Unit 3, the level of difficulty and rate of progression had increased unrealistically, and they found they had too much to learn in too little time. Nevertheless, it was a rewarding course to teach and some at least went on to O Level. Unfortunately it was not an entirely adequate foundation for A Levels.

Following my usual practice, I became an O Level examiner so as to see how to improve our performance and get some idea of how other schools were coping. The difficulties faced by some state schools, teaching in break-times and after normal hours made my own difficulties seem somewhat less compelling. At the heart of the problem, however, was the fact that under modern conditions classics was too hard a subject except for the very bright, and the only hope for those interested but less able was to study it in translation, whether as classical civilisation or ancient history. They would then hope to take up the languages at university, helped by the wonderful crash courses run by the JACT summer schools at Cheltenham. In the medium-term I could see little hope for the subject in schools except at a few centres of excellence. I taught the classical civilisation course later at St Mary's Wantage, and found it most rewarding – indeed, teaching the whole of Homer in translation, instead of two or three set books in the Greek, meant that almost for the first time I could teach it as a complete work of literature. To that extent the crisis in the classics has been beneficial.

I also covered for a year as a stand-in careers master for an ill colleague. I found it a most interesting experience. I knew too little to be of any real help to pupils, beyond running the office, helping with the ISCO careers assessments, setting up interviews with ISCO advisers, but it certainly taught me a lot about careers choice and advice. It had not even existed in my school-days, but has advanced dramatically, and now skills and aptitudes testing can help to steer a pupil into a realistic assessment of the most promising options for his or her abilities and interests. It was an area that caught my interest and encouraged me when I got to Campbell College to try to set up really good work experience projects, to join the British Institute of Management, and to serve on local committees of school heads and industrialists.

I had promised Simon that I would serve at least three years at Eastbourne, provided that, if Sedbergh came on the market, I could apply for the headship without recrimination. I had always wanted to return as head. The chapter on my experiences there as a boy will make clear that I felt it was ripe for change and that I would have liked to try and lead that change. My old house tutor and friend, the school's senior chaplain, Austin Boggis, wrote to me and urged me to have a go. He was a lovely man, though not everybody's cup of tea. He had introduced me by osmosis and a very loud radiogram to Gigli and *La Bohème* years before, and remained a friend till the end of his life. When Sara and I discovered Malham for short holidays, we used to visit him in later years at Beamsmoore, his nursing home near Sedbergh. He was largely incapacitated, but wonderfully philosophical about his situation, and I felt an affection for him, which I had felt for few others at that school. I applied for the headship; was interviewed; disliked the committee of rather grizzled old governors as much as they clearly disliked me; and that was that. Given the problems of the ensuing years, which were shared by many independent schools, I was probably well out of it. But I am glad to learn of its improving fortunes and coeducational character under Chris Hirst, yet another head from the Radley stable.

Towards the end of my time there was only one major excitement, for want of a better word, which genuinely disturbed the even tenor of our way. It was a major policy decision, with which I wholeheartedly agreed, but which massively upset the traditionalists. The decision was taken by Simon and the governors to close Ascham, the very successful college prep school, and to sell off for development the entire estate in the Meads, the most fashionable and expensive end of Eastbourne. The proceeds of the sale would be enough to finance the ongoing development of the college and provide a substantial endowment for future years. When I see the number of houses that have been crammed into the area, I am sure both college and builder made a small fortune. There was a second no less successful and marginally more fashionable prep school in the town, St Andrew's, also in the Meads, and a good relationship existed with them. The fear of a loss of pupils could therefore be discounted. At one time an attached prep school could be a reliable source of new pupils, but there was an increasing tendency, for perfectly good financial reasons, for parents to be rather more flexible about their loyalties than in the past and the old arguments did not carry as much weight as once they did. The event (which took place largely after my time) seems to have justified a brave decision.

After the Sedbergh setback, I completed my promised minimum of three years and really loved every minute of it. We were a happy family, living and working among friends, in a pleasant seaside holiday town with good amenities, and in a school that was clearly progressing. I was in no hurry to move, but I kept my eye on *The Times* (never the ghastly and depressing *Times Educational Supplement*) for advertisements for the headship of likely schools. Almost the first one to catch my eye was Campbell College, Belfast.

Surprisingly, I had only once set foot in its grounds, and that was when (introduced by a mutual friend) I went to talk to John Cook, the headmaster, about my own future and the possibility of a classics teaching post. He was a lovely man, and a fellow classicist, and I liked him instantly. But he said that though he would like to offer me a job, he would advise me very strongly against accepting it. He very wisely did not expand upon his reasons. Beyond that brief encounter, I knew very little about the place. Mourne Grange, my prep school, played matches against Cabin Hill, the college prep school, in every possible sport – and we were usually soundly beaten, since they were a far larger school with better resources. We all knew from legend and old magazines of a famous defeat at rugger of 120–0. They always seemed fearsomely large and well coached to all of us. But my only knowledge of the senior school was the typical snobbery of prep school boys at Mourne Grange, whose clientele usually headed for England or Scotland, that 'you only go to Campbell if you can't get in anywhere else'. Only later was I to learn of Samuel Beckett's cruel observation that 'Campbell boys were the cream of Ulster – and like cream, rich and thick'. It certainly was not true of the school I was to join, where there were some very bright students, thanks to the fact that it now had a grammar school intake.

Certain factors seemed likely to be favourable to my candidature. Campbell was, to the best of my knowledge, the leading public school in Northern Ireland (I will briefly describe the Ulster Grammar School system later); it would be a good launch pad after seven to ten years for what I ultimately wanted, which was a major English public school (Ronald Groves had gone on to Dulwich, for example). I was an Ulsterman who knew the province; I had worked in the independent sector in England and had reasonably good experience on both the pastoral and the academic side, which I assumed would be attractive to them; I was fully aware of the Troubles, then at their height, but had continued to visit my family in Helen's Bay and knew that the east (Protestant) side of Belfast was relatively peaceful – I was therefore less deterred than many potential English competitors would have been; the field was likely to be less competitive than under more normal circumstances; at a personal level, my parents were not getting any younger, and it would be nice to be a bit closer after a lifetime of working 'across the water'. I had discharged my side of the bargain with Simon and could apply without feeling that I had let him down. It looked to be, if not providential, at least something worth exploring further.

I was a bit naïve and had I known then what I gradually learned later, I would have done a lot more homework before committing myself. I should perhaps have been mildly surprised at the speed with which everything happened, with no first round interviews – simply a 'final'. But for the governors time was obviously short and it seemed perfectly understandable. The post was advertised late in the summer term of 1976 and interviews took place in the summer holidays, without the presence of the incumbent head to brief the candidates; the appointment was for January 1977.

For good or ill, I threw my hat in the ring, my references were taken up, and Sara and I were summoned for interview – Sara with a cruelly infected knee, heavily bandaged and taken to the plane in a wheelchair, which encouraged a degree of gallant sympathy from our hosts. Fellow competitors, of whom there were five I think, included myself, Gerald Vinestock, a fellow and contemporary old Sedberghian; Robin Tughan, the Vice Principal of the College, who later went on to a very distinguished career as head of the Rainey Endowed School in Magherafelt; and Luther Vye, the head of the college prep school, Cabin Hill. The field, as I had suspected, had been limited. Luther Vye was, I believed, the candidate to beat, an Oxford Hockey Blue, who had taught at Rossall and then been a very successful head of Cabin Hill for a number of years, much loved by all who knew him, and in Margaret, blessed with a wonderfully supportive wife. I saw a lot of him and Robin Tughan in the succeeding years, and it is a mark of their generosity of spirit that we remained good friends and they were never less than totally supportive.

We were shown round the school before the interviews and I must admit I was pretty shaken by its run-down condition and general dilapidation, and especially by the inadequacy of accommodation for boarding housemasters. The presence of ten 'temporary' classrooms making a sort of hutted encampment on the main square was unappealing. But they had been brought in to replace those lost by the sale of the junior boarding house, Ormiston, as a police headquarters, because its location on the wrong side of a busy main road was unsafe and unsatisfactory. So there were at least good reasons for their presence. A long Nissen hut on the far side of the square was an ugly hangover from the war, when Campbell had been a military hospital, but that was now thirty-two years ago, and it was still being used as a base for the CCF; the general state of the paintwork everywhere was poor; the courtyard leading to the boys' main entrance was a mud patch; the 'dump' which must have occupied five or six acres of potentially valuable land was a mess; the lake and its surrounds neglected – all these things were suggestive of poor finances and inevitable economies. I have a tendency to be brutally direct, when tact may be the better approach, but when asked my impressions of the school I said, honestly, that I thought it looked pretty run-down. It may well have been the answer the governors wanted.

I was asked about discipline and replied – naturally – that I was in favour of it (my homework having told me that local gossip suggested the school had a poor reputation for discipline). But I remain cautious about school reputations for indiscipline for reasons I have given before. I read, I think, in the history of Radley under Denis Silk – surely one of the most efficiently disciplined schools in the country in that period – that there were worries at one time about discipline even there. All schools have similar complaints virtually all the time, especially from governors who spend too much time listening to golf-club bar gossip, and from a certain sort of weak parent, who seeks to excuse his or her own failings in this area by blaming the school. In our society, parents have largely abandoned any attempt to control their children; the lawyers and civil rights campaigners have removed most of the means whereby they or anyone else can do so, should they want to. As for governments, they always blame anyone but themselves for the failures of society, and in this regard schools make the most convenient of scapegoats. One should not take complaints about indiscipline in a school at face value. Nevertheless, like motherhood and apple pie in America, in this country we are all in favour of discipline, though I prefer the more neutral phrase 'an orderly community'.

What else I was asked about at that interview I have no recollection. Had I known what I soon learned, I would have wanted to press them very hard on the relationship with the Department of Education (NI), which remained a problem to us throughout my time at the school. They appeared to have some hostility to the four type B grammar schools in the province, which they clearly found anomalous. No civil servant likes anomalies, especially if they bring with them a degree of independence from the dictates of central government. By contrast, the schools inspectorate were wonderfully supportive and interested, a source of good ideas and advice. Because they were routinely involved in dealing with grant applications for equipment, they were often in and out of the school on what were perfectly lawful occasions. Their presence therefore was natural, not threatening, but I have no doubt they had a very good sense of how well the school was doing, without the necessity of formal inspections like the diabolical visitations of OFSTED, which have done so much damage to teacher morale and confidence on the mainland.

I should explain that though there were seven HMC schools in Northern Ireland, we were all technically grammar schools. Campbell and the Royal Belfast Academical Institution were the only Protestant B schools; the rest were A. When the system was set up in around 1948, it consisted basically of grammar schools and secondary schools. Entry to the grammar schools was by the dreaded

Eleven-plus exam, an IQ test which to many seemed to dub as 'failures' those who did not pass. There were two types of grammar school and all their tuition fees were covered by the direct grant. But type A also received 85% (I think) of their capital expenditure as grants from the Department of Education. In return they had to accept central control of intakes and expenditure, and could only charge parents a minimal fee, £40 a year in my time. By contrast type B schools received no capital funding at all, but could set their own fees, though these had to be agreed with the Department. Such fees would be sufficient to enable them to fund their capital expenditure. They could also decide on their own intake, including the proportion of eleven-plus candidates they would accept. Boarders were subject to no restrictions, though their tuition fees were paid as if they were day pupils provided they had passed the Eleven-plus. So boarding was relatively cheap compared with English and Scottish counterparts, while day education at a good HMC grammar school like Methodist College would cost about £40 per annum.

It has always seemed to me that this remarkably flexible scheme had effectively abolished the independent sector. There was no hope of operating as a genuine independent school in the province. One independent prep school existed, Rockport, of which I became a governor, but not a single secondary school of any kind. I always wondered why Labour governments had never tried to introduce some variation of the system. I suspect it would have eliminated all but the most financially powerful of the public schools in a generation instead of doubling the size of the independent sector by their doctrinaire decision to abolish the grammar schools, the one truly egalitarian element in British education and a proven source of social mobility for its ablest young people.

When the interviews were over, I was surprised to find that the candidates and their wives all had to sit uncomfortably together in the head's study waiting for the result, making forced polite conversation and waiting for the summons to the boardroom. I had had a couple of previous attempts at headships before going to Eastbourne and was always impressed by the care with which it was made sure that no candidate met a competitor. This was about as uncomfortable and embarrassing a wait as any I can remember.

Came the summons; if offered the job would I take it? No chance had been offered to reflect upon what I had seen or to think about the day or the school in tranquillity. I took a deep breath and said 'yes'. And that was it. I had caught the tide and achieved my ambition before my fortieth birthday. Whether the current would lead on to good fortune remained to be seen. Thrilled, adrenalin charged, and unable quite to believe it, I was charmed by the kindest touch of all, when the Vice Chairman of the Board, Basil Walmsley, said it was ridiculous for me to order a taxi and he personally drove me and Sara home to Ballycrenan, where my parents were the first to know.

Mother was pleased.

CHAPTER 23

Campbell College I

School Motto: Ne obliviseeris *(Do not forget)*

I REMARKED IN MY INTRODUCTION THAT 'those who write their memoirs tend to be politicians seeking to carve their niche in history by an exercise in self-justification'. This chapter will inevitably lay me open to a similar charge, not only because headmasters are by the very nature of their calling politicians to some degree, but also because any account of his tenure of office written by the holder thereof will inevitably read like an *apologia pro vita sua*.

In the interests of a more dispassionate assessment I would refer the interested reader to the official history of Campbell College, published in 1993 to celebrate the first centenary of the school's opening on September 3, 1894. Entitled *neither Rogues nor Fools* (sic) it was written by Keith Haines, a very able historian whom I regularly but unsuccessfully urged to complete his PhD. He joined the staff as head of history on the same day as I did, and what he says offers a useful corrective to any extravagant claims or special pleading that I might be tempted to make.

Keith is extremely generous, but he records, correctly, that I 'did not develop a warm relationship with many of my staff'. As I saw it, the reason was not just because I 'found inconsequential conversation irksome' (if I do), but because – to my surprise – I found that my colleagues (as I thought of them) seemed uncomfortable with informality, preferring to call me 'Headmaster' where 'Brian' would have sufficed, and unable to relax into the sort of easy professional relationship with the head, which I had got used to at Eastbourne. I was quite certain that it would be a mistake to look for a kind of cheap popularity by trying too hard to be 'one of the boys'; but after the initial rebuffs it became easier to play the game according to rules which staff appeared to want and my senior vice principal recommended. The fault has to be mine; but there was another side to it.

There were other factors at play too. I came into a situation where there had been internal problems – probably exaggerated by gossip, but real none the less, and a source of disharmony. Of this I knew almost nothing, until faced with an assertion by a member of staff which I could not challenge; I had to send for the chairman and demand to know the truth, which he confessed with some embarrassment he had deliberately withheld in the hope that the fall-out would evaporate. Of others I learned in due course, especially from a former board member who became a good friend and was a discreet source of support to me over many years.

There was a staff bar, as in all civilised common-rooms, but it was for me a matter of some delicacy. For reasons of geography and history the staff room (which was a functional and working area) had to double as a social common-room, and was rather more publicly situated than those at, say, Eastbourne and Radley. It would have been nice to simply drop in and socialise, but I was particularly sensitive in this area, because my father had always explained to me that in Northern Ireland he would never drink in public, least of all at the bar of his own golf club. Gossip too often and too easily ran rife and was sometimes malicious; for a surgeon to be seen drinking in public, however moderately, could be enough to destroy his reputation. For similar reasons I felt it was important for me to tread very carefully and to some extent to keep my distance, at least until I had a clearer sense of how the land lay. A reputation for austerity, at least initially, would be no bad thing; but inevitably, barriers once established became difficult to break down. Instead Sara and I set ourselves to entertain to dinner within our first year all members of the teaching staff, together with their wives. Sara in addition invited all wives who did not have work commitments to coffee mornings. Initially it meant one dinner party a week, which was for Sara as cook and hostess quite demanding. But at least it suggests that our intentions were of the best.

Nevertheless, Keith's charge must stick. But I hope the explanation offered here is somewhat more complex than a dislike of inconsequential conversation.

With the boys there is a similar charge – and it too was probably deserved. I came in with a very strong brief to improve discipline, and it was reinforced by everything staff as well as parents, and gossip also, said to me before I arrived, despite my own scepticism about such allegations generally, as already explained. As a result, I was probably regarded by the boys, initially at least, as 'the enemy', to be handled with caution. But that simply is the price one has to pay – it comes with the territory. There is, too, a natural reserve about the Ulster boy, which contrasts sharply with the easy and sometimes insincere charm of his southern English counterpart. My instinct was to respect it and not to try too hard to be chummy. But as well as teaching a half timetable (to enable me to economise on teaching staff when a classicist retired), I helped where I could with coaching hockey and cricket and tried to follow Newell's example by watching games whenever possible. I hope that those pupils who had more direct dealings with me would acknowledge, as Keith does, that there was another, more approachable side to my public persona.

In life you have to strike many such balances. Inevitably some will think I got it wrong, and I fear they may be right. The nature of the office inevitably imposes a degree of loneliness upon its incumbent.

What Keith does not mention, but it was in a way an equally difficult problem, was that my dealings with the Old Campbellians were sometimes awkward. Again, it was part of my brief and the inevitable unpopularity is also something that comes with the territory. I was strongly urged (not least by Chesley Boyd, an ex-chairman of the governors and an OC) to 'rein in' the OC Sports Club. They ought to have been the most powerful elements of support for the school, but seemed to be engaged in a progressive take-over of its amenities in the evenings, claiming (inaccurately, I was told) that they had paid for 'most' of them in the last appeal. I felt that if we were to encourage the appeal of boarding at a difficult time, one of the areas where we could allow boarders to enjoy themselves and let off steam was in the evenings, even after prep. But by then the OCs were well encamped in the sports hall, swimming pool, and squash courts and were not readily amenable to persuasion on this point. This sort of tension is nothing special – all heads confront similar dilemmas all the time. But the policy was unlikely to win me friends and it was a battle to be fought on my own, since it would be little short of pathetic to blame the governors for a policy I agreed with.

Whenever you try to manage an organisation, it is important to be aware of your allies as well as your enemies. That is what I mean when I say that all heads are to some degree politicians. My inherent contempt for the breed (politicians, not heads) hardly helps when political skills are needed to gather allies in time of adversity. In this I think I am my father's son – and content to be so. He was unbending in his determination to do what he thought was right and popularity was not a consideration. But there came a time when the attempt to merge with Ashleigh House Girls' School meant that we needed all the support we could get. In both common-room and old boys it was my perception that there was some opposition to the project, whether out of genuine love for the school as it was, or dislike of the idea of coeducation, or for a few at least out of fear of the unknown.

In all our discussions I was bound by an agreement to absolute secrecy, which as usual in Ulster was not uniformly adhered to by all the parties. Such secrecy may well have been a mistake, and certainly unhelpful rumours developed which I felt unable to counter.

The idea of coeducation had predated my arrival and was already the policy of my predecessor and of the governors. But it was something I had wholeheartedly supported and the failure made a sad ending to something that had seemed so full of opportunity and was the greatest disappointment of my professional career. I had had a vision of a school of about 800, with boys and girls in equal numbers, on our beautiful campus for which our architects had devised a most imaginative set of buildings. There was ample space and enormous potential and our plans had the makings of a great school, which might have rivalled Methody. If everyone had kept their nerve and their cool, we might have succeeded in time in persuading the Department of Education, which had initially encouraged us and assured us that our plans were in line with their policies. But we were overruled at a political level, not an educational one, by a Minister of Education for whom I had little respect.

For all those reasons, once the attempt to merge had failed, I was inevitably identified with the failure, and felt I had lost a fair degree of support in several important areas. It seemed politic to move on if I could and I made a number of attempts to go back to another headship in England. I was, I think, the runner-up for Rugby, as well as having preliminary interviews for Winchester, Westminster, Oakham, Haileybury, and Wells Cathedral School, which in the light of our subsequent move to Somerset I particularly regret not being appointed to. The Winchester interview was so delightful and the governors so charming that I told Sara that there at least I cannot have been a serious contender. In fact they made an internal appointment.

In the end, after eleven years' service and on reaching the age of fifty, it seemed right to bow out gracefully in the best interests of the school. I asked for early retirement, which was legitimate and available, and it was granted. The governors must have felt that, like the Rump Parliament in the words of Oliver Cromwell, I had been there 'long enough for aught good I might do'. But my impression was that many parents, who were always my best supporters, regretted my departure, and their farewell gifts and generous comments were enough to make me feel my labours had not been entirely in vain.

In a short farewell speech of thanks at a presentation by them I took as my brief theme the lovely inscription from William Hazlitt's essay 'On A Sundial', '*Horas non numero nisi serenas*' (I count only the sunlit hours). For me and my family many of our hours at Campbell had indeed been sunlit, and my outstanding head boy, Colin McClean, the last of a marvellously talented family of Campbellians, converted the inscription into a small collage of line drawings of school life, which still hangs upon my wall.

So with that preliminary as a corrective to any extravagant claims for my own virtues, I can see no better way to give a broad account of my time at Campbell than to set out a final account of my stewardship, which I wrote for my own personal record in the last weeks of my time in office. It has at least the merits of freshness and recent memory, rather than the probably stale and rose-tinted perspective of some twenty years later. This is how I remembered it at the time. Others will, doubtless, beg to differ. To this account I shall append additional comments as quasi-footnotes to the text, together with assorted jottings and recollections in the following chapter to add some flavour to the basic stew.

One man's perspective – June 1987

During my time at Campbell we have been through a period of great difficulty. Politically there has been, above all, the problem of violence in a divided community and all that that implies. Political extremism has contributed to the sense of tension, even in schools. Yet for many pupils they have been oases of stability and normality – and it has been a major priority to keep them so.

Initially I found myself much involved in the campaign to resist the wholesale imposition of comprehensive education upon a system which the local community felt was tried, proven, and successful. We succeeded. Later came the demographic crisis (which we share with the rest of Britain) of declining birth rate and falling school rolls – in our case complicated further by population movements, as the religious communities retreated into their traditional strongholds (or out of the province altogether). Consequent government-imposed quotas on the intakes of schools have had a severe impact on relatively small schools such as ours. More recently, and perhaps worst of all, the government policy of cash limits has put desperate constraints on the management of all schools, and we are facing cuts in both staff and current expenditure as a result – a total loss of some £150,000 per annum revenue at 1985 prices. The quality of educational provision is declining – and will continue to do so as a result. A very weak local economy has also made things worse.

When I arrived in 1977 it seemed to me, even then, that we would be unable to sustain the school's traditional character in the particular circumstances prevailing. To one trained and reared in boarding schools it was a hard decision, but the best policy seemed to me to be to make a dash for growth on the day-boy side – a decision fully vindicated, I believe, by later and unforeseen events. As a result my eleven years have seen a marked shift away from our character as a boarding school with a fairly large day side, to a day school with a strong enough boarding side to still influence much of the corporate ethos. It has been a change which was, I believe, sad but unavoidable.

Our numbers when I arrived were down to 414 and there was much anxiety in the staff about redundancy. In the innocence of youth I announced to my first staff meeting that I did not believe in redundancy, and it is a matter of relief that I shall leave without having to implement any. The ensuing growth of the years 1977–84, in which our numbers rose to their highest ever figure of 515, proved invaluable in weathering the storm of unexpected financial crises (such as that provoked by the need to rewire the whole school) and in funding out of revenue the massive refurbishment and general improvement of our facilities which we so desperately needed and which has been a considerable feature of the period.

Yet this change of character, which was the only possible source of growth, was not a source of unalloyed pleasure to the traditionalists, especially the Old Campbellians, who failed to appreciate the enormity of the problems we faced. But it may have helped to bring the school somewhat closer to the local community, from which it had always been regarded as standing somewhat aloof. That at least has been a gain.

As change worked its way through, we tried very hard to maintain and develop the sense of identity of houses, on the day and boarding sides, and to ensure that the now preponderant day side picked up the torch of corporate commitment so characteristic of boarders traditionally. Three extra day houses were created and helped to keep the units of care down to reasonable numbers. I suspect we need one more. Boarding houses were given geographical identity; and as boarding numbers fall towards 100, plans are now in train to concentrate them in an area of their own, self-contained, with new loos and showers, and housemasters' residences clustered around for care and control.

At the same time the everyday regimen of the more senior boarder was somewhat liberalized. Too often he compared his lot, most unfavourably – and with justification – with that of his day-boy contemporary, whose considerable social life and freedom contrasted markedly with his own constrained existence. Relaxed self-discipline increasingly replaced imposed magisterial discipline – with beneficial effects for the majority, though as always a small minority abused the increased responsibility and trust placed upon them. This is a boys' boarding school after all, and not a convent.

The less perceptive elements saw this as a weakening of Discipline, with a capital D, a judgement which I found ironic in view of the considerable indiscipline with which I had to contend when I first came, and the generally favourable view of my success in dealing with it. I saw it (because I had to deal with the occasional lapses and defaulters) as a vast improvement in corporate behaviour and civilised community living. And it is a source of real pride to me that for eleven years we have been almost entirely spared the horrific misdemeanours (often involving drink, drugs or sex), which have made headlines in a number of independent schools across the water. Corporal punishment was dispensed with, informally from about 1981, and formally in 1984, with no deleterious consequences whatever.

Religion has also been 'modernised'. This is a delicate matter in the context of Northern Ireland, but an excess of compulsory worship and long services does nothing to create a sense of sympathy with or belief in Christianity. The pattern of family services, school services, and a modest number of parish services to keep boys in touch with the parish life of their own denominations, has produced as acceptable an arrangement as I think could be found for an adolescent community where sympathy with religion is unlikely to be excessive in the best of circumstances. Morning assembly has been retained entirely, and uncompromisingly, as an act of corporate worship, without school notices or other such extraneous matter; they have been remarkable for their decorum and sense of calm. The congregational singing remains awful. In all this the chaplain and I have aimed always to adhere to the requirements of the school's charter, that we provide 'a liberal Protestant education'. We have sought to offer a Christianity that is intellectually respectable and in the mainstream of liberal religious thought, yet one that is not partisan or overtly pious. RE is taught always without dogma and certainly without any covert proselytising.

On the academic side GCSE is about to bring considerable changes. But much has been done already to bring the curriculum more into line with modern requirements. In the last ten years, as well as RE at A and O Level, we have introduced political studies, economics and commerce, technology, increased provision for CDT and graphic communications, links with industry and business games, job experience for the whole of the Lower Sixth, computer studies to at least hands-on experience for all, and from next year we will be part of the first group of schools involved in the new CBI/City & Guilds Computer Studies Initiative. Industrial Society Conferences have been held every year and in this we led the province. UCCA applications have reflected some of this by a marked growth in those applying to read engineering and business studies to degree level.

The engine of change has been the formal curriculum and a massive increase in the provision for careers education and counselling. Improved statistical analysis, more internal exams, and better reporting systems have given us an improved control and monitoring of academic performance. And despite a relatively modest level of ability in our intake, we have sustained A Level results at about an average pass rate of 85/90%, with A, B, C grades at about 60%. O level averages have been raised to 70% overall and almost 80% for qualified pupils.

In the arts we have instituted, most successfully, an annual Arts Festival of Music, Art, and Drama, which has become the focus and climax of our year's activity in this field. It is now a firmly established part of our calendar and an effective vehicle for encouraging creativity and cultural life in the school. The expensive purchase by the Headmaster's Fund of a bleacher rake system has enabled us for the first time to seat our audiences safely and with a proper view of the 'stage', thus creating a genuine sense of theatre.

Sporting opportunities have been extended, choice widened, facilities improved, and the traditional games like rugby and cricket supplemented by increasing opportunities and success in sports such as athletics, cross-country, hockey, tennis, and archery, without I think significant detriment to other games like squash, swimming, sailing, and shooting where our record has long been excellent. Over the last ten years we have, I think, been Ulster champions at least once in almost every sport and at almost every level. For a small school the quality of performance and success at the highest levels of competition has been a tribute to the devoted efforts of a most talented and dedicated staff, and a solid vindication of the policy of diversification.

Meanwhile the Cadet Force has continued, with enormous success and a national reputation, to provide an umbrella organisation, within which all forms of adventure and initiative training can take place, and leadership, self-confidence, and initiative developed. The pipe band has gone from strength to strength, with ever-increasing public performances. It was also, at last and at great expense, kitted out in the Campbell tartan, which was of course the only appropriate dress. Meanwhile for those with a different inclination, an expanded social service organisation has done remarkable work for the handicapped, the under-privileged, and the elderly in our community, and won golden opinions for our pupils.

Building and development has been sustained throughout, even though there has been little cash to spare, and the Board has felt unable to allow me to run an appeal, because their previous one in 1972 was such a disappointment. This was a major waste of opportunity, as was the rejection of my initial plans for upgrading the whole boarding environment at a cost, which with hindsight looks absurdly modest. The result has been to make the marketing of our expensive boarding increasingly difficult.

Nevertheless, by internally generated revenue, considerable ingenuity by a brilliant bursar, and my own personal approach to parents, which has raised some £65,000 for the Headmaster's Fund, we have done a lot. We have managed to build – or create by re-allocation of space – an all-weather area for three hockey pitches and a 400-metre athletics track, a new chemistry laboratory, a new biology laboratory, a large art room, extended workshops and drawing offices, an eight-classroom teaching block formed from the Ormiston junior house, a sixth form centre for day-boys, a computer suite with a networked BBC system, a careers suite, enhanced library, renovated sports pavilion (with four self-contained changing and shower units for visitors) new changing rooms and lavatories for boarders, two new day-boy locker-cum-changing rooms, three new four-bedroom residences for boarding housemasters, four new hard tennis courts, and the rewiring of the whole school (which alone cost £200,000). The main school was repainted throughout, inside and out. We are now committed to a major uplift of the boarding provision, and the re-organisation of space within the main building, so as to create more classrooms and better amenities for the day-boy side. I look forward to the day when the 'temporary' classrooms will be eliminated.

We made two attempts at coeducation – both thwarted we believe for political not educational reasons by the Department of Education. We took sixth form girls for three years, with great success, before being required to phase them out. We then planned a merger with a local girls school with (we thought) the approval of the Department of Education, whose permanent secretary described our plan as 'ambitious and imaginative'. But they lost their nerve at the last minute and the development plan was aborted when the planning stages were well advanced. That was, I think, the greatest disappointment of my time here, and the greatest tragedy for Campbell. Not all would agree.

Much work has also been done to rescue our beautiful 100-acre estate, which must surely be one of the loveliest school campuses in the land. It had been sadly neglected for years, but as a result of a massive tree-planting operation, the dredging and re-landscaping of the lake, the new wall on the Hawthornden Road, and a general clean-up of the most offensive areas, the next two centuries should see us with a splendid amenity, provided at least that we keep up the momentum of tree replacement.

Finally, in terms of marketing, a much acclaimed prospectus, recently produced, has sought to bring these developments to the notice of OCs, friends, and parents, actual and prospective. Scholarships for Eire boys have sought to attract back to

Campbell a valuable element in the school, which has been totally lost to us as a result of the Troubles. And a second International Prospectus (produced jointly with other Northern Ireland boarding schools and grant-aided by the Industrial Development Board) has – largely on Campbell's initiative, but much helped by Professor Jim Magowan of the University of Ulster – publicised Northern Ireland's educational attractions all over the world.

> Cast a cold eye
> On life, on death,
> Horseman, pass by.
> (At this point the retrospective element of the document ends.)

It has always seemed to me that the essential duty of leadership is to look ahead, to plan strategy. If you know where you are going and why, the problem of getting there is never too difficult, unless you are dealing with government and civil servants, for whom obstruction of other people's ideas often seems irresistible. In various papers, usually written for my own purposes to clarify my thinking, but often shared with the Board, I had tried to set out some of my thoughts for the future. Almost from the moment of my arrival I had had my eye on the centenary (1994), and had mentally mapped out a programme to cover the intervening decade. A few extracts of varying dates illustrate the way my mind was going.

Structure

'Campbell must look very seriously at becoming an 11–18 school, like all others in the province ... Holiday courses, evening classes, entrepreneurial skills for pupils and staff – all these need developing. I suspect that the Community College model with specialist separate provision for boarders may well represent one way forward, reinforced perhaps by some form of continental TT and a modular pabulum of non-academic activity.'

Public schools

'In Northern Ireland people don't want a public school in sufficient numbers to sustain a market. On financial grounds alone there is already a case for recognising that our future lies either in being the best grammar school in the province, or, at high risk going independent and becoming a high quality, independent, coeducational public school. This would necessitate considerable capital expenditure.'

Social attitudes

'Are heavily in favour of day schooling; coeducation (I think); a five-day working week; family weekends; secondary schools starting at 11+; avoiding another change at 13+. There is also a limited specialist demand for boarding facilities, not boarding schools as we have always understood them. Price will count for more than quality in Ulster.'

Girls

'By hook or by crook we should seek to introduce girls to the school, whether as boarders in New House or as sixth formers, or by merger. It could all be funded by a major appeal, which should have been launched five years ago, as I advised. A second major source of funds would be to sell the two fringe areas of the estate for housing development, which would generate I suspect at least £150,000 (in 1987; perhaps double in 2006). This would also give us increased security on our very vulnerable boundaries without loss of cherished amenity.'

Marketing

'People tend to utter this word like a magical incantation, as if it were a panacea. But modern marketing is not an exercise in persuading people that they want what they manifestly do not want; rather it seeks to establish what they actually want, and then offer it to them at the highest quality consistent with a price they can afford.'

The Board

'I do not believe that the Board will function really effectively until it has reorganised itself further. It lacks coherence and consistency at the top. In eleven years I have served no less than six chairmen. HMC pamphlets of guidance lay great stress on the key relationship in the management of a school between the Chairman, The Head, and The Bursar. In our case the Chairman has barely time to learn his role before he is replaced.'

DENI

'The Department of Education is schizophrenic about us. There is some genuine goodwill at senior levels among those with enough perception to see that we are not snobs or out for privilege for its own sake, but that we are concerned to offer quality education. But there are two pressures for them: a. cash limits; b. equity – they (the DENI) must be seen to be fair. There is legitimate concern to help the so-called traditionally low-cost schools and we can only expect further pressure to curtail our running costs.'

The decline of boarding

'Is due to: costs; the Troubles; demographic trends; changing social attitudes; decline in the NI economy; ending of the five-mile limit, from outside which previously we would not accept pupils as day-boys; failure to upgrade our plant adequately. Campbell is a small school with a large and antiquated building to heat and maintain. The decline of boarding means that its space is under-utilised and inefficiently utilised. We need a quantum reduction in the price of boarding if we are to expand it.'

Expansion of the day-side

'Is likely to go into reverse unless we can keep the growth trend by new policies, which match the requirements of new markets. The two most likely to be effective are a) the abolition of Saturday school; and b) taking pupils into CCB at eleven-plus not thirteen-plus. The implications for Cabin Hill should then be explored. If this suggestion is rejected, let's not fudge the issue – the decision is to preserve Cabin Hill at the expense of Campbell.'

Reducing costs

'The only major solution is to increase the divisor by spreading the overhead costs among a significantly larger number of pupils. I feel increasingly that we are in a position of responding to events rather than being master of them. This is a crisis not so much of numbers only as of finance and social attitudes. It would not surprise me to find our numbers at about 80 boarders and 320 day-boys in three years' time (ie. September 1989).'

Specialist markets

'We might over a period produce a small specialist market in a number of areas of excellence such as music, sport, art, girls' boarding, remedial, and sixth form studies.'

In this connection, one idea, which I was beginning to think about but revealed to no one, was to try also to become a centre of excellence for music, by seeking an alliance with Daphne Bell's Ulster College of Music and offering them a home on our campus. They were, I gathered, under pressure for accommodation; we needed a new music school; Daphne Bell's achievement and work for Ulster music was absolutely outstanding. It seemed to me that there could be enormous benefits for both parties. But it was little more than a twinkle in my eye. Meanwhile I contented myself with sowing the seeds of the idea that the music departments of Campbell and Cabin Hill should be integrated, the choirs amalgamated, and subsidies offered for string players so that we could develop a decent orchestra.

I find it interesting to see what exercised my mind in that very difficult period. I have no idea whether I just got it all wrong or whether events proved me reasonably prescient; probably a bit of both. But the fascination of doing the job lay in the intellectual challenge of trying to think clearly and without emotion about profoundly difficult problems, in which pupils' education, people's livelihoods, and the destiny of a great school were at stake. I hope these excerpts from my memoranda will supplement the limited account in the school's official history of the many serious problems we faced.

Once I had departed, the kindest thing I could do for my successor was to stay out of sight and out of mind. Though for the next two years I lived within half a mile of the school, I made no attempt to stay in touch, nor did I make any attempt to visit it. Since my return to England I have lost touch entirely and in twenty years I have never set foot inside the school estate. Once my secretary Rona McAlpine died, very sadly much too young, there was no one around to keep me in touch.

'Swift as a weaver's shuttle fleet our years', as the poet Browning once wrote. Sometimes one forgets that one is growing old. In late 2005 I was startled as well as delighted to hear that Jay Piggott, an early pupil of mine at Campbell, had been appointed its headmaster. I hope he will relish and enjoy the challenges of the task as much as I did.

CHAPTER 24

Campbell College II – Familiar Matters of Today

> *Will no-one tell me what she sings? –*
> *Perhaps the plaintive numbers flow*
> *For old, unhappy, far-off things,*
> *And battles long ago:*
> *Or is it some more humble lay,*
> *Familiar matter of today?*
> *Some natural sorrow, loss, or pain,*
> *That has been, and may be again?*
>
> Wordsworth, 'The Solitary Reaper'

WHAT WAS IT LIKE TO LIVE IN Northern Ireland during the period 1977–1989?

It all feels a long time ago, and as the years roll by the horrors tend to grow dim within the memory. In addition, we have all become more accustomed to living with terrorism since that time, and the events of 9/11 in New York, and the London tube train atrocities more recently, have made us all more sensitive to the miseries of such emergencies. But it was a bad time for everyone living there, and very difficult for those of us who were 'exiles' yet retained our affection for the province and the love of our families still over there.

For me ancient history serves as a constant reminder not just of how terrible civil war – or its near equivalent – can be, but also how the patterns of violence and civil strife repeat themselves through human history. Thucydides described the *stasis* (civil strife) in Corcyra with a kind of harsh detachment, hoping that his readers would learn the lessons of history. Yet, as another wise historian remarked, the only lesson that history teaches us is that it teaches us nothing. Rome endured nearly one hundred years of civil war, until Augustus, a great statesman and subtle politician, finally brought peace, and earned from Virgil the poetic expression of a people's gratitude: '*deus ille, deus haec otia fecit*', 'A god is he, truly a god that brought us this time of peace.' There was no Augustus available to Northern Ireland, certainly not in the largely second-rate politicians sent across from England as Secretaries of State, though Jim Prior was, I felt, a notable exception. Augustus had been in his early days, if not a terrorist, most certainly a paramilitary leader. He was responsible for the assassination of his chief opponent, Cicero, Rome's greatest orator-statesman and champion of the rule of law, and many years later confessed to his nephew, when he caught him in the library reading Cicero's works, that 'he was a good man, who loved his country well'. I often wondered, rarely aloud, whether the real hope for the province might not lie in a ex-terrorist, so called, as it had in a number of other countries which Britain had once ruled.

Meanwhile, violence breeds violence, and we were all its victims. As usual, Shakespeare sums it up so well:

> A curse shall light upon the limbs of men;
> Domestic fury and fierce civil srife
> Shall cumber all the parts of Italy;
> Blood and destruction shall be so in use,
> And dreadful objects so familiar,
> That mothers shall but smile when they behold
> Their infants quartered with the hands of war,
> All pity choked with custom of fell deeds;
> And Caesar's spirit, ranging for revenge,
> With Ate by his side come hot from hell,
> Shall in these confines with a monarch's voice
> Cry 'Havoc!' and let slip the dogs of war.

One cannot but feel that, even if he had not himself experienced such things, the memory of them was still strong in the folk memory of the people among whom he lived.

The most powerful emotion which such situations generate, I think, is the feeling in ordinary people of sheer helplessness. Atrocities are random, directed against innocent civilians as much as the security forces, and blind chance rules one's chances of survival. Governments appear helpless – or indifferent. I never forgave Maggie Thatcher for barricading herself safely into Downing Street at a time when her fellow citizens were afforded no such protection by her government. It seemed like crass insensitivity and the self-interest so characteristic of all politicians.

After helplessness comes hatred, which spawns too easily a desire for revenge, tit-for-tat, and with it a willingness to tolerate, or at least tacitly condone, all kinds of retaliatory lawlessness by the forces of one's own side, because they claim to be the forces of law and order. To those who counsel moderation extremists rapidly assert that the fault lies with the other side. This is a typical old playground claim after any fight that 'the other boy started it'. The Israelis and Palestinians are still at it. Nationalists and Loyalists certainly feel it, even if they are less aggressive now in asserting it. Peace never comes until both sides agree to bury the hatchet, accept that there is fault on both sides, and subscribe to some sort of 'settlement'. I often suggested, without winning any converts, that if we wanted peace, in the end an amnesty was inevitable. The ancient Athenians did it by passing a law that forbade any mention of the events of their own reign of terror under the so-called Thirty Tyrants. In the case of the Romans, for the sake of peace, all parties acquiesced in a largely spurious political fabrication, under which they could all pretend that constitutional republican government had been 'restored'. In fact Augustus simply disguised his dictatorship sufficiently for all sides to agree, tacitly, that a 'fudge' was better than a fight. I even did a 'Thought for the Day' on the subject, suggesting that if you 'are seeking to reconcile the irreconcilable, you need to recognise the virtues of what I would call "creative dishonesty"; a willingness to blur the edges – not to leave your opponent totally deprived of room for manoeuvre or excuses for past misdemeanour'.

Well, pigs might fly, but not in Northern Ireland.

Compounding all the turmoil comes Rumour. Rumour abounded all the time. Given that every organisation from government downwards leaked like a sieve, partly because almost everyone had dual loyalties, the rumour mill worked overtime, compounding fears and apprehensions about what 'they' were planning. Virgil again, in a memorable passage, albeit in a different context, describes Rumour as a winged monster, whose effects are catastrophic:

Rumour, than which no evil is more swift.
Speed gives her force; she gains strength as she flies;
Though small at first, through caution, soon she climbs the heavens,
Walking on earth, but her head buried in the clouds.
A monster she is, horrific, huge; and every feather on her body
Is matched by a watchful eye beneath, and just as many tongues,
As many mouths to shout, as many ears pricked up to hear.
At night she flies 'twixt earth and heaven through the darkness,
Screeching, alert, oblivious to sweet sleep,
Clinging to lies and falsehoods, yet harbinger of truth,
And bringing terror to the cities of mankind.

In the midst of this 'terrible state of chassis' (to borrow Sean O'Casey's phrase) Britain not for the first or last time in her history had to hold the ring. The Nationalists who initially welcomed the arrival of British troops with open arms and cups of tea soon felt themselves let down, because they did not get everything they wanted – and turned to arms of a different sort and bombs instead of teacups. On the Loyalist side an increasing sense of betrayal by Britain became the prevailing emotion. Even among friends and relations, who were certainly moderates politically, I found this sense of betrayal total.

My attempts to understand and express what I saw as the difficulties and dilemmas faced by governments were rarely appreciated. Fair-mindedness became a mark of weakness. The fact that the Loyalist politicians were totally out-gunned (if one may use such a metaphor) by the skilful advocacy of their cause on the Nationalist side (with the characteristically naïve support of too many US politicians) simply meant that viewed from England Loyalists were intransigent and unreasonable and it is impossible to calculate how much harm Loyalist leaders and representatives did to their own side. Britain, doubtless trying to be fair to both parties, satisfied neither and became the focus of hatred from both. Conflict inevitably tends to deprave and corrupt, until the situation so vividly described above by Shakespeare became the norm. Relatively safe in my ivory tower within the grounds of Campbell, I was less affected than many. Even so, it was uncomfortable.

It is thirty years ago now, but I still remember vividly the sense of anxiety (almost paranoia) that prevailed in many places. Personal security was a very real issue for many people, especially judges, prison officers, and the security forces, but also senior business men, who were targets of the IRA because economic disruption was part of their strategy, and small business men if they dared to compete with the businesses 'protected' by the paramilitaries on both sides. The security forces could not possibly guard them all. Indeed my mother, who was a magistrate in the juvenile courts, neither sought nor was offered protection of any kind. But then she was a tough old girl – and very brave. Even I was licensed to carry a weapon for personal protection. But I saw no evidence that schools were ever targets and I quickly abandoned this somewhat dubious privilege.

I was always aware of a state of heightened alertness in myself – it was not fear, because I was pretty certain that I was never a target; but certain habits are still with me, though I have been away from the province for nearly twenty years. I always park my car facing outward, ready to go – 'always secure your exit' was a family saying. At a time when a bomb warning might occur at any time, the ability to make a short sharp exit could be valuable. Wherever I am I still scrutinise the surrounding area for unattended baggage, though of course that is no help when you are faced with suicide bombers. I assume, always, that my phone is tapped (more likely by the government than by a terrorist). I remain obsessed by punctuality – over there, if I was late or the children failed to honour a rendezvous on time, immediate anxiety overtook us. For a time, Emma tells me, Paddy used to laugh at her automatic habit of opening her bag at the door to any store in England for inspection by security. Conditioned reflexes die hard.

I greatly admired the security forces, both army and especially the RUC, as it used to be called. The IRA and their political front men ran a skilful but disgraceful campaign of denigration of a body of men and women who served the whole community at serious risk to their lives. Of course there are rogue elements in any organisation; the mainland is not entirely faultless in this respect either. But for me they always seemed to be a bulwark against a general descent into anarchy, such as we are now seeing in Iraq, and the whole community is forever in their debt.

It is remarkable what you can get used to. Roadblocks, traffic jams, checkpoints, searches – all these were normal everyday occurrences. The nightly sound of explosions and sometimes gunfire remains a vivid memory. And yet Sara reminds me that sometimes when the children were worried by it, she found that their real anxiety was whether someone was letting off fireworks. She would comfort them by telling them 'not to worry. It's only another bomb.' I myself was sitting at my desk one day and heard what sounded like a load of timber planks falling off the back of a lorry on the main road, about 200 yards away. I thought no more of it, until I heard later that it was an unfortunate prison officer, who had been assassinated.

I never felt personally threatened, though for everyone there was the constant sense that you might be in the wrong place at the wrong time. But in fact the most overt threat I faced was when the UDA (the Ulster Defence Association) called a general strike and I received a demand to close the school, 'or else'. I consulted the police and their advice was that I could safely ignore it. They were right. But I was a little more careful where I went for the next week or two.

In general, despite my conspicuous car with its English number-plate, I felt reasonably able to go even into mildly dodgy areas. When friends (not many!) visited us from England I used to take them on what I called my 'terror tour'. This was a long circuit up into north Belfast and across into west Belfast and back down the Falls Road. I wanted them to understand that there were other factors than militant nationalism and religious bigotry behind the troubles – poverty, unemployment, and dereliction, born of discrimination. Terror feeds on many factors, but without doubt poverty and hopelessness encourage it directly among those who feel they have nothing to lose and no hope of improvement by conventional means. I suspect that similar motivations exist among the Palestinians of Gaza and South Lebanon. It also ensures tacit support for insurgency among many who are themselves largely law abiding. Such 'tours' reminded me, too, of just how uncomfortable was the situation of many of my fellow citizens.

How do people cope in such a situation? Whether Protestant or Roman Catholic, religion never seemed to me a cause of the Troubles – rather it was a convenient badge with which to tag and identify your own side and your opponents, as well as a stick with which to beat them. For obvious and historical reasons, the Roman Catholic church had a fine record of supporting its downtrodden and depressed people during the centuries of English rule in Ireland, a rule that was not entirely creditable and whose failings undoubtedly fanned the flames of nationalism and desire for independence. But Protestants also felt threatened – and rightly so. The intolerance of the recently formed Irish Republic was no encouragement to them to think that they would be fairly treated, if union with the south came about, and northern Nationalists were manifestly indifferent to the democratic wishes of the majority of their fellow citizens when it came to questions of a United Ireland. The fear was real and justified; Protestant Britain was their best defence. So on each side, religion offered the labels, not the causes.

In the ordinary conduct of ordinary lives, however, my impression was that on every side Christians emerged with far more credit than discredit, for their capacity to forgive, for their heroic efforts at reconciliation, for the comfort and support they brought to those in trouble, sorrow, need, sickness or adversity. I have no doubt that on the Nationalist side there were a few naughty priests, who forgot their Master's injunction to forgive, to love your enemies, and to be peacemakers. Equally, on the Protestant side there were clerics, as well as their adherents, who seemed willing to encourage or condone intolerance and hatred of their fellow Christians, who 'dug with the wrong foot' (ie belonged to another branch of the one faith). 'Are you a Mick or a Prod?' the story goes, of a question directed to a stranger who found himself in the wrong street at the wrong time. 'Neither', came the reply. 'I'm a Jew.' 'Yes. But are but are you a Protestant Jew or a Catholic Jew?' In a climate of religious intolerance, there is no answer to such a question. But in general I felt that Christian people of all persuasions were a credit to their calling.

I greatly admired the sheer fortitude of the ordinary population. Time and again disaster struck, whether in the form of death or economic calamity; time and again they would pick themselves up, rebuild and start again, often dismissing their dire setbacks with the black humour which the Ulsterman had developed to help him cope with his misfortunes. The heartbreak of bereavement brought out extraordinary qualities of Christian forgiveness, of which Gordon Wilson (no relation) was but one example. He held the hand of his dying daughter, a nurse, amid the rubble of the Enniskillen explosion, heard her last words, 'Daddy, I love you very much', and later declared memorably in a heart-rending interview that he could carry no hatred in his heart for those who did the deed. After doing a 'Thought for the Day' I would sometimes find myself speaking on the phone to someone who had rung up in utter distress, because something I had said had touched a chord or stirred a painful memory. My prevailing impression was never of hatred or bitterness; always of heartbreak and helplessness, and there in my comfortable surroundings I had nothing to offer beyond a sympathetic ear.

They were a good people and a heroic people, served on the whole by too many contemptible politicians and undermined by fanaticism. As Yeats observed,

> Too long a sacrifice
> Can make a stone of the heart.
> O when may it suffice?

Well, maybe at long last, violence and horror has sufficed and they are building for a new day. I hope so.

So let us turn to more cheerful thoughts and change the mood from that of Milton's 'Il Penseroso' to his 'L'Allegro', amidst more 'familiar matters of today'. Like Wordsworth's 'solitary reaper', I suspect that too often one finds oneself reaping and singing by oneself and often in too melancholy a strain.

> Hence loathed Melancholy
>   Of Cerberus and blackest midnight born,
> In Stygian Cave forlorn
>   'Mongst horrid shapes, and shrieks, and sights unholy,
> Find out some uncouth cell . . .

But come thou Goddess fair and free,
In heav'n yclept Euphrosyne.

Amidst the mayhem, Campbell was a lovely place to work, a lovely spot in which to live and move and have your being. The source of such delight is hard to put your finger on, but in the end much of it comes down to pleasant people sharing a similar commitment to the school and working wholeheartedly for its good. Nothing illustrated this better than the Queen's Jubilee celebrations.

One of my first tasks was to plan for the Queen's Silver Jubilee. I had always thought that King's Week, the Arts and Music Festival at King's Canterbury, was one of the best things that happened there. It would take many years, if ever, before we could hope to match it for scope and quality; but the Jubilee gave us a chance to see what we could do at relatively short notice. The Festival Week Souvenir Programme, designed if I remember rightly by Chris Gailey, who later also took on the honorary task of college archivist, was a handsome product. The front cover consisted of a superb reproduction of the college's arms and crest, granted after it was incorporated by Royal Charter in 1951, when the charter was personally presented to the college by Queen Elizabeth, on behalf of her husband, King George, who was absent through illness. The official description by the Garter King of Arms was on the back. The programme inside showed that there were two performances of *Waiting for Godot* – a memorable production, as I remember it – and one of John Barton's *The Hollow Crown*; there was a grand fête, opened by Lady MacDermott, wife of the Lord Chief Justice, himself an Old Campbellian and former chairman of the governors, who famously led the defeat of the government by taking an appeal by the college all the way to the House of Lords; a cricket match against the Old Campbellian Jubilee XI; the CCF band beat retreat, and on the final day there was a commemoration service, a Jubilee ball, and a tree-planting ceremony. The weather as I remember it was superb.

The tree-planting ceremony was entirely my own idea. I hoped it would be a start to the regeneration of the estate, but more immediately would also serve as a reminder to us all of the remarkable number of staff and support workers who had served the school for very long periods. This is one of the things that immediately struck me on arrival. There was a loyalty and pride in so many of those who worked there and who gave to the school a commitment far beyond the call of duty. I wanted their commitment, which in its own way mirrored that of our Queen to her nation, to be the focus of our celebrations. A tree planting seemed exactly right. It symbolised our commitment to a future which none of us would see, and a willingness to think for the long term, since the beech avenue almost certainly still had another 100 years of life in it; and a new beginning.

In my forward to the programme I wanted to try and express all this. I wrote:

> It is right to make this Jubilee as memorable as we can, because few of us are likely to see more than two in our lifetimes; because we owe to our Queen a deep debt

of gratitude for a life of unsparing dedication, leadership, wisdom, and high principle that contrasts gloriously with much of what we see of public life about us; because as loyal subjects we should rejoice with her upon a great occasion. The tree planting is to express our gratitude to those who have served Campbell well, and to symbolise our faith in the future by planting for generations yet unborn.

We planted a new line of specimen beeches in front of the school and a twin line of oak trees down the avenue, behind the beech trees that gave the school such a stately entrance. Everyone who had worked for the school for twenty-one years or more planted his or her tree. It caught the imagination particularly of our remarkable band of support staff (office, medical, maintenance, domestic, and ground staff alike), for whom the fact of equal recognition with teachers in the ceremony was hugely appreciated as a symbol of how important they were to us. No less than thirty qualified, and each planted a tree – as did the governors. The sergeant major of the CCF, Harry Bradshaw, who died a few years later, asked that his ashes be buried under 'his' tree. They were.

It made a very happy start to my time there and the care of the estate remained always something which mattered to me very much, some would say to the point of eccentricity, I suspect. But when you inherit beauty, you have a sacred duty to preserve it if you can. And in an Old Campbellian, Jack Duff, whose firm was a large contractor for landscaping and sports fields, I found a wonderful ally, who pared all his estimates to the bone to help me in the task.

An even more significant ally in this, and in everything I tried to do, was Jim Devlin, the bursar. Of all the omissions from the official history of the school, it is the failure to acknowledge his achievement that I found the most regrettable. In 1973 he was appointed bursar, as successor to the much-loved Sam Caghey, for whom the ever-increasing burdens of the post were becoming intolerable. Through steady and patient planning, budgetary controls, and financial discipline, he ensured our strength and stability through some of the very difficult times that lay ahead. It was a thankless but absolutely critical task and the school's debt to him is immeasurable. I hope they acknowledged it generously when he retired; had I been there we'd have certainly done him proud.

He simply loved the school, and outside his home and his family the college became his prime *raison d'être*. Prior to coming to Belmont he had had a very successful career and won a considerable reputation, not least in the vital role he played in the development of the Ulster College of the Northern Ireland Polytechnic (later to become part of the New University of Ulster), during its formative years at Jordanstown – a most daunting undertaking for any man. But when he was appointed bursar in 1973, he just knew that Campbell was where he wanted to be and where he wished to finish his career. And so he did. The school was singularly fortunate to have got him. As time passed he seemed to know every single individual involved in the day-to-day running of the school, including the contractors and their squads, and everyone about the campus – not to mention most of the pupils and their parents. He loved the school – and lived for it.

In me he found a willing ally. The reason was simple. I never forgot the lesson taught me while still an undergraduate by Barry Trapnell, one of those brilliant ex-members of the Cambridge University Fives Club, who had gained first-class honours and several blues. He was already headmaster of Denstone College and moved on later to Oundle, in succession to Dick Knight, another similar ex-member of the Fives Club. Trapnell told me over a club dinner one night that, 'if you get the money right as a headmaster, everything else follows, and you can do almost anything'. I always remembered the comment, and I made it my business from the start to understand our finances and to work as closely as possible with Jim, to clear my ideas with him if they involved costs, and to see that he understood my thinking.

Among other things, he had to negotiate our fee levels every year with the Department of Education, and few appreciated how his reputation for absolute integrity and financial discipline ensured that, when he explained our needs they were rarely challenged, and the authorities were as helpful as they could be. He also introduced one very important change, which eliminated potential divisiveness (not uncommon), which can develop between ancillary and teaching staff, by linking their salaries to points on the teachers' grades. If teachers got a pay rise, so did the rest, and in the same proportions – without the hassle, and for some the embarrassment, of negotiations. It made a useful statement of parity of esteem and reduced petty jealousies.

No bursar can really hope to be popular. His is always a lonely task. It inevitably involves saying 'no' to people, and demanding adherence to budgets and planned expenditure. It is essential to his business to know what is going on and why. This can of course lead to accusations of being a control freak, but provided that he understands the broader aims of policy, a good bursar will be a tremendous help to any head. Jim was remarkable in this regard and always maintained that it was his job, if possible, to give me what I wanted. He was no 'typical' accountant, the bean-counter type who adds up the pennies, says 'no' to everything, and loses sight of the bigger picture. He was totally supportive and utterly loyal. We worked closely together and I trusted him totally.

I would like to think that I earned his trust in return, and that I was a help to him on the financial side, even if only in trying to set an example of frugal living and minimal demands for my personal comfort. I soon took over the care of the head's garden, dispensing with the need for a gardener; Sara also decided after a while that she could do without domestic help; my entertainment allowance was, by English standards, pathetic; we sought no improvements to the head's house. In matters of school expenditure, I tried to make sure he always understood my thinking and the reasons for spending money. The result was that despite some severe problems and threatening government-inspired crises and periods of rampant inflation, the school's finances were always in pretty good shape and we regularly achieved a modest surplus. The achievement was his. But I think I helped.

In this we both had a wonderful supporter in Charles Adams, another of the unsung heroes of the financial stability of the college, who deserves a similar accolade. As the long serving chairman of the Governors' Finance Committee, he and Jim worked closely together, to develop financial policy, in such a way as to give their headmaster as much of his head as they dared. Charles, an ex-golfing blue from Oxford (where I believe there is a university of some mild repute) was another of the 'right' kind of accountant – master of detail, of course, but never one to lose sight of strategy for the sake of mere tactical gain, and always an enabler, not an obstructer. He was unafraid of a debt, provided he could see clearly the means of repaying it; he had a wonderfully flexible mind; he enjoyed ideas. Above all, as an old boy, he loved the school and was utterly committed to its service. He gave of his time and expertise unstintingly, and was one of the governors for whom I felt total respect and affection. His public-spirited commitment to the service of the wider community as well earned him a richly deserved OBE in the Honours lists. My greatest regret was that his stint as Chairman of Governors could not be extended beyond the statutory two years. Buggins' turn began to operate – never a very satisfactory principle of management – and the loss from the Board of two faithful old hands, Dick Pink and Charles Stewart, did not help. In the untimely death of Charles in particular I lost a wise old friend and strong supporter, whose counsels carried great weight in our discussions.

Another remarkable figure, almost an institution, was Rona McAlpine. She was appointed at the tender age of twenty-six by John Cook, and worked for four successive headmasters of Campbell. She had an excellent mind, sadly denied the education it deserved by the fact of having to leave school early on the death of her father, but triumphantly crowned late in life by the award of a first-class honours degree by the department of extramural studies at Queen's University. She had a remarkable memory, which probably accounts for a somewhat idiosyncratic filing system, reinforced by an absolute refusal to spend any money on her office. She must have spent much of her career in the school while finances were very tight. She was highly protective of, and loyal to, each of her charges in turn, albeit usually with a time lag of a couple of years, while she got used to the new pharaoh. When she retired her three former charges each wrote a farewell appreciation of her in the Campbellian magazine. This was mine.

Rona McAlpine

> There is a nice story told of Mrs Thatcher that, when some Tory minion asked a minister anxiously what would happen if she was run over by a bus, he replied, 'Impossible. It wouldn't dare.' I feel rather the same writing about Rona's retirement: it's impossible – a thought no sane man would contemplate.

To describe a lady as an institution runs the risk of misconstruction – it sounds less than chivalrous, a two-edged compliment. Yet if the qualities of an institution are that it is always there, inspires affection and respect, is a timeless part of the landscape, and impossible to contemplate the absence of, Rona was indeed an institution.

All institutions generate their own mythology – was she, on appointment, the youngest headmaster's secretary in the HMC? The youngest ever? The ablest? Was she the only one with a first class honours degree? Did she carry the whole of the OC Register in her head as well as the details of all the boys in the school? Certainly I used to worry sometimes that if Mrs Thatcher's bus ever carried her off, I would never solve unaided the mysteries of her (almost superfluous) filing system.

When I first arrived she told me that a good secretary learned to mimic the style of those she worked for. I never dictated a letter – some, inevitably, I wrote out long hand; most I simply scrawled a comment on and signed the impeccably finished article on delivery. On spelling and punctuation honours were even – I thought I was infallible; she knew she was. I think I once defeated her on a question of fact; but rarely did I dare to issue a challenge. (Even Mrs Thatcher's bus knew its limitations). My personal obsession that correspondence should be dealt with by return of post was matched by her extraordinary productivity amid the multitude of other equally important calls on her time. She kept the whole show on the road.

She was utterly selfless. Her love of Campbell was absolute; her loyalties ferocious; her discretion total. Those qualities perhaps are no more than one might expect of anyone at the top of her profession. But beyond the call of school duties, she loved and lived for her family – both her mother, whom she cared for devotedly, and her brother's family, which was never far from her thoughts. Such was her generosity of spirit that she half-adopted mine as well. She kept up with the news of our children and even kept an eye on us in Eastbourne, where once we found a note on the windscreen of our car, parked in some street along the sea-front: 'we are staying at the Landsdowne – come for tea'. Amidst the trials of her own illness she was totally self-forgetful in her interest and concern for those of my family, long after we had left the scene.

If it is a measure of human greatness 'to give and not to count the cost, to toil and not to heed the wounds', Rona is indeed a great lady and I am privileged in our association and in laying this humble tribute at her feet.

She it was who bought for me and sent me as a gift a copy of Keith Haines' *History of the College*. It remains a treasured keepsake.

Then there was Albert Maxwell. He had joined the school in May 1929 as the boot boy, whose job it was to polish the 'young gentlemen's' shoes. Now he was the head porter and even more of an institution than Rona. He was one of nature's gentlemen, adored by the boys and admired by all. Among his many duties such as handling the post, running the tuck shop, acting as the school's receptionist from his porter's box in the front hall, which he kept superbly polished as the first thing a visitor would see, he also climbed the clock tower – a long way – once a week to wind the clock. I always thought it must be the secret of his remarkable health and fitness. On 1 May 1979 we planned a special surprise for him. We held a school assembly without telling him and then the vice principal called for him in his box, saying that the headmaster needed him urgently in assembly. There I read out his school report, carefully concocted for the occasion, and amid a standing ovation from the whole school, he was presented with 'The Albert Clock' (the real one being Belfast's Big Ben) and, utterly unprepared, he gave a lovely five-minute talk about his fifty years' service. He was also guest of honour at the common-room dinner. To my great delight, my own private (and necessarily secret) initiative also bore fruit, and he was recognised in the Queen's Birthday Honours. He was a wonderful man and a symbol of the loyalty and service of so many to the school they loved.

I made a similar attempt to get an honour for David Young, our long-serving vice principal, and coincidentally an old boy of King's Canterbury, who was a distinguished teacher of English and a wonderful coach of rugby football. Some famous names in the world of that sport had passed through his hands. I was unsuccessful, why I know not. How the labyrinths of power and patronage work is beyond my powers to penetrate. Vice principals, almost by definition, embody the best traditions of any school. Robin Tughan, already mentioned, Ronnie Caves (a very fine housemaster also) and Raoul Larmour (a fine scholar and much-loved teacher of modem languages) were each in their own way outstanding in this role, deeply respected, great servants of the school, and of invaluable assistance and support to me.

There were so many others, that it is invidious to try and name them all, but I shall allow myself a few, in particular one happy coincidence of time, place, and personality. John Hull, the college engineer, who led the maintenance team and kept the boilers going, was another of those wonderful people for whom nothing is too much trouble and who ask for little or nothing in return. It turned out, and I wish I had known it before my father died, that he had been the hospital engineer at the Lagan Valley Hospital, Lisburn, when my father was the senior consultant. He, and his wife Meta, and Rory, his lovely Airedale whom our children adored, were really friends of the family, and whenever I came back to Belfast after he had retired I would try to visit them in their retirement bungalow in east Belfast. He was a dear man, the salt of the earth, whom I always felt it was a privilege to know.

I was singularly fortunate in the two chaplains who served the college in my time. David Erskine and his wife, Moira, seemed always able to treat me as a normal human being and a friend, rather than 'the Head', and he was always 'David' to both the children. He was wonderfully human, and though a father of boys, he showed a really fatherly understanding of our girls. When Emma was in hospital, after crashing her bicycle on Stormont Hill, he visited her regularly there and at home, and introduced her to the *Bunty* magazine, which Sara and I had never even heard of. Emma read it avidly thereafter, together with the *Bunty Annuals*, which became a kind of regular Christmas gift. He was the epitome of a real Christian, sincere and devout in his religion, but blessed with robust common sense and utterly lacking in the pious persona of the ostentatiously 'religious'.

He was an ex-soldier who had been an Italian prisoner of war and escaped from POW camp. His account of his experiences, which he once allowed me to read, was a fascinating story and I wish he had published it, as I urged him to. English literature was a great love and we could happily talk books and poetry together. He supported all my efforts to 'modernise' our religious arrangements, and his support was important. At Campbell we always had to tread a fine line between the Presbyterian and Anglican traditions. He was a Presbyterian; I an Anglican. Fortunately I had a second Presbyterian ally in the Rev John Young, the liberal minister of our local Presbyterian church; he was no less supportive, and so I think I managed to keep both traditions reasonably content with what we were doing.

John Nelson, David's successor, was a Methodist, intellectually and theologically progressive, and very much a supporter of the Irish school of ecumenics, if I remember rightly. From him, too, I got great friendship and support, as well as reassurance and instruction, and I like to think that all we did was in accordance with the college's commitment to offer a liberal approach to religious education.

I have tried over the years to buy a picture from every artist personally known to me. It makes a nice collection, not least for the associations each picture carries in my memory. Robert Bottom, who ran the art department, was I always felt an artist of considerable potential and if his duties had allowed him to develop it to the full I thought he might have gone far as a landscape painter. I bought several of his pictures and they have been a source of great pleasure over the years. Michael Benington also, son of a well-known Ulster artist, was no mean artist himself, though he joined the staff from industry to teach biology. I have two of his pictures, one a tiny study of a badger, the other a fine study of herons on the front lawns of Campbell under the beech trees on a misty morning.

The teaching staff as a whole were able and highly committed, very concerned to maintain the school's traditional ethos of an English public school. Most symbolic of that was the willingness of almost all staff to support and coach games and run extracurricular activities, to an extent that will have seemed hard on their families and exhausting on their own reserves of energy. Many will have felt, too, the contrast between ourselves and the ordinary run of the mill of Ulster schools. Even in England it was becoming more difficult to sustain this 24-hour, seven days a week commitment; and the issue of Saturday schooling regularly raised its ugly head as a source of tension. I could see that in time it was going to have to be abolished and I gather that my successor has done so. To a boarding school it would be a serious loss; but Campbell is largely a day school now, and the loss is less significant.

But when things like the Arts Week Festival occurred, or even the teachers' strikes, they were admirably loyal to the school and on the only occasion when some members felt compelled by their union to withdraw their labour, they contrived to do so in such a way that I doubt if the pupils even realised it was happening. I am only sorry that I was clearly felt to be less approachable than I would have wished to my colleagues, who were such admirable servants of the school.

Inevitably a fair number of them went on to headships. Alan Acheson, our head of history, went to Portora Royal School. As well as an historian he was deeply interested in politics, and it was at his instigation that I once hosted a meeting of the Conservative Party's Northern Ireland team while they were still in opposition to discuss their attitude to the proposed change to a comprehensive system of our grammar school system, which we opposed and on which they seemed to be ambivalent. Airey Neave was there, a silent but dominating presence – he said nothing but clearly counted for everything. It seemed to me that the brains behind the operation was Stuart Sexton. I wrote to him later, when the Tories were back in government, and were imposing quotas on the grammar school intakes, to ask him what sort of sense it made for me to have to refuse all applications from primary schools other than our own prep school, and to be forced even to expel a number from Cabin Hill (where they normally stayed till thirteen) at the age of eleven, because it was over its authorised number of eleven-plus pupils. His advice was to refuse to do it; which was also my intention. But Tory educational policy in Northern Ireland was inflexible to the point of absurdity and it left me convinced that as a party they preached freedom and individual initiative, but were in fact far more *dirigiste* and centralised than their opponents – as it turned out, when we tried to follow their policy and merge with Ashleigh House. My final words to Stuart were simply: 'Isn't it terrible to be already half-yearning for a return of Lord Melchett.'

On another occasion Rhodes Boyson (once a highly successful headmaster, before going into politics) came to stay overnight and I still remember his comment on our political situation, which seems to hold true for all such conflicts. 'You will never get compromise from the centre.' It seems tragically true that only extremists carry sufficient credibility to bring their followers with them into negotiations, which inevitably require give and take. In times of conflict there is no room for reasonable people. Thucydides noted much the same thing in his account of the *stasis* (revolution) in Corcyra, to which I have referred above.

Other members of staff who moved to headships included Robin Tughan, our vice principal and head of day-boys, who took over Rainey Endowed School, Magherafelt; Jack Ferris, a superb teacher of maths and multi-purpose coach of sports, who went to Downpatrick; Tom Patton to Bangor Grammar School; Norman Eccles to Lurgan College; Dermott MacDermott to Elphin in Roscommon – and last but not least, an internal appointment, Ivan Pollock, a very able member of our own chemistry department, succeeded me as headmaster at Campbell. It is not a bad tally – and there were probably others, but memory fades with time and distance. It was always sad to lose some of our best staff, but it is immensely important that one should encourage and support those who want to seek promotion, and it always gave me great pleasure when such able men achieved their ambitions. It was good for the school's reputation too.

There are so many memories that even highlights would prove tedious. But one of the best was the opening of the all weather pitches, which had been built with Jack Duff's help on top of the old rubbish dump along the Castlehill Road. Behind it lay a long saga of discussions about location and (naturally) finance. My original thought had been to settle for a 300-metre track and one hockey pitch on the field beside the Hawthornden Road. It would have been more affordable and would put to good use a derelict area which was much more visible to the public gaze. Michael Caves, who ran PE and athletics, was adamant that we should try to afford a proper facility and in the end with the help of the Headmaster's Fund and the bursar's skills, we managed to produce a full-size athletics track for the summer, which converted to three hockey pitches in the winter.

The opening ceremony was an athletics match against Blackrock College, Dublin. Dublin schools and parents had become very chary during the Troubles of coming north for matches; but 'the Rock' were by unanimous vote the opponents of choice for this event; and as Julius Caesar might have observed, '*venerunt; viderunt; vicerunt*' – they came; they saw; they conquered. Who actually won the match I genuinely cannot remember and it could not matter less. It was certainly close. But the charm of our visitors conquered us all and I hope did a little for the goodwill between future generations in our absurdly divided island. When I was later invited to attend their prize giving in Dublin, I was applauded by parents and guests for simply being there – and I still have the tie to prove it. Goodwill abounds; but to our media goodwill is not good news, and rarely reported.

The Headmaster's Fund mentioned above was my only solution to the problem of the governors' refusal to risk another appeal. I cribbed the idea from King's Canterbury, and asked parents, entirely voluntarily, to round up their term's accounts by whatever sum they felt they could contribute. We put the proceeds into the Headmaster's Fund, and used it as seed-corn money to part-fund future ventures. The bursary would give me a list of donors each month and whether the sum was 5p or £50, I wrote personally to each parent by hand to thank them. Other parents ran events, of which I remember with the most gratitude Mrs Hazel Graham's regular bridge evenings in the Great Hall, which always proved useful money-spinners. After a couple of years writing individual letters became too onerous to continue and I asked their forgiveness if I sent them a standardised letter of acknowledgement instead. Twice I received £1,000 from one particularly generous parent. Once, when I wrote and thanked a parent for 5p, he was so taken aback that he added a fiver by return of post. Parents are usually more generous to appeals than old boys – and I still believe that there was such enormous goodwill that, had we launched one, we could have found the funds for much more substantial developments. As it was, with the bursar in support, we achieved a surprising amount with the Headmaster's Fund.

At Campbell, the sixth form dance was one of the great social occasions of the year. I always issued strong warnings that drinking and smoking were absolutely forbidden. But it became apparent one year that both were present to an unacceptable degree, with smoking among the girls who were the boys' partners complicating the issue. I had always insisted that boys were responsible for their partners' conduct. It was, of course, the last night of the term, so I had to wait till the first assembly of the following term to announce that there would be no dance the following year. There was predictable consternation and for a year I was subjected to every kind of pressure, from charming pleas from staff, to promises of good behaviour from the boys, to fairly strong appeals from the Old Campbellians, whose dance was consequently also cancelled, because each year they used the hall and its decorations on the night after the boys' dance for their own. But the effect of one severe sanction was that for several years after, boys would come up anxiously during the dances to ask whether everything was all right, and the problem was reduced – never, I suspect eliminated. Even in those emancipated days, boys seemed to need a touch of Dutch courage on such social occasions.

I had long felt that schools ought to do more to encourage their pupils to take industry seriously in making their career choices, and not simply turn unthinkingly to the professions. The Industrial Society had been staging one-day conferences in English schools for some time and with the help of David Oldfield (an outstanding head of economics and careers) we staged the first such conference in Northern Ireland. This brought me into useful contact with leading industrialists like Philip Foreman of Shorts Aerospace, Bill Slinger of Rothmans, and Stan Craigs of Courtaulds, who was already a parent. We worked very hard to set up some worthwhile work experience, and two firms especially were particularly helpful, till costs in senior management time forced them to abandon the attempt. Richardson's Fertilisers, a subsidiary of ICI, produced a wonderful scheme for six boys to spend a week there shadowing middle and senior managers. Sadly the economy moved into a down phase and they could not sustain the effort. Phil Foreman came up with another scheme at Shorts Aerospace in the form of a competition for would-be engineers to be given access to appropriate departments to enable them to spend a week on a significant project, possibly for their A Levels. As with all these initiatives, they are extremely costly for the host firm, and with a sixth form of nearly 100 in each year we had to settle for less than a Rolls Royce approach. In this area David Oldfield and Doris McGuffin worked wonders and our work experience week was a worthwhile activity for many.

This interest in industry led me into two committees. One called ACSIL (Advisory Committee for Schools Industry Liaison), was set up by Arthur Brooke, the former Permanent Secretary at the Department of Education, with whom I had crossed swords (and even got a mention in Parliament) during the war against the change to a comprehensive system. He had moved over to industrial development, and suddenly we found ourselves on the same side. We got on well and had useful discussions on the wellnigh intractable problem of encouraging able pupils to take a serious interest in industry – especially engineering. The engineering profession are their own worst enemies in this regard, and the speakers they put up to address school conferences were sometimes depressingly uninteresting. One thing led to another and I then found myself co-opted to NISTRO, the local branch of SATRO, the Science and Technology Regional Organisation which was operating across Britain. For a low tech classicist the experience was educative and interesting; I only wish I could say that we made a significant difference. I do not think we did, but the numbers of boys applying from Campbell to read engineering did I think begin to rise. (I am all in favour of any initiative that helps to rid the world of lawyers.)

In all my work Sara was a constant source of support and encouragement, indefatigable in helping to entertain and make a lovely home for us all, a wonderful mother of our children, and yet characteristically determined to carve out for herself a method of serving the wider community in wholly practical ways. Not for her the conventional committees and coffee mornings of the more social kind; she volunteered for the nurse-bank at the Royal Victoria Hospital and worked there until the stresses and trials of the work combined with problems of cross-city travel forced her to give it up. She then volunteered as a tea-lady at the newly formed Northern Ireland Hospice, which she described as a truly wonderful institution, and with which she has always tried to remain in touch. When they discovered that she was a nurse, they rapidly recruited her onto the staff and she became a senior staff nurse. She remained there for some six years in all, and loved it, finding almost a new vocation in her care for the terminally ill – so much so, indeed, that when we returned to England she continued with the work at the Sue Ryder Home in Nettlebed. Such commitment defies comment.

Of my entry into broadcasting I will write later. The idea and the initiative came entirely from John Young, the Minister at Belmont Presbyterian Church. He gave my name to someone who passed it on to someone else, and they rang me up and asked if I would do a 'Thought for the Day' series. If you profess and call yourself a Christian and something like that drops into your lap, you have to ask yourself if it is 'intended'. Anyhow, I thought I had better give it a go, and for nearly twenty years I have been a regular occasional contributor to BBC Northern Ireland, Radio 4, and the World Service. I even did one TV address, without notes, live, straight to camera from the shores of Strangford Lough – the longest five minutes of my life. In the end and in retirement I found I had so much material, I put it all together into a book, *A Faith Unfaithful*, published in 2004. In it I included some of my longer addresses on religious matters to various church groups, and my side of correspondence with like-minded friends lamenting the limitations of traditional theology and the modern church's presentation of it. I made no attempt to market the book, but have distributed something over 100 copies to friends and other interested parties who asked for copies.

Broadcasting was a whole new world; I enjoyed it; made good friends; and was forced to think out my own position on the faith of my fathers. 'All experience is an arch . . .'

CHAPTER 25

An Evin Macha – The Navan Fort Initiative Group

ELEVEN YEARS OR SO IS LONG ENOUGH for any headmaster; probably seven or eight is ideal. If nothing else came up, I had always planned to retire at fifty-five; fifty was a little earlier than expected, but sixty would have been too late. Most people (even prime ministers) hang on to office for too long and outlive their usefulness, partly because the inefficiencies of pension schemes make it unavoidable. In some ways fifty was perfect. I had worked hard all my life, ferociously hard for the last eleven years, and I had never had a break or sabbatical from that or any other any post I had held. I was glad of a temporary respite, but was certain I had energy enough for one more substantial task, if I could find it. There was also the small matter of supporting my family at the most expensive period – their mid- to late teens.

Once again providence seemed to drop something into my lap. Bill Slinger, of Rothmans, and a key figure in the local British Institute of Management, to whom I shall be eternally grateful, rang me up one day soon after I retired and told me that the recently established Navan Fort Initiative Group (a sort of independent quango, if that is not a contradiction in terms) were looking for a project manager to produce a feasibility study and a set of proposals for the future of this ancient monument and its surrounding area. Had I thought of applying? I had not even heard of them, though I knew of Navan Fort. But it was somewhat outside my area of expertise, because classical ancient history does not really take much heed of the Celts, except as a by-way in the study of Roman Britain. So my ignorance was almost total.

But it sounded like the kind of thing I wanted to do. It was totally different from schoolmastering; it would take me into the 'real' world of commerce as well as academe; it was on the fringes of my own academic subject, because I had taken Roman Britain as a special subject in my finals at Cambridge; it would involve commissioning a series of studies from experts in their field; and from these I would have to try and pull the threads together, analyse the issues, and formulate a coherent body of recommendations – a task that I found intellectually appealing.

The group (NFIG from now on) was rather high-powered, being chaired by the indefatigable Vice Chancellor of Queen's University, Gordon Beveridge, and including representatives of the Historic Monuments Inspectorate, the NI Tourist Board, the Department of the Environment, the Historic Monuments Council, the National Trust and the Ulster Museum. Peter Addyman, with whom I had been at school at Sedbergh and who had been the moving spirit behind the York Archaeological Trust and the Yorvik Museum, was the lead consultant. As usual with interviews, I cannot remember a word of our discussions, nor have I the slightest idea why they chose me. But I am absolutely certain that it led to two of the most interesting and enjoyable years of my working life.

My greatest regret was that, when my task was over, the report submitted, and a prospectus published, my task was at an end. The group would then have to decide whether the report made sense financially as well as conceptually, and then 'sell' the idea to interested parties and raise the funds needed to turn the recommendations into reality. Only then could they give it all the go-ahead. That intervening period was likely to be the better part of a year. Nothing would have given me greater pleasure than to hang on and try to help with the implementation, when and if it came about. But neither I, nor the group, could possibly tell whether that would happen; nor was there any evidence that I would be the right sort of person with the right qualifications to implement the proposals. There would certainly have to be a new advertisement and further interviews. A year's unemployment was unrealistic and so I had to look elsewhere.

It was a matter of the greatest sadness, but nothing could detract from the pleasure of those two years, which were like a sabbatical in many ways, and brought me into working contact with an extraordinarily pleasant and highly talented collection of people, as well as requiring me to spend a certain amount of time in my beloved Armagh, where Des Mitchell, a dynamic chief executive, and an enlightened council were just beginning to plot the resurrection of an historic and beautiful city, which had been economically and physically devastated by IRA terrorism. I found the whole commission inspiring, appealing as it did to my intellect and an idealistic desire to 'do something' for my own community.

So what was it all about?

Navan Fort, near Armagh, was by general consent Northern Ireland's most important ancient monument, so important indeed that an attempt was made (sadly unsuccessful) to get the whole area designated a World Heritage Site. At the heart of the site was a large quarry, and in the preceding years its steady expansion had caused increasing anxiety, which was brought to a head by an application for planning permission to extend it further. This led to worldwide protests and a public inquiry, the longest ever held in the province's history, culminating in a ministerial decision that all extraction of stone from the quarry should cease. This was hard on the owner, with whom I got on very well, partly because I admired his efforts over a long period to build up what was now an impressive operation. But the minister's decision was undoubtedly right. Two key central monuments were seriously threatened.

The NFIG was set up in early 1987 to consider the best future for the monument and its surrounding area. The issues were complicated by the fact that, though the DOE owned Navan Fort itself and the King's Stables, the quarry and all the surrounding land was in private ownership. Any attempt at purchase would send land values rocketing well beyond any likely capital sum that could be raised for the project. Yet how could a tourist attraction be developed without control of the landscape? It was a dilemma.

There were further complicating factors: Armagh was economically a depressed area, thanks largely to the fact that it was close to the border and the IRA 'homeland;' the city had suffered severely from their bombing campaign; inevitably the security forces were active in the whole area. It was not a place where anyone in their right mind would go for a quiet holiday. Yet tourism was increasingly seen as one of the more promising routes to economic revival, especially if the security situation began to improve. Any scheme proposed must add economic value to the area, primarily through tourism.

There was then a further dilemma. If the area was to be popularised for tourism, there was a risk that its archaeological integrity could be damaged. Purists would regard this as academic sacrilege; practical advisers might feel that some commercially-oriented development was necessary, if any scheme was going to succeed. Numbers of visitors, and repeat visits, were essential. The DOE Inspectorate of Ancient Monuments was naturally protective of the integrity of the site; the more commercially minded were going to want 'attractions'.

And what was to be done with the quarry? It is very large, very ugly, and not public property. Its machinery was a terrible eyesore and obtruded on the view of anyone standing on the monument.

Finally, the site itself was not immediately riveting. A modest drumlin and a grassy mound, some earth ramparts, a hideous quarry, a contracting ritual lake, an invisible hill fort, and a small ritual pond, and all spread out over quite a large area, did not appear to constitute the most promising material for a tourist honey-pot. Against that, a clear linkage with Armagh, which is a beautiful and very historic city, the mother city of Christianity in Ireland, blessed with two cathedrals and some fine Georgian buildings, could well offer a total package, which just might attract visitors.

Whatever the consultants from whom reports were commissioned came up with, any plan was almost bound to involve a degree of compromise between costs and proposals, purists and the commercially aware. The chances of raising the sort of money needed for a really satisfactory scheme seemed likely to be problematical.

Nevertheless, it was a fascinating assignment. As well as enjoying the challenge, I developed a tremendous love of the place, and learned a lot about the legends and mythology of my native land that I never knew before. Occasionally I had to give talks on the subject, and once the proposals were made public, there was a fair amount of interest and even a few requests from groups to come and talk about Navan. It is fair to say that except among the *cognoscenti*, there was limited knowledge of the subject in the province at large.

It was an important monument and I hope that the abbreviated version of my standard lecture on the subject which follows explains why. I make no apology for offering it at some length.

An Evin Macha – The Navan Fort at Armagh

Navan is Ulster's premier historic monument. That is a judgement which will surprise anyone who has visited the site. To the casual eye there is very little there. A pleasant landscape; a distant view of Armagh; an enormous hole in the ground – the notorious quarry; a mound on a small hill; a small lake (Loughnashade); a pond (the King's Stables); and an invisible iron age fort called Haughey's Fort.

Yet in the field of Celtic studies Navan has a powerful resonance – it is in its own way as important as Troy in the epic poems of Homer, which are part of the world's literary heritage. It has something of the same power to set the spine tingling and the imagination dancing as King Arthur's Camelot, from whence one day – so tradition tells us – in the hour of England's greatest need, the once and future king will come again riding to his country's rescue with the knights of the Holy Grail about him. Navan is a Celtic Camelot, or for those of a more classical frame of mind, a second Troy. Better than Camelot, we know where it is; like Troy it is an archaeological site of rare potential; like both it is rich in legend.

There are two things that appeal to almost every child and which he often carries into adult life: the lure of buried treasure and the magic of mythology. I was reared on the *Tales of Troy and Greece* by Andrew Lang, and to a lesser extent on the tales of King Arthur and his knights. It is a matter of great regret that Irish legends were not part of my childhood, since it is a mythology almost as rich as that of Greece. Achilles and Agamemnon, Hector and Paris, the rape of Helen, the adventures of the wily Odysseus, Jason and the Argonauts, Medusa of the snaky locks, Theseus, Heracles, Orpheus and Eurydice, and so on. They were great tales, which have shaped the European imagination and peopled its literature ever since. To a lesser extent King Arthur and his knights have done the same, though the poverty of the English folk imagination has left it more to the literary and educated to give those stories their more formal style. But of their power as stories there can be no doubt. Sadly Irish legends have a more restricted audience – but to those who know them their appeal in no less strong.

But weren't they mere fantasy, all right for children but hardly adults? You might have thought so; but in fact I discovered as a student that what I enjoyed as a child, and then came to regard as mere legend and fantasy, was firmly rooted in fact. The tales were exotic plants if you like, but growing in a bed of solid earthy actuality. Troy was real. As with Greek legends, so too with Irish.

This brings me to that second childhood attraction – the lure of buried treasure. Archaeology has a quite extraordinary appeal to many people. Not only modern scientific archaeology, with its painstaking scraping away of layer upon layer of soil as it slowly reveals the secrets of the past, but also the idea of digging somewhere and discovering treasure. In the last century the great German archaeologist Heinrich Schliemann did precisely that. He started from the premise that Homer's tales of the Trojan War were true and with his Homer in his hand he explored the plains of the Troad, just south of the Hellespont, and lit upon a mound at Hissarlik. And *eureka!* – he found the ruins of a city whose seventh occupation layer had been burned to the ground in about 1200 BC. The right time; the right place; though in fact, when even further down in the layers of about 2000 BC he discovered the treasure that in his heart he sought, he made the regrettable mistake of announcing that this was Homer's Troy and the treasure Helen's jewelry. In the end he was proved wrong and was forced to admit it – but nothing should detract from the glory of his original discovery.

He then made his way to the Greek Peloponnese to look for Homer's Mycenae, rich in gold, and found a citadel overlooking the main north/south communication lines of southern Greece. He found great tombs, an impregnable fortress, and in a circle of shaft graves below the citadel he uncovered a body wrapped in gold and with a golden death mask on his face – and sent a famous telegram to the King of Greece. 'I have looked upon the face of Agamemnon.' It wasn't – of course. The dates were wrong. But he had found Mycenae and, as Homer had said, it was indeed 'rich in gold' as the treasures unearthed there made clear.

Mythology and archaeology had come together. And though we have no evidence that the heroes of those days could really eat a whole ox for breakfast or throw boulders the size of chariots, or run as fast in full armour as any Olympic sprinter, nevertheless clear evidence emerged of an aristocratic or heroic culture very similar to that reflected in the songs of Homer. Further research has suggested that the adventures of Odysseus reflect very accurately the trade routes of the early Greek merchants as they opened up the Mediterranean to trade. Expert sailors like Tim Severin and Ernle Bradford have sailed the Mediterranean in the footsteps of Odysseus and claim to have identified the home of the Cyclops, the location of Scylla and Charybdis, the land of the lotus eaters, the island of Aeolus, god of the winds, and so on. More recently Robert Bittlestone (*Odysseus Unbound*) has produced a superbly documented and illustrated reinterpretation of Homer's account, which suggests very plausibly, that 'Ithaka' was originally an island but is now a peninsula of the island of Cephalonia.

In fact, mythology and archaeology can combine to reveal quite different aspects of a civilisation: the one its material remains and artefacts, by which we can assess something of its wealth and technological development; the other something of what made it tick – its value systems and codes of conduct, its dreams and aspirations, and the power of its collective imagination. That is why Navan is so important. We have there our equivalent of Homer in the tales of the Ulster Cycle and in particular of the *Tain bo Cuailgne* (*The Cattle Raid of Cooley*), as important for students of Celtic literature as Homer is to classicists, since outside of the classics it is the oldest written heroic literature in Europe. We have our equivalent of Troy or Camelot at Navan, the ancient capital of Ulster's King Conchobor, home of the King's boy troop and the Red Branch knights, and the location of the early exploits of Cuchulainn, the Hound of Ulster. The heart of the site is the Navan Fort, so called, whose Irish name was *An Evin Macha* – The Twins (or possibly The Brooch) of Macha. The corruption of *An Evin* to Nevin and thence to Navan is easy to envisage. Locals have never called it Navan Fort, but more correctly and simply The Navan, *An Evin*. It was never a fort – but of that, more anon. *En passant* I would add that Armagh, which is only a mile away, is *Ard Macha*, Macha's Height.

We have yet to find King Conchobor's palace. But it was clearly quite a place. 'Three houses had King Conchobor' says the bard, to wit 'the *Croeb-ruad* (Ruddy Branch), the *Teite-Brecc*, and the *Crob-derg* (the Red Branch).' In the Red Branch they kept the heads and the spoils; in the *Croeb-ruad* the kings lived; in the *Teite-Brecc* they kept the spears and shields. The *Croeb-ruad* had nine compartments, each thirty feet high; they were decorated with red yew carvings within and a roof of tiles above; there were boards of silver and pillars of bronze, whose headpieces glittered with gold, and a plate of silver hung above the king to the rooftree of the king's house; there were a hundred and fifty rooms, with space for three couples in each . . . etc.

So it looks as if, according to tradition, there was a royal residential complex of three major buildings: the palace, known as the Ruddy Branch, but usually referred to in popular usage as the Red Branch; which confuses it with the second building, *Crob-derg*, the genuine Red Branch, where the skulls were stored; and the *Teite-Brecc*, where the weapons were kept. The Irish word for Ruddy Branch is *Craeb-ruad* (Creeve-ruad) – and to this day the townland and drumlin next to the Navan is called *Creeveroe*. Is it possible that King Conchobor's palace is still waiting to be found beneath the hill to which his own knights gave their name? The possibility is exciting. That is why I have laboured the connection between the stories told by mythology and the facts exposed by archaeology. In heroic literature, there always seems to be a kernel of fact behind the exaggerated deeds of heroic derring-do. There are certainly some kernels of fact behind the legends of *Evin Macha*.

Which brings me to the Ulster Cycle. This is the name given to some eighty stories, some of them variants of the same story, about the early Irish heroes, especially Ulstermen, who were regarded in those days as models of heroic behaviour. *Evin Macha* has a central role, as the capital of Ulster and royal seat of King Conchobor. Indeed it is so well known to the story tellers as to require no discussion or explanation of its location.

Dating the events described is more difficult. The tales themselves date in written form from the seventh century AD, but appear to reflect a political situation which predates St Patrick (c. AD 390–460). The heroes are kitted out in the dress and weaponry of the early Christian or Viking period, but their behaviour such as head-hunting or competing for the champion's portion must be a lot earlier. As for cattle-rustling, which is the ostensible subject-matter of its principal tale, the Cattle Raid of Cooley, that has remained a traditional Irish pastime down to the present day, I am told, much helped by the border between north and south, and must therefore be deemed timeless and undateable.

All this mixed chronology is typical of oral as opposed to written heroic literature everywhere. Bards hand on the traditions from generation to generation. Each generation improves the tale adding their own particular embellishments, while clinging to the central core of the sacred story. You can see it in Homer where the heroes use chariots for warfare, even though it is quite clear that the later poets hadn't the slightest idea how a battle chariot was used. But the tradition had chariots; so chariots there had to be. The heroes ride in them out to battle as if they were taxis, and then dismount so as to fight in the appropriate manner of Greek hoplites. The poet knew about hoplites — but not chariots. Chariots in bardic literature over the centuries became as irrelevant to warfare as a modern sports car, but they had to be retained. In Russian folk epic, I believe, you have similar anachronisms, with heroes for example surveying dragons through telescopes before going off to slaughter them with swords.

The Ulster Cycle tales existed in oral form long before being written down, somewhere between the seventh and fourteenth centuries AD. And they certainly reflect an earlier era than that. *Evin Macha*, for example, is still the capital of Ulster, even though we know that by the fourth or fifth century AD it had fallen to Ulster's enemies and the original Ulstermen had been pushed eastward to Down, Antrim, and North Louth.

The tales are many and varied — those that have a close connection with *Evin Macha* include the aetiological tale of the origins of its name. Crunniuc, a wealthy widower, found one day that an unknown woman had come to care for his house, his children, and him. For a long time they lacked for nothing. Then, once, he attended a fair in Ulster and was overheard to boast that his wife could outrun the horses that pulled the king's chariot. The king ordered Macha to attend the fair under threat of executing her husband, and she was forced though pregnant to run a race against his horses. She won, but the effort killed her. As she lay dying she gave birth to twins (Old Irish: *emuin* = twins = *Evin*, as in *Macha*) and then laid a curse on all Ulstermen that in the time of their greatest need they would be as weak as women in labour for a period of nine days. Only three classes were free of the pangs: young boys, the women, and Cuchulainn. And those of us that know the women of Ulster know that Macha's curse (though only imposed for nine generations) holds good to this day. If you want something done, get the women to do it. If you want strength of character, look to the women.

The central tale of the cycle is the *Tain Bo Culaigne*, the Cattle Raid of Cooley, and Cuchulainn is the central figure of that tale. He is an Ulsterman only by adoption, since he comes from the plain of Murtheimne, in the area about Dundalk. This is why he was spared the pangs of Macha, and was available single-handed to defend the Gates of Ulster against the forces of Queen Maeve of Connaught, when she led her armies to try and steal the Brown Bull of Cuailgne.

Sadly the men of Ulster recovered from their pangs just too late to help defend the kingdom and save him from death. But like Achilles in Greek mythology, he too had chosen fame and a short life in preference to long life without a name.

The trouble began with a woman – it always does! The Trojan War was the same, you'll remember, when Paris fell for Helen. But this woman, Queen Maeve, was the first feminist and she could not bear the thought that a man should be superior to her in anything. When she failed in her attempts to borrow or hire the great brown bull of Ulster, the only match for her own Finnbennach, she decided to take him by main force. The great raid began and as usual in a crisis, the men of Ulster suffered from their pangs and Cuchulainn had to defend the province on his own until they recovered. It's a good story and no doubt a better one in the original Irish. And it all happened at the gates of Ulster, the hill range known as the Fews, *Slieve Fuait*, south of *Evin Macha*.

The archaeology is no less interesting. We know that *Evin Macha*, Navan Fort so called, was never a fort but rather a pagan religious site, superseding an earlier one further west in the area of Haughey's Fort. It may well, like New Grange, have begun life as a burial site and later come to be thought of as the home of the gods, in Navan's case these gods being the heroes of the Ulster Cycle. Archaeology confirms what legend has already suggested, that *Evin Macha* was indeed an ancient centre of religion. For the Navan landscape is full of religious remains. A huge temple; a ritual lake with evidence of human sacrifice; a ritual pool with evidence of votive offerings; a druid's circle; probably a mass of inter-drumlin lakes and streams – and we know the Celts were devotees of water. The natural development of a lake is to turn gradually into a bog and bogs are very much a feature of the area.

And if the place was a centre of religion, there is nothing odd in its becoming a seat of royalty as well, since amongst early peoples the king is often also the high priest or central figure in religious ritual, because he is the embodiment of the tribe. So it makes good sense to find that in the great period, round about 100 BC, the hill of Navan itself is crowned by a massive temple, while the king and his nobles dwelt (we assume) on the next door hill at *Creeveroe*, the Ruddy Branch.

We tend to talk of Navan as if it was a single monument. It is nothing of the kind. It is a complex. The whole area is potentially an archaeological treasure house, though so far archaeology has only scratched the surface. Such a landscape also needs a date. Navan is first occupied from around 3000 BC and I will deal briefly with that early period of occupation in due course. But for the purpose of describing its importance as a complex of monuments I would rather stop the clock and focus on a particular period and one particular date, 94 BC, when the great temple was complete.

Irish legend refers to the Celts as the three sons of Mileadh of Spain (Meela Spaunya) who together ushered in a Gaelic ascendancy, which culminated in AD 100 with the final suppression of the native Irish Firbolgs.

There followed a thousand years of Gaelic rule under Conn MacArt and his descendants, who created the central kingdom of Meath and Connacht, based on the royal seat of Tara, in about AD 200. Our period around 94 BC is still for Ireland a period of tribal conflict; territory is still a matter of contention; and great boundary works such as the Dorsey, the Black Pig Dyke, and others are being thrown up.

Within the Navan archaeological landscape there are four key individual sites: Navan itself, Loughnashade, the King's Stables, and Haughey's Fort. Navan itself has three distinct earthworks:

1. A large circular ditch with an external bank.
2. A ring work, much reduced by ploughing, but still visible.
3. A large mound, 150 feet in diameter and 20 feet high.

The large mound was excavated by Dudley Waterman between 1965 and 1972, but sadly he died in 1979 before he could publish his results. A colleague, Chris Lynn finally published them in 1989. It was a brilliant excavation. The story he unfolded was as follows:

The site had been occupied from the Neolithic period, when the first farmers came to Ireland. From this period (3000–2000 BC) came pottery, flints, and ploughmarks, which are evidence of cultivation. Then in the late Bronze Age (say 700 BC) a circular ditch was made in the area later occupied by the mound, inside which was a round structure with a larger one attached on the north, and approached by a fenced droveway.

These remains suggest a large house with an attached yard and Waterman showed that the houses were replaced nine times and the yard six times between 700 and 100 BC. This is clear evidence of continued occupation through the period, while the sheer scale of the structure suggests a royal or aristocratic resident. They also found from this period the skull and jawbone of a Barbary ape, a species to be found in Gibraltar or North Africa. Again this is significant. Gift-giving was a feature of aristocratic society and such a gift, coming from far afield and highly prized, says something of the prestige and international connections of the occupants. It is regarded as one of the most remarkable finds from the site. Another is the Navan brooch, an Iron Age brooch-type, so called from its discovery at the site.

In 94 BC, as dendrochronology has now established, they levelled the whole area and built a monstrous structure, 125 feet in diameter. It had an outer wall of upright posts and horizontal timbering, and inside it five concentric rings of massive posts, 275 in all. When you think that the temple of Artemis at Ephesus, one of the seven wonders of the ancient world, had only 127 columns (admittedly of marble) and yet was described by the Roman author Pliny as having a veritable 'forest of columns', the 275 posts of Navan must have been absolutely awe-inspiring.

At the centre Waterman found the well-preserved stump of a massive oak post, possibly as much as forty-five feet high. It was probably a sort of totem pole, since the archaeologists do not think it supported the roof. The fact that it fitted inside suggests that the roof must have been at least fifty feet high at the centre. For comparison, the columns of the temple of Artemis were unusually high at sixty feet; those of the famous Parthenon a mere thirty-four feet high. Impressive it most certainly was.

Yet within a few decades it was all gone. They filled it with limestone boulders to make a cairn. Then they set it on fire. The black layer of burnt material was clearly visible. Then they heaped a mound of turf above it and there it stayed till 1961.

What can we say about it? It was probably a temple. Its building and destruction were probably ritual acts. The building of a cairn and the ritual firing was the Celtic way of dedicating a place to the Otherworld. Though possibly rushing in like a fool to speculate where angels fear to tread, I could suggest an analogy. The building of the great cathedrals of England in the Middle Ages was a great act of community commitment – a religious act calling for the sacrifice of resources and application of great skills and requiring a massive organisation of manpower and materials, such as only a prosperous and highly developed civilisation could afford. Imagine building Canterbury Cathedral – what a glorious achievement. Imagine, within thirty years of completing it, you deliberately burn it down, as an act of true sacrifice – dedicating of your best to God, before you are tempted either to the sin of pride or mere idleness, to preserve instead of constantly renew your handiwork. Is it not the mark of a superior religion that they chose deliberately not to be encumbered by the weight of their own achievement?

Religion and ritual take us on to Loughnashade. To get there we must fly across the quarry and use a certain amount of imagination. Loughnashade is now a small, circular lake and, if left to nature, will in a few hundred years have probably become little more than a bog. It is surrounded by reeds and full of wild life. Its extent is now just over one acre. It 1835 it was five acres. At some point in the post-glacial period, so our palaeo-ecologists tell us from their core samples, it was some twenty to twenty-five acres in extent. Its greatest claim to fame is that on its shores at some point in the last century were found four great, bronze horns, some six feet long, curved into a semicircle, and decorated in the Celtic style. They were found by a farmer digging a drainage ditch and all but one is lost. The sole survivor, the Loughnashade trumpet, is in the National Museum in Dublin and remains a priceless treasure of Ireland's heritage. To track down the missing three would be a glorious thing. They are probably somewhere, unrecognised for what they are. The location of the find suggests that Loughnashade was a ritual lake – as far as we know the only one definitively identified as such in Ireland. As well as the trumpets, they also found evidence of animal and human sacrifice, all of which accords well with the known Celtic tendency to practise their religion close to water – whether streams or lakes – and to cast ritual offerings into them.

The Celts also had a particular affinity for skulls, not least as military trophies – the Ulster Cycle legends, you remember, refer to the Red House (Crob-derg) at *Evin Macha* as the place where Conchobor's knights kept their skull trophies. It will not surprise you when I say that the evidence of human sacrifice at Loughnashade included skulls of victims who had been ritually beheaded.

The quarry prevents either the eye or the feet making the direct connection between Loughnashade and the great ritual centre on Navan. But there can be no shadow of doubt that the two were closely connected and it is not difficult to imagine the great procession winding up the sacred way to Navan and down to Loughnashade, which at that stage probably lay close to the foot of the hill, with the victims going gladly to their death and the votive offerings being cast, as the worshippers imagined, for all eternity into the sacred waters. There they lay for nigh on 2,000 years – only to surface in the boggy fringes of the much diminished lake, to offer tantalising clues to the archaeologists as they painstakingly pieced together the story of a vanished people.

We now move westwards and somewhat back in time, to the King's Stables and Haughey's Fort, which both date from an earlier period than the Navan temple and the Loughnashade trumpet.

The King's Stables evoke different responses from different people. I first visited it before the DOE had launched a necessary blitz upon the surrounding trees and vegetation. Growth and greenery were rampant. It was a fine evening in high summer. The fields were white unto the harvest. The only sounds were those of nature. Magic was in the air. And when my daughter found a tiny frog about the size of a thumbnail, you would not have found it hard to persuade me that at any moment it would turn into a handsome prince. Yet another friend, on another occasion, described it to me as the sort of filthy pond you'd find at the bottom of a particularly ill-kempt Irish homestead. Chris Lynn, who excavated a segment of the site, describes it as a unique and puzzling earthwork, one of the few sites where even the hardened archaeologist is struck by a strange feeling of the unknown. Local tradition has it that the pool is occupied by a dragon, which defends the sanctity of the place.

Swinburne, in this extract from his poem, 'The Garden of Proserpine', catches something of the atmosphere of such a place, which is so redolent of ancient gods, green, mysterious, faintly sinister, but magical also.

> Here, where the world is quiet;
>   Here, where all trouble seems
> Dead winds' and spent waves' riot
>   In doubtful dreams of dreams;
> I watch the green field growing,
> For reaping folk and sowing,
> For harvest time and mowing,
>   A sleepy world of streams.

> No growth of moor or coppice,
>   No heather-flower or vine,
> But bloomless buds of poppies,
>   Green grapes of Proserpine,
> Pale beds of blowing rushes
> Where no leaf blooms or blushes
> Save this whereout she crushes
>   For dead men deadly wine.

Radiocarbon and other finds dated the pool to the late Bronze Age (1000–500 BC). Finds included sherds of coarse pottery, a spatula made from an antler, clay moulds for the manufacture of bronze swords, various animal bones and – you've guessed it – the facial part of a human skull, which had been deliberately severed from the cranium. All this pointed to the same conclusion: here was another ritual pool and the finds were ritual offerings, similar to those made all over north-west Europe by the Celtic peoples of the late Bronze Age to the water spirits of lakes and rivers. What makes the King's Stables especially remarkable is that in Ireland at least it is the only purpose-built monument of its kind.

Immediately up the hill to the south-west lies Haughey's Fort. It is invisible from ground level, but it persists in the local folk memory as a hill fort. Aerial photography shows an oval field boundary, where all the rest are rectangles, as well as suggesting the existence of an enclosing ditch. Jim Mallory of QUB ran a trial excavation there in the summer of 1987 to try and confirm what had hitherto remained a mixture of folklore and hypothesis. From this he concluded that it was indeed a fortified site of the late Bronze Age, dating from 1250–1000 BC, which is almost precisely contemporaneous with the King's Stables and also (as a matter of interest) the great final period of Troy. It seems reasonable to suggest that those who built the fort created the pool and used it for their ritual activities. For reasons that can only be speculative, there seems to have been an eastward drift towards Navan from about 600 BC, though Haughey's Fort may have continued to be occupied. And one may note, in passing, that the eastwards drift continues into the Christian era, when in time Armagh succeeded Navan as the spiritual focus of the area.

They found pits filled with charcoal and other debris of human occupation; a ditch and evidence consistent with an inner embankment appropriate to fortification; pottery sherds, animal remains, carbonised cereal, and remains of hazel, ash, birch, and alder. In some ways the most interesting discovery which happened quite by chance was the skull of what appears to be the largest domestic dog recovered from any site in the British Isles – about the size of a large Alsatian. Some of the cattle too were very large, one estimated at a height of 129.5 cm (4 ft 4 ins) to the withers.

So much for the immediate area of Navan and its environs. Further out we have the Dorsey and the Black Pig's Dyke, otherwise known as the Worm Ditch and the Black Pig's Race. One of the more interesting things to have emerged from recent excavation has been the relationship between these earthworks and Navan. If you stand on the mound of Navan, one of the most extraordinary things is the view. You look south to the Fews and the Dublin Mountains; west to the Sperrins and, on a clear day, I am told, to Slieve Muckish in Donegal; north to the hills above Coleraine and to Slemish mountain. In fact, from the top of the mound on this really very modest drumlin you can see most of the kingdom of Ulster, which it once controlled.

One of the ways in which ancient peoples delineated their territory was by building ditches or walls or both. The Chinese did it with the Great Wall; the Romans with Hadrian's and the Antonine Walls in Britain; the Welsh did it with Offa's Dyke. So did the Irish. Formidable works they were too and in later centuries their still visible remains gave rise to legends and superstition. The Devil was, naturally, credited sometimes with the work. So were the Danes, because in Irish folklore they were seen as a superhuman people, often responsible for building mottes and raths. Worms and devilish serpents, Danes and other supernatural beings, all these are remembered in the popular titles of these Irish earthworks. But the most popular of all is the schoolmaster and the Black Pig.

Once upon a time far away from wherever it is we are now, there lived a cruel schoolmaster who was a magician who trained the children at his school in witchcraft. He would turn them into animals, especially hounds, so they would hunt their own food and he didn't have to feed them. Sometimes he would turn some into hounds and others into hares and set them to chase each other – but the hounds never caught the hares. Then once he took into his school a very clever boy who watched him carefully and learned how he performed his magic. With or without the aid of his mother (according to choice) the lad turned the tables on the schoolmaster and turned him into a black pig. Then he and all the other children chased him out of the district and over hill and dale until they killed him. And as he went he churned up the earth to make the great dykes and sometimes valleys, which to this day carry his name. And in the end they killed him anywhere you choose from Mourne to Carrickmacross to Limerick to Oughterard.

Sadly archaeology reveals a much more pedestrian tale. These great linear earthworks are tribal boundaries. Though it is visible only in places along the route, the Black Pig's Dyke seems to have run from coast to coast, roughly from Lower Lough Erne south to Lough Allen, and then eastward through County Monaghan, having passed just south of Clones, where an excavated section has been preserved at Scotshouse, and then on to the Dorsey (not far from Crossmaglen) where another excavation has taken place, and up to the Bann somewhere a little north of Newry.

The Dane's Cast is the name given to a different set of Iron Age earthworks, a section of which crosses the same route as that defended by the Dorsey – but further north, and another four-mile intermittent stretch some five miles south-east of Scarva. The word Dorsey means 'doors' or 'gates', and the earthworks at the Dorsey are indeed the gates of Ulster. Combined with the natural fortifications represented by the Fews, the hill range south of Armagh, their purpose was probably to channel communications through a controlled causeway across the ditch into an enormous enclosure, whose purpose was still a matter of speculation until 1977, when by a lucky chance archaeologists working there discovered an oaken palisade and ditch, which gave strong evidence of the Dorsey's defensive function.

By now dendrochronology or tree-ring dating had come into its own, coupled with the information technology so essential for its effective use. As a result it was shown first that all the timbers had been cut down in the same year, and secondly that it was the identical year as that in which the massive central pillar of the Navan Temple had also been cut down. It is now almost certain, therefore, that the Dorsey was constructed as a routeway defence for the political and tribal area of which Navan was the capital. Radiocarbon dating has shown also that a burnt palisade from the Worm Ditch – or Black Pig's Dyke – supports the suggestion that several – or all – of the scattered lengths of earthwork in South Ulster were built at the same time as part of a system of frontier demarcation or for the defence of vulnerable points.

I hope that this lengthy account gives some indication of why the powers-that-be decided to commit so much effort to the Navan project and why for me it is such a special place. In September 1988 on 'Thought for the Day', I even managed to make Navan my theme for three talks.

Suffice to say that we commissioned a series of studies – the main concept study from Queen's University School of the Built Environment; a financial management study; a tourism and marketing study; an archaeological and mythological study. Ann Hamlin, the wonderfully scholarly Principal Inspector of the Historic Monuments Department of the DOE, kept her eye on me at all times and ensured that I did not stray too far from the straight and narrow path of academic rectitude, while Gordon Beveridge himself devoted hours of his precious time to encouraging, coordinating, and inspiring us all in the cause.

Out of all this I produced an analysis of the issues, technical and archaeological, economic, financial and managerial, conceptual and presentational, all of which had a bearing on our final proposal, which was that a major development should be established in the form of a 'high tech' visitor facility centred round Navan Fort and designed to present the complex of monuments and their landscape to a wider public in such a way as to reflect their importance and generate employment.

Following the work of the NFIG, the visitor and interpretation centre was set up, with funding from Europe, the government, the Tourist Board, and the

International Fund for Ireland. When I paid my first visit to it while on holiday, it gave me the most enormous lift to feel that in a small way I had helped to bring this about and to see it employing a significant number of staff both servicing the centre and doing research. Sadly, after a very encouraging first year, the project proved unsustainable in the face of the continuing Troubles, which prevented visitors from coming in the numbers projected. But this year (2006) I heard the glad tidings that the Armagh Council has taken over control of the Centre and are planning to reopen it one more. I also derived a certain pleasure from the fact that recently the British and Irish Prime Ministers met there during one of their many attempts to revive the Northern Ireland Assembly. As a symbolic choice of venue it will not have pleased everybody; it delighted me.

Armagh, as the place where St Patrick first established his church, remains the spiritual capital of Ireland both north and south. Navan, its pagan predecessor, is an important part of our heritage.

Navan will always be special to me, not only for the magic of place, but also for the delight in shared endeavour and the privilege of working with talented and committed colleagues. It also allowed me to re-connect with the ordinary (dare I say 'normal') community of working men and women away from the ivory tower of a boarding school establishment. Being self-employed, as a consultant, and free from the sometimes frenetic existence of a schoolmaster's life, I discovered almost for the first time how much more comfortable are the rhythms of more conventional lifestyles, where weekends are free, working hours are normal office hours, and professional relationships seem to be able to be conducted without the emotional intensity that seems too often to characterise common-room life.

It was in every way a good time for me and the family. I suspect that to some extent I rediscovered my own humanity.

CHAPTER 26

St Mary's, Wantage – The Female of the Species . . .

> *When the Himalayan peasant meets the he-bear in his pride,*
> *He shouts to scare the monster, who will often turn aside.*
> *But the she-bear thus accosted rends the peasant tooth and nail.*
> *For the female of the species is more deadly than the male.*
>
> Rudyard Kipling

IN THE ABSENCE OF ANY OTHER obvious source of gainful employment, I was going to have to return to my first love – teaching. While working for the NFIG, I had kept my hand in so to speak by continuing to mark A Levels, having accepted at short notice just before I retired a request from the NI Schools Examination Council to act as their Chief Examiner in A Level Latin. I had in the past set ancient history papers for Cambridge Locals; this was my first experience of setting Latin papers – I enjoyed the experience, which reassured me that my two-year sabbatical with NFIG had not made me unduly rusty. But I have never liked going back over familiar territory. As far as boys' schools were concerned I had been there, done that, and got the T-shirt.

> All experience is an arch wherethro'
> Gleams the untravelled world . . .

I wanted something different; but at fifty-two I suspected that I was a little old for another headship, and even if I got one, the inevitable stresses would probably shorten my life by a decade or more.

Again blind chance dropped a rather different challenge into my lap. St Mary's School, Wantage advertised for a deputy head. I knew of it by name and reputation; in addition my cousin, Christina Somerville had been a pupil there. I suspect that there had been school dances against them while I was at Radley, since some boys had sisters there. Having brought up two daughters myself, under Sara's expert instruction, I thought to myself that whatever else, it would be a novel experience. Again, I was summoned to interview, and rather like the immortal Eric Morcambe, when demonstrating to André Preview (Previn to his friends) how to play Rachmaninov, insisting that he was using 'the right notes, but not necessarily in the right order', so too I was in the right place for the interview and at the right hour, but not necessarily at the right height. In fact I was about 20,000 feet too high, since my plane, delayed by fog, was high above Wantage and only then on the approach path into Heathrow.

Full marks to the school. As soon as we touched down I rang and apologised; they were totally unphased, re-jigged the timetables, and when I arrived we had a very good discussion with the headmistress and the delightful vicar of Wantage, Robert Wright, now chaplain to the House of Commons. As a father of daughters, I could say with complete sincerity that I felt it was important in an era of gender equality that men should be seen to be willing to work as deputies to women. Girls need role models just as much as boys, so schools are an important area where they should see women in the 'top' job, especially since it was then relatively rare for it to happen anywhere else. I hope this was a factor in their brave willingness to take on a male as deputy head. Certainly I liked my interviewers from the start; they certainly pretended to like me; and I was hardly back in Belfast the same evening, when I got a phone call offering me the job.

As a family it was our sixth move in twenty years, but the business of packing up and moving lock, stock and barrel has one great merit – it forces you to discard unwanted baggage and reduce the clutter of your possessions. (This gave me an idea for another 'Thought for the Day' – suggesting that the Christian churches should do the same, not to their physical, but their intellectual and mythological clutter). We settled into Alfredston Place, which I have already described, a new development fifty yards from the school's front gate.

Wantage is a delightful, small market town at the foot of the Berkshire Downs, with strong associations with King Alfred and the old kingdom of Wessex. Within 100 yards of our front door we could be in open countryside and a two-mile uphill hike would bring us up to the Ridgeway, probably the oldest road in Britain and dating back to prehistoric times. It linked the Avebury region with the Thames, where it joins the Icknield Way, to continue north-east towards Norfolk, and all along it were monuments of the past of varying degrees of antiquity. I walked the length of it in stages over the next year from the Thames to Avebury Rings, and though it was occasionally disturbed by mud-pluggers on their motorbikes and even a few drivers of 4x4s, there was little else to disturb the sense that civilisation was far away. There were always larks and yellowhammers in summer, mad March hares in springtime, latterly kites as well as smaller birds of prey, bird life and insects. Only the lack of butterflies betrayed the environmental pressures that were already developing. Sara and I walked there regularly, and it was an area of sheer delight. Segsbury had an Iron Age hill fort, the White Horse Hill had another and a Roman encampment; Wayland's Smithy was a magical spot, with an Iron Age burial mound surrounded by ancient beech trees, and undoubtedly a haunt of ancient gods; Alfred's Castle seemed almost lost in deep countryside; from the Downs above Letcombe Regis you could still see the view of Christminster (Oxford) which first confronted Jude Fawley in Thomas Hardy's novel, *Jude the Obscure*. And just to keep your feet on the ground and remind you that it was the late twentieth century, the cooling towers of Didcot power station were always there, steaming sedately on every horizon and visible from twenty miles around.

It was also the constituency of Robert Jackson, a highly intelligent Tory MP, a Fellow of All Souls, a government minister, who was later to resign from the Tory Party, and a convinced Europhile, like his wife Caroline, who was the local MEP. He rang me up one day, out of the blue, having got my name from some unknown source, and asked me if I would give him lessons in classical Greek. It turned out that because he was with the Department of Trade and Industry, he was at the same time learning another modern language as well – Polish, I think it was; all this while also doing his job as an MP and a government minister. The intellectual energy was phenomenal. His progress in ancient Greek was startling; his approach highly systematic, and would be regarded nowadays by the educational *fashionistas* as totally outdated: grammar, vocabulary lists, and syntax learned by rote; plus masses of translation for consolidation, but with little interest in the more literary features. I am certain that within a year his grammar was more secure than mine; his vocabulary impressive; and only in the mercifully eccentric flexibility of Greek syntax was I able to demonstrate my superior knowledge and be of some use to him. I was a strong Eurosceptic, so at a conversational level there was plenty of scope for disagreement, but he dissented from my views in a benignly superior sort of way, always more in amused sorrow than in anger. He also told me to my great surprise what a nice person he thought Tony Blair was – and this while the Tories were still in power. Was it a sign of the defection to come? It never occurred to me that I had a small scoop at my disposal.

St Mary's School itself had an interesting history. It was founded by the Rev W J Butler, the Anglican vicar of Wantage, who was active in the Oxford Movement, the High Church wing of the Anglican communion, led by Oxford University dons such as Newman, Keble, and Pusey, whose aim had been to revive the religious life of Anglican England by emphasizing the catholic (which is not synonymous with Roman Catholic) principles on which it rested. Butler had started by setting up an Order of Teaching Sisters in 1848, known as the Community of St Mary the Virgin, ultimately the largest order of Anglican nuns in Britain. In 1873 they opened St Mary's School with fifteen boarders and sixty day-girls on the site of their old convent, when their new one had been built. The school steadily expanded and by 1900 it was entirely a boarding school. In the late 1980s, under the dynamic leadership of my future boss, Pat Johns, formerly a housemistress at Gordonstoun, their numbers reached over 300 boarders, too many for the accommodation but a measure of her success.

The sisters withdrew from any formal involvement in the running of the school in 1975, but its tradition and ethos remained Christian and Anglican. They continued to nominate three governors and were always sympathetic, interested, and supportive. They also owned the property, but charged the school only a peppercorn rent. The community itself developed worldwide and set up daughter houses in India and Australia, and though the numbers of applicants to join them has steadily declined, it remains an important Christian foundation. Finally, in a notable gesture of goodwill, the sisters gifted the ownership of the school to the governors soon after I left in 1997.

Two years ago the governors announced that they were selling the property and moving to a new site on the outskirts of Wantage, where they planned to build a brand new school from the proceeds of the sale. They had found that increasing regulation under health and safety legislation made the old plant too expensive to run and they had no option. This exciting initiative came to a sad end in March 2006 when they announced that instead, because of planning delays and escalating costs, they had decided to close the school and amalgamate with Heathfield School, Ascot, which itself had a long history as a girls' public school, having been founded in 1898. The new foundation would be known as Heathfield St Mary's. It is a sad ending, but one that is not uncommon these days. I am only glad that I was long gone before it all happened.

> When the early Jesuit fathers preached to Hurons and Choctaws,
> They prayed to be delivered from the vengeance of the squaws.
> 'Twas the women, not the warriors, turned those stark enthusiasts pale.
> For the female of the species is more deadly than the male.

I had long known the punch line of Kipling's poem, which I had read but never studied. I should have, for my own better education. On a superficial reading its sentiments are a disgrace to a more enlightened age, which preaches – even if it does not fully practise – emancipation and equality for women. In fact it catches something of their essential nature in a series of superficially offensive but fundamentally sympathetic observations, based on acute observation and understanding, despite the light-hearted tone in which it is written (jest, he acknowledges, is a 'male diversion').

> She is wedded to convictions in default of grosser ties;
> Her contentions are her children, heaven help him who denies! –
> He will meet no suave discussion, but the instant, white-hot, wild,
> Wakened female of the species warring as for spouse and child.

I can feel the claws sharpening and the Maenad sisterhood gathering to tear their prey limb from limb and to 'rend me tooth and nail'. My own dear sister and my blissfully happy marriage had given me a wonderfully idealised view of womanhood. For me women were sweet perfection. My two daughters, even during the supposedly tempestuous teens, rarely gave me cause to remember that grisly warning from the old hands, when they said that 'when your children are four they are so delicious, you could eat them; when they are fourteen you will wish you had'. At St Mary's occasionally (not often), I began to see what they meant, though I would have put it at a year older.

The most notorious events that occurred during my time took place with depressing regularity, during one of those exasperating periods when modern youth suddenly feels free to kick over the traces and run amok. The post O level period, when tensions are released and the need for disciplined endeavour has evaporated, has become a particularly difficult time for authority in many schools. The media, if they discover the news, fan the flames and encourage all kinds of mindless misdemeanour, while affecting a totally hypocritical shock and dismay at the results. The normal sanctions have suddenly lost their capacity to control the recalcitrant.

At Campbell College, in celebration of the end of the exam period, the boys had contrived a number of such activities which, though tiresome, usually revealed a sense of humour and imagination entirely devoid of malice. On one occasion a set of enormous footprint appeared across the front lawns and driveways and straight up the side of the main school tower. I shudder to think how it was done; had an accident occurred, I suspect it might have been a resigning matter. But it was clever, original, daring. On another occasion the small car of a member of staff was carried bodily into the locked school during the night and placed on the steps of the school chapel. Not quite as difficult as putting a car on the roof of the Senate House in Cambridge, which the engineering students of my year contrived to do as a brilliant demonstration of their craft – but very much along the same lines.

But the girls showed no such imagination or humour, and their post-exam shenanigans tended to be little more than mindless vandalism, destructive of school property and very difficult to control under modern conditions, when the law sides with the lawless in the name of human rights, and with pupils against teachers similarly. On one occasion my boss earned massive headlines in the gutter press by suspending the whole of the fifth year. On another the lavish distribution of horse manure, probably acquired from conniving parents, rendered parts of the school site slippery and potentially dangerous, while the hysterical screams and yells in the early hours will have (metaphorically at least) frightened the horses and appalled the locals. There was no way of physically controlling such madness, and despite the mounting of all night patrols by staff, once evaded and the 'revels' launched, one had to be content to stand and observe and try to ensure the pupils' safety.

It was the near-animal hysteria that I found so fascinating – in retrospect. I could not but remember the production of Euripides' *Bacchae*, with which my career at Radley had culminated. The tragedian was a master of psychology, particularly female psychology, and it earned him the reputation of a misogynist. Yet one has only to watch the behaviour of female fans and their hysterical adulation of film stars and pop musicians to see how differently their group dynamics work and how close they are to mass hysteria half the time. Euripides caught the flavour of such events very accurately in his play, and the Messenger's speech might have been written for these occasions. Abbreviated, and loosely translated into prose, not iambic blank verse as in the Greek, it goes something like this:

We cowherds and shepherds gathered together, arguing with one another at the amazing things these women did. We hid ourselves in ambush, and as we watched the women waved their thyrsus wands in preparation for their celebrations, shrieking aloud with one voice, and calling on the name of Iacchus, Bromius, the Son of Zeus. The whole mountainside and all the animals went mad with bacchic revelry along with them. And as they ran, all creation seemed to run beside them. Agaue, Pentheus' mother, ran close by where I lay hidden watching; but when I leapt up hoping to take her prisoner, she cried aloud, 'Come my hunting dogs, these men are hunting us; follow me and use your thyrsus wands for weapons.' We fled, every one of us, and narrowly escaped being torn limb from limb by the bacchanals. Instead they fell upon the herds of cattle grazing on the green meadow grasses. They had no weapons, but you would have seen a single woman with her bare hands and nothing else tearing apart a fatted calf as it bellowed aloud in terror; others tore young heifers in pieces alive; ribs and hooves were scattered everywhere, tossed in the air, and scraps of flesh hung from the trees, which dripped bright red with blood. Angry bulls, with anger mounting in their horns, were slain before they could attack, falling to the ground dragged down by this myriad horde of womenfolk, stripped of their skin and flesh, and scattered in pieces far and wide, before you could even blink your eyes. Buoyed by their own momentum they flew, like birds, across the plains below beside Asopus' streams ... Like an invading army they ravaged everywhere, swooping up and down to pillage everything, and even snatching children from their homes ... Enraged, the local villagers flew to arms, but their sharp weapons drew no blood; the women's thyrsus wands propelled like javelins caused grievous injuries. The men turned tail and fled, routed by womenfolk.

The Greeks even had a word for the activities thus described – *sparagmos*: a tearing apart; and *omophagia*: raw flesh eating. Well, sometimes it felt as if we were not far from it. Describing the events later to a fellow classicist, the husband of one of our governors, and himself the governor of other schools, I said to him two words: 'Euripides' *Bacchae*.' There was no need for more. He knew exactly what I meant. It was far from funny at the time; recollected in tranquillity it made me realise the degree to which control of a school, any school, really amounts to one colossal bluff by the authorities; or, at best, government by consent reinforced by mutual self-interest.

Riot and mayhem were mercifully rare, confined to one night of the year, when briefly the Lords (and Ladies) of Misrule ran temporarily amok. Shakespeare again would have recognised the syndrome and indeed reflected it in his *A Midsummer Night's Dream*. The Romans acknowledged a similar phenomenon, and with a wise recognition of the psychology of suppression, in the festival of the Saturnalia allowed a short release to the pent-up emotions of their slaves. Kipling seems to have seen this clearly also.

I have flirted with danger long enough. Let me appease the sisterhood by saying, categorically, that my eight years at Wantage were in fact a delight. Yes, there were problems and difficulties, but they were sources of interest and professional challenge, not pain and grief. I found my bosses (both of them) extremely good to work for, rational (*pace* Kipling), intelligent, highly skilful managers, and utterly dedicated, determined to get the best from and for their pupils. The girls were talented and charming, and mainly alarmingly hard-working; the staff likewise. The girls were brilliant at networking and the St Mary's Old Girls Association (superbly run by Victoria Humphries), showed that skills, already well honed at school, remained in place for years afterwards. SMOGs were always good friends and their regular emailed newsletter a model of information and mutual assistance.

I taught classical civilisation and Latin, rediscovering from the latter the pleasures of the Cambridge Latin course, and from the former finding how much additional insight one gets from studying a complete text even in translation. One very civilised arrangement for staff on the boarding side, which I had never come across before, was the timetabled day-off. It was an enormously humane source of restoration of energy and recovered sense of proportion. Sara and I used it for escape to many of the places of interest round about, such as National Trust properties, Westonbirt Arboretum, the WWT at Slimbridge (though our interest in birds was still in its infancy), or even just walking on the Downs.

Certain duties proved interesting. As safety officer I crawled all over the place trying out escape ladders and seeking to ensure that common sense, at least as much as legislation, would keep the girls safe in an emergency. Fire practices were frequent – at least as much because some idiots found it entertaining, even late at night, to set off the alarms, as for any attempt by me to rehearse emergencies. As a result I rarely had to organise official practices at strange times; we held one early each term to ensure that the drills were understood, but could rely mainly on the lunatic fringe for the rest.

As at Campbell, I found myself trying to work out ways of making better use of available space, not least because the school was very full. It is something I enjoy doing; I think I have an eye for spatial possibilities, and I much enjoyed trying to find ways to cram quarts into pint pots. My colleague in the senior management team, Cathy Old, the senior mistress, was superbly efficient in all administrative matters and brilliant at defusing the small tensions and squabbles inevitable in any busy staff room and I rarely had to offer my services in this area. Women are far more realistic and usually much tougher than men at managing their own kind, but they also possess a sensitivity to special circumstances that will often pass us by.

Cathy and her husband, Fraser, a retired engineer and senior manager from Harwell, became great friends and have continued so to be despite our removal to distant Somerset. Cathy, a modern linguist and brilliant teacher, shared my admiration for Pat Johns and I like to think that we made an effective and supportive team. Fraser, a pillar of the Ocean Youth Club (and in the distant past, I think, of the Oxford University Cruising Club) used to help with the school sailing club and even tried to instil into me some rudiments of nautical lore, hitherto derived largely from my beloved Arthur Ransome and occasional outings as a crew member for John Deane in his Dragon. His patient instruction during a couple of days sailing on the Solent remains one of my most pleasurable memories. We shared an interest in the stock market, but it was my admiration for his formidably logical and lucid mind (he was a scientist after all, and such people have little truck with arts' men's woolly waffle) when we talked of theology and other such matters, that made me wish that our paths had crossed much sooner.

My biggest single assignment, which devoured every waking hour and spare minute for about three years, was the regeneration and computerising of the school library. For a small school with limited resources, the governors gave me a formidably generous budget for the task. I bought new stacks; new furnishings; increased the purchase of books massively; and then single-handed re-catalogued and put onto computer some 6,000 volumes, literally sticking the label and Dewey code number onto and into every single book, and entering it into the computer records. It was immensely tedious and often felt immensely thankless also. I am sure I became a bore on the subject; I am sure too that some colleagues were grateful that it kept me well out of the way; a few that they always knew where to find me.

In researching the subject and then asking several firms to tender for the task of supplying the computers and the software, I was extraordinarily lucky to discover, from a colleague at the Dragon School in Oxford, a small computer firm called DTE (Down to Earth) Software Systems. Mike Gay, founder, owner, and managing director, wrote programs and supplied equipment, and he had devised specifically for schools a library program, which seemed exactly suited to our purposes. Because he also knew about hardware, he ensured too that I avoided basic errors in the field. For example, he insisted, rightly, that the future lay with the pc, not the Apple, and advised against an Apple-based system. The school for its own computer studies went the other way. But for its secretarial teaching, it stuck to pc's, like most of industry and commerce. As a result girls gained experience of both systems, but in the end the school computer staff changed their minds and came back into the pc fold.

It was a highly satisfactory association with DTE, and Mike's back-up and general support for trouble-shooting was wonderfully prompt. I commissioned his system, he installed it, I worked the program for about four years, until I retired, and found it most effective. Had I been technically more proficient I am sure I could have put its wide range of facilities to even better use. But I was too old a dog to be taught many new tricks, and he showed exemplary patience when technical incompetence reduced me at times to fury or despair. He remains my IT guru to this day, and even got me a fascinating small assignment to do the voice-over for a training CD for sommeliers, which was being commissioned by a specialist distributor of high quality brandies. I am told my voice may be heard at least as far afield as Dubai pontificating on the mysteries of that exotically expensive lubricant.

Pat Johns, my boss, was one of that brave band of women who had applied to take holy orders in the first wave of recruits to the priesthood, when at last the deplorably chauvinistic and deeply conservative Church of England dared to put its head above the parapet and ordain women. They have transformed the church and the priesthood for the better, though a minority continues to deny both the fact and the validity of their orders. She was robustly practical, a very good organiser, blessed with a logical and sharp intellect, as you would expect of a mathematician, and a wicked sense of humour, allied to a considerable talent for gossip. The school had not altogether prospered under her predecessors and she was utterly determined that she would give them the stability of a lengthy tenure of office and consistent management. She did, sometimes at considerable cost to her own popularity.

My unspoken task was to give her total support during that difficult period when her training and new commitment seemed to clash with her current task. It very rarely did, but I hope that my experience as a head had given me a degree of insight into the challenges and problems which heads face and that I was able to some degree at least to share the burden. That I hugely enjoyed working for her and with her goes without saying. She was a remarkable woman and a great head. She transformed the school and my farewell 'obituary' to her in the school magazine was my sincere tribute to her achievement.

One stated commitment that I had given in my interview was that I would stay long enough to see Pat Johns' successor safely into post. I worked with Pat for five years and her successor, Sue Bodinham (later Sowden), for three and so honoured the promise I had made some eight years earlier.

It was all very good experience, less stressful than being a head, but in its own way probably almost as difficult. Had I done it earlier in my life and before becoming a headmaster, I would have felt very tempted to apply for the headship of a big coeducational boarding school as my final ambition. As it was, still lacking the St Mary's experience, I had tried for the headship of Oakham while still at Campbell, but unsuccessfully. It would have been a fascinating assignment.

The other lovely thing that happened was that when Anne Marsden, the school nurse of St Mary's, retired, Sara applied for and was appointed in her place. She had been working at the Sue Ryder Home in Nettlebed, and though she very much enjoyed the work, it involved commuting a long way, and given the vagaries of the weather at times it was uncomfortable and stressful. This seemed like a wonderful opportunity. A new sick bay was instituted in a former gardener's cottage in the school grounds, suitably modernised and refurbished, right beside the main school building, and Sara was given a clear brief to heal the sick, of course, but also to cherish and comfort the afflicted, and in general to act as a kind of mother figure to all the girls. It was a task for which she was ideally suited by temperament, training, and character, involving as it did counselling skills almost as much as medical. As well as being a highly-trained nurse, Sara is a wonderfully patient listener, a brilliant diagnostician, and knows a thing or two about teenage girls. Even her apparent tendency sometimes to believe malingerers too readily derives from the thoroughly sensible proposition that there is probably an underlying problem, of which malingering is only the symptom – this is best investigated under the pretence of having been taken in.

What she was less well equipped to handle was the opposition which she encountered from some of the boarding staff, who worked hard to defend their territory, as they saw it, by challenging her policy and complaining about her for being too kind and too soft on discipline. Sometimes I found myself holding the ring uneasily between the parties, not always finding it easy, because I understood and agreed with her strategy and was in part responsible for her brief taking the form it did. She brought a gentle humanity to the constraints and discomfort of a boarding school. It would be my impression, prejudiced of course, that for the girls she was an enormous influence for good and her labours for them massively appreciated. But then 'he would say that, wouldn't he?' She absolutely loved the work and for both of us it made a tremendously happy end to our professional careers that we should be working together in the same school and at the same time.

We retired together in July 1997.

CHAPTER 27

In Retrospect

*Unarm Eros; the long day's task is done
And we must sleep.*
                    Shakespeare. *Antony and Cleopatra*

We try; we err; we try again. And in that way we give history meaning.
                    Karl Popper

RETIREMENT IS A SOLEMN MOMENT. My old friend Jim Devlin observed to me once, as we said farewell to a retiring colleague, 'You know what the next big step is, don't you?'

The final reckoning comes on the Day of Judgement. But the Day of Retirement is not a bad rehearsal for that big day. What the world sees as your useful life is over; you have had your opportunity. Could you have done better? Would you have set yourself the same targets and ambitions the second time around? If you could have your life over again, would you have done it differently? To ask such questions is to presume that you have by now formulated some sort of a view about the purpose of life. If you cannot say what you are here on earth for, then you cannot possibly assess whether you should have done differently or better.

One of the wise men who influenced me at Cambridge, a devout Christian, always surprised me when he asserted that the only purpose of living is to be happy. Epicurus might have said that; but I would have expected my Cambridge mentor to have suggested that we are here to serve God, or to 'do good', or something a little more obviously virtuous.

But he was in good company. I am told that Kant argued that 'it is not God's will merely that we should be happy, but that we should make ourselves happy', that John Stuart Mill declared that to maximise the welfare of all sentient creatures is the aim of our existence, and that their welfare consists of happiness, while Schopenahuer, the supreme pessimist, argued that escape from the misery of existence is possible through ascetic living, appreciation of art, and charity for our fellow men, and that the real symptom of unhappiness is the pursuit of wealth. All these great thinkers seem to assume that happiness is the ultimate purpose of existence. Thomas Jefferson in the American Declaration of Independence of 1776, while acknowledging the existence of the Creator, seems to have moved in the same direction:

> We hold these truths to be self-evident, that all men are created equal, that they are endowed by their Creator with certain inalienable rights, that among these are life, liberty, and the pursuit of happiness.

For him, life and liberty are prerequisites, but happiness the goal of human life; and all three are the gift of our Creator.

Our view of the purpose of human life must, of course, depend in part on our religious or philosophical beliefs. To a believer the true purpose in living must be to find his way home to God. Taking that as read, the ultimate purpose of living may well be said to be to seek happiness. But as the boring old schoolmaster always remarks, 'It all depends what you mean by happiness.' Define happiness and it may well turn out to be the same as goodness or God or ultimate reality. Plato would have agreed, I suspect, in that he saw all good as participating in the one reality, which is God.

As for the sources of happiness, men will argue about that till the cows come home. Certainly it cannot be anything as simple as riches, because whatever you have, you want more; and though aspiration is admirable, unrealised aspiration can only sour the soul. Bertrand Russell, in the lovely prologue to his autobiography, tells us that throughout his life three passions governed his existence: a longing for love; the desire for knowledge; and an overwhelming pity for the sufferings of mankind. To work to satisfy those three would be enough to give most of us golden slumbers. And though he was, I think, a convinced atheist, his three passions would not seem inappropriate for a believer either.

Happiness, indeed, seems a sensible objective for any mere mortal, even if he lacks the wisdom of a Russell, the certainties of a prophet, the insights of a saint, or the communion with God of a mystic. And it must be sought on earth. But of one thing I am absolutely certain: if anything on earth can give us an inkling of the joys of heaven, it has to be the love of family. Of my blessed marriage I have probably said enough; of my children likewise. But with hindsight, if I had been granted one wish by my fairy godmother, it would have been to be given what indeed I have received – a wife and children whom I love beyond all telling. However imperfect a husband and father I have been, my love for them has always been unconditional and unequivocal. I hope it has also brought out what there is of my better nature – and that surely is what all religion seeks to do as well, to inspire in us the immortal, the godlike part. Love on earth is our only paradigm for love of God; and certainly the reward for me has been a happiness of the profoundest kind.

Set against this, success – especially as the world seems to judge success, which is little more than wealth or celebrity or both – is an unsatisfactory source of happiness. I remember reading once the biography of a great classical scholar, W Warde Fowler, and being much struck by the testimony to his broad humanity in the comment of his biographer, who said of him that, 'though he may not have been a great man, he was great as a man'. That is not a bad epitaph. Success, as the world sees it, may bring fame or wealth or even a degree of satisfaction at a job well done; I am not sure that it brings happiness. But to be a success as a human being, a creature made for loving, that seems to be well worth striving for and might well bring happiness in its train.

Such happiness derives, I suspect, from a sense of fulfilment, completion, a feeling that you have accomplished what you are here on earth for, and can therefore live at peace with God and your fellow men. Jesus even said it on the cross – *tetelestai*: I have reached my *telos*, my goal; hit the mark. The conventional translation, 'it is finished' hardly quite conveys the full message. Somewhere a sense of purpose is implicit in any definition of happiness that I can offer. But this brings us back to the problem of belief: if you cannot believe that you are on earth for a purpose, but are simply the creature of blind chance and a random association of atoms, then you must find what happiness you can from simpler pleasures, such as a big salary or a large car or extravagant lifestyle. But this is to confuse enjoyment or pleasure with happiness, for I suspect that such things cannot bring true happiness. But all such discussion is ultimately futile, because each person ends up begging his own question, using his own definition of happiness to answer the question of what it is.

The Jews offer useful insights. Their two great commandments, as Jesus reminded them, required them to love God and their neighbour, not just their wife and family. He may well have disturbed them by extending the definition of neighbour to include all mankind. To love God you must know Him; to know Him you must find Him and to find Him you must seek Him; and one of my regrets is that I have never got beyond the seeking stage. Nevertheless, even in the seeking one is to some degree fulfilling a purpose, and through it a degree of happiness may be found, not least when we are vouchsafed the occasional glimpse of knowing.

George Herbert in this extract from his poem, 'Prayer', suggests something of the totality of happiness derived from a life lived for God, through prayer.

> Softness, and peace, and joy, and love, and bliss,
>   Exalted manna, gladness of the best,
>   Heaven in ordinary, man well drest,
> The milky way, the bird of paradise,
>   Church bells beyond the stars heard, the soul's blood,
>   The land of spices; something understood.

As for the love of my neighbour, I suspect that my track record does me little credit. All I can offer in my own defence is the proposition that the teacher's calling is a kind of loving of one's neighbour, because it is an invitation to the young to share our own enjoyment of some of the glories of man's past achievements, and a commitment to help them to find for themselves some of the resources needed for their own pursuit of happiness. It is better than nothing; it is a kind of giving, not entirely selfish; and with that defence I must rest my case and take what mild degree of comfort from it that I can.

But commitment to vocation and commitment to family was never enough for that most demanding of religious teachers, Jesus of Nazareth. Consider this fearsomely demanding prayer addressed to him, in language which still has all the resonance of Elizabethan verbal rhythms and poetic quality. I quote from memory, probably with less than total accuracy:

> Teach us good Lord to serve Thee as Thou deservest, to give and not to count the cost, to toil and not to seek for rest, to fight and not to heed the wounds, to labour and not to seek for any reward save that of knowing that we do Thy will.

Measured against that exacting standard, no man could claim success or rest content.

Happiness, however, may be a modern aspiration. For the ancients happiness seems more limited, consisting as it did of the ability to withstand the slings and arrows of outrageous fortune undismayed and undeterred. To cry, 'Fate cannot harm me; I have lived today', was for them sufficient. Without the insights of the great monotheistic religions, the Greek heroes faced their human destiny with a clear-sighted realism. Here is Homer's Achilles, speaking to King Priam, whose son he has just killed in single combat.

> Two urns stand upon the floor of Zeus, one filled with his evil gifts, and one with his blessings. To any man that Zeus who rejoices in lightning deals a mixed lot, that man meets sometimes with evil fortune and sometimes with good. But any man to whom Zeus gives only gifts from the evil urn, him he brings to scorn, famine pursues him all over the good earth, and he becomes a wanderer honoured by neither men or gods ... Keep courage and lament not unceasingly in your heart. For you will achieve nothing by grieving for your lost son, nor will you bring him back to life before you suffer fresh misfortune.

The Stoics could hardly have put it better. It has a bleak realism far removed from our idea of happiness. Yet even Lucretius, propounding the Epicurean philosophy – conventionally regarded as the opposite of Stoicism in advocating the undiluted pursuit of pleasure – achieves a similarly realistic tone. In fact it was not pleasure he advocated, but happiness, and to that end a healthy moderation in all things. Meanwhile make the best you can of the life you have.

> *Sic aliud ex alio numquam desistet oriri,*
> *Vitaque mancipio nulli datur, omnibus usu.*
>
> Thus one thing will never cease to be born of another;
> And life is given to none as a freehold, but as a tenancy to all.
>
> Lucretius, *De Rerum Natura*

Grit your teeth and soldier on. *Que sera, sera*. It is all of a piece with the old Greek proverb, 'Call no man happy till he is dead', which was cited by Solon, the greatest of the Seven Sages of the ancient world, to King Croesus. Croesus had invited him to admire his treasure stores as proof that he was the happiest man alive, and the tale is recorded by Herodotus. André Maurois even used the proverb as the title of his autobiography, *Call No Man Happy*, which is a minor classic of the genre.

Croesus, King of Sardis and the richest man in the world, asked Solon, statesman philosopher and the wisest man in the world, whom he thought was the happiest man in the world. 'Tellus, the Athenian', he replied. 'And what are his qualifications?' asked the king sharply, somewhat miffed that Solon had not chosen him. 'He lived at a good time in his country's history; he had sons, who turned out well; he lived to see them all have children of their own, who all survived him; by our standards he had a perfectly adequate income to live on; and to crown all this he died a really glorious death, serving in the Athenian army at the battle of Eleusis. He was killed fighting gallantly, and was given a state funeral, with a hero's burial where he fell.'

Herodotus *History*

Most of us are driven, to a greater or lesser degree. I certainly, without prompting or pushing by my parents, felt driven to 'succeed' by my admiration for my grandfather; yet there was never a chance that I would match him, whether in scholarship, achievement, goodness, or greatness. So if happiness is to be found, it must be found in an honest recognition of one's limitations, an acceptance of them, and a willingness to be content that we have tried. Like Chief Inspector Morse, all our second given names should be Endeavour.

I would certainly like to have made riches, because I persuade myself (but I suspect I mean deceive myself), that with riches you can do so much good by giving them away. But they may also make you miserly, or greedy, or even more selfish than before. That is a risk, certainly, but I have always thought it something of an affectation to assert that money isn't everything. As a means to an end, money is a great resource. It fails only when it is seen as an end in itself, for though it may offer physical comfort, I have rarely seen evidence that in itself it brings spiritual comfort or inner happiness. However much you have, it is never quite enough and there is good sense in the words of Andrew Carnegie that 'he who dies rich dies disgraced'. He was certainly better qualified than most to know. In fact, the price of making money is too high and though I may have regrets about my failure in this area, I am at least grateful to have achieved enough to be comfortable. I see no evidence that grinding poverty was ever a source of happiness for anyone. Like William Smith, the father of geology, I am glad to have discovered for myself that 'calmly to enjoy retirement with the never failing resources of a well-stored mind is the sweetest pleasure (not happiness, please note) of a full-aged man.' Well, one of the sweetest pleasures, anyhow. It is possible, too, that a sufficiency of different pleasures may amount to happiness.

There is an inherent paradox about money. Until man developed sufficiently to be able to organise himself as an economic species to generate surpluses he made little progress. Surplus wealth is the real source of his creature comforts and the high culture, which is one measure of civilisation. Art, music, literature, religion all contribute to quality of life and are for this reason potential sources of happiness. But these all need high level patronage; and that requires very rich individuals with resources to spare, or a state which acts as the supreme patron of all cultural activity – which, on the whole it is not very good at. The Athenian state is the exception that allows us to test the rule; but the rule holds good on the whole. Surplus (or profits) may not bring happiness of itself; but (however much left-wingers dislike the idea) surplus is essential for wealth, patronage, and high culture. Thus indirectly it is the source of happiness. That is the paradox to which I refer.

If I am happy, perhaps it is because I failed as a wealth-maker. I take that thought to my comfort. In old age other things come to matter more. Some of the last words my mother said to me, not long before her death and after I had returned to England, took the form of the simple question, 'Are you happy?' To which, endeavouring in true Greek fashion to give her an honest answer, I replied, 'I am content. I have had so many blessings.' I don't think I was splitting hairs; contentment is not happiness, but it is certainly a major staging post upon the way. I would like to think that my reply was sufficient for her to feel that she could finally let me go.

> I have had worse partings, but none that so
> Gnaws at my mind still. Perhaps it is roughly
> Saying what God alone could perfectly show –
> How self-hood begins with a walking away,
> And love is proved in the letting go.
>
> C Day Lewis (on seeing his son's first faltering footsteps)

I do not think I ever quite came to terms with my father's savage dismissal of the teaching profession, 'A man among boys; a boy among men.' It left a kind of bitter taste in the mouth ever after, for all my pleasure in what I believe was a worthwhile calling. Certainly it is hard for any of us to compete with the profession of healing, whether as doctor, surgeon, or nurse, as the one human activity which is unambiguously committed to doing good for others. And apart from its nurses, society rewards it accordingly. By contrast the teacher's calling brings few financial rewards and in too many schools little but stress, ingratitude and government-inspired harassment. Of the two, I would be inclined to argue that teaching is the more sacrificial profession – and therefore certainly no less admirable.

Both professions, it seems to me, have been wantonly destroyed by government-inspired mismanagement, which has created a culture of box-ticking and target-focus which is a denial of professional judgement and an insult to the commitment of those who practise these two vocations. I saw it happen in the mid-eighties when a Tory government brought in the 1,285-hour rule for teachers. This laid down that teachers must work a minimum of 1,285 hours in a year. Innumerable teachers, dedicated to their vocation, used to work innumerable extra hours, unpaid and far beyond the 1,285 hours or any contract agreed with management, simply because they were dedicated to their work and loved it. Almost overnight Mrs Thatcher destroyed their sense of vocation and their commitment to their calling. I suspect, but cannot prove it, that she thought that London-based, left-wing teachers who dominated the unions, probably needed to be brought under control, and this was her chosen method. The doubtless unintended consequence was to generate justifiable resentment across the whole work force and to destroy commitment.

Similarly, and more recently, a Labour government has done the same to doctors. They are no longer allowed simply to consider what is best for the patient, but how best to tick government boxes and deliver unnecessary treatments, thus earning a larger income for their practice or themselves. Hospital priorities are distorted and patients kept off waiting lists to ensure that the lists are not too long, so that the government can claim to have shortened them. Again, professional judgement and doctors' vocation are both insulted and we are all the poorer for it. The big-brother mentality of this government has superseded the nanny-knows-best mentality of the last. Centralisation and standardisation are the curse of our society. Targets, sensibly used, can be an effective management tool. Once they become the be-all and end-all of the workplace, they are disastrous.

My father told me not to go into medicine; I would now advise children not to go into teaching in the state sector, if they can avoid it; the independent sector still has something to commend it.

So if I had my time again, would I go into teaching? Somehow I doubt it; certainly nowhere that the state has anything to do with. But if you then ask what I would do instead, I have to hesitate. More than anything else I would like to have written a great book, or a set of great poems, or painted a few great pictures. These are all deeply selfish pursuits, but they all have the great quality of leaving the world a richer place than we find it. But once I put it like that, I would like to think that the schoolmaster's calling at its best is not dissimilar. It has a creative dimension to it; and like the artist, the test of the teacher's achievement may well not be seen for half a century or more. The rubbish that passes for great art in our modern galleries will soon, I hope, be forgotten if not forgiven; but great art stands the test of time and the artist may well die before he can have the satisfaction of knowing that he did well.

So too with teaching. The effects of what you do endure unseen; but like the mustard seed in the parable, you hope that one day it will grow to a mighty plant. But there is no knowing – and precious little thanks. I have lost my copy of the play, but somewhere near the start of Robert Bolt's *A Man for All Seasons* Thomas More urges Thomas Rich to 'be a schoolmaster. You'd be a good one, Thomas; possibly a great one.' 'Yes', replies Rich. 'But who would know?' More's reply went something like this – I wish I had the exact words. 'Yourself, Thomas. Your pupils; their parents; your friends; and God. Not a bad audience that.' Not a bad sales pitch for teaching either.

Failing that, I would like very much to have helped to run a major organisation. My various interactions with the world of industry made me realise the tremendous fascination to be found in what I call the 'challenge of complexity'. To see an aeroplane taking shape upon the factory floor and to contemplate the multitude of skills and the huge variety of pieces of equipment that go into fashioning this miracle of modern technology is to realise that managing such an undertaking requires skills, imagination, organising power, and sheer intellectual energy. I would have enjoyed it.

Nevertheless, '*je ne regrette rien*'. I have had much enjoyment; earned enough for my family to keep the wolf from the door; lived (as Solon puts it) at a good time in my nation's history, when Christian ideals became in many ways the ideals of the country I live in, implicit in the welfare state, which for all its failings has taken on the role of the churches in a previous age in supporting the weak, defending the afflicted, cherishing the young, caring for the old, and striving for a just society. For twenty years or more I have argued that the churches may be dying, but that is in part because their task is done and they must find a new role. They have won the argument on love of one's neighbour at least, and so one of the principles on which our faith is founded is also the principle by which our country strives to live. In that respect 'The strife is o'er, the battle done.' But now, I believe, the search for God must begin in earnest.

Like Solon's Tellus, I have indeed lived at a good time in my nation's history. I have had two children, who turned out very well, and through them I have been granted the immortal gift of grandchildren. We have had enough to live on comfortably, but without extravagance (as required by that first entry in my first commonplace book: *meden agan*, nothing in excess). The final ingredient in Solon's recipe for happiness, which I would prefer to be spared, is that I should die gloriously fighting for my country. Too many of my parents' generation did that for me to see it as a fitting finale, and the present government's latest foray in this direction affords us little grounds for pride. I would ask rather to fall asleep quietly and without fuss on a golden autumn afternoon in a ripe old age, without distress to family or friends, and before I become a real nuisance to those close to me through ill health or senility.

That would be the final blessing and I would ask no more.

Grow old along with me!
The best is yet to be,
The last of life, for which the first was made:
Our times are in His hand
Who saith 'A whole I planned,
Youth shows but half; trust God: see all nor be afraid!' . . .

Then welcome each rebuff
That turns earth's smoothness rough,

Each sting that bids nor sit nor stand but go!
Be our joys three-parts pain!
Strive, and hold cheap the strain;
Learn nor account the pang; dare, never grudge the throe! . . .

Therefore I summon age
To grant youth's heritage,
Life's struggle having so far reached its term:
Thence shall I pass, approved
A man, for aye removed
From the developed brute; a god though in the germ.

From Robert Browning's 'Rabbi Ben Ezra'

CHAPTER 28

Retirement – Rejoining the Community

To every thing there is a season, and a time to every purpose under the heaven: a time to get and a time to lose; a time to keep, and a time to cast away; a time to keep silence, and a time to speak . . . Wherefore I perceive that there is nothing better, than that a man should rejoice in his own works; for that is his portion.

Ecclesiastes

THE MOST REMARKABLE FEATURE of my life has been, I think, the fact that every decade has seemed an improvement on its predecessor. I do not count the first, since childhood happiness cannot really be weighed in the scales against the later years of self-awareness. The innocence of childhood does not lend itself to reflection; no child sits down and asks himself whether he is happy or content. Sensation is immediate; emotions momentary; desires instant. It was an immensely happy childhood – exactly as all childhoods should be. But for the rest my claim holds good. Retirement has been so far the best decade of all.

'The chief purpose of being busy is to be idle.' So said the great Dr Samuel Johnson for whom sloth, one of the seven deadly sins, was an enduring source of temptation. If anything I found the opposite. For almost the first time in my adult life I found time to pursue the hobbies and interests, which working in boarding schools had always denied me, and to try and make myself mildly useful to my community. In addition, Sara and I avoided what I believe to be the fatal mistake of those who retire, which is to move away from where we had lived and worked. Our eight years in Wantage had been extremely happy; we had made friends and got to know local people. Now it was possible to become involved in local life in a way which my work had always prevented me from doing.

I joined the West Berkshire Golf Club and found a regular playing partner with a similar handicap of about 20 in Ian Campbell, our local optician. He was also an enthusiastic bird-watcher and from him I learned to recognise the willow warbler's descending song, as it sang regularly from the willows along the third and fourth fairways, and began to develop what became an ever-growing interest, which I could share with Sara.

Golf is the most infuriating of games; I once played to a handicap of about 12, but my lack of application always made me unreliable and inconsistent, a reasonably long hitter but cursed with a permanently wayward slice at the end of my long shots and a deep reluctance to take a divot on my approaches, which is I suspect the key to accuracy. I played increasingly sporadically, and since retiring to Somerset not at all. It is a great shame, since of all games it can be most happily pursued into old age, and the handicapping system enables one to compete on level terms with far better players.

There is a charming passage in Cyril Alington's biography of that fine scholar and athlete, Edward Lyttleton, which offers comfort of a kind to exasperated golfers like myself. It goes something like this:

> Golf he took to late in life. But his habit of composing Latin verses in his mind during a round showed that he did not take this most exacting of games too seriously. And when for the second time his clubs were stolen by some simple-minded thief – for to tell the truth they were rather a job lot – he had no difficulty in seeing the finger of Providence in the matter and, with an equanimity indistinguishable from relief, abandoned the links for the garden.

Providence never came to my aid like that, but I was never good enough to really need its help and I found my own way to the garden.

By contrast I would have given anything, almost, to find a way to continue playing geriatric or village cricket. Of all games it remains my first love, whether playing or coaching. But the combination of a slipped disc, acquired when coaching junior hockey at Campbell College, and a kind of reserve, which made me hesitant to join a local club when my advanced age would, inevitably, make me more a passenger than a player, meant that I was never able to satisfy this longing. I have always felt, too, that sporting interests are deeply selfish activities for married men. Cricket especially is enormously time consuming and I have seen too many loyal wives bored out of their minds watching from the boundary the antics of their husbands, who never seem to have asked themselves whether they should not be offering mutually agreeable entertainment to their better halves.

Instead Sara and I found activities that we both enjoyed. Walking, the National Trust with its stately homes and gardens, birds, woodlands and countryside have given us unending pleasure over the years. Theatre, sadly, which we both enjoyed in our earlier days, we largely abandoned. The expense on a pension is now prohibitive and my ambition to see the whole range of Shakespeare's plays at Stratford foundered on the two rocks of cost and what seemed to me their gimmicky modernist productions, poor speaking, and eccentric choices of emphasis, which seemed to be in fashion at the time.

By sheer chance, soon after we returned to England, Sara spotted in the *Nursing Times* a promotion for Sparth House, a small hotel in Malham in the Yorkshire Dales, which was offering nurses and their spouses special reductions. We went, we saw, and we fell in love with Malham itself and all the Yorkshire Dales in general, and time and again we returned to Sparth House, where David and Lesley Oates ran a lovely establishment with fabulous cooking and the warmest of welcomes. When they sold up and moved on, we ceased to go, but by then we had our time-share in Bowness-on-Windermere, purchased in 1992 for £5,000, for three bedrooms and two bathrooms, and a very comfortable living-room. Current prices seem to be about £15,000 plus for similar facilities. Maintenance charges seem high; but low enough compared with a week in a hotel or the going rental for that same cottage.

It was sheer lunacy, of course. Sara on her own would never have done it. I was inevitably still captivated by the childhood fantasy of Arthur Ransome's Windermere, and fell for what seemed a lovely opportunity. Initially, too, we were somewhat overwhelmed by the classic, high-pressure sales pitch, when we attended a 'presentation' in Abingdon. But the law saved us, because we had a fortnight's cooling-off period. The more we thought about it, the more convinced I was that it was a con trick and that the time-share did not even exist. There was something deeply suspicious about the way in which the salesmen worked on us, and we suffered almost immediate buyer's remorse. We handed it back three days later and cancelled the deal.

But then, on our next holiday in Malham, we thought we would drop in on Burnside in Bowness, just on the off chance to see if it really did exist. We were bowled over; there was no pressure; we liked the set-up and the associated option of using the hotel's facilities instead of having to cook; and we bought a week on the spot, straddling the end of May and the start of June, sometimes coinciding with half-terms and bank holidays, sometimes not. The western side of the Yorkshire Dales (including Sedbergh) was just over half an hour away; Malham only an hour, Hadrian's Wall an hour and a half. So we had got ourselves a perfect base for walking in wonderful countryside, exploring either the Lake District or the Dales. It has proved a godsend, and a year later I bought a second week in mid-October (for a slightly lower price) to allow us to enjoy the autumn colours. Though we have occasionally exchanged, nowhere we have been can begin to match the glories of the area or the comfort of our two cottages, the second also sleeping six but possessed of its own sauna as well. Wherever else we go, those two weeks have given us a constant stream of perfect holidays. Our exchanges did produce one lovely week in Madeira to celebrate our silver wedding; another in Clowance, Cornwall. But most proved disappointing.

We joined the Wildfowl and Wetlands Trust at Slimbridge and subsequently became life members there too, thus gaining access to their various sanctuaries across Britain, including Castle Espie in Northern Ireland, though Welney is our favourite, being wilder and wetter than Slimbridge, which was contemptuously dismissed by one of the Welney members we talked to as 'little more than a bird zoo'. Membership of the RSPB inevitably followed and this too has added interest to our holidays. At Leighton Moss, just south of the Lakes, we saw our first bittern and bearded tits; at Titchwell Marsh in Norfolk we enhanced our skills in recognising waders and saw Sammy the black winged stilt (very rare indeed); at Cley marshes near Blakeney wonderful displays of marsh harriers, golden in the slanting sunlight; at Haweswater we saw the only resident eagle in England, sadly still waiting for a mate to fly down from Scotland to join him on his demesne; above Bassenthwaite we have watched the ospreys and their chicks.

At Shapwick and Ham Wall on the Somerset Levels we now walk regularly, watching without success so far for bitterns and regaled by choruses of Cetti's warblers, whose call is best remembered by a naughty mnemonic, for which I must refer you to Simon Barnes' lovely book on *How to be a Bad Birdwatcher*. We are not twitchers; our expertise is severely limited; but the pleasure of recognition of sound as well as sight adds so much to the pleasure of any walk, that it is hardly surprising that the RSPB are probably the largest single leisure organisation in the UK, with over a million members.

At Ham Wall another memorable day came on a cloudy afternoon in late April. As we left the car we heard our first cuckoo of the year calling from half a mile away across the reed beds. Our arrival at the first viewing station was greeted by a chorus of marsh frogs that would have delighted the heart of Aristophanes, while Cetti's warblers by the hundred exploded into song; out in the reed beds, well hidden from view, the mocking laughter of the little grebes rose and fell in ululating symphony. Then, as we walked along a rhyne, a second cuckoo started to call just above our heads. At the same moment I spotted my first Cetti ever; they are usually the opposite of Victorian children, heard and not seen. This time there were three or four and, unable to identify what looked like any other LBJ (Little Brown Job), I said to Sara that they must be wrens, except that I had never seen one with a white patch under its chin. But there were no wrens singing or clicking, but Cetti song abounded. The bird book later confirmed my Cetti diagnosis.

Meanwhile we turned again to inspect the cuckoo, and for some twenty minutes fired by a frenzy of frog music and cheered by a chorus of Cettis, and laughed at by little grebes, we played grandmother's footsteps with our cuckoo all along the rhyne. It flapped from tree to tree; perched; dropped to the ground to grab a comforting worm; returned to its perch, with that lazy, drooping wing posture that is a give away. Each time we approached, it would let us get to about thirty yards and then fly off a little further. He never opened his mouth, confirming what some elderly twitcher told us the previous year, that they only sing in flight; a 'fact' denied by the experts, who assured us that they never sing in flight.

To score two firsts in a single afternoon is the stuff of magic for mere amateurs like us. But our latest and greatest achievement to date has been to see and hear five bitterns at Minsmere in Suffolk. One for about two minutes on a long feeding flight; two challenged by a third in a territorial dispute; and two more settling near our hide, one about three feet off the ground on a cluster of reeds (which our RSPB guide assured us 'never' happens), and the other in classic camouflage pose with beak pointing skyward, motionless, but visible because we saw him take up position. Wonderful.

We also became life members of the National Trust, thereby ensuring that for a quite significant one-off payment we would have for the rest of our lives an unending source of pleasure and interest. We have visited almost every property in whatever area we have lived and a fair proportion of those in the areas where we have taken our holidays. Sara can educate me on art; I sometimes can offer information on literary matters, though she is better read than I. Great houses, famous gardens, lovely landscapes all have their associations and from it all we have derived a shared delight. The Lake District, and Cornwall with its gardens, have been two particularly rewarding areas to visit. Neither of us have any horticultural expertise, but a shared delight in beauty is sufficient for us both. The British have always been a nation of gardeners and, as Francis Bacon once observed in his famous essay, 'God Almighty first planted a garden (eastward in Eden), and indeed it is the purest of human pleasures. It is the greatest refreshment to the spirits of man; without which buildings and palaces are but gross handyworks.'

We also became members of the Friends of Westonbirt Arboretum. At almost any time of the year and in almost any conditions we have found it a place of quiet restoration for the spirit. It was about an hour from Wantage and is now an hour from Cleeve, which is near enough to be convenient, far enough to feel you are going out for the day. Every year since we joined it seems to have developed or improved new areas, and the new acer garden in the midst of larch woods (much loved by goldcrests) is a particular delight. The whole arboretum has an extraordinary capacity for absorbing people, so that whatever the state of the car park, it never feels crowded. Someone once pointed out to me that trees are the longest living organisms in the world, and certainly one of the pleasures in planting trees (which I have tried to do wherever I have lived) is the thought that you are planting for future generations, since you will barely see your saplings into their adolescence. The pleasure of walking amid gnarled oak trees, those 'green robed senators of mighty woods', is incomparable, and the fact that they were probably planted in the time of Henry VIII or Elizabeth I to provide timbers for the future British navy is a wonderful thought. Pine woods have their own appeal – a kind of deeper silence and mysterious gloom, with 'mossy winding ways', but for me deciduous woodlands carry the day, and oaks especially, not least for the fact that they sustain more different species of animal, bird, and insect life than any other.

The stock market has been a hobby since my time in Canterbury, when I inherited a small legacy from my uncle John and found in Brian Turner, who was later to teach Anna economics, and Denis Ball, a couple of colleagues who shared my interest. I wish I could pretend that over the years by shrewd management and skilful investment I had turned my £500 into £500,000. Alas no. As my mother used to observe, 'you have to buy your experience'. I did, but not to such an extent that my wife and children had recourse to the poorhouse or myself to leaping from the upper storeys of the stock exchange.

But for a schoolmaster the stock market is a hobby which has use as well as interest. In following the fortunes of innumerable companies and risking a few pounds on some of them, I gained a familiarity with the economic life of the country and the progress of its economy in a way that I could never have done by simply reading the newspapers. I found, too, when talking to parents – who often affect a supercilious condescension to the dusty old pedagogues who teach their children – that I could demonstrate some knowledge of their particular field and ask intelligent questions about it in a way that would sometimes take them aback and show that I was not totally confined to my ivory tower of academic irrelevance.

In the family stockbroker, Hilary Morrison of William F Coates in Belfast, I also found not only a source of wise advice, but also a friend who shared my own interest in theology and was a long-standing adviser to the Church of Ireland synod. His best single piece of advice, which certainly helped to spare me the horrors of the 2000 meltdown in technology stocks and shares, was very simple, but surely valid: 'look after the growth of dividends and the growth of capital will take care of itself'. In that sense I have always been a value investor, refusing under normal circumstances to invest in any company that failed to deliver regular and rising dividends. I also discovered for myself the merits of a contrarian approach, not least because it suited my own temperament, which to an extent is that of any Irishman – mildly bloody-minded and inclined almost on principle to resist the opinions of the herd. Certainly I know that whenever the City columns talk of 'new paradigms' or 'unmissable opportunities', it is time to take to the hills. When the unit trust industry is purring, you know the crash is about to come. When investment companies feature their star managers in advertisements, find out how long they have been there, and in most cases assume they will soon be gone. Above all, put not your trust in the professionals. It really does appear that they can do little better than the amateurs and sometimes rather worse than a monkey with a pin. Invest in solid companies with long histories and steadily rising dividends and you can't go far wrong.

In retirement I was lucky enough to be able to join GHORIC, a local investment club, largely made up of retired scientists from Harwell, and there I found a shared interest, friendly company, and a willingness to learn our trade through mutual education. Its purpose was both social and financial, and though we were not one of the more successful of such groups, it was a source of interest and amusement and drew my attention to the possibilities of smaller companies. Greatly daring, after a while I also joined (though not for long) a much more high-powered association called SIG, the Serious Investors' Group, whose expertise was so formidable that I could only maintain a kind of awed silence at the few meetings I attended, and whose techniques of analysis were so refined that I was quite incapable of following them. I saw little evidence that their overall results were significantly better than anyone else's, since everyone boasts about their gains; few confess their losses. Objective judgement is well nigh impossible.

I never found a chess club, a game I have always enjoyed and might have become reasonably proficient at. I was once challenged to a game in a railway carriage by someone heading off to compete in a tournament and to his great chagrin defeated him. But as in so much else you need challenge and opportunity. I found neither. Instead I bought a computerised opponent who offered to play me at no less than 75 levels, ranging from fun levels, through novice, to intermediate, stronger, and finally at level 72 advanced. To my considerable satisfaction I have managed to improve steadily and have beaten it at level 50 and thus qualified as 'stronger'. But I have always played white, and therefore am probably deluding myself as to the quality of my performance. It is certainly better than Sudoku.

As for gardening, that was a joy to come, and one that I was unable to indulge until we moved to Somerset. Our house in Alfredston Place had a small garden, triangular in shape and about twenty-five feet by fifty. In it I planted too many shrubs and several trees, including a beech, which will certainly cause problems one day unless the owners prune it. But I comforted myself with Madame de Pompadour's famous remark, *'après nous le deluge'*. It grew like Topsy and made a very nice focus for the garden, drawing the eyes up to the hills behind. I was already working to my basic formula for a low-maintenance pensioner's garden: shrubs, tubs, and lawn. Though small, it was surprisingly attractive.

In describing these pursuits and hobbies, I am reminded of a quotation, which I recorded in my first commonplace book, though its source is unknown to me, about Georgiana, Duchess of Devonshire: 'her life was now as full as only an empty life can be'. Mine must seem similar, because so far I have reported only pleasures and frivolities. There was a more serious side.

I found myself, I am not sure how or why, inveigled back into the JACT orbit, and became the Treasurer of the Ancient History Bureau, which aimed to service in particular those teaching ancient history at O Level. Old friends were still on the committee and new stars had entered the firmament. Moses Finley and Peter Brunt were gone, sadly, but in Robin Osborne (then Professor of Ancient History at Oxford, but since translated to a superior university) they had found a dynamic and brilliant chairman. He told me that a companion volume to *Res Publica* was needed for the A Level Augustus period, and asked me whether I would be willing to do the translating. John Rich, of Nottingham University, had agreed to take on a similar role to Pat Lacey by planning the overall structure of the work, making the selections, and providing the scholarly notes. It was to be the biggest LACTOR yet produced, ending up at something over 400 pages. In Chapter 17 I have already said all that needs to be said on the subject. I love translating; it kept my ageing brain working; it made me read things I had never read before; and the links with the JACT committee kept me in touch with my own subject. Above all, and in retirement I am sure this is absolutely essential, it gave focus and purpose to my daily life, and a routine of work, which prevented me lapsing into the sloth so greatly feared by Dr Johnson.

I continued to examine ancient history at A Level and have to confess to a degree of smug satisfaction in finding the gobbet questions in the papers still featuring *Res Publica* after thirty years, and now adding excerpts from *The Age of Augustus* as well. I would love to have been a university academic and was never quite good enough. These small pleasures were a kind of compensation. I also enjoyed another quasi-academic activity, as a guest speaker on the Swan Hellenic cruises, so much so that I have devoted to them a chapter of their own, which follows. They brought me six years of varied travels through the antique lands of a lifetime's study, kept my mind busy, expanded my knowledge, and brought new friends. In a sense they rounded off my career with a slightly different kind of 'teaching' and closed the circle of my working life.

Conventional wisdom has it that the church and politics should not mix. In this conventional wisdom is wrong. If the people of the church refuse to sully their hands with politics, they leave the battlefield open to those whose motives may be less worthy. I shall devote a later chapter to my church activities, because they overlapped with what I did at Cleeve, but local politics had also caught my attention.

What the Greeks called *ta politika*, the affairs of the *polis* (the city state) should be the concern of every citizen. Wantage was in size very similar to an ancient city state – about 10,000 strong. I had been for some years a paid up but inactive member of the Conservative party. I had always felt that for a teacher to be interested in politics is legitimate; but I would have found it difficult to be active therein, without bringing my politics into the classroom, however inadvertently – and this would be wrong. But the political process had always been of interest, not least because I had regularly taught the evolution of Athenian democracy and had admired its robustness and surprising effectiveness. Pericles, in his funeral speech, perhaps along with David's lament for Saul and Jonathan, the finest and most famous of all laments for the heroic dead, says of his fellow Athenians that 'here each individual is interested not only in his own affairs but in the affairs of the state as well . . . we do not say that a man who takes no interest in politics is a man who minds his own business; we say that he has no business here at all'. In an age of justified cynicism about politics and politicians it sounds a remarkable assertion. But for the vigour of the body politic there is much to commend such an approach.

Suddenly an interesting opportunity dropped into my lap. Like many others I was pretty disenchanted with the Tory party. They seemed to have been in power too long; the accusations of sleaze and generally disreputable conduct seemed increasingly well-founded. Mrs Thatcher had held on for two years beyond her sell-by date; her successor, though a nice man, seemed to have no coherent vision of the future; altogether they were a pretty depressing lot. In the meantime I was happy to send contributions to the Referendum Party (later the Independence Party), because I viewed Europe as a disaster for Britain, bureaucratic, deeply socialist, corrupt, self-serving, undemocratic, sinister, and imperialist in the sense that it was out to create a single highly centralised European state, ruled by unaccountable faceless commissars. They had destroyed our fishing industry; weakened our agriculture; damaged our legal system; and were determined to destroy all the members' economies by their insistence on outdated socialist rules and regulations and a rigid adherence to discredited economic *dirigisme*. Any organisation unequivocally committed to helping us to escape from its strangulating meshes was to be supported. I toyed with offering to stand as a candidate, but decided it would require more commitment than I could offer and as yet they were a movement more than a national party.

I found, however, that at the local level the Liberal Democrats were both effective and a rather pleasant collection of people. Europe apart, I was sympathetic to their general philosophy and belief in decentralisation and local autonomy. I had had a number of friendly conversations with Jim Moley, the leader of the local party, an intelligent and interesting personality. As a result, he persuaded me to stand as a candidate in the local elections. He assured me that my views on Europe were no impediment. I explained that I was not really a political beast and that I would be no good at canvassing. This too he assured me was no impediment. They had a good local team and a very well managed central organisation, whose computerised information on every constituency gave a good indication on where to place the emphasis of our effort. Despite my low expectations, I was elected, and a new phase of my political education began.

There were two main surprises for me. The first was how little power and what a tiny budget (£10,000, if I remember rightly) the local council had. Car parking charges enabled it to raise a little more. Yet here they were, responsible for the immediate management of a town of some 10,000 people, but with few resources with which to do anything significant. I became chairman of the planning committee; but all we could do was to inspect proposals and make recommendations to the district council, where all the decisions were made. Some town council members were also members of the district council, and when the party had a majority there too, our recommendations could carry some weight. Wantage (Thomas Hardy's Alfredston, so named from the association with King Alfred) is a lovely old market town, but there was little contentious in the planning committee, since everyone wanted to keep it beautiful. But it was interesting to see how strong feelings could be generated over relatively small matters. I was only in office for about two and a half years before moving to Cleeve and resigning. So I missed some of the more exciting later issues, as three new areas of development opened up and negotiations took place with the developers for the enhancements to the site most advantageous for the local community. Going back some five years later, I was pleasantly surprised to find how much had been done – little of it offensive aesthetically, and some I hope beneficial to the town's declining economy.

One sure sign of such decline was the increasing number of charity shops occupying prime positions in the town centre. It was a matter of concern, but I was never able to establish to my own satisfaction the reasons for this increase, which was not a phenomenon confined to Wantage. My analysis is probably faulty, but what seemed to lie at the heart of the problem was a matter of accountancy rules, to be summed up in the simple sound-bite: 'no rent is better than low rent'. If the landord charges a low rent for a property, its capital value to an accountant must also be low, since it will based on a simple formula of x times the annual rental. In his accounts, therefore, the landlord may have to show a capital loss, if in time of economic decline he lowers his rent. But if he lets a charity occupy the property for nothing, he can maintain the capital value in his books, while at the same time keeping the property occupied and maintained. But such properties paid no council tax. As a result there was a positive disincentive to landlords to lower their rents to attract new tenants. This seemed to me a manifest nonsense, but it would require legislation at the national level to change it, and that required politicians with time and inclination to challenge the whole series of vested interests involved.

So charity shops will continue to bleed the life out of the centres of small towns, ably assisted of course by the big national chains and the out-of-town shopping malls. The only thing I can find to say in favour of the process is that first, charities do so much good for our society that we should be careful not to discourage them; and second, in an era of recycling, they are the recyclers of unwanted goods *par excellence*, and we should be grateful to them. Nevertheless, there must be a better way.

My second surprise was how small a team was required to run the town and how hard the individual councillors worked. Among other things we were the managing authority for the town's graveyard. To pay a contractor to prune trees and do one-off maintenance, as opposed to regular grass cutting was expensive. So we did it ourselves, despite the usual anxieties about accident insurance and all the other impediments to local initiative and volunteering which mad governments continue to impose. Councillors and the (modestly paid) town staff seemed to devote hours of time to resolving local problems, looking into disputed matters, and servicing or serving on committees, with no reward beyond the satisfaction of doing the job they had offered themselves to do. If that is the typical pattern across the country, we are extraordinarily lucky. I have ceased to be critical of local politicians, reserving my strictures now for those who work at the national level. They seem to have acquired for themselves a very cushy number, with long holidays, vast expenses, big perks and pensions, and salaries that increase at about ten times the rate of those of the rest of the population. It is little consolation to observe that it is probably true that throughout history it was ever thus.

I also found myself, by virtue of my chairmanship of the Planning Committee, elected Chairman of JET, the Joint Environmental Trust for Wantage. This was

Two Wilson Weddings

Anna Jane Illingworth Wilson marries Dr Robert Adams, July 2003

Emma Margaret Wilson marries Patrick Hales, April 1998

Granny Sara Wilson (2001) – with Imogen (aged one hour)

Our Grandchildren. L to R: Arthur Gregg Hales, Imogen Brianna Hales, Molly Sara Adams (plus Anna)

The Sara Wilson Tapestry

Audrey (my sister) and Alistair Macafee

A happy coincidence of Academic Honours, 8 July 1949. Grandfathers-to-be, J.A.F. Gregg (2nd from left) and C.G. Lowry (3rd from left), receive honorary doctorates from Queen's University, Belfast

The Macafee Cousins at Anna's wedding.
Clockwise from top left: *Jeremy, Margaret, David, Barbara,*

Campbell College, Belfast (an antique print by Cresswell Boak). A gift to the author from the family of Charlie Stewart, Governor who died in office.

Horas non numero nisi serenas – *'I count only the sunlit hours.'* Drawn by my last Head Boy. Colin McClean, as a farewell gift on my retirement

A Ripe Old Age. In Donegal with L to R: Kay Deane, Alistair Macafee, Audrey, Sara and John Deane (my best man)

a small group, which met every other month, on which members of local environmental groups sat. We tried, with very limited financial resources, to offer seed-corn financing to local initiatives, to keep under review the preservation of the built environment, put up blue plaques on buildings of local and historic interest, and to suggest enhancements to areas where it seemed desirable. The Letcombe Brook, a small but pretty stream flowing through the lower town, was one obvious source of concern, since it seemed to be regularly disfigured by local vandals and was crying out for a riverside walk as a local amenity. Again, as a simple initiative, which gave a focus for local activists, JET did no harm and tried to do some good. Again, though there were strong feelings, I found it an agreeable body with which to work.

Along similar lines I became, *faute de mieux*, Chairman of the Friends of Wantage, a body conceived with the best of intentions to act as a pressure group to defend the local heritage and to foster interest in it. Sadly, I have to confess, that despite my best efforts, I was unable to get it off the ground. It was occasionally helpful to be able to make statements in the name of the Friends in support of environmental initiatives, but honesty would compel me to admit that we served little other useful purpose. But one learns from failure as well as success, and for me the lesson was simple: pious talking-shops without the capacity, energy, and finance to take action too often generate little but frustration – as they did in this case.

I also became a governor of a local primary school in Charlton village. I attended the required largely futile but statutory induction course, and sat on its various committees. As in almost all the local committees I joined, I was left with a profound admiration for the good people who serve on them and strive to better their communities. But in this case, with my experience of independent (or in the case of Campbell semi-independent) schools, I could only feel a growing sense of frustration at the total lack of power to do anything except implement government wishes. The governors were little more than unpaid administrators, government hacks; they had no power to make policy or to control finance. They were there to do what they were told by reading innumerable government circulars and responding to enough bumf to create a paper mountain every year. Apart from acting as a comfort to the excellent but over-worked headmaster and his staff, we could do little. The chairman laboured ceaselessly to support them and to implement the wishes of a micro-managing government, which has never discovered the extraordinary energy and sense of excitement that can be released by genuine local autonomy. When we departed from Wantage for Somerset, I vowed that I would never again be associated with school management, and I have no doubt my decision was correct.

Nevertheless, those three years between retirement and our departure for Somerset were good years. I really felt I had rejoined my local community; I had tried to put a little back into it, despite the frustration involved. It left me absolutely certain that the first political party that can really decentralise and give local communities their heads by abolishing huge swathes of legislation imposed upon us by fashionable political correctness or European bureaucratic madness will set the people free and give them a sense of commitment to and pride in their communities to a degree unimaginable by those who have made themselves the *apparatchiks* of centralised government or the lobby fodder of their political masters. 'Set the people free' has been used before as a political slogan – but sadly those who have done so have failed to deliver. It will require a Federal United Kingdom, led by a statesman with the courage and determination of a Margaret Thatcher (without her nanny-knows-best instincts), combined with the love of freedom of a Thomas Jefferson, before we can hope to reach such a desirable end. It will not happen soon. What politician who once acquires power is going to be willing to relinquish it?

CHAPTER 29

Swan Songs – Cruising with Swan Hellenic

> *Swans sing before they die, 'twere no bad thing*
> *Did certain people die before they sing*

ALMOST AS SOON AS I RETIRED, I found a second source of pleasure in another semi-academic activity. Encouraged by Diane Webb, the popular, energetic, and highly successful head of history at St Mary's Wantage, who had heard that they were looking for speakers, I wrote to Swan Hellenic to ask them if they had any use for me as a guest speaker on their Mediterranean cruises. I was sure the answer would be 'no'. After all, I had never been on a cruise, since the price was well beyond the resources of a schoolmaster, and their guest speakers seemed to be largely distinguished academics – which I was not. But I thought it just possible that if they were short of university dons in term-time, they might have a use for me. I was invited to interview in London; liked my interlocutor very much; and to my great delight was invited to join a cruise 'on trial', as it were. They told me what they wanted me to speak on, and though the list was somewhat daunting, because there was nothing precisely within my range of specialities, it was in some ways easier than on subsequent occasions, when I had the more uncomfortable problem of making bids for cruises and offering my own ideas, without really knowing if they were what the company required.

The cruise was called 'A Greek Anthology' and took place in late October and early November, and for any classicist was well nigh perfect. From Piraeus and Athens through the Corinth Canal to Delphi and Olympia, down the west coast of the Peloponnese to Messene and Gythion (Sparta's naval base, where Paris and Helen spent their first night of elopement together), up to Nauplion for Mycenae, where thirty-five years before I had sat, like Schliemann long before me, watching the sunset under the eucalyptus trees outside La Belle Hélène, and sipping *mavrodaphne* served by Agamemnon and his son Orestes. Thence we crossed the Aegean via Delos (the largest slave market in the ancient world) to Kos, the home of Hippocrates, father of modern medicine, and on to Rhodes, which I had last visited during some crisis (associated with Cyprus I think) and had endeared myself to Greek soldiers heading out and expecting trouble by reciting in my best public school Greek the 'Epitaph on the Spartan Dead at Thermopylae'. With hindsight it was probably not the most tactful choice, but they applauded me for my good intentions rather than the implicit sentiments. On then to Fethiye for Xanthos, Bodrum (ancient Halicarnassos, home of Herodotus) and Kusadasi for Ephesus, where for me the most memorable moment was, inevitably, seeing the great theatre in which St Paul had addressed the crowds and started a riot with Demetrius and the silversmiths.

There are of course many other special places, but for a first cruise it covered an awful lot in a fortnight and put some flesh on the bare bones of a subject which I had always loved but largely visualised in the eye of imagination, for nearly forty years since my first youthful ventures into that glorious country.

The talks were challenging: 'Greek Architecture and the Parthenon' was reasonably familiar territory, though I lack formal training in art appreciation; 'Homer's Heroes and Heroines' likewise; he is one of my great favourites. But 'Rhodes and the Crusades' was not my period at all, and 'Ephesus, as a Masterpeice of Ancient Town Planning' verged on the esoteric. I bought a lot of books – something which I rarely have had such a compelling excuse for doing – and worked up all four talks over about six months. I am not a natural speaker, and for people like me the only thing is to deliver the talk as if it were an academic paper, reading it but trying to incorporate some light relief, and aiming to be sufficiently familiar with the text to enable one to appear to be looking at one's audience while actually reading.

In those for me early days with Swan Hellenic, it seemed that the audience were educated people with a genuine interest in the subject and a desire to learn more; over some seven years I would suspect that there was a slow decline in the level of interest, if not necessarily of education, and a change in the type of clientele. I was warned initially that in any of my audiences there would be one or two at least who knew a lot more about my subject than I did; but that they would never embarrass a speaker or attempt to show off. It was absolutely true. Even the real experts were appreciative, interested and interesting, and extremely friendly. I have little doubt that I tried to cram too much into every talk, and I would have given anything to have that easy gift of conversational lecturing, which my more expert colleagues showed. But it all seemed to go all right. My best moment came, I think, after my talk on 'Homer and his Heroes', which I closed with a reading of Cavafy's famous poem, 'Ithaca'. At the end the most terrifyingly knowledgeable of all the Greek guides came up, gave me an emotional hug, and kissed me, and said it was wonderful. I knew then that for someone at least that talk had worked and my own love for Homer's epics had got across. It boosted my confidence no end. The closing lines could serve as a theme for any man's memoirs:

> Have Ithaka always in your mind
> Your arrival there is what you are destined for.
> But don't in the least hurry the journey.
> Better it last for years,
> So that when you reach the island you are old,
> Rich with all you have found on the way . . .

I think Tennyson's Ulysses would have understood what he meant.

Among the passengers were always some remarkable people, usually ladies, remarkable for their age, agility, and powers of endurance. Doubtless toughened by years of travelling with Swans, they skipped about the landscape like somewhat elderly goats, impervious to heat, formidable in their determination to go everywhere and see everything. In some ways they resembled those wonderful old Victorian explorers and lady travellers who wandered fearlessly all over the known – and unknown – world putting the fear of God into the savages and compelling respect if not awe from local potentates.

We were worked quite hard. As well as four talks, each of forty minutes, we had to give short ten-minute talks at several sites, describing the wider context of their importance. The Greek and Turkish guides then took over, with their terrifying – and sometimes rather exhausting – knowledge of the detail of every site. In my first essays at this less formal but necessarily unscripted exercise, I had to talk about Gythion, Claros, and Sparta. Of the first two I knew nothing; of the last, the site was so disappointing that one felt there was little to say. But I certainly increased my knowledge of my subject. Then there were the deck talks, given over the ship's public address system, usually as we docked in some idyllic harbour. Sometimes it was necessary to find out beforehand from the captain where we planned to dock and which direction the ship might be facing, so as to get the landmarks correctly identified.

For me the whole cruise was a great experience, and a wonderful renewal of old acquaintance; for Sara it was less easy, since she had no role really, except that like all the spouses she helped with the excellent ship's library. But she endured it all and was a tremendous source of comfort to me, as I tormented myself with doubts about whether it was 'going all right'. That it all went well enough was made clear to me by a second invitation to cruise the following year, at relatively short notice, standing in for a speaker who had fallen ill.

This took me into far more unfamiliar territory, though I was able to use a couple of the talks again and added one on ancient religion, which it was not too difficult to recycle on a future occasion. The cruise was themed as 'Autumn in the Levant' and instead of travelling west from Piraeus, we went steadily eastward, ending up in Cyprus via Turkey, Syria, and Lebanon. These really were new horizons for me: after Ephesus, again, there was Priene, that small gem of a Greek city looking out over the flat valley plains of the Maeander, whose name was familiar from my classical reading but I had never seen; it was immediately clear why the river had acquired the nickname of 'the Great Worker' as one contemplated the amazing amount of silt it must have washed down from the high plateau behind to create a richly fertile coastal plain where once there was sea and a harbour, but now horticultural produce was grown in lavish abundance.

There were visits once again to Xanthos and Claros, but also to new places such as Kas, Myra, Perge, and Phaselis, a magical site with its twin harbours and a view of distant hills where dragons roamed at night and you could see the fire from their nostrils. Hitherto it was known to me only because the Phaselis decree was a key inscription in my Greek history texts; now it remains always a favourite memory. Aspendos, with its amazing Roman theatre followed, and Termessos, dramatically situated high in the mountains, the only stronghold which Alexander the Great decided not to try and capture, Uzuncaburg, Antakya and ancient Antioch, where I took a photograph of St Peter's first church, set in a cave in a precipice high above the city. I later incorporated the picture into the cover design of *A Faith Unfaithful*.

Thence into Syria, which was very welcoming on the surface, with small bouquets of flowers handed to each of us, but somehow mildly sinister also, with security officers highly visible. We visited Saladin's Castle (utterly dramatic) and the glorious crusader castles of Krak des Chevaliers (where my talk was rained off by a cloudburst of unbelievable intensity and bitter cold) and Margat. After that we sailed to Beirut, the Lebanese capital, and had a somewhat scary bus ride up the Bekaar valley to Beit Eddine, as well as an exciting guided tour on foot round the gradually resurrecting city of Beirut itself. It was a whole new world and my first and only encounter with the Middle East, where all the news seems to have come from ever since.

In 2000 we were off again for another cruise, which combined now familiar places with some further novelties. Ephesus (again), Bodrum, Delos, Nauplion for Mycenae, Piraeus, Delphi, Olympia were old friends; but the Nauplion visit was also memorable for the fact that all the speakers and their wives were the guests at dinner of Ken Swan, eponymous founder of the Swan Hellenic line. This was to be the last time we saw him before his death. It was in a typical Greek café on the waterfront and suitably atmospheric, though the menu was not entirely easy for palates trained on the more conventional fare to be found on the ship itself.

And then came magical Ithaka (loved long since and lost awhile, where I would dearly love to own a small house and a good boat) rich in its associations with my favourite hero, many-wiled Odysseus, but now after two and a half millennia possibly to be displaced as his 'far-seen' island, 'harsh but a good nurse of men', by a newcomer, a promontory of Cephallenia, which in Homeric times was in fact an island off its western coast, but has since been united to its larger neighbour by earthquakes and the works of the mighty Poseidon, Enosigaios, the Earth-shaker. If this is finally confirmed there will be hell to pay! The second half of the cruise was all new: Corfu, Dubrovnik, Korcula, and Venice, this last sadly something of a disappointment because of poor weather and very high tides. We must visit it again.

The happiest cruise of all was in 2001, when Sara invited Anna (not yet married) and her old friend Alison Hurst together with Emma (pregnant with Imogen) plus Paddy to join us and hear the old buffer rambling on once at least before he popped his clogs. Swan Hellenic offered generous discounts to family and friends, which helped somewhat with the formidable costs. The theme was 'Easter in Greece', and the only disappointment was that we saw rather less than we had hoped of the Easter celebrations, for which the Greeks are famous.

The first half of the cruise took us from Cyprus (through which the spring bird-migrations were coming) back along the southern coast of Turkey to Rhodes. They aimed to show us something of the countryside, the bird life, and the spring flowers, as well as the more conventional ruins, so there was a richer mix of activity than sometimes, which suited us well. Thence to Athens, where Emma and Paddy joined us for the second half of the cruise, which took us to the holy island of Tinos (where sadly, strong winds and bad weather prevented us from docking and visiting the Easter celebrations), Bodrum, Patmos (very atmospheric, especially the grotto of St John), Ephesus of course, then Pergamum (phenomenal), and on to Troy. This was another of those famous cities, which I had never seen, but which had been the focus of my childhood imagination in Andrew Lang's *Tales of Troy and Greece*, in Homer's *Iliad*, and then in the ever-remembered and evocative lines from Tennyson's 'Ulysses', where the hero tells of how he had

> ... drunk delight of battle with my peers,
> Far on the ringing plains of windy Troy.

To see where Schliemann had dug and wrongly claimed to have found King Priam's treasure; to stand upon the Scaean gate, where old Priam had watched the Greek army with Helen at his side and she had pointed out the heroes to him by name; to imagine Hector's last desperate flight around the walls, pursued to his death by Achilles; and to see the gate through which the wooden horse brought death and disaster into the city ... all this was magical, and could not be spoiled even by the execrably-contrived replica of the wooden horse installed outside the gates by the local tourist board. For me it was as memorable as, I am sure, the visit was for Paddy to Gallipoli, where so many allied soldiers lost their lives in Churchill's ill-fated attempt to shorten the war. We finished up in Istanbul, another first, and we found much enchantment in that amazing city. It was all a very happy family experience.

In 2002 we were genuine paying passengers on a one-week cruise to Egypt and the Red Sea, as part of Sara's recuperation after an operation. 'Riches of the Pharaohs' was the theme and despite ultra-long coach journeys, the blistering heat, the tight security, and a slight sense of insecurity when we remembered the massacre at Luxor, it was a splendid week. It was lovely to be spared the strain of entertaining others and to feel that we were there simply to be spoiled. Sharm-el-Sheik itself was unspeakable – glitzy, soulless, with a miserable beach, and wholly lacking in charm. Why the Blairs go there I cannot imagine, unless perhaps it is a fact that 'like cleaves to like'. Everything else was wonderful: Petra, that 'rose-red city, half as old as time' was not particularly rosy, but in location and atmosphere very impressive. The weather was again unkind, and the combination of a violent wind out of the desert and a bitterly cold rainstorm made us glad to reach the shelter of our coaches.

At Luxor in a single day, after a cruelly long coach trip and under military escort, we 'did' Karnak, the Valley of the Kings, the temple of Queen Hatshepsut – all of them superb, literally and metaphorically out of this world – plus the Colossi of Memnon and the temple of the goddess Hathor. The colossi seemed a perfect evocation of Shelley's great poem, 'Ozymandias'.

> I met a traveller from an antique land
> Who said: 'Two vast and trunkless legs of stone
> Stand in the desert . . . Near them, on the sand,
> Half sunk, a shattered visage lies, whose frown,
> And wrinkled lip, and sneer of cold command,
> Tell that its sculptor well those passions read
> Which yet survive, stamped on those lifeless things,
> The hand that mocked them, and the heart that fed:
> And on the pedestal these words appear:
> "My name is Ozymandias, king of kings:
> Look on my works, ye Mighty, and despair!"
> Nothing beside remains. Round the decay
> Of that colossal wreck, boundless and bare
> The lone and level sands stretch far away.'

Later we learned that these were not the statues that inspired Shelley. In fact it was at the temple of the Goddess Hathor at Dandarrah, I think, that we saw the real thing. There I photographed Sara standing beside another 'colossal wreck', just a pair of enormous feet and a pair of colossal hands about the same height as herself. I was going to comment that they were a powerful reminder of the decay of all mortal things, but then realised she might take this amiss. Suffice to say that Solon would have deeply approved of Shelley's sentiments.

Another long day took us to Cairo, the pyramids at Giza, and a special opening of the Cairo museum, solely for Swan Hellenic. We were hugely privileged to be able to observe the treasures of King Tutankhamun without a horde of other visitors pressing around us, and to have the sole access to the whole museum and its amazing collection. It was, I think, a public holiday, but Swan's prestige was such that we were accorded special treatment. The pyramids were impressive, but even more so was the price I was offered for my wife by an Arab gentleman, who took such a fancy to her that he offered me one hundred camels in exchange. Sara was less than flattered, so I deemed it prudent to refuse his price as being wholly inadequate. We failed to solve the riddle of the Sphinx, perhaps because we were not allowed near enough to hold converse with her.

In its own special small museum was the solar boat of Cheops, one of the famous pharaohs and builder of the Great Pyramid. Herodotus says that he ran short of money while building it, but 'was such a villain that he hired out his own daughter to a brothel and gave her strict instructions what to charge'. Apparently, he says, she did so well that she went into the business on her own account as well, demanding not only her personal fee but also one block of building stone per client, with which she was able to build her own (somewhat smaller) pyramid in front of that of her father. Quite a family. But Cheops' truly beautiful solar boat was in some ways almost more memorable than his great pyramid. And I would have quite liked to meet his daughter!

The old aficionados of Swan's early tours speak fondly of the first ships, chartered merely for the summer season or individual cruises and holding something under 200 passengers. Those who had not been on the *Orpheus* and her predecessors really felt like tiros, compared with the seasoned adventurers from those more robust times, when I believe the ladies and gentlemen slept in dormitories – is that really true, or has my imagination taken an unwarranted leap? – and the old insult ('I am a traveller; you are a tourist; he is a tripper') could be applied genuinely to the lesser mortals who followed in their footsteps. At some point a ship built as a Russian ice-breaker came on the market and at a price no one could afford to refuse; so Swan Hellenic bought and converted her and she became *Minerva*, a vessel whose robustness was assured, and whose stately progress across the wine-dark seas of the Aegean was somewhat more comfortable than speedy. She held when jammed to bursting point some 350 passengers, at which point she was almost uncomfortably crowded. Her swimming pool was little more than a plunge bath, though I have vivid memories of a distinguished American senator, clearly a fitness fanatic, with weights clutched in both hands 'swimming' relentlessly backwards and forwards across it in the early mornings. Three strokes each way sufficed. The lounge where lectures were held had limited technology, but always generated a sense of occasion, especially when crowded out. The post-lunch talks could be challenging, for audience almost more than speakers, but it was an accepted fact of life that Morpheus, the god of sleep, would always overtake some of the more elderly members. No one minded. There was a sort of camaraderie about the whole undertaking that made passengers, cruise staff and crew feel very much in it together and enjoying it together. As an exercise in civilised living and joint exploration, I fear that we shall never see its like again.

To my great sorrow they traded in *Minerva I* for *Minerva II*, a rather larger vessel, somewhat faster, and capable of holding I believe nearly 700 passengers. I had more sense than to bid for the maiden voyage, which I was sure would be reserved for the most prestigious speakers; but I was invited as a speaker on her second cruise, 'A Portrait of Spring', which took us to many of the old familiar places, but included Crete and Santorini, the first of which I had longed to revisit, and the second I had never seen. My great regret was that grandmotherly duties meant that Sara could not come, since Emma was having a miserable time in the early stages of her second pregnancy. I would love to have shared both Crete and

Santorini with her. Knossos had been remarkably developed, and improved, since my previous visit forty years before; the walk up the Samaria Gorge after a landing from the sea was a novelty for me and memorable for the sheer drama of the scenery, for the evocation of Allied landings and escapes during WWII, and the incipient vertigo from which I suffered during the alarming coach trip across the central mountains *en route* to our embarkation point. It was a wonderful day. As for Santorini, scene of the most apocalyptic eruption in recorded history (including Krakatoa), that was awe-inspiring. The trip concluded with a long dash overnight to Thessaloniki in northern Greece and a visit to the royal tombs of Macedon and the burial treasures of Philip of Macedon, father of Alexander the Great. It was a splendid climax to a wonderful cruise.

Sadly, it turned out also to be my last. Why one was selected or not for these cruises was never entirely clear. Classicists are two a penny, I suspect, and plenty of competitors exist. Audiences may well have become bored with my information overload or my somewhat ponderous delivery, since I am not a natural or gifted speaker. As a result I may have scored low marks on the post-cruise feed-back ratings received from the clientele.

I had made no secret to the cruise staff – though not to the audiences – of my disappointment with the new *Minerva II*, which was too large, rather glitzy, and lacking in atmosphere. Of necessity, for economic reasons, they had to market it much more intensively to fill it, and the clientele was perhaps somewhat less – I search for a suitably tactful word – discerning, or (shall we say?) academically inclined, than their predecessors. The managers made what I was sure was a tactical error in recording all talks and then piping them on a loop system for twenty-four hours to the cabins. As a result there was no incentive to attend the formal delivery and the sense of occasion was seriously reduced. The original *raison d'être* of the Swan's cruises was being eroded.

Since it was my swan song and because I so love the island of Crete, and in order to put at least one fragment of my talks on the record, so to speak, I give here the opening ten minutes or so of my introductory lecture on Crete, loveliest of islands, the birthplace of Greek, and therefore European, civilisation.

Swan Hellenic Cruise M 309 (April/May 2003)
A Cretan Hors d'Oeuvre
(Myth or Reality?)

I have called this talk 'A Cretan Hors d'Oeuvre', ladies and gentlemen, in the hope that it will serve something of the same function as its gastronomic equivalent by stimulating your taste buds before the real feast, which is Crete itself, without leaving you so replete with stodgy information as to render you incapable of any further movement or interest for the next twenty-four hours.

Crete is special – it is, by common consent, the birthplace of Greek civilisation and therefore also the birthplace of European civilisation as well. It has a special place in English hearts for its heroic struggle for freedom against the Germans in the last Great War. And for British archaeology it has an even more particular interest, because it was at Knossos that Arthur Evans, Keeper of Oxford's Ashmolean Museum, launched his excavations on the 23 March 1900 and began to unearth an unknown civilisation, which had hitherto been regarded as entirely mythical. And his successors, who had between the wars been peacetime archaeologists and scholars were the ones who later helped in wartime to lay the foundations of the classic resistance movement, which was only the last of the many struggles of the Cretans to defend their ancestral freedoms against invaders. Fittingly it was the Villa Ariadne, built by Arthur Evans as his headquarters and home during his excavations of Knossos, which was the scene of the final surrender of the German occupying forces. I have jumped ahead, ladies and gentlemen, but as I say, Crete is special.

To begin at the beginning – I rather like the story of the little girl who said to her mother one day, 'Mummy, why are you getting so fat?' A slightly disconcerted mother explained that 'Well, you see, Daddy has given me a baby for Christmas.' Apparently satisfied with this answer the child went away, only to corner her father later that evening, like a good examiner, with a rider to the original question. 'Daddy, you know that baby you've given Mummy for Christmas?' 'Yes . . .' came the cautious reply. 'Well, she's eaten it.' It reminds me of the immortal comment of an exhausted parent of teenagers that when your child is four she is so delicious you could eat her. And when she's fourteen, you wish you had. As you can see I have returned to my gastronomic theme – and with a deliberate purpose, because in the beginning Crete was the stage on which an act of divine as opposed to merely human cannibalism was played out. It is a land full of legends and stories, a place where storytellers abound and every Cretan is a creative artist in his own right, with a genius for re-working stories to a point where truth and fiction blend into myth and thus acquire immortality – and it still goes on, as Dilys Powell makes clear in her affectionate account of the scholars of the Cretan resistance, in her book about the Villa Ariadne.

St Paul was typically disapproving of this characteristic, and in his letter to Titus (1.12) the first Bishop of Crete, in about AD 90 he says that 'The Cretians (*sic*) are always liars, evil beasts, slow bellies', this last gloriously vivid if meaningless expression being the literal translation of the Greek *gasteres argai*, which the New English Bible renders more accurately but certainly more prosaically as 'lazy gluttons'. That Paul had probably been dead for nearly thirty years when this letter was written rather spoils the story. Lawrence Durrell, who did not have the benefit of recent biblical scholarship, light-heartedly suggests that St Paul's ill-humour must be due to the fact that he slipped into a café in Chanea for a quick *ouzo* with a bundle of controversial epistles under his arm and was given short shrift by the natives, who have a tendency to be suspicious of foreigners. He points out that they have lived through countless crises in their long history and have emerged perhaps a little like the Scots, dour at first but improving on further acquaintance, indomitable friends, deadly enemies, but above all with a tradition of hospitality whose rules are cast-iron and generous to a fault. Even today, he says, it is dangerous to express admiration for any of your hosts' possessions. You will almost certainly find it in your baggage as a farewell gift when you leave. You cannot refuse. They will be adamant. Indeed, he concludes, 'I knew a lady, once, who got a baby this way'.

To begin at the beginning. *Arkhe tou paramythiou, kalispera sas* – 'the fairy tale begins; good evening to you'. With such stately formality, the Greek equivalent of 'Once upon a time', all the best stories should begin. So to borrow from Kipling, let me tell you that 'In the High and Far-Off Times, O Best Beloved, in the beginning of years, when the world was new . . .' (and many years before 4004 BC, which was the date assigned to Creation by Archbishop James Ussher, who drew up the articles of doctrine for the Irish Protestant Church in 1615) the god Chaos ruled over the darkness and none could describe him, since in the dark he was invisible. He shared his throne with his wife, Nyx, Night, whose black robes and countenance did little to alleviate the surrounding gloom. Wearied in the end of their rather drab sovereignty, they summoned their son, Erebus, Blackness, to assist them. Like any good Freudian, he immediately dethroned his father and married his mother. Later their children, Aether (Light) and Hemera (Day), in turn dethroned them both and seized power. With the help of their own child, Eros or Love, they created Pontus, the Sea, Gaea, the Land, and as the crowning glory of creation, Ouranos, the Heaven. Gaea and Ouranos soon seized power and thereafter ruled from the summit of Mount Olympus, which is situated as you know in northern Greece. They had twelve children, the Titans, six male and six female, who were so gigantic and powerful that they had to be imprisoned in Tartarus, or hell, to keep them under control.

Gaea, Earth, was a bit put out by this savage treatment of all her children and urged them to revolt. But only Kronos, Time, who devours all things, had the courage to do so. So Gaea armed him somewhat improbably with a scythe and sent him off to defeat his father – which he duly did by castrating him, presumably with the aforementioned agricultural implement, though the mind boggles at the mechanics of such an operation. Thereafter, in the decorous language of the Oxford Classical Dictionary, Ouranos (Heaven) 'no longer approached Gaea (Earth) but left room for the Titans between them . . .', and this presumably accounts for the fact that Kronos was said to have married his sister, Rhea, incest not being a problem in those innocent far off days, possibly due to the influence upon early Cretan culture of Egypt, where it was customary for the royal family at least. They produced a string of children whose names will be familiar to you from the Olympic pantheon. But Ouranos had cursed Kronos when he defeated him and prophesied that one of his own children would in time defeat him. Determined to prevent such an outcome, as each of his children in turn was born, Kronos swallowed them alive; but since they were immortal that was not the end of them and one wonders how he coped with what must have become a painful problem of cosmic indigestion.

Rhea obviously took a poor view of this policy, which rendered her succession of pregnancies rather pointless. So finally she wrapped a big stone in swaddling clothes and offered it to Kronos for consumption in lieu of her youngest newborn child, Zeus. Intellectually Kronos was clearly a few leptas short of a drachma and proceeded to devour the offering without further ado. Rhea – here at last we get back to Crete – entrusted her baby to the care of the Melian nymphs who carried him off to a cave on Cretan Mount Ida and recruited the goat, Amalthea, to be his nurse – for which her reward was to be set in the heavens as a constellation. The cave is still there, described by Dilys Powell as 'black in the grey face of the mountain with a dead empty look, its huge arched mouth belittled its visitors; only the cracks in the lips showed life, where flowers grew white, virginal, springing from brilliant green leaves; striated rocks showed their teeth; patches of scrub and a clump of stunted trees grew in front of it; inky birds flapped and scattered. Oozing and slippery the entrance sloped down sharply but I was disinclined to explore far.' (*Villa Ariadne*, by Dilys Powell).

To prevent Kronos hearing the baby's cries, Rhea's priests, the Coretes or Corybants, screamed and clashed their weapons and danced and chanted rude songs. Given his intellectual track record, it is not entirely surprising that it took Kronos some time to rumble the significance of all this unusual noise. By then it was too late. Zeus defeated him and seized power. Then he forced Kronos to vomit up all his devoured children – Poseidon, Hades, Hestia, Demeter, and Hera – plus the stone in swaddling clothes, which was later preserved at Delphi. After that Zeus ruled from Olympus, took his sister, Hera, to wife, and sensibly shared his kingdom with his brothers and sisters, while retaining a sort of chairman's overall power, reinforced by a high tech line in thunderbolts, manufactured by the Titans. Kronos himself, whom the Romans called Saturn, retired to the islands of the far west and lives out time in a permanent golden age, for which mankind has yearned ever since.

And if you believe all that, ladies and gentlemen, then you are well on the way to being good Cretans.

Zeus had something of a roving eye and a particularly suspicious wife. Such things go together – I am told – but which comes first is probably as difficult to determine as the order of precedence between the chicken and the egg. Anyhow, the next connection with Crete came about when he fell for Europa, daughter of Agenor, the King of Tyre in Phoenicia. He turned himself into a friendly and uncharacteristically gentle bull and paid a visit to Europa while she was picking flowers in a spring meadow, and enticed her to go for a ride on his back. As soon as she had got her leg over (if I may be so indelicate) he charged off into the sea at enormous speed and carried her off to Crete, where he had his dastardly way with her. She bore him three sons, Minos, Rhadamanthus, and Sarpedon. Minos became King of Crete with the help of Poseidon, god of the sea, who sent him a fabulous white bull from the sea as a sign that he should be lord of all the island. A grateful Minos promised to sacrifice the bull to him in return. Rhadamanthus did not die but was carried off to Elysium and rules in the afterlife as one of the judges of the dead – later to be joined in a similar role by Minos himself. Sarpedon died in the Trojan War, fighting against the Greeks, to Zeus' manifest distress and his wife Hera's barely concealed satisfaction – as Homer tells us.

Minos married Pasiphae, daughter of Helios, the Sun. But he so admired the white bull that Poseidon had sent him that he broke his promise to sacrifice it to the god. Poseidon punished him by making his wife, Pasiphae, fall in love with it. She managed to consummate this somewhat unusual passion with the help of Daedalus, Minos' own resident master-craftsman, and the child of this liaison was the Minotaur, a monster, half man half bull, which was kept concealed in a labyrinth – also built by Daedalus – to conceal the queen's shame.

Theseus, son of the King of Athens, was one of seven youths and seven maidens sent by the Athenians each year as tribute to King Minos, at that time probably their historical as well as legendary overlord. They were incarcerated in the labyrinth as a sacrifice to the Minotaur. Theseus, however, unravelled its secrets, with the help of Minos' daughter Ariadne, whose name is suggestive of the Greek word *arachne*, meaning spider. She gave him a long reel of silken thread so that he could find his way out when he had slain the monster. Armed with this key to the labyrinth, Theseus himself killed the Minotaur and eloped with Ariadne to the island of Naxos, where he abandoned her. She was later found by the god Apollo, who also seduced her, but at least he gave her a decent recompense by turning her into another constellation. Minos punished Daedalus for his part in the Pasiphae affair by locking him and his son Icarus up in prison, whence they escaped – as you doubtless remember – by making themselves wings of feathers and wax and flying off to Sicily to take refuge at the court of Cocalus, a local king. Icarus, as you will know, never got there. Minos pursued Daedalus to Sicily and demanded his surrender, but was tricked by the king into taking a bath at the hands of his own daughters – in the best traditions of Homeric hospitality. But they poured boiling water all over him and killed him.

. . . And so it goes on and on and on . . . like all good Cretan stories.

A hundred and fifty years ago you would have dismissed all such tales as pure poetic fantasy, figments of a popular imagination. You would of course have done the same with the Homeric epics. Then came Schliemann and between 1870 and 1890, with his Homer as a guidebook, he discovered and then excavated Troy and Mycenae, and a number of other sites around Greece. He wanted to excavate Knossos, too, but by then the authorities were wise to his methods and would not let him. Thanks to him, no one now doubts that there was a Troy, a great and prosperous city much as Homer described it, one which controlled the entrance to the Dardanelles and grew rich on the proceeds. Few doubt that a historical reality lies beneath the heroic superstructure, and that Homer's long catalogue of cities which fought in the Trojan war bears a close resemblance to what the archaeologists have revealed of the Mycenaean world of around 1250 BC, when Troy fell.

Later still, only a hundred years ago, people, would have similarly dismissed the references to Homer's Crete. Yet in the catalogue of the Greek army at Troy, Homer tells us (2.740) that

> . . . the great spearman, Idomeneus, led his Cretans,
> the men who held Knossos and Gortyn ringed in walls,
> Lyctos, Miletus, Lycastus' bright chalk bluffs,
> Phaestos and Rhytion, cities a joy to live in.
> The men who peopled Crete, a hundred cities strong –
> The renowned spearman Idomeneus led them all in force,
> with Meriones, who butchered men like the god of war himself.
> And in their command sailed eighty long black ships.

Only Nestor of Pylos with ninety ships, and Agamemnon of Mycenae with 100, surpassed the Cretan navy in size and these are two of the great Mycenaean palace cities, which were destined to supersede the empire of Cretan King Minos. As for Homer's 100 cities, what sounded once simply like a figure symbolic of a great number no longer looks improbable. Knossos we shall of course be visiting; archaeology has established Gortyna as the home of Europe's oldest written constitution; Phaestos was probably the summer palace of the rulers of Knossos. So Homer's description of it as a joy to live in may be no mere empty epithet.

And so on . . .

I shall remain forever grateful to Swan Hellenic for the whole experience of their cruises, for the privilege and excitement of visiting all sorts of places I would never otherwise have seen, for the way they helped to bring alive what had been for me the study of a lifetime, and for the sheer pleasure of meeting interested and interesting people.

These included Don and Liz McClen, with whom by that strange alchemy that makes some friendships almost immediate, we instantly got on. Liz is the daughter of an RAF family – her father too was a pilot – and she has a wonderful gift of focused interest in and sympathy with whoever she is with. She also, like me, adores Greece. Don is a man of action, his activities multifarious, his distinctions genuine. He flew fast jets for the RAF and was a member of the Central Flying School formation aerobatic team, the Red Pelicans, based at Little Rissington, shortly after the time when I was at Radley negotiating for the loan of those same Red Pelicans for our general's inspection (see Chapter 15). It would have been fun to think that our paths had crossed so long before. We did share what must have been a common experience of children in wartime – Don, as a boy, was evacuated from Newcastle to Bretherdale, in Westmoreland (Cumbria), in a hidden valley between Tebay and Shap, not far from Sedbergh. He stayed with a farming family and kept in touch with them until they died. His memories of that period are delightfully enshrined in his book, *Bretherdale: A Childhood Odyssey*. He was up there this year, too, fighting (successfully I am glad to say) to prevent the location of a hideous wind farm development along their lovely skyline. Shortly after commanding RAF Binbrook, one of the bases for Britain's air defence Lightning squadrons in the Cold War, he left the RAF and went to work for British Aerospace, among other things lobbying (successfully) for the European Fighter Aircraft, and ultimately as chief executive for the Al-Yamamah project in Saudi Arabia.

He is no mean athlete, thinking nothing of a twenty-mile walk along the Bretherdale skyline to protest about those windmills, but also a county squash player and a fellow member of the Jesters Club. But he is no less a man of letters than a man of action – he too has kept a commonplace book for many years as I mentioned in Chapter 2, and my copy of his *The Heart of Things* holds an honoured place on my 'special' bookshelf beside his *Bretherdale*. He is literary executor for Cecil Lewis, who was like St Exupéry one of the celebrated writers on flying in its early days, and a lover of theatre and music as well as books. We exchange excerpts from our respective commonplace books, we correspond especially on matters theological, where we see very much eye to eye, and his robust as well as knowledgeable views on the Middle East accord surprisingly often with my own prejudices, which are largely born of ignorance. Sara and I meet him and Liz more rarely than we would like, to walk and talk; their company does us both a power of good. I look forward eagerly to the forthcoming publication of his memoirs, provisionally entitled *True Riches*.

Swan Hellenic were taken over by P & O and I felt that things became a bit different thereafter. P & O were themselves taken over by Carnival Lines, a vast American company, who would have found it difficult, I suspected, to accommodate something like Swan Hellenic in their scheme of things. And as if in confirmation, I heard just recently that *Minerva II* will end her career next year and her cruises will be absorbed into the normal programme of their various ships. The Swan Hellenic brand is to be sold. I have to confess that I am not entirely surprised that *Minerva II* has been dispensed with; but if that is also the end of Swan Hellenic as we knew it, I shall be extremely sad. They were somewhat different and a wonderful company.

In the meantime I have recently received an invitation from Saga to be a guest speaker on one of their 'Spirit of Adventure' cruises. They seem to making a pitch for the old Swan Hellenic market. The early itinerary includes Egypt, Lebanon, and Syria, and about a week after I had accepted the invitation the latest flare-up in that sad corner of the Middle East erupted. I fully expect to be diverted. But it is nice to have another opportunity to travel in that area and it will be fun to see how well the two cruise lines compare.

I find it interesting to observe that the more the study of classical languages dies out, as an illiterate generation abandons its respect for the structures of its own language, which owes its origins in large part to Greek and Latin, and at a time when media personalities often seem almost unable to speak the Queen's English, the interest in ancient history in its widest sense (not just classical archaeology) seems to have grown to a level unprecedented in my lifetime. Countless programmes on TV describe and interpret the past to vast audiences at varying levels of scholarship and sophistication. Books associated with such programmes then reinforce that interest.

In illustration of this point, I can report that with a group of volunteers the other day I was digging a trench to make a culvert in a rhyne round a local SSI. It was an entirely mundane and tedious task. Everyone there was offering their own variation of the 'Timewatch' archaeological programmes from TV, as part of the light-hearted banter which accompanied this otherwise tedious operation. Clearly everyone had seen them. The lure of buried treasure is of course part of the attraction; the unravelling of mysteries of any kind has all the natural appeal of any detective story; the past will always exercise a kind of fascination, especially for those who see no future for their kind; authorities of every sort are so discredited that most of us have become obsessed with the idea of conspiracy and cover-up – to such an extent that even the most improbable and entirely fanciful novel about the 'secret history' of Jesus can take on the quality of a scholarly academic study, and be denounced by the Archbishop of Canterbury, thus enhancing its popular appeal.

Sadly what we seem incapable of producing is the disciplined evaluation of evidence; we are trained to leap to conclusions, rather than to think through problems. Careful textual study; rigorous analysis; precise use of language – these belong to the old academic subjects like maths, science, and the classics. They are all falling out of favour and I see little prospect of their return.

I wish I thought that the effect of so much popular archaeology would be a return to favour of the subjects I love. But sadly TV programmes give totally the wrong impression. They eliminate all the tedium, all the drudgery entailed in proper academic study. We are producing a generation that expects instant results and easy answers. Real life is different. The classics are very difficult – like the natural sciences. But the sciences still have the huge advantage of being useful as well as interesting. Classics is only interesting, save for a few scholars and the students of language.

> *Sic omnia fatis*
> *In peius ruere ac retro sublapsa referri,*
> *Non aliter, quam qui adverso vix flumine lembum*
> *Remigiis subigit, si bracchia forte remisit,*
> *Atque illum in praeceps prono rapit alveus amni.*
>
> Fate's law decrees that all things
> Rush towards the worst, fall back, decline,
> Just as an oarsman barely drives his craft upstream
> Against the current; if he relaxes for a moment,
> Headlong downstream his vessel carries him away.

I begin to sound like Virgil (*Georgics* 1.200), writing in the early days of Augustus' reign, before his genius had restored peace and order to the Roman state. For him the darkest moment came before the dawn. Here's hoping!

CHAPTER 30

Church Activities – Parishes and Religious Broadcasting

God made man in His own image. And man chose to return the compliment.
G B Shaw

AND THAT IS HALF THE TROUBLE with the church. Whatever churchmen tell you, the church is a human construct, built upon the imperial power of the Roman Empire and structured to resemble it. It was designed by men for men, and to an extent for the exploitation of women in an era when, inevitably, a woman's place was largely in the home. God I believe had very little to do with it. I am absolutely certain that Jesus did not say to Peter that he was 'the Rock on which he would build his church'. I see no evidence in the gospels that Jesus had any idea of building a church in our sense; he told his followers to go out and preach the gospel. And they did – in the synagogues, as I suspect Jesus intended. The split between Judaism and Christianity probably dates to around AD 100, certainly to the period after the fall of Jerusalem and well after the death of Christ. For Jesus it seems much more likely that his gospel was for the Jews of the Jewish synagogues certainly, and of the Diaspora perhaps, but not for Gentiles generally – until St Luke and St Paul got to work. The gospel stories, three of them certainly written post-AD 70, after the fall of Jerusalem, were fashioned to accommodate the Christian story and its expanding mythology to the Jewish liturgical calendar, and to placate the dominant Roman superpower. They were interpretative, not historical, and their inconsistencies are accounted for by the intentions of their authors. For me biblical truth is not, and cannot possibly be, literal or historical truth; it is religious truth, symbolic and metaphorical truth – which is arguably something even more profound.

The leadership of the church is well aware of this, but so distrusts its own followers that they dare not tell them of the discoveries of modern scholarship and the new insights gained through modern biblical studies. In the long term their dishonesty will help to bring about the downfall of the very institution they are striving to preserve; the faith they seek to defend will come to seem increasingly indefensible, because it is incredible to educated audiences. Honesty is nearly always the best policy, in the long run, but honesty is not what ordinary congregations are being given. When Grandfather once observed to a friend that 'it may be that the true mission of the church is to disappear', he showed himself at least willing to contemplate a possibility, which those with a vested interest in their own power and status derived from the power of the church seem wholly unwilling to contemplate. To me the churches, as institutions, are regrettable necessities, not divine creations. In human society, wherever there exists a need for coherent and purposeful activity, some form of organisation is inevitable. That is how the churches evolved, backed after 300 years by the formidable power of the Roman state under Constantine, in an era when religion and superstition were not easily distinguishable and religion was always an instrument of policy.

Someone always has to try and run the show, and so here on earth we need organisation and leaders. But this makes neither the organisation nor its leadership divine or divinely appointed. Such assertions are born of tradition and reinforced by superstition. Men like power and status – more so than women – and have long struggled successfully to protect their power, to keep women out of the ranks of the clergy, and lay people out of the sacramental side of the liturgy. The ordination of women has been a great blessing, reinforcing the declining ranks of male clergy and bringing a warmer, more inclusive ethos to the ministry. Once we have female bishops and archbishops, it is at least possible that things may get better still. That the Episcopal Church of the US now has a female president (equivalent of an archbishop) and the Church of England has taken an important step towards female bishops is for me a significant sign of returning health in these bodies.

By contrast the so-called ministry of the laity still seems to be a contrivance to get the dreary jobs that clergy don't like or can't be bothered to do carried out by someone else. In the absence of an ordained minister, I personally would have no problem in accepting Holy Communion from any layman (or woman) who conducted the service with a proper reverence, nor would I feel it lacked validity. Worship is worship and it is the intention, not the paraphernalia, that determines its validity. If one day we get a real ministry of the laity, again a new dynamic may enter the church. Meanwhile, like every priesthood there ever was, ours struggles to protect its privileges by preserving its mystique. Closed shops are no monopoly of the trades union movement.

But in the meanwhile we must make do with what we've got. The church, for all its limitations, is the only one we have; Jesus is the founder of our faith, to which the different churches bear witness in their different ways. For all my reservations I was, and remain, a communicant member of the Anglican branch of Christianity, finding in it because of my upbringing and my culture the least unsatisfactory vehicle for expressing my worship of a God whom I seek always through what the mediaeval saints called 'the clouds of unknowing'. I could never become a Roman Catholic, which seems to me to require exactly the sort of intellectual surrender, which I have described above. Grandfather's little classic, *The Primitive Faith and Roman Catholic Developments*, charts the incremental development of superstitious elements added to the early faith across the centuries by that particular branch of the Christian church. No one with a mind of their own could possibly take them seriously. Educated Roman Catholics seem to operate a kind of Orwellian double-think, which enables them to live with the incredible assertions which their faith has acquired over two millennia.

But each to his own taste; those that are not against us are for us. Our disagreements are insignificant compared to what unites us.

It is usually best to try to support change and reform from within, especially in an age when fundamentalism runs rife and seems to be leading us back to another dark age of primitive superstition, rather than an adult and intellectually coherent faith. Where (rare) opportunity offered, I was always interested in making what contribution I could to church life, but when you work in a boarding school it is always difficult. I confess I was surprised, as well as flattered, when Archbishop Michael Ramsey invited me to serve as a member of a Canterbury Diocesan Commission on Education, Mission, Evangelism and Pastoral work. It sounded immensely important; its outcome proved otherwise. As an experience, however, it introduced me to the Church Administrative, as opposed to the Church Militant, Triumphant, or Sacrificial – an experience that was revealing of deficiencies rather than inspiring. I was disappointed to find that I had so little to contribute to the discussions, positively disillusioned to feel that the 'professionals', the clergy, seemed caught up in minutiae and lacking in any serious ideas of how best to confront the growing challenge of presenting the gospel to an increasingly secular and uninterested world. As ever in such circumstances, we had recourse to discussions of structures, systems, and resources – those last refuges of the unimaginative.

Later, when headmaster of Campbell College, I was invited to be a member of CRAC, the Central Religious Advisory Committee, which advised the BBC and ITV jointly on matters connected with religious broadcasting. Again I was disappointed to find that we seemed to discuss, endlessly, the rather arcane principles governing the 'Godslot', the protected period of Sunday evening broadcasting during which the rival broadcasters agreed not to compete with each other by scheduling genuinely popular programmes against religious broadcasts of (to be honest) rather varying quality. The broadcasting executives seemed determined, however slowly, to erode the Godslot; the 'religious' representatives to defend it. We did also discuss more general issues of religious broadcasting, including whether religious programmes might be able to take their place in the schedules in their own right without such 'protection'. But there seemed little meeting of minds; vested interests on both sides were all powerful; over the years (predictably) the broadcasters pretty well got their way; but some remarkable programmes have shown that the worst fears of the religious side were unjustified.

I was sure that the broadcasters viewed us with complete cynicism, as a necessary evil to be endured in order to placate religious pressure groups, *Daily Telegraph* readers, and our old friend Disgusted of Tunbridge Wells. In my three years' service I don't think I ever felt we managed to change their minds on any issue or to achieve any significant improvement in the quantity or quality of religious broadcasting. As our title implied, our role was advisory; those we advised were fully entitled to ignore our advice. And they did.

But once I retired, it was a genuine pleasure to be able to offer my assistance at the more mundane level of the ordinary parish, where real people wrestled with real problems in real communities. I told our vicar that if there was anything useful I could do to help, I would be willing to give it a go. I explained that I was not too good at chummy activities, or overt manifestations of piety, like prayer meetings and hugging people; but practical things I would happily endeavour to help with. I was not entirely comfortable with the high church tradition of Wantage parish church ('bells and smells'), but its daughter church, technically a Chapel of Ease, in Charlton village on the other side of the town offered perfectly 'normal' worship and we happily went there on Sundays. Anyhow, such things are hardly part of one's faith, simply the flummery of the drama of its rituals, attendant trivialities, which matter very little.

How it happened I do not know, but I found myself made secretary to the PCC (Parochial Church Council). Needless to say this was an area where I hoped I could be useful. Words are my profession; I have never found administration difficult; I was comfortable with word-processing at a modest level; writing minutes and memoranda I have had to do all my life; I liked John Salter, the vicar, which is important, and from what I heard and saw, thought he had been doing a very good job. By temperament I was only too happy to be of service in the background, and was comfortable acting as the recording scribe rather than a leading light. As so often, we had excellent churchwardens and a dedicated fabric and works committee, and a vicar who knew where he was going and what his priorities were. One thing he was absolutely determined to do was to clear out the clutter of decades and renew the church physically as well as spiritually.

As a result I was a witness rather than an active participant in the struggle to restore and refurbish the parish church. The procedures of the established Church of England and the Oxford Diocese beggared belief and seemed designed only to waste time and fill the pockets of the lawyers, not to assist a vicar and his PCC to realise their plans for modernisation. If you wished to move a pew, it seemed as if you needed a faculty; if a member of the parish objected to any proposed course of action, whether through ignorance, malice, or honourable intention, even if he or she was a lone voice, then a costly procedure had to be followed. It took months to achieve what a sensibly constituted organisation would have achieved with a phone call. The patience and perseverance of all concerned on the PCC was little short of saintly. I wrote letters, recorded resolutions, wrote minutes, listened to mainly temperate and reasonable discussion, despite the frustrations, and by the time I left I had come to admire the qualities of the vicar and his PCC to a high degree. There was also a complicated proposal to develop the church primary school, whose ramifications I never fully grasped and whose resolution I am sorry to say I missed, because I had moved by then to Somerset. But their limitless energy and enthusiasm for their varied responsibilities were amazing.

The vicar and I disagreed on only one issue, but it never came between us: I was in favour of women priests; he was opposed. I assume that to those of the high church tradition the idea is unacceptable; I could not see why. Even Michael Ramsey admitted that he could see no biblical objection, while admitting that he hoped it would not happen in his lifetime. I am only sorry that they feel unable to accept the view of the majority of their colleagues and congregations. In the end I go along with Queen Elizabeth I: 'There is but one faith – the rest is dispute about trifles.' It is only when faith becomes confused with superstitions that feelings run high and disagreement escalates into quarrels. I acknowledged his views, though I could not agree with or even respect them; but that was no ground for a quarrel. Returning after some five years, I found the church a delight. It had been beautifully refurbished; there was a new organ; a reduced number of pews made the effect spacious and more appropriate to a modern congregation; the stonework had been cleaned and new lighting installed. It was a joy to behold and I am glad I was there to see the start of it all. As for the vicar, *si monumentum requiris, circumspice.*

I continued to do a little broadcasting. Though I was asked occasionally to go back to Northern Ireland to offer a 'Thought for the Day', the mechanics of the operation were never easy for reasons of timing and expense. But once they found the technical means to let me record my talks at Oxford Radio, it became much easier. That led to invitations to do similar talks for the local radio station, where the traditional three minutes of 'Thought for the Day' were curtailed to seventy seconds. I have always relished the discipline of working through an idea in a brief space of time; this was a new challenge. It kept my hand in and imposed further constraints upon my natural prolixity. But I did not do many, because we soon moved to Somerset, possibly to the relief of my local audiences.

And so, after about twenty years my broadcasting 'career' had also come to an end.

It had been a privilege and a pleasure. Rightly or wrongly – and some may well say hypocritically – my more radical views on the faith I espouse were not something that I felt required to parade before my radio audiences. I dislike controversy; I hate quarrels. I did not feel that it was part of my brief to ride my own hobby-horses in that brief moment of peaceful contemplation amid the mildly frenetic momentum of the morning news programmes. I was not there to capture headlines; if anything, to reflect upon them. So I was happy to try to produce the odd ear-catching turn of phrase; but I sought to avoid distressing or affronting those who listened to me.

I have occasionally joined in studio 'discussions', but I am not well suited to such activities. I like to think out my position before declaring it; studio discussions require the opposite – a willingness to speak off the cuff, preferably dogmatically and with a view to cheap victory in an argument, rather than reaching the truth through discussion – something reflected in the male chauvinist joke about the woman who was asked what she thought about some pressing issue of the day. She replied, very sensibly: 'How do I know what I think till I've heard what I've said?' In studio discussions, everyone has to have a turn, so there is no time to develop an idea or refine a position or grope towards a viewpoint. The group must be balanced, which also means there is no chance of getting agreement on anything. And too often, the producers have an agenda of their own towards which the 'discussion' is slanted. Without controversy, too, the viewing is dull. In all this truth is the casualty.

The short radio talk, by contrast, was a form of discourse which suited me, both temperamentally and in terms of such skills as I possess. I am not an orator, but I would like to think that I am a wordsmith. The radio is my most natural medium, since I can read my script without feeling compelled to look at the audience and fearful of losing my place or their attention. I have a reasonable delivery, and a voice which some have been kind about, though others have described it as 'plummy'. I think my producers found me a reliable performer, at least, and Father Jim Skelly, my first producer, nicknamed me 'one-take Wilson' – which I regarded as a huge compliment.

I began to broadcast because I was asked to. I would never have had the nerve to offer my services. But one thing led to another, and in due course I found myself doing 'Prayer for the Day' on Radio 4, always recorded rather than delivered live as sometimes in 'Thought for the Day'. This was very humane, since the talk went out at 6.30 in the morning. Then came an invitation to do some late night talks for the BBC World Service, called 'Reflections'. Other series followed, 'Pause for Thought', 'Words of Faith', and 'Meditations for Holy Week'. All of these were short – never lasting more than five minutes, all meditative in character, though to some degree over the years 'Thought for the Day' became rather more focused on secular matters and the daily news, albeit from a religious standpoint – a development I regretted, but which probably reflected the increasing secularisation of society and the requirement placed on broadcasters to be balanced, religiously neutral, and politically correct.

As the programme evolved, instead of a speaker for the week, they had two, one giving a series of three talks mid-week, while another focused on current affairs on Monday and Friday. For a time I was asked to do the Monday and Friday slots, which again I took to be a compliment and expression of confidence in my reliability. The talks could not be written until the day before. My producer would ring me at about 10.00 at night and get me to read my piece and then I would go in and deliver it live the next morning. I well remember how once, two weeks in succession, I had to ditch my prepared piece and write another, because first came the news of the Anglo-Irish Agreement, and then the news of the

Reagan-Gorbachev summit. They were both significant moments in our history, so it seems worth recording my own initial reactions to them, as given on a public forum.

Announcement of the Anglo-Irish Agreement
15 November 1985

If I was living in Columbia now, where a volcano has just erupted killing some 15,000 people in a real disaster, I doubt if I would be very interested in the volcano erupting here in Ulster over the subject of the Anglo-Irish talks.

It is difficult, and indeed pointless, to talk about an agreement – if such it is – whose details as yet we do not know, but I have to confess that I have not been impressed by the tone or quality of the comments I have heard or read, even from those who sought my vote for the privilege of calling themselves my representatives.

After all, we have lived for sixty years here in Ulster with a difficult, if not impossible, problem of community division. Whose fault it is seems to me to matter not at all, since in any quarrel there are always faults on both sides. And if you want a quarrel patched up, both sides must show magnanimity and generosity – and learn to keep their voices down.

Nor is it right in 'Thought for the Day' to take any sort of sides in the political argument. But I have asked myself, as a Christian, where my duty lies at this very difficult time and what my attitude should be once we know the facts.

I cannot escape, first of all, the absolute injunction of our Lord: 'Blessed are the peacemakers.' And I have to acknowledge that, however misguided their motives may seem to have been to some, the two governments do appear to have been trying to be peacemakers, to reach an agreement to patch up an old quarrel, and to make progress. I may or may not like the direction in which they wish to progress – that is my business. But I must at least believe that when two parties to a dispute reach agreement, then given goodwill on all sides, there is potential for good.

I remind myself that our Lord also ordered us to 'Render unto Caesar the things that are Caesar's'. My government is the sovereign government of Westminster, freely elected by democratic process; and its duty is to govern **all** the country in the interests of **all** the country when once it has been elected by a majority. In so doing it has a claim to my obedience under the law – at least, that is how I interpret our Lord's saying.

Then again, I have to remember that Jesus lived out all his days under an occupying power, an alien government if you like, without apparently having very much to say about it. He certainly refused, steadfastly, to follow the way of violence, and in this he disappointed some at least of his more zealous followers. Yet from those unpromising circumstances he managed to launch a moral and religious revolution which still rocks the world. In fact he turned apparent disaster into triumph.

Finally I must ask myself – as he did – 'What shall it profit a man if he gain the whole world and lose his soul.'

So let us reserve judgement here at home until we know the facts – and spare a thought for the dead and dying in Columbia.

And here for completeness' sake is my talk on Reagan/Gorbachev meeting, surely one of the most momentous events in modern history, marking as it did the beginning of the end of the Cold War.

Reagan/Gorbachev Summit
22 November 1985

We have had two summits in the last week, and the more recent one in Geneva has probably generated even greater hopes and fears, even greater media build-up, than the one at Hillsborough.

But in another corner of the globe there has been another peace mission going on. Earning less publicity than the two summits, but considerably more than he would probably have liked, Mr Terry Waite, the Archbishop of Canterbury's envoy, has been delicately picking his way through the minefield of Middle Eastern politics.

Now I am not primarily concerned to discuss the substance of the various discussions, whether between Terry Waite and the Lebanese kidnappers, or between the two prime ministers, or between the leaders of the two superpowers, beyond observing that for all of them the objective was peace and reconciliation. But they all seem to me to have something else in common too. If – and it is a very big IF – if there has been any progress made in any of these areas, then that progress has been due largely to the personal relationships built up between the key personalities involved. And I find it interesting, indeed encouraging, that even in this era of superpowers and experts and PR men and permanent officials, in the end progress can still best be made person to person; and that two statesmen, sitting by the fire, seem to achieve something in two days that their officials could not achieve in years.

And this seems to be true whether you look at Mr Waite's mission to secure the rescue of a few kidnap victims, or Mr Reagan's mission to secure the future of the whole world.

I've never met Mr Waite, but it is quite clear that he is a remarkable person, with a capacity to inspire trust in all sorts of people from Archbishops to paramilitaries. His public demeanour is quietly friendly, modest, very calm and rational, and sweetly reasonable. He doesn't shout or make a protest – but he certainly achieves results where no one else can. He inspires confidence.

And again, at the Reagan/Gorbachev summit we find the same thing. Anyone who expected instant results or decisions was deceiving himself. But with the blessed help of a media blackout, the discussions seem to have led to a considerable rapport between the two men, a mutual respect and recognition by each leader of the sincerity of the other. They inspired confidence in each other and as a result the climate seems to have changed overnight. And if that is so, then the political will to move towards peaceful coexistence once more, through gradual disarmament, will have been strengthened.

In each case personal relationships have been the key. And it seems to me from my limited reading of modern theology that the new discovery – if I may call it that – of the past ten years or so, has been the emphasis placed on relationships as the model for the way in which God works in the world, through the power of the Holy

Spirit. 'Where two or three are gathered, there am I in the midst' said Jesus. Or again, if I may borrow the title of Bishop John Taylor's book, the operation of the Holy Spirit is the operation of what we might call the 'go-between God'.

Perhaps we might pray today that the go-between people, the quiet people, who work in difficult and dangerous situations to build trust and mutual confidence through personal relationships at all levels, whether high or low, may find power (even if they are atheists) through the Holy Spirit to bring safety and peace to others and a new hope to suffering humanity.

Well, they are still trying; and it has not all been a story of failure.

A whole new dimension opened up when Jim Skelly summoned me to discuss his idea for a Lent series of forty-minute meditations round a common theme, leading towards Easter. He had a great love of literature and music, and he wanted to blend the meditations, music, and readings into a coherent whole, using five or six different speakers for the series, each developing his own ideas. This was exciting and demanding. I wrote the text for the first of them, selecting the readings and with his help choosing the music. If my memory is right, it was delivered live, because he thought that a recorded programme lacked naturalness and a certain vitality. I did several of these, but the first remains most vividly in the memory. The theme for the series was 'Into the Wilderness' and mine was entitled 'The Outcast', introduced of course by the only possible choice, Chesterton's 'The Donkey', one of my favourite poems, which I can still recite after being made to learn it sixty years ago.

The meditation went out in 1982, I think, and the series evolved into a regular series of studio services, sometimes free-standing, sometimes part of a series, but based similarly on a theme, and sometimes with the addition of recorded music from one of the many excellent church choirs to be found around Northern Ireland. It was as nearly creative as anything I had done, and it gave me, if no one else, enormous pleasure. My meditations and short talks like 'Thought for the Day', and some of my longer addresses and sermons, I was able to incorporate into a book of collected sermons and addresses, *A Faith Unfaithful*, which I published in November 2004. But these studio services were too long and they remain in my files, unread and doubtless long forgotten.

Here as a token reminiscence is Chesterton's 'The Donkey'.

> When fishes flew and forests walked
>   And figs grew upon thorn,
> Some moment when the moon was blood
>   Then surely I was born;
>
> With monstrous head and sickening cry
>   And ears like errant wings,
> The devil's walking parody
>   Of all four-footed things.

The tattered outlaw of the earth,
  Of ancient, crooked will;
Starve, scourge, deride me: I am dumb,
  I keep my secret still.

Fools! For I also had my hour;
  One far fierce hour and sweet:
There was a shout about my ears,
  And palms before my feet.

In 1984 I did an Advent service; another, 'Swords into Ploughshares', in 1985; a Holy Week service in 1987; a Good Friday service in 1988, and another for Advent in the same year; a post-Christmas New Year service in 1989, and an 'ordinary' studio service in July 1991; a Lent service, 'Betrayal', in 1997. One rarely got any feedback, but the continued use of the format suggests at least that our producers felt the series worked.

I never ceased to be amazed by the quality of my two producers, Fr Jim Skelly and Dr Bert Tosh. For men whose lives must have been lived under the constant pressure of deadlines and time schedules (and broadcasting is unforgiving and unrelenting in this respect), they always seemed unbelievably calm, controlled, patient, flexible, and skilled. Such quiet, unflustered expertise is far more impressive (and reassuring to amateurs like myself) than the frenzied posturing of media so-called 'personalities'. They were a pleasure to work for.

If you profess and call yourself Christian, then you have a duty to proclaim your calling and explain your beliefs by whatever means you think appropriate. By virtue of my office, I had to preach fairly regularly, but I was also invited to address meetings or conferences. Here it was possible, sometimes, to let my more radical ideas show through. I doubt if they made much impact on those I spoke to, but evolution, whether biological, intellectual, or theological, is a slow process and almost invisibly incremental. Thirty years ago I felt at times that my ideas were outrageous, drifting in the direction of blasphemy. Now I know that many others were doing far more pioneering work and that I was, at best, perhaps slightly more sensitive to the changing mood of the times than others. Where Bishops John Robinson and David Jenkins seemed to have led the way, I discovered in time that others like Bishops Jack Spong in America and Richard Holloway in Scotland were beginning to offer much more radical (and to me persuasive) ideas for a 'modern' view of the Bible and Christianity.

I talked to sixth formers at an SCM conference; I spoke to a diocesan synod at the invitation of George Quin, our bishop, and to a Parish study group; at the invitation of Samuel Crooks, the dynamic Dean of Belfast whose drive and commitment finally brought to completion the building of the city's lovely cathedral, I gave a Lent address on 'The Whining Schoolboy', one of seven in a series themed as 'The Seven Ages of Man'. In retirement I preached occasionally in English public schools, and in Cleeve I gave a talk – my most provocative – to a parish colloquy entitled 'Towards a Christology for the 21st Century' in conjunction with Francis Miles, a diocesan clergy trainer. At the end of this, memorably, a member of the audience came up and told me it had been the best day of his life, as a thinking Christian.

To join in amicable discussion with thoughtful Christians, of whatever conviction, is a constructive way to develop and refine ideas, which in my case are largely shaped by my reading. That reading has moved me steadily towards a conviction that the current formulation of the faith simply will not do, and that unless we modernise our ideas and render them compatible with the discoveries and insights of modern science, the faith community will face increasing ridicule, and slowly decline into the absurdities of creationism and biblical fundamentalism, populated by the naïve, the superstitious and the ignorant.

We moved to the village of Cleeve in North Somerset in the diocese of Bath and Wells in the summer of 2000. It was in a small way symbolic that we should transfer to a new home for a new millennium. It was also for me theologically a new phase. I was reading more, and steadily clearing my mind on where I stood on the historical validity of the Bible, the truth of the gospel story, and my beliefs generally. Once I began to think about it, I found the divinity of Jesus an almost meaningless proposition, beyond the sense in which we are all alike 'God's children'. The factually indisputable crucifixion had long seemed a far more powerful focus for belief than the resurrection, which has a degree of emotive power symbolically, but none for me as a literal, physical fact; virgin birth was a biological nonsense and even my mother's generation had abandoned it in the 1920s, while my father's dry observation that 'I can't help feeling that Joseph had something to do with it' was a comforting reinforcement of my own views, given his otherwise conventional approach to religion. The fact that Grandfather could commend the views of Simone Weil who 'came to Christ through God', not vice versa, as usually suggested, and could remark that 'belief in God was possible for many years before ever Christ appeared' gave similar comfort to me in my inability to respond to the conventional emphasis among the more pious of my acquaintance on 'knowing the Lord Jesus'.

We were singularly blessed in our vicar, Cathy Horder, a wonderfully open-minded thinker but a deeply spiritual pastor, who tolerated (and even occasionally sympathised with) my dangerously heretical views. I was delighted to be asked to serve on the PCC as their secretary; I came to admire greatly the devoted service of a small but admirable congregation to the life of their whole village community, and not just that of the church; the sincerity of their faith and the sheer kindness and goodness of their membership was a living testament to their commitment to their Lord. We were part of the Yatton Moor group of churches, which were all highly active and extremely vigorous, under the leadership of our talented vicar, Ian Hubbard, a former headmaster, school inspector, and composer of church music.

But the more I found my ideas developing, and increasingly incompatible with the conventional teaching of the church, the more I felt it was dishonest (if not dishonourable) to remain a member of the PCC, as a representative of a congregation whose views would be so very different from mine. As usual, I had enjoyed making my modest contribution to the work of the church community in a task where I felt reasonably competent; but I was sure it was wrong to continue. So after what was the normal four-year stint, I resigned as secretary to the PCC and did not offer myself for re-election.

Since then I have renewed the active correspondence with friends on matters religious and otherwise, which has been a feature of the last ten years. My side of some of that earlier correspondence can be found in the final section of *A Faith Unfaithful*, and it illustrates the preoccupations of my declining years. It has been interesting to discover how many of them share my disappointment with the church of our fathers and yearn for some intellectual leadership from those who would claim to be our spiritual guides. For me it has been reassuring to discover that in my doubts and explorations I have not been alone and I explore it more fully in my penultimate chapter.

CHAPTER 31

Cleeve, Somerset – Grandchildren and Other Commitments

Lo, children are an heritage of the Lord:
And the fruit of the womb is his reward.
As arrows are in the hand of a mighty man:
So are children of the youth.
Happy is the man that hath his quiver full of them.

Psalm 127

Never have children; only grandchildren.

Gore Vidal

IF, AS I HAVE SUGGESTED ELSEWHERE, happiness is the true goal of human living, then children and grandchildren are beyond peradventure the surest way in which to find it.

St Augustine maintained that happiness lies in the possession of an invulnerable good which cannot be lost to misfortune, and that the only such good in the universe is God. Therefore happiness lies, he says, in the vision of – or union with – God. But to be possessed of an invulnerable good is to be certain of it, so much so that you can safely take it for granted. You hardly have to work for it, though the worthy saint ('Make me virtuous, Oh Lord, but not yet') has it both ways, by insisting that in order to be sure of it you must lead a moral life. My own classical background suggests to me, yet again, that far more precious is that which is precious precisely because it is uncertain, forever vulnerable. How much more precious therefore are those blessings which we have and hope to keep, but can never quite be sure of. The malice of fate and misfortunes of blind chance are always lurking in the background, threatening to rob us of them. Of all such impermanent blessings, none I can think of can begin to match a blessed marriage and the gift of children who, as my psalmist rightly observes, are 'an heritage of the Lord'.

In the year 2000 Sara and I decided to move to Somerset. The fact that Anna and Emma were now both teaching in Bristol and seemed likely to remain there was the primary factor. Rob was hardly even a gleam in Anna's eye; and if Paddy and Emma knew something when they pressed us to move westward, they weren't letting on. Both our children, however, seemed to be keen to have us nearer, though we were hardly yet so utterly decrepit as to be unable to look after ourselves; nor did we wish ever to be dependent on them. Moving, however, is never easy and as one gets older it becomes increasingly unattractive. As Macbeth observed, while screwing up his resolve to slaughter King Duncan, 'If it were done when 'tis done, then 'twere well/It were done quickly:'.

The opportunity arose through the sad circumstance of the death of Sara's father, Ted Hollins. He had finally come to accept that he could not manage to continue looking after himself in his beloved Robin Hill and for some months had been in a very civilised and comfortable nursing home in Midhurst, where he seemed relatively happy with his lot. Sara would visit him once a week, and the drive, though long enough, was manageable in a way it would not have been from Bristol. Sometimes I went with her, but not often, since I was never quite sure that I was welcome. He had never been easy, but as he declined he seemed somewhat more at peace with himself and even with me. His final release, though painful to observe, brought him I am sure a blessed relief.

Again we found ourselves running with the tide in our affairs, which 'taken at the flood' might lead on, if not to fortune, at least to the happiness of being nearer to our children and in one of the loveliest counties of England – and some would say one of its best kept secrets. We moved with a speed and decisiveness which in retrospect surprises me. We got lists of possible houses from estate agents. We came down for the day to inspect three properties within the radius of about ten miles which we had agreed upon, saw one in Kingston Seymour, near Clevedon, made an offer which was accepted, and waited upon the inevitable tortoise race conducted between solicitors, agents, and vendors. The vendors were eager for speed and we were happy to go along with them. But the more we sped, the more reluctant they became, until finally they reneged on us and we were back to square one. There must be a better way to win a war or buy a house – to me it sounds as if the Scots may have it, but I have not had a chance to test my thesis. Meanwhile, in an age of global warming and rising seas, there was a corner of me glad to seek a house on higher ground. Kingston Seymour had been flooded in the past, long ago, in the seventeenth century, I think, and the mark of the high water level is still to be found in the village church. It all seemed relatively close to the substantial but not so very lofty sea defences.

Back to square one: particulars, short list, prices, distances, one day-visit to inspect three more houses; 30 Warner Close in Cleeve was the last of three. The village itself, sitting on the A370, and at first glance an unappealing bit of ribbon development, looked unprepossessing. But the house was the right size; it was a good location in a small close, a reasonably new (1990) development, which had replaced an old garage (we always buy new houses). There was a relatively large garden. We walked into the drawing room, saw the garden and the view – and that was it. We barely looked at the rest of the house, made an offer of the full asking price on the spot, and had it accepted next day. The owners were unusually honourable. They later received a higher offer, but refused it. Not everyone gazumps.

We bought with an enormous bridging loan, and then had to sell 60 Alfredston Place. There was no mortgage, since I had paid it off in 1997, but the new property was significantly more expensive (different in design, though similar in size and amenity, apart from the garden) and it was important to make a good sale. We were lucky. Our next-door neighbours had friends who wanted to get out of London. The market was relatively buoyant, though not yet overexcited. We sold for the price originally demanded by the developers in 1989, which like the rest of the market had come down by a third by the time we bought in 1992. It was a sad moment. We had been very happy there, and it was where our children had passed from teenage to adulthood.

But 'all experience is an arch wherethro'/Gleams that untravelled world'. We remember with gratitude; we move on in hope. And for us the hopes have been abundantly fulfilled.

The modern village has little to commend it visually; but some of the houses in the older part are full of character, built from the red-brown local stone or painted in strong brick colours. There used to be eleven dairy farms just after the war; now there are none. But sheep and cattle remain the primary industry, with residual orchards whose trees are profusely hung with mistletoe. We are surrounded by pastureland. The country lanes are pleasant for walking, and all around us are the Mendip foothills, densely wooded, part of the Avon Forest in the making. From our front door we can walk in every direction directly into countryside or woodland, while Goblin Combe and Cleeve Combe are magical under snow or in their summer greenery, and both the haunt of innumerable song thrushes, whose evensong would require the genius of a poet to celebrate. The dawn chorus heard from our bedroom at 4.00 in the morning is truly memorable, with blackbirds competing with thrushes and the robin, who seems unwearied by his long night of non-stop singing from the top of the local lamppost, which never goes out, so that he thinks it's always daytime. I am writing this in April, which combined with the mention of song thrushes makes recourse to Browning's 'Home Thoughts from Abroad' inevitable.

> O to be in England
> Now that April's there,
> And whoever wakes in England
> Sees, some morning, unaware,
> That the lowest boughs and the brushwood sheaf
> Round the elm-tree bole are in tiny leaf,
> While the chaffinch sings on the orchard bough
> In England – now!
>
> And after April, when May follows,
> And the whitethroat builds, and all the swallows!
> Hark, where the blossomed pear-tree in the hedge

Leans to the field and scatters on the clover
Blossoms and dewdrops – at the bent spray's edge –
That's the wise thrush; he sings each song twice over,
Lest you should think he never could recapture
The first fine careless rapture!
And though the fields look rough with hoary dew
All will be gay when the noontide wakes anew
The buttercups, the little children's dower
– Far brighter than this gaudy melon-flower!

He has not told the half of it, but he's caught the spirit of the place, and that surely makes a good start.

There are two or three Iron Age fortresses within a mile; there may well be a Roman villa (unexcavated) in the field above us; the local environmental group (YACWAG) is extremely active and brilliantly led by Tony and Faith Moulin, and Trevor Riddle of the RSPB; it has managed to buy up quite an acreage for preservation as wildlife reserves. In our garden, thanks to Sara's ever generous bounty of peanuts, sunflower seeds, and fat bars, we have been visited (mostly regularly) by green and great spotted woodpeckers, jays, magpies (alas), mallards from a neighbour's pond (blast them!), crows, rooks, starlings, pigeons, pheasant, collared doves, wrens, dunnock, robin, tits (great, blue, and coal), blackcaps, blackbirds, thrushes, nuthatches, chiffchaff, wheatear, bullfinch, chaffinch, greenfinch, siskins, brambling, goldfinch, treecreepers (sometimes), a red-legged partridge (once), swallows and martins (mainly overhead and certainly in April not May – *pace* Browning), buzzards always floating high above, and often mewing in the woods, and a sparrowhawk (on the off chance of a free meal) from our avian guests. We also see too much of the local tree rats (grey squirrels to you) that eat birds' eggs and steal the bird food. Overhead, and an ever-present reminder of Campbell, the herons commute to the Severn estuary from their mighty rookery in Cleeve Wood, a protected site, but you can watch them on a closed-circuit TV in the local garden centre.

We eliminated a parade of enormously lofty *leylandii* along the fence at the bottom of the garden (which made it gloomy and gave little protection); both neighbours have followed suit, in whole or in part. Shallow rooted, I was glad to see them gone, before they succumbed to the strong south-westerlies which often plague us. Most of them had already developed a certain inclination to the north-east, as evidence of their vulnerability. Instead we have planted deciduous trees – oak, maple, beech, copper beech, chestnut, ash, field maple, larch, silver birch, whitebeam, red-leaved oak, Aetna broom, Californian red-leaf, rowan, cherry, hawthorn, amelanchier, willow, wisteria, and weeping willow. Following my easy-management principles, the lawn occupies centre stage (for croquet of course) and all around the edges are shrubs (including nearly twenty different acers), whose variegated and differing leaves and flowers give us variety and colour pretty well all the year round. Apart from a few tubs, my only concession to flowers in the conventional sense is my ever-increasing collection of snowdrops, daffodils, crocuses, primroses and cyclamen – none of them need any attention and simply spring up and slowly spread. Apart from regular mowing, a week's blitz in the late spring and another in the autumn is enough to keep it under control. It is, so far, a pleasure not a burden. A large conservatory, added soon after we arrived, allows us to enjoy both birds and garden all the year round and makes a useful playroom for the grandchildren.

For the arrival of each new grandchild I planted a tree in celebration: a chestnut for Imogen, with pink flowers of course; a copper beech for Arthur, suitably manly; and a flowering cherry for Molly, pretty as a picture. It was pure sentimentality, but I had always been attracted to Godfrey Marshall's story of how, in Patterdale, his father planted for him at his birth a whole plantation. This is hardly in the same league – but the best I could do. I hope the children will enjoy watching them grow, as I do them.

If, as we plan, we see out our days in this lovely and enchanted place, it will probably be the longest we have lived in any home. Campbell and Wantage hold the record so far, at eleven years apiece, but otherwise we seem to have moved too regularly to put down roots in any one spot. Canterbury, Eastbourne, Campbell, Wantage, Cleeve – in their different ways we have loved them all. Yet none has afforded us that sense of permanence we crave; in that I envy the Macafees who have lived at Stramore for three generations, and I understand the sentiment in Yeats' 'Prayer for My Daughter', which I quoted in my chapter on Sara.

May she live like some green laurel
Rooted in one dear perpetual place.

Bill Golding, our neighbour, a retired builder who has lived in the area all his life and has a fund of tales about life between the wars, as well as during and after WWII, has told us all about the rooting powers of laurels; they grow deep and long and very strong, and will destroy the foundations of any building you let them near. His knowledge gave added vividness and force to Yeats' metaphor.

We settled in; we joined the parish church where everyone was extraordinarily welcoming; we found no truth in the myth that you have to be in an English village for thirty years before you qualify even as a newcomer; the local shop was run by Ron Bebe, another exile from Northern Ireland; we explored the walks and woodlands; we contributed to the National Trust's exciting new multi-million pound purchase of nearby Tyntesfield; I made a half-hearted attempt to see if I could join the local cricket club, but it came to nothing. Instead I joined a gym to try and keep myself in reasonable shape. I have yet to find a better way to put on weight rather than remove it. I volunteered to be the local street coordinator for Neighbourhood Watch.

Briefly I also became a co-opted member of the parish council, when they asked for volunteers to fill a place between elections. Unlike Wantage, this council was entirely unpolitical. Though technically our status as a local council was the same as Wantage's, we were of course an infinitely smaller operation. Richard Whittaker, who also ran the local post office in Claverham, our next-door village, was a superbly efficient part-time clerk and our only employee; Wantage by contrast had a full-time clerk, council offices, and several supporting staff. But the task was the same: to care for the village and protect its interests as best we could. We were as powerless as Wantage, able only to make representations to the district council. Bristol Airport was a permanent source of frustration and irritation, with planes causing pollution by noise and (we believed) exhaust particles, and late night flying, with the airport managers largely indifferent to our complaints and representations. Their promises of an extended flight path away from the village have so far come to nothing.

But after years of effort we have recently got a pedestrian crossing with traffic lights, to enable elderly people, of whom we have many, to cross the busy A370, where the speed limit is regularly abused. Of such small victories are community triumphs made.

An enjoyable effort was the production of a village statement – another Blairite idea, one suspects, designed to keep the natives quiet by occupying as much of their time as possible to minimum effect. We worked hard to interview as many local people as possible and to record what we felt was the character of our village and things we wished to see preserved. The theory was that this would be incorporated in the district plan, which would shape planning policy for the next quinquennium. My particular job was to talk to farmers and see what they felt about things. It was an excellent way of getting to know some of the local people, who had a particularly strong commitment to the place, where some of their families had lived for generations. It made me even more aware of the difficulty of being a small farmer in modern Britain, and much more sympathetic to their plight. Producing the statement was the least of our tasks. Getting it accepted by the bureaucracy proved wellnigh impossible – procrastination, staff shortages, and probably a degree of wilful obstruction went on and on. But it was finally accepted in July 2006 and if in the end it helps preserve our precious green belt status against the barbarians of John Prescott's ministry, the effort will have been worthwhile.

Again my membership of the parish council foundered on impatience with probably necessary but tiresome procedures, the inescapable bureaucracy of anything touched by government, and the consequent late nights entailed in meetings. My stamina by day is good; come ten o'clock at night I can think of little else but sleep. When the elections arrived I did not offer myself as a candidate.

Instead, encouraged by Sara, I allowed my name to go forward as a possible chairman of the North Somerset Neighbourhood Watch Association. I felt that I had some experience in running an organisation and a reasonably clear mind in developing strategy, so I hoped I could be of use. Ian Sheppard, my predecessor, had done a remarkable job for a number of years chairing this rather amorphous and somewhat disparate body, which sought to coordinate the activities of all the local schemes across the district of North Somerset, which stretched from Portishead and Abbots Leigh (where Emma is a street coordinator) in the north to Weston super Mare and Bleadon in the south, and across to Langford and Dundry to the east. We represented some 26,000 households grouped into some 1,250 local street schemes. At a national level the numbers must be incredible and as a force for good in every kind of local community the potential of the movement is inestimable.

But there were problems. It is an entirely voluntary organisation and determined to remain so; its structure is resolutely local and no two localities have the same concerns, needs, or constituents – united effort is therefore almost impossible; it is studiously unpolitical, and therefore reluctant to get too close to government, though it is so large that only government could really make it truly effective; when I became chairman, the National NW Association lacked money and manpower and looked as if it was about to go broke, when its main sponsor pulled out; it was somewhat undemocratic in its structures, and had difficulty establishing a relationship with more local organisations – indeed the consensus within our own association was that they were useless. There were several tiers of organisation in the system – and the higher you got, the less effective they seemed to be.

At individual street level NW works well; and a group of such street schemes within a single locality served by an area coordinator, who distributes the newsletter, attends meetings of the district association, also makes good sense. Above that it is all pretty messy. The district association, of which I now became chairman, because no one else was foolish enough to volunteer, met four times a year and its executive committee a further four times. The association tried to act as a forum for discussion of issues, to disseminate information, liaise with the police, and formulate policy (if that is not too pretentious a word) and agree good practice. We had some good meetings, but for perfectly valid reasons, they were attended by a faithful band of regulars but failed to attract a consistent turnout by a fully-representative spread of the association. The district was, in theory, represented on the national association, but again for perfectly understandable reasons rarely had any feedback from its representative and never had any influence on the national policy – if there was such a thing.

With a general election coming in 2005, the government must have seen a chance to make a splash as a way of appearing dynamic and concerned for local communities and began to take an interest and promise initiatives. But it was seen by the movement as a covert attempt by the Home Office to take them over, the promised initiatives failed to materialise, and resistance mounted. As soon as the election was over and they were safe, the government's interest evaporated. Yet I remain convinced that, if the potential of the movement could be harnessed by government to work for the whole community in a totally unpolitical way, its potential for good is enormous. It needs a great deal of money, the resources of government, and high-powered management expertise to make it work properly.

Had I been twenty years younger and blessed with a private income so that I did not need to earn my living, it would have been a fascinating challenge to try to join the national association and work to pull the whole thing together. As it was, though my colleagues on the district association were generous about my efforts, I felt that I was not helping to make it effective or to develop its potential. I was also finding myself, somewhat to my surprise, I confess, increasingly stressed by the effort to make the thing work, and decided I must resign. I much regret it, because it was a thoroughly worthwhile activity, I enjoyed the company of my colleagues, and I could see what huge possibilities the movement offered in an era when crime and disorder were increasingly significant issues in society. I would have liked to serve on the national body as well as the district and try to make it effective.

One thing impressed me enormously and that was the commitment of the police to the whole concept of Neighbourhood Watch. Our own district of North Somerset had two dedicated full time civilian NW administrators, as well as designated police officers whose job it was to liaise with us. Avon and Somerset Police had another development officer in their headquarters for the whole police authority area. There were other organisations with which we had relations, not always harmonious, such as the local action teams (whose activities were much more up-front and in-your-face). There were also the CSDATs, the community safety and drug action teams, whose meetings I attended twice a year, and found rather impressive for their quiet resolve to get things done locally to make things better.

It was part of my feeling of inadequacy that I could rarely offer the services of Neighbourhood Watch in active support of any particular initiative. But that was the nature of the beast – we were a set of low visibility, voluntary, local groups committed to crime prevention by local alertness and quiet support of our neighbours – we were not really designed for action. Of our two really useful functions, one was the distribution of a quarterly newsletter, which reported on the state of crime, warned people of current trends and risks, and publicised ways of reducing risk to property; the other was the excellent ringmaster system, run by our two civilian administrators. Any event or information which might be useful in alerting local people to a crime or the presence of criminals in the area was sent out by phone or email to local coordinators, whose job it then was to spread the news. A crime thus prevented is, of course, impossible to measure, since it never happened. So one cannot know how effective NW is, because its task is prevention rather than response. If 'spin' was my trade, I suspect I would be arguing that the less you hear about NW, the more successful it is.

I continue as the local street and area coordinator because it is a splendid concept. I remain sad that its huge potential seems impossible to realise and that the association has found it impossible to replace me and is suspending its activities as an association.

I also agreed to sit as a member of the Schools Appeal Panel for parents whose children had failed to get into the school of their choice. I found that North Somerset had evolved an impressive and meticulously careful and fair appeals system and felt privileged to be a part of it. Some of the decisions we had to make were cruelly hard; some of the special circumstances behind the appeals were heart-breaking. But I felt the process was painstaking and the outcomes as reasonable as human frailty could make them and that I was making a small but worthwhile contribution to the local community.

Sara and I jointly became wardens of Littlewood, a local nature reserve of some six acres on nearby Kenn Moor, which by sheer chance I was instrumental in persuading YACWAG to purchase, when I spotted it was for sale but found the price beyond my range. Its fascinating range of species of flora, fauna and insect life leaves me feeling speechless and incompetent to guide others round it.

Sara, meanwhile, threw herself into a range of different good works. We both joined the rota for reading in the church; but she took on the regular cleaning task as well. For a couple of years I helped to mow the churchyard, but found it increasingly troublesome for my back, on which a strimmer makes heavy demands, not least because it is not the fastest way to cover a considerable quantity of ground. My stint took about two hours and I paid the penalty for several days afterwards. Sara was also much better than I at joining in the Lent courses, which were provided every year. I am not too good at holy huddles; she is more tolerant, more willing to become engaged, and probably more open-minded.

Following her successful foray into voluntary reading help in Wantage, which she had hugely enjoyed, Sara continued with it in Cleeve, helping weak readers in the local church primary school. There was no local branch of VRH, but they were willing to let her take advantage of the facilities of the Bristol branch. However access was difficult and her own expertise rendered it largely unnecessary.

To this she added another interesting assignment, acting as a mentor in the local authority's scheme for Education Other than at School. Unmotivated pupils, served by a combination of volunteers and teachers (who sometimes seemed defeated and demoralised) was an unpromising combination, but she persevered until the demands became too much for her.

She also acted for a time as a visitor at the local nursing home for the elderly.

More creatively, she set herself to complete one and launch out upon the second of a pair of glorious tapestries, each about four foot square, and each ultimately destined for one of our two daughters. Designed by Elizabeth Bradley, there are four central panels in each, depicting four different garden flowers; round the edges run continuous borders, in one a garland of flowers and butterflies, in the other garlands depicting the four seasons. The colours are rich and deep. They are simply beautiful and a labour of great love. I tried to calculate the number of stitches involved and decided that approximately a million in each was about the figure. I hope they will pass down the families as treasured heirlooms. Of one thing I am certain: they will endure far longer than my books! As I said before,

> A thing of beauty is a joy for ever:
> Its loveliness increases; it will never
> Pass into nothingness . . .

Increasingly grandchildren have come to be the focus of her wonderful skills with children and she has had to withdraw from most of these other commitments. But she still continues to work for a splendid local charity called Springboard, which takes in disabled or disturbed children and works with them to overcome their learning difficulties. Some are distressingly handicapped, whether mentally or physically, and require one-to-one attention, so volunteers to support the professional staff are essential to the operation. The patience and resilience required to do this work is enormous and I have to contrast my own comfortable existence somewhat shamefacedly with the work she does.

The arrival of our grandchildren has, of course, been the source of our greatest joy. To be a parent is the supreme pleasure here on earth, but it brings with it concomitant discomforts and anxieties, sleepless nights, worries about irrevocable damage – rarely realised, thank goodness, since children are remarkably resilient in the face of all the ills that flesh is heir to. But such things torment us none the less. But to be a grandparent, to share the pleasure and enjoy the love and then hand back the child to its mum or dad is a luxury undreamt of in that earlier phase.

To be allowed, even asked, to help out; to be trusted to care for them so as to give their mother a brief spell of peace and opportunity to get things done; to be treated, when they are young, as both surrogate parent and just another playmate; to have the sacred duty of spoiling them just a little and loving them a lot; to live out once again the wonder of childhood as well as the anxiety of parenthood, while yet absolved from real responsibility – all this is to enter the seventh heaven of old age.

Ratty, in *Wind in the Willows*, observed to Mole, I think it was, 'Believe me, my young friend, there is nothing – absolutely nothing – half so much worth doing as simply messing about in boats.' He was wrong. There is one thing much more worth doing, by a hundred miles, and that is enjoying the company of one's grandchildren. To be allowed by our children to have such easy access to them is like being let loose in a sort of pensioners' permanent sweetie shop.

They are each so different and each equally delightful – parents may not entirely agree all the time. Imogen has the sweetest and gentlest of natures, richly imaginative, and a joy to read to or talk with. Happiest moments have been sitting watching Walt Disney's *Fantasia* with her and noting how extraordinarily appreciative she is of the music and the story line. She dances at the slightest opportunity and Sara's gift of her own CD player has introduced her to classical music, which she clearly genuinely enjoys. Arthur is a real boy (despite his predilection for the colour pink!), into dumper trucks and tractors, solidly built and destined, I suspect, for the Welsh front row, though secretly I hope not. But he too has that sweetness of nature I observe in Imogen. When I once fell over a sofa and it took me a moment to recover, his consternation and heroic attempts to elevate me to an upright position was evidence of real concern. Our video of *Thomas the Tank Engine* currently devours all spare moments not devoted to the railway line in the conservatory, where a 'real' Thomas has his empire. Molly gave her mother hell at birth and a very tough first few months. But now she is the greatest fun, crawling everywhere at high speed and blessed with an infectious chuckle and a winning smile, designed to melt the heart of any soupy grandparent. We are so lucky – I really can't believe it.

As I am increasingly confronted by what Churchill called 'the surly advance of decrepitude', I should dearly like to achieve a level of tranquillity and physical inactivity, which would perhaps enable me to turn my hand to poetry. I have never felt that I have the imagination of a real poet. Yet I once heard Robert Graves, while Professor of Poetry at Oxford, describe the poet's calling as 'a profession of private thought reinforced by craftsmanship of words'. I was sufficiently struck by the definition to inscribe it in my commonplace book, among the many I have collected, and I might try to measure up however inadequately to that particular description of a poet's trade.

'Turning blood into ink' was T S Eliot's phrase, I think; Ortega y Gasset describes it as 'a tool for creation which God forgot inside one of his creatures when he made him;' Ezra Pound says that 'poets are the antennae of the race' – I thought it was Shelley, but my quotation book says otherwise; 'language working under stress', 'A moment's monument' (specifically of the sonnet), 'emotion recollected in tranquillity' and so on – I keep collecting definitions and descriptions, and would love to think that somewhere, just once even, I might manage to produce something mildly memorable that met some of their requirements.

I was moved, quite recently and entirely out of the blue, to write a tiny poem to Imogen, simply expressing the sheer delight of being a grandfather and yet so welcome in her own small world. I sent it to a friend to ask if it was any good; the reply was generous and he told me that his wife read it and burst into tears. Reassured by such a verdict, I offer it from a full heart to 'Immy', as the senior representative of all my beloved grandchildren, Imogen Brianna, Arthur Gregg, and Molly Sara.

Here it is:

Imogen

'Pappa' she calls me,
Taking my hand
And issuing her stern command
To 'come up and see' . . .
Her picture, or doll, or teddy bear,
Or shells, or Play-doh fantasies,
And all those myriad joys
We grown-ups call 'toys'.

So then, obedient
As befits my age,
Accorded equal status in
A child's democracy
And thus sublimely honoured,
I obey,
And meekly follow up the stair
To view the wonders waiting there.

Thus gently and sweetly, we
Rehearse the moment when
Another voice commands
'Come up and see . . .'

In both I sense my immortality.

CHAPTER 32

The Arch of Experience – Gleams that Untravelled World

I am a part of all that I have met;
Yet all experience is an arch wherethro'
Gleams that untravelled world, whose margin fades
For ever and for ever when I move.

As I approach my eighth decade, I am tempted to wonder what new untravelled worlds may open up beyond the archway of experience. If every decade of my life is to continue to be happier than its predecessor, as I have tempted Fate by suggesting, the challenge to improve upon my seventh will be considerable. The ageing Ulysses, in Tennyson's great poem from which my title and the above quotation comes, continues,

> How dull it is to pause, to make an end,
> To rust unburnished, not to shine in use!
> As though to breathe were life. Life piled on life
> Were all too little, and of one to me
> Little remains: but every hour is saved
> From that eternal silence, something more,
> A bringer of new things . . .

Unable to simply sit back and enjoy the fruits of a lifetime's memories, he leaves Telemachus, his beloved son, to wield his sceptre and to rule his island kingdom of Ithaka. His son is blessed with a more placid temperament, well-suited to the routine tasks of governance and 'centred in the sphere of common duties'. But Ulysses is of a different kind; he 'cannot rest from travel', and wants only to 'drink life to the lees', determined always to 'follow knowledge like a sinking star', even if it means that he must 'sail beyond the sunset and the baths of all the western stars' until he dies. So he summons his old comrades to one last adventure.

> There lies the port; the vessel puffs her sail:
> There gloom the dark broad seas. My mariners,
> Souls that have toiled, and wrought, and thought with me . . .
>
> Death closes all: but something 'ere the end,
> Some work of noble note, may yet be done
> Not unbecoming men that strove with Gods.
> The lights begin to twinkle from the rocks:
> The long day wanes: the slow moon climbs: the deep

Moans round with many voices. Come my friends,
'Tis not too late to seek a newer world.

Ulysses was for Dante, as for Tennyson, a symbol of that restlessness, physical and intellectual, which some call 'divine discontent' while others would deny it the defining adjective. Dante pictures him in one of the lower circles of hell, forever consumed by fire, symbolic of his consuming 'itch to rove and rummage through the world, exploring it', as Dorothy Sayers so wonderfully translates it. Even Homer portrays him as similarly consumed by a desire to know, so much so that he even longed to hear what songs the fatal sirens sang. He made his men stop their own ears with wax, but tie him to the mast of his ship and ignore all his pleas to be released, so that he could hear their song but not succumb to it. I suspect that this lies at the heart of his inability to settle down ever after.

Of all the heroes of ancient Greek mythology, Odysseus (Ulysses is his Latin name) is for me the greatest. I lack all his heroic qualities, his courage and endurance, his strength of will, his bravery in battle. But two things I would like to share in some small degree: his famed fidelity to his beloved wife, Penelope, and something of his restlessness of mind, his abiding interest in the world around him, and desire to explore it. Within the limitations of my wholly unscientific education and the enormous advance in human knowledge of every kind, which puts the bulk of it beyond the reach of any one person, I think I retain an interested mind, and reading will always be one of my particular pleasures. The great Professor E T Salmon, whose famous work, *The Infallibility of the Church*, denied the Pope's claim to any such capacity, was said by his contemporaries to 'know more about everything than anyone else knew about anything'. Such a quality will never again be possible in the modern world; one can do no more than be interested and strive to be aware, and then restrict one's reading and thinking to a narrower compass.

It is presumably a symptom of old age, as one contemplates the strange mystery of eternity, that theology, at a relatively low level, has become the focus of my interest. Ever since Jock Burnet at Cambridge told me that every educated man should read theology as a sideline, I have tended to have some sort of theological work 'on the go'.

O world invisible, we view thee,
O world intangible, we touch thee,
O world unknowable, we know thee,
Inapprehensible, we clutch thee!

Francis Thompson's great poem, 'In No Strange Land', seems to have been with me all my life – another legacy of compulsory learning by heart from the Sedbergh Classical Sixth. It expresses as vividly as any I know the strange dilemmas of faith and belief in the existence of God. Of that existence – whatever we may mean by God – I am more confident than sceptical, my conviction being based on a perception of the probabilities, man's capacity for goodness, his varied but universal intuition of the existence of a divinity, and his belief in meaning and purpose, without which the unending, ever-expanding universe seems a ludicrously pointless and improbable joke. That I should have slightest idea of what form such a Being may take or how he chooses to operate within the sensible world seems to me mere folly, futile speculation at the best. As we are to the ants that will inhabit the globe long after we are gone, so perhaps is God to us, a being beyond, above, beneath, and around us, but inscrutable, untouchable, unknowable except in metaphor – or, as my wise old mother once put it to me, 'My generation saw God as an unending Mind, expanding ever to elude.' All we can do is go about our business like the ants, as best we can, and acknowledge that blind chance or deliberate action may sometimes bring us into contact with that Great Unknowable.

It may be nothing more than the residual pantheism of my youth, but yet at times, like Wordsworth, and more in youth than in old age,

> I have felt
> A presence that disturbs me with the joy
> Of elevated thoughts; a sense sublime
> Of something far more deeply interfused,
> Whose dwelling is the light of setting suns,
> And the round ocean and the living air,
> And the blue sky, and in the mind of man.

Sometimes I have been surprised by that joy and 'turned to share the transport', which is predictably indistinguishable from that more general happiness of the kind I have already described. I take refuge in Socrates' wise observation that either death is no more than a sleep and a forgetting, in which case there is nothing to worry about; it comes to us all and is (as Benjamin Franklin observed long ago) as inevitable as taxes (if not more so). Or else it is a journey to another place, where characteristically he was, of course, immensely looking forward to interrogating the wise men of the past and even more all his contemporaries who had evaded his questions here on earth. And of this I am sure, he concluded, 'that no evil can happen to a good man. So have a care for your soul.'

And that observation reminds me of Tony Bridge, former atheist and artist, later to become Dean of Guildford, giving a talk at Radley when I was a young don there, and saying that 'if there is a God, we are one kind of creature; if there is not, we are another. So it is pretty important to try and find out which.' And that is what throughout my life I have tried to do, assessing the evidence and arguments put to me in sermons, books, and conversations as honestly and dispassionately as I can, less tormented by doubt than challenged by it to seek the truth.

I have never ceased to be a communicant member of the Anglican church and a reasonably regular churchgoer. My reasons were simple, some would say simplistic. If one day you are going to have to play a cricket match 'out in the middle', then it is essential that you constantly keep up your practice in the nets. The fact that more and more I found myself out of sympathy with what went on in church and the increasing banality of its services has no bearing on the broader argument about the reality of God and the search to find Him. The essential thing is to keep yourself in practice, sensitised to the possibility of divinity, and to hold the doorway open to revelation and the insinuating influence of the Holy Spirit – though heaven knows He sometimes makes it very hard and His servants, the churches, even more so.

Much of the process, and my growing scepticism about the traditional mythology of the Christian faith, I tried to reflect in the introductory passages to each section of my collected broadcasts, talks, sermons and correspondence, published in *A Faith Unfaithful*. Putting it together was a useful exercise, forcing me to review my ideas as they had developed over the last twenty-five years. I found that in broadcasting I had few reservations about expressing those ideas in traditional language, since for myself I was satisfied that I was speaking metaphorically, poetically if you like, while for my listeners I was using language and concepts with which they were familiar and comfortable. God welcomes His children by whatever road they come.

What did surprise me was the remarkable sense of relief I felt as, at a personal level, I found it ever more easy to acknowledge that the literal truth of the Christian story was no longer credible. Even the gospels were less a record of historical events than what the Greeks would have called myth-history, expressive of profound truths about God, but not precise records of historical events. Of course there is history in the gospels, as there is in the Old Testament and in the epics of Homer. Jesus certainly existed and was crucified by the Roman authorities in Jerusalem. He was manifestly a prophetic figure endowed with a deep sense of God, and at a time of high Messianic expectation he may even have been associated with key figures in the Jewish resistance, who would have hoped to exploit his charisma to spark their nation into open revolt against Rome. But it seems clear that he would have nothing to do with violence, though it is perfectly possible that the Roman authorities were unaware of this and treated him as 'just another troublemaker'. Whatever their motives, he was from their point of view expendable.

Whether he was tried in the manner described in the gospels is debatable; whether he died in the manner described must remain a matter of faith not fact; that the details of the crucifixion occurred as described seems at least unlikely, given the gospels' inconsistencies and their admission that the disciples 'all forsook him and fled'. Incontrovertible is the effect of Jesus' life and death upon his followers, so much so that in time the myth of his physical resurrection developed, as the Jewish concept of exaltation was replaced in the Graeco-Roman world through which the faith was spreading by the more familiar myth of escape from Hades, or resurrection, which was common enough in the mythologies of many lands. But that it was myth, not a physical fact I am certain, just as I am equally certain that he was begotten of an earthly father and born of an earthly mother, that the miracles are myth-historical, and that his teaching has been edited by his chroniclers to some unspecified degree. I am now persuaded that over several centuries the believing community continued to develop its doctrines and refine its narrative, and that it was not until the end of the fifth century and the start of the Middle Ages that our foundation myth was broadly fixed in the form which we have inherited. The evolution of the cult of the Virgin Mary illustrates the process, as Bishop John Shelby Spong demonstrates so convincingly in his compelling work, *Born of a Woman*, in which he suggests that Mary Magdalene was gradually 'airbrushed' out of her central place in the gospel narrative by the mother of Jesus, in order to 'prove' her son's divinity.

I did a 'Thought for the Day' once on the joys of moving house, suggesting that the sense of relief one feels as one discards the accumulated clutter of the years is not unlike the relief one finds in discarding the unwanted clutter of belief. I now think of Jesus as in every way similar to the founders of other great world religions – a prophet, a profound and compelling teacher, a wonderful human being with a close (and, if you insist, unique) relationship with the Being we call God, and a remarkably original mind, which worked to refashion the Jewish faith in which he was reared. He introduced to the religion of his time a whole new concept of divine love for man, of man's duty of sacrificial love for his fellow men, of the inclusiveness of God's care for all His creatures, and what we would now call a re-branding of his own inherited Jewish religion, which in time became so changed in emphasis and content that it evolved into something entirely different, which we now call Christianity.

In all this development of my ideas, over the last few years two writers have influenced me most: John Shelby Spong, the retired Episcopal Bishop of Newark, USA, and Richard Holloway, former Episcopal Bishop of Edinburgh and Primus of the Scottish Episcopal Church. For those whose thinking inclines in this direction I commend their writings as a source of comfort and liberation. These men are professional theologians and profound scholars; I am not. I am at best an intelligent and I hope thinking layman. To find that I had reached a similar position to them on the tenets of my faith, without the knowledge and intellectual equipment and background that they had, was an enormous relief and the source of real liberation. More and more also, I felt that over the years I had been betrayed by the clergy and senior figures of my own church, to whom these ideas are perfectly familiar and possibly even acknowledged, but who through timidity or a misguided sense of obligation to the fearful faithful have not dared to challenge their congregations to rethink their own beliefs. Bishop Spong's books, especially *Born of a Woman* and *Liberating the Gospels*, have certainly liberated me. Holloway's *Doubts and Loves* and *Looking in the Distance* have encouraged me to continue the search for understanding.

Of course behind these relatively recent influences lie many others over the years, which have paved the way – *Honest to God, Soundings,* and the *Myth of God Incarnate* spring to mind. But authors like Paul Tillich, Teilhardt de Chardin, Ian Ramsey, Don Cupitt, Karen Armstrong, A N Wilson, Arthur Peacocke, Bertrand Russell, John Wilson, John V Taylor, and others have always had to jostle with more traditional writers such as J B Phillips, C S Lewis, Michael Ramsey, George Simms, William Temple, Alister McGrath, Wolfhardt Pannenberg, John Austin Baker, Rudolph Bultmann, C H Dodd and many others, whose thinking was no less interesting and served as a corrective to my more radical inclinations. I have tried to read traditionalists as well as radicals, but increasingly I have found the traditionalists wanting and some of their arguments unconvincing.

I wrote in my introduction to *A Faith Unfaithful* that, 'finally it became clear to me that religion, like everything else, was the product of evolutionary forces, and developed in conjunction with the human societies to which it belonged. While this is not the same as saying it is untrue, one does not have to be an aggressive Darwinian to see that failure to evolve is the shortest route to untruth and the surest guarantee of extinction.' The problem has been that the faith of my own church is failing to evolve in any but the most superficial way. Hence my disenchantment with the institutional church . . . What interests me is to find how many among the educated and thinking laity seem to think like me and to express their disillusion with the leadership of the church for its failure to give a lead in this area.

Just as the authority of Aristotle effectively blocked the development of European science for the next 1,500 years, so too the emergence of a central religious authority based on Rome fossilised the development of our Christian faith for a similar period. There is a rich irony in the possibility that the Enlightenment and the rebirth of science (which to an earlier generation seemed likely to destroy all forms of religious belief) may well prove to be the source of a revival of our faith, by enabling it to redefine its traditional mythology, so ushering in a new stage in its evolution and saving it from the general scepticism which its obscurantism has earned.

In a later passage I commented that, 'there is much wailing and gnashing of teeth among the church's hierarchy about the flight from belief and the drift of the laity from conventional churchgoing. All sorts of reasons are offered, from the legalisation of Sunday shopping to the loss of clerical vocation, from economic incompetence to the decline of moral standards in an increasingly secular world, from the incomprehensible language of our sacred texts to the spiritual emptiness of their replacements. Solutions are offered from every side, most of them well-intentioned. My own reservations about most of them is that they tend to tinker with structures rather than grapple with fundamentals.'

In John Shelby Spong's *Born of a Woman* I found the following statement, which profoundly comforts me. 'Long ago I decided that I could no longer sacrifice scholarship and truth to protect the weak and religiously insecure. I see another audience that the church seems to ignore . . . I want them to find in the Christian church a gospel that takes seriously the world of their experience, that does not seek to bind their minds into pre-modern or ancient forms, that is not afraid to examine emerging truth from any source, whether from the world of science or the world of biblical scholarship.' That speaks to me with clarity and conviction. *O si sic omnes* – if only they were all like that.

In the end, provoked by a competition on the BBC, I tried to write a Creed for the twenty-first century, with which I could feel comfortable. I made it my entry and sent it in. Since it was not even acknowledged, I assume that it was unacceptable to the judges. Here it is:

A Personal Creed for the 21st Century

I believe in one God,
Source of creation, expanding ever to elude,
Whose essence is one and manifestations infinite,
Whose love embraces all that is.

I honour his Prophets, of every faith and creed,
Whose teachings and example
Brought faith to the world,
Understanding to the mind,
Enrichment to the spirit.

I honour especially the Prophets of the kindred faiths
of all the Peoples of the Book,
Moses, Jesus the Christ, and Mohammed.

I hold sacred above all the memory of Jesus,
By whose life and witness
God's nature was revealed and
His love made manifest,
By whose death
Love's victory over evil was made certain,
And by the triumph of whose spirit
Redeemed humanity received the hope of life eternal.

I believe in the loving spirit of God,
Working for good in ways beyond our understanding;

I pray for strength
To live my life in the service of God and all humanity.

The heart of the failure of the Christian churches lies, it seems to me, in the failure of their leadership to render the faith, and the worship through which believers seek to give expression to that faith, credible in a modern age. The imagery of its worship is no longer believable or effective – the concept of sacrifice (whether for sin or anything else) is redolent of a more primitive age of religion, when gods were tyrants who required placating; eating Christ's body and drinking his blood is a less than attractive image for the uncommitted, suggestive of the pagan idea of consuming elements of animals so as to acquire something of their *mana*, or life-force. In fact, the whole Christian 'narrative' (to use the modern jargon) or, as I would prefer to call it, the Christian myth (using the term as it should be used, to mean 'sacred story, seen as an expression of a profound religious truth') is simply incredible, given the discoveries of science, archaeology, the evolution of biblical scholarship, and our wider understanding of how such sacred stories develop and take on a life of their own.

The failure to educate the faithful to this deepening understanding of the real nature of our sacred literature is the cause of an aggressively fundamentalist view of the Bible as 'the Word of God' on the one side (wholly unacceptable to any thinking individual) and on the other side an ever-growing scepticism in an increasingly well-educated public about all the claims of the Christian faith, whose chief exponents have for centuries seemed wholly resistant to new ideas. As for the church and its structures, its tradition of male (and in some cases compulsorily unmarried) clergy, its hierarchies and power structures – all seem far more characteristic of political systems designed to reinforce the status and authority of those already in office (usually men) than the vision of a servant church whose founder washed his followers' feet as an example of humility and love.

Striving to reconcile in my mind the church and the faith in which I was reared with what I now believe it must become would, I suspect, keep me reading and arguing happily for a hundred years. I have for some time conducted correspondence with a number of intelligent and like-minded friends, some of very long standing, and they too help and provoke me to further thought. I enjoy writing, letters as well as books, and as I decline into my anecdotage I shall doubtless continue to afflict them with my ramblings. I have signed on as a subscriber to John Spong's weekly newsletter and joined for a trial year the PCN (Progressive Christian Network). It should serve to keep me intellectually alive, if nothing else.

I found this poem in my grandfather's anthology book. The author is unknown to me, but I like the thought and am rather happy to end with something that appealed to him as well.

I Go a Journey

I go a journey on an unknown day
Into an unknown land.
I only know
That I must go,
No more – but that is planned
By the one power I cannot disobey.

Shall I be heedless or shall I prepare?
What baggage shall I take?
Possessions here
So runs the fear
A useless load will make:
Rumours are rife of different values there.

Will those I love go with me? Or, alone,
Must I be venturesome?
Why trouble so?
Surely I know
To that land all must come:
I welcome, or am welcomed by, my own.

And Time – so rumours reach me – may be new,
A tyrant robbed of power;
What circles here
Into a year
May there be not an hour;
What if these rumours happen to be true?

Certain it is that I must journey there –
That at least I know:
Should I not teach
Myself the speech
Before I have to go?
I think it would be wisdom to prepare.

CHAPTER 33

In Conclusion – *Respice; Prospice; Sursum corda*

IN APRIL 1991, FOR A SERIES called 'Words of Faith', I gave three short broadcast talks, whose theme was an inscription in my Uncle John's Greek Testament. It was dated Advent 1918, and signed by his Shrewsbury Headmaster, H A P Sawyer. World War I was dragging to its agonising close with the Armistice of 11 November, so it must have been a time of painful memory but also dawning optimism. And so for a young prizewinner, aged fifteen and full of hope and promise, he wrote those four Latin words, *Respice; Prospice; Sursum corda*, 'Look back; look forward; be of good cheer (literally: lift up your heart)'. I have slightly edited the talks to reduce the repetition. But it seems as good a way to end this memoir as any I can think of.

I

When my uncle died, alas too young, while a prisoner of the Japanese and far from home, my grandfather gave me his Greek Testament, a prize from his schooldays. In the front there was a simple inscription in Latin from his old headmaster: '*Respice, Prospice, Sursum corda*' – 'Look back, look forward, lift up your heart'. How much the words meant to a young schoolboy long ago, I don't know. But I find increasingly that they have something to say to me as I move gently through late middle age.

Fourteen years ago in late winter I took my father's ashes for burial in a tiny churchyard in the very heart of Ireland. Very recently I brought my mother's ashes there to join his. There was a timelessness about the place: the trees were gaunt against the wide horizon; crows and jackdaws, squabbling round their nesting places in the high beech trees, alone gave promise of the spring to come; fields and bare hedgerows were as I always remembered them from my childhood. And enfolding all, there was a deep peace, engendered partly by the quiet of the countryside, but partly too by the sense of belonging when the heart comes home. It stills the restless soul, offering balm for sorrow, a calming of desire.

I am reminded of the tale of a wise old doctor, whose patient suffered for many years from a chronic but undiagnosable illness and indefinable lassitude. When she asked him for the umpteenth time to tell her what was wrong, he had to admit that he simply did not know. 'But I may have a cure', he said. 'Tell me, where were you born?' And she named some awful slum in the old industrial north of

England. 'Sell up', he said, 'and go back home and live there.' So she went, and in due course over the years her letters told him of health restored and strength renewed.

So too with our religious faith. It is rooted and grounded in the timeless wisdom of past insights and revelation, recorded by the wise and holy, tested by the experience of the ages, and always waiting like the timeless countryside for rediscovery by succeeding generations, when their hearts are ready to come home once more.

If we are rootless wanderers, as increasingly our modern way of living compels us to become, sometimes our hearts fall sick for love of home. And if our faith is rootless, as increasingly our modern way of thinking forces it to be, sometimes our souls fall sick, forgetting the roots and well-springs of belief, and we feel lost and far from home.

Nostalgia is a dangerous emotion, if it means no more than clinging to the past for fear of facing the future. Too often here in Ireland, whether in religion or politics, that sort of dangerous nostalgia prevails. Whether through cowardice or idleness or self-interest, people cling to their old familiarities; and the dead hand of the past snuffs out the light of future possibility. But just as young people grow to maturity, when encouraged by parents and teachers and wise friends, so too do ideas, when wise and holy men and women are allowed to bring their influence to bear. And then the past becomes the seedbed of the future, a home from which we venture forth to build our lives, and to which we return to find the peace and wholeness for which we always yearn.

So the instruction in my uncle's Testament – 'Look backward' – is nothing to do with a rosy nostalgia for a vanished past that never was, but sound advice for a young man setting out on life's long journey, not to forget, whether literally or metaphorically, the soil from which he sprang.

II

Looking backward, I suggested in my previous talk, is a healthy activity, if it serves to remind us of the roots from which we spring, literally, intellectually, and in our religious faith; unhealthy, if it is mere nostalgia and a sign of our reluctance to face the future. That is why looking back must always be balanced by looking forward. *Respice*, 'look back', the first imperative, needs its counterpart, *Prospice*, 'look forward'.

If there is one thing that seems to distinguish humanity from the rest of the animal kingdom, it is its capacity for looking into the future – the capacity to plan, to hope, and to aspire. Where other animals react, we anticipate. Indeed one might go further: as far as we can judge, animals live only in the present, meeting their immediate needs to survive and reproduce. If they plan, they plan only unconsciously, by instinct. But man lives in at least three worlds: those of the past, the present, and the future. In terms of survival value, obviously the ability to remember and learn lessons from the past brings considerable advantages, though as a species we do not appear to learn very much from past mistakes, judging by our almost infinite capacity for repeating them. But we are, of course, in evolutionary terms, still in our infancy. We have a long way to go.

Likewise, the ability to plan for the future offers us the possibility not just of preparing for future emergencies – even squirrels do that – but of conceiving great plans, organising our societies for mutual advantage, and ultimately cooperating for the betterment of the whole planet, which we share. Here too, however, we are still at the beginning of our evolutionary journey.

These twin capacities, of seeing the future and remembering the past, between them offer great possibilities for human progress. Each capacity seems particularly associated with a different sector of society. It is the old who remember and whose perspective on the past seems most perceptive. They treasure its inheritance and transmit it to the next generation. Some human societies set a higher store by this than others, and societies where reverence for age is most developed seem perhaps more stable and orderly than others. Traditional values count for more.

By contrast, looking to the future seems more a quality of youth – that time of restlessness, energy, and a desire to do great things, without quite knowing what they are. It is perhaps true that societies which admire these qualities show a greater dynamism, perhaps at the price of stability. The challenge of youth to age is always a source of tension; but it is also a guarantee of future vigour for the species.

But as well as the worlds of present, past, and future, there is a fourth world, which, as far as we can see, only man inhabits. It is a world that is not the prerogative of old or young, though by temperament old age seems best adapted to its exploration. It is a world that blends the wisdom of the old with the imagination of the young, while those blessed with the innocence of childhood seem best equipped of all to cross its boundaries. This is the world of eternity, outside of time, a world not built by hands, the world of the spirit. Since none has seen it, none can describe it. The intuition of the visionaries, the mystics, and the prophets are no more than pointers, signposts to that great and ultimate reality, whose glory can only be conveyed in the language of metaphor and symbol.

That's the world on which the old headmaster urged my uncle to fix his eye, when he wrote *Prospice* – look forward – in his Greek Testament.

III

Looking back and looking forward are capacities unique, as far as we can guess, to humankind among the animals. Each capacity has a survival value for the species, since it offers humankind (uniquely) the capacity to learn from experience and to plan ever more effectively for the future. But we also have a fourth capacity: the ability to move, however inadequately, into that eternal world of spirit, which represents the culmination of our mortal existence. One outward sign of this capacity is joy. Thus the three imperatives listed by that old headmaster, 'look backward, look forward, lift up your heart', encapsulate the best advice that old age can offer youth, as it enters the journey into adult life.

Today, as then in 1918, many might argue that this third imperative, 'lift up your heart', is sadly misplaced in a world where war, famine, pestilence, brutality, tyranny, greed, crime, and evil flourish as never before. If we look back we see only what the historian Gibbon called 'a dull uniformity of abject vices, neither softened by the weakness of humanity nor enlivened by the record of memorable crimes'. If we look forward we can see only the mixture as before, to which we must now add the devastation of our planet by the forces of greed, indifference, and exploitation. Why should we lift up our hearts?

Well, my answer would go like this. Joy is a religious duty, the outward expression of our faith. We are commanded to put our trust in God, not to let our hearts be troubled, to rejoice in the Lord always, and to set our hearts in heaven, where true joys are to be found. It is a command which, heaven knows, is hard to obey: yet where I meet those whose faith seems most strong, there I seem to find a serenity that is wellnigh radiant, and a peacefulness of spirit that renders all contentiousness preposterous, all worries trivial. There indeed I find joy.

Such joyfulness is a true expression of a living faith in God. But there is another side to the argument. Joy may be a sign of faith; but faith can also be a product of joy. Out of a determination to be joyful, a deeper faith may develop. For faith is not merely a gift of heaven; it is also the product of our wills. If, through faith, we set our wills to honour God by joyousness, God's reward is to compound that joy and reinforce our faith. It is a sort of religious virtuous circle.

And despite the catalogue of woes I listed earlier, there are good reasons for joy as we contemplate both the past and the future. Across the long perspectives of history, as well as disappointment we can see great advances, as religion passes from gross superstition to enlightenment, from being a weapon of the strong and privileged to one that offers protection to the weak; from the arrogance of power to the humility of service.

After the triumphalism of the scientific revolution and the so-called Age of Reason, we have moved into a period of rediscovery of religion. It is true that its immediate effects are sometimes depressing and uncomfortable, since fundamentalist zeal too often mars the good which religion does. Yet time always tames the zealot; moderation overtakes extremism in the end. All will be well and all manner of things will be well. And meantime we can rejoice in the rediscovery of the world of spirit, which binds the wisdom of the past with the promise of the future, when God in His own good time will pour out His spirit upon all flesh.

So, my beloved children and grandchildren all, for whom this book is written, look back; look forward; and be of good cheer. *Respice; prospice; sursum corda.*

Just as it was in Advent 1918, it is still good advice for a young man or woman setting out, from an old man heading home.

Chapter 34

Envoi – Final Thoughts; Last Words

Morte d'Arthur

And slowly answered Arthur from the barge:
The old order changeth, yielding place to new,
And God fulfils Himself in many ways,
Lest one good custom should corrupt the world.
Comfort thyself: what comfort is in me?
I have lived my life, and that which I have done
May He within Himself make pure! But thou,
If thou shouldst never see my face again,
Pray for my soul . . .

. . . Long stood Sir Bedivere
Revolving many memories, till the hull
Looked one black dot against the verge of dawn,
And on the mere the wailing died away.

Alfred, Lord Tennyson

Crossing the Bar

Sunset and evening star,
And one clear call for me!
And may there be no moaning of the bar,
When I put out to sea,

But such a tide as moving seems asleep,
Too full for sound and foam,
When that which drew from out the boundless deep
Turns again home.

Twilight and evening bell,
And after that the dark!
And may there be no sadness of farewell,
When I embark;

For though from out our bourne of Time and Place
The flood may bear me far,
I hope to see my Pilot face to face
When I have crossed the bar.

Alfred, Lord Tennyson

Socrates on Swansongs

Do you think I have less divination than the swans? For they, when they know that they must die, having sung all their lives sing louder than ever, for joy at going home to the god they serve. Men, who themselves fear death, have taken it for lamentation, forgetting that no bird sings in hunger, or cold, or pain. But being Apollo's, they share his gift of prophecy, and foresee the joys of another world.

Plato, *Phaedo*

Appendices
Family Trees and Connections

Unvisited tombs

The growing good of the world is partly dependent on unhistoric acts: and that things are not still with you and me as they might have been is half owing to the number who lived faithfully a hidden life, and rest in unvisited tombs.

George Eliot, *Middlemarch*

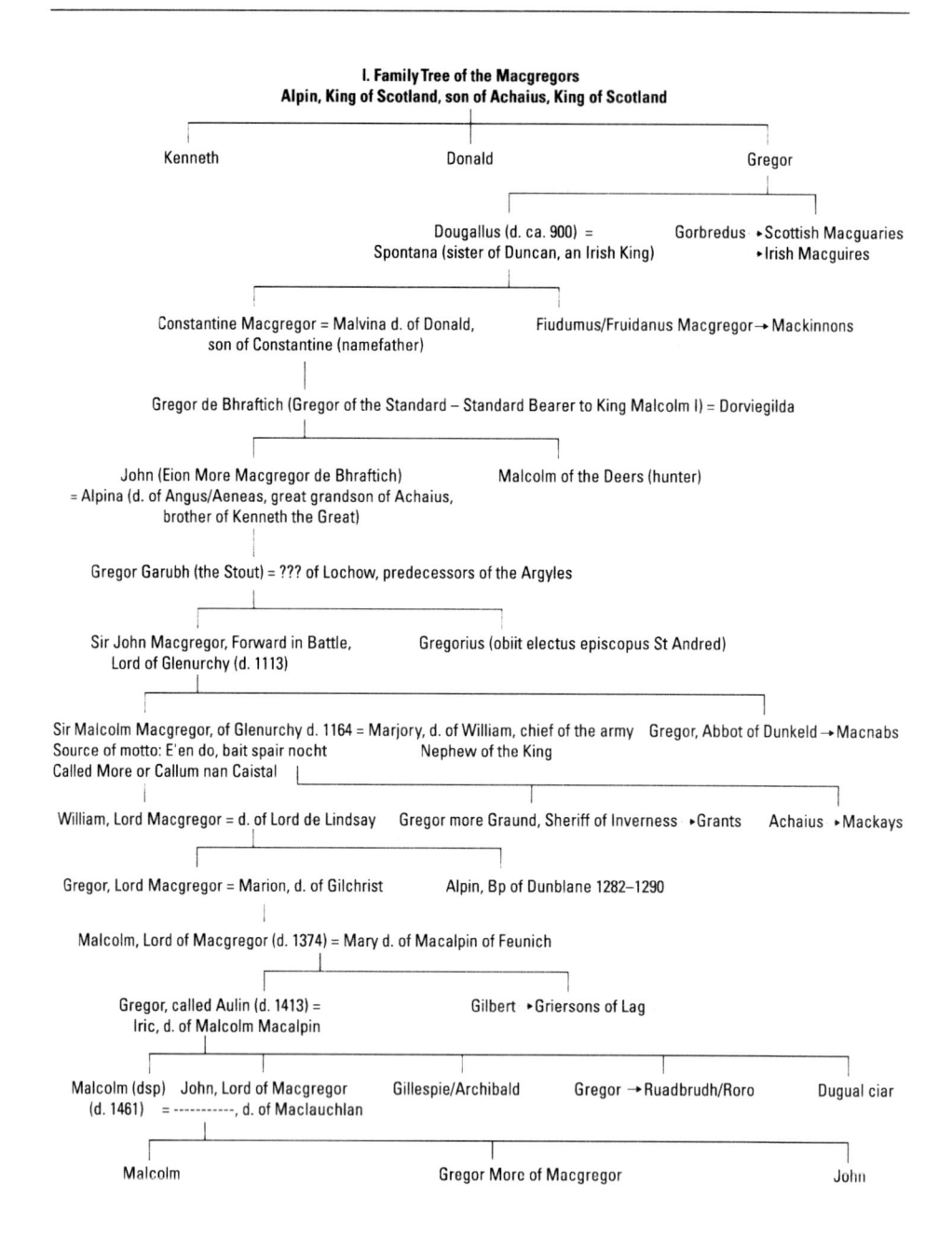

I. Family Tree of the Macgregors
Alpin, King of Scotland, son of Achaius, King of Scotland

- Kenneth
- Donald
- Gregor
  - Dougallus (d. ca. 900) = Spontana (sister of Duncan, an Irish King)
    - Constantine Macgregor = Malvina d. of Donald, son of Constantine (namefather)
      - Gregor de Bhraftich (Gregor of the Standard – Standard Bearer to King Malcolm I) = Dorviegilda
        - John (Eion More Macgregor de Bhraftich) = Alpina (d. of Angus/Aeneas, great grandson of Achaius, brother of Kenneth the Great)
          - Gregor Garubh (the Stout) = ??? of Lochow, predecessors of the Argyles
            - Sir John Macgregor, Forward in Battle, Lord of Glenurchy (d. 1113)
              - Sir Malcolm Macgregor, of Glenurchy d. 1164 = Marjory, d. of William, chief of the army Nephew of the King
                Source of motto: E'en do, bait spair nocht
                Called More or Callum nan Caistal
                - William, Lord Macgregor = d. of Lord de Lindsay
                  - Gregor, Lord Macgregor = Marion, d. of Gilchrist
                    - Malcolm, Lord of Macgregor (d. 1374) = Mary d. of Macalpin of Feunich
                      - Gregor, called Aulin (d. 1413) = Iric, d. of Malcolm Macalpin
                        - Malcolm (dsp) (d. 1461)
                        - John, Lord of Macgregor = ----------, d. of Maclauchlan
                          - Malcolm
                          - Gregor More of Macgregor
                          - John
                        - Gillespie/Archibald
                        - Gregor → Ruadbrudh/Roro
                        - Dugual ciar
                      - Gilbert ▸ Griersons of Lag
                    - Alpin, Bp of Dunblane 1282–1290
                - Gregor more Graund, Sheriff of Inverness ▸ Grants
                - Achaius
                - Mackays
              - Gregor, Abbot of Dunkeld → Macnabs
            - Gregorius (obiit electus episcopus St Andred)
          - Malcolm of the Deers (hunter)
    - Fiudumus/Fruidanus Macgregor→ Mackinnons
  - Gorbredus ▸ Scottish Macquaries
    ▸ Irish Macguires

APPENDICES

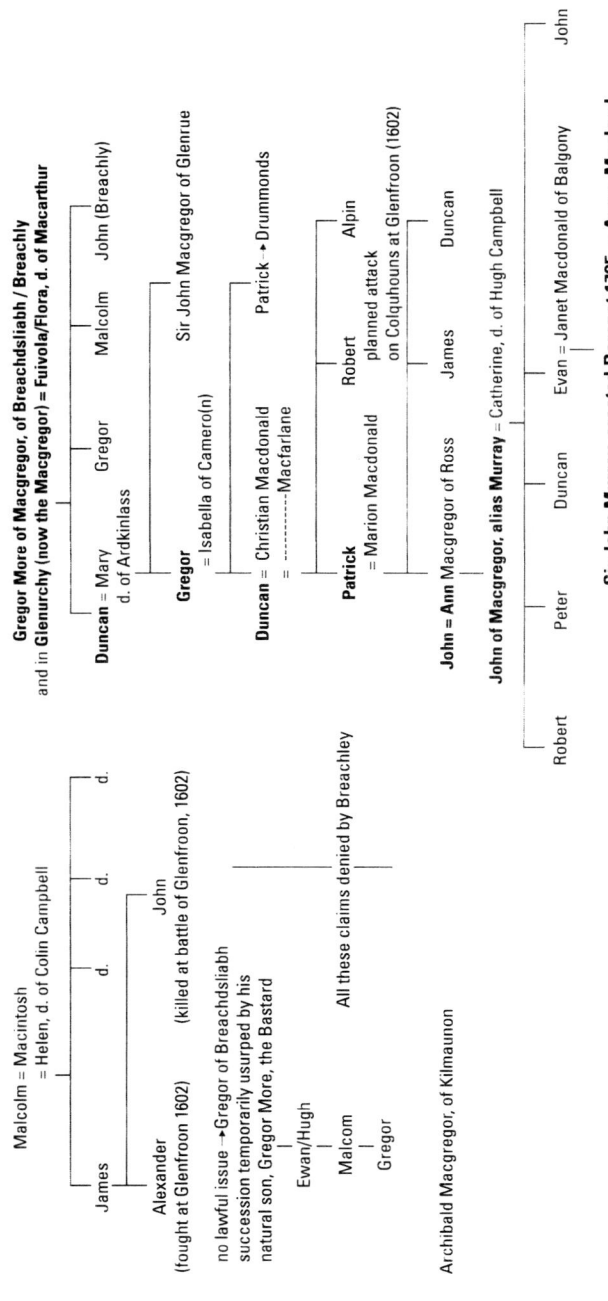

Gregor More of Macgregor, of Breachdsliabh / Breachly
and in **Glenurchy (now the Macgregor)** = **Fuivola/Flora, d. of Macarthur**

- **Duncan** = Mary, d. of Ardkinlass
- Gregor
- Malcolm
- Sir John Macgregor of Glenrue
- John (Breachly)

Gregor = Isabella of Cameron
- Patrick → Drummonds

Duncan = Christian Macdonald = ...Macfarlane

Patrick = Marion Macdonald
- Robert — planned attack on Colquhouns at Glenfroon (1602)
- Alpin
- James
- Duncan

John = Ann Macgregor of Ross

John of Macgregor, alias Murray = Catherine, d. of Hugh Campbell

- Robert
- Peter
- Duncan
- Evan = Janet Macdonald of Balgony
- John

Sir John Murray, created Baronet 1795 = **Anne Macleod**

Malcolm = Macintosh
= Helen, d. of Colin Campbell

- James d.
- Alexander (fought at Glenfroon 1602)
- d.
- John (killed at battle of Glenfroon, 1602)
- d.

no lawful issue → Gregor of Breachdsliabh succession temporarily usurped by his natural son, Gregor More, the Bastard

- Ewan/Hugh
  - Malcom
  - Gregor

All these claims denied by Breachley

Archibald Macgregor, of Kilmaunon

II. The Greggs of Cappagh/Capa

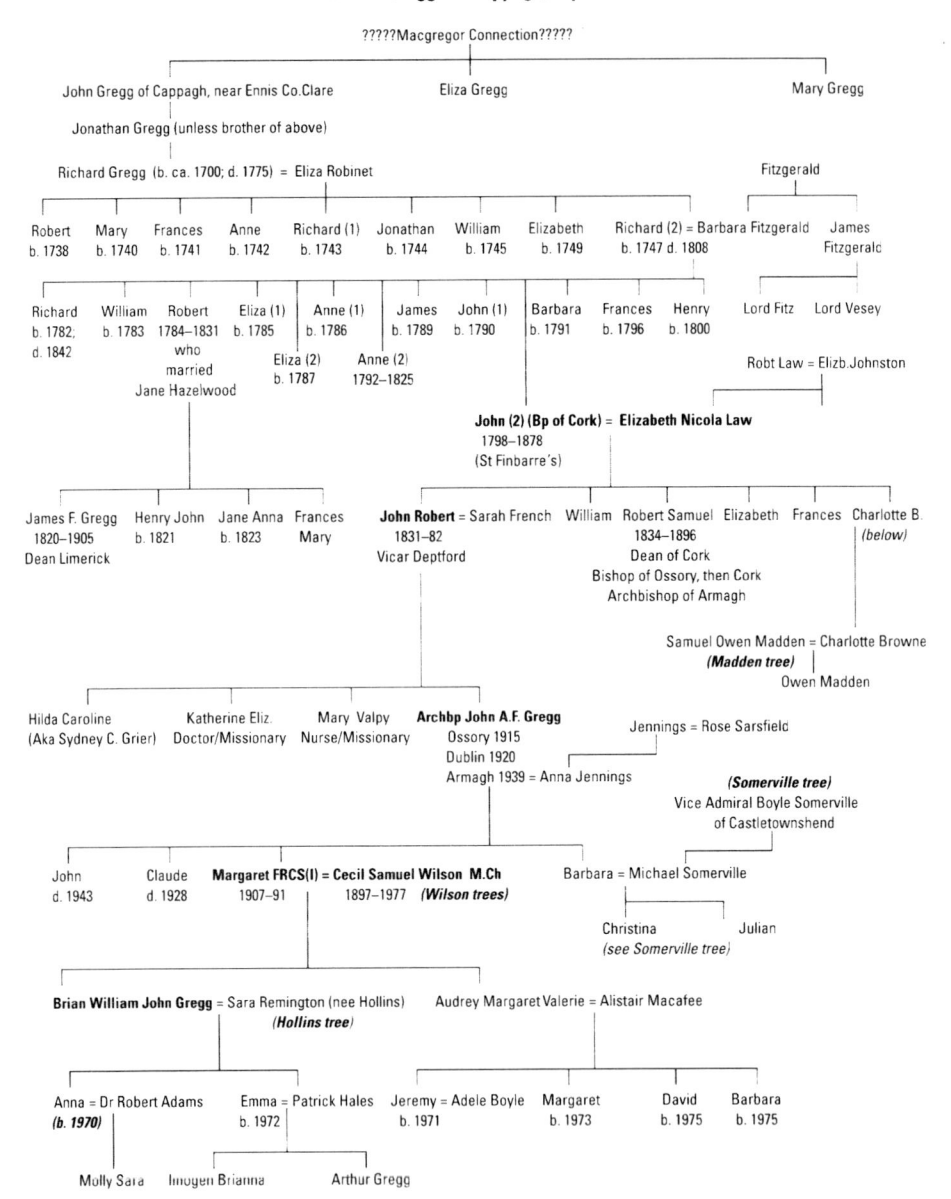

?????Macgregor Connection?????

- John Gregg of Cappagh, near Ennis Co.Clare
  - Jonathan Gregg (unless brother of above)
    - Richard Gregg (b. ca. 1700; d. 1775) = Eliza Robinet
- Eliza Gregg
- Mary Gregg
  - Fitzgerald

Children of Richard Gregg and Eliza Robinet:
- Robert b. 1738
- Mary b. 1740
- Frances b. 1741
- Anne b. 1742
- Richard (1) b. 1743
- Jonathan b. 1744
- William b. 1745
- Elizabeth b. 1749
- Richard (2) b. 1747 d. 1808 = Barbara Fitzgerald
- James Fitzgerald

Children of Richard (2) and Barbara Fitzgerald:
- Richard b. 1782; d. 1842
- William b. 1783
- Robert 1784–1831 who married Jane Hazelwood
- Eliza (1) b. 1785 / Eliza (2) b. 1787
- Anne (1) b. 1786 / Anne (2) 1792–1825
- James b. 1789
- John (1) b. 1790
- Barbara b. 1791
- Frances b. 1796
- Henry b. 1800
- Lord Fitz
- Lord Vesey
  - Robt Law = Elizb. Johnston

John (2) (Bp of Cork) 1798–1878 (St Finbarre's) = **Elizabeth Nicola Law**

Children:
- James F. Gregg 1820–1905 Dean Limerick
- Henry John b. 1821
- Jane Anna b. 1823
- Frances Mary
- **John Robert** = Sarah French 1831–82 Vicar Deptford
- William
- Robert Samuel 1834–1896 Dean of Cork Bishop of Ossory, then Cork Archbishop of Armagh
- Elizabeth
- Frances
- Charlotte B. (below)

Samuel Owen Madden = Charlotte Browne **(Madden tree)**
  - Owen Madden

Children of John Robert and Sarah French:
- Hilda Caroline (Aka Sydney C. Grier)
- Katherine Eliz. Doctor/Missionary
- Mary Valpy Nurse/Missionary
- **Archbp John A.F. Gregg** Ossory 1915 Dublin 1920 Armagh 1939 = Anna Jennings

Jennings = Rose Sarsfield

(Somerville tree)
Vice Admiral Boyle Somerville of Castletownshend
- Barbara = Michael Somerville
  - Christina
  - Julian
  (see Somerville tree)

Children of Archbp John A.F. Gregg and Anna Jennings:
- John d. 1943
- Claude d. 1928
- **Margaret FRCS(I)** 1907–91 = **Cecil Samuel Wilson M.Ch** 1897–1977 **(Wilson trees)**

- **Brian William John Gregg** = Sara Remington (nee Hollins) **(Hollins tree)**
- Audrey Margaret Valerie = Alistair Macafee

Children:
- Anna = Dr Robert Adams **(b. 1970)**
- Emma = Patrick Hales b. 1972
- Jeremy = Adele Boyle b. 1971
- Margaret b. 1973
- David b. 1975
- Barbara b. 1975

- Molly Sara
- Imogen Brianna
- Arthur Gregg

APPENDICES 369

III. Wilson / Martin / Ronaldson / ? Cody Connections

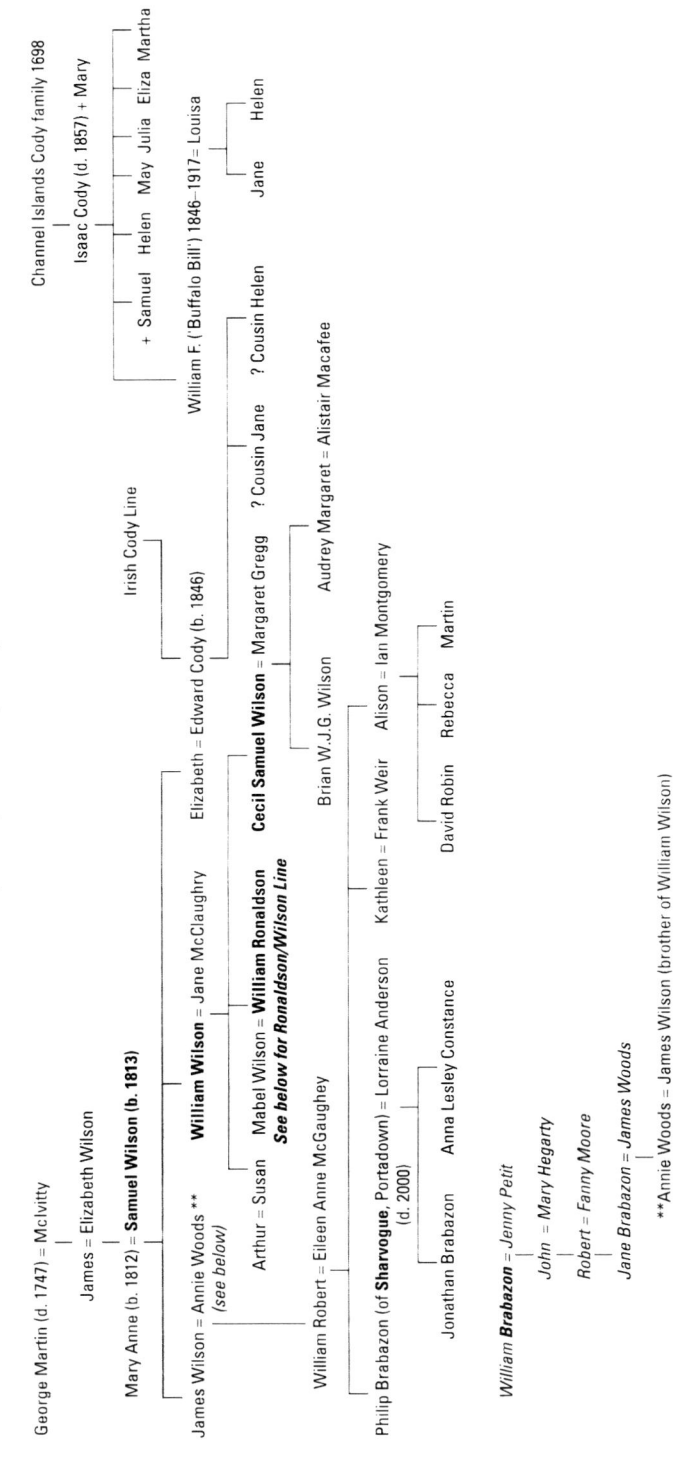

Channel Islands Cody family 1698

Isaac Cody (d. 1857) + Mary

+ Samuel   Helen   May   Julia   Eliza   Martha

William F. ('Buffalo Bill') 1846–1917 = Louisa

Jane   Helen

Irish Cody Line

Elizabeth = Edward Cody (b. 1846)

Cecil Samuel Wilson = Margaret Gregg   ? Cousin Jane   ? Cousin Helen

Brian W.J.G. Wilson   Audrey Margaret = Alistair Macafee

George Martin (d. 1747) = McIvitty

James = Elizabeth Wilson

Mary Anne (b. 1812) = **Samuel Wilson (b. 1813)**

James Wilson = Annie Woods **   **William Wilson** = Jane McClaughry
(see below)

Arthur = Susan   Mabel Wilson = **William Ronaldson**
See below for Ronaldson/Wilson Line

William Robert = Eileen Anne McGaughey   Kathleen = Frank Weir   Alison = Ian Montgomery

Philip Brabazon (of **Sharvogue**, Portadown) = Lorraine Anderson   David Robin   Rebecca   Martin
(d. 2000)

Jonathan Brabazon   Anna Lesley Constance

*William **Brabazon** = Jenny Petit*

John = Mary Hegarty

Robert = Fanny Moore

Jane Brabazon = James Woods

**Annie Woods = James Wilson (brother of William Wilson)

IV. Wilson / Ronaldson / Strong Line

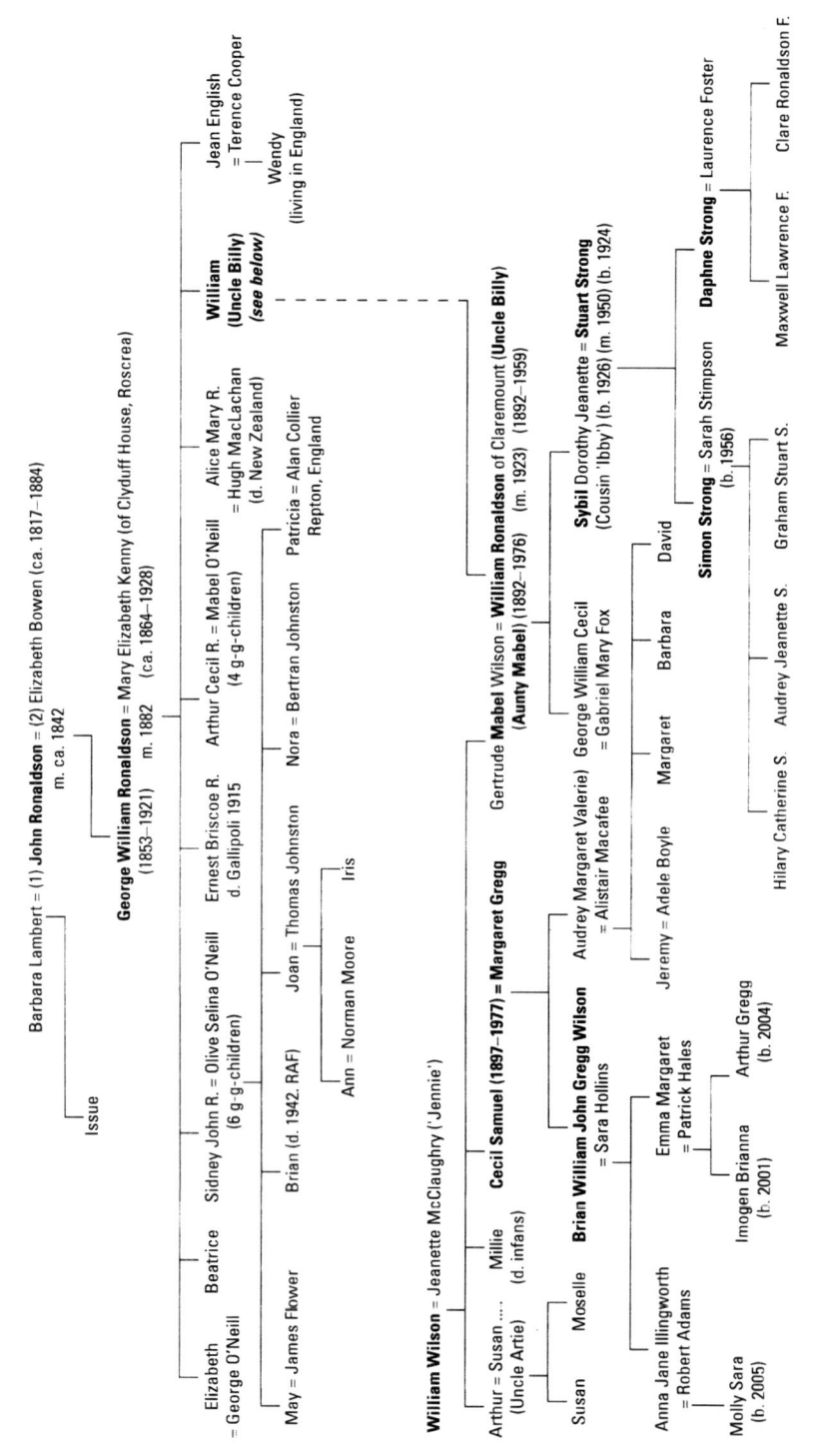

Barbara Lambert = (1) **John Ronaldson** = (2) Elizabeth Bowen (ca. 1817–1884)
m. ca. 1842

Issue

George William Ronaldson = Mary Elizabeth Kenny (of Clyduff House, Roscrea)
(1853–1921)   m. 1882   (ca. 1864–1928)

Elizabeth	Beatrice	Sidney John R. = Olive Selina O'Neill	Ernest Briscoe R.	Arthur Cecil R. = Mabel O'Neill	Alice Mary R. = Hugh MacLachan	**William (Uncle Billy)** *(see below)*	Jean English = Terence Cooper
= George O'Neill		(6 g-g-children)	d. Gallipoli 1915	(4 g-g-children)	(d. New Zealand)		

May = James Flower   Brian (d. 1942, RAF)   Joan = Thomas Johnston   Nora = Bertran Johnston   Patricia = Alan Collier Repton, England

Ann = Norman Moore

Iris

William Wilson = Jeanette McClaughry ('Jennie')

Arthur = Susan.....	Millie	**Cecil Samuel (1897–1977)** = Margaret Gregg	Gertrude **Mabel** Wilson = **William Ronaldson** of Claremount (**Uncle Billy**)	**Sybil** Dorothy Jeanette = **Stuart Strong**
(Uncle Artie)	(d. infans)		(**Aunty Mabel**) (1892–1976) (m. 1923) (1892–1959)	(Cousin 'Ibby') (b. 1926) (m. 1950) (b. 1924)

Susan   Moselle   **Brian William John Gregg Wilson** = Sara Hollins

Audrey Margaret Valerie) George William Cecil   **Simon Strong** = Sarah Stimpson   **Daphne Strong** = Laurence Foster
= Alistair Macafee   = Gabriel Mary Fox   (b. 1956)

Anna Jane Illingworth   Emma Margaret   Jeremy = Adele Boyle   Margaret   Barbara
= Robert Adams   = Patrick Hales

David

Molly Sara   Imogen Brianna   Arthur Gregg   Hilary Catherine S.   Audrey Jeanette S.   Graham Stuart S.   Maxwell Lawrence F.   Clare Ronaldson F.
(b. 2005)   (b. 2001)   (b. 2004)

Wendy (living in England)

V. Wilson / Other Wilsons / Woods / Brabazon

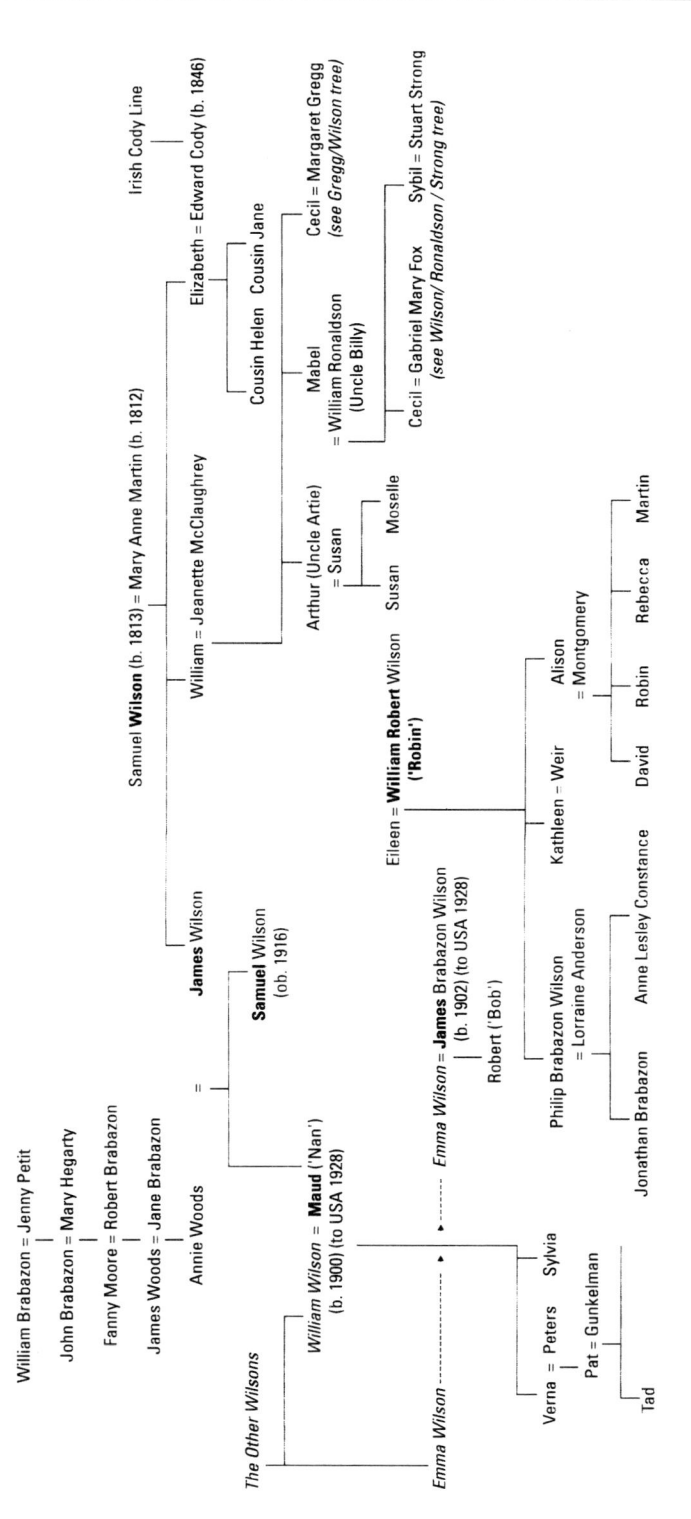

```
William Brabazon = Jenny Petit
         |
John Brabazon = Mary Hegarty
         |
Fanny Moore = Robert Brabazon
         |
James Woods = Jane Brabazon
         |
      Annie Woods                         Samuel Wilson (b. 1813) = Mary Anne Martin (b. 1812)                                     Irish Cody Line
              =                                              |                                                                             |
         Samuel Wilson                        William = Jeanette McClaughrey                                   Elizabeth = Edward Cody (b. 1846)
         (ob. 1916)                                       |
                |                              ┌──────────┼──────────┐
           James Wilson                   Arthur (Uncle Artie)    Cousin Helen   Cousin Jane
                                            = Susan
                                         ┌─────┴─────┐                  Mabel              Cecil = Margaret Gregg
                                       Susan     Moselle          = William Ronaldson      (see Gregg/Wilson tree)
                                                                     (Uncle Billy)
                                                                                    Cecil = Gabriel Mary Fox    Sybil = Stuart Strong
                                                                                    (see Wilson/Ronaldson / Strong tree)

The Other Wilsons

Emma Wilson ┄┄┄┄┄┄┄┄┄  William Wilson = Maud ('Nan')  ┄┄┄┄┄┄  Emma Wilson = James Brabazon Wilson              Eileen = William Robert Wilson
                       (b. 1900) (to USA 1928)                                (b. 1902) (to USA 1928)                     ('Robin')
          ┌─────────┐                                       ┌──────────────┬──────────────┐              ┌──────────────┬──────────────┐
    Verna = Peters  Sylvia                         Robert ('Bob')   Philip Brabazon Wilson                        Kathleen = Weir        Alison
       |                                                              = Lorraine Anderson                                |            = Montgomery
   Pat = Gunkelman                                                              |                                        |                |
       |                                              ┌──────────┬──────────┐                                         David    ┌────┬────┬────┐
      Tad                                     Jonathan Brabazon  Anne  Lesley Constance                                       Robin Rebecca Martin
```

VI. Hollins / Fennell / Brontë Connection

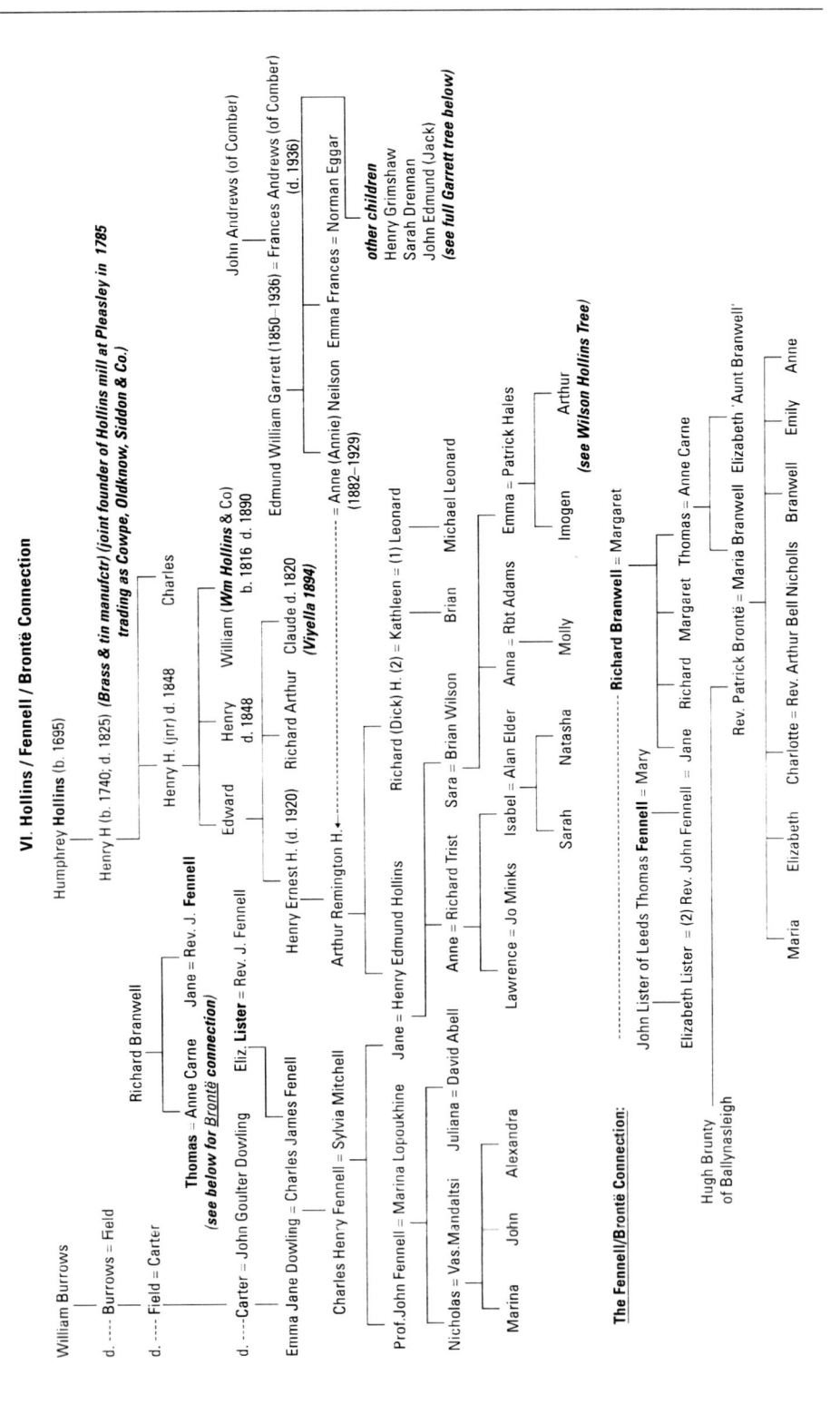

Humphrey **Hollins** (b. 1695)

Henry H (b. 1740; d. 1825) *(Brass & tin manufctr) (joint founder of Hollins mill at Pleasley in 1785 trading as Cowpe, Oldknow, Siddon & Co.)*

Charles

Henry H. (jnr) d. 1848   William (***Wm Hollins*** & Co) b. 1816 d. 1890   John Andrews (of Comber)

Edward   Henry d. 1848   Claude d. 1820 (***Viyella 1894***)   Edmund William Garrett (1850–1936) = Frances Andrews (of Comber) (d. 1936)

Richard Arthur   Henry Ernest H. (d. 1920)   = Anne (Annie) Neilson   Emma Frances = Norman Eggar (1882–1929)

other children
Henry Grimshaw
Sarah Drennan
John Edmund (Jack)
(see full Garrett tree below)

Arthur Remington H.   Richard (Dick) H. (2) = Kathleen = (1) Leonard   Michael Leonard

Jane = Henry Edmund Hollins   Anne = Richard Trist   Sara = Brian Wilson   Brian

Juliana = David Abell   Isabel = Alan Elder   Anna = Rbt Adams   Emma = Patrick Hales

Lawrence = Jo Minks   Molly   Arthur
                                        (see Wilson Hollins Tree)

Sarah   Natasha   Imogen

William Burrows

d. ---- Burrows = Field

d. ---- Field = Carter

Richard Branwell

Thomas = Anne Carne   Jane = Rev. J. **Fennell**
(see below for Brontë connection)

d. ----Carter = John Goulter Dowling   Eliz. **Lister** = Rev. J. Fennell

Emma Jane Dowling = Charles James Fennell

Charles Henry Fennell = Sylvia Mitchell

Prof. John Fennell = Marina Lopoukhine

Nicholas = Vas. Mandaltsi

Marina   John   Alexandra

The Fennell/Brontë Connection:

Hugh Brunty
of Ballynasleigh

John Lister of Leeds   Thomas **Fennell** = Mary

Elizabeth Lister = (2) Rev. John Fennell = Jane   **Richard Branwell** = Margaret

Maria   Elizabeth   Charlotte = Rev. Arthur Bell Nicholls   Rev. Patrick Brontë = Maria Branwell   Elizabeth 'Aunt Branwell'

Jane   Richard   Margaret   Thomas = Anne Carne

Branwell   Emily   Anne

APPENDICES

VII. Hollins, Lennox, Andrews, Garrett, Drennan, Eggar, Duffin

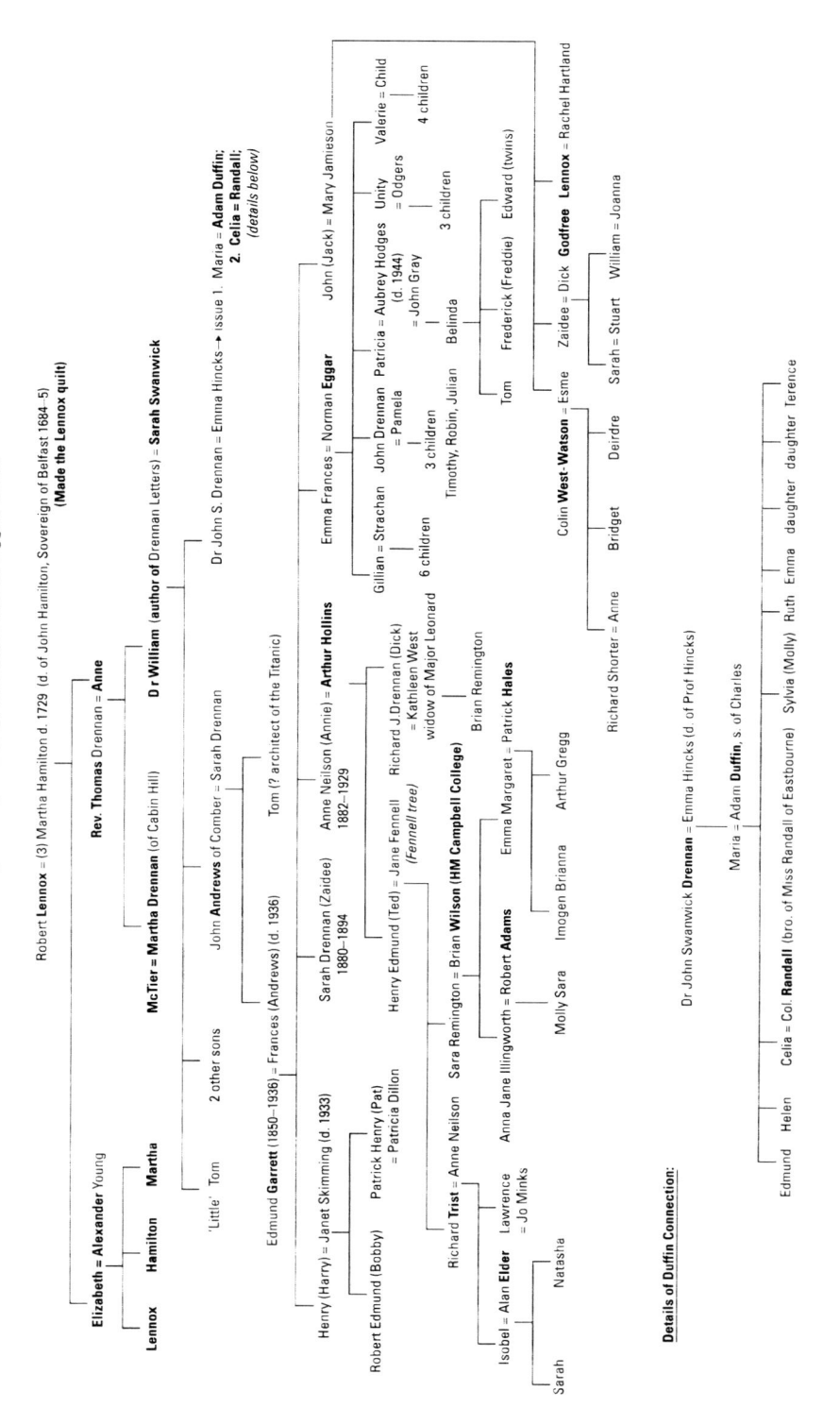

Robert **Lennox** = (3) Martha Hamilton d. 1729 (d. of John Hamilton, Sovereign of Belfast 1684-5)
(Made the Lennox quilt)

Children:
- Elizabeth = Alexander Young
  - **Lennox**
  - Hamilton
  - Martha
- **McTier** = Martha **Drennan** (of Cabin Hill)
- Rev. Thomas **Drennan** = **Anne**
  - John **Andrews** of Comber = Sarah **Drennan**
    - 'Little' Tom
    - 2 other sons
    - Edmund **Garrett** (1850–1936) = Frances (Andrews) (d. 1936)
      - Henry (Harry) = Janet Skimming (d. 1933)
        - Robert Edmund (Bobby)
        - Patrick Henry (Pat) = Patricia Dillon
          - Richard **Trist** = Anne Neilson
            - Isobel = Alan **Elder**
              - Sarah
            - Lawrence = Jo Minks
              - Natasha
          - Anna Jane Illingworth = Robert **Adams**
            - Molly Sara
            - Imogen Brianna
          - Sara Remington = Brian **Wilson** (HM Campbell College)
          - Emma Margaret = Patrick **Hales**
            - Arthur Gregg
          - Brian Remington
    - Tom (? architect of the Titanic)
  - Sarah **Drennan** (Zaidee) 1880–1894
  - Anne Neilson (Annie) = **Arthur Hollins** 1882–1929
    - Henry Edmund (Ted) = Jane Fennell *(Fennell tree)*
    - Richard J. **Drennan** (Dick) = Kathleen West, widow of Major Leonard
- Dr **William** (author of Drennan Letters) = **Sarah Swanwick**
  - Dr John S. **Drennan** = Emma Hincks → issue 1. Maria = Adam **Duffin**; 2. Celia = **Randall**; *(details below)*
    - Emma Frances = Norman **Eggar**
      - Gillian = Strachan
        - 6 children
      - John **Drennan** = Pamela
        - Timothy, Robin, Julian
      - Patricia = Aubrey Hodges (d. 1944) = John Gray
        - Belinda
        - 3 children
      - Colin **West-Watson** = Esme
        - Bridget
        - Deirdre
        - Richard Shorter = Anne
    - John (Jack) = Mary Jamieson
      - Unity = Odgers
        - 3 children
      - Valerie = Child
        - 4 children
      - Tom
      - Frederick (Freddie)
      - Edward (twins)
      - Zaidee = Dick **Godfree**
        - Sarah = Stuart
      - **Lennox** = Rachel Hartland
        - William = Joanna

Details of Duffin Connection:

Dr John Swanwick **Drennan** = Emma Hincks (d. of Prof Hincks)

- Maria = Adam **Duffin**, s. of Charles
  - Edmund
  - Helen
- Celia = Col. **Randall** (bro. of Miss Randall of Eastbourne)
  - Sylvia (Molly)
  - Ruth
  - Emma
  - daughter
  - daughter
  - Terence

VIII. Somerville Family Tree

Rev. William Somerville (1641–1694) = Agnes Agnew, d. of Sir Patrick Agnew of Lochinver bart.
Fled persecution in Scotland in 1692 and went to Ireland with family in an open boat

Rev. Thomas I (1689–1752) Rector of Myross & Castlehaven. Educ. TCD 1706-11

Thomas II (1725–1793) = Mary Townsend of Rosscarberry (3 sons and 8 daughters)
Known as Tom the merchant; made fortune trading in commodities in W. Indies and elsewhere. Built the tower on Horse island as a beacon for his ships.
Built Drishane about 1790.

Thomas III (1760–1811) = Elizabeth Becher Townsend of Shepperton, Co. Cork

Thomas IV (1797–1882) = Henrietta Townsend of Castletownshend

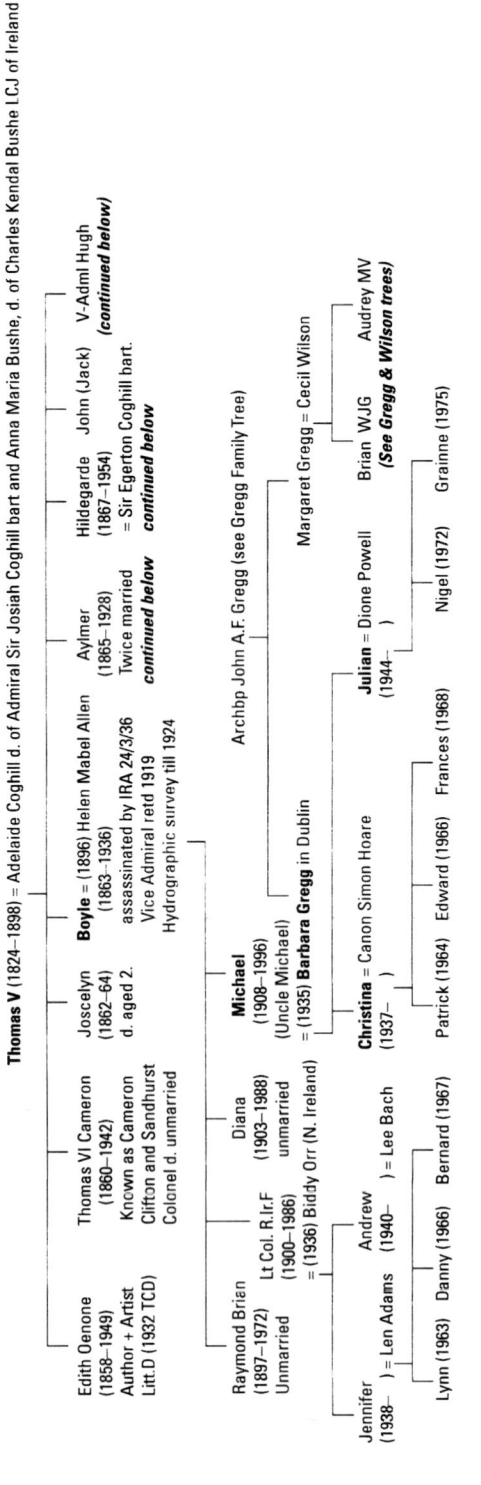

Thomas V (1824–1898) = Adelaide Coghill d. of Admiral Sir Josiah Coghill bart and Anna Maria Bushe, d. of Charles Kendal Bushe LCJ of Ireland

Edith Oenone	Thomas VI Cameron	Joscelyn	**Boyle** = (1896) Helen Mabel Allen	Aylmer	Hildegarde	John (Jack)	V-Adml Hugh
(1858–1949)	(1860–1942)	(1862–64)	(1863–1936)	(1865–1928)	(1867–1954)		*(continued below)*
Author + Artist	Known as Cameron	d. aged 2.	assassinated by IRA 24/3/36	Twice married	= Sir Egerton Coghill bart.		
Litt.D (1932 TCD)	Clifton and Sandhurst		Vice Admiral retd 1919	*continued below*	*continued below*		
	Colonel d. unmarried		Hydrographic survey till 1924				

Raymond Brian   Lt Col. R.Ir.F   Diana   **Michael**
(1897–1972)   (1900–1986)   (1903–1988)   (1908–1996)
Unmarried   = (1936) Biddy Orr (N. Ireland)   unmarried   (Uncle Michael)
                                                   = (1935) **Barbara Gregg** in Dublin

Archbp John A.F. Gregg (see Gregg Family Tree)

Margaret Gregg = Cecil Wilson

Jennifer   Andrew   **Christina** = Canon Simon Hoare   **Julian** = Dione Powell   Brian WJG   Audrey MV
(1938–) = Len Adams   (1940–) = Lee Bach   (1937–)   (1944–)   *(See Gregg & Wilson trees)*

Lynn (1963)   Danny (1966)   Bernard (1967)   Patrick (1964)   Edward (1966)   Frances (1968)   Nigel (1972)   Grainne (1975)

Somerville Family Tree (Continued)

Thomas (V) Somerville

(fifth child) Aylmer (1865–1928) = (1st wife) Emmy Sykes

- Desmond (1889–1976) = Moira Roche d. 1976
- Sir Nicholas (1924–) = Jennifer Nash
  - Christopher (Dan) (1921–) = Celia Dent
  - Harriet (1950)
  - Thomas (1952)
  - John (1956)
  - Pippa (1953)
  - Penny (1954)
  - Robin (1959)

Aylmer (1865–1928) = (2nd wife) Natalie Turner

- Elizabeth (1905–1959) = Paul Chavasse
  - Timothy (1931–) = Philippa Roche
    - Kate (1959)
    - Christopher (1967)
  - Isobel (1935–) = Robert Stileman
    - Mark (1967)
    - Patrick (1969)
    - Elizabeth (1972)

(sixth child) Hildegarde = Sir Egerton Coghill (see below)

- Gillian (1890–1983)
  = (1) F. Bonham-Carter (divorced) → son Simon (1914)
  = (2) Prince Lobkowicz of Czechoslovakia
  - Martin
  - Dominic
  - Oliver

  all in the USA

- Gilbert (1907–1980) = Jacinth Lillingstone
  - Twin daughters Susan and Judith (b. 1930)

(seventh child) John (called Jack) 1872–1955 (see below)

(eighth child) Hugh Vice Admiral, CB, DSO = Mary Hancock

- Nugent (1904– ca. 78) = (1) Lois Spicer = (2) Molly Byrne (no children)
  - Clodagh (m. 3 sons)
- Philip (1906–42) DSO & Bar DSC & Bar unmarried

Seventh child of Thomas V Somerville

John Somerville (called Jack) = (1) Vera Cooper-Key (d. 1938)

- Tony (1911–34)
  = (2) Mildred McCheane (1883–1984) no children

Hildegarde Somerville (1867–1954) = Sir Egerton Coghill (5th bart) (1853–1921)

- Patrick (1896–1980) Unmarried
- Neville (1899–1979) = Elspeth Harley
  - Faith (1928) = James Garson
    - Carol (1928)
    - Nerissa (1961)
  - Lucy
  - Rachel
  - Jeremy
  - Laura
- Ambrose (1902–1984) = (1) Betty Atkins
  - Sir Toby (6th bart) = Gay
    - Patrick
    - Lisa
- Katharine (1906–) = Terence Johnston no children

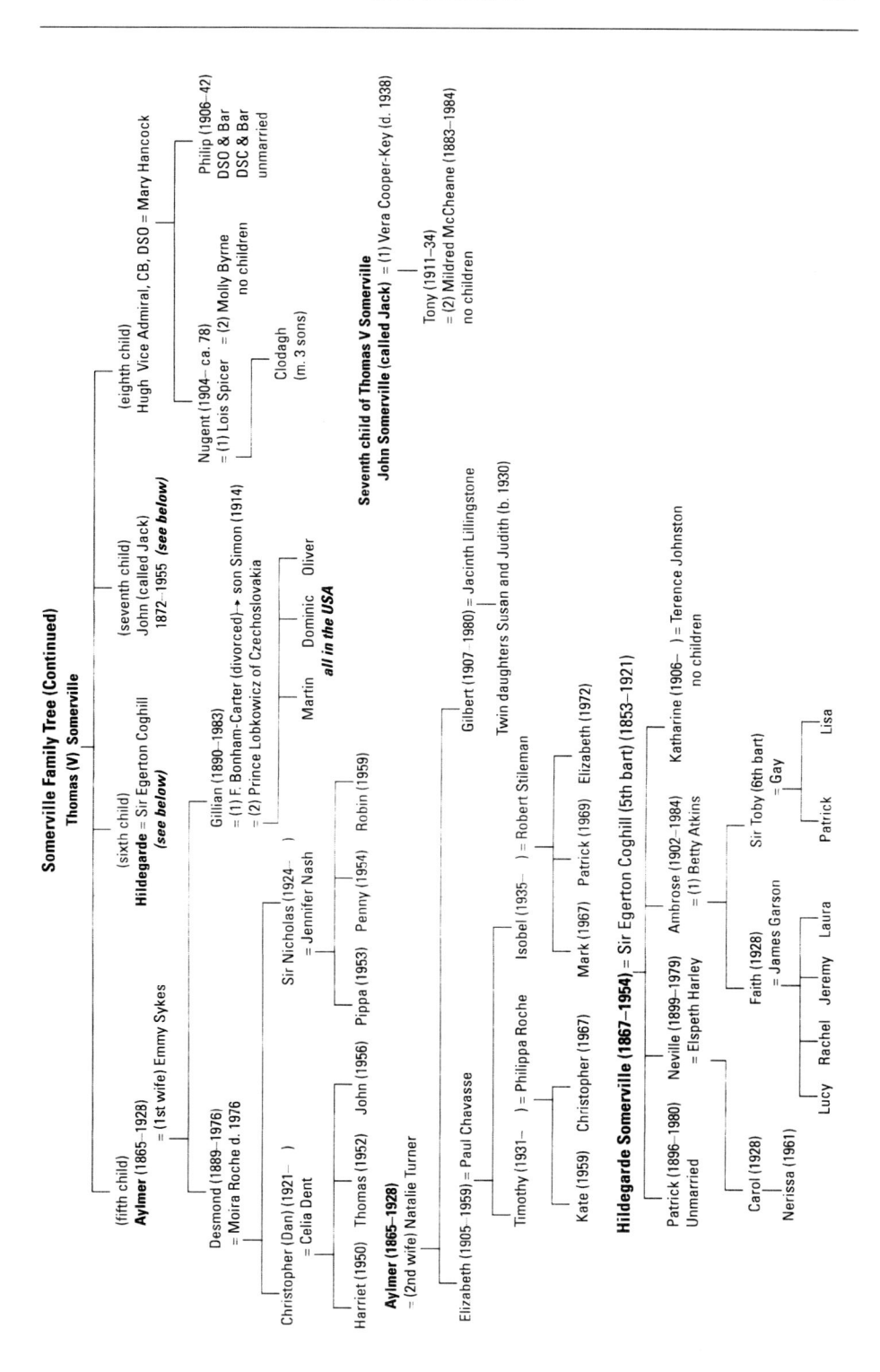

IX. The Maddens of Mallow

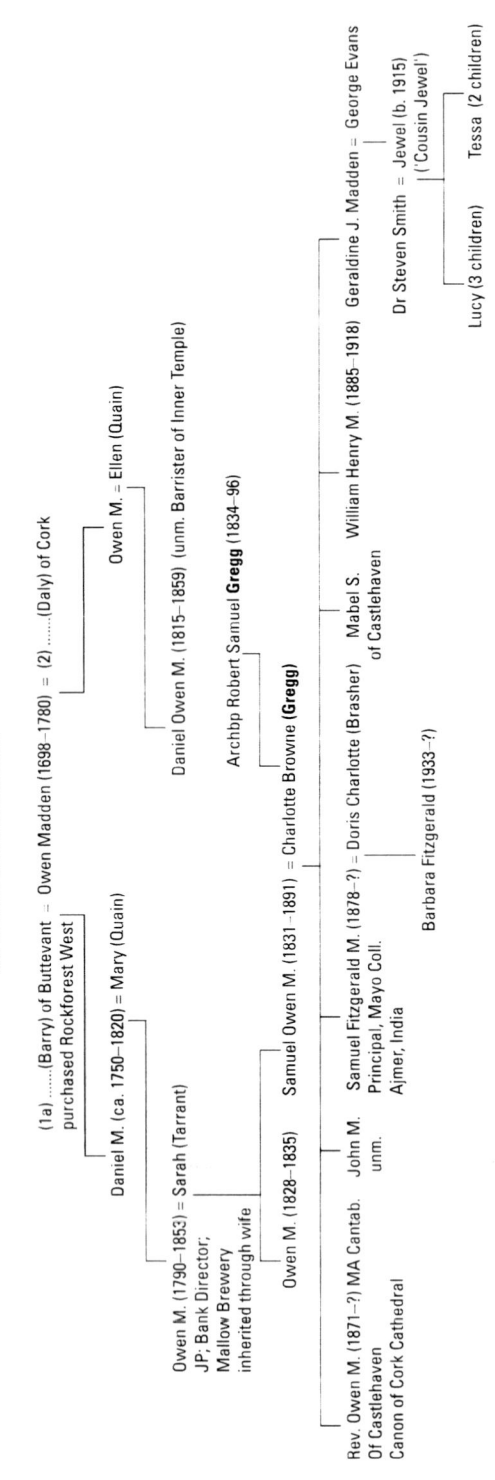

(1a) ......(Barry) of Buttevant = Owen Madden (1698–1780) = (2) ......(Daly) of Cork
purchased Rockforest West

Daniel M. (ca. 1750–1820) = Mary (Quain)

Owen M. = Ellen (Quain)

Daniel Owen M. (1815–1859) (unm. Barrister of Inner Temple)

Archbp Robert Samuel **Gregg** (1834–96)

Owen M. (1790–1853) = Sarah (Tarrant)
JP; Bank Director;
Mallow Brewery
inherited through wife

Owen M. (1828–1835)

Samuel Owen M. (1831–1891) = Charlotte Browne **(Gregg)**

John M.
unm.

Samuel Fitzgerald M. (1878–?) = Doris Charlotte (Brasher)
Principal, Mayo Coll.
Ajmer, India

Mabel S.
of Castlehaven

William Henry M. (1885–1918)

Geraldine J. Madden = George Evans

Dr Steven Smith = Jewel (b. 1915)
('Cousin Jewel')

Rev. Owen M. (1871–?) MA Cantab.
Of Castlehaven
Canon of Cork Cathedral

Barbara Fitzgerald (1933–?)

Lucy (3 children)   Tessa (2 children)

Index

Acheson, Alan 260
ACSIL 262
Adams
    Anna (*née* Wilson) 32, 163, 168, 170f, 201ff, 314, 338
    Charles Kingsley 213
    Michael & Judy 213
    Molly Sara 214, 342, 347
    Dr Robert (Rob) 213f, 338
Adams, Charles 256
Addyman, Peter 265
Alexander, Bolo 93
Allen family of Australia 68
Andrews
    Frances (*see* Garrett)
    John 195f
    Sarah (*née* Drennan) 195
    Tom (i) 196
    Tom (ii) 93
Armagh 74, 75ff, 112, 266f, 270, 276
Armagh Girls High School 80
Armagh, The Palace 68, 75ff, 215
Ashleigh House School 220, 237, 260

Ball, Dennis 166
Ballycrenan 21, 27, 221, 234
Barraclough, James 145
Barry, Canon John 60
Bates, Harry 112
Batten, James 141
Beale, Mr (Steward) 77
Bell, Daphne 245
Benington, Michael 259
Beresford, Archbp Lord John 76, 80
Beveridge, Dr Gordon 265f, 278
Biddle, George 85ff
Birley, Sir Oswald 77
Blackrock College 261
Bland, Christopher 93
Blakeney, Bobby 94
Boggis, Rev A.T.I. 101, 230
Bottom, Robert 259

Bowles, Duncan 209
Boxall, Richard 135
Boyle, Adele (*see* Macafee)
Boyson, Rhodes 260
Brett, Charles 27
Bradshaw, Sgt Major Harry 254
SS *Brittanic* 72f
Bromley, Richard 7, 150, 155
Brooke, Arthur 262f
Brown, Canon John S.147, 164
Bruce Lockhart, J.H. 17, 106
Brunt, Prof. Peter 173ff, 305
B Specials 87
Buffalo Bill (*see* Cody)
Burnet, Jock & Pauline 129, 132ff, 140, 158
Burnside in Bowness, Windermere 300ff
Butterworth, Arthur 89

Cabin Hill 195f, 231
Caghey, Sam 254
Callimachus 155
Campbell College 17, 28, 38, 205, 219, 225, 228ff, 235ff, 247ff, 328, 342
Campbell, Ian 299
Carey, Alan Sausmarez & Florence 85f
Carey, Patrick S. 85ff
Carey, Jeremy 159
Castell, Mrs (Headmistress, Armagh Girls High School) 81
Castletownshend 3, 32, 35, 63ff
Caves, Ronnie 258
Caves, Michael 261
Changi 2, 72
Chaudhuri, Nirad 14
Chavasse family 67
Christ's College, Cambridge 7, 35, 61, 74, 78, 109, 114, 121ff, 147, 177
Clarke, A.B.D.E.A. 93
Clarke, Euan 209, 211
Clayton Jones, Rev Roger 212f
Cleeve, N. Somerset 338ff
Cocks, Theo 142, 144

Cody
- Edward & Elizabeth (née Wilson) 42
- Helen & Jane ('Cousins') 41f
- William (Buffalo Bill) 41f

Coe, Mark 127
Coghill, Nevill & family 66
Combined Cadet Force (CCF) 150ff, 241f
Cook, John 231, 256
Cook, Peter 139
Cooley, Melvin 174, 178
Craig, Sir James 195f
Craigs, Stan 262
Crawford, Michael, 176
Cricket 146, 148, 168, 300, 342
Crooks, Dean Samuel, 335
Crymble, Margaret (see Macafee)
Cullen, Cpl (Piper) 118
Cunningham
- James 93
- Josias (Joe) 90, 93

Cunningham, Nicola 170
Cuss, Martin 135, 177

Davies Jill (see Dreyfous)
- Roy 204
- Susan (Sue) 203f

Deane, John & Kay 183, 287
DENI (Dept of Education, N. Ireland) 216, 233, 237, 242, 244, 255
de Valera, President Eamon 36f
Devlin, James 254ff, 290
Drennan
- Dr John 196
- Maria (see Duffin)
- Sarah (see Andrews)
- Tom (Little Tom) 195
- Dr William 195

Dreyfous, Etienne & Jill (née Davies) 204
Duff, Jack 254, 261
Duffin
- Adam 196
- Celia (see Randall)
- Maria (née Drennan) 196
- Sylvia ('Molly') 196

Eastbourne College 148, 164, 169, 202f, 208ff, 222, 224ff
Eaton Hall OCS 114ff

Eccles, Norman 260
Edgar, Willy 89
Eggar
- Emma Frances (née Garrett) 196
- Patricia (see Gray)

Elder, Alan & Isabel (née Trist) 185
Erskine, Rev David 258f
Evans
- Dr George 64
- Geraldine (née Madden) 63
- Jewel (see Smith)

Evans, John J. 144f, 204
Ewan, Vicky 222
Ewing, Bob 127f, 135, 183, 203

Fairservice, Colin 165f
Falkner, Ninian 18
Fennell
- Jane (see Hollins)
- Prof John & Marina (née Lopoukine) 32, 198
- Sylvia (née Mitchell) 199f

Ferris, Jack 260
Finley, Prof Sir Moses 123ff, 144, 173ff, 177, 305
Fitzgerald, Lords F. & Vesey 59
Fives (Eton, Rugby, Winchester) 91, 101, 132, 146, 226
Fleming, Bp. Launcelot 133
Forbes, Duncan 145
Foreman, Philip 262
Fortnight Magazine 22
Foster
- Daphne (née Strong) 16, 47
- Clare 16

Fox, Gabriel Mary (see Ronaldson)
Fox, Yvonne (née Gaunt) 213
Fraser, Ian 18
Friendly Brothers of St Patrick 15

Gailey, Christopher 253
Gardiner, Peggy & Tony 142f
Garrett
- Anne Neilsen (see Hollins)
- Edmund 195f
- Emma Frances (see Eggar)
- Frances (née Andrews) 195
- John (Uncle Jack) 196, 200
- Lennox 196
- Mary (née Jamieson) 196
- Rachel (formerly Hartland) 196

Gaunt
  Ernest 213
  Louise 213
  Yvonne (*see* Fox)
Gaunt, Jonathan 145
Gay, Mike 287f
Gedge, Bernard & Muirne 30, 64
Gertrude, (Hollins housekeeper) 197
Gibson
  Jo (formerly Hollins) 193
  Mary Anne 193
Gilliatt, Ivor 139
Godfree, Dick & Zaidee (*née* Garrett) 196
Gow, Ian MP 37f
Golding, Bill 342
Golf 299f
Gould, Arthur 212
Gower, David 166
Graham, Billy 206
Gray, John & Patricia 196
Graham, Mrs Hazel 261
Great Ormond Street Children's Hospital 185f
Greenhous, Guy 145
Greenstock, Mark 176
Greenwood, Clodagh 63
Gregg family 49ff, 60ff
  Anna Alicia, (*née* Jennings) 29, 31, 76
  Claude 2, 35
  John A.F. (Archbp. of Armagh) 7, 11f, 24f, 33ff, 60ff, 75ff, 88, 109, 125, 132, 164, 177, 187, 326ff, 357, 359
  John F.F. (Uncle John) 2, 11, 25, 35ff, 71f, 109, 303, 359
  Lesley (*née* McEndo), ('Aunt Lesley') 77
Gregg
  Frances (Fanny) 62
  Hilda (Sydney C Grier) 65
  Katherine, Dr 64
  John, Bp. of Cork 28, 62
  John Robert, Vicar of Deptford 62
  Mary Penelope Valpy 65
  Richard (of Cappagh) 59, 61
  Robert Samuel, Archbp. of Armagh 62
Grey, Ethel, (Headmistress, Bloomfield Collegiate) 81, 207
Grier, Sydney C. (*nom de plume* of Hilda Gregg)
Griffith, Margaret 63
Grose, Sidney 123
Gunkelman, Pat 47

Haines, Keith 235ff, 257
Hales
  Arthur Gregg 213, 342, 347
  E.J. Hales 212
  Emma (*née* Wilson) 27, 83, 149, 169f, 201ff, 229, 258, 314, 338, 344
  Imogen Brianna 213, 314, 342, 347, 348f
  James Patrick (Paddy snr) & Mary 212f
  Patrick (Paddy jnr) 212f, 314, 338
Halliday, Alexander 205
Hamlin, Dr Ann 278
Hannon, Bp. Brian 93
Hardy, David 140, 148
Harington, Roger 145
Heather, Harry 89
Henley, Mrs 171
Heracleitus 122f
Herodotus 177, 293, 316f
Hibbert, Christopher 138, 141
Hinds, Joe 77
Hirst, Chris 230
Hoare
  Christina (*née* Somerville) 3, 68, 76, 83, 280
  Canon Simon 68
Hogarth, A.C. 106
Hollins
  Anne (*see* Trist)
  Brian 197
  Henry Edmund ('Ted') 32, 184, 190ff, 339
  Jane (*née* Fennell) 32, 184, 198f
  Richard (Uncle Dick) 195, 197
  Kathleen (formerly Leonard) 197
  Sara (*see* Wilson)
Hollins
  Anne Neilsen (*née* Garrett) 196
  Arthur Remington 191ff
  Henry I, II, III, IV 190-5
  Henry Ernest 192f
  William 191f
Hollins, William & Co. 190ff
Holloway, Bp. Richard 187, 335, 354f
Holt, Jeremy 148
Homer 99f, 127, 137, 229, 268f, 271, 293, 312, 315, 321ff, 351, 353
Horder, Rev Cathy 213f, 336
Hough, Graham 123f
Houston, John 94
Howard, Ronnie 140, 142, 151
Hubbard, Rev Ian 337

Hudson, Antony 140
Hudson, Nicholas 93
Hull, John & Meta 258
Humphries, Victoria 286
Hutchinson, Peter 103

Industrial Society 241, 262
ISCO (Independent Schools' Careers Organisation) 134, 228ff

Jackson, Miss (Theatre Sister) 19
Jackson, Robert MP 282
JACT (Joint Assoc of Classics Teachers) 125, 173ff, 229, 305
Jennings
  Anna Alicia (*see* Gregg)
  Eithne (*see* Pope)
  Rose Margaret (Cousin Meg) 29, 64
  Muirne (*see* Gedge)
  Tom 29f
Johns, Rev Pat 282ff, 288

Kelso, Sally 216
Kennedy, Geordie & Tommy 83
Kerr Muir, Ronald 134
Kidd, T. 94
Kilmorey, Earl of 85
Kilroy, Richard (Dick) 23
King, Raymond 143
King's School, Canterbury 68, 156, 158ff, 208ff, 220, 225f, 228, 253, 261
Kinnear, Nigel 18
Knight, Dick 255
Knox, Monsignor Ronald (Cousin Ronnie) 65

Lacey, Prof Pat 124f, 177f, 305
Langdale
  Diana 226
  Philippa 133, 226
  Simon J.B. 133, 140f, 144, 146, 164, 169, 203f, 224ff
Larmour, Raoul 258
Latin 6f, 9, 229
Law, Capt. John 111
Law
  Elizabeth Nicola 28, 61
  Barbara 61
  Robert 61
  Stephen & Ida 61

Leonard, John 118
Leonard
  Kathleen (*see* Hollins)
  Michael ('Micky') 197
Lewis, Tony 126
Liberal Democrats 307
Lowry, Lord 220
Lowry, Prof C.G. 220
Luce, Richard 135
Lynn, Chris 273, 275

Macafee
  Adele (*née* Boyle) 222
  Alastair 215ff, 342
  Anne (*see* Mahood)
  Audrey (*née* Wilson) 3, 15,19, 25, 27f, 81f, 136, 180f, 183, 215ff
  Barbara 221f
  Charles H.G. ('Prof') 219f
  David 211, 222
  Jeremy (snr) 220
  Jeremy (jnr) 221f
  Margaret (snr) (*née* Crymble) 220
  Margaret (jnr) 61, 221
McAlpine, Rona 246, 256f
MacArthur, Brian 2
McCann, Archbp. James 60
McClean, Colin 238
MacGregor, The Clan 49ff
Macrory, Cardinal 60
Mahood, Anne (*née* Macafee) & David 220
McClen, Don & Liz 9, 14, 323f
MacDermott, Dermot 260
MacDermott, Lord & Lady 253
McEwan, Ian 7
McGahern, John 14, 17
McGuffin, Doris, 262
McIldowie, Eric 98f
M'Tier, Martha 195
Madden
  Geraldine (*see* Evans)
  Samuel Owen (snr) JP 63
  Owen of Castlehaven 28, 63,65
  Samuel Owen, Dean of Cork 63
  Charlotte Browne (*née* Gregg) 63
Mallory, Jim 276
Marriott, Peter 108
Marshall, Rev Godfrey 144, 148, 342
Matthew, Mary Josephine (*see* Hales)

Maugham, Somerset 160
Mavitty, Norman 93
Maxwell, Albert 257f
May, Nigel 93
May, Sheila 63
Meredith, Michael 42, 140
Meredith
   James 167
   Richard & Hazel 167f, 178
Meyer, Michael 148f
Miles, Rev Francis 336
Miller, Chris 169
Miller, David 177
Milligan, Wyndham 133, 137ff, 164, 204
Mills, Bertie MC 150
Milton, John 121f, 125
Mitchell, Des 266
Moley, Jim 307
Money, Tony 142
Moore, Dr John 140, 175
Morgan
   Margaret 133
   Richard M. 133, 140
Morrison, Hilary 304
Moulin, Tony & Faith 341
Mourne Grange Prep School 21f, 63, 85ff, 99, 224, 231
Mullen, Karl 89
Munro, Alan 135

National Trust 342
Navan Fort (Evin Macha) 135, 265ff
Neave, Airey 260
Neighbourhood Watch 342, 343ff
Nelson, Rev John 259
Newell, Canon Peter 6, 104ff, 158ff, 202, 225
NISTRO (N. Ireland Science & Technology Regional Organisation) 263
N. Ireland Hospice 263
N. Somerset District 343f, 345f

OFSTED 233
Old, Cathy & Fraser 286f
Oldfield, David 262
O'Lone, Edith 26
Orr, Rose (Aunt Biddy) (*see* Somerville)
Osborne, Prof Robin 305

Paisley, Rev Dr Ian 81

Pannett, Juliet, 185
Parkes, Fred 206
Patton, Tom 260
PCN (Progressive Christian Network) 357
Peck, Arthur 123
Penrose, Maggie 157
Pinker, Steven 3
Pittman, Robin 159, 167
Plato 121, 129, 291
Plumb, Sir Jack 123f, 131
Poetry 7ff, 348
Pollock, Dr Ivan 260
Pope, Eithne (*née* Jennings) 30, 64
Power, Bridget 76
Pratt, Dr C.L.G. 125ff, 131
Prentice, Richard 131

Quin, Bp. George & Nora 218, 221

Radley College 90, 105, 132, 136, 137ff, 150ff, 225, 233
Ramsey, Bp. Ian 125, 147, 355
Ramsey
   Joan (*née* Hamilton) 31f
   Michael, Archbishop 31f, 164, 328, 330, 355
Miss Randall ('Rannie') 187, 203, 220
Randall, Celia (*née* Duffin) 196
Reacher, Mark Henry 169
Reynell, Anthony 105
Rhodes James, Robert 99
Rich, John 174, 178, 305
Riddle, Trevor 341
Roberts, John 176
Roberts, Timothy 94
Robinson, Archbishop 76
Ronaldson
   Cousin Cecil & Gabriel Mary Fox 2, 46
   Mabel 2, 15f, 43f
   William (Uncle Billy) 2, 43f
Ross, Sheena 180
Rowse, A.L. 174
Royal Irish Fusiliers 110ff
RSPB 301f, 341
Runcie, Archbp. Robert 133
Rye, Mrs 171

St Columba's School, Rathfarnham 137
St Fin Barre's Cathedral 28, 62
St Leger, Alicia 30

St Luke's Home, Cork 30, 62
St Mary's School, Wantage 144, 157, 176, 280ff
St Paul's Cathedral, Lisbon 61
St Thomas' Hospital 180, 185f, 217f
Salter, Rev John 329f
Salter-Townsend family 28f
Salts Mill, Saltaire 194, 198
Schliemann, Heinrich 268f, 311, 315, 321
Seaver, George 11, 24, 29, 59, 61
Sedbergh School 6f, 19, 94f, 97ff, 230, 323, 351
Sewell, William 137f, 142
Sexton, Stuart 260
Sey, 'Nanny' 28, 219f
Sharwood Smith J. 173f
Shirley, Canon Fred 159ff
Shrewsbury School 19, 86, 95, 129, 132, 144, 160, 359
Silk, Dennis 141, 204, 233
Skelly Fr Jim 334f
Skipper, David 151
Sligo Grammar School 18
Slinger, Bill 262, 265
Smith
    Cousin Jewel xi, 28, 31, 63ff
    Cousin Steven 63
Smuts, General Jan Christiaan 74, 125
Solon 293f, 297, 316
Somerville
    Barbara (née Gregg) 3, 33, 35ff, 39, 63, 66ff, 76
    Biddy (Aunt Biddy) 29, 32f, 63
    Boyle, Admiral 33, 66
    Brian 111
    Christina (see Hoare)
    Dione (née Powell) 68
    Edith Oenone 3, 33, 66
    Julian 3, 68, 76
    Michael 3, 111
Sopwith, S.S. 9, 160ff, 165
Spong, Bp. Jack 187, 335f, 354ff
Springboard 347
Stephens, Annie (née Rycroft) 29
Stewart, Charles 256
Stockwood, Bp. Mervyn 129
Strachan
    Gillian (née Eggar) 196
    Rosemary (see Wilson, Tim)
Strong
    Stuart 18, 42f, 46f

Sybil (née Ronaldson) 2, 16, 43, 46
Simon, 47
Daphne (see Foster)
Swan Hellenic 306, 311ff
Swetenham, Margaret 191
Synge
    Edith 63
    John 63

Tain, The (*The Cattle Raid of Cooley*) 269f
Templer, General Sir Gerald 22, 117
Thompson, Norman 135ff
Thorneley, Michael 106f
Tosh, Rev Dr Bert 335
Totten, Mr (Chauffeur) 76
Trapnell, Barry 255
Trinity College, Dublin 17, 25ff
Trist
    Anne 184f, 191ff
    Isabel (see Elder)
    Lawrence 185
    Richard 185
Troy 268ff, 315
Tugendhat, Christopher 135
Tughan, Robin 232, 258, 260
Turner, Christopher 140, 143f
Turner, Isabella (Matron, St Thomas') 217

Usherwood, Dick 140

Valpy, Richard 65
Virgil, 10, 44f, 99, 127, 247, 249, 325
VRH (Voluntary Reading Help) 346
Vye, Luther & Margaret 232

Walker, Bond 89
Walmsley, Basil 234
Wantage 281f, 299, 306ff, 329ff, 342f, 346
Ward, P.E. 94
Waterman, Dudley 273
Webb, Diane 311
Weldon family 188, 203
Westonbirt Arboretum 286, 303
West Watson
    Colin & Esme (née Garrett) 196, 200
    Zaidee (see Godfree)
Whidditt, Mrs 171
Willis, Canon Andy 95
Wills, Madeline 76

Wilkes, Vaughan 137, 141
Wilson
   Sara (*née* Hollins) xii, 4f, 168ff, 178, 179ff, 190ff, 201ff, 207, 232, 236, 255f, 263, 288, 300f, 316, 339
   Anna (*see* Adams)
   Emma (*see* Hales)
Wilson
   Cecil Samuel (Father) 2, 13ff, 26, 39, 41ff, 103, 106, 111, 134, 216ff, 236f, 359
   Margaret (*née* Gregg) (Mother) 3, 18f, 24ff, 45, 71f, 149, 222, 303, 352, 359
   Arthur (Uncle Artie) 2, 15, 42f
   Jeanette, 'Gan', (*née* McClaughry) 13ff
   Millie 15, 43
Wilson
   James 47
   James Brabazon 47
   Philip Brabazon 47f
   Susan 43
   William 13f
   William Robert ('Robin') 47
Wilson
   Bishop Leonard 22f, 196
   Tim & Rosemary (*née* Strachan) 196
Wilson, Pipe Major RIrF 157
Wilson's Hospital, Mullingar 17
Woctor, US Army 76
Wright, Edred 165
Wright, Rev Robert 281
Wrinch, Charles 105, 144f
WWT (Wildfowl & Wetlands Trust) 301f

YACWAG (Yatton & Congresbury Wildlife Action Group) 341, 346
Young, David 258
Young, Rev R.J. 259, 263